Reclaiming the Gospel

and

Reforming Churches

———

Twenty years of the Southern Baptist
Founders Conference
1982 – 2002

THOMAS K. ASCOL, EDITOR

Cape Coral, Florida
FOUNDERS PRESS
2003

Published by
Founders Press
Committed to historic Southern Baptist principles
P.O. Box 150931 • Cape Coral, FL 33915
Phone (239) 772-1400 • Fax: (239) 772-1140
Electronic Mail: founders@founders.org or <http://www.founders.org>

Printed in the United States of America.
ISBN 0-9713361-1-3

Typeset and Scripture Index by G. Wm. Foster, Jr.
Strait Gate Publications
Charlotte, North Carolina

CONTENTS

CONTENTS

Contents

PREFACE
THOMAS K. ASCOL

THE late James Boice once pointed out that we tend "to overestimate what God will do in one year and greatly underestimate what He will do in twenty." I have discovered that tendency in my own thinking about reformation and revival. It is hard to believe that the Southern Baptist Founders Conference has been around twenty years. The euphoria of that first conference caused some of us who were there to think that we were on the brink of a fresh outpouring of God's Spirit that would sweep across the nation and around the world in a matter of years if not months. By the time the fourth or fifth conference had come and gone, the organizing committee had to fight disillusionment and even entertained suggestions that what we were trying to do simply could not be done.

Now, twenty years later, we can look back with thanksgiving and praise to God for what He has done among us. During those years thousands of students, pastors and church leaders have participated in the annual conference. Before moving in 1991 to the campus of Samford University in Birmingham, Alabama, the conference met for eight years on the campus of what is now Rhodes College in Memphis, Tennessee. Many additional ministries have also emerged out of the conference since its inception.

Six regional conferences are currently meeting across the country. Founders Fraternals have been organized to encourage pastors in a more regular way and meet in 18 different locations. The *Founders Journal* is in its twelfth year of publication. Founders Press has published fifteen books. Our web site attracts over 200,000 hits each month. The Founders Internship ministry has provided for church-based training for several men who were preparing for the pastorate.

vii

In addition to all this, Founders Ministries has also had a part in inspiring conferences and reformation efforts in several nations around the world. A growing number of pastors and churches are being encouraged to pursue biblical reformation in local congregations. That has been the goal of Founders from our inception—to see healthy churches joyfully and wholeheartedly pursuing that new life in Christ that the Bible clearly sets before us.

By God's grace, this is happening. The gospel of God's grace is being rediscovered in our day. Churches are being renewed and reformed according to the Word of God. A whole generation of younger pastors is being raised up by God to keep pressing forward in this great cause. The Lord has indeed done far more in the last twenty years than we could have imagined at the start. The advance of reformation transcends geographical and denominational boundaries. It is humbling and gratifying to look back and see how God has been pleased to use the efforts of Founders Ministries to make His truth known. That He has done so illustrates His revealed *modus operandi* of using "foolish," "weak," "base" and "despised" vessels to accomplish His purposes on the earth (1 Corinthians 1:27-28).

The publication of this volume celebrates the twentieth anniversary of the Founders Conference. The first conference was planned and organized as the result of a prayer meeting that took place on November 13, 1982. On that occasion seven men gathered in a motel room in Euless, Texas to consider what could be done to call pastors and church leaders back to the historic, biblical principles that had characterized Southern Baptist church life at the founding of the convention in 1845. After spending half of the day in prayer, those men agreed to plan a conference that would be based upon the doctrines of grace as they had been historically articulated by our Southern Baptist forebears.

It was an interesting collection of men in that room. Ernie Reisinger was the senior voice of experience. He was then serving as Pastor of North Pompano Baptist Church in North

Pompano, Florida. Today he is retired and living in Cape Coral, Florida. R. F. Gates was a full-time evangelist from Shreveport, Louisiana. He still lives there, serving as an elder and evangelist in the Heritage Baptist Church. Tom Nettles was a Professor of Church History at Mid-America Baptist Theological Seminary in Memphis, Tennessee. Today he is a Professor of Historical Theology at Southern Baptist Theological Seminary in Louisville, Kentucky. Fred Malone was preparing for Ph.D. studies at Southwestern Baptist Theological Seminary in Ft. Worth, Texas and planting Heritage Baptist Church in that city. Today he is Pastor of First Baptist Church in Clinton, Louisiana. Bill Ascol was Assistant Pastor at Broadmoor Baptist Church in Shreveport. Today he is the Pastor of Heritage Baptist Church in that same city. Ben Mitchell was an M.Div. student at Southwestern and was helping Fred with the church plant. Today, he is a professor of Ethics at Trinity International University in Deerfield, Illinois. I was also there that day. I was an Assistant Pastor at Spring Valley Baptist Church in Dallas and an M.Div. student at Southwestern. Today I pastor the Grace Baptist Church in Cape Coral, Florida.

Ernie Reisinger was the one who had given the most careful thought to our deliberations before we met. He made all the arrangements and prepared for us to read selected Psalms and hymns along with our prayers. Ben Mitchell chaired the meeting and led us through the agenda that Ernie had prepared. After several hours of considering concerns and challenges we agreed to organize a gathering for pastors and seminary students who were interested in seeing theological and spiritual renewal take place within the churches of the Southern Baptist Convention.

A Statement of Principles was drafted, assignments were made, and the result was the first Southern Baptist Conference on the Faith of the Founders (quickly—and mercifully—shortened to "Founders Conference").

Following is the original Statement of Principles that was drafted in that hotel room:

THE MOTIVE

The motive of the conference is to glorify God, honor His gospel, and strengthen His churches by providing encouragement to Southern Baptists in historical, biblical, theological, practical, and ecumenical studies.

THE PURPOSE

The purpose of the conference is to establish and continue an annual meeting under the oversight of a local Southern Baptist Church for Southern Baptist ministers, elders, deacons, and theological students.

THE NATURE

The desire is to be a balanced conference in respect to doctrine and devotion expressed in the doctrines of grace and their experimental application to the local church, particularly in the areas of worship and witness. This is to be accomplished through engaging a variety of speakers to present formal papers, sermons, expositions, and devotions, and through the recommendation and distribution of literature consistent with the nature of the conference.

THE SUBJECTS AND PROCEDURES

The theological foundation of the conference will be the doctrines of grace (election, depravity, atonement, effectual calling, and perseverance) and specifically related truths. These subjects will be presented doctrinally, expositionally, homiletically, and historically. Each conference will concentrate on the experimental and pastoral application of the respective doctrines.

After six years the conference was moved from the oversight of a local church to being governed by a board of trustees and supported by several local churches. Other than that, those same principles that were articulated to guide the conference continue to guide the expanded work of Founders Ministries today.

A word about the content of this book is in order. More than 250 presentations have been made at the National Founders Conference over the last two decades. Thirty-four of them are included in this volume. The most difficult task in editing this book has been the work of exclusion. One of the great blessings of God on the Founders Conference through the years has been the rarity of presentations that fell flat. This is all the more amazing when one considers the variety of topics that have been addressed.

Over the years whole conferences have focused on such themes as Sanctification, Law and Gospel, World Missions, Biblical Evangelism, Preachers and Preaching, Pastoral Ministry, The Puritans, Baptist History and Heritage, The Invitation System, Ecclesiology and The Sufficiency of Scripture. A review of all the conferences and individual messages would immediately dispel the myth that Founders Ministries is only concerned with Calvinism. Our burden and aim has been and remains the reformation and revival of local churches.

The messages that constitute the chapters of this book represent that burden quite well. If you have never attended a Founders Conference then reading them will give you a small taste of what goes on in those meetings (though nothing can begin to describe the singing!). If you are familiar with the conference then the content of the following chapters will be no surprise to you but will provide you, in a more permanent form, some of the rich content which has been delivered the last twenty years.

A word about style is in order. All of these chapters were originally delivered verbally. Many of them were preached. Keep this in mind when reading. We have endeavored to preserve each speaker's unique manner of address (what Ernie

Reisinger calls his "Ernieisms") while adapting the spoken word into the written word. Thanks to all the contributors who trusted us with this process. A book like this could never be produced without the faithful labors of dozens of people. All who have worked behind the scenes in planning and organizing the Founders Conference have helped make it possible. Those thousands of pastors and church leaders who have attended the conference and encouraged its continuance have a part in this book. Without the warm initial reception of these messages there would be no reason to have them in printed form.

Some people who have specifically worked on this volume do deserve mention. Cindy Kemp, Mark Singleton, Pat Barley, Sarah Loson and Heather Olive all helped with transcribing many of the messages. Matthew Allen did a Herculean job in editing many of the manuscripts. Bill Ascol and Phil Newton lent editorial assistance and Don Reisinger helped proof read. Bill Foster's diligent work in formatting the book has been deeply appreciated. His kind patience over the many months of compiling material has been admirable.

Sam Hughey graciously designed the cover for the book and the layout of pictures from past conferences. His contribution to the book is also appreciated.

A very special thanks to Barb Reisinger, my administrative assistant, whose organizational gifts, tireless efforts of coordinating various phases of the project and passionate commitment to the work of Founders Ministries have been indispensable.

Finally, I am grateful to my precious wife, Donna. Not only has she encouraged me in the completion of this book she has also welcomed the work of Founders as an important part of our life together. Only the Lord knows the sacrifices she has gladly made to see the cause of reformation advance the last twenty years through Founders Ministries.

CONFERENCE PERSONALITIES

THE LAST FRONTIER (1999)
Anonymous

A missionary under appointment of the International Mission Board of the Southern Baptist Convention. Because he is serving in a high risk mission field, the details of his training and ministry are being withheld for security purposes as well as to protect the lives of those indigenous believers with whom he labors, taking the gospel of Jesus Christ to the last frontier.

A BIOGRAPHICAL SKETCH OF JOHN A. BROADUS (1989)
CHURCH DISCIPLINE IN THE LOCAL CHURCH (1999)
Bill Ascol

Bill Ascol is a graduate of Lamar University (B.A.) and Southwestern Baptist Theological Seminary (M.Div.) in Fort Worth, Texas. An original member of the Founders Conference Planning Committee, he presently serves as Chairman of the Board of Founders Ministries, Inc. He is also the Coordinator of the Southern Baptist Founders YOUTH Conferences. Bill is active in the conservative resurgence in the Louisiana Baptist Convention, serving as the Editor of *LIFe Line*, the official newsletter of the Louisiana Inerrancy Fellowship. He is also a member of the Executive Board of the Louisiana Baptist Convention. Bill is the founding pastor of the Heritage Baptist Church in Shreveport, Louisiana, where he has served since 1992.

When he preached at the 1989 conference, he was serving as pastor of the First Baptist Church of Clinton, Louisiana. In 1999, Bill was in his seventh year as Pastor of the Heritage

Baptist Church where he continues to minister.

REFORMATION AND MISSIONS (1999)
Tom Ascol

Tom Ascol is a graduate of Texas A&M University and also a Ph.D. graduate of the Southwestern Baptist Theological Seminary in Fort Worth, Texas. He is an original member of the Founders Conference Planning Committee and presently serves as the Executive Director of Founders Ministries, Inc. He has also served as the Editor of the *Founders Journal* since its inception. Tom has spoken throughout the USA as well as internationally. He has edited and contributed to several works and written *From the Protestant Reformation to the Southern Baptist Convention: What hath Geneva to do with Nashville?*

When he preached at the conference in 1987, he was in his second year of his ministry as Senior Pastor at the Grace Baptist Church in Cape Coral, Florida.

THE SUFFICIENCY OF SCRIPTURE AND EVANGELISM (1994)
Walter Chantry

Walter Chantry was ordained to the Christian ministry in 1963 after receiving a B.A. degree from Dickinson College and the M.Div. degree from Westminister Theological Seminary in Philadelphia, Pennsylvania. He was called to the pastorate of Grace Baptist Church in Carlisle, Pennsylvania in the fall of 1963 and continued his labors there until his retirement in 2002. He is an Associate Editor of the *Banner of Truth* magazine and a contributor to other evangelical publications, as well as the author of six books.

A HISTORY OF SOUTHERN BAPTIST PREACHING (1995)
Mark Coppenger

Mark Coppenger is a graduate of Southwestern Baptist Theological Seminary (M.Div.) in Fort Worth, Texas and Vanderbilt University (Ph.D.) in Nashville, Tennessee. He has been a college professor, an army officer, a seminary president, a magazine editor, a denominational executive, and a pastor. He has been involved in short-term mission endeavors in South America, Europe, Africa, and the Middle East. Mark has published two books in ethics, and contributed to several journals and edited volumes. He currently serves as a church planter for the Southern Baptist Convention.

When he preached this message in 1995 he was serving as President of Midwestern Baptist Theological Seminary in Kansas City, Missouri.

THE VALUE OF THE PURITANS FOR SBC MINISTRY (1995)
Mark Dever

Mark Dever is a graduate of Duke University (B.A.), Gordon-Conwell Theological Seminary (M.Div.), the Southern Baptist Theological Seminary (Th.M.), and Cambridge University (Ph.D.). He is a former member of the Board of Trustees of Founders Ministries, Inc. He presently serves as the Senior Pastor of Capitol Hill Baptist Church in Washington, D.C. In addition to his pastoral responsibilities, he serves as the Senior Fellow for the Center for Church Reform. Mark is a popular conference speaker, both in the USA and abroad. He has contributed to several journals and edited volumes, and has authored several books, among them, *Nine Marks of a Healthy Church.*

When he preached this message in 1995 he was serving as Senior Pastor at Capitol Hill Baptist Church, where he continues to minister.

THE PROVIDENCE OF GOD IN THE TEACHING OF JESUS (2000)
J. Ligon Duncan

J. Ligon Duncan, III is a graduate of Furman University in Greenville, South Carolina and Covenant Theological Seminary in St. Louis, Missouri (M.Div. in 1986 and M.A. in 1987).

In 1995 he graduated from the University of Edinburgh, Scotland (Ph.D.). He has served as Chairman of the Department of Systematic Theology at the Reformed Theological Seminary in Jackson, Mississippi. Since 1996 he has served as Senior Minister at the historic First Presbyterian Church in Jackson, Mississippi. Ligon serves on several boards, among them the Council for Biblical Manhood and Womanhood and the Alliance of Confessing Evangelicals. He has authored numerous articles in various magazines and journals.

When he preached at the conference in 2000 he was in his fifth year of ministry at First Presbyterian Church where he continues to serve.

CLOSING WITH CHRIST (1998)
Jim Elliff

Jim Elliff is a graduate of Ouachita Baptist University (B.A.) in Arkadelphia, Arkansas and Southwestern Baptist Theological Seminary (M.Div.) in Fort Worth, Texas. Jim has served as a teaching pastor or in pastoral staff positions in churches across Florida, Arkansas, Texas, and Oklahoma. In 1985 he undertook an itinerant ministry as the founder and president of Christian Communicators Worldwide. He has since spoken across America and in several foreign countries. Jim has written several valuable resources for the church, including *Wasted Faith, How Children Come to Christ*, and *Led by the Spirit*. Until recently he served as the first consultant for the new Center for Biblical Revival at Midwestern Baptist Theological Seminary in Kansas City, Missouri. During this time he was instrumental in planting a new church in the Kansas City area.

When he preached at the 1998 conference, he was ministering in Kansas City through the North Pointe Baptist Church where he is still an elder.

SHEPHERDING THE FLOCK (2001)
Roger Ellsworth

Roger Ellsworth is a graduate of Southern Illinois University (B.A.) and Midwestern Baptist Theological Seminary (M.Div.) in Kansas City, Missouri. Roger is a former President of the Illinois Baptist Convention and served as Chairman of the Board of Trustees of the Southeastern Baptist Theological Seminary. He is the author of several excellent works published by the Banner of Truth Trust and Evangelical Press, including *Strengthening Christ's Church* and *How to Live in a Dangerous World*. He has been serving as Pastor of the Immanuel Baptist Church in Benton, Illinois since 1988.

THE VALUE OF PILGRIM'S PROGRESS IN PREACHING (1983)
Jim Gables

Jim Gables is one of the living authorities on John Bunyan's classic *The Pilgrim's Progress*. He has traveled extensively preaching and teaching God's Word. His series on Pilgrim's Progress still stands today in a class all by itself. For the past eighteen years he has served as Pastor-Teacher at the Oakland Baptist Church in Birmingham, Alabama.

When he preached at the conference in 1983, he was serving as the Pastor of the First Baptist Church in Osceola, Missouri and conducting a multi-faceted ministry known as Grace Abounding Ministries.

THE SPIRITUAL STATE OF THOSE WE EVANGELIZE (1984)
R. F. Gates

R. F. Gates is a graduate of Centenary College in Shreveport, Louisiana and Southwestern Baptist Theological Seminary in Fort Worth, Texas (Th.M. and M.Div.). He has pastored churches in Oklahoma and Louisiana. For more than thirty years he has been engaged in an itinerant ministry of evangelism through the R. F. Gates Evangelistic Association. During this time he has preached in almost every one of the fifty states as well as several foreign countries. He has served as Associate Pastor of the Heritage Baptist Church in Shreveport since 1992.

When he preached at the 1984 conference he was engaged in a very active itinerant preaching ministry.

THE LIFE AND MISSION OF WILLIAM CAREY, PARTS 1 & 2 (1992)
Timothy George

Timothy George is a graduate of the University of Tennessee (A.B.) at Chattanooga and Harvard University (M.Div. and Th.D.). He pastored churches in Tennessee, Alabama and Massachusetts, and formerly taught historical theology at the Southern Baptist Theological Seminary in Louisville, Kentucky. In 1988 he became the founding Dean of Beeson Divinity School in Birmingham, Alabama, where he continues to serve. Timothy is an Executive Editor of *Christianity Today* magazine and serves on the following editorial advisory boards: *The Harvard Theological Review*, *Christian History*, and *Books and Culture*. He has also served on the Board of Trustees of Lifeway Christian Resources of the Southern Baptist Convention. A prolific author, he has written more than twenty books, among them, *Theology of the Reformers*.

When he preached at the conference in 1992, he was serving as the Dean of Beeson Divinity School, where he continues to minister.

A DEVOTIONAL PSALM (1998)
Steve Haines

Steve Haines is a graduate of the Southwestern Baptist Theological Seminary in Fort Worth, Texas, where he received his M.Div. and Ph.D. degrees. Steve has served on the foreign mission field as a church planter and theological educator under the auspices of the Foreign (now International) Mission Board of the Southern Baptist Convention. His fields of service include Colombia, Ukraine, and Paraguay. He is presently serving as a church planter and theological educator in South America.

When he brought the devotional Psalm in 1998 he was serving as Associate Pastor of the Grace Baptist Church in Cape Coral, Florida.

THE PURITANS AND THE RECOVERY OF THE LORD'S DAY (2002)
Erroll Hulse

Erroll Hulse is a native of South Africa and has been a resident of England for almost all of his adult life. In addition to his being the Editor of *Reformation Today* magazine and Carey Publications, he currently serves as one of the elders of the Leeds Reformed Baptist Church. He is a prime mover behind the International Fellowship of Reformed Baptists and serves on the board of directors of Evangelical Press. He is a prolific author, having written such titles as *Give Him No Rest* and *Who Are the Puritans?* Erroll is widely traveled, having ministered extensively throughout North and South America, Africa, Europe, Asia, and Australia.

MINISTERIAL DEPRESSION (1990)
David Kingdon

David Kingdon was converted at fifteen years of age while living in an orphanage that was originally founded by Charles Spurgeon. He later studied at Spurgeon's College and ultimately succeeded Spurgeon's grandson as the Principal of the Irish Baptist College. He currently serves as Visiting Lecturer in Baptist Principles and Practices at the London Theological Seminary. David has written extensively in various magazines and journals. His book *Children of Abraham* is a tremendous discourse on the Baptist covenantal position of believers' baptism.

When he preached at the conference in 1990, he was engaged in ministry in London.

REDEEMED FROM THE CURSE OF THE LAW (1993)
John MacArthur

John MacArthur is a graduate of Talbot Theological Seminary in La Mirada, California and Pastor-Teacher at Grace Community Church in Sun Valley, California where he has served since 1969. In addition to being a prolific author (more than 100 titles in print, including the bestseller, *The Gospel According to Jesus*), he is President of The Master's College and founder of The Master's Seminary. He is President and featured teacher of "Grace to You," the nonprofit organization responsible for developing, producing, and distributing John's books, audiocassettes, and the "Grace to You" radio program. "Grace to You" airs more than 800 times daily, reaching all major population centers in the United States, as well as Canada, Europe, India, New Zealand, the Philippines, and South Africa. In its three-decade history, "Grace to You" has also distributed more than 11 million audiocassettes.

When he preached at the 1993 conference, he was in his twenty-fourth year of ministry at Grace Community Church, where he continues to serve as Pastor-Teacher.

THE MAN IN ROMANS 7 (1986)
Fred Malone

Fred Malone is a graduate of Reformed Theological Seminary in Jackson, Mississippi (M.Div.) and the Southwestern Baptist Theological Seminary in Fort Worth, Texas (Ph.D.). He is an original member of the Founders Conference Planning Committee and is the Secretary of the Board of Trustees of Founders Ministries, Inc. Fred has served as the Pastor of the First Baptist Church in Clinton, Louisiana since 1992. He is the author of *A String of Pearls Unstrung* and has a forthcoming book on believers' baptism. He has served as a member of the Board of Trustees of the Southern Baptist Theological Seminary. He also serves as a member of the Board of Trustees of Louisiana College and is active in the work of the Louisiana Inerrancy Fellowship.

When he preached at the conference in 1986 he was serving as the founding Pastor of the Heritage Baptist Church in Crowley, Texas.

THE DOCTRINES OF GRACE AND WORLD MISSIONS (1996)
George Martin

George Martin is a graduate of Florida State University (B.S.) and New Orleans Baptist Theological Seminary (M.Div. and Th.D.). He served with the Foreign (now International) Mission Board of the Southern Baptist Convention in Indonesia from 1988 to 1994. He was Professor and Academic Dean at the Jakarta Baptist Theological Seminary. In addition to this he taught at the Asia Baptist Graduate Theological Seminary. He was an Associate Professor of Religion at North Greenville College before joining the faculty at the Southern Baptist Theological Seminary in Louisville, Kentucky, where he serves as Professor of Christian Missions and Associate Dean of the Billy Graham School of Missions, Evangelism, and Church Growth.

When he preached at the conference in 1996, he was making the transition from North Greenville College to Southern Seminary.

THE LORDSHIP OF CHRIST (1985)
David Miller

David Miller is the founder of Line Upon Line Ministries and the former Director of Missions for the Little Red River Association in Heber Springs, Arkansas. His itinerant ministry has taken him throughout the country where his expositions have been used by God to bless multitudes. He is recognized as a preacher without peer. David served on the Board of Trustees of the Southern Baptist Theological Seminary at a crucial time in the transitional life of the Southern Baptist Convention.

When he preached this message in 1985 he was Director of Missions for the Little Red River Association in Heber

Springs.

THE LIFE AND LABORS OF PATRICK H. MELL (1983)
C. Ben Mitchell

Ben Mitchell is a graduate of Southwestern Baptist Theological Seminary (M.Div.) in Fort Worth, Texas and the University of Tennessee (Ph.D.) in Knoxville. He was an original member of the Founders Conference Planning Committee. Ben has taught ethics at the University of Tennessee and the Southern Baptist Theological Seminary. He is presently a Professor of Ethics at Trinity International University in Deerfield, Illinois. He is a consultant on biomedical and life issues with the Ethics and Religious Liberty Commission of the Southern Baptist Convention. Ben has been published widely in bioethics and is the author of numerous articles and reviews.

When he preached at the 1983 conference, he was a student at Southwestern Baptist Theological Seminary.

PREACHING AND IRRESISTIBLE GRACE (1990)
Tom Nettles

Tom Nettles is a graduate of Mississippi College (B.A.) and Southwestern Baptist Theological Seminary (M.Div. and Ph.D.). He is widely regarded as one of the foremost Baptist historical theologians in America. He previously taught at Southwestern Baptist Theological Seminary in Fort Worth, Texas, Mid-America Baptist Theological Seminary in Memphis, Tennessee, and Trinity Evangelical Divinity School in Deerfield, Illinois, where he was Professor of Church History and Chair of the Department of Church History. Since 1997 he has served as Professor of Historical Theology at The Southern Baptist Theological Seminary in Louisville, Kentucky. Along with numerous journal articles and scholarly papers, Tom is the author or editor of nine books. Among his books are *By His Grace and For His Glory* and *Baptists and the Bible*, the highly influential volume which he co-authored with Russ

Bush.

When he preached at the 1990 conference, he was teaching at Trinity Evangelical Divinity School.

A DEVOTIONAL PSALM (1997)
Phil Newton

Phil Newton is a graduate of the University of Mobile, New Orleans Baptist Theological Seminary (M.Div.), and Fuller Theological Seminary (D.Min.). He is a former member of the State Board of Missions with the Alabama Baptist Convention. He serves as an adjunct professor at Crichton College in Memphis and the Institut Theologique de Nimes in France. He is a member of the Board of Trustees of Founders Ministries, Inc.

When he brought the devotional Psalm in 1997 he was in his tenth year at the South Woods Baptist Church in Memphis, Tennessee, where he continues to serve as Senior Pastor.

THE ATONEMENT, PART 1 & 2 (1991)
Roger Nicole

Roger Nicole is a native Swiss Reformed theologian with an M.A. from Sorbonne, a Th.D. from Gordon Divinity School and a Ph.D. from Harvard University. He has long been regarded as one of the precminent theologians in America. A renowned bibliophile, his personal library includes *Calvin's Commentaries on the Gospels and Acts* published during Calvin's lifetime and many other rare volumes from the 1500s and 1600s. He was an associate editor for the *New Geneva Study Bible* and a corresponding editor for *Christianity Today*. He assisted in the translation of the *NIV Bible*, is a charter member and past president of the Evangelical Theological Society, and was a founding member of the International Council on Biblical Inerrancy. He has written over 100 articles and contributed to 50 books and reference works. Some of his works have recently been published with the title, *Standing Forth*.

When he preached at the conference in 1991, he was serving on the faculty of the Reformed Theological Seminary in Orlando, Florida, where he continues to minister.

THE GLOBAL PRIORITY OF MISSIONS (1999)
John Piper

John Piper is a graduate of Wheaton College (B.A.), Fuller Theological Seminary (B.D.), and the University of Munich (Th.D.). He taught Biblical Studies at Bethel College in St. Paul, Minnesota for six years, and since 1980 has been Senior Pastor at the burgeoning Bethlehem Baptist Church in Minneapolis, Minnesota. John's passion for God's glory is contagious. He is a prolific author whose usefulness in the cause of Jesus Christ has been greatly extended through Desiring God Ministries.

REFORMING CHURCH MUSIC (2001)
Ken Puls

Ken Puls is a graduate of Southwestern Baptist Theological Seminary in Fort Worth, Texas where he received the M.M. and Ph.D. degrees in Church Music Ministry. He taught church music and classical guitar at Dallas Baptist University, and also served as Music Minister at Heritage Baptist Church in Mansfield, Texas. He has composed over 40 hymns, including hymns in *Psalms, Hymns, and Spiritual Songs*, the hymnal of the Southern Baptist Founders Conference. Currently, Ken works full time with Founders Ministries.

When he preached at the conference in 2001, he was serving the Heritage Baptist Church in Mansfield.

DOCTRINE AND DEVOTION (1983)
Ernest Reisinger

Ernest Reisinger is a retired pastor and author residing in Cape Coral, Florida. He is an original member of the Founders Conference Planning Committee and continues as a member of the Board of Trustees of Founders Ministries, Inc.

He has served as a member of the Banner of Truth Trust, and is the author of several books, including *The Law and the Gospel*, *Whatever Happened to the Ten Commandments*, and *Lord and Christ: The Implications of Lordship for Faith and Life*. Ernie was the prime mover behind the reprinting of James P. Boyce's *Abstract of Systematic Theology* and John L. Dagg's *Manual of Theology and Church Order*. He has been singularly used by God to advance the cause of reformation throughout the Southern Baptist Convention by means of the distribution of literature.

When he preached at the 1983 conference, he was serving as the Senior Pastor of the North Pompano Baptist Church in Pompano Beach, Florida.

DEPRAVITY (1988)
Pat Stewart

Pat Stewart is a graduate of Southeastern Bible College and Southwestern Baptist Theological Seminary in Fort Worth, Texas (M.Div.). He also engaged in doctoral work at Mid-America Baptist Theological Seminary in Memphis, Tennessee. Since 1992 he has served as Pastor of the First Baptist Church in St. Charles, Illinois. He has served as a member of the Board of Trustees of the International Mission Board of the Southern Baptist Convention.

When he preached at the 1988 conference, he was serving as Pastor of the North Pompano Baptist Church in Pompano Beach, Florida.

REDEEMED BY THE SON (1996)
Geoff Thomas

Geoff Thomas is a graduate of the University College in Cardiff, Wales as well as Westminster Theological Seminary in Philadelphia, Pennsylvania. He has pastored the Alfred Place Baptist Church in Aberystwyth, Wales since 1965. Geoff was an Associate Editor of *Evangelical Times* for ten years and has been Associate Editor of the *Banner of Truth* magazine for thirty years. He is the author of *Daniel: Servant of God Under Four Kings* as well as the soon to be published biography of Ernest Reisinger.

When he preached at the 1996 conference, he was in his thirty-first year of ministry at the Alfred Place Baptist Church where he continues to serve as Pastor.

THE LIFE AND DEVOTION OF DAVID BRAINERD (1985)
John Thornbury

John Thornbury is a graduate of Lexington Baptist College (B.A.), Gettysburg Theological Seminary (Th.M.), and Drew University (D.Min.). He has served as Pastor of the Winfield Baptist Church in Union County, Pennsylvania since 1966. John has written several books and articles, including *David Brainerd: Pioneer Missionary to the American Indians* and a forthcoming biography on Spencer Cone. He has been involved in training pastors in the Crimea and Belarus.

RICHARD FULLER: HIS LIFE AND PREACHING (1991)
Don Whitney

Don Whitney is a graduate of Arkansas State University, Southwestern Baptist Theological Seminary in Fort Worth, Texas (M.Div.), and Trinity Evangelical Divinity School (D.Min.) in Deerfield, Illinois. He is a member of the Board of Trustees for Founders Ministries, Inc. In 1980 he began a fif-teen-year pastorate at the Glenfield Baptist Church in Glen Ellyn, Illinois. In 1995 he became Associate Professor of Spiritual Formation at Midwestern Baptist Theological Seminary in Kansas City, Missouri. In 1996 he helped to plant the North Pointe Baptist Church in Kansas City. Don is the author of several excellent works, among them *Spiritual Disciplines for the Christian Life* and *Spiritual Disciplines Within the Church*.

When he preached this message in 1991 he was serving as Senior Pastor at the Glenfield Baptist Church.

A Devotional Psalm (2000)
Hal Wynn

Hal Wynn is a graduate of Luther Rice Seminary. He is a member of the Board of Trustees of Founders Ministries, Inc. and serves as the Chairman and Conference Coordinator of the Founders Conference. Hal has served in various capacities in the Royal Palm Baptist Association, including Moderator and President of the Pastors' Conference.

When he brought the devotional Psalm in 2000 he was in his nineteenth year as Senior Pastor of the Northside Baptist Church in North Fort Myers, Florida, where he continues to serve.

DOCTRINE

1.

DOCTRINE AND DEVOTION
ERNEST REISINGER
1983 Southern Baptist Founders Conference

FOR our text tonight, I've chosen a passage from Titus chapter 2:

> But as for you, speak the things which are proper for sound doctrine: that the older men be sober, reverent, temperate, sound in faith, in love, in patience; the older women likewise, that they be reverent in behavior, not slanderers, not given to much wine, teachers of good things—that they admonish the young women to love their husbands, to love their children, to be discreet, chaste, homemakers, good, obedient to their own husbands, that the word of God may not be blasphemed. Likewise, exhort the young men to be sober-minded, in all things showing yourself to be a pattern of good works; in doctrine showing integrity, reverence, incorruptibility, sound speech that cannot be condemned, that one who is an opponent may be ashamed, having nothing evil to say of you. (Titus 2:1–8; NKJV).

These verses, like many, many more in the Bible bring together what should never be separated: our belief and our practice—our doctrine and our devotion.

The first verse speaks of doctrine. There, Paul tells Titus, this young preacher, to "speak the things which are proper for sound doctrine." This is the foundation. In

verses 7 and 8, he talks about the other side of the coin—
devotion. "In all things show yourself to be a pattern of
good works." There, Paul talks about the house you build.
He is talking about the Christian life.

This subject, doctrine and devotion, is dear to my own
heart. My deepest desire is to see sound doctrine and then
a devotional house built on that doctrine. It's my burden.
One reason why that is so is I have seen (and I'm sure
you have seen) many who are sound in doctrine, but they
are so sound, they are sound asleep. They've forgotten devotion. Another reason why it is my burden is that I have
also seen others who are feverishly building the house,
putting in windows, putting on doors, nailing on the roof,
but they've forgotten the foundation. They've forgotten
doctrine.

Years ago, in the early 1960s, I recall the first letter I
wrote to my great, esteemed friend, Dr. Martyn Lloyd-
Jones. There was a young man graduating from college in
whom I had a great interest. He wanted to go to seminary
and he often talked to me about which seminary to attend.
Well, that wasn't an easy question to answer back then;
nor is it an easy one today. I thought I would write to the
Doctor and ask him his opinion. I think I would do a bit
better in my descriptive language now, but then I didn't
know any better. I asked, "Is there a school over there in
England that has some Pentecostal power and Presbyterian doctrine?" Well, believe it or not, that question en-
deared me to the Doctor. I've had many hours with him
and meals with him since then, and he always remembered the way I tried to express what I was looking for and
what I am still looking for. That combination, doctrine and
devotion, is my topic tonight. Only out of that rare combination of sound doctrine and true Christian devotion will
the church experience long-expected, long-prayed-for
awakenings. Revival will come only by a combination of
doctrine and devotion.

A DOCTRINAL FOUNDATION

The Importance of Doctrine.

True knowledge of things and felt power of things; it's a rare combination. There are those who cry down doctrine and cry up experience. You are as familiar with the phrases as I am: "Christ is our creed!" "The Bible is our textbook!" They sound so pious. However, I wonder which Christ is their creed. We live in a day when there are a thousand christs on the religious market. Only the person with a doctrinal foundation can say which Christ we are talking about. In addition, all the cults in the world claim that the Bible is in some way their textbook. Somebody has to say what it means. That, of course, gets us into doctrine.

It is not enough to speak of mystical experience with God without some doctrinal knowledge. We worship God in truth, the Bible says, as well as Spirit (John 4:23). Truth is stated in words, in real words, and in Bible words. When you speak truth in real words, what is that? Why, that's doctrine!

This effort to be a practicing Christian without knowing doctrine, without knowing what Christianity is all about, will always fail. The true Christian must have a doctrinal foundation. The conflict between our Lord and the Pharisees was over doctrine. To savingly believe in Christ means to believe right things about Christ. Who he was—not any Christ, but the virgin-born Son of God. What he did— suffer vicariously on a Roman cross. Why he did it—to redeem an innumerable company of sheep from every tribe and nation and tongue.

What is true religion? Is it some mystical, nebulous thing floating around in the sky? Of course not. True religion cannot be anything less than right thinking in relationship to God, right feeling in relationship to God, and right acting in relationship to God. True religion must reach the whole man. It must reach his mind, because that's what he thinks with. It must reach his emotions, because that's what he feels with. It must reach his will because that's what determines his actions. What is Christian experience? Christian experience is the influence of sound doctrine, biblical teaching, and applying it to the mind, the affections and the will, by the power of the Holy Spirit. I like what J.C. Ryle said about this:

> You can talk about Christian experience all you wish, but without doctrinal roots, it will be like cut flowers stuck in the ground. It will wither and die.

It is impossible, therefore, to overemphasize the importance of sound doctrine in the life of the Christian. Right thinking about spiritual matters is imperative if we would have right living.

You may ask yourself, or someone may ask you, "Well, how do I test this Christian experience you are talking about in the midst of so much spurious religious experience and religious confusion in the world, confusion among Baptists and among Southern Baptists, in particular. Let me throw out three tests that you can use if you are asked:

> Is the experience produced of God and blessed of God?
>
> Is the experience regulated and governed by biblical truth?
>
> Do the subjects of this professed religious experience manifest a general and cordial love for the Bible?

With respect to the third element, ask yourself (or the other person asking you this question): What are your views about the character of God? What are your views about God's holy law? What are your views concerning sin? What are your views about our acceptance with respect to our Christian hope? These are elementary questions, but they deserve to be asked and answered.

Like Bones to the Body.

Biblical doctrines are more important than most ministers and church members realize, because doctrine not only expresses our experiences and beliefs, doctrine determines our direction. Doctrine shapes our lives and our church programs. Doctrine to the Christian and to the church is what my bones are to my body. It holds the flesh together. I'd hate to have all flesh and no bones. That's what doctrine is to the Christian and to the church; what bones are to your body.

Biblical doctrine, I say, is more important than most people think. The preacher that neglects to teach sound doctrine weakens the church's membership. He works against unity. He invites instability into the fellowship. He lessens conviction and stalemates true progress in the church

The Doctrines of Grace.

I suppose that, at this point, many Baptists would not disagree with what I have said. That's fine. But I don't want to just speak in general terms. I wouldn't get into any trouble if I were content to speak about doctrine in general terms. Indeed, to keep the conversation at the general level would be meaningless. So I want to get specific. I want to talk about those doctrines that are the heartbeat of this Founders Conference. I want to talk about those doctrines that were believed by James P. Boyce, John A. Broadus, B. H. Carroll, John L. Dagg, Luther Rice, P. H. Mell, John Bunyan, Charles Haddon Spurgeon, William Carey, and Andrew Fuller. I want to talk about those doctrines expressed by the Philadelphia Convention from which the Southern Baptist heritage sprang. Certain doctrines were the foundation of their devotion. They were the foundation of their worship. They were the foundation of their witness and all of their service to Christ and His church.

Before I tell you what these doctrines were, let me make one very important point. It's simple but important, and I hope that every young preacher here will write it on his heart. The doctrines that I am about to talk about were believed and preached by these men, some of whom sealed their life's blood for it. If these teachings were true then, they are equally true tonight! The Bible has not changed! Men have minds like sieves; they change their minds and let things leak out and errors seep in to dilute the truth. But truth has not changed!

What doctrines am I talking about? I'm talking about the doctrines of grace—those doctrines that were set forth, defined and defended in the Synod of Dort and later expressed in the Westminster Confession of Faith and the London Confession of 1689. That's what I am talking about.

Now you can go around the Southern Baptist Convention and talk about doctrine, doctrine, doctrine and be fine, but if you start talking about these doctrines, you will not always be welcome.

What doctrines am I talking about? I'm talking about doctrines that set forth a God who saves people! Not a little god who just helps men save themselves. I'm talking about the doctrines that reveal the three great acts of the Triune God in recovering poor, helpless, lost men. Those acts are: election by the Father, redemption by the Son, and calling by the Spirit. All these acts are directed to the sinner, securing his salvation infallibly. I mean those doctrines that make salvation depend on the work of the Triune God and give all glory to God for the saving of sinners. There is no dividing of the glory for salvation between God and man.

Election by the Father.

I'm talking about the doctrines that see the Creator as the source and end of everything, both in nature and in grace; the doctrines which say history is nothing less than the working out of God Almighty's predetermined plan. These are doctrines which set forth a God who is sovereign in creation and sovereign in redemption, both in planning and perfecting it.

Redemption by the Son.

The doctrines of grace set forth a Redeemer who actually saves, not one who just makes salvation possible, but actually saves sinners by grace and by power. The Trinity works together for the salvation of sinners: the Father electing, the Son redeeming, the Spirit applying. Isn't that beautiful?

On the other hand, some people preach a frustrated God. They have the Father planning one thing, the Son purchasing something else, and the Spirit applying it somewhere else. I have enough trouble with understanding the Trinity (that's a heavy doctrine) but when I hear preachers that have a frustrated God it disturbs me even more.

Well, God saves sinners, and we cannot weaken this great truth by disrupting the unity of the work of the Trinity or by dividing the achievement of salvation between God and man! Jonah had it straight. He had to go into the belly of that fish for a few days to find out, but he discovered that salvation is of the Lord! (Jonah 2:9).

The doctrines of grace show the cross as revealing God's power, not his impotence. The cross is not just a place to make salvation possible with poor, little, impotent Jesus standing idly by waiting to see what these powerful, sovereign sinners are going to do. No, no. The cross is a place where God's power is manifest. It is a place that does not merely make salvation possible, but actually secures the salvation of sinners, fulfilling the words of the great evangelical prophet Isaiah, "He shall see the labor of His soul and be satisfied." (Isaiah 53:11). God is not confused, nor defeated. He is satisfied. The cross was not an accident. God did not take a vacation that day. He was the Master of Ceremonies.

William Cowper put it best in that hymn we all love, "There Is a Fountain Filled with Blood": "Dear dying Lamb, Thy precious blood shall never lose its power, till all the ransomed church of God be saved to sin no more." You know, some people sing this hymn all their lives and never see the doctrinal implications. How many of your people sing that hymn and don't have a clue what it means? It's your job to tell them. If you have been pastoring a church for a while and your people can still sing that hymn and not know what it means, there is something wrong with your ministry.

Called by the Spirit.

The doctrines of grace set forth a Holy Spirit whose work is not just an enlightening work; it is also a regenerating work. The Spirit takes away men's hearts of stone and gives them hearts of flesh. He renews their wills and by His own mighty power, He determines and causes them to come to Christ. Not against their will! They come most freely, being made willing by His grace and by His power. The Psalmist put it well when he said, "Blessed is that man whom Thou choosest and causes to approach unto Thee, that he may dwell in Thy courts" (Psalm 65:4). And in this sense, grace proves to be irresistible because it destroys the power to resist.

Toplady put it like this:

> What tho' I cannot break my chain
> Or e'er throw off my load,
> The things impossible with men
> Are possible with God.
>
> Who shall in thy presence stand,
> Or match Omnipotence;
> Unfold the grasp of thy right hand
> And pluck the sinners thence?
>
> Faith to be healed I fain would have,
> O might it now be giv'n;
> Thou canst, thou canst the sinner save,
> And make us meet for heav'n.

Although salvation is the sovereign work of God, let us not

suppose God's decision to save a man by a decree leaves him
passive or inert. Listen! The very opposite takes place! The
covenant of grace does not kill man; it doesn't regard him as
a tin can or a piece of wood or a robot. It takes possession of
the man! It lays hold of his whole being with all his faculties
and power of soul and body for time and eternity. It doesn't
annihilate his powers. It removes his powerlessness. It doesn't
destroy his will; it frees his will from sin. It doesn't obliterate
his conscience; it sets the conscience free from darkness. It
regenerates and recreates man in his entirety, renewing him
by grace, causing him to love and consecrate himself to God
most freely.

A DEVOTIONAL HOUSE

There's much more to say about a doctrinal foundation, but
I want to get on to the other side of the coin. I want now to talk
about the devotional house. The doctrinal foundation is just
that—a foundation, not the house. Many never get off the foundation. They make the foundation an end in itself. We stand
on the foundation to preach Christ and build the house. When
we preach Christ it should be from the doctrinal foundation.

As I said, many, of course, never get off that foundation;
they make it an end in itself. But God didn't send preachers
out just to preach election (although if you preach the Bible
you will preach the truth of election).

The things I want to say about a devotional house are
drawn from what I have observed in other ministers, what I
have read in biographies, but most of all, what I have drawn
from my own painful acquaintance with my own deficiencies,
my own temptations.

Hear the Scriptures: "Take heed therefore unto yourselves,
and to all the flock, over the which the Holy Ghost hath made
you overseers, to feed the church of God, which he hath purchased with his own blood" (Acts 20:28). Take heed to yourself—and to your doctrine.

John wrote to the church at Sardis (not John, but our Lord
Himself): "I know thy works, that thou hast a name that thou
livest, and art dead" (Revelation 3:1). You have a living name

but a dead experience. Though in name you live, you are dead! I ask you tonight: What is your experience? Is it a dead experience? Are you what people think you are? How awful to preach and witness an unreal Christ! You see, it is the devotional house that gives unction and power to the commission. Our Lord, in his great prayer in John 17, prayed that the Father would send those He gave to the Son into the world even as Christ Himself was sent. But that's not all He prayed. He also prayed that they would be sanctified. "Sanctify them through thy truth: thy word is truth" (John 17:17).

You see, and I'm convinced of this, if I cannot persuade myself and if you cannot persuade yourself to be holy, we will have no success with others. You must taste and see that the Lord is good. You've got to taste it yourself. You must bear the message that is written on your heart as did blessed John when he said:

> That which was from the beginning, which we have heard, which we have seen with our eyes, which we have looked upon, and our hands have handled, of the Word of life—we have seen it, and bear witness, and shew unto you that eternal life, which was with the Father, and was manifested unto us; that which we have seen and heard declare we unto you, that ye also may have fellowship with us: and truly our fellowship is with the Father, and with his Son Jesus Christ. (1 John 1:1-3).

That's reality! A thousand wonderful sermons on holiness will not counter a cold, carnal, careless life! A holy sermon is but for an hour, but a holy life is a perpetual sermon. Richard Baxter is a great example for ministerial diligence. He said, "A minister's life is the life of the ministry." Do you have that? I'm talking about the house now. A devotional house. A minister's life is the life of the ministry. The Christian's life is the life of his Christianity.

Devotional life is personal religion. This is strongly brought out in another letter from our Lord to the seven churches in Revelation, the letter to the church at Ephesus. Do you remember His word to that church in Revelation 2:1-6? Christ commends the Ephesian church for many things. He commends them for their service. He commends them for their sacrifice. He commends them for their suffering. Oh, how they suffered! He also commends them for their separation. They were ecclesiastically separated; they hated the works of the Nicolaitans. And yet He also said to them, But I have just a little problem with you, you have left your first love (Revelation 2:4).

This devotional life—you don't need a lot for it. You need a quiet place. That's not hard to find. Most of you can find a quiet place. You also need a quiet hour. That's harder to find. I'm going to tell you, I know it is quite hard to get a quiet heart, because I'm not blessed with patience. I don't seem to have time for anything. It's hard to get a quiet heart.

Note well Paul's deep personal hunger in his words to the church at Philippi:

> Yea doubtless, and I count all things but loss for the excellency of the knowledge of Christ Jesus my Lord: for whom I have suffered the loss of all things, and do count them but dung, that I may win Christ, And be found in him, not having mine own righteousness, which is of the law, but that which is through the faith of Christ, the righteousness which is of God by faith: That I may know him, and the power of his resurrection, and the fellowship of his sufferings, being made conformable unto his death; If by any means I might attain unto the resurrection of the dead (Philippians 3:8-11).

When I read this passage it does something to me. I've prayed this passage time and time again. Here he is, the great apostle Paul, who suffered much throughout his life—but as great as he was, listen to him express his personal hunger! "That I may know Him and the power of His resurrection and the fellowship of His suffering, being made conformable unto His death." That's not some carnal Christian trying to be a spiritual Christian! That's a spiritual Christian talking! Again, thinking of the devotional life and a concern for men, I know some people who want to take you to Romans 9 right away, and they are quick to point out, "Jacob have I loved, but Esau have I hated." They are quick to take you to God's words, "I will have mercy on whom I will have mercy." But these people miss the first four verses of Romans 9:

> I say the truth in Christ, I lie not, my conscience also bearing me witness in the Holy Ghost, That I have great heaviness and continual sorrow in my heart. For I could wish that myself were accursed from Christ for my brethren, my kinsmen according to the flesh: Who are Israelites (Romans 9:1-4).

Don't ever dive into the later verses in Romans 9 if these opening verses of the chapter haven't gripped your heart. If the first four verses don't mean anything to you, be quiet about the other verses! Paul said he had great heaviness and continual sorrow for the Jews! He wished he could be anathema from Christ for his brethren's sake. That's not the foundation, that's the house.

Did you ever try to comfort somebody that was jilted by his love? He had the engagement ring, the wedding set, and then he got one of those "Dear John" letters? He wants her, he wants her to love him, but it's past his reach. He can't turn a little button and require her to love him. He wants it with all his heart; it's grieving him; he's pained; he's deeply hurting, but the thing he desires is beyond his reach. But if he really desires love and he really wants it, that which is past his reach will have a profound effect on him. It will cause him some of this sorrow of heart and unceasing pain that Paul felt.

Listen, there are people in my church that have been sitting there for six years listening to me preach, and they are as lost today as they were the day I preached my trial sermon. My heart's desire is that they would know God!

I'm talking about Romans 9! There is a danger of covering truth with error. There is a danger in holding tenaciously to the truths of the doctrines of grace and then covering them with the error of "do nothing" because you can't save your people anyhow. Solomon said, "They made me keeper of the vineyard, but my own vineyard have I not kept" (Song of Solomon 1:6). My brothers, I am talking about keeping the vineyard now. I'm not talking about what you believe in your head. The New Testament corollary to the Song of Solomon passage I just quoted is 1 Corinthians 9:27: "But I keep under my body, and bring it into subjection: lest that by any means, when I have preached to others, I myself should be a castaway." In other words, watch the weeds in your own garden. Never be satisfied with being the instrument of grace without being the subject of grace.

WHAT DOES IT COST?

Well, what does all that cost? What does a doctrinal foundation cost? It costs a little study, a little seriousness with the Bible. What does a devotional house cost? It requires a disciplined life. I remember some years ago, there was a Scottish preacher, Glen Walters, who came to Westminster Seminary to speak. Some of us went down to hear him, and I remember part of his message as if it were yesterday. He was warning young preachers and doing it with a heart of passion. He warned them of laziness, looseness, levity and lethargy. When I got back home, I wasn't sure what lethargy meant so I got *Webster's* out. "Lethargy," it said, is "morbid drowsiness, profound sleep, a state of inaction or indifference." And Noah Webster listed a synonym, "languor." I had to look that up, and its definition was "inertia arising from soft living." That's what languor is—inertia arising from soft living.

What does it cost to be sound in doctrine? What does it cost to have a devotional house? It costs some of that pill my brother told me about once. You know the pill you take to lose weight? SELF-A-DENIAL. Some people think self-denial is putting away your sin, but that's not it. That's not optional. Setting aside indwelling sin is not optional; it does not come under the head of Christian liberty. What comes under Christian liberty are those things that are indifferent. Self-denial involves denying yourself the use of things that are legitimate. That's the character of the cross! Self-denial is subordinating every secondary point to the primary objective. It's singleness of mind!

Let me tell you something—whatever experience you have, whatever experience chills your fervor, dissipates your mind, diverts your attention or time or interest, that's the right eye that needs to be plucked and cast out. I'm not talking about the other extreme. An old Puritan said, "You render the bow useless by always keeping it bent." Some people need to take the string off the bow once in awhile. That's not what I am talking about. I don't mean have no diversions, but I do know this: The good men that I know who've gone down in usefulness did not succumb to the big dangers that kill most ministries—women, money or pride. They went down because of legitimate things—their family, their home, their position, sports, television. These are all legitimate things. I want to suggest a little test about building the devotional house. This is what it takes. Ask yourself: Do I have an idolatrous relationship with my family? Do I have an idolatrous relationship with sports and other legitimate things?

What has the supreme place in your affections? What is the dominating power of your life? What has the molding influence on your heart right now? When we think about legitimate things we need to remind ourselves of those three great biblical principles: Is it edifying to God, others and myself? Is it expedient? Does it manifest love for the lost and love for my weaker brother? Never have I known a case of apostasy from the faith, either in doctrine or practice, when the person has been committed to a prayerful and diligent study of God's Word.

Well, those great doctrines that I mentioned at the beginning—the doctrines of grace—if they do not produce and develop in you a true heavenly zeal, a holiness, a measure of self-denial, some evangelistic concern for the lost, you can be sure of one thing—they are not held right. They are not held in a biblical way; they are not Pauline.

You must have the doctrinal foundation, the things we believe concerning God and ourselves. But you also must have the devotional house. That comes from a disciplined life. When we have occasion to deal with infidels, skeptics, and the unconverted, we cannot operate with cold metaphysical reasoning or dry scientific arguments. We must deal with them by preaching the whole gospel and living the whole gospel! We must spread the whole gospel by life and lip. We must be living epistles. Living epistles, known and read, are better than all the scholarship in the world. Oh, for some men and women who know gospel truth and live gospel lives!

I pray that this conference will be used to sharpen us doctrinally and shape us devotionally and make us conformed to the image of Him whose we are and whom we serve.

2.
THE MAN IN ROMANS 7
FRED A. MALONE

1986 Southern Baptist Founders Conference

INTRODUCTION

THE seventh chapter of Romans is teeming with important pastoral and theological insights. A careful study of it yields help for Christians who are confused or despondent over their remaining sin. Paul's comments in 7:14-8:4 contain important practical principles which dispel many erroneous and superficial depictions of the Christian life.

Consider the following theological questions as we approach this text:

> 1. What is the function of God's law for the unconverted? What is the function of the law for the converted? And which law is God's law? The Ten Commandments; the Nine Commandments; more or less?

> 2. Is the man in Romans 7:14-25 regenerate, unregenerate?

> 3. If the man is a Christian, is this his entire Christian experience? Is it a periodic lapse from which he recovers? Or is this only a normal part of the daily Christian walk? Does one ever get out of Romans 7 into Romans 8?

> 4. Does the Christian have one nature or two natures? Is the Christian an old man and a new man butting heads? Or is the Christian one unified nature? Where does sin come from in the

Christian life? The old man, the new man, or the bodily flesh?

These vital questions, which have implications for evangelism, sanctification, pastoral care, assurance of salvation and more, must be answered in the light of the seventh chapter of Romans. Specifically, verses 14-25 should be studied.

THE NEW COVENANT CHRISTIAN

By delineating the biblical characteristics of a new covenant Christian and comparing them to Romans 7:14-25 we recognize that the kind of person which Paul has in mind is nothing less than a believer.

From Jeremiah 31:31-34 (fulfilled in Hebrews 8 and 10), we learn that a new covenant Christian has two main characteristics: 1) a new record and 2) a new heart. His new record through the work of Christ is described this way: "And their sins and their lawless deeds I will remember no more." And this is the new heart provided by the work of the Spirit: "I will put my laws upon their heart, and upon their mind I will write them." This is what it means to be born again by God's Spirit.

One of the major differences between the Sinai Covenant and the new covenant is this: God's law has been internalized in every covenant believer by the regenerating work of the Spirit. The Christian has a new attitude toward God's law as well as having the forgiveness of sins and the knowledge of God.

Which law? The same law which Jeremiah understood when he prophesied; the same law the Israelites understood when they heard the prophecy; and the same law the Jewish readers of Hebrews understood. It is the only law which God Himself wrote: the Ten Words, specifically called "the covenant" in Deuteronomy 4:13. Old Testament exegesis demands this understanding of law in Hebrews 8:8-12. Further, Paul illustrates his meaning of moral law in Romans

7:7-25 by describing the tenth of the Ten Words in 7:7. God's moral law has not changed between the old and the new covenants. Rather, it has been internalized in the heart of every new covenant believer.

In Romans 7:7-13, Paul uses the first person, past tense to recount his pre-conversion state. Before conversion, he was blameless as a law-keeper in his own eyes and before his countrymen (Philippians 3:6). However, when the Tenth Commandment came to his conscience, "Thou shalt not covet" (7:7), it killed Paul before God. It stirred up his heart, revealed coveting before God, and killed his self-righteous soul sometime before (or when) he looked into the righteous face of Christ on the Damascus road.

Romans 7:7-13 perfectly parallels Paul's past tense description of every Christian's pre-conversion state in 7:5: "For while we were in the flesh, the sinful passions, which were aroused by the law, were at work in the members of our body, to bear fruit for death." In Paul's unconverted state, God took the sword of His holy law and pierced his heart, unleashing all manner of filth and degradation which killed him before God. There was nothing wrong with the law. Paul was the problem.

In Romans 7:14-8:4, Paul moves to the first person, present tense. This is a perfect parallel to the shift from the past tense in 7:5 to the present in 7:6: "But now we have been released from the law, having died to that by which we were bound, so that we serve in newness of the Spirit and not in oldness of the letter." The shift from the past pre-converted state of every believer in 7:5 to the present converted state in 7:6 is illustrated by Paul's personal experience in 7:7-13 and 7:14-8:4 respectively. The man of 7:14-8:4 is described in the first person, present tense. He is Paul as a Christian.

What characterizes this Christian man? In 7:14, he believes that "the law is spiritual." In 7:22, he "joyfully concurs with [delights in] the law of God in the inner man." In 7:25, he serves the law of God with his mind inwardly and spiritually in a way that he did not before. The law, described as one

of the Ten Words in 7:7, is no longer written only on tablets
of stone. Now it is written on Paul's heart by the Holy Spirit.
This is exactly the description of the new covenant Christian
above.
I once asked Dr. J. I. Packer if he really thought that Paul's
use of the present tense in Romans 7:14-25 refers to Paul as
a believer. Dr. Packer's learned and scholarly reply to me was:
"Of course!" The man in Romans 7:14-8:4 is a Christian.

OBJECTIONS TO THIS VIEW

The main objection to this view argues that Paul uses a first
person, historical present tense in 7:14-25 to describe his pre-
Christian state. This position states that surely no Christian,
much less Paul, could say "I am carnal, sold under sin ...
nothing good dwells in me, that is, in my flesh ... wretched
man that I am! Who will set me free from the body of this
death" (7:14, 15, 25). Rather, the argument goes, this must
be the non-Christian of 8:7-8, who is hostile to the law of
God.
The problem with this objection is that it refuses to let 7:14-
25 be admitted as evidence for the Christian life. The man of
7:14, 25 delights in God's law and he is not hostile according
to the objection. This objection is presuppositional. This word
"carnal" is used in 1 Corinthians 3:1-3 of Christians caught
in particular sins and acting as "babes in Christ." How were
they carnal? They were arguing over the best preacher and
his baptism. They were not totally "carnal" as is popularly
conceived in the erroneous, so-called "carnal Christian"
doctrine. Neither were they treated as non-Christians
because they acted "carnal" or " fleshly" in this area of
division over preachers. There is no such thing as a totally
"carnal" Christian nor a totally "spiritual" one.
Paul's claim, "I am carnal, sold into bondage to sin," is explained by Horatius Bonar in the following way:

This is not the language of an unregenerate or

half-regenerate man. When, however, he adds, "I am carnal, sold under sin," is it really Paul, the new creature in Christ, that he is describing? It is; and they who think it impossible for a saint to speak thus, must know little of sin, and less of themselves. A right apprehension of sin; of *one* sin or *fragment* of sin (if such a thing there be), would produce the oppressive sensation here described by the apostle—a sensation 20 or 30 years progress would rather intensify than weaken. They are far mistaken in their estimate of evil, who think that it is the multitude of sins that gives rise to the bitter outcry, "I am carnal." One sin left behind would produce the feeling here expressed. Who can say, "I need the Word less and the Spirit less than I did 20 years ago"?[1]

The true Christian knows very well that every time he falls into sin that "The law is spiritual ... [but] I am carnal, sold into bondage to sin."

The same man who cries, "Wretched man that I am! Who will set me free from the body of this death [of this body of death]?" also cries, "Thanks be to God through Jesus Christ our Lord .... There is therefore now no condemnation for those who are in Christ Jesus" (7:25-8:1). This man is not convicted under the weight of his sin's condemnation. He is groaning as a regenerate man convicted under the weight of his remaining condition of sin. He cries out to Jesus Christ for help because he wants to be free from the condition of indwelling sin.

Granted, this is not all that there is to Christian experience. The man in Romans 7:14-25 is also the man in 8:1-4 at the same time. He repents (7:14-25) and believes (8:1-4) daily. Romans 7:14-24 is but one aspect of the mature Paul and every Christian. All Christians feel within the inward struggle

---

1 Horatius Bonar, *God's Way of Holiness* (Hertfordshire: Evangelical Press, 1979), 91.

against remaining sin. This is the man in whom God has written His law upon the heart and who mourns over his daily failures to please the God of grace. If you see yourself in 7:14-25, you are in the company of an Apostle of Jesus Christ.

PRACTICAL LESSONS

First, every Christian delights in the law of God in the inner man, agreeing that it is spiritual and good. To put it another way, you cannot have Jesus as Savior unless you bow to Him as Lord. By the very definition of the new covenant, the covenant law of Sinai (the Ten Words) is written upon the Christian heart by the Holy Spirit (Hebrews 8:8-12). While we may be ignorant in many ways of the implications of those laws, failing in many ways to keep them, still the saint has a disposition to walk in the commandments of God. And he is grieved and hurt and he mourns when he fails daily. Yet every mourner has this hope: "Blessed are those who mourn, for they shall be comforted."

No passage in the Bible better enables the saint to look within and know that he has come to know God (1 John 2:4). If he cannot say, "I do all the good that I wish," he can always say, "the good that I wish, I do not do." This is not excusing sin; it is dealing with the reality of remaining sin honestly and biblically. Pastors ought to open up God's Word in Romans 7:14-25 and read to struggling saints their spiritual condition so that they might know that God has not left them to hardness of heart. They must learn from 7:14-25 that repentance is still at work in their soul and is deepening. They must understand the Romans 7 comfort that "He who began a good work in you will bring it to completion in the day of Christ Jesus" (Philippians 1:16). This is not "negative preaching" and "joyless experience." It is the binding up of the broken-hearted. Should not every Christian say of every remaining sin: "I am carnal, sold into bondage under sin," yet "I delight after the law of God in the inner man?" Should not every Christian yearn to be free from this body of death?

Second, this passage teaches that sin remains in the new covenant Christian. Some have tried to teach that there is no sin in the new creature and have been driven to distorted views of the Christian's nature and life. This has resulted in the spiritual bondage of many. This error usually quotes Romans 7:16-17 as a proof-text to divorce the existence of remaining sin from the new creature: "So now, no longer am I the one doing it, but sin which indwells me." In other words, some say that when the Christian sins, he does not sin with his new heart. Rather, sin has a separated existence in the Christian. This path inevitably leads to irresponsibility, laxity, and antinomianism. This error takes several different forms.

One form of this teaching says that the Christian has two natures within—the sinful old man and the perfect new man.[2] Each is in a continual battle for supremacy. Sometimes the old man wins and sins. Sometimes the new man wins and does righteous acts. They butt heads in Romans 7:14-25. Theoretically, in this view, if one can "make Jesus Lord" and surrender to Him in an act of absolute faith and total commitment, He will take control and live His life through the new man. Some proponents of this view go so far as to claim that perfectionism (of a limited kind) is possible.

However, if this line of reasoning is correct, when (not if) the Christian sins, who is responsible for the sin committed? In this view, the new man cannot be responsible because he is "perfect" and "cannot sin." The true saint who has surrendered all to Christ has to figure out how the old man (or Satan) became stronger than Christ who controls the new man. How did Christ fail to prevent sin once He took over? This confused teaching causes doubt, despair, depression, lack of assurance of salvation, and even suicidal thoughts in some. Others will not examine themselves. They overlook sin since the new man is not responsible. The result is a prideful, arrogant, spiritual elite who will not deal seriously with God's

---

2 Charles Caldwell Ryrie, *Balancing the Christian Life* (Chicago: Moody Press,1969), 34-35.

law. Because of these errors the pastor who teaches holiness and obedience to God's law should expect despair from some and opposition from others.

Further, if this teaching is true, when one sins, who needs the forgiveness? It cannot be the new man for he is perfect and needs no forgiveness. It cannot be the old man, for he cannot go to heaven or repent or change.

Finally, who is it that makes progress against sin? Not the new man, for he is perfect. Not the old man, for he is beyond change. The two-nature view does not explain adequately the responsibility for sin in the Christian life, nor the need of forgiveness, nor the truth of progressive sanctification.

Another form of this view is that of David Needham in his work entitled *Birthright.* Needham rightly contends for a one-nature view of the Christian against the confusing two-nature view. However, he advocates that the new man is perfectly new and does not sin. Rather sin resides in the bodily flesh of the Christian in his brain patterns, thoughts, and desires.[3]

The problem with Needham's view is that he does not explain satisfactorily how one can separate one's sinful thoughts and desires in the bodily flesh from the new man's pure thoughts and desires, especially since the will of the Christian cooperates in the sin. Further, how can the sinful flesh overcome the perfect new man, yielding sin? The practical effect of Needham's one-nature plus sin-in-the-flesh is the same as the two-nature view. Either the Christian must deny full responsibility for sin when he sins or he must be cast into despair and confusion when he feels guilt for sin.

The truth that sin is found in the new man is revealed in Romans 7:14-8:4. Paul identifies sin as the culprit, but it is sin which indwells his new nature when he sins. "I do it," he says, over and over. Paul summarizes and clarifies himself in 7:25, saying: "So then, on the one hand, I myself with my

---

3 David Needham, *Birthright* (Portland: Multnomah Press, 1979), 36, 44, 49, 52, 65, 75, 78-79, 82-85, 125, 135, 139.

mind am serving the law of God, but on the other [I myself] with my flesh am serving the law of sin." "I myself" is the new man who serves both the law of God with his mind and the principle of sin with his flesh at the same time.

How can this be? Romans 6:6 explains: "Our old man was crucified with Christ, that our body of sin might be done away with, that we should no longer be slaves to sin." The two-nature view above tends to say that the old man is only judicially dead, that he still exists, and must be reckoned as crucified daily by faith. But Paul states that our old man—our former pre-Christian nature—dominated by sin and hostility to God and His law, has been done away with through the work of the cross and its application to us by the Holy Spirit in the new birth. Now the Christian is a new man: "If any man is in Christ, he is [not has] a new creature (2 Corinthians 5:17). "Since you have laid aside the old man with its evil practices, and have put on the new man who is being renewed..." (Colossians 3:9-10). No longer are Christians slaves to sin as when they were old men. Now they are new men, dominated by slavery to God and grace and righteousness and delight in His law. The old man is dead.[4] Our slavery to sin is broken. However, the sins which once dominated us remain in the imperfect new man.

This position is not popular. "Has God made the new man imperfectly? Has He done an imperfect job? But God does nothing imperfectly," say the objectors. This objection is full of emotion, not biblical argument. The fact is that God has chosen to make the new man so that the sinner's (not God's) sins remain. When Thomas Boston described regeneration in his *Human Nature in its Fourfold State,* he said:

> It is a universal change; "All things become new."
> It is a blessed leaven, that leavens the whole lump, the whole spirit, and soul, and body.... Yet

---

4 John Murray, *The Epistle to the Romans* (NIC) (Grand Rapids: William B. Eerdmans, 1968), 219-221.

it is but an imperfect change. Though every part
of man is renewed, there is no part of him perfectly renewed.[5]

John Murray clarifies this state in his *Principles of Conduct*:

The believer is a new man, a new creation, but he
is a new man not yet made perfect. Sin dwells in
him still, and he still commits sin. He is necessarily the subject of progressive renewal; he needs to
be transfigured into the image of the Lord from
glory to glory.[6]

Romans 7:14-25 teaches that the Christian has one nature
now dominated by service to God but in which remains sin.
His mind seeks to know God's ways, his affections seek to
please God, and his will seeks to obey God. Slavery to sin is
broken. But the existence of sin remains in his mind, his
affections, and his will so that "the flesh lusts against the
Spirit, and Spirit against the flesh, for these are in opposition
to each other, so that you may not do the things that you
please."

Who then is responsible for obedience to God's law? It is
the new man who loves Christ and seeks to keep His commandments. He cries out to Christ for help and deliverance
from his remaining sins by the power of the Spirit. He
cooperates with God's Spirit in obeying Christ and fighting
against sin.

Who then is responsible for sin? It is the new man who
grows in sensitivity to remaining sin, who is grieved when he
finds it each day, who confesses his sin and finds God faithful
and just to forgive him his sins and to cleanse him from all

---

5 Thomas Boston, *Human Nature in its Fourfold State* (London: The Banner of Truth Trust,
1964), 208-209.
6 John Murray, *Principles of Conduct* (Grand Rapids: William B. Eerdmans, 1981), 219. See 202-228
for a full explanation.

unrighteousness. He continues to repent of his sins and deepens his repentance. He continues to believe and when he sins, he flees to His Advocate, Jesus Christ the Righteous. He is not surprised by sin anymore. He knows he needs Christ daily. He knows that he must guard and keep his heart every day until he sees Christ in glory.

Romans 7:14-25 teaches that the Christian has one nature. A new work has begun, but it is not yet perfected. There is hope here for those who struggle with sin, yearning to be free of it. There is assurance here for those who mourn over their remaining sins. And there is joy here for convicted ones because "there is therefore now no condemnation for those who are in Christ Jesus" (Romans 8:1).

A third lesson which Romans 7:14-8:4 teaches is that the Christian life is not so much a stairstep by degrees to holiness nor a dramatic second experience, but it is an increasing dynamic of repentance and faith daily exercised. The Christian never gets out of Romans 7:14-25 into 8:1-4 because he always lives in both chapters! Faith increases on the upper plane though sometimes weaker and sometimes stronger as we live by grace. We increasingly depend upon the blood and righteousness of Christ. We increasingly love Him and seek to keep His commandments. Moreover, repentance deepens on the lower plane, though sometimes weaker and sometimes stronger as we discover more sins that need putting to death. Daily we mourn and cry out, "I am carnal." Daily we rejoice in the truth that "there is therefore now no condemnation for those who are in Christ Jesus." Daily we die to sin. Daily we live to righteousness. Daily by the Spirit we "put to death the deeds of the body that we might live." Daily we put aside anger, wrath, malice, and slander while the inner man is being renewed day by day.

Romans 7:14-25 and Romans 8:1-4 speak of the Christian from different aspects. The first is the Christian's inward battle against remaining sin and his imperfect obedience to God's law. The second is the Christian on the counterattack with faith in Christ and the Spirit's assistance to fulfill the righteousness of the law. Both aspects are a continual dynamic in Christian experience. This is a mark of true conversion. Romans 7:14-25 is our guide to point out remaining sins, to deepen our hatred of them, and to increase our heart love for Christ and His graces (for he that is forgiven much loves much). Romans 8:1-4 is our teacher to lead us in the paths of righteousness by the power of the Spirit. For "He condemned sin in the flesh in order that the righteousness of the law might be fulfilled in us, who do not walk according to the flesh but according to the Spirit." If you live in Romans 7 and find repentance deepening and live in Romans 8 and still flee to Christ for redemption and the Spirit's help to fulfill the righteousness of the law, it is enough.

CONCLUSION

Do not deny that Romans 7:14-25 is the Christian. You will despair if you are honest with your soul. Do not think that you will ever get out of Romans 7 into Romans 8. If you do, you will chase a figment of men's theological imaginations which will destroy your assurance of salvation and blind you to the work of God in your soul, or else it will foster a spiritual pride and antinomianism which may end up destroying your soul in hell. Rather, look into Romans 7:14-25 and see the work of God begun in the Christian soul and rejoice that He has not left you alone to harden your conscience against sin. Rejoice that the dominion of sin is broken and He is leading you into deeper repentance, increased holiness, and greater dependence upon Christ and joy in His free and ever available grace. Then do with your people what Bunyan did: "I preached what I smartingly did feel."

There will be a day when faith will be needed no more. For then faith will become sight in His beautiful face. And repentance will be no more, for the need of it will be gone—eradicated from our glorified soul. But until then we live in need of deepened repentance and increased faith every day as we endeavor to love Him and keep His commandments. Learn the lessons of Romans 7. "Happy are those who mourn, for they shall be comforted."

John Newton has expressed it well:

> I asked the Lord, that I might grow
> In faith, and love, and every grace;
> Might more of His salvation know,
> And seek more earnestly His face.

> I hoped that in some favoured hour
> At once He'd answer my request,
> And by His love's constraining power
> Subdue my sins, and give me rest.

> Instead of this, he made me feel
> The hidden evils of my heart;
> And let the angry powers of hell
> Assault my soul in every part.

> Yea more, with His own hand He seemed
> Intent to aggravate my woe;
> Crossed all the fair designs I schemed,
> Blasted my gourds, and laid me low.

> "Lord, why is this?" I trembling cried,
> "Wilt Thou pursue Thy worm to death?"
> "'Tis in this way," the Lord replied,
> "I answer prayer for grace and faith."

> "These inward trials I employ
> "From self and pride to set thee free;
> "And break thy schemes of earthly joy,
> "That thou may'st seek thy all in me."

3.
THE BIBLICAL DOCTRINE OF DEPRAVITY
PATRICK T. STEWART
1988 Southern Baptist Founders Conference

INTRODUCTION

WE live in a time in Southern Baptist life where theology is almost a dirty word. I often tease people by telling them, "If you want to scatter a covey of Southern Baptist preachers faster than any other way, discuss doctrine. They will fly." Frequently that is the case, but it appears to be changing. I rejoice in the grace of God that we are seeing a change in our own day. What an exciting time it is in which to live and praise our God and King!

There is the biblical doctrine of total depravity and then there is a teaching about total depravity that is anything but biblical. We need to be aware of that distinction. I am convinced that if you understand the condition of man as set forth in the doctrine of total depravity, you will welcome all the doctrines whose five points make up the acronym "TULIP" for they are interconnected. I came to grasp the subject of total depravity as I read God's Word. It was the connection between evangelism and the sovereignty of God that convinced me. I saw that I could not stand and rely upon anything but God's sovereignty and His work of grace within my life because I saw that I was totally depraved. It is only by God's mercy and His grace that I trusted in Jesus Christ. Of course I came to observe that this was true as well in the lives of others whom I would evangelize. Soon I began to adjust my methodology of communicating the gospel message. Understanding the biblical doctrine of total depravity will bring about a greater understanding and a greater reverence of our God and King. We desperately need that within our lives.

THE DEFINITION OF TOTAL DEPRAVITY

I would like for us to consider the biblical definition of total depravity. This will not be an exhaustive definition, but I hope it will be one that will have application in our hearts and minds as we consider God's Word. All the descendants of Adam have been affected and infected by Adam's fall. Each human being conceived by the seed of Adam and his descendants inherits a nature which is sinful. We must conclude that from God's holy Word. This is true of adults; it is true of young people; it is true of children. Yes, it is even true of infants. They are conceived in sin. Many of you will be familiar with the passages to which I will turn as we trace the thread of this doctrine through God's Word.

In Psalm 51:5 we read: "Behold, I was brought forth in iniquity, And in sin my mother conceived me." David was a sinner at the point of conception. The implications of that for us today, concerning many things, are apparent. I think of the ethical question of abortion. Certainly when we look at the Word of God there is no question that at the point of conception man is a sinner. But if he is a sinner, that means he is a living soul at that point. How can he be a sinner and not be alive? Man is a sinner and he is totally depraved at the point of conception. He is conceived in sin.

I've had some people tell me that babies are innocent. When I look at Scripture I do not find that kind of testimony. In Psalm 58:3 we find that "the wicked are estranged from the womb; these who speak lies go astray from birth." That does not sound like innocence to me. It sounds to me like infants as well as adults are in need of the mercy and grace of God. Praise the Lord that He provides it. We describe man's sinful condition as total depravity.

What Total Depravity Is Not.

We first must understand what total depravity is not. Total depravity does not mean absolute depravity—that man is as bad as he possibly can be. We know that. We have observed that in our own lives. We've observed it in the lives of non-Christians. Not every non-Christian, given the opportunity, kills or steals. Not every non-Christian does every evil thing that he possibly could do.

I remember, before I experienced the grace of God in my life, running around with my friends in Lawton, Oklahoma. We thought it was really neat to go to the store, buy balloons, and tie them to the sides of our bicycles. We would tuck them into the spokes and disturb everybody in the neighborhood as they made a noise like a motorcycle. But we ran out of money one day and we couldn't get the balloons. The desires of our hearts and our affections were for the pleasure of the noise and the experience, so we went into the store and stole the balloons. We had gotten away scot-free. We had pulled it off. We even did it once or twice after that but didn't make a habit of it. A few months later a friend of mine was called to the office at school. This was one of the boys who had stolen the balloons with me. There were a couple of police officers there. They were questioning him because they thought he had broken into a church, which was not true. But when they asked him if he had done anything wrong recently, the confession came forth. He didn't want to suffer alone so my brother and I and others were named also and we suffered together. My father was overseas at the time and my mother has never spanked me so hard in all my life as that time. What an embarrassment it was to her. It was sin. It was evidence of the fact that I was totally depraved and not concerned about the things of God. I did it. I forgot about it. The Lord reminded me of it. I stole the balloons, but I did not continually steal. I did not continually kill. I didn't do everything bad that I possibly could do, yet I was totally depraved in keeping with the scriptural definition of it. Total depravity is not that the lost sinner has no knowledge of God or no consciousness of right and wrong.

Many of us here are pastors and we have seen religious church-goers who are totally depraved. They do not know the Lord. They come to church and yet they do not give testimony or evidence that God has changed their hearts and lives. They come Sunday after Sunday, but until God changes their hearts we know that they are totally depraved.

The only reason total depravity in lost man is not absolute depravity is that the Holy Spirit of God still carries on a restraining ministry toward sinners. It is true that man is not as bad as he can be. But I am convinced, as I look at the description of man in God's Word, that if it were not for the restraining ministry of the Holy Spirit toward sin, the streets would be filled with murderers, rapists, and thieves. We could not even gather together because of it. That would be the condition. As difficult as things have become and as little morality as we see in this country, the fact that we can still walk about is only because the Holy Spirit of God still restrains sin. It would be impossible to live if it were not for the providence of God still overseeing His creation.

We see evidence of that in Genesis 6:3: "Then the Lord said, 'My Spirit shall not strive with man forever because he also is flesh. Nevertheless, his days shall be one hundred and twenty years.'" We know that God was bringing the flood at that time, but what we find here is that the Holy Spirit was striving with man. God was sharing with us that He will not always strive with man. What was the condition? Verse 5 tells us, "The Lord saw that the wickedness of man was great on the earth and that *every* intent of the thoughts of his heart was only evil *continually*" (emphasis mine). Folks, it can get worse than it is right now, and the Holy Spirit will still be restraining sin. God has not turned loose of His creation. We do not need to despair. He is the God who by His mercy and grace chose Noah. Genesis 6:8 says: "But Noah found favor in the eyes of the Lord." Did he find favor because he was a good man? No, he found favor because God had worked in his life. God was the difference in the life of Noah. It was the mercy and the grace of God. God was righteous and just in rewarding everyone else for their evil, and He would have been just as righteous and just to have judged Noah. But in His grace, love and mercy, He ministered to Noah.

What Total Depravity Is.

Next we need to understand what total depravity is. It means that the corruption of man's nature extends to every element and faculty of his being—his thoughts, his affections, his wants. Everything about him has been affected and infected by sin. The fall has overwhelmed him. He is characterized by it. Romans 1:18-23 says:

> For the wrath of God is revealed from heaven against all ungodliness and unrighteousness of men, who suppress the truth in unrighteousness, because that which is known about God is evident within them, for God made it evident to them. For since the creation of the world His invisible attributes, His eternal power and divine nature have been clearly seen, being understood through what has been made, so that they are without excuse, for even though they knew God, they did not honor Him as God, or give thanks, but they became futile in their speculations and their foolish hearts were darkened. Professing to be wise, they became fools, and exchanged the glory of the incorruptible God for an image in the form of corruptible man-and of birds and four-footed animals and crawling creatures.

Even though God has clearly revealed Himself in creation and nature, man's depravity still requires the grace and mercy of God. His thoughts, his affections, his wants all lead him away from God and into corruption. He needs God's mercy. It is his only hope.

Total depravity means that there is no spiritual good in man. Man does not meet God's standard. Any good in man can only be spoken of from an anthropocentric (man-centered) viewpoint because the minute we put our eyes upon the God of the universe, there is no good in man. He falls short at every point without exception.

Total depravity is the fact that by his very nature man does not meet God's approval. Man cannot meet God's approval, though he is totally responsible to the God of the universe to do so. He is responsible, but he does not desire to meet it and he cannot meet it. He is totally depraved. He is a sinner in the sense of the definition that we find in the Word of God.

TOTAL DEPRAVITY IN THE LIFE OF ADAM

Turn with me to Genesis. I want us to see next that total depravity was first evidenced in the life of Adam. I think in order to see a contrast we must first consider man's innocent state.

> So God created man in His own image; in the image of God He created him; male and female He created them. God blessed them, and God said to them, "Be fruitful and multiply; fill the earth and subdue it; and rule over the fish of the sea, over the birds of the sky, and over every living thing that moves on the earth." And God said, "Behold, I have given you every plant yielding seed that is on the surface of all the earth, and every tree whose fruit yields seed; it shall be food for you. Also, to every beast of the earth, to every bird of the sky, and to everything that moves on the earth, which has life, I have given every green plant for food," and it was so. Then God saw all that He had made, and behold it was very good [even with reference to man]. So there was evening and there was morning, the sixth day (Genesis 1:27-31).

God's creation was good. Man was good. He was in an innocent state. That is our reference point. Adam and Eve are the only two humans who have experienced innocence. Since then depravity has come from the seed of Adam, yet many talk today as if all of us are born innocent. We are not born and made as they were made.

> Then the LORD God took the man and put him in the garden of Eden to cultivate it and keep it. And the LORD God commanded the man, saying, "From any tree of the garden you may freely eat; but from the tree of knowledge of good and evil you shall not eat, for in the day that you eat from it you shall surely die." Then the LORD God said, "It is not good for man to be alone; I will make him a helper suitable for him." Out of the ground the LORD God formed every beast of the field and every bird of the sky, and brought them to man to see what he would call them. And whatever the man called each living creature, that was its name. And the man gave names to all the cattle, to the birds of the sky, and to every beast of the field. But for Adam there was not found a helper suitable for him (Genesis 2:15-20).

Of course we know that God made Eve. But what about this innocent Adam? What about this man that God said was a product of His creation? As I've read and studied the accounts in Genesis, I have become more and more convinced that Adam must have been the healthiest, physical specimen of a man ever to exist. He came from the very hands of God. We've been given a lie in our age. Our children have been lied to as well: "Ancient man, ignorant man? Inadequate man?" I don't believe so. I believe ancient man is intelligent man. I believe Adam was a healthy, physical specimen. He named all of the animals. God made him right. God gave him ability. God equipped him for the design and the purposes for which

He had created him. Adam was innocent. He was good. Adam enjoyed the creation of God. He understood it in its right perspective. He looked at it from God's viewpoint. He communed with the God of the universe.

However, when the fall occurred, how radically things changed! Many today are trying to convince us that man still has all the abilities of Adam. We don't find that taught in God's Word. What about man's fallen state here as we consider this evidence of total depravity? Turn to Genesis 3:6-12:

> When the woman saw that the tree was good for food, that it was a delight to the eyes, and that the tree was desirable to make one wise, she took from its fruit and ate. She also gave to her husband with her, and he ate. Then the eyes of both of them were opened, and they knew that they were naked; and they sewed fig leaves together and made themselves loin coverings. And they heard the sound of the LORD God walking in the garden in the cool of the day, and the man and his wife hid themselves from the presence of the LORD God among the trees of the garden. Then the LORD God called to the man and said to him, "Where are you?" So he said, "I heard the sound of Thee in the garden, and I was afraid because I was naked; and I hid myself." And He said, "Who told you that you were naked? Have you eaten from the tree of which I commanded you not to eat?"
>
> Then the man said, "The woman whom Thou gavest to be with me, she gave me from the tree, and I ate."

In verse 7 we see a radical change in the condition and the disposition of man—in his desires, affections and will. All of a sudden their eyes were both opened and they knew that they were naked. They sewed fig leaves together and made themselves loin coverings. Why the change? Now they were looking at things from a man-centered position rather than through the perspective of the God of the universe. Perversion had come. Instantaneously it had come, and they were trying to rely upon their own abilities to cover their guilt. We've been doing it ever since, haven't we?

In verse 8 we find that now, instead of communing with God and looking forward to the presence of God, man hides from God. What a radical change. Now he's moving away from God. Personally, I think this settles the total depravity question. The first man doesn't seek after God here; he hides from Him. This isn't a man who has only known a fallen state. This is a man who existed in innocence with the God of the universe, and he is hiding from Him because he has fallen. I don't understand the conclusions of men today who say that they see sinners seeking after God.

There's more here. We see that man now blames another for his sin. Man makes excuses for himself continually. He points the finger at others and will not look at himself, nor admit his guilt and sin. The cover-up continues. But this Adam, who had known innocence, goes even beyond that. He doesn't just say it is the woman, he says it is the woman whom *Thou* gavest to me. "It's your fault, God," that's what Adam is saying here. Total depravity brought out a radical change in man. Now man blames God. Certainly we find evidence of total depravity in the life of Adam. We need to remember that Adam had a reference point in that state of innocence in his life. Yet, still he sinned. He tried to cover his guilt. He hid from the God of the universe. He blamed another human being and then he blamed God for his sin. The fall of Adam has had, and continues to have, a devastating effect upon all of humanity. The example and evidence that we have in the life of Adam is still true. It is still happening.

TOTAL DEPRAVITY EXPANDED AND EXPOUNDED

We not only see the evidence of total depravity in the life of

Adam, but we also see the doctrine of total depravity expanded and expounded in the Scriptures. We find the depravity of man taught throughout God's Word. Consider Romans 3 where in verses 10-12, man's ability, resulting from his depravity, is assessed:

> What then? Are we better than they? Not at all. For we have already charged that both Jews and Greeks are all under sin. As it is written: "There is none righteous, no, not one; There is none who understands; There is none who seeks after God. All have turned aside; together they have become useless; There is none who does good, no, not one. Their throat is an open grave; With their tongues they keep deceiving; The poison of asps is under their lips; Whose mouth is full of cursing and bitterness. Their feet are swift to shed blood; Destruction and misery are in their paths; And the path of peace they have not known. There is no fear of God before their eyes" (Romans 3:9-18, NKJV).

In verse 3:10 is a statement concerning man's condition. "There is none righteous, not even one." Man is not right before God. He does not meet God's standard. He is not holy. There is none righteous. This is man's condition. We see in the first part of verse 3:11 concerning man's mind that there is none who understands. In his mind he is fallen and totally depraved. He cannot understand the things of God. His mind is darkened.

We see in the second part of verse 11 the truth about man's disposition or his desire. There is none who seek God. Man is not interested in pursuing God. He is just like Adam in the garden—he is still hiding himself and running away. He does not seek after the God of the universe. That's his sinful condition. It is what he is and what he does, by nature.

What do we find in the first portion of verse 12 concerning

man's spiritual direction? "They have *all* turned aside" (emphasis mine). They are not going the way of God. They don't want to go the way of God. The second part of verse 12 concerns man's value. What is his value in this condition? "Together they have become useless." What about man's good works (verse 12)? "There is none who does good." Do you understand that we are looking at the person of God and comparing man in light of the Holy God of the universe? Man doesn't seek after God. Man doesn't understand and man doesn't do good when it comes to comparing him to the God of the universe. Man is a sinner and totally depraved.

But if that were not enough, God in His revelation, through the Apostle Paul, decided to paint a portrait of man. We need to get a glimpse of the portrait. Our people need to see the seriousness of total depravity and the seriousness of sin. What is it that God sees? It is hard to perceive the portrait in all its depth. How does God see the totally depraved? According to verse 13 concerning the throat, God sees an open grave. Let your imagination go for a moment. Think of an artist on a canvas. He's painting the condition of a man. He's illustrating his sinful condition. When you think of the throat of man you see an open grave with all of its decay and rotting bones. That's the picture of man that God gives to us. What about the tongue? How does God, with His painter's brush, show the tongue? He says, "With their tongue they keep deceiving." He paints the tongue with deceit. In verse 13 we see that, as He paints the lips, He paints them poisonous. God describes the mouth as cursing and full of bitterness. This is the portrait of man. Totally depraved.

As God moves to the feet of the man, He paints them with bloodshed because "they are swift to shed blood." On the canvas God begins to paint the path that man walks in this totally depraved state—destruction and misery. As He continues, He looks at the knowledge of man, and He paints the knowledge of the totally depraved man without peace: "And the path of peace they have not known." If there is any question concerning man with reference to the God of the universe, when God comes to the eyes, the statement is clearly set forth in verse 18: "There is no fear of God before their eyes." They don't reverence God. They don't care about the things of God. They are in rebellion against the God of the universe. There is no fear of God in their eyes. Their eyes pursue the things of their own desires.

You say, "What about those who come to church or those who demonstrate some concern about God?" God is the one who tests the heart. God investigates the motives of man. If He says there is no fear or reverence toward Him in their eyes, we must accept it. Man is totally depraved, and the picture is serious. I know that it gets almost depressing as you study through these passages, but I think it is healthy and helpful for us to see the depth of what mercy and grace have done in our own lives. This was us. This was Pat Stewart in the past, and the God of the universe put fear in his eyes and reverence toward the Holy God. That which I did not want, did not seek and did understand, God provided. Yet we still hear the proclaimers of man's abilities, his freedoms and his spiritual desires. Many cry out that lost man is seeking God. How many preachers have you heard say, "Well the reason he is an alcoholic is that he is looking for God." "The reason he is perverted in how he deals with his sexual desires is that he is looking for God." Man is not seeking God! He is running away from God as fast as he can run and in as much perversion as he can seek. God's Word says, "No man seeks after God."

There are multiple other Scriptures that proclaim man's nature. In Ephesians 2:3 we find the statement: "By nature we are children of wrath, even as the rest." By nature! That is the way you and I were before we experienced the grace of God and before He had mercy on us. Ephesians 2:1 tells us: "And you were dead in your trespasses and sins." That was our condition— dead! We were in sin against the Holy One. Verse 3 tells us that we were "indulging the desires of the flesh and of the mind." Why? Because we were by nature children of wrath. We indulged sinful desires because we were totally depraved. We were fallen in Adam.

The Scriptures reveal the condition of man's depraved will. The battleground in our day around the gospel is being focused right here at this point. This is the battleground—the condition of man's depraved will. Some say that sin has infected and affected every aspect of man except his sovereign will. The evidence doesn't demonstrate that, but men so badly want to believe it that they continue to preach it and proclaim it. The first objection that we get when we talk to people about the sovereignty of God, His mercy and grace and the work of Christ, is "What about the free will of man?" They don't mean free agency and free will in the way that you and I do. They mean with every option open to them. They want to be in a state of innocence though they are not and cannot be. But that is what they are espousing.

Let's look at some passages in the gospel of John. It took me a number of years to realize that I didn't have to go to Ephesians 1 to share with people about God's sovereignty and His work and man's need and the condition of man's will. John 1:12-13 says of man's will: "But as many as received Him, to them He gave the right to become children of God, even to those who believe in His Name." Then it is as if the Holy Spirit said, "Okay, John, there is going to be some confusion over this so we need a little bit of commentary here." Some folks are going to misunderstand the truth. How were they born? "Not of blood, nor of the will of flesh, nor of the will of man, but of God." How clear can you be? Man does not have a sovereign will.

But, if man's will in exercising faith is not what brings about regeneration, what does? In John 3:3 we find Jesus' answer to Nicodemus, "Truly, truly I say to you, unless one is born again he cannot see the kingdom of God." Nicodemus was confused by this answer. "That which is born of flesh is flesh and that which is born of Spirit is spirit" (John 3:6). Why do men think that a will born out of flesh will pursue spiritual things? Only a will that is transformed in spirit and receives the new birth, that experiences regeneration, will pursue the holy things of God. Jesus was making it clear to Nicodemus.

You would think by the teaching that goes on today that everyone is willing to be saved. Jesus didn't indicate so. He saw the impact of depravity and understood man's fallen nature. Today we talk to men, and they don't see Jesus physically in their presence, but I want you to observe the statement of Jesus with men who were looking at him face-to-face as He spoke to them:

> And the Father who sent Me has born witness of me. You have neither heard His voice nor seen His form, nor does His word abide in you, for you do not believe Him whom He sent. You search the Scriptures because you think that in them you have eternal life. And it is these that bear witness of Me. And you are unwilling to come to Me that you may have life. I do not receive glory from men, but I know you, that you do not have the love of God in yourselves. I have come in My Father's name, and you do not receive Me; but if another shall come in his own name, you will receive him. How can you believe when you receive glory from one another, and you do not seek the glory that is from the one and only God? (John 5:37-44).

They did not seek God's glory. They were unwilling to hear Jesus and come to Him. That's where man's will is—captivated by his depravity and under the dominion of his fallen nature. But there is more.

Does depraved man seek Jesus for any reason? Certainly not in terms of a relationship with Him or with reference to the glory of God. But otherwise the answer is yes. Man will seek after God for reasons other than spiritual ones. Notice what Jesus said in John 6:24-26:

> When the multitude therefore saw that Jesus was
> not there, nor His disciples, they themselves got
> into small boats and came to Capernaum seeking
> Jesus, and when they found Him on the other
> side of the sea they said to Him, "Rabbi, when did
> you get here?" Jesus answered them and said,
> "Truly, truly I say to you, you seek Me not be-
> cause you saw signs [evidence of His deity, His
> person and His power] but because you ate the
> loaves and were filled."

Jesus let them know that their motives were wrong.

I had a professor at Bible college who once said, "All they
wanted was some more Big Macs and that's all that Jesus was
to them—One who could give them fast food." But they were
not interested in His person, His power, His work, or His
salvation. They did not have concern for that. They wanted
more food. They sought after Him, but it was for the wrong
reason.

Who of the depraved will have eternal life? In John 6:36-40
Jesus said:

> But I said to you that you have seen Me and yet
> do not believe. All that the Father gives Me shall
> come to Me, and the one who comes to Me I will
> certainly not cast out. For I have come down
> from heaven, not to do My own will, but the will
> of Him who sent Me. This is the will of Him who
> sent Me, that of all He has given Me I lose noth-
> ing, but raise it up at the last day. For this is the
> will of My Father, that everyone who beholds the
> Son and believes in Him may have eternal life;
> and I Myself will raise him up at the last day.

Who is going to be raised? The ones believing. Who are the
ones who are going to be believing? The ones that God has
given. Jesus will not lose a single one of them. They are the
ones who will have eternal life. They are the ones who have

experienced the grace of God in their hearts and lives as God works in them. How is it that the depraved come to Jesus since they will not seek after Him? Why do they come to Him? John 6:44 tells the story: "No one can come to Me unless the Father who sent Me draws Him; and I will raise Him up on the last day." How do the depraved come to Jesus? By the power and the drawing of the God of the universe. Because they are depraved sinners, they will not seek after God. They follow their own affections in their hearts and they are unrighteous. They do not love our Jesus.

TOTAL DEPRAVITY AND PRACTICAL APPLICATION

The doctrine of depravity does have practical application to our understanding and conduct. If you want your theology to be on target, you had better be right in your understanding of total depravity.

The Priority of Regeneration to Faith.

This doctrine is practical in addressing the most important issue confronting us today regarding the gospel. It should affect our understanding of the relationship of regeneration to faith. It must affect it. A spiritually dead man does not exercise a faith which, by his nature, he does not and cannot possess. That is all there is for that subject. He does not possess it. It is outside of his nature to have it.

Many self-acclaimed evangelists today are masquerading as "Calvinist" or "Calvinistic" or as those who believe in total depravity, when in reality they are nothing but semi-Pelagian to the core. They say faith has become that one small contribution that man makes in bringing about regeneration. But since when can a spiritually dead man conduct himself spiritually? It is a work when it is presented in that way. There are brethren whom we love and appreciate who have taken that position. Luther would cry for another Reformation. We need a modern-day Luther and we need a new Reformation. This is our battlefield today. When you understand the doctrine of total depravity you must understand the necessity of regeneration to faith.

Many in Southern Baptist ranks have become Roman Catholic in their concept of the will of man because they have missed out on the doctrine of sin and total depravity. They don't even understand it. Luther said that *The Bondage of the Will* was his most important work. I want to quote a section of Dr. Packer's introduction which touches the heart of the matter. The context is Luther dealing with Erasmus. Dr. Packer shares his own insight concerning the pointedness of the difference between semi-Pelagianism and Pelagianism and how semi-Pelagianism is really worse than Pelagianism. The excerpt from Packer's introduction begins with Luther saying,

> "This hypocrisy of theirs results in their valuing and seeking to purchase the grace of God at a much cheaper rate than the Pelagians. The latter assert that it is not by a feeble something within us that we obtain grace but by efforts and works that are complete, entire, perfect, many and mighty; But our friends here tell us that it is by something very small, almost nothing, that we merit grace. Now, if there must be error, those who say the grace of God is priced high, and account it dear and costly, err less shamefully and presumptuously than those who teach that its price is a tiny trifle, and account it cheap and contemptible." To be an inferior kind of Pelagian in this way, however, is not, as Luther points out, to approach any nearer to the Augustinian position; it is merely to advertise to the world that, in addition to holding an unwarrantably high opinion of the natural powers of man, one also holds a shockingly low opinion of the moral demands of God's character.

We need to grasp that. Listen closely as I continue to read:

The semi-Pelagian compromise, says Warfield, amplifying Luther's thought at this point, "while remaining Pelagian in principle yet loses the high ethical position of Pelagianism. Seeking some middle-place between grace and works and fondly congratulating itself that it retains both, it merely falls between the stools and retains neither. It depends as truly as Pelagianism on works, but reduces those works on which it nevertheless depends to a vanishing point." Pure Pelagianism is bad enough, for it tells us that we are able to earn our salvation, and this is to flatter man; But semi-Pelagianism is worse, for it tells us that we need hardly to do anything to earn our salvation, and that is to belittle salvation and to insult God.[1]

That is what is being proclaimed today in most of our pulpits across America. Many have set forth faith as that little thing that man does in bringing about regeneration. "God has done all that He can do, and now if man will just add his faith to it, he will be changed." Luther would call them an Erasmian Roman Catholic to their face. According to Luther, there is a line of truth that exists, and wherever the battle rages along that line of truth, to not stand in the gap at that point is compromise. When the battle rages over inerrancy and infallibility, will we have the courage and integrity to stand in the gap at that point? But if the battle rages over the truth of the necessity of regeneration to enable faith, in keeping with the biblical doctrine of total depravity, we must stand at that point and give testimony, declaring the depravity of man and proclaiming the grace and mercy of God as being man's only hope.

Total Depravity and Evangelism.

In a practical sense, the doctrine of total depravity also

---

1 J. I. Packer, Foreword to *The Bondage of the Will,* by Martin Luther (Cambridge: James Clarke and Co., Ltd., 1973 reprint), 50.

should affect the way we witness. If your hope in sharing the gospel with a lost man is in his response, your hope is ill-placed. But when you understand the doctrine of total depravity you understand that he is dead. He is totally depraved. Though there are many people who get "responses" they get dead responses. There is no life in them. It is demonstrated over and over again in our churches. There may be hundreds going in the front door but there are equal hundreds going out the back.

I have seen it right here in a local association of which I was a member for six years. The population in this county and in this association more than doubled in the last twenty years. But the number of Southern Baptist churches remains the same. The number of members in those churches is only different by a thousand, though there have been hundreds and thousands who supposedly have trusted in Jesus Christ during that time. There is "something rotten in Denmark" and we better start facing it. The methodology must be checked. It is bankrupt and it's killing us. As we witness we must be motivated by the very person of God and hope in the mercy and grace and power of God. He is our *only* hope as we go out with the gospel upon our lips. Our hope should certainly not be in the will or the response of a totally depraved man.

The Weight of Our Depravity.

The third practical item is that we need to consciously perceive the seriousness of our own previous fallen and totally depraved condition. Total depravity is so serious that an angry, righteous, and wrathful God sent His own Son to stand in the place of His elect. The price was high. God spared not His own Son. Jesus Christ the Righteous came, and the weight of our sin and God's wrath fell upon Him. He sweat drops of blood. As they hung Him on the cross, He suffered on our behalf. He shed His precious blood. The sun was darkened. The infinite God-man was suffering and groaning and dying on a cross because our sin is so serious and so weighty. Christ died for us.

We need to understand total depravity because it gives us a grasp of the death of Jesus Christ. It helps us perceive the glory of our God. May our understanding of this doctrine lead us into right doctrine in other areas. May it lead us into right practice as we go out and share the gospel. And, oh, may it lead us into right worship as we focus upon our God, our King, our Lord and Savior, who shed His blood on the cross on our behalf. He is the author and the finisher of our faith. May our hope and our worship rest in Him and in His power and His strength.

4.
THE ATONEMENT—PART 1.
ROGER NICOLE
1991 Southern Baptist Founders Conference

INTRODUCTION

I PLAN to make certain observations today concerning the nature of the atonement in its place in the total orbit of the Christian faith. Tomorrow I would like to discuss something about the scope or extent of the atonement and attempt to validate the proper reformed doctrine of definite atonement.

THE CENTRALITY OF THE ATONEMENT

The first remark about the nature of the atonement is that it is indeed at the very center of the Christian faith. This centrality can be proven perhaps in three different ways.

The first way is to go through the Scripture of God and to see what kind of reference there is to atoning sacrifice. This surely is emphasized strongly in the Old Testament with the whole sacrificial system. The prophets, who at times protested against abuses in the sacrificial system, never meant to set aside the prescriptions that God had given, but protested against improper attitudes of people who were going through the motions, so to speak, without having a real allegiance to God. There were "no-lordship" worshipers in that day, and the prophets had good occasion to protest against them.

When we come to the New Testament we notice the enormous amount of space given by the Gospels to the death of our Lord Jesus Christ and His resurrection. In fact, I once counted the number of pages discussing the last week of Christ's life compared to the first thirty-three years of his life.

I counted that two-fifths of the pages of the four Gospels are dedicated to the last week of Jesus' life, from His entrance into Jerusalem through His resurrection. When you examine the epistles you find again, that the death and the resurrection of Jesus Christ have taken the central place. There are not many allusions to events in His life. Instead, what is put to the fore, in a very pungent manner, is the death and the resurrection of Jesus Christ, so much so that Paul could say, "I have determined not to know anything among you, save Jesus Christ and Him crucified." How could you have something hit a bull's eye more than this? It definitely indicates that Paul understood well that the death and resurrection of Christ, His atoning work, was the very heart of the gospel that he was presenting.

Even in the book of Revelation the Lord Jesus appears again and again as the Lamb, and that once more bears witness to His sacrificial work. So, if you examine the Scripture, you will find that there is a red thread that goes from Genesis to Revelation which emphasizes the principle of sacrificial service, the principle of salvation by grace through faith in Jesus Christ our Lord, particularly through His death and resurrection.

Another way of showing the centrality of the atonement is to show how closely it ties in with many other doctrines of Scripture. In this you could open a well-organized systematic theology and take the headings of all the main chapters. I would be prepared to show you how each of those chapters has a close relationship to the death of Christ, I would not do that here. However, I am letting you know that I have in fact done this, and therefore, it is not an idle boast that I am presenting. For the sake of brevity I will not go into that.

The third way of proving the centrality of the atonement is to reflect upon the nature of the Christian faith. We can summarize it as follows: Christianity is the revealed, redemptive religion centering in the mediatorial ministration of the God-man, Jesus Christ, the second person of the Holy Trinity. Created in the image of God, humanity has, in the Father's gracious plan, a glorious destiny, forfeited by sin, but restored and even enlarged in Christ for the redeemed, through the work of the Holy Spirit.

Now, I am not attempting to summarize all of the Christian faith in two sentences like this, but it represents some of the major elements, at any rate, that you would find in our faith. Surely the redemptive color of Christianity is something that must be underlined. Christianity is a redemptive religion; therefore, it is a religion that addresses itself to people who have the consciousness of being lost. They do not expect to climb by their own power, but do expect an administration of God's grace to lift them up. That is what is characteristic of Christianity, but then it is also the revealed, redemptive religion. Other religions may attempt to be redemptive, but they do not provide redemption, while the Christian faith does provide the redemption that God Himself has appointed. Therefore this redemption is at the very heart of everything that is Christian.

So much for the centrality of the atonement.

THE VARIETY OF LANGUAGE USED TO DESCRIBE THE ATONEMENT

The second point I would like to make relating to the nature of the atonement is that, in the Scripture, we have quite a variety of language that is used in order to describe what it is that Jesus has done for us. I find that you have, at least, five major lines of approach, all of which must be validated in order to have a proper, biblical doctrine of the atonement.

The Language of Friendship.

The first is the language of friendship, or proper relations with others. Here we have the word "reconciliation" that comes so strongly to the fore in Romans 5 and then again in 2 Corinthians 5. In Romans 5, in two verses, we have the words "reconcile" and "reconciliation" three times. In 2

Corinthians 5:18-20, in three verses, we have it five times. These are the most important passages in this respect. Reconciliation is that process whereby two parties, who were at first in harmony, but who have severed their relation of affection, are brought back together into a normal relation of affection and mutual confidence. Here indeed, the one who has a major grievance is not we humans, but God. Therefore, reconciliation relates particularly to the process whereby God, instead of visiting us in His just anger against our sin, has found a way, without damage to the majesty of His own nature and of the law which reflects His nature, to bring us back into a position of fellowship through Jesus Christ our Lord.

This is reflected by the word "propitiation" that fits in that same category. Propitiation is the act by which someone who is angered is brought back to peace, is appeased, so that His anger is set aside, and he or she can deal with another person in terms of friendship and acceptance instead of anger. The anger of God, the wrath of God, is a just wrath and hatred of our sins. It is necessary that this wrath, and distaste and disgust of God at our sins, should be expressed. And it is expressed indeed for the redeemed in the substitutionary work of Jesus Christ who has accepted to take our place as sinners, to bear our punishment and, therefore, to satisfy the full demands of the law.

The Language of Sacrifice.

The second form of language used to describe the nature of the atonement is the language of sacrifice or ritual, or we might say the language of the laundry. This involves the notion of purification, or washing, or being cleansed by blood, of being made acceptable by an erasing or removal of the stain that sin has caused upon us.

Here again we have a very strong emphasis in Scripture. The word "blood" is used 297 times in the Old Testament, and some 100 times in the New. In some cases, this does not relate to our relationship with God, but about half of the passages do relate to the approach of the worshipper to God. The blood is a sign of a life forfeited because of sin, and cleansing is an indispensable condition for an appropriate approach to God whose eyes are too pure to see evil (Habakkuk 1:13).

The whole sacrificial system in the Old Testament bore witness to this, and the New Testament never expresses the slightest disrespectful comment with regard to the Old Testament sacrifices. What has come closest to it might be some statements in the Epistle to the Hebrews. That epistle magnifies the Old Testament as a revelation from God and does not in any way disparage what was done in the past. The author of that epistle says, "without the shedding of blood there is no forgiveness," (Hebrews 9:22) but he also makes the comment that the blood of bulls and goats could never be sufficient (Hebrews 10:4) because the value of these animals, even in numerous quantity, could never amount in total to the value of one single human life. Therefore, that offering is manifestly insufficient to replace a life forfeited by sin. It was necessary that the Lord Jesus Christ Himself, God incarnate, should offer Himself.

There the value is infinite. He alone is able to cover a multitude of humans, all the human race, if He so intended, and a thousand races beside if He intended so. The question, however, remains. For whom did he intend to offer Himself? That will be considered in the second part of this study.

So the language of ritual sacrifice, or if you want, the laundry, is very prevalent in Scripture because there is a cleansing, something that is red becomes white. This is language that is very important for our understanding of the conditions under which we can approach God and expect acceptance from Him.

The Language of the Law Court.

Then there is the language of the court of law. Here God is

presented as a judge. We as His creatures, created with responsibility and the ability to make decisions in view of motives, are called upon to give an account unto God of what we have done with this great gift that He has given to humanity. If we are to give account unto God, in relation to our performance, we are all undone for the Scripture says, "by observing the law no-one will be justified" (Galatians 2:16). There is no way in which we can escape the judgment of God, if there is not an intervention that God Himself provides, by which He would rescue us from the inevitable consequences of our own sinfulness.

It is in this point especially that our Lord has come to take upon Himself the sanctions of the law against us and provide for us the ability to be declared "not guilty." This is what the word "justify" means. It's a declaration of "not guilty." It is not a statement about our present condition. But it is a declaration about our relationship to law and to God as the lawgiver and the One who will be the judge of all humanity (Genesis 18:25).

It is a wonderful thing to know, that God will be the judge because, so very often, we run afoul of the judgment of others. Even our human courts, established with great care to preserve the rights of the accused, may fail in various ways. But with respect to the judgment of God there will be no excuses, there will be no lawyers, there will be no legal loopholes, through which anybody can escape. There will be no suspended sentences, there will be no probation, there will be no release, but everything will be done in a perfect manner, according to the strictest standards of justice. So everyone will receive his or her come-uppance. Except, of course, those whose burden has already been born in this respect by the Lord Jesus Christ. They will be acquitted on account of their Savior, their Substitute.

The Language of the Marketplace.

The next form of language used is that of the marketplace.

Here the Greek New Testament is very emphatic. There are three different roots from different Greek verbs which are used to indicate that there has been a purchase and that this purchase has been very costly. The term "redemption" comes here.

"You were bought at a price" (1 Corinthians 6:20; 7:23). "For you know that it was not with perishable things such as silver or gold that you were redeemed from the empty way of life handed down to you from your forefathers" says the apostle Peter (1 Peter 1:18). So the purchasing, by God of our lives, and the cost incurred by our Lord Jesus Christ in order to effect this purchase, are brought into sharp focus in this kind of language.

It is difficult for us to understand substitution at the legal level. Our courts do not accept substitution. If somebody has committed a crime, and in compassion I say to the judge, "Please, judge me and punish me instead of that person," the judge is bound to respond, "No sir, we cannot accept your offer. We've got our man. You go home and think further on the importance of the judicial system in which it is the guilty party that gets punished and not somebody else." So in the case of Christ, there is something that is unusual, not reflected ordinarily in human affairs. Therefore, substitution is difficult for us to understand at this level, and some people have thought it repugnant.

But at the level of payment, substitutions can easily be arranged. If I am in arrears on my rent, and some gracious person comes forward and says, "I'll pay your rent for you," the landlord has no right to say, "You are still in arrears." The moment the money has come into his pockets I am in order. Substitution is very easy at the payment level. Perhaps some of us have realized that to our own detriment. Some of our children may have made expenses for which we had to pay!

So the Scripture does emphasize the payment principle, both in order to show us a range of life in which substitution is common and also to bring to the fore in a special way the enormous cost unto God of the redemptive process.

The Language of the Battlefield.

In the fifth place, I say the work of Christ is represented in the language of the battlefield. That is, there is a great struggle between Satan and ourselves, and Jesus Christ has come as our Champion. In one place He is called "the Captain of our salvation" (Hebrews 2:10, NKJV). That does not mean that His rank was just that of a captain, and that there were colonels and generals over Him. Rather, it means that He, as a Captain, leads His troops into the fray.

Our Lord has taken the place of maximum vulnerability for us, in order to fight against Satan, and at one point, He said, "I saw Satan fall like lightning from heaven" (Luke 10:18). In Colossians 2:15, the apostle Paul emphasized that Jesus Christ "disarmed the powers and authorities, He made a public spectacle of them, triumphing over them by the cross." So our Lord has used the language of battle in order to show us that, in the great struggle engaged between the forces of God and the forces of evil in this world, He has enlisted us in this battle in which He Himself has taken such a vigorous part.

Now, if we are to have a well-rounded biblical doctrine of the atonement, every one of these elements must be validated. If there is one place in which our presentation fails to round it up like that, then we have a truncated view of the atonement, which lacks the full advantage of the biblical presentation. It would appear to me that God has done this precisely in order to concentrate our attention on the great deeds of the Lord Jesus Christ, so that not only one line of illustration be used, but a variety of lines of illustration, in order to make us understand what it is that God has done for us.

I would like to read to you a statement by Alexandre Vinet about this subject, and I translate it from a very long French sermon which he wrote on "looking to Jesus." He says,

> One should not say: "Together with many other truths, we find this one in the Gospel"; One

should not even say: "This truth is the most important one of the Gospel"; one should say "This truth is the Gospel itself," and all the remainder of the Gospel, if I may use this expression, is either the shape that this doctrine assumes, or its translation, or its applications. This truth is everywhere present in the Gospel as blood is everywhere present in the human body. Everything reminds of it, everything reproduces it in the eyes of whoever has understood this primary truth; even where any other would not even suspect it's presence, he sees it, he feels it: wherever he may look, whatever detail he may examine, whatever application he may consider, everywhere he meets, and recognizes the cross ... Erase from the Gospel, I do not say the cross, but the evangelical meaning of the cross, and you will make these eighteen centuries absurd or impossible."[1]

THE RELATION OF THE ATONEMENT TO THE DOCTRINE OF SIN

The doctrine of the atonement is very closely related to the doctrine of sin, because the atonement is precisely God's message to give us deliverance from sin. In order to understand the nature of deliverance we need also to understand the nature of the predicament.

People who think lightly of sin think also lightly of redemption. If I lose a quarter in three inches of water, it is not difficult to pick it back up, but if I drop it from a ship in the middle of the Atlantic, and it goes down six thousand feet or more, then there is real problem, and most people will say it isn't worth picking up. It would be too great an enterprise.

So I say, if you have a weak doctrine of sin, you will have a

---

1 Alexandre Vinet, *Etudes Et Méditations Evangéliques*, II (Lausanne: Payot, 1952), 248, 255 (translation mine).

slighting of the doctrine of redemption; if you have a realistic doctrine of the enormous gravity of sin, by that very fact, you will be compelled to have a very serious view of the doctrine of the atonement. Many of the popular doctrines of the atonement are faulty precisely at that point—people have not stopped to think seriously of the gravity of sin.

This is marvelously expressed as early as Anselm of Canterbury, who lived in the eleventh century. In his great work, *Why Was God Made Man?* the master makes this remark with respect to the people with whom we have a dialogue. He says, "You have not yet considered the fearful gravity of sin" (I. xxi). You just have six words there in Latin, but it goes like a hammer to destroy ineffective views of the atonement. It is like the ball of the man who is razing a building; it just sweeps away inadequate views. If we want to have a truly biblical doctrine of the atonement, we will have to have a biblical notion of the gravity of sin.

Now, it is true that the thought of sin and the language of sin offends some people. Perhaps there may be ways in which, in an attempt not to offend at first, we may circumvent being too direct about it. I know this is the approach of Dr. Schuller, who avoids the language of sin in his radio and television ministry, and the reason for that, as he said to me in person, is not that he does not believe in sin, but he thinks that people will turn off their TV if he is talking that way. So he attempts to accommodate himself to the taste and situation of his hearers.

Now some accommodation is certainly desirable and we need, when we address anybody, to take cognizance of the audience we address. Otherwise, we don't communicate and what we say goes for naught. At the same time, personally, without wanting to be unduly critical of Dr. Schuller, my impression is that this particular method of handling the matter has been damaging to the total gospel presentation that he has. And there have been people watching or listening who may not sufficiently comprehend their predicament. He is a little bit like a doctor who has diagnosed cancer, and says, "I think you have a little pimple on your forehead."

I think you need to awaken people to the fearful gravity of sin. Surely if you read the newspaper it is not difficult to find evidence. A lot of people read the newspaper and see the stories of heinous crimes and they say, "I am not like that." But one way in which the matter can be stated is, "You have in your pocket the nails that put Christ on the cross." People ought to understand that. The root of sin is right there in the best living people, in the most honored citizens, in good husbands and obedient children. We all have the same dastardly orientation which calls for a drastic remedy. So we cannot provide a proper description of the glory of the atonement if we have not understood the depths of our predicament as sinners.

THE RELATIONSHIP OF THE ATONEMENT TO ADAM

I would like to make a comment about the relation of the atonement to Adam. This is grounded particularly in Romans 5. In that chapter, it is made quite plain that in Adam there is a representation, and actually a substitution, that parallels the substitution of Jesus Christ.

Now a moment ago I said our courts do not permit this. The substitution like the one of Jesus Christ does not occur in the ordinary affairs of human life. But the substitution of precisely that order occurred in the case of Adam and all his descendants by natural generation.

It is this same principle that provides our condemnation and visitation in Adam that also provides the way of salvation for our redemption and restoration by Jesus Christ. We may rebel against the fact that God considers us as a guilty nation, a guilty people, by virtue of Adam's sins, quite apart of our own sins. But it is by virtue of that unity of grace, that corporate responsibility, that Christ could also enter into our race and then by His marvelous grace extend that same type of substitution to those whom He desires to save. So in discussing the doctrine of the covenant, we have a discussion of that principle of representation which is not found elsewhere.

Now I know that the covenant is invoked by some people as a means of justifying infant baptism. So there are some Baptists who, in order to protect believer's baptism, have decided to discard the covenant doctrine altogether. This is a frightful mistake in my judgment; this is throwing the baby out with the bathwater. We are the ones who really have bath water and who really ought not to throw it away. We ought to be proud to represent the Scriptural concept of the covenant of God.

It is a principle that goes from the Old Testament to the New, "We are under covenant with God." It is by virtue of the covenant of grace that we can in fact be covered by Jesus Christ. He is the head of the covenant, and His mediatorial office is particularly accomplished toward those who are encompassed by God's grace and choice in His covenant. Therefore, it is true, that at times it is difficult for us to explore and fathom this relationship with Adam. We have no sense of his own guilt. It is difficult for us to see that Adam was a sinner, and there I, as part of him when he rejected God, was also constituted a sinner. He stood as my substitute and, therefore, I am rightly held responsible for what he did.

That is difficult for us, but if we reject that out of hand, then we undermine the way of salvation in which Christ stands as our substitute. That is something very precious and it is with this that I will close. I want to emphasize substitution.

A substitution of persons is the very heart of the atonement. There is no other way to explain the intensity of the sufferings of Christ, no way that is magnifying to God. Unless there is a very real reason why Christ had to suffer so much, then God stands accused as having abandoned the one person in the whole world that really lived in accordance with His law.

In some way it has to be that Christ on the cross is the substitute for sinners and not merely someone who shows how God would punish a man if He were a sinner. Showing how one would punish a man by inflicting pain on one who is not a sinner is, in fact, an act of injustice. Somebody who is not a sinner may not be punished like a sinner, and no one could say that this magnifies justice. Thus, in a very real way, Christ must be seen as laden with our sins.

I will not say the sins of the whole world, but the sins of the redeemed. Those are the sins, in a particular way, which our Lord bore, and it will do no good to accuse the Jews or Pilate or Judas, saying they are the ones who crucified Jesus. Reformed people, with a profound grief in their own hearts, must see: "I am the one who crucified Him."

A very vivid illustration of this was given by Becky Pippert. She was talking about two young people who had been very vigorous in their advocacy of the gospel in their church. They were very gifted leaders, a young man and a young woman, and they were engaged to be married and exercised together a wonderful ministry. Becky saw this young woman at a later point in life, and she had become very despondent. She said, "I don't believe God can forgive me for what I have done."

"Well," Becky said. "What is it that you feel is so bad that God can't even forgive you?"

The woman responded, "My fiancé and I had sexual relations before we were married and I became pregnant. Then the question was, what I am going to do? If people in the church know that I became pregnant before marriage it will ruin my testimony and I will be too ashamed even to appear there."

So she said, "I had an abortion. I killed my own baby. I don't think God can forgive me for that."

Becky said, "Have you ever thought that this was not your first murder?"

The woman responded, "What do you mean?"

Becky responded, "When Jesus Christ died, why do you think he died? He died for your sins, and He has forgiven you of that murder and He can forgive you of this one too."

Now this is not an encouragement for people to have an abortion, but it shows that really when we come down to it, we are the ones who are mainly responsible for the death of Christ. It is for us that He died.

> What Thou, my Lord, hast suffered
> Was all for sinners' gain:
> Mine, mine was the transgression,
> But Thine the deadly pain;
> Lo, here I fall my Savior!
> 'Tis I deserve Thy place;
> Look on me with Thy favor,
> Vouchsafe to me Thy grace.[2]

---

2 Paul Gerhardt, 1607-1676, "O Sacred Head, Now Wounded" based on a Medieval Latin poem; tr. James W. Alexander, 1804-1859.

5.
THE ATONEMENT—PART 2.
ROGER NICOLE
1991 Southern Baptist Founders Conference

INTRODUCTION

IS the atonement effectual or is it universal? I emphasize the fact that it cannot be both. If it is universal and effectual, then all people should be saved. If it is universal, but not effectual, then perhaps it was made for all, but then, effective only in some. If it is effectual, then surely it is not universal, since all people will not be saved. So the issue is really quite crucial, although the subject as we approach it is somewhat delicate. There are many who don't understand at all what you mean or what you profess when you have what they call (and sometimes unfortunately we also call) limited atonement.

DEFINING THE ISSUE

In order to prevent confusion and be clear on this matter, let us discuss three issues which are not in view.

What Is Not In View.

In the first place, it is not a question as to what is the worth of Christ in His death. Those who hold to definite atonement are in no wise interested in restricting the value of Christ in His death. In fact, somebody asked me what ground I had to say that the value of the death of Christ is infinite. I told him John 1:1, "In the beginning was the Word and the Word was with God and the Word was God." The One who died is God and, therefore, the value of His death is absolutely infinite.

67

There is nothing in the whole universe that could even begin to equate the value of the death of Jesus Christ. So it is not as if those who hold to definite atonement have a limitation on the value of the work of Christ. We do not say that if another person had to be saved, Christ should have shed another drop of blood or have some other pain added to the torment which He underwent. There is no such speculation at all, and the death of Christ is recognized as strictly able to save as many as God would be pleased to save.

The second issue not in view is whether those who are not saved gain some benefit from the fact that Christ died. Those who hold to definite atonement are not interested in saying Jesus Christ is of no value whatsoever for people who are not saved. We will say, on the contrary that, because of the death of Christ, there are benefits that come down on humanity and that affect some people who are not saved and will not be saved. These benefits are short of salvation and they don't involve the substitutionary ministry of Jesus Christ for those people. One of the benefits, in fact, is that there is a proclamation of the gospel that is spread throughout the whole world, and without the death of Christ there could not have been a universal proclamation of the gospel. The previous economy was centered very strictly on the Jewish people. It is the ministry of Jesus Christ and of the Holy Spirit that has opened wide the doors, so that people from every category, even those from outside the Jewish nation, could enter. We could say also, since God has His elect, and the Second Coming of Christ will not take place before all the elect are gathered in, that the wicked "unbelieving world" has a respite from the final judgment. This they would not have short of the saving work of Jesus Christ and God's gathering of His elect from the whole world. So we do say that there are blessings that any member of the human race receives by virtue of the death of Christ, but this does not include the blessing of salvation.

The third issue that is not in view, is whether all people of the human race, every man, woman, and child, in the end will be saved or not. The people who contest definite atonement are not ordinarily outright Universalists. There is a lot of outright universalism in our day, even in the Roman Catholic Church. But the people with whom we deal ordinarily recognize that a bifurcation of destiny is clearly outlined in Scripture, and that there will be those angels and humans who in the end will not share in the blessings of heaven but will be separated from God in grief and in hell. So nobody with whom we are presently dealing, none among the evangelicals anyway, would move to a doctrine of outright universalism.

What Is In View.

Now, the question is, what is at stake? What is the subject we are dealing with when we talk about the extent or the scope of the death of Christ? This issue can be defined very simply in saying the question is: "For whom did the Father send the Son, and for whom did the Son deliver Himself unto death, enduring the pains of hell in substitution for sinners?"

There are those who answer: "For every member of the human race." These are the so-called "Universalists." They hold to universal atonement, although not universal salvation. Then there are others who say, "It is only for those who will in fact be saved." These are those who hold to "definite atonement" or "particular redemption."

Now, we need to consider at this point the language to be used. The language of "limited atonement" is very common, so much so that some people who hold to this view actually use that term. In my judgment the matter is not one of limits and, therefore, to talk about limited atonement is really a misnomer. In some way, anybody who says that all people will not be saved recognizes that the work of Christ is not so universal that all people in the end will be saved. So no one who is not an outright Universalist fails to acknowledge a limit. Some people limit it in breadth and others in depth, but limits are there and the term limited atonement does not apply more readily to a reformed view than it applies to an Arminian or an Amyraldian view. Therefore, it is unfortunate to use a term which really does not define clearly what is at stake.

Furthermore, we put ourselves at a psychological disadvantage when we talk about limited atonement. Because immediately, those who are not in agreement with us will say, "I believe in an unlimited atonement," and that will sound good. It would seem that they are the ones who truly exalt the grace of God and that we in some novel and stingy way are wrongly limiting and restricting it.

For this reason, I have disciplined myself and encouraged my students to use the term "definite atonement." Definite implies that the work of Christ was defined—was intended—precisely for those people that it saves. This gives us a psychological advantage, because if we say, "I believe in a definite atonement," what will the other people say? "I believe in an indefinite atonement"? That doesn't sound so good.

Now, if they want to talk about limited atonement, I cannot prevent them from doing so, although I can take issue with them that this doesn't really describe my view. What is unfortunate, though, is that people who believe in definite atonement use the word "limited" at that point and put themselves at a disadvantage. If we have the choice of words, let's use a word that is effective.

Now another word formation that is appropriate is "particular redemption." This is especially interesting for Baptists because in the early Baptist movement in England, there were two factions, the General Baptists and the Particular Baptists. It was exactly on this issue that those terms rested. The General Baptists held to a universal atonement, and the Particular Baptists held to definite atonement. That is where they are called "particular."

Now, the Southern Baptist Convention historically derives largely from the Particular Baptists. Therefore, we modern Particular Baptists are rightfully and fully Southern Baptists. We are those who have gone back to the roots better than others; therefore we are not to be hesitant to let our flag flap in the wind, trusting that it is the wind of good doctrine.

REASONS FOR HOLDING TO DEFINITE ATONEMENT

Now, my purpose is to indicate some basic reasons for holding to definite atonement. Then I plan to consider some objections raised by those who do not believe in it and to address the Bible verses that are involved.

Scriptures Describing the Intended Objects of the Atonement.

The first argument that I want to mention is the language of Scripture in relationship to those for whom Christ worked atonement. We are told that Christ came to free or redeem *His people* from their sins (Matthew 1:21). He came to give His life *for His friends* (John 15:13). The Good Shepherd gives His life *for His sheep* (John 10:15). Here, surely the context indicates, He did not give His life for goats. So definiteness here is very plain. He came to give Himself *for His church* (Ephesians 5:23-26). God hath placed you overseers *over the church of God* which He purchased with His own blood (Acts 20:28). "He gave His life for many"—you have that expression in Isaiah 53, but then again in Matthew 20:28, Mark 10:45, and in the institution of the Lord's supper in Matthew 26:28. He gave Himself *for us* (Titus 2:14). "He gave Himself *for me*," says Paul in Galatians 2:20.

Now all of these expressions indicate a particular intent for people who, in fact, will be saved. That does not necessarily exclude the rest, although with the sheep, the rest seemed to be in view and not under the blessing involved. This is particularly the case when Paul says, "He gave Himself for me." It is quite plain that he does not mean to eliminate all the rest of humanity. And so these Scriptures do not, by themselves, constitute a sufficient basis for saying that the atonement is not universal. Rather, they constitute a formulation which is best in keeping with an atonement for people who will be saved, but they do not constitute, by themselves alone, a proof for definite atonement. They constitute only a presumption in that direction.

Scriptures Describing God's Specific Purpose In the Incarnation.

Now in the second place, there are some Scriptures that emphasize the specific purpose of God in the incarnation. We have perhaps the most notable passage in John 11:51-52, where John, in connection with Caiaphas' statement, tells us why Jesus came. John says, "He did not say this on his own [Caiaphas], but as high priest that year, he prophesied that Jesus would die for the Jewish nation, and not only for that nation, but also for the scattered children of God to bring them together and make them one." So, here you have a statement that God's children are scattered through the world, but it is not for those who are not children of God that Jesus would die.

Then again in John 6:38-39 where Jesus Christ is the Bread of Life, He is giving Himself and giving His flesh to eat. There again, it is only those who eat His flesh and drink His blood that have the benefits that are involved. In Titus 2:14, Christ has come "to purify for Himself a people that are His very own." Here again, the purpose of the incarnation is to gather a people unto God.

Scriptures Describing the Nature of the Work of Christ.

A third argument comes from the nature of the work of Christ as it is described in Scripture. That is a very important argument which, in my judgment, not only creates a presumption, but actually gives a demonstration of the definiteness of the atonement.

The work of Christ is described as reconciliation. Reconciliation is, as I described earlier, the process whereby two people who are at odds are brought again into a relationship of friendship and closeness. Now, we are told that "Christ is the reconciliation"; in Him, "God reconciled the world unto Himself." We plead—"be reconciled with God." This does not show simply that God has now been made reconcilable, that some obstacle for reconciliation has been removed, but that reconciliation has now been effected. I have to ask, what kind of reconciliation is this, when people are still at odds? If reconciliation is taking place, then, indeed, the enmity is stopped.

The work of Christ is also described as redemption, and redemption is the deliverance of captives by virtue of payment of a sum, which in this case is very considerable. It might be considered like "bail out money" in our system of jurisprudence. Well, suppose now that I have come to the help of a friend, and I give money to bail him out when he has been accused of some crime. And the next day I ask, "Where is my friend?" I hear, "Oh, he is in prison." In prison? I paid the money for the bail, he should have been freed. And I say, "what kind of redemption is this when the people continue to be captive? If you really have redemption, they have to be liberated. If you have redemption, the price has been paid, the debt cancelled, and people will be freed. Therefore, the work of Christ applies to people who, in fact, will be free. They will not be freeable. They will not be merely redeemable. They will be redeemed. That is what the Scripture implies.

In the third place, the Scripture presents the work of Christ as propitiation. Propitiation is the process whereby the anger of someone is appeased, specifically, the righteous anger of God is appeased by virtue of an appropriate substitution. I have to ask, "what kind of propitiation is this when God continues to be angry, and so angry, in fact, that He casts people into hell? How can it be said that they have been propitiated?"

So, if you analyze the Scriptural language for the nature of the work of Christ, it shows that it is something that is effectual. It reconciles, it redeems, it propitiates.

If this is so, obviously, the only ones who are the beneficiaries of it are those who are saved, the ones who are in fact reconciled, redeemed, and toward whom God is propitiated. Those who are not saved are not reconciled, they are not redeemed, and God is not propitiated toward them.

Scriptures Describing the Substitutionary Nature of the Atonement.

A fourth argument for a definite atonement comes from the nature of penal substitution as the work of Christ. In fact, in a sense, what I said before is only a preface for what I have to say now because I want to hammer strongly the nail of substitution. If you don't have substitution, you don't have a real atonement. If you don't have substitution, all the theories on the atonement that try to bypass substitution are immediately, by that very account, inadequate and incomplete. In most, if not all cases, theories that deny substitution destroy even that part of the truth that they were meant to emphasize.

Most theories of the atonement are mainly incomplete. They are not exactly false in themselves. They have picked one element of the truth that they sought to put into light, but they may have undermined the very existence of that truth by denying what happened in fact—that Christ became the substitute for those whom He saved.

Now, if Christ is a substitute for people, then what will be left to condemn at the judgment? Obviously, nothing. The very idea of condemnation at the time of judgment is immediately contrary to the idea that Christ has in fact borne the punishment due unto the sins of these people. So, substitution, if the atonement is universal, will lead us, of necessity, to universal salvation. But this is the very thing that all of us together deny—Arminians, Amyraldians, as well as Calvinists.

In response, some people say, ok, they will not be punished for original sin, and they will not be punished for sins other than unbelief. The one sin that remains and that makes the difference, is unbelief. To this there are two very serious objections that arise at once.

The first one is that in biblical descriptions of judgment it is not true that unbelief is the only thing that is incriminating. People will be punished for the evil deeds they have accomplished. "The LORD examines the righteous, but the wicked and those who love violence His soul hates" (Psalm 11:5). They will give an account "for every careless word they have spoken" (Matthew 12:36). The variety of sins that human beings commit is presented as a charge in the judgment (Romans 2:2; 2 Peter 2:9; Revelation 6:9, etc.). This could not be if Christ has already suffered for them. Therefore, those who will be condemned will be condemned for their sins unless Christ intervenes.

The second great objection is that some lack of faith remains on the charge of those who have shown belief. Then I have to say, nobody will be saved, because there is nobody in the whole world who has all the faith that God is entitled to require. I don't dare to go to God and say, "OK, Lord, I am coming to You on the basis of my faith. My faith deserves to receive Your acceptance." Even believers need to be forgiven for their imperfect faith.

Nobody has shown the connection between substitution and the definiteness of the atonement more emphatically than the great John Owen, who wrote a whole book on the subject, *The Death of Death in the Death of Christ*, a great theological classic (Carlisle, PA: Banner of Truth, 1959, or in John Owen's, *Works*, volume 10). Anybody who reads this book and holds to universal atonement, in my judgment, is entitled to it. Anybody who holds to universal atonement and does not read this book has not made the utmost effort to test his position. So I would recommend the book, although at times, it's reasoning is so compact as to require a considerable effort.

Owen makes a statement that shows definite atonement in a very remarkable way (op. cit. pp 61-62). I abridge it just a little yet retain its main point: "God imposed His wrath due unto, and Christ underwent the pains of hell for, either all the sins of all men, or all the sins of some men, or some of the sins of all men."

Now there would be another possibility, that Christ died for no sins of anybody, but it's not really worth considering. So here are the three possibilities: 1) all the sins of all men, 2) all the sins of some men, or 3) some of the sins of all men.

If the last one is true, that Christ died for some of the sins of all men, then all of us will be lost. Owen said, "All men have some sins to answer for, so shall no man be saved."

On the other hand, if Christ died for all the sins of some men, he says, that's the truth, and definite atonement. Christ dies for all the sins, past, present and future, of all the elect in the whole world.

But let's consider the first option, that Christ died for all the sins of all men. Then, Owen said, all men must be saved, since there will be nothing to hold against them at the day of judgment. So, substitution leads to universal salvation. The response is, "they will not believe." They are condemned because of unbelief. And Owen says, "This unbelief, is it a sin or is it not? If it is not a sin, why should they be condemned for it? If it is a sin, Christ died for it or He did not. If He died for it, why should they be condemned for it since it is already condemned. If He did not, He did not die for all their sins and that is contrary to the premise. So, he finished, "Let them choose which part they will."

It is an irresistible argument. This is what I call Owens's vise. You can turn the screw as much as you want.

Scriptures Describing Christ's Work of Intercession and Oblation.

A fifth argument, the priestly work of Christ consists of two elements: intercession and oblation. Now, it is plain from John 17:9 that the intercession of Christ does not extend to the whole world, at least not in the way in which He intercedes for His own. For in John 17:9, Jesus said, "I pray not for the world, but for those whom You have given me."

So the question is, would Christ refuse to pray for those for whom He shed His blood? Would Christ the priest exercise a ministry of a different scope in intercession than He did in oblation? It is very unlikely, and the consistency and unity of the priestly work of Christ demands an oblation that is coextensive with His intercession, and goes no further.

The Unity of Purpose In the Trinity.

A sixth argument for definite atonement is drawn from the unity of purpose in the Holy Trinity. According to those who would hold to universal atonement, God the Father, in His own wise purpose, has elected some people out of humanity unto whom salvation would be applied. He allowed some people to be passed by. So, the original purpose of God is to save some and not others. Now then, the Son would say, "Father you have not been very generous. I am going to come into this world and I would offer myself for absolutely all human beings." Then the Holy Spirit would appear, and He says, "Well, I am not going to give repentance and faith to anyone but the elect. So it is two to one, and the Son loses."

You see, things don't go like that in the Godhead. Anybody who has that view of the Trinity needs to have another course in Junior Systematics. The Godhead has absolutely one purpose. You could not find a hair's breadth of difference between the purpose of the Father, and the purpose of the Son, and the purpose of the Holy Spirit. Therefore the unity of the Godhead, since there are only so many that are saved, in fact, demands definite atonement and a specific intention of Christ for the redeemed which is not given to others.

These are just six arguments out of twelve or fifteen that could be advanced. I believe that the strongest ones have been mentioned.

RESPONDING TO OBJECTIONS

Now I would like to consider with you the objections that are raised by those who do not believe in definite atonement.

Passages Suggesting God Wants To Save Everyone.

The first objection is that there are passages in Scripture that show us a universal, saving will on the part of the Godhead, that God wants to save all people. This causes at once a difficulty with the doctrine of election because if He wants to save all people, the question is, why doesn't He do it? For surely He could do it. So the passages need to be considered with care and this already has been done in the history of the church, very manifestly in the writings of Augustine. One of those passages is 1 Timothy 2:4, where the apostle Paul tells that we should pray "for kings and all those in authority." "This," he said, "is good and pleases our Savior who wants all men to be saved and to come to a knowledge of the truth." The way in which this passage is interpreted by our friends is that God wishes that every member of the human race should arrive unto salvation.

In this passage the word "all" in Greek does not have the article. It is not reflected but Greek has a way of saying "all," and another way of saying "all kinds of." The form that is used here is "all kinds of." You have *pantas* without the article. Therefore Augustine in Enchiridion 103 (NPNF III, 270) made it very plain. I would summarize it as follows: "Here Paul does not declare that God wants everybody to be saved, but He wants people of all kinds and categories to be saved, including even kings who are very unlikely candidates for salvation."

Unlikely candidates, God has shown us often, are still the object of His saving love. If there was one person who was an unlikely candidate, it surely was Paul, and yet he was elect, so you ought not to go on the basis of some presumption that "this person can't be elect, he's just too wicked." Instead, you ought to say, "This is a potential elect." In fact, that is the very strong emphasis we should have as reformed Baptists. Every person of the human race that is living and that we can reach ought to be considered as a possible elect. What closes out election is death, or the sin against the Holy Spirit, but in all my life I have not seen a single person about whom I felt absolutely convinced that he or she had committed the sin against the Holy Spirit, so I hope we don't go to precipitous judgments in this matter.

Augustine said, "He wants the rich and the poor. He wants the great and the small, the old and the young, the learned and the ignorant." And He has about twenty different categories that he uses at that point in his writing, in more than one place incidentally, to explain that passage and show its harmony with the doctrine of election. So, the passage does not assert a universal, saving will; it asserts that God wills to gather His elect from all kinds of human categories running across all the differences that we make of race, or sex, or age, or culture, and otherwise. All of these are crossed over by the purpose of election.

Another passage of that type is 2 Peter 3:9, which says that God does not postpone His promise, but "is patient with you, not wanting anyone to perish, but every one to come to repentance." Well, you notice the word "you" here. The apostle Paul addresses himself to Christians. The second coming of our Lord did not seem to appear as quickly as the Christians expected, and they were impatient about it and asked, "Did God forget His promise?"

"No," said Peter, "He did not forget His promise. In fact, He shows His love and patience to the church, not willing that any of His elect people should perish, but wanting to have a full church with everybody in it that belongs there." And so He does not want any of those who are elected to salvation to perish, but that all of them should come to repentance. This has nothing to say about God's attitude toward humanity at large. It relates to God's people, as the word "you" surely should have led us to recognize.

Then, there is the passage in John 3:16, "God so loved the world, that He gave His one and only Son." That passage is often quoted and for many people, it seems to carry immense conviction. One has only to read the passage with care to see that the particular reason is imbedded in it. He said that "Whoever believes in Him shall not perish." So then, the love here is meant for the salvation of those who will be saved.

Now some people are clumsy when they attempt to replace the word "world" with the words "the elect." But it doesn't say the elect, it says the world. What does the "world" mean in this passage? Well, it means that God has oriented His love toward this earth of ours in which humanity dwells. This love is manifested in that He has determined out of this fallen humanity to draw a multitude of people whom He would save by His mighty arm and by the work of Jesus Christ. The fact that the word "world" is found here does not mean that God has an equal love for all members of the human race.

In the United States we have what is called a Rhodes Scholarship. The Rhodes Scholarship holds some very important gifts of money which are provided to very promising students in the United States so that they could go to some of the best schools in England, Cambridge and Oxford, to carry out their studies there. Now, it is a remarkable thing that Mr. Rhodes should have made such a disposition of his fortunes because he was living and flourishing in the first part of the nineteenth century. It is from him that Rhodesia in Africa had been called. South Rhodesia and North Rhodesia have become now, respectively, Zimbabwe and Zambia, but they were first called by the name Rhodesia. Lord Cecil Rhodes was the governor there, and that is where the term came from.

Now you could have expected an Englishman at that time to devote his fortune to the culture of English people. The United States, at that time, was not an ally; they were really still the enemy. As recently as 1812 there had been battles between English forces (or British forces) and American forces. So it is a remarkable thing that Rhodes would devote a large amount of his fortune to provide for the best training for American people. So I could say, Rhodes so loved America that he gave his immense fortune so that citizens of the United States of America could have the benefit of the best training that England can provide. That doesn't mean that every citizen of the United States can go out to Oxford and Cambridge on a Rhodes scholarship. This is something done for some special people, but the affection of Rhodes was bent toward America and then particularly focused on some people, who, in the course of time, would receive this magnificent scholarship and study in these magnificent universities. Now, let me take my parallel with God. God so loved the world, this earth, this humanity, that He gave His only begotten Son for the salvation of His elect that He draws out of humanity. That's what it means. It's not necessary to be afraid in any way whatsoever of John 3:16. I can preach on John 3:16 with as much conviction as any Arminian I know. In fact I can preach with greater conviction because I believe the salvation God provides is effective.

The passages of Ezekiel 18 and 33:11 repeat several times that God does not want the death of the wicked. "He does not take pleasure in the death of the wicked, but rather that they turn from their ways and live. Turn! Turn from your evil ways! Why will you die, O house of Israel?" So, the question would be: If He wants the wicked to repent and live, why doesn't He make them do so? Well, the point of Ezekiel, it seems to me, is not to penetrate behind the elective purpose of God to second guess God, so to speak, but to show to us the enormous generosity of God.

When we have people who have terribly damaged us and hurt us, we want to get even with them. Our tendency is to say, "Ok, you slapped me, I will give you two slaps."

In fact, our tendency is to let the thing snowball, with constant aggravation and retaliation. Surely, the feeling that most of us have when we have been hurt is to get even. Ezekiel portrays the marvelous generosity of God, who, instead of saying, "Well and good. They are getting what they deserve," rather says, "Come unto me. Repent. I want to give you the chance, the opportunity, and in fact the reality, of a renewal of fellowship with Me." Instead of showing His fist, God extends His hand and that is what causes the Christian to rejoice. So those passages which allegedly represent a universal, saving will do not in fact counter those passages representing a particular will of salvation in the process of predestination or election.

Passages Suggesting That Some of Those For Whom Christ Die May or Will Perish.

There are four passages that are asserted to uphold universal atonement by stating that some people for whom Christ died may perish or will perish.

All four of those passages relate to people who are distinguished from the mass of humanity by certain privileges. So at the very best, those passages will not prove universal atonement. They consider particular cases of people already enlightened, assimilated in the church in various ways. They might prove an atonement that goes beyond the range of people who actually will be saved, and therefore, if considered in that light, they could be damaging to definite atonement. Therefore, we need to consider them with care.

First of all, there is Romans 14:15 (which is very similar to 1 Corinthians 8:11), where Paul says, "Do not by your eating destroy your brother for whom Christ died." Another passage is Hebrews 10:29, where the author of Hebrews says that there are people who will be punished, they will not have salvation because they have "treated as an unholy thing the blood of the covenant that sanctified them." In that context, there is no hope of salvation for the people in view—they are irremediably lost. Similarly, in 2 Peter 2:1, there is a statement that there are doctors who come and spread malicious and false teachings, "denying the sovereign Lord who bought them," and for them also there will be swift retribution. There is no hope left for them, according to that passage of Scripture.

So the first two passages, Romans 14 and 1 Corinthians 8, indicate that people might perish, but it is not said they will perish. Hebrews 10 and 2 Peter 2 say that people will perish, and in all four cases the reference is made of some work of Christ done for those people.

How can we understand this group of texts? The first two speak of brothers for whom Christ died. The statement is made specifically in Romans 14:4 that, though they might perish, they will not in fact perish because God will cause them to stand.

If you hold that these passages relate to real Christians that may really or will really perish, then obviously the doctrine of the perseverance of the saints is negated. So, here, in Romans 14, Paul makes it very plain that God will see to it that a brother will not perish.

So why does he say, "Will you for your meat cause your brother to perish for whom Christ died?" What he remonstrates against is the hard-heartedness of a Christian, or somebody who claims to be a Christian, who would show so little concern for a weak brother or sister.

The only reason why Christians might want to buy meat sanctified to idols was to realize some minor saving of money. Now, there were people who thought that to eat such meat was to participate in idolatrous worship. Obviously, if they did that, it would be a very serious sin. Paul remonstrates against a lack of consideration, an irresponsibility, on the part of the Christian who says, "Never mind what the effect is of what I am doing. I want to use my Christian liberty irrespectively of what other people do or think about it." His emphasis on the fact that Christ perished for this one brings simply to the fore the difference in attitude between Christ, who was ready to die for the salvation of such a person, and the attitude of the one who claimed to be His disciple, who was disregarding entirely the spiritual welfare of the other. Therefore there is no asserting here that perishing will in fact occur, but it would be the implication if God did not intervene. Paul remonstrates with a hard-heartedness of people who act irresponsibly toward others who are weak.

In Hebrews 10 and 2 Peter 2, the matter is different because here we are told they will perish. We note that what is stated of them does not imply a true regeneration, but rather the claim that they made. These are people who are not true believers but are merely professing the Christian faith. They may have perhaps joined the church, may be listed among the membership, even among the eldership or in the ministry of the church, but they are not really saved. We may have a kind of attitude, therefore, which goes directly contrary to the fruits that would be expected on the part of a truly saved person.

In Hebrews 10, the reference probably appears to be to participation in the Lord's Supper. For in the Lord's Supper people participate, partake of the cup which is a symbol of the covenant of grace and of the blood of the covenant, whereby those who believe in Jesus Christ are in fact, sanctified. Somebody who takes the Lord's Supper without being a Christian yet, makes by this act a claim of being placed under the blood of Jesus Christ. Now, this is something that can occur, and unfortunately, it is at times done by people who take the Lord's Supper lightly. Therefore, it is wise, according to 1 Corinthians 11, to declare before the Lord's Supper is administered that this is a sacred ordinance and that people may eat and drink a judgment against themselves if they are not truly sharers in the new life that God has provided in Jesus Christ.

Similarly in 2 Peter 2, the people denied the Master that bought them. It is not that Christ actually did buy them in divine redemption, but they had merely claimed to be bought by Christ. Peter said that they were not now, nor ever before, true disciples of Him whom they now deny. Their claim was spurious and their condemnation irremediable. The subjects of the passages have entered in an irreparable manner the path of ultimate rebellion to God.

Passages Suggesting That the Work of Christ Is Intended For Every Man.

This third group of passages is the most important. They are passages which seem to indicate that the work of Christ is intended for all, for the world, for every man, and for whomever. Here, without going through the complete list, I will give you some of the passages that are advanced, quoting them without a comment at first, and reserving the comments for the end of the quotation.

Let's take "all" first. We have Isaiah 53:6, "We all, like sheep, have gone astray, each of us has turned to his own way; and the LORD has laid on Him the iniquity of us all"— especially that last statement. Romans 5:18: "As in Adam, death and condemnation came upon all, so in Jesus Christ justification of life comes unto all." 1 Corinthians 15:22, which is a parallel to Romans 5:18 where we have "as in Adam all died, so in Christ shall all be made alive." Romans 8:32: "He who did not spare his own Son, but gave Him up for us all—how will He not also, along with Him, graciously give us all things?" 2 Corinthians 5:14-15: "For Christ's love compels us, because we are convinced that one died for all, and therefore all died. And He died for all, that those who live should no longer live for themselves but for Him who died for them and was raised again." 1 Timothy 2:5-6: "For there is one God and one mediator between God and men, the man Christ Jesus, who gave Himself as a ransom for all." Titus 2:11: "For the grace of God that brings salvation has appeared to all men."

Let's take the word "every." Hebrews 2:9: "He might taste death for everyone."

Then we have the word "world." John 1:29, the statement of John the Baptist: "Look, the Lamb of God, who takes away the sin of the world!" John 3:16: "God so loved the world." John 4:42: "... this man really is the Savior of the world." John 12:47: "I did not come to judge the world, but to save it." This is a statement of our Lord. 2 Corinthians 5:19: "God was reconciling the world to Himself in Christ." 1 John 2:2: "He is the atoning sacrifice for our sins, and not only for ours, but also for the sins of the whole world." 1 John 4:14: "... Savior of the world."

Then finally, "whosoever." John 3:16: "... that whoever believes in Him should not perish" (NKJV). And also "whosoever will" in Revelation 22:17 (KJV). The text doesn't have "whosoever," but says "the one willing." There is, however, no need to quibble on that.

This is a considerable list of passages. I have not omitted intentionally any one with which I have any difficulty. I try to play fair with people with whom I do not agree, and acknowledge the best weapons they can advance. My list includes some passages that very badly boomerang. These are advantageous for me, especially when dealing with people who quote such passages without realizing that they do not support their view. What I am going to say may serve as a warning for people who want to espouse the Arminian view or the universalistic view not to quote certain passages because they work at cross purpose.

Let's start with Isaiah 53. In Isaiah 53, when you realize that Isaiah is talking to the Jewish people, it is very difficult to imagine that when he says "all" he is thinking of the whole of humanity. His message obviously is related to the Jewish people to whom he refers with "we and "our." Several things stated there are very obviously particular. For instance, he says: "He was pierced for our transgressions, crushed for our iniquities, the punishment that brought us peace was upon Him." Only His people, not all humans, are now at peace. And then, "By His wounds we are healed." That could not be said of people who are not saved. So, it is the saved people who have found peace and who are healed. Then again, we read, "He bore the sin of many" in verse 12. We are told there that He made intercession for the transgressors, and now the intercession of Christ is borne in direct connection with the salvation that is mentioned (cf. John 17:9). "By His knowledge my righteous servant will justify many and will bear their iniquities." Only those saved are justified. So Isaiah 53 is fairly filled with particularistic expressions. To pull out the verse, "All we like sheep have gone astray," and isolate it because it can apply to humanity at large is really not dealing fairly with the text. We need to consider the text in its context and the reference is obviously to people whom God will save and does save.

Let's take Romans 8:32. We read, "He who spared not His own Son but gave Him up for us all, how will He not with Him, give us all things." Well, on the face of it, right away we note the passage does not apply to humanity at large because God does not give all things to all men. Particularly, He does not give salvation to some of them. Obviously, there must be something wrong here and what is wrong is made very patently plain in the context. Verse 28 starts by saying, "And we know that in all things God works for the good of those who love him, who have been called according to his purpose." Then verses 29-30 have that marvelous, golden chain, "Those God foreknew, He also predestined to be conformed to the likeness of His Son, ... and those He predestined He also called; those He called, He also justified; those He justified, He also glorified." Five golden links in that chain without a loss of anyone in the process. Then it says, "What then shall we say in response to these things? If God is for us, who can be against us?" But God is not for those who remain against Him. God is for those whom, by His grace, He leads to be for Him as well! Then comes the passage in question. Then immediately after that, "Who can lay anything to the charge of God's elect?" Here is the crucial word "elect." It says, "It is Christ who justifies." Here is justification which is a blessing that no one receives except those who are saved. And it is completed by that marvelous hymn of joy, "That nothing can separate us from the love of God, not even life." So in the midst of this strongly particularistic passage, and context, if you pull out one text which itself does not fit too well, and try to develop universal atonement out of that, it is in my judgment simply nonsense. When people do that, I believe that the Lord has delivered them into my hands. It's really not difficult to make a proof of that point.

Take 2 Corinthians 5:14. "Christ's love compels us, because we are convinced that one died for all, and therefore all died." How can the all be interpreted as all human beings? Did all human beings die in Christ? No, this is obviously something that applies to Christians. Again the pronouns should have warned us on that. "The love of Christ constrains us." Us believers. Us unto whom has been committed the ministry of reconciliation. This is not a privilege of the clergy; this is the privilege of the people of God. That is what the priesthood of all believers means among other things. So the reference is clearly to Christians and not to non-Christians. The passage proves nothing for universal atonement.

Hebrews 2:9: "He tasted death for everyone." What is the context of that? Well, it is the context that deals with people who are sanctified (v. 11). They are people who are brothers of Jesus Christ (v. 11). They are people who are children of God. He comes forward, "Here I am with the children God has given me" (v. 13). There is plenty of evidence that the reference is not universally to humanity but to people who are in a saving relationship with Jesus Christ.

"Behold the Lamb of God that takes away the sin of the world." Surely, there is no other way of taking away sins than through the Lamb of God. That does not mean that all the sins of the world will be taken away. If I see a garbage truck I say, "Here is the truck that takes away the trash of Birmingham." Yes, but that doesn't mean that one truck goes to all the streets and actually takes all trash. So, the reference is to the uniqueness of the work of Christ in taking away sin, but does not suggest that all the sins of the whole world are taken up by Christ to be atoned by Him.

In that sense, He is the Savior of the world, not in the sense that all the world is saved by Him, but in the sense that outside of Him, there is no Savior. That is what is stated by Peter, "There is no other Name under heaven given to men by which we must be saved" (Acts 4:12).

All right, so we go to 1 John 2:2, which is the best passage that can be advanced for indefinite atonement. If you want to hold to universal atonement, that's the best you can advance since it is both positive and negative. It says, "He is the propitiation for our sins and not only for ours, but for the sins of the whole world." Now, on the face of it, once again I would say, it's very unlikely that you would have here universal atonement, and this for two reasons.

First, the strong term propitiation. So, obviously, if He is the propitiation of the whole world, the whole world in the sense that John mentioned must be propitiated with God. But that is not going to happen since some people will be condemned at the last day, at the last judgment.

Second, this is placed in immediate relationship to the intercession of Christ. "If anybody does sin, we have one who speaks to the Father in our defense—Jesus Christ the Righteous One. He is the propitiation..." Then the question is: how can we understand this passage? What did John mean by "the whole world"?

There are three explanations that come forward. I am following John Murray on this who has summarized the matter admirably (cf. John Murray, *Redemption Accomplished and Applied*, Carlisle, PA: Banner of Truth, 1961, pp. 72-75). The first, is that John had in view a small group of people, probably narrowly defined, perhaps Jewish Christians, for indeed one of the great discoveries of the early church was that the message was not confined for Jews, but was to be delivered to people of all parts of the world. So the point would be, para phrasing now, "He is the propitiation for our sins, not only for us who are gathered in this small company, or just as Jewish Christians, but for people who are believers throughout the whole world, and there will be an extension of the message of the gospel into the whole world." In fact, this is how a statement in an early writing *The Martyrdom of Polycarp* has been interpreted. In *The Martyrdom of Polycarp* there is a statement, almost a quotation of 1 John 2:2, where we read, "He died for our sins, and not for ours only, but for those of the saved people in the whole world." That I think might very well be the meaning of 1 John 2:2.

Then a second suggestion is that the emphasis of John is on exclusivity. That is, He is the propitiation for our sins, but not for ours only, as if we had this method of propitiation, while others had other means of propitiation. But in the whole world, there is no propitiation available at all except in Jesus Christ. A paraphrase would be this, He is the propitiation for our sins, and not in such a way that we have recourse to this propitiation while others have recourse to another propitiation. No, He is the only propitiation in the whole world which is effective before God.

A third suggestion which is not as good because I think the word *"aeon"* should be used instead of *"cosmos"* if that were what John meant. The point might be that John is relating the matter to time so that there is not only one time in which Christ is the propitiation, but that His propitiation covers people from Adam even unto the end of the world. The paraphrase would be this, "He is the propitiation for our sins, and not only for ours, people who live at this time, or after the coming of Christ, but He is the propitiation for people who have lived in all ages of humanity whatsoever." Well, as I said, I think if that was the meaning exclusively in the passage, I would think that John would have used the word *"aeon"* instead of *"cosmos,"* therefore I am not pressing this as the single, legitimate interpretation.

Those however, can be taken in combination.

So let me put side by side the Arminian interpretation and the other which is a combination. The Arminian interprets, "He is the propitiation for our sins, and not only for ours as Christians, but for the sins of every man, woman, or child who ever lived in the world." The Calvinist interprets, "He is the propitiation for our sins, and not only for us who are a narrowly defined group, like the Christian Reformed, and not only for us, while others had another approach to God, not only for people who lived as contemporary to us, while others would have to go another way, but He is the propitiation for the sins of people recruited out of the whole wide world in all categories of humanity. It is the only propitiation available either in time or in space." That, I think, is what John meant. I don't have a bad conscience with this passage. I think I can say with honesty what Calvin said on his death bed, "I have never twisted knowingly any passage of Scripture."

The Atonement and the Universal Offer of the Gospel.

There is at last one more rather important objection, and

that is this: "If you hold to definite atonement, it is urged, then you are undercutting the universal offer of the gospel and therefore stultifying evangelism and missions." There are many people who agree with that, and they say that in order to offer the gospel you have to tell people, "Christ loves you with redemptive love." "Christ died for you." If you can't say that, they say, you can't make an evangelistic appeal. It is based on the belief that a well-meant offer does demand a co-extensive provision, that is, you cannot offer anything from God unless God has actually provided for it in advance.

So the question is, what is really required for a legitimate, well-meant offer? I say to you, what is required is not a coextensive provision, but only the assurance that if the terms of the offer are complied with, that which is offered will actually be tendered. That's all that can be required.

Here by the courtesy of a brother I have a copy of *The Birmingham News* and in it I have an offer. It's an offer made by Macy's of things that they plan to sell. Here's an interesting sale: "of all sizes, renaissance cutwork lace duvet sets." This is available for $139.99. This is *The Birmingham News*, a very reputable paper, obviously, and I imagine since Birmingham is a large city, it must appear in 200,000 copies. Shall I gather that Macy's has gathered 200,000 renaissance cutwork lace duvet sets. Well, if they did, they must have some very large warehouse somewhere that I did not notice when I came here. Of course, this is not the only offer you have in this newspaper, but there are all kinds of other things that are offered: refrigerators, automobiles and very expensive cameras.

This really is ridiculous. You know very well, that there are not as many of those sets as there are papers. Nobody can be mad at Macy's for having made a judgment that all people will not in fact flock to their store to buy just this one item. You ask them, "Well, how many did you set aside when you printed this?" Obviously they must have had some because otherwise they would not have spent their money in putting this in the paper.

Now, in some cases, I think there are some dishonest

business people who have what is called a "come-on." They seem to have a very generous offer, but they have only one or two objects of the kind, and they want to attract people to the store and sell them something else. That I think is not a well-meant offer, but all that you can really require of Macy's is that if you come forward to them with $139.99 plus the tax you will be delivered a lace duvet set of this type.

Now, it is plain as the nose on the face that a coextensive provision is not necessary. All that is necessary, I repeat, is that if the terms of the offer are complied with, that which you request will in fact be delivered. I am in the position to say to you that there is not one single example in all the history of mankind where people coming to God and to Jesus Christ on the basis of repentance and faith, claiming His atonement, have heard the answer, "Sorry fellow, there is nothing for you, you are not in the Book of Life." And how do I know that? Well, I know that because Jesus said it. He said, "Whoever comes to me I will never drive away" (John 6:37). So I am taking Jesus at His word, I know He's not going to go back on it. So this idea that you need to have a coextensive provision in order to have a well-meant offer is a piece of sophistry. There is no truth to it.

AGAINST THEIR OWN CONVICTIONS

In closing let me read to you some fine hymns which speak of definite atonement.

> And can it be that I should gain
> An int'rest in the Savior's blood?
> Died He for me who caused His pain....

The author? Charles Wesley.

> Arise, my soul, arise; shake off thy guilty fears;
> The bleeding sacrifice in my behalf appears:

> Before the throne my surety stands,
> Before the throne my surety stands,
> My name is written on His hands.

And who wrote this? Charles Wesley.

> Plenteous grace with Thee is found, grace to
> cover all my sin;
> Let the healing streams abound; make and keep
> me pure within.

And who is the author of this? Charles Wesley.

> He breaks the power of cancelled sin,
> He sets the prisoner free;
> His blood can make the foulest clean,
> His blood availed for me.

Who is the author of this? Charles Wesley.

> What Thou, my Lord, hast suffered was all for
> sinners' gain:
> Mine, mine was the transgression, but Thine the
> deadly pain.
> Lo, here I fall, my Savior! 'Tis I deserve Thy
> place;
> Look on me with Thy favor; vouchsafe to me Thy
> grace.

Who was the author of this? Bernard of Clairvaux, a Roman Catholic who held to universal atonement. The hymn was translated into German by Paul Gerhard, a Lutheran who believed in universal atonement.

> Jesus, Thy blood and righteousness—
> My beauty are, my glorious dress;
> Lord, I believe Thy precious blood
> Which, at the mercy seat of God

Forever doth for sinners plead,
For me, e'en for my soul was shed.

That was written by Zinzendorf, who was a Moravian (and the Moravians are Arminians) and translated into English by John Wesley.

So you see when the Arminians start writing hymns, the beauty of Scriptural truth takes hold of them, and they write against their own convictions. And when they pray, they also come to God as if everything depended on Him (as it does indeed) rather than on the unsaved sinner who has not yet been converted! So, instead of bashing them, let's rejoice for some of their inconsistencies. This may be the way in which you can start with them, with something we have in common. Then move them from there to here, to the full understanding of the glorious work of Jesus Christ which is effectual. Amen.

6.
REDEEMED FROM THE CURSE OF THE LAW
JOHN MACARTHUR
1993 Southern Baptist Founders Conference

WHATEVER HAPPENED TO SIN?

SEVERAL years ago, Dr. Carl Menninger, a world-famous psychiatrist and head of the Menninger clinic, wrote a book called *Whatever Happened to Sin?* The book gained some prominence, although its impact on society is questionable. In it Menninger tried to have people face the reality that their problems are related to sin. This is an interesting perspective for a psychiatrist because today, in our culture, sin is not an acceptable diagnosis of anything. There is much talk about "values," and we are called to stand up for "traditional values," but that is impossible to do without a clear definition of sin. I'm not so concerned about the cultural aspect about it, but what burdens me so much about man's refusal to diagnose himself as a sinner is that he cuts himself off from redemption. If he doesn't assess the problem, he doesn't know the cure.

Ann Melvin is a writer for the *Dallas Morning News*. In August she had an interesting column. She wrote it about sin. She said that most sins have gained respectability through politics or profitability. They are legalized, advertised, organized, supervised and taxed. She wrote that clearly we are foundering as a society, preoccupied with values and hopelessly vague on sin. Sin doesn't really fit into the "self-esteem cult," and it certainly doesn't fit into the "victimization syndrome." All the people-helpers that are floating around—the

95

counselors, psychiatrists and psychologists—are championing a re-definition of human behavior, a definition sans iniquity. I have read a relatively new book by Wendy Kaminer entitled, *I'm Dysfunctional, You're Dysfunctional.* In the book, Wendy confronts the new "anthropology/psychology/theology" trend. She is incredulous and skeptical about it, and concerned that it is an effort to deny personal responsibility for sin. She wrote, "No matter how bad you've been in the narcissistic 1970s and the acquisitive 1980s—no matter how many drugs you've ingested or sex acts performed or how much corruption you've enjoyed—you are still essentially innocent: the divine child inside you is always untouched." These new definers of man's nature say that no one is inhabited by evil or unhealthy urges because inside every addict (a new clinical title for sinners) is "a holy child yearning to be free." Wendy Kaminer wrote,

> Inner children are always good-innocent and pure-like the most sentimentalized Dickens characters, which means that people are essentially good ... evil is merely a mask—a dysfunction. The therapeutic view of evil as sickness, not sin, is strong in the co-dependency theory. ... "Shaming" children ... is considered the primary form of child abuse. Both guilt and shame are not useful..."[1]

To put it bluntly, sickness is much more marketable than sin. I assume that some of you have been exposed to the recent writings—probably the flagship book along this line is *The Diseasing of America*—advocating the reclassification of every human behavior in quasi-medical terminology which puts the church basically out of business. We don't do medicine.

---

1 Wendy Kaminer, *I'm Dysfunctional, You're Dysfunctional* (Reading, MA: Addison-Wesley, 1992), 18-20.

As long as people deny sin, like the rich young ruler, they are unredeemable. A failure to understand our sinfulness, then, ultimately is the supreme gospel tragedy because it obscures the need to understand redemption and the Redeemer. I'm so concerned because this trend to stop talking about sin has found its way into evangelicalism. But if we don't admit and confront the disease then people don't know the cure —or even feel they need a cure. Charles Sykes writing in his new book, *A Nation of Victims: The Decay of the American Character* said,

> Unfortunately, that is a formula for social gridlock: the irresistible search for someone or something to blame colliding with the unmovable unwillingness to accept responsibility. Now enshrined in law and jurisprudence, victimism is reshaping the fabric of society, including employment policies, criminal justice, education, urban politics, and, in an increasingly Orwellian emphasis on "sensitivity" in language. A community of interdependent citizens has been displaced by a society of resentful, competing, and self-interested individuals who have dressed their private annoyances in the garb of victimism.[2]

Everybody has a disease. Everybody has an addiction. Everybody has a disorder. Everybody has a syndrome. The quasi-medical terminology, I believe, is carefully calculated to put the church out of business in dealing with human calamity and human iniquity. It is a satanic counterfeit of the true condition of man with intent to cut him off from the truth of redemption. People will pay a terrible price for absolution. The price is damnation. The glory of a Redeemer is lost to them.

---

2 Charles Sykes, *A Nation of Victims: The Decay of the American Character* (New York: St. Martin's, 1992), 15.

CHRIST OUR REDEEMER FROM THE CURSE OF THE LAW

We read in Galatians 3:10-13:

> For as many as are of the works of the law are
> under the curse; for it is written, "Cursed is
> everyone who does not continue in all things
> which are written in the book of the law, to do
> them." But that no one is justified by the law in
> the sight of God is evident, for "the just shall live
> by faith." Yet the law is not of faith, but "the man
> who does them shall live by them." Christ has
> redeemed us from the curse of the law, having
> become a curse for us (for it is written, "Cursed
> is everyone who hangs on a tree"), that the bless-
> ing of Abraham might come upon the Gentiles in
> Christ Jesus, that we might receive the promise of
> the Spirit through faith.

I want to focus on that statement in verse 13, "Christ has
redeemed us from the curse of the law."

THE CURSE OF THE LAW

Do you remember what the response of the people of Israel
was when God originally gave His law?

> So Moses came and told the people all the words
> of the LORD and all the judgments. And all the
> people answered with one voice and said, "All the
> words which the LORD has said we will do." And
> Moses wrote all the words of the LORD. And he
> rose early in the morning, and built an altar at
> the foot of the mountain, and twelve pillars ac-
> cording to the twelve tribes of Israel. Then he
> sent young men of the children of Israel, who of-
> fered burnt offerings and sacrificed peace offer-
> ings of oxen to the LORD. And Moses took half
> the blood and put it in basins, and half the blood

he sprinkled on the altar. Then he took the Book of the Covenant and read in the hearing of the people. And they said, "All that the LORD has said we will do, and be obedient" (Exodus 24:3-7).

I like their spirit! They made a promise. What was the promise? "We will obey." So Moses took the blood and threw it all over the people (Exodus 24:8). Half the blood went on the altar and half the blood went on the people. He said, "This is the blood of the covenant which the LORD has made with you according to all these words." That is the sprinkling of blood that Peter refers to in 1 Peter 1:2 when he talks about us being chosen and sanctified by the Spirit—"for obedience and sprinkling of the blood of Jesus Christ." But it is not the sprinkling of the blood of Christ related to salvation to which he refers; it is the covenant of obedience attached to salvation that he references.

In the Old Testament, the children of Israel said, "We'll obey. We'll obey." God came right back to them and said, "You had better. Because if you don't, I'll kill you." Is that right? God would kill them? Not only that, but when you die, you'll go to hell. If you are going to live by the law, you must keep it all.

Christ redeemed us from the curse of the law, having become a curse for us. Galatians 3:10 contains a quotation from Deuteronomy 27:26: "Cursed is everyone who does not continue in all things which are written in the book of the law, to do them." God says He will curse you if you don't keep the whole law.

I think most people probably think the law of God—God's moral code, summarized in the Ten Commandments—is a good ethical system and something to strive for, adherence to which makes one a very religious and somewhat noble person. It is a nice standard for general conduct but not really deadly. Certainly the Judaizers of Paul's day were banking on the fact that you didn't have to keep it all, all the time. Just every now and then would work. But Deuteronomy 27:26 says you must keep it all or God will curse you and you'll die. Cursed are all who do not persevere in doing all that is written in the law. John 7:49, mocking the Jewish leaders, echoed this: "this crowd that does not know the law is accursed."

Moses brought that reality into really clear focus. Remember Deuteronomy 27:9? He declared triumphantly, "O Israel: This day you have become the people of the LORD your God." To dramatize that, Moses reiterated their covenant responsibility which harks back to Exodus 24. He also inaugurated a very special ceremony. Six tribes went to Mount Gerizim (symbolizing blessing) and six tribes went to Mount Ebal (symbolizing cursing). God basically said, "People, keep the law and I'll bless you. Break it, and I'll curse you."

Do you remember some of the extracts from Deuteronomy 28? They are amazing. Let me just remind you of them.

> The Lord will send on you cursing, confusion, and rebuke in all that you set your hand to do, until you are destroyed and until you perish quickly, because of the wickedness of your doings in which you have forsaken Me. The Lord will make the plague cling to you until He has consumed you from the land which you are going to possess.
>
> The Lord will strike you with consumption, with fever, with inflammation, with severe burning fever, with the sword, with scorching, and with mildew; they shall pursue you until you perish...
>
> The Lord will cause you to be defeated before your enemies; you shall go out one way against them and flee seven ways before them; and you shall become troublesome to all the kingdoms of the earth. Your carcasses shall be food for all the birds of the air and the beasts of the earth, and no one shall frighten them away...
>
> The Lord will strike you with madness and

blindness and confusion of heart. And you shall grope at noonday, as a blind man gropes in darkness...

You shall betroth a wife, but another man shall lie with her...

Your sons and your daughters shall be given to another people, and your eyes shall look and fail with longing for them all day long; and there shall be no strength in your hand....

So you shall be driven mad because of the sight which your eyes see...

And you shall become an astonishment, a proverb, and a byword among all nations where the Lord will drive you...

Moreover all these curses shall come upon you and pursue and overtake you, until you are destroyed, because you did not obey the voice of the Lord your God, to keep His commandments and His statutes which He commanded you. And they shall be upon you for a sign and a wonder, and on your descendants forever. Because you did not serve the Lord your God with joy and gladness of heart, for the abundance of everything, therefore you shall serve your enemies, whom the Lord will send against you, in hunger, in thirst, in nakedness, and in need of everything; and He will put a yoke of iron on your neck until He has destroyed you....

The tender and delicate woman among you, who would not venture to set the sole of her foot on the ground because of her delicateness and sensitivity, will refuse to the husband of her bosom, and to her son and her daughter, her placenta which comes out from between her feet and her children whom she bears; for she will eat them secretly for lack of everything in the siege and desperate straits in which your enemy shall distress you at all your gates.

If you do not carefully observe all the words of
this law that are written in this book, that you
may fear this glorious and awesome name, THE
LORD YOUR GOD, then the Lord will bring upon
you and your descendants extraordinary plagues
—great and prolonged plagues—and serious and
prolonged sicknesses. Moreover He will bring
back on you all the diseases of Egypt, of which
you were afraid, and they shall cling to you. Also
every sickness and every plague, which is not
written in this Book of the Law, will the Lord
bring upon you until you are destroyed...
Then the Lord will scatter you among all peoples, from one end of the earth to the other, and
there you shall serve other gods, which neither
you nor your fathers have known—wood and
stone. And among those nations you shall find no
rest, nor shall the sole of your foot have a resting
place; but there the Lord will give you a trembling
heart, failing eyes, and anguish of soul. Your life
shall hang in doubt before you; you shall fear day
and night, and have no assurance of life. In the
morning you shall say, "Oh, that it were evening!"
And at evening you shall say, "Oh, that it were
morning!" because of the fear which terrifies your
heart, and because of the sight which your eyes
see. And the Lord will take you back to Egypt in
ships, by the way of which I said to you, "You
shall never see it again." And there you shall be
offered for sale to your enemies as male and female slaves, but no one will buy you.

The psalmist said, "God will wound the head of His enemies" (Psalm 68:21). "Let there be none to extend mercy to
him, Nor let there be any to favor his fatherless children"
(109:12). "Happy the one who takes and dashes Your little
ones against the rock!" (137:9). C. S. Lewis said, "In some of
the psalms the spirit of hatred is so strong it strikes us in the

face like the heat from a furnace mouth." In 1901, R. M. Benson wrote a book entitled *War Songs of the Prince of Peace*, and in it he said there are no less than 39 psalms that are war songs of God. One English study in 1974 concluded that 84 psalms were not fit for Christians to sing.

Do you remember the words of the prophets? The Lord is a jealous God and avenging. The Lord is avenging and wrathful. The Lord takes vengeance on His adversaries and keeps wrath for His enemies. The Lord is slow to anger and great might. The Lord will by no means clear the guilty. Who can stand before his indignation? Who can endure the heat of His anger? His wrath is poured out like fire and the rocks are broken asunder by Him. The Lord is good, a stronghold in the day of trouble. He knows those who take refuge in Him. But with an overflowing flood He will make an end of His adversaries and pursue His enemies into the darkness. Woe to the bloody city.

Listen to Isaiah: "Behold, the day of the LORD comes, Cruel, with both wrath and fierce anger, To lay the land desolate; And He will destroy its sinners from it" (13:9). "Their children also will be dashed to pieces before their eyes; Their houses will be plundered and their wives ravished" (v. 16).

In the New Testament we hear Jesus say in Matthew 25:41: "Depart from me, you cursed, into everlasting fire." Jesus also pronounced a damning curse on Chorazin, Bethsaida, and Capernaum. And you hear the Apostle Paul echo the Word of God, "Vengeance is mine, I will repay" (Romans 12:19).

Let me tell you something, folks. If you don't keep the whole law of God, you're in some serious trouble. God's law curses us. It is a holy, righteous, just law, but we can't keep it. So it damns us, it curses us. That's what Paul says in Galatians 3:13 when he references "the curse of the law." Did you ever stop and think why the law curses us? Let me give you some reasons.

First, the law requires behavior contrary to human nature. Do you know what the law asks you to do? Precisely what you can't do. It demands us to do what we hate. It demands us to do what we loathe. It calls on us to function opposite to all our longings, passions, desires, and lusts. It asks us to go against our natural inclinations. We can't do it.

Second, the law requires behavior impossible to human nature. It requires behavior not only against our will, but even if we could will it, we couldn't do it. Sinners cannot do holy deeds. We don't have the ability or the desire.

Third, the law requires perfect performance of every part. The Judaizers were wrong. God wasn't satisfied with just "a good shot." The law is a severe creditor that demands perfect compliance. It demands nothing less than absolute perfection. It asks what is unwanted, what is impossible, and asks us to do it perfectly, so perfectly that Jesus could say, "Be ye perfect, even as your Father in heaven is perfect" (Matthew 5:48, KJV).

Fourth, the law refuses to accept good intentions as any consolation. Even if there were some good desires, even if there were some good deeds, even if there was some effort toward morality, if there were some effort to please whatever god in which one believes, intention counts for absolutely nothing. "Nice try" means nothing. There's no consolation bracket in the law. Trying doesn't count.

Fifth, the law accepts no payback plan. You can't offer the law some payback scheme by which you somehow pay off the debt you have accumulated. You can't go to God and say, "I've been racking up sin for a long time and what I'd like to do is work it off. I'd like to give you a little down payment of righteousness and a few good deeds every week and maybe we can get that baby paid down." No, the debt is never discounted and it's never repayable. In fact, if, hypothetically, you were to break the law once in the beginning of your life and do righteous deeds for the rest of it, all the accumulated righteous deeds of your entire life would never pay back the debt incurred by the one violation. If you were to live righteously your entire life and violate the law once before your death, your accumulated righteousness wouldn't satisfy God. There's no accumulated merit plan and there's no payback scheme.

Sixth, the law is an unrelenting taskmaster. It never eases up. It never lightens the load. It never relaxes the requirements. It never says to the sinner, "Take a day off, today, your sin won't count. It's a freebie." Never! Twenty-four hours a day, every single moment of our lives the inexorable law is working. No days off. It is stringent, unbending, unrelenting, and we never get any relief from its imposition.

Seventh, the law shatters happiness. The law hits our lives like steel rods on a clay pot, or like a hammer on a thin pane of glass. It disintegrates life. Sinners live in shame, guilt, restlessness, sorrow, fear, pain, futility, frustration, dissatisfaction, doubt, and hopelessness. The law just can't provide relief. The law shatters happiness. Just when you think you've got it, you lose it.

Eighth, the law requires the severest penalty: hell with no parole. Do you realize that God is so offended by our sin that an eternity in hell doesn't pay back God?

Ninth, the law only demands, it doesn't help. The law never comes alongside and says, "I know this is tough, let me help you." The law never helps. It offers no strength, no power, no method, no plan, no assistance of any kind at all, ever.

Tenth, the law offers no salvation. No deliverance. No restoration.

Eleventh, the law never listens to anybody's repentance. It couldn't care less. It doesn't matter how much you weep and groan and moan. It doesn't care about your sorrow. It doesn't care about your grief. It has no concern for your remorse. It isn't interested in your penitence. It doesn't care at all about your desires to make amends and change. The law is utterly, totally indifferent to all repentance.

Twelfth, the law offers no forgiveness, no grace, and no mercy.

Thirteenth, the law offers no hope at all. The law can never say there'll be a better day. There's no brighter tomorrow coming. There's no happy future out there.

REDEMPTION FROM THE CURSE OF THE LAW

Now you understand why the Bible says we're under the curse of the law. Everyone who has ever broken the law is cursed by it. If people don't understand this, then they won't know what it means when verse 13 says: "Christ has redeemed us from the curse of the law." He brought us out from under the curse. Like slaves we were brought out of the marketplace.

Paul said He did it by giving Himself a ransom for all. He told Titus in Titus 2:14 that He gave Himself for us, being cursed for us. Try to fill up that concept with everything I've been saying to you about what it means to be cursed. When witless, ignorant, pagan Caiaphas said, "It is expedient that one man should die for the people that the whole nation should not perish" (John 11:50), he had no idea what he was saying. He was thinking Jesus would be a political scapegoat to quiet Rome's hovering suspicion, but God was speaking through his wicked lips the truth of redemption.

Certainly this is in the heart of Paul and the rich and profound truth of Romans 5:6-9:

> For when we were still without strength, in due
> time Christ died for the ungodly. For scarcely for
> a righteous man will one die; yet perhaps for a
> good man someone would even dare to die. But
> God demonstrates His own love toward us, in that
> while we were still sinners, Christ died for us.
> Much more then, having now been justified by His
> blood, we shall be saved from wrath through Him.

We are delivered from the curse. All the full fury of God's wrath fell on the Lord as He took our place to pay the price for our deliverance from the curse of the law.

Paul uses a symbolic and graphic way to illustrate this great truth in Galatians 3:13: "It is written, 'Cursed is everyone who hangs on a tree.'" Quoting from Deuteronomy 21:23, he refers to the fact that criminals sentenced to die under the Mosaic law usually were executed by stoning. After being stoned they often then were tied to a post. Being tied to a post was to display the shame and the consequence of sin, to generate fear among the people so they would not do the same thing. The tying to the post made public display of the fact that this person had been cursed by God.

Paul looked at the cross and he saw Jesus tied to a post, cursed by God, on our behalf. What was the purpose of that? Verse 14 tells us. It was in order that, in Christ Jesus, the blessing of Abraham might come to the Gentiles. That's justification by faith, so that we might receive the promise of the Spirit through faith. That's sanctification by faith. The purpose is two things: justification by faith and sanctification.

We are given this message to preach, this message of redemption. Do we understand that there is no need for a Redeemer unless people understand they are under the curse? If we understand that, how can we remove the proclamation of man's hopelessness and sinfulness from the message? We can't do it without assaulting the glory of the redemption. This week a man said to me, "You know, my pastor is an evangelical, but he says you must never mention sin or confront sin from the pulpit. It offends." God help that man!

Let me wrap this up with Titus 1. All of salvation, including election, justification, sanctification, and glorification which are referred to in Titus 1:1-2, comes about because God, who can't lie, made a promise long ages ago. I want you to understand this. Literally the Greek says "before the times of the ages," or in eternity.

Back in eternity God made a promise. To whom did he make the promise? According to 2 Timothy 1:9: "[He] has saved us and called us with a holy calling, not according to our works, but according to His own purpose and grace which was given to us in Christ Jesus before time began." Now we know who made the promise. The Father made the promise to the Son. Hebrews 13:20 calls it the eternal covenant. What was the promise? John 17:24 says: "Father, I desire that they also whom You gave Me may be with Me where I am, that they may behold My glory *which You have given Me; for You loved Me before the foundation of the world"* (emphasis added).

Do you get the picture? Before the foundation of the world the Father loved the Son. Love must give. Love must express. At some point in eternity the Father covenanted with the Son to give Him a gift of love—a redeemed humanity. The Father covenanted to give to the Son a redeemed humanity who would come into their presence in eternity and give the Son glory. Glory, forever and ever and ever because the Father so loved the Son, He wanted Him to have that.

Do you think people are running around this world willy-nilly, deciding whether they want to love Jesus? I'm telling you, folks, we are a part of something so vast and incomprehensible that sweeps us back into eternity past. John 6:37 says: "All that the Father gives Me will come to Me." That means there are some people that God has chosen in eternity past to give to the Son as a redeemed humanity to praise Him forever and ever and ever. The Father has already identified who they are and they're all going to come. In John 6:38 Jesus said He had come down from heaven, not to do His own will, but to be the Redeemer. The Father said, "It's My plan. It's My love. It's going to be My gift. Will You go down there and redeem them?" And Jesus said, "So I came down from heaven, not to do My own will, but the will of Him who sent Me. This is the will of Him who sent me, that of all that He's given I will lose none. I will raise them up at the last day. For this is the Father's will, that everyone who beholds the Son and believes in Him will have everlasting life." Here we were, damned to hell, under the curse, and Jesus came because the Father sent Him to redeem His own.

Just thinking about belonging to God that way is absolutely mind-boggling. Why me? What is darkness to my intellect is sunshine to my heart. Someday all redeemed humanity is going to be together with Him, and something absolutely wonderful is going to happen. 1 Corinthians 15:28 says, "When all things are made subject to Him," that is, when the whole re-deemed humanity and everything else in the universe is brought to Christ, then "the Son Himself will also be subject to Him who put all things under Him, that God may be all in all."

I believe that when the Father's love gift is complete and given to the Son, the Son will turn right around and give it to the Father. This whole redemptive plan, beloved, is all hap-pening because of love in the Trinity. To think that we are so privileged to come to Christ because God chose us to be a part of the love gift—is it any wonder that the man who plowed the field and found the treasure sold everything? Is it any wonder that the man seeking pearls found the pearl of great price and sold everything? Is it hard to understand why Paul said in Philippians 3 something like, "I used to have this column and in that column I had credits, credits, credits, gain, gain, gain. Religious heritage, zeal, keeping the law, tribe of Benjamin, people of Israel, circumcised, all that gain, and then I sought Christ. I then counted the rest as manure." He sought the surpassing value of knowing Christ.

I close with this note. He was precious at the moment of salvation. The question we need to ask our own hearts is this: "Is He still that precious?" Is Christ still the treasure for which you'll sell everything, and the pearl for which you'll give up everything? Can you cry with the apostle Paul, "I know Him but I want to know Him more? I want to know the power of His resurrection. I want to know the fellowship of His suf-ferings." What does that mean? I want to commune with somebody who understands my pain. Is He as precious now as He was when you found the pearl? You see, I don't think people will ever understand the glory of the Redeemer if they don't understand the curse of the law. They'll never under-stand the immense and inexplicable privilege of belonging to Christ if they don't understand that this is all of God's grace in a vast and eternal love gift to the Son. It's way beyond them. This is what we need to preach.

Prayer:

"*Father, we can say nothing but thank You. We don't understand. We're just cursed and You sent Christ. You decided that we should be redeemed. We don't understand that, but we thank You. We just want to say all over again, everything else is manure. Christ is everything. Help us to know. We want intimacy. We want relationship. We want power, the power of Your resurrection working in our lives. We want fellowship, deep and sweet communion, even in the hard things of life. We want to be made conformable unto His death. We want to go as deep as we need to go to be faithful men. We are overwhelmed by all of this. Lord, help us in cultivating that exhilarating and exuberant gratitude and joy, to somehow translate that into our preaching and to preach the glories of the Redeemer, which means we have to preach the curse of the law. Make us faithful and may You be pleased as You gather in Your redeemed humanity to use a few of us humble servants to help You collect them, and we'll give You thanks. In the Savior's name we pray. Amen.*"

7.

REDEEMED BY THE SON: PARTICULAR REDEMPTION

GEOFF THOMAS

1996 Southern Baptist Founders Conference

G OD, who at various times and in various ways
spoke in time past to the fathers by the
prophets, has in these last days spoken to us
by His Son, whom He has appointed heir of all
things, through whom also He made the worlds;
who being the brightness of His glory and the
express image of His person, and upholding all
things by the word of His power, when He had by
Himself purged our sins, sat down at the right
hand of the Majesty on high, having become so
much better than the angels, as He has by inheritance obtained a more excellent name than they
(Hebrews 1:1-4).

WHO IS THIS SON?

God has a Son! The Lord Jesus Christ is the only begotten
Son of God. He is the One through whom God has spoken to
us and He is the One who speaks in creation. "The heavens
declare the glory of God; and the firmament shows His handi-
work" (Psalm 19:1). This Son also speaks through your conscience, the great divine monitor that He has set within every
single person who is made in His image and likeness. This
same Son has spoken through the prophets, as he rises early
in his eagerness to tell men all they need to know. He bids
them come into His presence, and reveals the deepest intentions of His heart and will to them. It is the Son who sends

111

them forth with His Word which burns in them like a fire in their bones.

Then this Son became incarnate and with His own voice He has spoken to us. His disciples came to Him and He taught them saying, "Blessed are the poor in spirit, for theirs is the kingdom of heaven. Blessed are they that mourn, for they shall be comforted. Blessed are the meek for they shall inherit the earth. Blessed are the pure in heart, for they shall see God. Blessed are the merciful, for they shall obtain mercy. Blessed are they who hunger and thirst after righteousness, for they shall be filled. Blessed are the peacemakers, for they shall be called Sons of God ..." (Matthew 5:3-9). How wonderful are those truths. Shakespeare never wrote any words like that. I've read much that's great in the literature of mankind, but there is nothing that compares to the speaking Son. "Come unto Me, all you who labor and are heavy laden and I will give you rest, take My yoke upon you and learn of Me, for I am meek and lowly in heart, and ye shall find rest for your souls, for my yoke is easy and My burden is light" (Matthew 11:28-29). How easy those words of Jesus recorded by Matthew trip off our tongues, yet there is nothing in the heart of John's Gospel so magnificent. This is the Son who has spoken; this is the Son who prayed, "Father forgive them for they know not what they do" (Luke 2:34); this is the Son who claimed identity with God, "I and my Father are one; ... if you've seen Me, you have seen the Father" (John 10:30; 14:9). He is God manifestly seen and heard and heaven's beloved One. This is the One of whom our text is speaking; this is the One who purged our sins.

Our text's context answers the question, "Who is this?" It tells us that He is greater than the angels because He made the angels, and He is the Lord of the angels. He is greater than the universe because He made the universe. At the beginning of the letter to the Hebrews these credentials of Christ are set out as they are also found at the beginning of John's Gospel, that by the Son of God every single thing was made that has ever been made. Nothing exists uncreated by

Christ. Paul sets these same credentials of Christ before the Colossians, that He made all things visible and invisible (1:16).

Man is so fascinated with origins. Where did it all come from? At one time there was nothing. It isn't that at one time there was space. There were no dimensions whatsoever, there was simply, absolutely unimaginable nothing. There was God alone and at one moment He spoke, and creation began; He commanded and all things stood fast like a totally obedient horse awaiting the next command of its master. Then creation develops step by step as God decrees. We Christians make a great claim, that this One who lived on this earth and at times was thirsty, asking a drink of a Samaritan woman; He made the universe. This One who held a child in His arms and blessed it, this One who was crucified on Golgotha, it was He who made the heavens and the earth in the beginning. He made the tree out of which that cross was shaped. He made the iron out of which the nails were formed which impaled Him on that cross.

These verses tell us who this Son of God is. He is the brightness of God's glory and the express image of His person. Do you remember the glory of God seen in the Seraphim and revealed to Isaiah in the Temple? Do you remember when Moses drew near to Him, how his face shone with that glory? Do you remember how, when Christ came, His glory was seen on the Mount of Transfiguration? Do you recall the brightness of His glory when He met with Saul on the road to Damascus, or when He appeared on the Isle of Patmos to the imprisoned and elderly John? But the glory of God, John tells us, is not so much the effulgence of His heavenly majesty, but the glory of His grace and truth, "And we beheld that glory," the apostle says on behalf of all those eyewitnesses, "in the incarnate Son of God" (John 1:14).

The Son has come in the apex of underived glory, not like the moon reflecting the glory of the sun. He is the very brightness of God's glory, not at all some kind of reflection of it. You can see that glory comprehensively in Jesus Christ. He is the express image of the only God there is. He is the exact representation of that eternal living God so that there is absolutely nothing in deity lacking in God the Son. There was a debate in the early church where some in the church were saying, "Jesus Christ is very like God." Others who were more mature and orthodox shot back, "No! He is not very like God at all, but He is very God. He is Jehovah. He is just as much God, as the Father is God, or the Spirit is God. He has all the names of God, all the titles of God, all the attributes of God, and all the prerogatives that are divine. They are all His, with no divine attribute omitted."

God is love and when we see Jesus on His knees, washing the feet of His disciples, we are seeing God's own love incarnate. Or when we see Him on the cross, in agony, we survey the whole likeness of God's sacrificial love in giving Himself. There is the heart of God. That was the most Godlike thing that God ever did. Calvary and the broken body of Jesus display the glory of God's grace and love most powerfully.

Who is this One of whom these verses speak? This is God the Son, greater than the angels as their Maker. The God of the prophets who spoke through them. The Creator who is the brightness of God's glory and the express image of His person.

WHAT DID THIS SON DO?

The writer of the letter to the Hebrews tells us that He purged our sins. To do this it was necessary for Him to come into the closest possible contact with men and women. He came into contact with them as they sinned. There was their failure to love God and to love their neighbors as themselves. They had other gods before Him; they made idols; they took His name is vain; they failed to set apart one day each week to Him; they didn't honor their parents; they killed; they committed adultery; they lied; they stole; they coveted. The Son of God was surrounded by people who behaved like this. They were His family, and the neighbors who lived on His street, and the boys He went to school with, and the customers who came to Joseph's carpenter shop for furniture and implements.

They were all sinners and their behavior defiled them. It made them dirty of spirit and heart, and so they needed more than a little washing—their very beings needed a purging. In other words, you sin, and you're unclean. You act in that way, and you are dirty. You say those cruel words, and you are defiled.

There was once an occasion where a man rang the bell at my front door. I met a stranger who wanted to see me. I brought him in and he said, "Will you baptize me?" I had never seen him before. He told me that he had been involved with a woman and she had conceived a child and had had an abortion. They had ended the relationship, but he was the one who felt defiled, dirty, unclean. He needed to be washed! I spoke to him, not of the sign of baptism, but what it signifies.

> I know a fount where sins are washed away,
> I know a place where night is turned to day.
> Burdens are lifted and blind eyes made to see;
> There's a wonder-working power in the blood
>   of Calvary.

Our sins have made us, the Bible says, as black as an Ethiopian, as spotted as a leopard, red like crimson, but the Son of God has come to do something about these sins. He has come to purge our sins. "Our sins" purged away, that is, totally removed. Whose sins? Who is he writing to? Hebrew Christians in the church. He is not writing this letter to the Sanhedrin. Is he writing it to Caiaphas or Annas the High Priests? Is he writing this letter to the persecuting Pharisees? Is he writing it to the rationalistic Sanhedrin? No, this is a letter to a certain constituency, a definite constituency, a particular constituency, a limited constituency. It is not a public letter; it's not a promiscuous letter. It's a letter to a church, the followers of the Lord Jesus Christ.

When Paul wrote to the Corinthians, he said, "Christ died for our sins" (1 Corinthians 15:3). He was effectively acknowledging that the death of the Lamb of God was as much his hope and the foundation of his pardon, as the youngest beginner, or the most menial slave who had confessed Christ in the Corinthian church. When he wrote to the Ephesians, he said, "Christ loved the church and gave Himself for it" (Ephesians 5:25). And when he wrote of God breaking into his own experience and shattering the shackles that bound him to sin, he said, "He loved me and gave Himself for me" (Galatians 2:20). Christ's work on the cross is always so particular; it is always as definitive as that. It is never for the anonymous mass. It is for those whose sins have once and for all been dealt with by the One greater than the angels, the mighty Creator who is the brightness of God's glory. Those who benefit admit and confess their sins, acknowledging that the total answer to their guilt and condemnation is found in this, "He purged our sins."

So this glorious divine Christ is set before us as One who has made an effective purgation for these people's sins. The consequences for those of us whose sins have been purged away are unbelievable. For me it means that my sins today are as though they never were. What a magnificent and incredible concept that is, that our sins do not control, or modify, our relation to God today. It is as if they were not there. There is no defilement, no dirt, it is all removed—every single speck of it. Christ has taken our sin, past, present and future, and He has put it away. He has provided purification for it so that all for whom He has died are whiter than snow. I am not sure my conscience believes it. I am not sure there is not in me some egotism that wants to cling in self pity to some remnants of guilt so that I may be able to feel sorry for myself. Aren't such feelings the whole basis of the invention of purgatory, that mythical place where one's guilt will be slowly cleansed away? Isn't there some pride in every human heart that wants to go bravely into that fantasy land to make amends for a messed-up, dirty life?

If only I can let this truth be the whole truth about the way things are between me and God, that there is no barrier whatsoever between God and me; that there is no impediment whatsoever. It is all forgiven. It is all blotted out. The only way I am permitted to look at my past sins is to see them as forgiven sins. It may even be that sometimes we use a vague assumption that all is not right between ourselves and God to justify a little less commitment, a little less discipleship, a little less purity because, we reason, all is not forgiven. But I am saying it is all forgiven! He has purged it; he has borne it all away—all the guilt, every spot, and every sin was laid on Christ by the Father. The glorious Son of God took the liability for my sin. The single determinant of your relationship with God today is what happened on the cross. Nothing else matters. Nothing else is relevant. There are only two factors in the equation: what Christ did and how God responded. How you might feel and how you struggle, and what you achieve, and how you'll fail in the future, all that is not relevant. The one and only thing relevant to my forgiveness is what Christ did on the cross.

I do not for a moment believe that the heart that knows this will take advantage of it and go from that to live a life without law, because that cross, that grace, won't allow it. On the other hand, I also believe that a bad conscience, a feeling that God has something against you, often serves as the basis of an unconscious grudge against God, and that idea will seek to justify our being less than perfect. It will try to justify a relapse here, and a shortcoming there. I want every Christian to know, in the depth of their hearts, that Jesus Christ has perfectly completed the work God gave Him to do. He has. No angel came to do it. No creature. The angels' Lord Himself did it. Jehovah Jesus has made a real purging of our sins. Consider who He is—the Creator of the heavens and the earth; the mighty Prophet that comes from God; the brightness of God's glory; the express image of God's person.

How focused He was from the moment His public ministry began. He set His face steadfastly towards Jerusalem. There was a task and an eternal vocation before Him. He was walking with destiny and His goal was Golgotha. There were those His Father had given to Him whom nothing would prevent Him from saving. There, in His great and royal death, He would deal with sin, our defilement, the way God hates our shame, the way it has created a gulf between God and ourselves, the way sin corrupts us, poisoning and perverting all that is good. The Son of God came to deal with all this, as the Almighty One who raised the dead. Christ appeared as the One who spoke and the winds and waves obeyed Him. Jehovah Jesus, the Messiah long prophesied, came, but there was one thing more He had to do before He could cry out, "It is finished! Father, into Thy arms I commend my spirit" (John 19:30). He had to purge our sins. He had to remove that defilement that corrupts every single thing we have done, and the guilt of every failure. This great Holocaust offering had to take the off-scouring of sinners into the cosmic incinerator that God had set up on Golgotha, and Himself choose to enter so freely that judgment of the fire that they deserve, embracing all that is unclean, absorbing it into Himself and standing, in solidarity with it, in the naked flame of God's holiness until it was all gone.

Christ had to be made sin for us, taking all our foulness to Himself, and then purge and wash it from us (every single atom of contamination), imputing Christ's righteousness to us. Because He has purged us from our sins, we can cry to the world, "Look! There is flowing a crimson tide, whiter than snow, you may be today."

Now you see one consequence of this, that the dying of Jesus is itself purgatory. Golgotha is the only purgatory in this world, or the world to come. There is no need of another purging because there is absolutely nothing left to purge, and no other purifier for sin can be found. The angels may scour the universe in vain to try to find one. Not all great Neptune's ocean can cleanse a sinner of his sin. But Christ the Lamb of God takes all the guilt of our sin away, a sacrifice of nobler name and richer blood than all the world's refiners. He has accomplished everything. He has undefiled a company of people more than any man can number. He has borne all their punishment. He has won for them eternal life. When they see Him, they will be like Him, for they shall see Him as He is. Until then He is able to keep us from falling and to present us faultless before the presence of His glory with exceeding joy (Jude 1:24).

The Lord could speak to the dying thief and He could say, "Today, thou shall be with Me in paradise" (Luke 23:43). He didn't do half a job on Calvary did he? "Ninety nine-and-a-half won't do," sang Dorothy Love Coates. Quite right! He didn't leave a little bit for us to do in suffering in this world, and then in some nebulous fantasy state of darkness and suffering in the world to come. If I should have some contribution to make in the purging away of my own sin then I am a lost man because I can never do anything without sinning. No! He by Himself purged our sins.

HOW DID THE SON DO IT?

The third thing we need to see is that He did it by Himself. We've talked about who He was and what He did. He was offering Himself without spot to God; He wasn't offering His sufferings only; He wasn't offering His blood only; He wasn't offering His obedience or His human nature. He was offering Himself without spot to God. He is the ransom price. The price then has been paid once and for all. Every penny. There is nothing at all left outstanding. We are free. He Himself is the propitiation for our sins. God's anger towards us is absolutely and utterly appeased. Now we are all welcomed as returning prodigals by our loving Father. See Him run to embrace each one of us. He will never let us leave Him again. O, love that will not let me go! Christ is the great Satisfaction rendered to God. He is the Price of our liberation. There is nothing overlooked for anyone, nor is there anything unpaid. The most hypocritical and deeply dyed stain that has seemed to drip on us all through our lives has been all washed away by Christ.

He made a comprehensive purging for sin, not trembling before any stain, and He did this, not by enabling you to do something, not by inspiring you to choose, not by encouraging you to repent, not by challenging you to discipleship, not by exalting you to faith, not by commanding you to live a holy life, nor by pleading with you to be compassionate towards your fellow men. If my standing before God today depended on my repentance, my faith, my compassion, my holy living, then I would have no hope at all before God. But He did something, and He did something by Himself.

Do you remember after the temptations when angels came to minister to Him in the wilderness? At His baptism God spoke to Him and assured Him of His love and flooded His heart with a divine affection. At His transfiguration towards the close of His ministry, again, that affirmation of Sonship was given by God Himself. In the Garden an angel came to comfort Him. But on Calvary, there was no voice of affection coming down from heaven. There was rather a cry of abandonment ascending from earth: "My God, My God, why hast Thou forsaken me?" (Matthew 27:46). He was all by Himself. There were no friends, there was no family, and no disciples there. They had all forsaken Him and fled. They were a broken group standing way off, none attempting to encourage, none trying to catch His eye and pour through a glance love and a wordless, intense look saying, "I know what You are doing and I love You for doing it."

You and I were no help to Jesus as He hung on that cross. You were no support to Him. He was His own support, and by Himself our brave Prince of Glory purged all our sins. What could be more glorious and liberating than that? There is a real and a total purging of sin which He Himself has accomplished. He did it by Himself. That is the great theme of the Bible from beginning to end, that the work of salvation is entirely (only and exclusively), the work of the Lord Jesus Christ. Nobody had any share in it. There was nobody with Him. All that has been done, He has achieved by Himself. Do not bring a scrap, or a shred of your righteousness (which is as filthy rags) anywhere near him. "He that glorieth, let him glory in the Lord" (2 Corinthians 10:17). Do not talk about your faith, your smartness in choosing Him, your goodness, your works and your efforts. Redemption is all accomplished by Him alone. Thank God it is. "I have trodden the winepress alone" (Isaiah 63:3). He could do it alone; He did it all by Himself.

WHAT IS THE SON DOING NOW?

The fourth thing we are told in Hebrews 1 is that after He purged our sins He sat down at the right hand of the Majesty on High. In other words, He is a sitting Savior. Now, what do we do with that? It means, of course, that He finished the work that He had been given to do in eternity, and He completed it on this planet in time. It is all over, and perfectly accomplished, so He sits down. You may remember that in both the Old Testament tabernacle and temple there were no chairs. There were tables and altars and candles and curtains, but no chairs. The work of sacrifice never ended, morning and evening, year after year, they were busy, busy, busy, doing, doing, doing. But now that this great High Priest after the order of Melchizedek has finished His work, He sits at the right hand of the Majesty on High. Just as God surveyed the original work of creation and pronounced it to be very good, so today, God the Father, God the Son, and God the Holy Spirit, look at the whole travail of cosmic redemption—all the pain and suffering, the accomplished work of the Servant, the obedience to the death of the cross—and the Triune God is utterly and completely satisfied. This is the most glorious thing in this world or in heaven itself, that Jesus Christ is completely satisfied with His own work. He looks at Golgotha and He says, "Very good," and He sits down and He now rests. God the Father looks at the work of His Son, and He rests in love for Him, and God the Holy Spirit looks at the work of Christ, and He rests in eternal delight. And the angels in glory look at that work and are filled with wonder, love and praise.

The fearful fact is that everybody is happy with it except you. You feel you must contribute a little bit of yourself. You must think, "Yes, but He couldn't have saved me unless I had agreed to cooperate." And you want to throw in a little bit of Christian experience, and you've got to present to God some gifts of yours. You've got to offer a little growth, and some progress, and a wee bit of suffering, and some witnessing, and a taste of pain and patience in providence. Then it will be absolutely perfect when you've made your contribution to the work that Christ has done. You won't sit down, you see. You won't rest in the work of Christ. Notice what God the Son did, how He sits and He is satisfied. Consider God the Father— He is thrilled, and God the Holy Spirit is delighted. All the angels in glory are overwhelmed by it, and the church that is glorified now in the presence of God, is singing: "Unto Him who loved us and washed us from our sins in His own blood, unto Him be glory and praise and dominion forever and ever." When they reach that destination, they are never thinking about what they did during their pilgrimage. Instead, they are saying, "Worthy is the Lamb! Thou art worthy to receive power and riches and wisdom and strength and honor and glory and blessing" (Revelation 5:12). They see that He has made a complete purging, and I am saying to you, there is nothing in the whole world more glorious than that.

That is why this Bible is such a magnificent Book! That is why you all have a Bible and you read the Scriptures, and you want the Word preached to you. "Feed me now and evermore," you say, because you live by these words that proceed from the mouth of God. I am saying that if you are a biblical Christian, you sit in awe at what Jesus did, when by Himself He purged your sins. You are filled with wonder, love, and praise.

WHAT SHOULD WE DO IN RESPONSE TO WHAT THE SON DID?

So, what do I want you to do? I want you to do nothing,

absolutely nothing. I don't want you to get out of your seats.
I don't want you to come to the front, I don't want you to be
baptized. I don't want you to join the church. I don't want you
to make any resolutions that after today and from now on you
are going to become more religious. I don't want you even to
think of what you are going to do. I want you to sit. I want you
to sit absolutely still. Don't move, don't plan, don't decide. I
want you passive.

> Jesus, my great High Priest,
> Offered His blood and died.
> My guilty conscience seeks no sacrifice beside.
> His powerful blood did once atone,
> And now it pleads before the throne.
>   (Isaac Watts)

Christ is absolutely satisfied with His accomplished redemption and the question is: "Are you satisfied with that?"
Are you completely and totally contented? When Satan comes
to remind you of one sad episode or another in your life do
you say, "But Christ, by Himself purged my sin"? When you
fall again for the thousandth time into the sins of omission, of
imagination, of thought, word and deed, do you say, "Christ
by Himself purged my sins"? Do you believe that?

When a man is drowning and a lifeguard swims alongside
him, he doesn't say, "Now look, see the shore? That's the way
to go. Good luck!" He doesn't do that. He saves him. He says,
"Stop struggling," and he holds him up and he keeps his head
above the waves and he powerfully delivers him from the
watery grave. So for you too, I don't want you to move until
that is settled. I want you to sit. I don't want you to bat an
eyelid. I don't want you to breathe. I want you to purge the
word "do" from your mind. I never want you to think in terms
of doing,

> Until to Jesus' work you cling by a simple faith.

Doing is a deadly thing; doing ends in death.

Sit, and consider what God the Son has done, and be absolutely satisfied with that. Let your conscience be satisfied with it. If God is satisfied with it, my friend, you and that tender conscience of yours can be satisfied with it. Here is the answer: The Lord of glory is satisfied with the work of Christ. So bring your past, your hope in death, your conscience, your intellect, to that work of Christ. Don't move a muscle, until you settle on this: "I am the chief of sinners, but Jesus died for me."

The world is full of religion. New religions appear every month promoting, "Do, do, do, ... do this, and do that." Christ tells us to sit and look. "Behold! The Lamb of God takes away the sins of the world" (John 1:29). Be satisfied with that. Beholding the life and death of Christ in faith, we find salvation. That is grace! That is eternal life! Neither is there salvation in any other, "for there is none other name under heaven given amongst men whereby we must be saved" (Acts 4:12). He invites you, "Look unto me and be saved, all the ends of the earth, for I am God and there is none else ... Let the wicked forsake his way, and the unrighteous man his thoughts" (Isaiah 45:22; 55:7).

The dying thief brought one plea to Christ, "Remember me." That man, as he contemplated the One who had all of heaven and the heaven of heavens under His authority, but Who was hanging next to him upon another cross, asked Jesus not to forget him while He was governing the universe. "I can do nothing but look at You. Please remember me." Make that your prayer.

Sit, and look to Him, that He might have mercy on you, that He might abundantly pardon, for He has, by Himself, purged our sin and is now seated at the right hand of the Majesty in heaven. Amen.

8.

THE PROVIDENCE OF GOD AND TEACHING OF JESUS

LIGON DUNCAN

2000 Southern Baptist Founders Conference

I COUNT it an enormous privilege to be here among like-minded brothers in Christ. My regard and hopes for the ministries of faithful, Bible-believing, Southern Baptists and their churches are unbounded. I am grateful to you for this invitation to an "interloping" Presbyterian, though I do have some good Southern Baptist roots. I not only grew up around streets named, "Boyce," "Manly," "Broadus," and "Williams," I have a cousin named, "Truett" (George W.). My mother taught at Furman University on the music faculty and studied at Southern Baptist Theological Seminary in the Church Music program. In fact, she was involved in cataloging the church music library in the late 1950s at Southern Baptist Seminary. So I have a special love in my heart for the Southern Baptists for a variety of reasons. I want to say that in God's providence He has ordained that the Southern Baptist churches are the vanguard movement of American evangelicalism. So, all of us who are reformed Evangelicals have a vested interest in the spiritual health of the Southern Baptist churches as well as the convention and all its constituent ministries. Therefore, we regularly pray for you in our pulpit prayers and elsewhere—that God would bless you and prosper the work of your hands. May the Lord bless His Word among His people and in your midst.

I have as my assignment this week to consider the providence of God. By providence we mean "God's most holy, wise, and all-powerful preserving and governing of all His creatures and all their actions." Our catechisms and our confessions (Baptist and Presbyterian) say this without a word's variation, I am happy to say.

Today, I want to look at the doctrine of God's providence in Jesus' teaching. I think you will find that, though the doctrine of providence is ubiquitous on the pages of the Old Testament, the New Testament is as at least as clear and forceful in its presentation of the comprehensive doctrine of God's providence. You will find it all over the teaching of our Lord and Savior.

OPPOSITION TO GOD'S PROVIDENCE

God's providence is under assault from a number of directions. When you attempt to preach God's providence in the churches, and even sometimes when some attempt to *believe* God's providence in the churches, you are likely to meet some form of opposition and disagreement. I would suggest to you that there are at least three areas or forms of opposition that we will encounter.

Arminian Opposition to Providence.

First, there is the popular Arminian opposition to God's providence which basically says this: "God knows, but He doesn't govern, because that would make us puppets."

Surely, you have heard this. My godly, Southern Baptist grandmother, who had the privilege of being ministered to under Calvinistic, Baptist preaching in the hills of east Tennessee, unfortunately, somewhere along the line, imbibed some of this popular Arminian teaching. When we were around Grandmother, we knew that this subject of God's providence, and especially the subject of God's predestination, was not one we were to talk about! One Christmas we were at Grandmother's and Grandfather's house, and we were reading our devotions that day as a family. We happened to be in Ephesians 1. I bit my tongue hard at the end of the reading and said *nothing*—even as a fifteen-year old Presbyterian. Nothing came out of my mouth, but my grandmother knew what I was thinking! After the reading she said to me, "Now son, you understand that we are Baptists and we don't believe in predestination." I said, "Well, Grandmother, you and I may disagree about what predestination means, but Paul uses the word. We both agree in predestination, you just think it means something differently from me." She responded, "No, son. You don't understand. We are Baptists and we don't *believe* in predestination." I said, "Grand-mom, the word is in the Bible. Calvin didn't write this passage. Paul said, 'predestined.' Now you and I disagree about what he meant when he used that word but we both believe in predestination." She responded again, "No, son. You don't understand." My grandmother had two control beliefs: The Bible was true and predestination was not. Therefore, anything you showed her in the Bible that said "predestination" could not possibly be true because predestination was not true and the Bible was true.

So often we run into precisely that kind of popular opposition to the doctrines of grace, in general, and the doctrine of providence, in particular. It is characterized by a control belief that has a firm appreciation for the authority of Scripture in the abstract, but when it comes to an uncomfortable doctrine—a doctrine which might challenge our own self-sovereignty—that particular doctrine is written out of the Scripture while the Scripture is, in the abstract, upheld as the final authority for our faith and practice. All of us know that kind of opposition—popular Arminianism, we might say.

Liberal Opposition to Providence.

Second, we have had much opposition to the traditional doctrine of providence from process theology and other kinds of liberal theology all this century long. As a matter of fact, this has been going back for some time. We could not only stretch back into the nineteenth century but even towards the end of the eighteenth century in some German, liberal, rationalist circles. But especially this century, in the English-speaking world via process theologians and other liberal theologians, we have seen frontal assaults on the doctrine of providence. Most of this opposition is motivated by alien philosophical and cultural influences. In other words, they are not derived from a desire to read the Scripture carefully. They come from a desire to re-understand the Scripture in light of something else—whether it is process philosophy or something similar.

These views of providence scale-down God. I remember the very first lecture I attended at the University of Edinburgh College. It was on the book of Job, and it was given by the eminent professor of Old Testament, Professor J. C. L. Gibson. Professor Gibson was the editor of a very important Old Testament commentary series and was in the process of re-translating the entire book of Job. I went to the lecture with some trepidation and was encouraged initially when, in his introductory remarks, he began to comment about the fact that he was disappointed that some of the more difficult sections of Job—some of those sections that sort of rub against our grain—were being taken out of the *Church of Scotland Book of Common Worship and Lectionary* and thus, being taken away from the regular hearing of the people of God. I thought, "Um, well, maybe he will have something good to say." Then he went on to share with us some of his radical re-translations of the book of Job. Of course, there was a total evacuation of any reference to our Lord and Savior Jesus Christ even in the famous passage, "I know that my Redeemer lives." But especially radical was his re-translation of Job 42 in which, instead of Job repenting before God, he has God repenting to Job. Gibson said that the book of Job teaches us two things: First of all, it teaches us that there are some people who do not need forgiveness. He suggested Job as such a person who needed no forgiveness and, therefore, he took a direct aim at the evangelicals in the audience and said, "You need to learn that there are people out in the world who don't need forgiveness." Secondly, he said, "The book of Job teaches us the triumph of the creature over the Creator. For in the book of Job, God has to confess to Job that there are some things in His creation that are outside of His control." I was glad that I was fourteen rows back just in case any stray electromagnetic activity in the atmosphere appeared at that particular moment. This is the kind of stuff that you will get in much liberal theology today opposing anything like an orthodox view of the providence of God.

Openness of God Opposition to Providence.

And now, breaking forth on the evangelical scene (of all places) in the last few years is a third opposition to the orthodox and biblical doctrine of the providence of God, that is, the "openness of God" movement. Openness theology is what I call, "Arminianism with a vengeance." The older Arminianism had the decency to leave the God of the Bible with at least foreknowledge—He knew what was coming, it's just that He didn't do anything about it. However, this species of Arminianism realized something Calvinists have been saying for a long time: If the future can be known then the future is fixed. So these neo-Arminians said, "Well, so much for the future being known." Out went God's knowledge of the future.

There is a particularly nuanced view of the openness presentation of God which is even more difficult to critique than, say, Clark Pinnock's view, and it is found in the position of Greg Boyd, for instance, in his book, *God of the Possible*. Boyd would say something like this: "Well, there are some things that God knows ahead of time. And, there are some things that He predestines. But He doesn't know all things, because the future doesn't exist unless He has predestined that particular thing and He has not predestined all things, only certain things." Therefore, if you say, "What about this passage which speaks of God predestining that?" He will say, "Oh, of course, God predestined that. It is just that He doesn't predestine all things." You can go through the entire Bible and show him thousands of verses in which God rules, exercises sovereignty, and predestines, and he will say, "I agree with all that. It is just that God doesn't do anything more than that." Or, "if he does do more than that, we can't know it." It is a very subtle and dangerous thing.

THE PROVIDENCE OF GOD IN MATTHEW 11

I want us to spend some time looking at Jesus' teaching about providence especially in Matthew 11:

> Then He began to reproach the cities in which most of His miracles were done, because they did not repent. "Woe to you, Korazin! Woe to you, Bethsaida! For if the miracles had occurred in Tyre and Sidon which occurred in you, they would have repented long ago in sackcloth and ashes. Nevertheless, I say to you, it shall be more tolerable for Tyre and Sidon in the day of judgment than for you. And you, Capernaum, will not be exalted to heaven, will you. You shall descend down to Hades, for if the miracles had occurred in Sodom which had occurred in you, it would have remained to this day. Nevertheless, I say to you that it shall be more tolerable for the land of Sodom in the day of judgment than for you."
> At that time Jesus answered and said, "I praise Thee, O Father, Lord of heaven and earth, that You didst hide these things from the wise and intelligent and didst reveal them to babes. Yes, Father, for thus it was well-pleasing in Thy sight. All things have been handed over to Me by My Father, and no one knows the Son except the Father. Nor does anyone know the Father except the Son, and anyone to whom the Son wills to reveal Him. Come to Me, all you are weary and heavy laden, and I will give you rest. Take My yoke upon you and learn from Me, for I am gentle and humble in heart, and you will find rest for

your souls. For My yoke is easy and My load is
light" (Matthew 11:20-30).

Matthew 11 and its depiction of Jesus' tribute to John the
Baptist, Jesus' warnings against these unrepentant cities, and
His evangelistic call is Matthew's follow-up to the account of
Jesus sending forth the disciples as ambassadors in Matthew
10.

We might have expected Matthew to give an account of the
disciples' activity in their mission after Jesus had sent them
out. But, in fact, what we find at the end of Matthew 10 and
throughout Matthew 11 is that Matthew focuses us *wholly* on
the glory and majesty of Jesus Christ. Though we might expect Matthew to speak about what the disciples were doing,
He turns our focus to the Lord Jesus Christ.

There is a hint in there to us as well. The Puritans used to
say, "The secret of soul-fatting Bible study is not to ask, 'what
does this text teach me about how I am to live today, but what
does this text teach me about my God?'" Matthew turns our
attention to the glory and the majesty of Jesus Christ. His
focus is clearly on Christ. Indeed, the events that are assembled here in Matthew 11 are all designed to witness to Jesus
as the Messiah. Matthew is showing us the majesty of Jesus
the Messiah. That is his real theme in Matthew 11. In verses
20-30, you will find the clearest expressions of God's sovereignty and man's responsibility laid side-by-side in all of the
Scriptures. And Jesus is right in the middle of it. In that regard, this is an excellent passage on which to meditate at the
beginning of a conference devoted to the subject of God's
providence.

Yes, the things about which Jesus speaks are a subset of the
totality of what we consider when we talk about God's providence. They are certainly a part of God's governing and ordering all His creatures and all their actions. We are going to focus on Jesus' words of praise to His sovereign Father and His
tender words of invitation and their implication for our understanding of God's providence and of the sovereignty of our

Lord and Savior Jesus Christ.

There are five things I would like you to see in this passage, bearing in mind that the theme is the majesty of Christ. It is in this passage that we see the majesty of Christ in regeneration, illumination, revelation, invitation and especially in providence. In this passage, Christ looks to heaven in thanksgiving to the Father for His providence, His sovereignty, the security of His eternal plan, and He looks to earth to overture all those who are burdened with sin, inviting them to partake of the privileges and benefits of the covenant of grace.

God is Sovereign.

First of all, Jesus emphatically asserts God's sovereign providence. Bible-believing Christians will joyfully acknowledge that God the Father is sovereign in salvation. In verses 20-24 the issues of sovereignty and responsibility have already been raised in Jesus' words of warning to the cities which had rejected Him. Jesus reminds us here that not everyone has the same exposure to the gospel. That is an issue of the sovereignty of God. Matthew Henry said, "Some places enjoy the means of grace in greater plenty, power and purity than other places." Jesus is saying this to the cities of Korazin and Bethsaida: "Sodom would have converted if she had seen Me, and you have turned your back on Me and all My miracles."

Then in verses 25-26, "Jesus answered and said, 'I praise You, Father, Lord of heaven and earth, that You have hidden these things from the wise and intelligent and have revealed them to infants. Yes, Father, for this way was well-pleasing in Your sight.'" Notice that Jesus explicitly asserts here that God has hidden spiritual truth from some. He is, for all practical purposes, speaking of the doctrine of reprobation. I agree with most of the reformed commentators that He is ultimately also lifting up praise for those who are humble of heart, despised in the eyes of the world, but who had responded to His ministry in spite of the rejection of those who were wise in their own eyes and self-righteous. It is interesting that the very form of words that He uses in the praise and prayer to His heavenly Father provoke us to think about the doctrine of reprobation. He lifts up a praise to His heavenly Father and explicitly asserts that God has done this according to His own good pleasure. It is unconditioned. His providence is His own. He has ordained it in His sovereignty.

I want to pause here and say that, however distasteful the doctrine of reprobation may be, it is emphatically not only the doctrine of Scripture, but the doctrine of our Lord and Savior Jesus Christ, and He couldn't have said it more clearly. So, if our reaction—and I understand the reaction of the heart—is to recoil initially from that truth, the proper response to that recoiling is to repent and bow the knee to Scripture. For, where the Scripture speaks, God speaks. Therefore, we see Jesus in His sovereignty telling us about the sovereignty of His Father in providence.

Behind all resistance to the sovereignty of God you will find two things. I want to be careful when I say this because I am not presuming to be able to look into the hearts of men and women who reject the doctrine of God's sovereignty and judge their motives or their sincerity. They may be very sincere in their belief that they are deriving their position from Scripture when they oppose God's sovereignty. But because the doctrine of God's providence and sovereignty is so painfully clear in Scripture, one must ultimately look to other origins for the rejection of that doctrine. What I share with you I share with you carefully.

The first is the idea that I will not believe what I cannot understand. By understanding, I mean that to which I cannot get *all* the answers. Those who reject God's sovereignty always have taken an epistemological starting point, and say, "If I cannot totally comprehend it and work out all the answers to all the questions, then I'm not going to believe it. There are problems there. There are unanswered questions there and until I have answers for those, I'm not going to believe it." My friends, that is Arian epistemology. That is preciously what the heretic Arius did with the doctrine of our Lord and Savior

Jesus Christ. He couldn't figure out the concept of the doctrine of the deity and the humanity of the Lord Jesus Christ in the incarnation and, therefore, he denied it. He came up with a solution that he thought was more intellectually coherent but which was actually heresy. Whenever we are in the posture of saying, "I will not believe what I cannot understand," we are rejecting much of that which is most precious in the Scripture.

Dare any of us say we can explain the relation between the two natures of our blessed Lord? Dare any one of us now stand and say that those are not Scriptural doctrines? The Arian has to say, "I will not believe what I cannot understand," and that is precisely what the Arminian does with the doctrine of God's sovereignty. Even though the Arminian says, "I'm wanting to be more biblical," the historical fact is that the Arminian is the one coming up with a rationalist solution to problems that he perceives being raised by the biblical doctrines of grace.

The second thing behind every resistance to the doctrine of the sovereignty of God is the sneaking suspicion on the part of an individual that he is more loving than God. "Oh, but God couldn't do that—that wouldn't be loving," he says. What's behind that statement? "Oh, but God could never ..." translates into "I'm more loving than a God that would do that." I'm standing in judgment upon the love of God.

The irony of this, my friends, is that apart from His grace we are hell-bound sinners. Every Christian would admit it. We are sinners and we sin every day. So, we have to ask the person who rejects God's sovereignty, "So, you're saying, you the sinner, are worried that the God of the Bible might do something wrong?" Interesting. Behind the rejection of the sovereignty of God is the sneaking suspicion that we have achieved a level of love and understanding that surpasses these rude, crude and limited presentations of the person and the actions of God which have been bequeathed to us from the ages of the church. So, now God needs to be updated so He can be as loving as we are? Those things are pernicious, my friends, and they can be soul-destroying.

We are talking about something in deadly earnest that is very important. When we say that Jesus emphatically asserts God's sovereign providence we must be concerned to take care that our people do not out of hand reject that truth because the acceptance of it is a significant part of our willingness to bow the knee and acknowledge that He is wiser than we are and that His ways are not our ways and we are called to trust in Him despite all evidence to the contrary, even in places which surpass our own finite understanding. In other words, it is a very important part of growth in faith to learn to trust in a God whose ways are sovereign.

I had the privilege of being an interim pastor in Yazoo City, Mississippi. The reason I was the interim pastor in that local congregation was because, on New Year's Day, returning from fellowship with his brother who was a minister in Memphis, Mike Sartelle and his family were involved in a terrible automobile accident. Mike and his youngest son, Nate, were killed instantly. His wife, Diane, was thrown from the car nearly dead and the other two children were in critical condition. When they awakened Diane at the hospital, she immediately started asking, "Where is Mike?" One of the family friends was there and knew that Mike was already dead and simply said, "He is alright, Diane. We need to worry about you right now." It took two days before they could tell whether she was going to make it through until they could bring themselves to tell Diane that Mike was dead. They told her the news and she asked, "Where's Nate? Where's my baby?" They said, "Diane, he has gone home to be with the Lord, too." Her words were: "The Lord is good in all His ways."

Ten years later, to the month, an elder in the church who had been so helpful in helping Diane through the recovery and the difficulties of being a widow with two children received a phone call one Sunday afternoon. "Bob, your niece Maggie was killed this morning on the way to church." Bob pulled His wife, Amanda, out of the Sunday School area at First Presbyterian, Yazoo City. He said, "Amanda, it is bad news." She asked, "It's Maggie, isn't it?" He replied, "Yes." And she said, "The Lord is good in all His ways." The doctrine of God's providence is among the most practical doctrines of the whole Christian life. We cannot afford to ignore it. To do so would be to ignore the directives of our Lord and Savior.

Second, in verses 20-24, I want you see that God's providence is consonant with and even conducive to the most urgent warnings of judgment. Bible-believing Christians will not bring two clear teachings of Scripture to oppose one another. Just as we cannot construe the attributes of God so that one is opposed to another—for example, God's justice versus His mercy—so too, must we not bring the clear teachings of Scripture to oppose one another. Even as the Bible tells us to urgently plea with those who are lost, so also the Bible tells us that God is sovereign in salvation.

Look at how Jesus addressed these cities. Look at the urgency with which he warned Korazin and Bethsaida. Jesus here makes rubbish of the charge that belief in God's providence robs a preacher of urgency in his witness. I defy you to find more importunate appeal to dying sinners than you find in the words of our Lord and Savior.

And in a few moments He is going to acknowledge that *God* has blinded the hearts of these people. Brothers, especially those of you who believe in the doctrines of grace, you must be *emphatic* in your dealing with sinners—in your calling of sinners by the gospel invitation, in your pleading with sinners and your warning of sinners—lest anyone be given any ground whatsoever for opposing the counsels, purposes, ends and means of God. You and I both know that is wrong to say that because God has ordained the ends, means don't matter. Arminians will constantly tell you that the idea that means don't matter is the logical result of your theology. And so, in all of your ministry you must be careful to emphasize both the means and the ends—both the sovereignty of God and the responsibility of man. Jesus does it beautifully right here. God's providence is consonant and even conducive to the most urgent warnings of judgment.

A third thing I would like you see in this passage is that, in verse 25, God's providence evokes and provokes praise. Jesus thanked God the Father for actually hiding spiritual truth from some people though He later invited all to come to Him. Bible-believing Christians should regularly and specifically contemplate God's providence and then worship Him for it.

Jesus' heart must have been downcast by their unbelief because you remember His words elsewhere, "O Jerusalem, Jerusalem! How often I have wanted to gather you as a hen gathers her chicks and you would not have it" (Matthew 23:37). His heart beat for those who were lost. And yet here Jesus lifts up a prayer of thanksgiving to the Father for the rejection of His ministry amongst these unrepenting cities. To contemplate God's sovereignty and wisdom and the preservation of a remnant in this little circle of disciples (humble though they were) would have been supremely comforting to the Lord Jesus' soul. "The wise of this world have rejected Me though I am the wisdom of the ages. The great of this world have rejected Me though I am the first born of all creation. Thank you, O God, for these humble, poor fishermen and their friends who in your counsel, before the foundation of the world, You gave into My hand. I love You for it. I love You for them, even as I love them."

When we are discouraged, we are to take encouragement in God's decree, His wisdom, His faithful, His goodness, and that is preciously what Jesus does here. Not only does He take encouragement but He thanks God and praises Him even in the face of rejection.

Thanksgiving to God, my friends, is the antidote. It is the answer to dark and disquieting thoughts. Why was Joseph not a bitter man? Because he believed in the providence of God and so had a thankful heart. Separated from the father of his heart for twenty years through the nefarious deeds of his brothers he could still say, "God meant it for good." The providence of God kept that man from bitterness. The providence of God leads Jesus to praise.

Notice specifically that Jesus thanks His Father for revealing His gospel to babes and acknowledges that He has hidden it from the wise. He glories in the fact that the Lord has revealed this mystery in the fullness of times, and that it will be the wise and the self-righteous who will reject Him, and the humble and meek sinners who will embrace Him. It shows the unexpected character of God's providence and His decree.

Those favors which distinguish us from the lost and are rooted in the goodness of God are those favors which most oblige us to praise God. The things that have nothing to do with us most oblige us to praise God. So often, even still, it is the intelligent, the educated, the self-sufficient who reject God and the gospel. "One thing, at all events," said J. C. Ryle, "stands out in Scripture, as a great practical truth to be had in everlasting remembrance: those to whom the gospel is hidden are generally 'the wise in their own eyes and the prudent in their own sight'; and those to whom the gospel is revealed are generally humble, simple-minded, and willing to learn." Jesus praises God for it. Have you ever been around those who are the wise of this world and marveled over their intelligence? You think, "He (or she) is so much smarter than me. Why didn't you bring him into the kingdom?" or "Why didn't you bring her into the kingdom?" "God opposes the proud but gives grace to the humble" (James 4:6).

This doctrine of God's providence is humbling. Though some say it results from spiritual arrogance, the truth is that anyone who really understands the doctrine of the providence of God is humbled to the dust. Again, J. C. Ryle said, "Let us watch against pride in every shape—pride of intellect, pride of wealth, pride in our own goodness, pride in our own desserts. Nothing is so likely to keep a man out of heaven, and prevent him seeing Christ, as pride: so long as we think we are something we shall never be saved. Let us pray and cultivate humility; let us seek to know ourselves aright and to find out our place in the sight of a Holy God. The beginning of the way to heaven, is to feel that we are in the way to hell." The doctrine of God's providence so conditions a man's soul to humility.

Do you contemplate those distinguishing favors? Do you contemplate that it was in God's providence that you were brought into the realm of the kingdom of His mercy?

Look in the Founders hymnal, *Psalms, Hymns, & Spiritual Songs,* and notice the meditation of distinguishing favors given to you by Isaac Watts in his hymn, "How Sweet and Awful Is the Place" (#17):

> How sweet and awful [the older word
>   for "awesome"] is the place
> With Christ within the doors,
> While everlasting love displays
> The choicest of her stores!
>
> While all our hearts and all our songs
> Join to admire the feast,
> Each of us cry, with thankful tongues,
> "Lord, why was I a guest?"
>
> "Why was I made to hear Thy voice,
> And enter while there's room,
> When thousands make wretched choice,
> And rather starve than come?"
>
> 'Twas the same love that spread the feast
> That sweetly drew us in;
> Else we had still refused to taste,
> And perished in our sin.

Listen to Watts meditate on the distinguishing favors of God. Do you see the slightest hint of pride? No, you see abasement. Look where it leads him—right to missions and evangelism:

> Pity the nations, O, our God!
> Constrain the earth to come;
> Send Thy victorious Word abroad,

And bring the strangers home.

We long to see Thy churches full,
That all the chosen race
May with one voice and heart and soul,
Sing Thy redeeming grace.

That is the heartbeat of a biblical Christian responding to the providence of God. Do you contemplate the distinguishing favors of God?

Fourth, in verse 27, we see that Jesus is the Steward of God's providence over all things, including the saving knowledge of God. "All things have been handed over to Me by my Father; and no one knows the Son except the Father; nor does anyone know the Father except the Son, and anyone to whom the Son wills to reveal Him." Bible-believing Christians will joyfully acknowledge that God the Son is sovereign in salvation. This sentence is a preface to the call or invitation which Jesus is about to issue. In it, He gives His authority and credentials. He asserts four things in this packed sentence.

First, He asserts His exclusive and absolute authority. "All things have been handed over to Me by my Father." This reflects the eternal covenant of redemption in which God, in His good purposes, pledged to the Lord Jesus Christ to give into His hands all of the created order in reward for His obedience in His saving work, in His fulfilling of the covenant of works on our behalf. It speaks of His ascension when He goes to the right hand of the Almighty and assumes the control of the universe. John Duncan of New College, Edinburgh, said, "Think of it. The dust of the earth now sits on the throne of heaven." A *man* is in the cockpit of the universe. The man God, the Lord Jesus Christ, and He is ruling the world for the sake of His people by His Word and Spirit.

Second, notice how He asserts the Father's exclusive relationship with Him. "No one knows the Son except the Father." He speaks here of the uniqueness and the intimacy of the relationship which the Father has with Him. He has just

given us, and is going to give us, a glimpse of His heart. Here
He is essentially saying, "No one knows My heart like My Father. We have a unique relationship and My desire is for you
to participate in that relationship." Someone has likely said
that all of New Testament redemptive history teaches us this
relationship between the Father and the Son and the call of
the Son for us to come and enter into that saving relationship
with His heavenly Father.

Third, notice He speaks of His exclusive understanding of
the Father and relationship with the Father. "No one knows
the Father except the Son." If Jesus were not divine and not
the providential Ruler, that would be the most arrogant statement ever made. Do you realize how completely that sentiment contradicts the pluralistic sensibilities of today? Talk
about the uniqueness of Christ. Do you think you know God?
He says, "*Nobody* knows God except Me."

Then He said, "If you want to know God, you come through
Me"—His exclusive ability to reveal the Father. "Anyone to
whom the Son wills to reveal Him"—He speaks here of His
own will, the will of the sovereign Son. This revelation about
Himself serves to give us confidence to believe the invitation
that He is about to issue. The true happiness of man lies in
the knowledge of God. To know God is to live and Jesus says
if you want to know God you've got to get that knowledge from
and through Him. You must apply to Jesus for that knowledge.

Bible-believing Christians rejoice in the fact that the Son is
sovereign in providence and salvation. All things have been
given into His hands. Think again of John 13. It is that
thought that gets Jesus through the night of betrayal and the
day of crucifixion. Remember John's words in chapter 13
verses 1-4? When He [Jesus] remembered that all things had
been given into His hands by the Father; He rose up, took off
His garments, wrapped the towel around Him and washed
their feet.

Finally, in verses 28-30, Bible-believing Christians will be
no more restrictive in their entreaties with unbelievers than
was our Lord. God's providence is consonant with and even

conducive to the fullest expressions of gospel invitation and overtures of mercy. Christ, the One who had just said that the Father blinds the wise, now says, "Come to Me *all* who are weary and heavy-laden and I will give you rest." He promises rest—spiritual, true, saving rest—to those who come to Him, those who are heavy-laden and burdened with sin. He calls them to Himself: "Come to Me." He promises blessing to all who come to Him—rest from sin's terror and guilt, peace of conscience, rest from sin's power, rest in God's love.

My friends, this is the most arrogant and preposterous thing that has ever been said unless Jesus knows their hearts' needs; unless He has what is required; or unless He is able to give them what they need. The Lord Jesus is standing before them and saying, "I got all three. I know your heart. I know what you need. I have what you need and I can give it to you. Come to Me." In this passage He calls us into His service and into His school. "My yoke is easy and my burden is light." It is the only place in the Scripture where Jesus' heart is described: "I am gentle and humble of heart." This gentle and humble Savior says, "Take the easy yoke of my commands—not the burdensome commands or traditions of men, not the burdensome commands of the Old Covenant ceremonial law—you take on *My* burden for it is easy and *My* yoke for it is light." The Apostle Paul could say that the momentary afflictions of this age could not match the surpassing glories of the blessings of the Lord Jesus Christ (Philippians 4:8-11).

God said, both at His baptism and at the Mount of Transfiguration, "This is My Beloved Son in Whom I am well pleased. Listen to Him." Listen to Him when He teaches you of a sovereign God whose providence is everywhere.

DEVOTION

9.
PSALM 97: THE LORD REIGNS!
PHIL NEWTON

1997 Southern Baptist Founders Conference

IN early March of this year, I found myself in deep con-
templation over international issues affecting one of our
church members. Kevin Millard started attending our
church shortly after it was planted and continued through
most of his years in seminary until he left for the mission field
in Albania. In one of our church services he had announced
publicly his call to vocational missions. Only months before
his departure in 1993, I had called to tell him of the need and
opportunity in Albania. He made an excursion trip and then
concluded that God's will for him was to begin serving in that
formerly atheistic country.

Now I sat with the disturbing prospect that something
terrible could happen to him or his wife and two children due
to the upheaval in Albania. Trouble had brewed in the country over failed pyramid investment schemes with those on the
losing end pointing fingers at the current government for
their crippling losses. In the southern portion of the country
of four million, rebels put feet to their words by overrunning
police stations and army depots, looting weapons and artillery.
Men and children who had never held guns before were now
playfully pulling the triggers and shooting in every direction.
Tanks were being driven through streets with their guns firing. Curious teenagers were firing bazookas and tossing gre-
nades at no-certain target. Stray bullets, many that fell from
the sky fatally striking innocent by-standers in the head, were
killing hundreds.

I followed the daily news reports, growing more anxious as

the rebel forces made their way from the south to the capital of the country, Tirana. That had been Kevin's home for over three years. We corresponded via e-mail and discussed the situation. He agreed to make contingency plans to evacuate the country in case the rebel forces got too close. In the mean time, it appeared that the trouble had slowed. Kevin secured plane tickets for his family and busied himself with tying loose ends, all the while listening to the gunfire surrounding the city. Then it happened. On the morning he and his family were scheduled to evacuate for safety, the only airport in the city closed! I received a phone call with a terse message on the recorder from someone who had been in contact with another missionary in Albania: "They can't get out!" Rebel forces controlled the roads; the seaport was facing modern-day piracy; and the small airport was shut tight.

Kevin and his family spent a night and a day lying on the floor in another missionary's apartment, as bullets zinged all around them. In a quiet corner where he retreated to seek the Lord all of the anxiety of the past month overwhelmed him. As he contemplated the hand of the Lord, His promises, the missionary call, and the rule of our Lord over all things, peace took over! There were still bullets in the air. The airport was still closed. There was still no way out. But God was still on the throne, reigning and ruling in righteousness! It is this reality, "The Lord reigns!" that has calmed the fears of many a believer through the difficulties and trials of life. This truth has strengthened the weak hands of Christian servants laboring for the furtherance of the gospel in our sin-darkened world. This truth has smitten the stubborn hearts of resistant sinners to bring them humbly before the cross of Christ. Let us be reminded, "The Lord reigns!"

How should this truth of the Lord's reign affect us as believers? The knowledge of the Lord's sovereign rule frees us in worship, corrects our fearful thinking and stirs us on in faithfulness. Let's consider three aspects of the Lord's reign as expressed in this psalm.

A STABILIZING PREMISE (VV. 1-6)

Old Testament scholars debate the authorship and time of this particular psalm, which maintains a theme similar to those of Psalms 93-100. Some place it during the time of David after his kingship was confirmed. The Septuagint and other versions ascribe it to David. Others place it during the post-exilic period as the nation contemplated the judgments of God against them and His continued mercies in their restoration. Though knowledge of the psalm's author and date might add a few insights of interpretation, the essential message of the psalm stands firm throughout all periods of time. The Lord reigns!

The Lord reigns! (v. 1)

How careless we are at times, forgetting the most basic truths God has revealed about Himself in His Word. It is as though the psalmist perceives our forgetfulness which, in this case, leads to anxiety. So he reminds us, "The Lord reigns; let the earth rejoice." Spurgeon calls this statement, "The watchword of the Psalm,"[1] for over and over the whole idea of His rule emerges out of the text.

The theme of the Lord's reign begins in Psalm 93, expressing the majesty of His reign. The next psalm shows that His reign declares the Lord to be the Judge of the earth who will surely take vengeance upon the wicked. According to Psalm 95, we, the people of God, should reverently rejoice and worship at the footstool of our Sovereign Lord. The greatness of the Lord is extolled in our singing and worship in Psalm 96.

Psalm 97 shifts the attention of His reign to the whole earth. The earth has cause to rejoice because Jehovah reigns over all! Is this not good news? What if the world was left to its own rule? Some would argue that this is exactly what is happening—that the Lord God blithely sits back in heaven, unable to lift a hand against the terrors of humanity. He waits

---

1 C. H. Spurgeon, *Treasury of David* (Peabody, MA: Hendrickson Publishers, nd.), vol. II, part 2, 194.

to see what the rulers of the earth will do next. Perhaps He holds His breath or wrings His hands at the sight of humanity's foolish ways and His inability to do anything about it. "NO!" cries the psalmist, "The Lord reigns; let the earth rejoice!" Yes, those who have bowed the knee to His saving authority and Lordship realize that He reigns over our lives. But the psalmist reminds us that His rule extends over the earth so that even the earth itself rejoices with delight that Jehovah reigns. His reference to "the many islands" being glad, points to what Derek Kidner calls, the "innumerable outposts of mankind."[2] In other words, all the lands that can be reached by ship—wherever people might live—the Lord reigns.

There have been many times in the past nineteen years of pastoring that I have found consolation and joy in knowing that the Lord reigns. When those circumstances of ministry turn sour, the Lord reigns. When some physical malady affects someone in my flock, the Lord reigns. When dreams and ambitions lie in the ash heap, the Lord reigns. This is not a grim resolution. It is a confident, assuring statement so that the psalmist could declare that in light of the knowledge of the Lord's reign, "let the earth rejoice." Even when we cannot understand the scope of His reign, we are to rejoice in it.

His reign is righteous. (v. 2)

Plenty of rulers in the world have reigned without righteousness over their nations: Pol Pot in Cambodia, Enver Hoxher in Albania, Fidel Castro in Cuba, and on the list could go. We must not confuse the reign of the Lord with that of mere human rulers. Even the best of earthly rulers is affected by the fall so that his reign performs injustices. While Cromwell, the great English protector of the Puritans, did so much to meet the needs of his Puritan subjects, he at the same time treated the Scottish and Irish subjects without similar cour-

---

2 Derek Kidner, *Psalms 73:150: Tyndale Old Testament Commentaries* (Downers Grove, PA: Inter-Varsity Press, 1975), 350.

tesy and justice.

But not so with the Lord! "Righteousness and justice are the foundation of His throne." There is never a moment when God's character fails or sags so that His rule is unrighteous or unjust. Indeed, His rule often mystifies us, for "Clouds and thick darkness surround Him." The psalmist harkens back to Mt. Sinai and God's revelation of Himself in the clouds that veiled the mountain. They trembled at the awesome holiness of the Almighty and the unapproachable presence on the mountain. While many things about the Lord are hidden from our understanding, we can be assured that every act of omnipotence has its foundation in His righteous and just character.

In the greatness of His love, our Lord purposed to save sinners. But He would not save even one apart from His righteousness and justice. For God to let our sins slide and admit us into His kingdom would be a violation of His holy character. The Fall demands His justice. Our sin and enmity against Him demands that God bring His entire righteous wrath to bear upon us in the fierceness of eternal judgment. So, for God to save even one sinner demanded that the righteous and just foundation of His throne be maintained through the incarnate Son. Paul records this truth for us in Romans 3:24-26:

> Being justified as a gift by His grace through the redemption which is in Christ Jesus; whom God displayed publicly as a propitiation in His blood through faith. *This was to demonstrate His righteousness,* because in the forbearance of God He passed over the sins previously committed; *for the demonstration, I say, of His righteousness* at the present time, *that He might be just* and the justifier of the one who has faith in Jesus (NASB, emphasis mine).

Rejoice in His justice in saving sinners who come to Him in faith, for His saving work is founded upon His righteousness and justice! Rejoice in His righteous judgment in damning sinners who spurn His light and invitation to come to Christ, for it is founded upon His righteousness and justice!

Some complain about their lot in life. They question, "Where is God?" Or assert, "God is unfair." The psalmist reminds us that when we cannot see the outcome or even disagree with God's wisdom, we can rest in the Sovereign Hand that reigns in righteousness and justice. He cannot do otherwise. It is impossible like that of putting all of the oceans of the world into one Coke bottle. It cannot be done.

His righteous reign demands that He devour His adversaries. "Fire goes before Him, and burns up His adversaries round about." There is no escaping the rule of God. The atheist who claims there is no God will be devoured in judgment just the same. For the religionist who charts his own course contrary to the revelation of God in His Word, wrath awaits his foolish ways. In salvation *and* damnation, our God reigns in righteousness and justice.

His reign is universal. (vv. 4-6)

We would expect that God's reign would be over His own people. Even a moderate unbeliever would acknowledge that the Lord is King over those who profess Him but he would deny that the Lord has any place in his life. So the psalmist directs our attention to the Lord's universal reign. He is not like the localized gods of the ancient east, with every little tribe having their own god or set of gods. His reign covers the earth, yes, even the universe!

"His lightnings lit up the world; the earth saw and trembled." The poetic imagery suggests that the entire natural realm is under the Lord's authority. Nature operates because of "the higher causality,"[3] as Leupold put it. At the Lord's pleasure, "The mountains melted like wax at the presence of the Lord, at the presence of the Lord of the whole earth." The

---

3 H. C. Leupold, *Exposition of the Psalms* (Grand Rapids, MI: Baker Books, 1969), 688.

most impregnable refuge of humanity, a mighty mountain, becomes as the tallow of a candle before the presence of the Lord. There is no hiding from the just reign of God, even if one flees to the highest mountain. As the writer of Hebrews expressed it, "And there is no creature hidden from His sight, but all things are open and laid bare to the eyes of Him with whom we have to do" (Hebrews 4:13).

I recall the stunning pictures in *The National Geographic* several years ago when Mount St. Helen melted like wax. The "before" shots captured a snow capped volcanic peak, covered with huge trees. The scenes after the eruption showed how the forests had been torched and washed away in a torrent of lava. "The mountains melt like wax before the presence of the Lord." It was a clear reminder that we do not rule this world. Even nature is subject to the pleasure of God. And He accomplishes His mighty purposes in His creation.

Even without voice the heavens speak declaring that all God does is righteous. "The heavens declare His righteousness. And all the peoples have seen His glory." The whole earth exists according to the design and symmetry established by the Lord. If He took His hand off of this planet for one second, the whole world would be thrown into chaos.

"The Lord reigns; let the earth rejoice." The eighteenth century preacher, Samuel Davies, clarifies what should be our whole attitude when thinking upon the reign of the Lord over the earth. "And how joyful a thought this, that we are not at the arbitrary disposal of our fellow mortals, and that affairs are not managed according to their capricious pleasure, but that our God is in heaven, and doth whatsoever he pleaseth! Psalm 115:3."[4]

AN ASTONISHING WARNING (VV. 7-9)

After contemplating the majesty and righteousness of the

---

4 *Sermons of the Rev. Samuel Davies* (Pittsburgh, PA: Soli Deo Gloria Publishing, 1993 reprint of 1854 volume), vol. I, 433.

Lord who reigns over all creation, the psalmist shifts his attention to the natural man—the "brute," as Spurgeon calls him. "When a man gravely worships what has been engraved by a man's hand, and puts his trust in a mere nothing and nonentity, he is indeed brutish, and when he is converted from such absurdity he may well be ashamed."[5]

The shame of idolatry. (v. 7)

The psalmist abhors idolatry. J. C. Ryle said, "Idolatry is a worship in which the honor due to God in Trinity and to Him only, is given to some of His creatures, or to some invention of His creatures." An idol is in reality anything or anyone that receives a person's devotion other than the Lord. The bent of human nature is toward idolatry. It is not simply reserved for the African or South American jungles. It is found in the towns and cities of our nation. For when men fail to acknowledge the Lordship of Christ over their lives, they are knowingly or unknowingly acknowledging another lord. They are exchanging the truth of God for a lie, and worshipping and serving the creature rather than the Creator through His Son, Jesus Christ (Romans 1:25).

In light of the Lord's universal and righteous reign, the psalmist goes on to show how foolish, even shameful, it is to bow to a graven image. Israel may have been regarded as an insignificant nation, but in her worship she did not fear chiding the idolatrous world about her, "Let all those be ashamed who serve graven images, who boast themselves of idols; worship Him, all you gods."

The nations around Israel were all idolaters. They crafted their idols of trees, silver, stone—all the work of men's hands. Idolatry was simply expected by the unbelieving world. But not so with God's people! They alone, of all the people in the world, are repulsed by the very idea of idolatry.

The Scripture offers numerous descriptions of idolatry and

5 *Treasury of David*, 196.

its foolishness. Isaiah describes the man who goes into the forest and cuts a tree for firewood to cook his food and for carving an idol. He burns the wood in the fire to prepare food and satisfy his hunger but with the balance of the tree he carves a graven image. Then, "He falls down before it and worships; he also prays to it and says, 'Deliver me, for thou art my god'" (Isaiah 44:17b). Isaiah goes on to point out the foolishness of this man in verse 19: "And no one considers in his heart, nor is there knowledge of understanding to say, 'I have burned half of it in the fire. Yes, I have also baked bread on its coals; I have roasted meat and eaten it: And shall I make the rest an abomination? Shall I fall before a block of wood?"

"Worship Him, all you gods." The marginal rendering of "supernatural powers" or "angels" is to be preferred in this case over "gods" (see Hebrews 1:6). What a marvelous reminder in our day when people are so preoccupied with angels! We have no business setting our minds and affections on angels when we have a Lord who reigns over all! By the way many professing Christians talk, you would think that God is somewhat paralyzed in His power without the angels running to His rescue. May I remind us all that the angels are nothing and less than nothing in comparison to the great glory of our God! The angels consistently point all worship aimed at them right back to the Lord. They shunned attention, seeking to give all glory to the Lord.

How can we think of worshipping idols? For that matter, how can we consider worshipping Jehovah in any way other than how He has revealed Himself in the Word? To do so is to slip into idolatry. When we proclaim the gospel of Jesus Christ, we are calling for idolaters to see their foolishness and turn to the wisdom of God in Christ (1 Corinthians 1:18-31). Certainly, we who have been redeemed from our bondage to idolatry by the precious blood of Jesus Christ cannot go on in idolatry. Yet in many Christian circles, professing believers are worshipping God through images created by men's hands. Others are constructing non-biblical concepts of God and applying their energies to worshipping such false images. This psalm serves as a reminder that any sort of idolatry, whether pagan or so-called "Christian," is shameful in light of the revelation of the exalted Lord.

The recognition by God's people. (vv. 8-9)

There is a profound effect upon God's people ("Zion" in this passage) when they come to the glorious recognition of God's sovereign rule over His people. "Zion heard this and was glad, and the daughters of Judah have rejoiced because of Thy judgments, O Lord." Unbelievers do not understand that the Lord reigns, for if that truth actually penetrated their depraved minds, they would flee to Christ for mercy. But we, who by grace have come to faith in Christ—the people of God, "Zion"—rejoice in the exercise of God's sovereign activity. We have no fear of the idols of the world that are worshipped by multitudes. They have no saving power. They have no righteousness. But all that the Lord does is righteous, whether in justifying sinners through the righteousness of Christ or judging sinners who do not believe. Therefore, we rejoice!

The joy of the believer can be seen in the confessional summary of this truth in verse 9, "For Thou art the Lord Most High over all the earth; Thou art exalted far above all gods." The Christian virtues of joy and rejoicing express the very essence of the redemption that we have experienced and the reign of the Lord over our lives. Because the Lord who reigns over all has saved us from His terrible wrath and brought us into a right relationship to Himself through His Son, we cannot help rejoicing. I believe that Martyn Lloyd-Jones was correct when he stated that the chief virtue that ought to characterize every believer is joy. We are joyous because of who our Lord is—"the Lord Most High over all the earth ... exalted far above all gods." Our joy is not in our performance but in the reign and righteousness of the Lord. That is why the Apostle Paul tells us, "Rejoice in the Lord, always, and again, I say, Rejoice" (Philippians 4:4).

THE FITTING RESPONSE (VV. 10-12)

Doctrine always demands response. The doctrine of the sovereign rule of the Lord over our lives cannot leave us with a neutral attitude. Something must happen in our lives as the result of recognizing and bowing before the Lord of the universe as Creator, Redeemer, and Sovereign. Since the Lord reigns in righteousness and since we have rejoiced in His reign through faith in Christ, then we must take action. All that we do in the Christian life, if our motives are proper, is simply a response to God's revelation and redemption toward us.

Hate evil. (v. 10-11)

"Hate evil, you who love the Lord, who preserves the souls of His godly ones; He delivers them from the hand of the wicked." The believer cannot have a neutral attitude, much less a condoning one, toward sin and evil. John writes of our God, "God is light, and in Him there is no darkness at all," which points to His absolute holiness and sinlessness (1 John 1:5). So to be comfortable with sin or to tolerate it or to ignore its presence in our lives is an affront to the Lord's holiness. Here, the psalmist shows us that it is a contradiction to loving the Lord. It is "you who love the Lord," who are to "hate evil." Richard Sibbes stated, "It is evident that our conversion is sound when we loathe and hate sin from the heart."[6] The only way that we can hate sin from the heart is to have a new heart that has been created in righteousness and holiness of the truth (Ephesians 4:24).

Since sin is contrary to the nature of God, it must be contrary to those who have become "partakers of the divine nature, having escaped the corruption that is in the world by lust" (2 Peter 1:4). God's determination to declare sinners righteous made Christ's death necessary. Our God's holy hatred of sin found its mark upon His Son at the cross. Can

---

6 *Treasury of David*, 205.

we love and desire that which caused the death of our Lord? "We cannot love God without hating that which He hates," commented Spurgeon. "We are not only to avoid evil, and to refuse to countenance it but we must be in arms against it, and bear towards it a hearty indignation."[7] This runs counter to the modern version of Christianity that eliminates repentance from the gospel and holiness from sanctification. John wrote, "And you know that He appeared in order to take away sins; and in Him there is no sin" (1 John 3:5).

One might ask, how can I hate evil and still live in this sinful world? The psalmist tells us that the Lord "preserves the souls of His godly ones." This is the Lord's keeping-power at work in our lives. "He that began a good work in you will continue it until the day of Jesus Christ" (Philippians 1:6). On your part, by the strength that God has given you, through the discipline He has nurtured in you, "hate evil." But realize that in the depths of your being, it is the Lord who is preserving you. When He preserves us He does not "pickle" us so that we are suspended in time until He gathers the church home. His preserving power works through all of the demands of life. Through every trial, He preserves us. Through every battle, He preserves us. Through every temptation, He preserves us. Thankfully, through every failure on our part, He preserves us! Ultimately, He will glorify us in His presence, when He "delivers" us from the hands of the wicked and the presence of sin.

Just in case we are feeling the pressures of darkness about us, the psalmist reminds us in this matter of hating evil, that the Lord is working all along the way. He reigns over all, so He is surely capable of bringing about His sanctifying purpose in our lives. "Light is sown like seed for the righteous, and gladness for the upright in heart." You can almost picture the despondent believer wrestling with sin, when in the midst of his trouble the Lord gives him the light of revelation of His goodness and joy in the assurance of being justified before

7 *Treasury of David*, 197.

God. Those words of the Apostle Paul ring home, "There is therefore, now, no condemnation to those who are in Christ Jesus" (Romans 8:1). He is liberated from the stupor of sin and brought to a fresh hatred of sin, and love of the Lord. The Lord sows light and gladness along the way as flowers lining the paths of life. He enables us to gather these refreshing bouquets to strengthen us in hating evil.

Be glad in the Lord. (v. 12)

Sadness and depression characterize our day. Stand in a public setting and watch people for one hour and you will be overwhelmed by the looks of despondency that seem to sour face after face. But we are to stand in contrast to such sadness. "Be glad in the Lord, you righteous ones." The attractiveness of "gladness" or joy in the Lord provides one of the clearest testimonies of the grace of God applied to sinners. Remember, our gladness or joy is never to be in our circumstances or accomplishments or even our own righteousness. These can change like the wind. But our joy is "in the Lord," that is, within the sphere of our relationship to the Lord.

The knowledge that "I am His and He is mine," produces an incredible sense of joy in the child of God. When we reflect upon the reality of His reign over our lives and over the world itself, we can look at our circumstances with the joyful knowledge that "the Lord reigns!" What right do I have to be discouraged when the Lord reigns? How can I live in despondency when I am a recipient of His saving grace and constant goodness to me? Oh child of God, "Be glad in the Lord!"

Give thanks to His holy name. (v. 12)

Our gladness should be followed by our gratitude to the Lord. "Give thanks to His holy name." What an important reminder to us who live in a nation in which ingratitude may be the most prevalent sin of our age.

Just think of how often you hear complaints during your

day. In virtually every kind of setting grumbling words complain about the weather, finances, sports teams, preaching, prices, government policies, etc. What the psalmist points out is that since the Lord reigns, since He sustains or preserves us, and since He constantly gives to us, then we are to ever give thanks to His holy name.

I've had the opportunity of meeting several Christian brothers from Kenya over the past few years. These men serve the Lord in difficult areas with very little reward of material possessions. The average pay they receive is around $20 per month. Most of them walk from church to church and house to house in their ministerial labors. The one thing I have noticed in every single one's conversation and correspondence is the common thread of "I thank God that...." By our standards, they have nothing. But to them, the richness of being in relationship to the living God through Jesus Christ causes them to give thanks.

CONCLUSION

Perhaps the demands of life and ministry have left a cloud hanging over your head. I want to give you a vital and simple reminder: "The Lord reigns." Think upon His reign over you personally and the world about you. Our great God will surely fulfill everything He has purposed, so rejoice in Him. Let this truth affect your sanctification, so that you hate evil. Let this truth affect your disposition, so that you are glad in the Lord. Let this truth affect your conversation, so that you give thanks to His holy name.

10.

PSALM 96: FROM PRAISE TO PROCLAMATION

STEVE HAINES

1999 Southern Baptist Founders Conference

INTRODUCTION

S ING to the LORD a new song; Sing to the
Lord all the earth. Sing to the LORD, bless
His name; Proclaim good tidings of His salva-
tion day to day. Tell of His glory among the na-
tions, His wonderful deeds among all the peoples.
For great is the LORD, and greatly to be praised;
He is to be feared above all gods. For all the gods
of the peoples are idols, but the LORD made the
heavens. Splendor and majesty are before Him,
Strength and beauty are in His sanctuary.

Ascribe to the LORD, O families of the peoples, Ascribe to the LORD glory and strength.
Ascribe to the LORD the glory of His name; Bring
an offering and come into His courts. Worship
the LORD in holy attire; Tremble before Him, all
the earth. Say among the nations, "The LORD
reigns; Indeed, the world is firmly established, it
will not be moved; He will judge the peoples with
equity."

Let the heavens be glad, and let the earth rejoice; Let the sea roar, and all it contains; Let the
field exult, and all that is in it. Then all the trees
of the forest will sing for joy before the LORD, for
He is coming. For He is coming to judge the
earth. He will judge the world in righteousness,

159

And the peoples in His faithfulness (Psalm 96:1-13, NASB).

Spurgeon called Psalm 96 the great missionary psalm, and indeed it is. It is the Great Commission in Old Testament dress. As we begin our look at this psalm, I want to cite a source probably not quoted before at a Founders Conference. That's Frank Zappa, rock musician of a generation gone by who said in *The Real Frank Zappa*:

> Missionary evangelism is the height of cultural arrogance. To go to somebody else's country and attempt through trickery, food, or medical treatment to capture souls for Jesus presumes that the guy with the travel budget or the hypodermic needle has a spiritual edge over the native he's going to save.

Now that same sentiment is still expressed by those who are better educated. As missionaries, we still occasionally hear people ask, "Do you know what you're doing? Why don't you leave them alone? Why do you insist that they hear the story about Jesus? Isn't their own religion good enough for them?" So the fact that Frank Zappa said it does not give credence to the complaint; it is commonly heard about missions. If you go to the *Instant Quotation Dictionary* on the internet, you'll find a much more biblical phrase by Fredrick Moore. He said, "Christianity is a missionary religion: Converting, advancing, aggressive, encompassing the world. A non-missionary church is in the bands of death." And so it is.

The setting of Psalm 96 is described in 1 Chronicles 16. The story is of David bringing the ark into Jerusalem, into the city of Zion, and we find this hymn repeated almost word for word in 1 Chronicles 16.

Psalm 96 is also joined in the *Psalter* with Psalms 95-100, all of which have phrases in common with Psalm 96. Look at Psalm 95 as I want to quickly give you the feel for the other psalms. What you will find in Psalm 95 is singing to God about our salvation, praise that God is a great God above all others. He is Creator and there is a need to worship Him. If you look past Psalm 96 to Psalm 97, you find a call to the earth to worship our reigning God and King. That psalm presents God as Judge. It provides a call to the heathen who worship idols to worship Him. It is a call for those who love the Lord to give thanks.

In Psalm 98 we see some of the same phraseology: "Sing to the LORD a new song." Sing of His works, His victory, His salvation. The call is for creation to praise God. Psalm 98 has the same ending as Psalm 96. The point is that God is coming as Judge to judge. In Psalm 99 we find the reigning God. There is a call to all peoples to praise and exalt Him. There we see the character of this reigning God. He is a righteous King. There is again a call to worship Him and a hint of His coming judgment. Psalm 100 calls all the earth to praise God and to serve Him, for He is Creator. And for all of this we give thanks.

Turn back to Psalm 96 so I can show you the structure briefly. It's not easy to do in a verse by verse process, because this psalm has three sections and three repeating ideas. Each section begins with a triple repetition of a call to praise. Notice verses 1-6: "Sing to the LORD, sing to the LORD, sing to the LORD." That starts one section. It's a call to praise. Verses 7-10 make up the second section. Three times we have a triple call to praise: "Ascribe (or give) to the LORD" (twice in v. 7); "ascribe to the LORD" (v. 8). And then the final section is in verses 11-13. "Let the heavens be glad" (v. 11); "let the sea roar" (v. 11); "let the field exult"(v. 12); and finally "the trees of the forest will sing" (v. 12). This is a call for all creation to praise our God, the Father of the Lord Jesus Christ.

So we find three divisions and each one begins with a triple call to praise. The movement of each of the three sections is the same. In the first section we have a movement from praise to proclamation. In the second section we also have movement from praise to proclamation. Then in the third section, we go from praise to proclamation to *parousia*, the return of the righteous King.

So we find a basic movement that is true, not only in the psalm, but also in the heart of the individual believer. We move from praise to proclamation. Out of the heart that overflows with joy and gratitude to God for His salvation, we move to the need to proclaim that joy, that grace, and that message to everyone. That is the fuel, the fire and the goal of missions.

SING TO THE LORD!

The *New American Standard Bible* puts a title to this psalm, "A call to worship the LORD, the righteous Judge." But in that title, there is one element missing that the title doesn't capture. The editors of that version didn't really do justice to the idea of it. The idea is a call to worship the LORD, the righteous Judge, together with all the nations and all creation. We need to put those phrases in there, too. The psalm is not merely for the individual believer to worship God and to proclaim Him. It is a call for all of us, individually first, and then together, to worship God, and to involve all the nations in God's worship, and to harmonize with all the creation as the entire universe praises its Creator. That is the thought to be conveyed by the title.

John Piper's words on the cover of the brochure advertising this conference captured extremely well the relationship of praise and proclamation. It says, "This truth more than any other I know seals the conviction that worship is both the fuel and the goal of missions." Do you catch that? Worship is both the fuel that fires the boiler and the goal toward which missions move. It comes out of worship, it proclaims the gospel, and it leads back to worship.

The deepest reason why our passion for God should fuel missions is that God's passion for God fuels missions. Missions is the overflow of our delight in God because missions is the overflow of God's delight in being God. And the deepest reason why worship is the goal of missions is that worship is God's goal. What does He want out of all creation? That creation should worship Him. All of us and all of the created order are to worship God.

I want us to see how the psalmist relates praise and worship to proclamation and evangelism.

First of all, praise and worship build the fire, stoke the boiler, for proclamation and evangelism. Look at the passion reflected in the start of each of the three sections. Psalm 96:1 says, "Sing to the LORD a new song; sing to the LORD, all the earth. Sing to the LORD, bless His name." Now jump to verse 7, "Ascribe to the LORD, O families of the peoples, ascribe to the LORD glory and strength. Ascribe to the LORD the glory of His name, bring an offering and come into His courts." Do you notice at the end of that verse that praise has led to corporate worship? Praise that overflows out of the heart has led to worship. Praise is a form of worship, but worship is more involved. Finally, in the third section, "Let the heavens be glad, and let the earth rejoice; Let the sea roar, and all it contains; let the field exult, and all that is in it; then all the trees of the forest will sing for joy" (Psalm 96:11-12). All of creation rejoices in God. Do you see the passion there? This is a very passionate appeal to believers to praise and worship God, to sing to His name.

Whenever I come to the Founders Conference, I am always struck by how well we sing. We feed off each other, and the volume, the depth, and the profundity of it are wonderful. Do you sing that well at home? Do you sing with that kind of joy? Do you sing with all your heart? A singing heart is a characteristic of a saved soul. The one who can't sing knows very little about the glory of God. Do you sing well at home, with enthusiasm? I don't mean sing well technically; I mean sing well from an overflowing heart, or do you find it difficult? A heart that doesn't sing does not have a musical problem, it has a spiritual problem.

Psalm 47:5 is a call for all of us to sing. It says: "God has ascended with a shout, the LORD with the sound of a trumpet. Sing praises to God; sing praises; Sing praises to our King; sing praises. For God is the King of all the earth; Sing praises with a skillful psalm." There is a call for the redeemed of the Lord to sing to Him. Martin Luther wrote, "I have no use for cranks who despise music, because it is a gift of God. Next after theology I give to music the highest place and the greatest honor."

Fannie Crosby was a blind composer of many hymns that we love and appreciate. An unknown poetic, moved by her hymns, wrote a tribute to her in poetic form: "Sweet blind singer across the sea, tuneful and jubilant. How can it be? How can she sing in the dark like this? What is her fountain of life and bliss? Her heart can see! Her heart can see!" There it is. Fannie Crosby's eyes were blind, but her heart could see the glory of her Lord. She couldn't see but she could sing.

The measure of your singing is a partial, though not entire, measure of how your heart is related to God. In his book *Psalms of the Heart*, George Sweeting illustrated a great truth from the experience of two Moody Bible Institute graduates, John and Elaine Beekman. God called them to missionary work among the Chol Indians of southern Mexico. Sweeting reported that they rode mules and traveled by canoes to reach the Chol tribe. They and other missionaries with them labored twenty-five years to translate the New Testament into the Chol language. Today the Chol church is thriving. More than 12,000 Christians are in the Chol community and the church there is financially self-sufficient. Sweeting commented that when the missionaries came, the Chol Indians did not know how to sing. They had no singing music. With the coming of the gospel, however, the believers of the tribe began to love to sing because they now have something to sing about. We of all people should be the most singing people on all the face of the earth. We have something to triumph! We have something to sing about. This hymn begins in praise, leads to worship, and flows out in proclamation. Missions is evangelism, and then it returns back to worship and praise, but bringing with it a whole train of the same. It's a wonderful progress.

ASCRIBE TO THE LORD GLORY!

Verse 8 says, "Ascribe to the LORD the glory of His name" and then it proceeds, "Bring an offering and come into His courts." The courts of God were the place where He has placed His name.

Now I want to spend a moment on that word, "Bring an offering." What is it that the psalmist wants us to bring? The word is *minchah*. It's the word for a blood offering, not the word for a burnt sacrifice. The word is used more than 200 times, almost entirely all of which reference what is called the meal offering. In the Old King James Bible, it's called the meat offering, but the word meat doesn't mean flesh; it means blood. This is the offering brought out of a grateful heart. It follows the burnt offering, the sacrificial offering, to atone for sins.

Now, that distinction is important. What's being commanded here is that the redeemed soul brings himself, person and property, to worship God, realizing he has been bought with a price. He's no longer his own; the blood of Jesus Christ has purchased him from the realm of Satan and darkness. But only after the blood sacrifice of Jesus Christ has been applied to the heart is the meal offering presented. The word is used in its secular context to refer to gifts to superior persons, particularly to kings. It conveys the attitude of homage and submission to the superior person.

You can see the word used in a secular sense in 1 Samuel 10:27. It's instructive. The Israelites despised Saul. Certain worthless men said, "How can this one, Saul, deliver us? And they despised him and did not bring him any present." That word for "present" is *minchah*. They brought him no offering. They despised him. That's how the word is used in a secular sense. In the religious sense, it's a gift of grain. It's never mixed with salt, honey, or leaven, but is mixed with frankincense and oil, representing the anointing of the Holy Spirit. It is the gift of what the believer has to bring to God. It is the gift of the believer's time and talents and all that we possess, recognizing that we've been purchased by One far greater than ourselves.

You can find another definition of it in Leviticus 2 and 6. The *minchah* was offered every morning and evening. It was a holy offering. It was eaten only by the priests, not by the worshipers. It indicated submission of the totality of life as God's people to the great King.

Here is where I want to make an application. There are more than 500 of us here. Certainly many of us have known each other for years and it's the gathering of old friends. But always in such a gathering like this, there are some who come for various motives. The Lord Jesus in His sovereign will has brought some of you here, perhaps out of interest, perhaps a friend has come, perhaps you've accompanied someone, and you've wondered, "What do these people do when they get together? I will just go." Perhaps your heart is troubled, and you thought, "If I go to a religious conference and I hear people talk from the Bible and about the Bible, it'll make me better." Perhaps some of you have thought you would give this time to God in order to calm what's going on in your heart.

Let me suggest to you, this is not what the Lord wants. He does not want your gifts of time or money or talent until the sin offering has removed your guilt. You do not need to bring your time and your money and your dedication to missions to the International Mission Board. You need to repent and come to the Lord. Now I say that not with any sense of looking down on anyone, but always in a group this large, there are those who, for one reason or another, are not at peace with Jesus Christ. You have not been born again, you're not quite sure what it is we're talking about, but you want to do the right thing. The right thing is not religious activity; the right thing is not sacrifice. The right thing is to come to the only One who made the blood offering to remove sin and that is Jesus Christ. If you come to this conference but you're outside Christ, it is not your time or your talent that Jesus wants. He invites you to repent of sin and to run to Him and be saved; to be born again by trusting in the only sacrifice for sin that God will accept. He will only accept the sacrifice that His Son rendered. He will not accept religious work performed to atone for sin. Pardon this digression, but it is always necessary in context of a large group to call people to Christ, because sometimes people want to do the right thing, but they think the right thing is religious work. That is not the right thing until the heart is right with God through Christ.

What's being called for in the *minchah* here is the offering of one who is already a believer. It is the offering of person and property by one who has been redeemed; who has been saved. Notice the call for praise and how that call for praise runs into worship. Thomas Aquinas, the Catholic theologian of the thirteenth century wrote: "We pay God honor and reverence, not for His sake, because He is of himself full of glory which no creature can add anything, but for our sake." We worship God not for His sake, but because in our hearts we must worship. We've been created to worship God. We are called to worship Him. Eugene Peterson said, "Worship does not satisfy our hunger for God. It whets our appetite for God!" We don't calm the hunger we have by worship; it stirs us up for an even greater appetite to know the ways of God.

Proclaim His Salvation!

Again, I want you to see the movement in this psalm from praise and worship to proclamation, missions, and evangelism. Look again at Psalm 96 and what happens, for instance, in the first section in verse 2. "Sing to the LORD; bless His name. Proclaim good tidings of His salvation from day to day." Do you see the movement from praise to proclamation? Praise fuels the fire and the proclamation of His glory is the result.

Notice in the second section verses 8-9: "Ascribe to the LORD the glory of His name; Bring an offering, and come into His courts. Worship the LORD in holy attire. Tremble before Him, all the earth." Notice verse 10 says, "Say among the nations"—not among the congregation, but among the nations. Once again, we go from praising God out of the overflow of our hearts to the proclamation of the saving work of Christ—the good news of what He's done.

And then in the final section: "Let the heavens be glad, and let the earth rejoice; let the sea roar." All of creation praises God. Verse 13 says that they do this "before the LORD" for He is coming. "He is coming to judge the earth. He will judge the world in righteousness, and the peoples in His faithfulness."

Not long ago in Plano, Illinois, the song leader stood up before his congregation and said to them, "Turn to page 654 in your hymnals. We'll sing till the whole world knows." What he meant was that we'll sing the hymn called "'Till the Whole World Knows." He didn't hear a young girl in the back say to her father, "I think we're going to be here a long time." There's more theological truth in that statement than the little girl knew. We'll sing until the whole world knows! And yes, we'll be here a long time though not nearly as long as we'll be there, on the other side of that great return, because then we'll sing to all eternity of the glory of our King. Proclamation follows praise and worship.

Who's going to do the proclaiming? Notice in this psalm that it is the people of God first, but ultimately it is all the earth. It starts with the people of God but then it embraces those who do not yet know and it culminates with all creation singing. It's a wonderful picture of the expansion of the gospel of Christ. It starts with the people of God. But notice who does the proclaiming in verse 1: "all the earth." In verse 7, it is all the families of the earth. In verses 11 and 12, we find that all creation will proclaim. A similar idea is in Psalm 98:7, where the culmination has all creation proclaiming God. "Let the sea roar, and all it contains, the world and those who dwell in it. Let the rivers clap their hands; Let the mountains sing together for joy." All of God's creation is designed to sing praises to the Creator.

Where are we going to proclaim it? Among the nations, according to verse 3, and among all the peoples. The gospel is for the ends of the earth.

It was my family's privilege to be the first SBC missionaries in Ukraine. When we got off the train in Kiev back in 1991, we did not know a single person in the city. Nor did we know a single word of Russian. All we had was the knowledge that someone would meet us at the train and "take care of us." My twin girls were 4 years old, and I wondered, "Lord, what have I put us into? What am I doing 900 miles from the nearest American friends back in Moscow?" But the Lord is faithful. His goal is that the ends of the earth should know of Christ.

An American volunteer team came over and together, with a Ukrainian pastor, we made provision to preach the gospel in a village called Zdvizhivka, about an hour's drive from Kiev. This village apparently goes back to the tenth century. It's a very old village, but recently it doubled in size when the Chernobyl refugees were moved in from the zone around the nuclear power plant. So there were about 800 people in this area. There was one family who we knew to be professing Christians. We took the volunteer team, brought New Testaments in Russian, and spent three days distributing them in the area, inviting them to come to what I called the Civic Hall. The Communists always built in every village a frame building big enough to hold virtually the whole population and that building was used for monthly political indoctrination. We got permission to hold a meeting there one Sunday morning. We arranged for a bus to take the Americans out there and the Baptist Union of the Ukraine supplied the pastors. We were excited about it because people had indicated that they would like to come. They were willing to come to hear the gospel. There had never been, in more than 1000 years, a church in the area of Zdvizhivka; none whatsoever. The people had never heard the gospel of Christ.

When the bus pulled in that spring morning, there was still snow on the ground, but it wasn't terribly cold. I pulled in with another group of people right behind the bus in a van. And all I could see was two old men sitting on a bench in front of the civic building. One was whittling and one was smoking a pipe. I was very disappointed. So I walked up to the two men, and said to them, "Where is everybody?" They laughed and said, "Everybody? Everybody is inside the building. They've been there for 2 hours waiting for you to arrive!" I exclaimed, "What?" And the Ukrainian pastor who was with me braced his foot against the door, shoved it open a bit and yelled inside, "Make room! We're the preachers." It was jammed. And under the frowning visages of Marx on one side and of Lenin on the other, the gospel was proclaimed. It had never been heard. When we gave away New Testaments, people were nearly killed in the stampede that it caused. Never did we give away New Testaments in that way again because the crowd just about trampled the old folks that were sitting in the front.

There is a wonderful privilege involved in the spread of the gospel where it has not been heard. It is a privilege reserved for those who will go to where the edge is. How many of you will be willing to go to the edge where the gospel has not been heard before?

It's frightening, but it is a wonderful privilege. It's a wonderful thing to do. Misha Vakhenko, whom I worked with, was a deacon assigned to that church in the village of Babintsi. There were 8 old members of that church; not one of them younger than sixty years of age. Misha went out to preach the gospel every time he could get his old car to start. He and his father dug the foundation for a new church in Babintsi. Having no money to build, they dug the foundation and laid the first layer of block for a church big enough to seat two hundred people. The local townspeople said, "Why are you doing this? You are a complete fool." And Misha said, "My God is a great God and He will supply." Now he had already laid that foundation when we came to the Ukraine. Through the generosity of others, money was provided to build that church and when the building was inaugurated, it was filled to overflowing. There is now a wonderful functioning church there with nearly 100 members and the church in Zdvizhivka has about 50 members. It is wonderful to be on the cutting edge, where the gospel is preached in freshness and in power.

When are we supposed to proclaim this gospel? "From day to day," as the psalmist said (96:2). It's our task for now and it is to be done now. What message shall we bring today? Shall we go up and tell them that God has a wonderful plan for their life, but they've messed up that plan by resisting Him? Look carefully at the content of the proclamation in Psalm 96. It is the character and the work of Almighty God. What are we going to proclaim to people? "Proclaim good tidings of His salvation from day to day. Tell of His glory among the nations, His wonderful deeds among the peoples."

Now look at His character: "For great is the LORD, and greatly to be praised." He is to be revered. He made the heavens. He is Creator. He is great in His splendor, majesty, strength, and beauty (96:6). This is the message to be proclaimed. The message is a message about God. It is not a message about men. It is not even the story of the greatness of how God has saved you or me, though that is a great story. The proclamation is of the character of God, the greatness of God and the work of God. This is a God-centered message.

The primary drive for missions is not compassion for a people group whose behavior, culture, background and traditions you will find somewhat repugnant as a missionary. You are not called to work up some kind of emotional tie to that people. You're called to have emotional ties to God! If you have that tie to God, out of love for His name and His glory, you will go to the ends of the earth to proclaim His message. Sometimes potential missionaries get the wrong idea. They look inside themselves and say, "The truth is, I don't really know if I like the people over there, and I'm pretty sure I don't like the customs, and I'm very sure I don't like the food! I guess I'm not called." I know that because that's how I thought. I can remember being at Southwestern Seminary in 1977, praying this spiritually profound prayer:

"Lord, I love you with all my heart. I will go anywhere and do anything for you in the Continental United States." Now I thought that was a fair offer—He had 48 to choose from.

Do you see the limit? Sometimes we think, "I have to work something up on the inside about the other people." No, that will come. First, see what you have in your heart towards God. Do you love Him? Do you love His name? His kingdom? His will? His glory? His character? His Son? That's where it starts. It starts vertically and it will flow out horizontally to the peoples. It is a God-centered message—that God's kingdom increase, that His name be lifted up, that His Son be glorified.

I want to tell you the problems I faced as a missionary and contrast them with a particular missionary that we all know about. Some years ago in Ukraine, three men from a very large Southern Baptist Church in Texas came as a group of volunteers to help plant a church. I said to them, "Yes, I think we can do that. There is a need for a church on the northern suburb of Kiev. There is no church there. We have the backing of the Baptist Union of Ukraine. We have the support of the North Carolina General Convention of Southern Baptists. We have a missionary on the field that will work together with you, and we have the three of you. Let's go see if God will bless our efforts in planting a church up there in that northern suburb." So we walked around, met people on the street, handed out flyers and invitations to come to the civic hall (again, under the frowning pictures of Marx and Lenin), to hear the gospel preached. It was a four-headed beast. Never had we put together a state convention, volunteers from an individual church, Southern Baptist missionaries, and the Baptist Union in a joint project. It was a colossal headache but it came together. We found that there was a nucleus of Baptists that didn't know about each other and they had been praying for a church for years! A church was founded and established. The place packed out and within six months that church was constituted as a participating church in the Baptist Union of the Ukraine. That's the fastest that any church has ever come into existence and been received by the Baptist Union.

It was a marvelous triumph of God's grace, for which the area secretary received a three-page complaint about what a bad job I had done. Yes, it worked out right, but the three men complained in their letter, "The missionary didn't let us tell our story."

I remember the situation. There was a time allotted to each of them to speak during this founding week of preaching. One of them said to me, the very first one, "What should I do?" I responded, "Let me put it like this: The majority of people here have never heard the story of Christ. They've never heard the gospel. They don't have the faintest clue about what the gospel is. I would suggest a simple message about the cross; about Christ."

What did he say in reply? "How about giving my testimony?"

And I said, "Well, you know your testimony probably won't be understood by the people, even through an interpreter, because all of the surroundings, all of the cultural trappings, are completely foreign to the Ukrainians. They would have no way to relate to problems with payments on a second car, and the PTA. It doesn't make any sense. I would suggest you preach the gospel to them." For that suggestion, I was criticized later. They didn't get to tell their story.

Let me ask you, whose story is more important? His story or your story? If you have only one story to tell, are you going to tell people about yourself and what God has done for you? Or are you going to tell them about Christ and what He has done? Now I hope you'll decide to tell them about Christ. There is a place for testimony but the story that compels is the story of Jesus.

I want to tell you what happened when Adoniram Judson returned from the mission field. He was invited to speak somewhere and a huge number of people gathered to meet him. He had just come from the ends of the earth (Burma) and when he got his chance to speak, he spoke for fifteen minutes on what great work the Savior had done. He spoke of how He had died and how He had purchased a people for Himself and then he sat down visibly affected.

The leaders came to him and said, "The people are very disappointed. They wondered why you didn't talk of something else." Judson said, "What else could I talk about? I gave them, to the best of my ability, the most interesting subject in the world."

"But they wanted to hear something different," the leader said. "They wanted to hear a story."

Judson replied, "Well I'm sure I gave them a story, the most thrilling one that can be conceived of."

"But," they continued, "they had heard that story. They wanted something new from a man who had just come from the ends of the earth."

Then Judson replied, "Then I'm glad to have it to say, that a man coming from the ends of the earth had nothing better to tell than the wondrous story of the dying love of Jesus. My business is to preach the gospel of Christ, and when I can speak at all, I dare not trifle with my commission. When I looked upon those people today and remembering where I should next meet them, how could I stand up and furnish food to Dame Curiosity, tickle their fancy with amusing stories, however decently strung together on a thread of religion. That is not what Christ meant by preaching the gospel. And how could I hereafter meet the fearful charge: 'I gave you one opportunity to tell them of me, and you spent it in describing your own adventures'?"

Now that's Judson. That's what it means to be a missionary. That's whose story it is to tell. Whose story are you telling? Are you telling the story of Christ or are you telling your own story? Your call is to be an ambassador for Christ.

Now I want to look, in passing, at the negative messages. There are at least three here and they would be offensive in many settings on the mission field.

First of all, the gods of the heathen are idols. Actually, in Hebrew, the meaning is worse than idols. They are useless; they are nothing at all. There is a play on words. Look down at the first part of verse 5: "For all the gods of the peoples are idols." What's happening in Hebrew, is it's saying all of the gods, the *Elohim* of the people (that's the standard word for gods in its plural form) are *elil*—worthless. So what the psalmist is saying is that all the supposed gods don't even exist. They are little nothings. They have no existence. Now modern theology says, "Well let's go out to the field and have a dialogue about what we can find out about what we believe in common. Let's sit down and share how the general God of all has revealed Himself to the heathen and to the Christian."

The call is to proclaim, not to dialogue. I don't want to pound a fundamentalist pulpit. I don't want to rabble-rouse. But it is not a call to waddle around in intellectual dishonesty, figuring out if there's something out there that they know that might remotely relate to God. They need to know about Jesus Christ. We are to proclaim that the idols, the nothings, that are worshiped afar, are indeed "nothings" at all. They do not represent a fragment of the truth, a piece of the truth, a bit of the truth, a spark of the truth. They represent lies, uselessness and falsehoods.

Notice also in this message that the Lord alone reigns, and there is no other. Only one God rules, and he rules everywhere. He rules not just in the church or just in the heart of the believer. He rules! He is sovereign. There is no other. His Word is not contravened. His will is not upset. His end is neither delayed nor detoured. It is absolute. Notice also that this Lord is coming as Judge to judge all the peoples. And when He judges, He will judge fairly by the light of Jesus Christ. He's coming as Judge. There's no room here for missiological dialogue with false religions; no search for common ground; no hope that the non-Christian might possibly be worshiping the unknown Christ. It is not so, it does not happen.

Speaking to the graduating seniors of the New Zealand Bible College, Brian Smith recalled the words of an old missionary he once heard who had come from India. This old missionary was reflecting on the phenomenon that we call

Hinduism. "When you see its temples, hear the throb of its drums, smell the fragrance of its incense and realize the tremendous hold it has upon the land, your heart sinks. And the consolation that I have is this: this too, this mighty construction of religion and faith and worship, will disappear like all those systems of the past. Where are now the ancient gods of the Syrians, the Egyptians, the Romans? Where now is Artemis, the great god of the Ephesians, to whom all Asia and the whole world worshiped? They are no more. False religions will die. They will die because the true God will kill them. He will triumph over them."

A girl returned home from Sunday School class displeased with the reaction of her class after the day's lesson. She told her mother, "We were taught to go into all the world and make disciples of all nations, but we just sat there." She had caught something. We are called to make disciples, but we just sit here. Now there is a contradiction.

Will you go? Will the Lord lay hands on you to further the gospel in a far away place? If He does you will find it to be the most glorious opportunity that ever could befall a saved sinner. It is without doubt the most honorable thing we could do.

Jesus sends us out in the highways and byways. What are we going to do about that? Dr. A. Scott Patterson, who lost his health while a missionary in Africa, said this: "If the doctors were to tell me I could not get well, I would still want to take the next boat and go back to Africa. Being a missionary isn't a sacrifice. It's a joy. It's a delight. It's a privilege!" And so it is.

When William Carey announced his plans to serve as missionary in India, his father tried to talk him out of it. He reminded his son that he lacked the academic qualifications necessary for that kind of work. Young Carey, however, was confident that God had called him and he responded, "I can plod. I can plod." Brilliance is not needed on the mission field. It would be welcome from time to time, but it's not needed. Some of my bosses would have said that about me, too. I'll tell you what's needed: faithfulness and plodding. Faithfulness to Christ and the willingness to gut it out; to plod. To rejoice in littleness. To testify of God where He's not been heard. What's needed is faithfulness and plodding, and many of you here can be faithful plodders. I know you can.

We will conclude with 1 Corinthians 4:1: "Let a man regard us in this manner, as servants of Christ and stewards of the mysteries of God. In this case, moreover, it is required of stewards that one be found trustworthy."

11.
A DEVOTIONAL PSALM: PSALM 33
HAL WYNN
2000 Southern Baptist Founders Conference

I WANT to speak about the providence of God under three headings from this Psalm: 1) rejoicing in God's providence; 2) reflecting on God's providence; and then in those last verses, 3) responding to God's providence. I believe that how we understand providence affects our everyday life. It affects how we think about life and how we respond to life.

A couple of days ago I read a story about Sherlock Holmes and his buddy, Watson. They were out on a wilderness camping trip, and while they were out there they had their dinner and a bottle of wine and then went to their tent for the night's sleep. Several hours later Holmes woke up and shook Watson and told him to wake up. "Look up to the sky, what do you see?" Watson looked up and said, "I see millions and millions of stars." Holmes said, "What does that tell you?" Watson replied, "Well, astrologically, it tells me that Saturn is in the constellation of Leo, and meteorologically, it looks like we're going to have a good day tomorrow. Theologically, it would appear that God is a great and awesome God, and we are very small and very insignificant. Horologically it tells me it's about 3:15 AM. What does it tell you, Holmes?" Holmes was silent for a few moments and said, "Watson, you nut, someone has stolen our tent!"

The providence of God has to do not only with the great theological questions that we might entertain, but it has to do with our tent. It has to do with the fact that we've come to this conference this week, and there's no bridge between our housing and the chapel so we have to walk around. Perhaps

179

there are a lot of little inconveniences that face us every day in our lives, but we believe that God is in control of everything, so with that belief we've learned how to rejoice even in the inconveniences of things.

I picked up *USA Today* and was looking at it this morning. The feature article on the front page is entitled "Why Everyone is So Short-Tempered." In this article the reporters are talking about the new epidemic of anger, sometimes deadly anger. They talked about two shoppers in Westport, Connecticut, who went to a supermarket and got into a fistfight over who should be first in the newly opened line. A Continental airliner had to return to Anchorage because one of the passengers took a bottle or can of beer and threw it at the stewardess, then went and bit the pilot. In Reading, Massachusetts, a father beat another father to death in an argument over rough play at their sons' hockey practice. Why are people becoming so angry? Why is rage the rage today? The article suggests this: Experts searching for causes blame an increasing sense of self-importance, the widespread feeling that things should happen my way.

We happen to believe that, no matter how difficult life is, life should happen God's way. We believe that God is in control of everything, so providence would tell us that we should trust God even with things we don't understand—the little inconveniences of life as well as the big things.

REJOICING IN GOD'S PROVIDENCE

Sing joyfully to the LORD, you righteous; it is fitting for the upright to praise Him. Praise the LORD with the harp; make music to Him on the ten-stringed lyre. Sing to Him a new song; play skillfully, and shout for joy (Psalm 33:1-3).

In the beginning of this Psalm the Psalmist invites us to rejoice in God's providence. As the Psalmist calls us to worship there are four things I want to bring to your attention.

First, notice the fervency of our worship. As you read these verses you see that we are to "sing joyfully to the Lord." Looking at the last part of verse 3, we are to "shout for joy." So the idea is that when we come before God to worship it is not with a lazy spirit. It is not with our minds occupied with every other thing, but rather to worship with a genuine fervency in our spirit as we seek our God. John Bunyan said, "When thou prayest, rather let thy heart be without words than thy words without heart." So it should be in our worship.

Second, notice our faith as we worship. "Sing joyfully to the Lord, you righteous." All of our worship ought to be directed to the Lord. The Bible tells us in Hebrews 11:6 that without faith it is impossible to please God. Those who come to God must first believe that He is and that He rewards those who diligently seek Him. So we believe that when we worship, we worship in the presence of a holy God. God is present and we come before Him with the eye of faith seeking Him. The Bible reveals to us the kind of God that He is, and we come with expectation, believing that He will reward those who diligently, and with great seriousness of mind, seek Him. So we sing joyfully, not to entertain one another, not because we happen to like that particular tune, but to worship, adore and glorify Him.

There is our faith concerning God as we worship, but there's also our faith concerning ourselves as we worship. "Sing joyfully to the Lord, you righteous." What business do you and I have before this holy God except we stand in the perfect righteousness of Jesus Christ? We've been accepted in the beloved, the Bible says, so as we come before God, though we know that we are sinners, we thank Him that He does not deal with us as our sins deserve. In Him there is forgiveness and there is therefore no condemnation to those who are in Christ Jesus. We can come to this gracious, forgiving, pardoning God, and though He is a holy God and sits upon a throne of grace, we can worship Him remembering that in Jesus Christ we are accepted in Him.

Third, there is the fitness of our worship. "Sing joyfully to the Lord, you righteous; it is fitting for the upright to praise

Him." The idea of the fitness of our worship certainly includes the idea that God delights in our worship. Jesus, talking to the woman at the well in Samaria, said, "The Lord seeks such as you to worship Him." I believe God is seeking worship and delights in worship. God made us to be worshipers and our hearts are most fulfilled when we are praising, loving, and glorifying God, and worshiping Him. There's nothing more fitting than God's people worshiping Him. There is nothing more unfitting than that God's people should not worship Him. "The donkey knows his owner and the oxen, but Israel does not know, My people have not considered it." What a contradiction in terms it is when Christians do not worship—when they do not enjoy coming before their God in worship as the Psalmist describes here.

Then there is the freshness of our worship. Verse 3 tells us to sing to Him a new song, play skillfully and shout for joy. We are invited to sing a new song. There is variety in the verses: ten-stringed lyre, or a harp. The Psalmist is not imposing limits here. He could have added a banjo, guitar or other musical instruments that may praise God. We are to praise the Lord with our harps and with the skills He gives us. I think we may praise God instrumentally without even necessarily singing words. All of the ministry of music belongs to God and we may praise Him with that which is appropriate for worship. There is variety here and skill. We ought not to come before God without being prepared, without offering the very best that we have to offer Him in our act of worship. In Malachi's day the people were bringing lame and blind sacrifices and God was repulsed with such worship and offerings. I wonder if God is repulsed whenever we come before Him in sloppy fashion, unprepared to come before His presence.

We are invited here to come with skills and fervency and faith, and this kind of worship is fitting before God. But this new song doesn't necessarily mean that it is a song we haven't sung before. I trust that many of you are familiar with the Founders Conference hymnal, *Psalms, Hymns & Spiritual Songs*, and rejoice in singing those songs. There are a lot of new songs being written today and all of them, obviously, are not of equal value theologically and biblically, but the new song does not necessarily mean a brand new song. It means that as God blesses us with fresh providences in our lives, every time we sing that song, though we've sung it a thousand times before, it is fresh to us.

The Psalmist has called us to worship but what is the ground for that call? On what basis is he making that call?

> For the word of the LORD is right and true; He is faithful in all He does. The LORD loves righteousness and justice; the earth is full of His unfailing love. By the word of the LORD were the heavens made, their starry host by the breath of his mouth. He gathers the waters of the sea into jars; He puts the deep into storehouses. Let all the earth fear the LORD; Let all the inhabitants of the world stand in awe of Him. For He spoke, and it was [done]; He commanded, and it stood fast. (Psalm 33:4-9)

In verse 4, the character of God is the basis for the call. We see the character of God expressed in the testimony of God's Word. That is why we ought to pray with faith, fervency, fitness and freshness. He is faithful to His Word, and He is a faithful God. That means His Word is true, and if His Word is true then it is also right. The Word of God ought to be the authority for everything that we do. If God's Word is true then it is right to follow it in terms of our worship. If it is true then it is right in terms of our evangelism. It is right in how we order our churches. In everything we do before God in terms of our Christian life and the church, we have God's Word to guide us and give us clear principles. The character of God as testified to in His Word.

Behind your doctrine of the Word of God is your doctrine of God. His Word is true and it is right and He is faithful in all He does. He was faithful to give us His inerrant Word and He is faithful to every promise that He makes in it. Therefore, we take God's Word seriously because God takes His Word seriously, and we can't separate Him from His Word. He has revealed Himself in His Word as a faithful God.

Verse 5 testifies of God in the world. The testimony of God's character in the world is obvious. The Bible says the world is full of God's love. God cares for the animals, He cares for us, He causes the sun to rise on the just and the unjust. Even our sins do not prevent Him from blessing us, either in common grace or in special grace. God's earth speaks to us of love as we look around it.

I wonder if people around the world look at the world and wonder how a good God could have created the kind of world we live in. Their question is, "Why do bad things happen to good people?" Of course, we would raise the question, "Why do good things happen to bad people?" That's the real question. If we got what our sins deserved we would all go to hell just for the sins we've committed since we walked into this auditorium this afternoon; because the wages of sin is death. Yes, God's love is evident, not only in His providential care of His creatures and the ordering of the cosmos, but even in His dealings with us and His mercy and grace towards us—sinful people, with whom He remains patient. There's a testimony of God's character in the Word and in the world.

The creation of God also gives rise to this joyful worship in God's providence according to verse 6. First we see the creative power of God's word: "By the word of the Lord were the heavens made, the starry host by the breath of His mouth." Hebrews says we understand by faith that the worlds were framed by the word of God. God spoke and the world came into existence, all the cosmos.

Consider the Milky Way galaxy. There are very conservatively, 100 billion stars like our sun. When we think of a number like 100 billion we just cannot really comprehend it; but I understand that if you filled up an average sized swimming pool with sand and you counted each grain of sand, that that figure would be approximately 100 billion. There are that many stars the size of our sun in the Milky

Way galaxy. These stars are great distances apart. If you shrank a star down to scale the size of a basketball, and you put that basketball in New York, the next nearest star would be another basketball in California. Think how many basketballs you can get in between. In the Milky Way galaxy you have 100 billion stars with great distances between them, and there are many galaxies like the Milky Way. It's incredible when we consider the greatness of our God and that He spoke all of these things into existence by His word and by His power. The breath of God! The Psalmist is moved by that realization and as modern men we should be even more moved than was ancient man since we understand more about cosmology.

There is the creative power of God that gives reason to this great worship and then there is the concern of God over His world, which we see in verse 7. Just as a farmer might gather his crops and store them up, or a woman in her kitchen might do some canning, so God is pictured as taking care of all of the created order, making sure that things are where they ought to be. As Jerry Bridges says, "There are no random molecules in the cosmos. Everything is being ordered by God." That ought to give us cause for praise as we come before Him.

Then there is the call to glorify God. In verses 8 and 9 there is wonder. The Psalmist can't help himself when he is speaking about the greatness of his God, or wondering about God. Augustine said, "Let others wrangle, I will wonder." Sometimes in our worship time we don't do a good enough job of exposition or of expressing the greatness of our God in the hymns we sing. There is a loss of wonder. We tend to minimize God, which is no doubt what the openness of God view is partly about—trying to make God more like us so that we can relate to Him a little better. But here is this great God of Scripture and that ought to move us to wonder and it ought to move us out into the world. The Psalmist can't help, as he considers this great God, but be jealous that all who are in the world should know this great God that he has come to know.

There is a call here to glorify God. Concern for the glory of God is what ought to drive missions.

I have people who visit my church and people that I visit every day. I am by nature not a very compassionate person, and you may be that way too, but God has changed my heart. Do you know what drives me? It's not people. It's not that I think people are so wonderful so I have to share with them because they're so valuable, though I think people are valuable. It's not because I have such a wonderful heart—that God has so moved in me that my heart is more sensitive than your heart is—but it is the concern that God has put in my heart for His glory. When I am faithful in my task but I'm not seeing what I would like to see from the results, I don't cheapen the message. I don't set out to resort to tricks in order to get good results, because my driving force isn't the result, it is God's glory. That is the thing that enlivens me. That is the thing that moves me into the world and keeps my fire burning. Worship ought to lead to witness. This is what happens with the Psalmist as he considered these things.

REFLECTING ON GOD'S PROVIDENCE

The LORD foils the plans of the nations; He thwarts the purposes of the peoples. But the plans of the LORD stand firm for ever, the purposes of His heart through all generations. Blessed is the nation whose God is the LORD, the people He chose for His inheritance (Psalm 33:10-12).

We began in rejoicing in the providence of God. We continue in reflecting on God's providence.

First, there is the futility of man's plans and purposes apart from God in verse 10. We don't need to look up the Hebrew to see and understand that God is foiling and thwarting the plans of people that are contrary to His. Remember Pharaoh in Egypt. How ironic that he was going to kill the babies by throwing them into the river, and it was from the river that Moses came (Moses name means "drawn from the river"). He who was raised in Pharaoh's own household became the deliverer. And so it goes. Balaam is hired by the king of Moab to curse Israel, but instead he blesses Israel. Joseph's brothers, out of envy wanted to murder him, yet their evil actions were actually used by God to work His plan and be the saving means of Israel. God is foiling and thwarting the plans of men. Our plans are futile apart from God.

In verse 11 we see the certainty of God's plans and purposes. God's plans stand firm, because God is perfect in His wisdom and efficiency. God never has thought a new thought. He has always known the end from the beginning and the beginning from the end. God does not have to go through some thought-process to figure out what He is going to do next. God is never contingent on waiting around to see what someone else will do before He acts. His plans stand firm and they are forever. God's plans are sure to be accomplished. Isaiah 46:9-11 says it this way:

> "Remember the former things, those of long ago; I am God, and there is no other; I am God, and there is none like Me. I make known the end from the beginning, from ancient times, what is still to come. I say: My purpose will stand, and I will do all that I please. From the east I summon a bird of prey; from a far-off land, a man to fulfill My purpose. What I have said, that will I bring about; what I have planned, that will I do."

God's plans stand firm and they are forever. That's at the heart of our understanding of providence, the fact that God's purposes are consistent with His love. At least that is suggested in the second part of verse 11—"through all generations." God is not some celestial iceberg, nor an unmoved mover but He is a God who reveals Himself as a God with a heart, if you will. His purposes proceed from His purposeful heart. We can be sure that everything that happens to us in our lives is a clear expression of God's divine love for us, though we may not understand why or wherefore at the time. The impassability of God does not mean that we have a God who doesn't have a heart. It means that He is not contingent. He has His own plans and purposes that will surely be fulfilled, but God has sovereignly chosen to enter into our lives and struggles and to deal with us, to condescend and speak with us. Because of these things we have a wonderful relationship with our God.

I spoke with a woman in our church last week who came to me when her 21-year old daughter was diagnosed with cancerous polyps. The doctor said he had never seen anyone with such a bad case. It will require very serious surgery. I asked her how they felt about this. She said they struggled through it when they heard the news, but as they thought about it and prayed about it, they realized that this is an expression of God's perfect love for them. That is to understand God's providence—to know that even the things that come into our lives that are inconvenient, and hard, and painful, are still an expression of God's perfect love for us. These are purposes that come from His heart.

Do you see the blessedness of faith in verse 11? Do you see the joy and the happiness of the nation whose God is the Lord? What nation would that be? Obviously, in the Old Testament Israel was a theocracy, but in the New Testament you look around and ask, "where is the nation of God?" Certainly America isn't a nation of God in the sense that Israel was. But we might say, according to 1 Peter 2:9, we constitute, as the church, a holy nation. So the blessedness that is intended here for us today is the blessedness of a people who are in covenant with God through Jesus Christ. As we consider ourselves God's people we are blessed. We know the joy and blessing that comes from God and we delight in His plans and purposes. We can say with Paul in Romans 8:28 that we know "all things work together for good to those who love the Lord, to those who are the called according to His purposes." I love his reasoning in Romans 8:32, "He that spared not His own Son, but delivered Him up for us all, how shall He not with Him also freely give us all things?"

That's the rationale as we consider God's plans and purposes toward us. Notice, not only is our delight in God but God's delight is in us. The Psalmist said, "Blessed is the nation whose God is the Lord, the people He chose for His inheritance." God's delight is in us. He has chosen me. Not because I am worthy, not because He saw anything in me that was worthy of His choice, but His choice of me was unconditional. It was His good pleasure to choose me. John Calvin said, "Lest it should be thought that men attain so great joy by their own efforts and industry, David teaches us expressly that it proceeds from the fountain of God's gracious, electing love that we are accounted the people of God."

God delights in us. Not because we're so delightful, but because nothing so clearly expresses the love, mercy and grace of God as sinful people like us, redeemed by His grace. He is glorified by such as us in our redemption. He is more glorified by the salvation of a sinner than by the thousands of galaxies that may exist. We find blessedness in God's plans and purposes.

God's providence also has to do with people.

> From heaven the LORD looks down and sees all mankind; from His dwelling-place He watches all who live on earth—He who forms the hearts of all, who considers everything they do (Psalm 33:13-15).

Notice the global perspective of God for people. God is looking down and sees all mankind. God's mandate hasn't changed from the Old Testament to the New Testament. It still has to do with all mankind. The Old Testament does not begin with Abraham, it begins with Adam, even though when Abraham comes along, He said, "I'm going to make you a father of a great nation, and all nations will be blessed through you." God's intention all along has been for all mankind. Then Jesus sends us out with the Great Commission to go into all the world and make disciples of all nations. We have to understand clearly the global perspective that God has for people and that should be our motive and incentive in the work of evangelism and missions.

God is personally in the lives of people as seen in verse 14. It's not just that God is a great God in keeping the cosmos going and doing the "big things," but here the Psalmist is suggesting that everything we do God pays attention to. He has formed our hearts.

There are a couple of thoughts I would share with you. First, He's the Creator and as the Creator nobody understands you like God. He is the One who knows your heart. As Savior He took on our heart. The Bible says in Romans 8 that He was made in the weakness of sinful flesh. It doesn't mean that He had any sin, but He came in humility as a man and was constituted and lived out His human life with all of the weaknesses attending fallen man, yet without sin. He had a heart, so we have not a high priest who cannot be touched with the feeling of our infirmities but in all points tempted as we are, yet without sin. We come to the throne of grace boldly and openly because God gives us grace and mercy and He understands us.

Then I think of the Spirit of God that is in us. Sometimes we don't know how to pray as we ought, Romans 8 says, and the Spirit helps us in our weakness. A passage says the Spirit searches our heart and He knows what the mind of the Spirit is and He makes intercession for us with groanings that cannot be uttered. God knows your heart. He made your heart. Coming in the person of Christ, He had a heart. The Spirit of God continually works in your heart. There is this personal involvement of God in your life at every level. I rejoice in that fact. I think it was a blessing to Peter on that seaside after the resurrection, after having denied His Lord three times, that Jesus asked three times, "Peter do you love me?" Each time, Peter replied: "Lord, I do." "You know I do."

Finally, "You know everything. You know that I love you." Even as we sin against God His perfect knowledge of us still sees that part of our heart that loves Him. There is personal involvement of God in the lives of His people.

RESPONDING TO GOD'S PROVIDENCE

No king is saved by the size of his army; no warrior escapes by his great strength. A horse is a vain hope for deliverance; despite all its great strength it cannot save. But the eyes of the LORD are on those who fear Him, on those whose hope is in His unfailing love, to deliver them from death and keep them alive in famine to deliver them from death and keep them alive in famine. We wait in hope for the LORD; He is our help and our shield. In Him our hearts rejoice, for we trust in His holy name (Psalm 33:16-21).

How do we respond to God's providence? It is a humbling truth that ought to lead us to repentance. Notice in verse 16 the foolishness of depending on others to save you. "No king is saved by the size of his army." Other people cannot save you; other people cannot deliver you, no matter how many there are. The context may not only mean spiritual salvation. Look at the terms that are involved here. We are talking about warfare. We're talking about death. We're talking about famine. These are matters of life situations that could happen to us so that we would have need of being saved out of them. Not only for salvation from our sins but the idea of being rescued, being helped by God, to do the things that God has called us to do or to face life with faith when things are happening to us. This is the idea then in responding to God's providence and doing so humbly. It is foolish to depend on others to save you.

I thought about Ahab here and my mind went to that passage where he had to have Naboth's vineyard, and so he killed

Naboth. Elijah confronted him and told him he was going to die and the dogs were going to lick his blood. In the battle with Aram, king Ahab of Israel told Jehoshaphat to wear his royal robes and he would go in disguise. The king of Aram said to his 32 chariot soldiers, "Don't fight with anyone, great or small, make a beeline for the king and get him." So the battle ensued, and they begin chasing Jehoshaphat because he is obviously wearing the royal garment. He cried out that he was not the king of Israel. The Bible says something very interesting in 1 Kings 22:34: "But someone drew his bow at random and hit the king of Israel between the sections of his armor." I love the way the word makes the point. At random? As though there could be such a thing? It finds it mark. In things that we think are at random, things we think are happenstance, God is ordering and it accomplishes His purpose. No king is saved by the size of his army.

Then there is the foolishness of depending on yourself for salvation. Look at verse 16: "no warrior escapes by his great strength." I thought of the tragedy of Samson. What a strong man he was but he confused the Lord's strengthening of his might and his own strength. When he went up to face the Philistines, as he had at other times, he did not know that the Spirit had departed from him, and you know the tragedy and humility that he experienced. It doesn't matter what our education or experience is. No man is saved by his own strength. What do we have that we have not received from God? How can we boast in it or trust in it?

Then there's the foolishness of depending upon methods to save you. Notice what the Psalmist says in verse 17: "A horse is a vain hope for deliverance." Despite all of its recognized, great strength the horse cannot save. There is nothing wrong with methods. We have to use methods, so obviously that is not what it is about. What He is talking about is what you trust in when you jump on the horse. Are you riding into battle or away from your enemies hoping on that horse? If you are, it is a dead hope. It is a tragic figure in Shakespeare's play who cries, "A horse, a horse, my kingdom for a horse!"

Richard was going to need far more than a horse to get him out of the mess he was in. So do we. Our methods are weak and useless to do what God would have us do. We need God as our help. He is our only hope. Methods are fine but they are only means that God may be pleased to use to accomplish His purpose.

This is a humbling truth, but it is also a hopeful truth when we look at verse 18. If the humbling truth brings us to repentance, this ought to bring faith to mind. God first helps those who hope in Him. That's what verses 18 and 19 say. Again, these terms used here are not terms that would refer to someone having an easy life. It is talking about someone who is facing death and needs to be delivered, or is in famine and is struggling for his life. Jerry Bridges' book *Trusting God Even When Life Hurts* is a good title because life often does hurt, and we do have to deal with the pain of life. He makes a great point in the book when he says it is easier to obey God than to trust God, because when we obey God it makes perfect sense to us.

God has promises associated to every command that He gives us. That makes sense. We do this and we have expectation of blessing. But when there is something that occurs in our life that has nothing to do with obedience—the baby dies, the plane crashes, illness afflicts us—it's a matter of trusting that God is at work even in that situation, bringing about His good purposes. That is hard to do. What are we to do at a time like that? Psalm 32:10 says that the Lord's unfailing mercy surrounds the man who trusts in Him. There we discover that the mercy of the Lord surrounds those who trust Him.

Not only is there great hope for those who hope in God, but we also see in this Psalm the determination of faith as a response to God's providence. There is no resignation in verse 20. Faith is their primary strategy: We will wait in hope, not with resignation, but with expectation that God is working here. In fact, God will indeed use these things in a way that glorifies Him and is for our good. So faith makes a determination: "I'm going to quit griping and complaining and grumbling about this … I'm going to quit feeling sorry for myself because of all the things that are going on. Instead, I am going to hope in God … I am going to wait for Him and hope for the Lord because He is my help and He is my shield."

Finally, there is the desire of faith in verse 21. Our hearts delight in our God, we trust in our God, we find pleasure in our God. He has made us for Himself and our hearts move toward Him as we consider who He is and what He has done. Notice the final verse. It's really somewhat of a sobering prayer. If the opening words of this Psalm speak of shouting for joy and singing, this is something of a different mood. "May Your unfailing love rest upon us, O LORD, even as we put our hope in You." We want to please Him by trusting Him because without faith it is impossible to please Him. So look to Him and hope in Him.

I want to close with a word from Spurgeon concerning our Lord and the reasons we ought to hope in Him.

> Our Lord Jesus is ever giving and does not for a solitary instant withdraw His hand. As long as there is a vessel of grace not yet full to the brim, the oil shall not be stayed. He is a sun ever shining. He is manna always falling 'round the camp. He is a rock in the desert, ever sending out streams of life from His smitten side. The rain of His grace is always dropping. The river of His bounty is ever-flowing and the wellspring of His love is constantly overflowing.

Because of that we can sing joyfully to the Lord. It is fitting to praise Him.

MISSIONS/EVANGELISM

12.
THE SPIRITUAL STATE OF THOSE WE EVANGELIZE

R. F. GATES

1984 Southern Baptist Founders Conference

INTRODUCTION

BEFORE I begin my exposition from Paul's letter to the Ephesians, let me say that the story of my life is one of pure grace from start to finish. I came out of a religious home. I think a person can be drugged on religion quicker than any drug today. I was a religious addict and I went to church Sunday after Sunday (just Sunday morning because only fanatics went back at night and I wasn't a fanatic). One Sunday morning I decided it was time to make my profession of faith so I walked to the front of the church building. I had to answer a series of questions such as, "Will you promise to uphold the church with your presence, your prayers, your gifts, your services?"—I nodded in the affirmative. Then I had a little bit of water sprinkled on my head and I was in. I thought I was now all right.

Later I was to realize that God's grace is truly amazing. Not only does He save, He sometimes saves by Arminian methods. I went to hear a man by the name of Billy Graham. He was a young preacher at the time. I was sitting in the end zone of the State Fair stadium in Shreveport, Louisiana. I do not recall a lot of what Graham said but I do know that God dealt severely with my heart, and I felt I was the chief of sinners. I only knew one thing to do, and that was to cry out to God for mercy. While everyone else was going forward, I got saved right there in my seat.

I didn't know what had happened to me. I was so ignorant that I didn't know what to call it and for several months I thought to myself, "I wonder if this will last through the week?" The way I finally began to understand this experience was through reading the Scriptures. I went home that night and read a Bible that my grandmother had given me. For the first time in my life I wanted to read the Scriptures. I had read it in the past as much as one or two verses without stopping, but this time I really wanted to read it and keep reading. I got up the next morning and thought, "Dear God, I don't know who You are and I don't know what You have done but whatever it is, keep it up." I was a high school senior and that was thirty-three years ago this past April.

I want to tell you it was all grace. As I have said, I didn't even know I was saved until I read about it in the Scriptures. I read in God's Word where it said, "If any man is in Christ he is a new creation." I said to myself, "You know, that sounds exactly like what happened to me. In fact, I think that *is* what happened to me." I am in Christ—however I got there. And today I can testify that living for Jesus has been thrilling and wonderful.

God called me to preach the unsearchable riches of Christ and I can only say, "Three cheers!" and "Hallelujah!" for what He is doing with many young preachers in this day in our Southern Baptist Convention. There are many who are coming to the realization that it is not by might, nor by power, but it is indeed by His Spirit. We cannot coax men out of the tomb. If they are called it shall be by the saving call of God's grace that ransacks the grave.

THE FULL TIME WORK OF EVANGELISM

Let's now turn to our text. I have been assigned to preach on the first chapter of the book of Ephesians, but I am going to go beyond that. I have been thinking about the book of Ephesians and how I could take hold of it in two sessions. You know, if you grab a tiger by the tail you never can let go of him, and I feel that way about laying hold of the book of Ephesians for two sessions. So I thought to myself, "Well I'll try to sneak up on it by using a practical approach." I greatly fear that in our day many preachers can be charged with the same charge that God laid against the prophets in Jeremiah's day. Let me read a few verses from Jeremiah chapter twenty-three. In that chapter, as God indicts the prophets, He makes two statements that have stuck solidly in my own throat. He says in verse 14: "I have seen also in the prophets of Jerusalem an horrible thing: they commit adultery, and walk in lies." Then He says, "They strengthen also the hands of evildoers, that none doth return from his wickedness: they are all of them unto Me like Sodom, and the inhabitants like Gomorrah."

God declared through Jeremiah that instead of helping bring the lost to Christ the prophets in that day had strengthened the hands of the wicked so that, rather than turn, they grew stronger in rebellion. The prophets had given the lost a false message.

Then the Lord said through Jeremiah in verse 17: "The prophets say unto those who despise me, the LORD hath said, Ye shall have peace; and they say unto every one that walketh after the imagination of his own heart, No evil shall come upon you." In other words, to these prophets it didn't matter if God was their Lord or not. "It doesn't matter if you have turned from your wickedness or not. You are all right because you made your profession of faith." I do not wish to be a preacher that goes after men with a misunderstanding of the condition that they are in. Nor do I wish to have a misunderstanding about what to expect when they get saved.

Look with me in the book of Ephesians with two basic thoughts in mind: First, what is the condition of those to whom God sends us as evangelists? Second, what is the result in those who are saved?

The Condition of Lost Man—Dead in Trespasses and Sins

I have been engaged in full time itinerant evangelism for several years now. But those of you who are called by God's grace to be pastors are, as far as I am concerned, also called to the work of full time evangelism. So what I say about myself applies to you as well.

When I share the gospel with people, I need to know something: Are those to whom I go sick, comatose, or dead? My remedy and my treatment for their condition will vary dependent upon what their condition actually is. Do they need treatment for an illness or do they need resurrection from the dead? If they need treatment I suppose I could do as well as any other man. But if they need resurrection, I could blow my breath in their faces with all the strength that is in my Southern Baptist lungs and it would do no good. If they need resurrection—then brother, recovery is out of my hands. Therefore, the first thing I need to know is: "What is the condition of those to whom God has sent me to preach?"

The next question is this: "What am I to expect to happen?" Shall I expect that if God does a work it will only be a partial work? Should I expect it to last only six weeks? If a man comes to church a few months and then drops out, should I give him the title of "carnal Christian" and let him go on his way while I pick up other dead carcasses? What am I to expect of those sinners to whom God has sent me to offer the balm of salvation?

When I was a young boy a doctor misdiagnosed my medical condition. The doctor came to visit me on my sick bed. I had been ill for some time. My mother was wringing her hands and saying, "Doctor, I don't understand what is wrong. He continues to lose weight. Nothing we do seems to strengthen him." The doctor checked me over as best he could and said, "I think he has got the flu." That was his diagnosis and here was his treatment: "Mrs. Gates, give this boy all the ice cream, malts and fattening foods he will eat. We have got to build him up." That was his purpose, to build me up. His prescribed treatment was to give me all the sweets I could handle. His diagnosis was that I had the flu. But it turned out that his diagnosis was completely wrong. I had developed juvenile diabetes. And because of the missed diagnosis and the accompanying inappropriate treatment, I came close to the Valley of the Shadow of Death. They took me to the Highland Hospital, and for twenty-one days I lingered between life and death as my blood sugar rose to almost 700.

Through the years I have often wondered have I, as a preacher, misdiagnosed the cases of those to whom God has sent me? How often have I moved among men thinking they will not be too hard to reach? For example, here is a man who has been in church all his life or here is a little boy or little girl who has shown spiritual interest toward God. I believe if I get with them and pray with them they will be saved. Or, if I just have a prayer with them and have them repeat the prayer after me and then baptize them, they will be alright. I fear that there are some to whom I have gone who will find themselves in hell because of my misdiagnosis and subsequent mistreatment. When I look back I shudder to think that I simply wanted to have them say a prayer so that I could pronounce them saved.

The apostle Paul has a lot to say about these things. I want to look briefly at the picture he draws in the book of Ephesians concerning the state of those to whom God sends you to preach the gospel. In the first and second chapter there is much said on this subject. It does not matter what day or in what age God sends a preacher to preach the gospel. Men and women, boys and girls, children and adults—we all start out in the shape we read about beginning in chapter 2, verse 1, of the book of Ephesians:

> And you hath he quickened, who were dead in trespasses and sins; Wherein in time past ye walked according to the course of this world, according to the prince of the power of the air,

the spirit that now worketh in the children of disobedience: Among whom also we all had our conversation in times past in the lusts of our flesh, fulfilling the desires of the flesh and of the mind;
and were by nature the children of wrath, even as
others. But God, who is rich in mercy, for His great
love wherewith He loved us, Even when we were
dead in sins, hath quickened us together with
Christ, (by grace ye are saved;) And hath raised
us up together, and made us sit together in heavenly places in Christ Jesus: That in the ages to
come He might shew the exceeding riches of his
grace in his kindness toward us through Christ
Jesus. For by grace are ye saved through faith;
and that not of yourselves: it is the gift of God:
Not of works, lest any man should boast. For we
are his workmanship, created in Christ Jesus unto good works, which God hath before ordained
that we should walk in them (Ephesians 2:1-10).

Throughout this book, much is said about the state of the
natural man.

The first statement this passage makes is that those to
whom I go are dead in trespasses and in sins. In the physical
world of living, death carries with it finality. There is hopelessness in death. There is no treatment for death. The only
remedy for death is resurrection.

I realize that those who are dead physically are completely
dead. Their heart is dead, their lungs are dead and their internal organs are dead. There is nothing they can do that will
cause them, by their own accord, to rise from the mortician's
slab. And when I am called to preach to men I must recognize
this fact. Spiritually speaking, lost men are dead. This extends
to their mind, emotions, and will. They are "dead in trespasses and in sins."

I must also understand that they will show no interest. The
dead have no appetite, no interest, and no concern. I must

not expect them to stand up and say, "Oh, we were just waiting for you to come." I believe that is the biggest lie in the world. I don't believe anybody is waiting for you to come. Jesus said, "I will call you to be fishers of men," and I have never heard of a fish that wanted to get into the boat. Water is natural to a fish and so is sin to a sinner. It is by God's amazing grace that He would bring any of the dead from death to life in Christ. Our job is nothing more than to go to the tomb and tell them, "Lazarus, come forth."

I realize that men are dead and I think that Paul put that first because it makes us realize that we can do nothing to make the dead come alive. Nothing! I don't care how many seminary degrees you have. There is simply nothing we can do to make the dead come to life!

Back in November my mother called me in the early morning hours and said, "Son, come quickly. Your dad is dying." I went and my 79-year-old dad, the man who had been such a gracious father to me, was passing away. I watched the ambulance crew come and work on him feverishly trying to keep him alive but finally when he died their efforts stopped and they did no more. As long as he was alive there was hope, but when he died they could do no more. I have to realize as God's preacher that those to whom God sends me are dead in trespasses and in sins. There is nothing I can do.

Not only are *they* helpless—*I'm* helpless. They can't get out of the grave nor can I get them out. They are helpless. Do you believe that? Do you believe that no matter where God sends you everybody is helpless? Whether it is in North Carolina, Louisiana, Arkansas, Alaska or New York—everybody you greet and meet who has not been saved is dead in sins. My verdict must start there. My diagnosis will be there.

Let me read a few other things our text says about those in the state of spiritual death. It says, "In times past you walked according to the course of this world, according to the prince of the power of the air, the spirit that now worketh." The word "worketh" is *energeo.* The devil is energizing those who are dead in trespasses and in sins. Satan is the force, the mover behind them. They follow the world bound in their sins, bound to their lusts, moved upon by the forces of darkness. There they stand—hopeless and without God or His Son. As a preacher, I must realize that I am dealing with people bound as Romans 6 says, "slaves of sin"—slaves of the world, slaves of the devil, slaves of their lusts, slaves of self. I have no way to loose them and let them go.

Look at something else the text says about those who are without Christ. They are the sons of disobedience. We know that. There is no question about that. A very interesting word employed here is *apeitheia*. We derive our English word apathy from *apeitheia*. Apathy is a simple way of saying, "Who cares?" Those to whom we are sent are people who have no concern or care about what God says. They are apathetic. They don't care. It doesn't matter to them. Many times I have tried to talk to a man and thought, "Surely that argument will cause him to come alive," and he just yawns in my face and says, "So what? I have heard that a thousand times."

As a preacher of the gospel, I need to realize that the apathy mentioned here is not a passive apathy but an apathy of hostility. The Bible says that we are "enemies in our minds by wicked works." "When we were enemies we were reconciled to God by the death of His Son." "The carnal mind is enmity against God." And that strong enmity rises up against that which God has called us to do. As a minister of the gospel, I must not be surprised that people do not get excited when I come to tell them of Jesus. The power of Satan in their lives, the lusts of their flesh, and the deadness of their souls produce in them apathy. They have no interest in what I have to say unless God plants that interest there. I want you to know and believe this because if you don't, you will start trying to pull people out of the tomb. Or, what you will do is try to manipulate people and work on them and tell them sad stories, giving them a lot of illustrations, and somehow end up asking them to bow their head forty times and raise their hand ten and then come to the front. God have mercy. Men are not interested. I don't care how many times they raise the hand—they must bow the heart. Lost men are by nature apathetic with hostility built in. Dead in their sins, bound by their lusts and this is true of everyone to whom you have been sent including the 10-year-old boy. He may not have been spiritually dead as long as his granddaddy but he is dead nonetheless.

Notice what else the text says: "We all had our manner of life in times past of the lust of the flesh and of the mind." In other words, Paul says that all of this inward corruption will belch forth by the activities of the flesh—by living life in a corrupt and diabolical way. Paul says that because by nature we are children of wrath.

So men are by nature under the wrath of God. We do not *become* children of wrath. Rather, we are *born* children of wrath. When did you get your nature? Whenever you got your nature that's when you became a child of wrath. We know from Psalm 51 that in sin our parents conceived us and at that point we became the children of wrath. Moreover, being children of wrath means we are under God's holy displeasure. We're there not primarily because of what we have done but because of what we are. Of course we are there also because of what we have done since we are told in Romans 1 that the wrath of God is displayed from heaven against all ungodliness and unrighteousness. The wrath of God is also displayed against us because of our unbelief. The Bible says that those that do not believe are under the wrath of God. We are all by nature under the wrath of God.

Sometimes I hear people say, "I am sure that little child went to heaven because he died in his innocence." There is no such reality as dying in your innocence. If you get to heaven, whether as a two-year old or ninety-two year old, you will get there by God's grace. There are not two parts to heaven—one place where the people go who got there by grace and then another place for those who got there by their innocence. I don't know what you think about babies dying in infancy. I personally think God takes them all home to glory by pure grace, just like He does you and me. It is all of grace.

But the question should be asked, "If all people are born in this condition, how can I pull them out from the wrath of

God?" What shall I do? I know that whosoever will, may come, but what about the ones who won't come? What do I do to get them out from under this plight? Oh, I'll tell you, I can either throw up my hands in frustration or I can look unto the heavens from whence cometh my help. My help cometh from the Lord. Bless God, I would have quit twenty-five years ago if it hadn't been for His grace. I didn't understand it. I just enjoyed it.

I want to say another word on this point. Throughout the book of Ephesians—not just in the opening pages, but throughout the book—Paul continues to remind us of our natural state. He does this, for example, in chapter 5 verse 8 saying "For ye were once darkness, but now are ye light in the Lord: walk as children of light."

You were darkness. That is reinforced also in other parts of the book. For example, in the fourth chapter verses 17-19:

> This I say therefore, and testify in the Lord, that ye henceforth walk not as other Gentiles walk, in the vanity of their mind, Having the understanding darkened, being alienated from the life of God through the ignorance that is in them, because of the blindness of their heart: Who being past feeling have given themselves over unto lasciviousness, to work all uncleanness with greediness (Ephesians 4:17-19).

Paul says here that, spiritually, all men to whom God sends us are in stark, awful, stygian, midnight darkness. They know not aught. They know not the kind of God of whom we speak. They are ignorant of God. They know not how holy God is. They use His name as a curse word. They make jokes about Him. They think of Him as if He were nothing more than a little human being, referring to Him as "the man upstairs."

Listen friend, the men to whom you go have no knowledge of a holy God—a God before Whom the angels cry, "Holy, holy, holy is the Lord God of Hosts." They don't know that.

They have no conception of the holiness of God. But they are also in darkness about themselves. They do not know that in them there dwelleth no good thing. Do you think they know that? No. Do you think they believe that their best acts of righteousness are as filthy rags? No. Do you think they believe they sit in darkness in need of a great light? No. They are dull about their own condition.

Not long ago I was speaking with a man and I said to him, "Sir, you need the Lord," and he said, "Oh, I'm not so bad. Granted, I drink a little. I run around with women. I tried a little dope and never go to church." "But," he said, "At heart I'm a good man." Do you think if I had simply stayed there long enough I would have convinced him that was a lie? No. For you cannot convince a blind man that the picture you have drawn is pretty no matter how pretty it truly is. I don't care if you preach the gospel so clearly that a little two-year-old could understand it. No one, unless God's saving light flashes into their souls, can see the glory of God in the face of Jesus Christ, nor can they see their own horribly filthy heart. Never. "I once was blind but now I see." So the men to whom you go will be stark blind. They will be able to hear nothing you tell them should God leave you to minister to them unless He graciously unstops their ears. Let me say another word or two, and then we shall think some positive thoughts and go into a period of praise.

I want to remind you of something that Paul brings to our attention as we move back to the second chapter of Ephesians. The apostle says in verse 12, "At that time," meaning before conversion, "ye were without Christ, aliens from the commonwealth of Israel, strangers from the covenants of promise, having no hope, and without God in the world: But now in Christ Jesus ye that once were far off are made near by the blood of Jesus."

What is the state of those people to whom you go? I know they are dead and I don't know how to make them alive. I know they are bound and I cannot break the chains asunder and set the prisoners free. I can't do it. I know they are children of wrath and I cannot find out how to get them out from under that great boulder of wrath that hovers over their head. I don't know how to do that. I can trick them. I can seek to persuade them. I can pull on them, but even if it appears that I am succeeding at getting them out into the light, they run right back under the rock and hide in the dark again.

I recognize the fact that the people to whom we are sent are living in darkness and I have never been able to give sight to the blind. Oh mercy, what can be done for them? God says that you can't give them what they need on your own. They are without Christ, the source and the root of all blessing. Every unsaved person with whom you will be dealing, from the smallest to the largest, will be without Christ. They will be aliens from the commonwealth of Israel. They will have no relationship with God's covenant people. No wonder they don't want to go to church. They don't have anything in common with God's people. They don't have any desire to be there. They are strangers from the covenant of promise. They have no relationship to God's saving promises. They are hopeless. In other words, they have no anticipation of anything beyond the grave.

Then Paul says they are without God in this world. The word translated "without God" is interesting because it is the word *atheos*, which means "atheist." The only time that God uses the word "atheist" in the Bible is right here, as far as I can tell. The word carries the impression not so much that the people with whom we have to deal will not be believers in God, but that they will be without God Himself. God is not as interested in whether you believe He exists but rather, if you really know Him. In the Scripture an atheist is a person who does not know God, not a person who does not believe that there is a God. You may even have atheists in your church— those still do not *know* God. What Paul is saying here is that those with whom you will have dealings throughout your ministry will be atheists in a practical sense and have not God—being without these great promises, without the people, without Christ, and without the hope.

But is this true of all? Oh yes. Throughout this portion of Ephesians the theme is that all who are lost are in this condition. There is no limitation to it. I must know this and be convinced of it. Everybody I go to is like this whether they seem to be so or not. If they are open at all to the gospel message, it is because of grace. But this is true of all who receive the gospel. Once again, there are no exceptions.

Now, that might be enough to make some people say, "Well, I guess the best I can do is just hide my head in the sand and wait for the lightning to strike." But no, bless God! Paul paints the picture so black in order to make us desperate to find even a pinpoint of light. The book of Ephesians is flooded with light. That is why the book of Ephesians is often called the "Book of Grace." Throughout this letter the message is that you, as a preacher, can't help sinners any more than they can help themselves. If they are saved it is of grace and if you have anything to do with it, that too, will be of grace. You need to know that. It was grace that saved you and if God ever lets you see one person saved it will be pure grace. Pure grace. That is what Paul tells us in the rest of the book.

THE CONDITION OF THE ELECT—MADE ALIVE IN CHRIST JESUS

What does Paul tell us in Ephesians about what God does for those in that condition who are His elect? He does have His elect among those who are dead in trespasses and sins. They are right there in that mess and that arena of horribleness. Paul repeatedly uses the direct object here. A direct object is a part of speech that depicts an action as having been taken and the action as having landed on an object. If I say, "I hit you," then you got the hit. That is an example of a direct object.

The first chapter of Ephesians is loaded with examples of the use of the direct object. In verse 3 we are told, "He hath blessed us." To whom does "us" refer? "Us" refers to "the saints . . . the faithful in Christ Jesus," later referred to as "chosen"—part of the elect. He hath blessed us. Isn't that marvelous? That's grace!

Notice also verse 4, which states, "He hath chosen us in Him." Verse 5 says, He "Predestinated us in His love." Then again in verse 11, "In whom we have obtained an inheritance being predestinated." What a blessed word. And then verse 6 states, "He hath begraced us in the beloved." Then verse 8, "He hath poured out lavishly upon us His grace." Then there is verse 1 of chapter 2, "He hath quickened us and made us alive in Christ Jesus." Then in verse 6, "He hath raised us." Also in verse 6, "Made us sit together." Verses 7 and 8 tell us what He has done for us by way of His grace and His love. And then in verse 4, "He hath loved us." Every one of these is a direct object. It is as if God were telling us that if those to whom I minister get any blessing at all they will get it through pure grace. They will be the objects of God's grace, the objects of God's actions, and the objects of God's mercy. God will do it.

I also like the passive voice verb used in the Greek New Testament in Ephesians chapter one and two. The passive voice means that the subject has been acted upon. If we take the example above and change it to reflect the passive voice, the sentence will now read as follows: "I was hit." I am the one who is on the receiving end of the hit.

Notice some of the passive verbs that are employed in the first and second chapters of Ephesians, telling us what has happened to us by the grace of God. In chapter one, verse 11, we read, "In whom also we have obtained an inheritance." The phrase "obtained an inheritance" is in the passive voice, which means that God has made you His inheritance.

In verse 13, we read, "After trusting because of His grace in whom after ye believed, ye were sealed." We who are trusting Christ are in that number too and were sealed—passive voice.

When you come to verse 5 of chapter 2, there is yet another passage. "For by grace ye were saved." See once again the passive voice? You received the salvation. You received the action. It was a passive operation.

Then again in verse 8, "For by grace," again, "are ye saved through faith; and that not of yourselves: it is the gift of God: not of works, lest any man should boast." There again is the occurrence of the passive voice. You were put into a state of salvation and it was all God's doing.

And then look at verse 13, "But now ye in Christ Jesus who were far off are made near." We see the passive voice, meaning you were *made* to come near—you didn't bring yourself near. God found you out there at a distance and He just picked you up and brought you near in Christ Jesus. The preacher didn't talk you near. God brought you near. Isn't that good? Isn't that great? You were dead and God made you alive. You had no inheritance and He made you an heir. God did it! Hallelujah! Oh, Praise God!

PASTORAL IMPLICATIONS

I want to close by asking you, "Does this message have any personal, pastoral, and practical implications for your life?" What does this have to do with me as a child of His and a preacher of the gospel, or a Sunday School teacher, or simply a Christian who cares about others?

The first pastoral implication is that in a very practical sense, this message of salvation ought to do something to my own spirit. My dear people, we're not just talking about sinners "out there" when we ponder this. We are talking about sinners in here—the church. Have you ever wondered why you are saved and some boys or girls that you went to school with are not? I am thinking of two young men with whom I went to school who were better behaved than I was at that time. Yet, as far as I know, one of them is in hell now and the other is caught up in a pagan lifestyle in New York City having no thought of God. All three of us went to that evangelistic meeting at the State Fair stadium. For reasons I don't pretend to understand, God in His grace picked me out. I didn't do it—He did it. Hallelujah, what a Savior!

I read not long ago about World War II veterans who went

back to Normandy on the fortieth anniversary of D-Day. *U. S. News and World Report* quoted one of the men as saying, "As I looked out there at that 170 acres of tombstones, 9,380 crosses and Stars of David, I thought in my heart, 'I wonder what kept me from being in those rows of white crosses?' I was there that day." I could have told him what kept him from those rows of white crosses—it was God's pure grace.

But it is the same way with me. Why am I not out there today moving towards hell, bound by the forces of this world, energized by Satan, fulfilling the desires of the flesh and of the mind, being by nature under God's wrath? Who or what caused me to differ? It is God's pure grace and I am going to rejoice and be happy about it. I want to keep that spirit. I want to be able to sit down and weep and say, "Oh God, you did it to me. 'Depth of mercy, could there be mercy, oh yet, reserved for me?' Thank you Lord for doing it for me."

Don't ever get professional, my beloved. Always weep when you think about grace, and think about every reason why you ought to be in hell today. Isn't that so? Why aren't you in hell? It wasn't the preacher. It was God's grace. That is the first implication I want to draw out for myself and I hope you will draw the same.

But there is a second implication. Knowing these things will help us to better assess the spiritual conditions of our day. Knowing these things helps us understand why some of our churches act like they do. They are full of corpses. I think perhaps what we've done is that we thought if people showed an interest in Christ that meant they were already saved, and so we dunked them and welcomed them into the membership. I understand the condition of some of our churches because I know that the people there were brought in by man and not by the Spirit.

A third implication is that we must fully comprehend and feel in our hearts our utter dependence upon the great sovereign God to see anything done in our ministries. I don't want you to get the impression that I am saying we shouldn't do anything to help people. I realize that Paul not only wrote many words of evangelistic exhortation to others, but he also actively engaged all those people in Rome who would listen to him in an intense evangelistic appeal. Do you remember that episode in the life of Paul recorded in the twenty-eighth chapter of Acts? "And when they had appointed him a day, there came many to him into his lodging; to whom he expounded and testified the kingdom of God, persuading them concerning Jesus, both out of the law of Moses, and out of the prophets, from morning till evening. And some believed the things which were spoken, and some believed not" (Acts 28:23-24).

There was a split between those whom God picked and those He did not. But listen to the text. "Paul expounded"— the word is literally "drew out," *ektithemi*. He just put the truth out and laid it right under their noses. But he could not cause them to take it. Luke records that Paul testified (the Greek word is *diamarture*). This word means "to testify to the very end." Paul went through all the Scriptures seeking to show them Jesus, but still only some believed. The same Paul who said that lost men are dead, gave all he had that they might be saved. And then Luke says he "persuaded them." Here it is the word *peitho*. Not *apeitho*, but rather *peitho*. It is saying that Paul was attempting to throw them out of their lethargy and make them give full attention to the gospel of Christ, but he knew he couldn't do anything more about it. He opened the Old Testament Scripture and then he just stood back and watched the Spirit do His deep and everlasting work.

Not long ago I was at a little church near Shawnee, Oklahoma. I learned something incredibly beautiful from one of the old saints of the faith. I stayed with an old deacon who told me the story of his conversion and it illustrates well the point I am trying to make—how you and I have to give it our all when sharing the gospel with others and then trust God to do His mighty work in the hearts of men. This old deacon's story went like this:

You know, when I married my wife I told her that I wasn't a child of God. But she was and she prayed for me and started imploring me to go to church with her until I finally started attending. We had an old backwoods preacher that didn't have a very good education. He used words like "aint" and misused other words, but bless God, he sure could preach—even with bad English. He just laid it on the line. I got so disturbed one day I kind of shook a little bit and thought maybe it's time for me to join the church so I went up after the service and I said, "Brother Dave, I want to talk to you." It seemed to me like that man stood there for fifteen minutes without answering and then he looked me in the eye and said, "No, I don't think you're ready yet." Why that just made me so mad. I waited about three more weeks and it seemed to me like every Sunday that preacher threw that old finger out and pointed at my heart and said, "Thou art the man." After about four or five more weeks I walked up the second time (this time a little more humbled) and said, "Brother Dave, I am concerned a bit about my soul." That dear brother looked at me again and he shook his head east and west and said, "I'm sorry, you're going to have to wait a little longer." Now this time I was a little peaked but I wasn't mad. I got back in my chair and thought, "Well that's a funny preacher that doesn't want anybody to join his church."

Bless God, he had a preacher who knew the grace of God. He wasn't scared that that fellow was going to get run over by a wild horse before he got saved. He believed God in His grace could do it. The old deacon continued with his story:

I sat through that another two months and the next time I came I took that preacher by his shoulders and said, "You're going to talk to me now!"

I asked, "Do you know what he was doing for you?" He answered, "I didn't know at the time but I do now." He said that preacher told him,

> "Well, I'll tell you what. Now that the service is over why don't I take your family and head home in my wagon and you take your wagon by yourself down that road and you think about it?" I got in that old cart and I started heading for home. Every time those wheels turned it seemed as if they said to me, "Thou art undone, thou art undone." I got within a hundred yards of home and pulled that old team of horses by the side of that dirt road and under an old tree I cried out, "God, have mercy on me, a sinner." I got those horses and you should have seen how fast I went the last one hundred yards. I ran to the house and the first person that met me was the preacher. He took me by the hand and he said, "Brother, doesn't it feel better now?"

That preacher knew exactly what he was doing. He was stepping out of God's way for the Spirit of God to do His saving work. You won't get as many "converts" that way, but when you get one, he or she will be a real convert and not just a number. That man is a deacon today and I would guess he hasn't missed ten worship services since the Lord saved him. I saw that man on his knees weeping for the souls of men and for forty years he has walked with King Jesus. Get out of God's way. You can't save sinners in and of your own power—sinners are saved only by grace. Just preach, pray, plead, and then move out of the way and watch God call Lazarus out of the tomb.

13.
THE LORDSHIP OF CHRIST IN EVANGELISM
DAVID MILLER
1985 Southern Baptist Founders Conference

INTRODUCTION

YOU have bestowed on me a great honor by allowing me to share in your fellowship today and preach on this occasion. I do not take this privilege lightly, but as a charge from the Almighty. The title of my sermon is "The Lordship of Christ in Evangelism." I think we can agree that Peter preached an evangelistic sermon on the day of Pentecost. In Acts chapter 2, Peter is preaching,

> Ye men of Israel, hear these words; Jesus of Nazareth, a man approved of God among you by miracles and wonders and signs, which God did by him in the midst of you, as ye yourselves also know: Him, being delivered by the determinate counsel and foreknowledge of God, ye have taken, and by wicked hands have crucified and slain: whom God hath raised up, having loosed the pains of death: because it was not possible that he should be holden of it (Acts 2:22-24; KJV).

In verse 32, he reiterates concerning the resurrection:

> This Jesus hath God raised up, whereof we all are witnesses. Therefore being by the right hand of God exalted, and having received of the Father the promise of the Holy Ghost, he hath shed forth

this, which you now see and hear (Acts 2:32-33).

He speaks of the resurrection again in verse 36:

Therefore let all the house of Israel know assuredly, that God hath made this same Jesus, whom you crucified, both Lord and Christ. Now when they heard this, they were pricked in their hearts, and they cried unto Peter and the rest of the disciples, saying, "Men and brethren, what shall we do?" Then Peter said unto them, "Repent, and be baptized every one of you in the name of Jesus Christ for the remission of sins, and you shall receive the gift of the Holy Ghost. For the promise is unto you, and to your children, and to them that are afar off, even as many as the Lord our God shall call." And with many other words he did testify and exhort, saying, "Save yourselves from this untoward generation." Then they that gladly received his word were baptized: and the same day there were added unto them about three thousand souls (Acts 2:36-41).

I have divided my sermon tonight under two general headings: First, an explanation of the Lordship of Christ in evangelism; and second, an example of preaching the Lordship of Christ in evangelism.

AN EXPLANATION OF THE LORDSHIP OF CHRIST IN EVANGELISM

Preaching the Lordship of Christ in evangelism is simply telling the truth about who Jesus is. In other words, preaching the Lordship of Christ involves expository preaching, that is, letting the Word of God say what it says about who Jesus is.

Preaching the Lordship of Christ in evangelism means presenting Christ as Lord in every aspect of His redemptive work. For example, when we speak of Him as our atonement we must let it be known that He is attractive, acceptable, and approved. If we speak of Him as our Advocate, we must let it be known that He is astute, articulate, and accredited before the Father. If we speak of Him as our expiation for sin, we must let it be known that Jesus Christ is the essence, the effulgence and the expressed image of the invisible God. If we speak of Him as Mediator, we must let it be known that He is mighty and marvelous and matchless. If we speak of Him as our Priest, we must let it be known that He is pure and perfect and peerless. If we speak of Him as our Redeemer, we must let it be heralded, clearly and unequivocally, that He is rich and royal and righteous. He is the Lord! If we speak of Him as our Savior, we must let it be known beyond any doubt that He is sinless, sovereign, and sufficient. He is the Lord! For you see, to speak of the Lordship of Christ is to proclaim that Jesus Christ possesses all of the divine attributes and authority. Preaching the Lordship of Christ in evangelism simply means to tell the truth about Jesus.

AN EXAMPLE OF PREACHING THE LORDSHIP OF CHRIST IN EVANGELISM

Now, with that aside, I want to share an example of preaching the Lordship of Christ in evangelism. The example is found in our passage in Acts 2. Peter understood that evangelism is not completed until three things have happened.

1. There must be a proper perception of Christ's Lordship.
2. There must be a proper profession of Christ's Lordship.
3. There must be a practice of Christ's Lordship.

A Proper Perception of Christ's Lordship.

Those who heard Peter preach at Pentecost perceived that Jesus Christ was Lord. Peter did not take it for granted that his audience understood who Jesus was.

Perception and reality are not always the same. At times, we might be preaching Lordship in reality, but the perception of our message may be something altogether different. Often people hear what they want to hear instead of what is actually being said.

If you don't think there is a difference between perception and reality in this regard, let me share an example. Several years ago, on a Sunday afternoon, I went to a church in the next county to preach at an associational stewardship rally. I got there about two minutes after the service had begun. A pastor friend of mine gave me assistance up the steps and to the pulpit. The brother who introduced me was eighty years old and he had been blind since the age of twenty-five. You could have heard a pin drop on the carpet during the introduction. The folks were wondering about me; they didn't know if I was going to make it or not. I told myself, "I must inject some levity into the situation so they can get their minds off my affliction and hear my address." In a moment of inspiration, some humor came to mind. When I came to the podium I asked, "Has anyone present been run over by a bulldozer?" No one had. I then said, "Well that's too bad, for if there was one then we would have the Scriptural precedent on the program today—'the maimed, the halt and the blind'." I thought there was a great deal of humor in my joke, but the folks didn't get it. They didn't laugh at all. My wife said to me on the way home, "David, I hope you'll have enough presence of mind never to do that again."

The next day, I traveled to eastern Arkansas to begin an evangelistic meeting. When I got there, the place was dimly lit, the few saints who were present sat in the back of the building, and the pastor had a hard time assisting me up the steps. The folks were tense. I thought, "I'll tell that same joke I told yesterday. It will help these folks relax and get their minds off my affliction so they will hear my address." I told the same story, and I thought I had told it marvelously well. Not only did they not laugh, they didn't even smile! They just stared at me. But the next morning at the pastor's home where I was staying, a lady called and, in the course of the conversation with that pastor, she remarked, "My, isn't it a shame that Brother Miller got run over by a bulldozer." Now I'll tell you, brethren, perception and reality are not always the same thing!

Peter didn't want to risk his audience confusing reality with perception. He wanted to preach the truth of Christ in reality, and he wanted the people to perceive the truth.

Peter recognized three elements in the salvation experience. Intellectually, there must be a proper Christology. Emotionally, there must be a profound conviction, and volitionally, there must be a powerful conversion. What an experience! It happens in time and space. You can get your hands on it and your teeth into it; you can know about it in your head and feel it in your heart. It's not something you just wake up with some morning, not knowing where it came from or how you got it or what you're going to do with it. I believe it's an experience. It is a soul-saving, life-changing experience.

Peter recognized that intellectually there must be a proper Christology. He addressed his crowd by proclaiming some facts. He said something like this, "Today I want you to know some things about Jesus of Nazareth. I want you to know that He is a man approved of God among you. Confirmation of His deity has been given by miracles, and wonders, and signs. He has set aside the laws of the universe and worked miracles in your midst. You know this. You have taken this Christ of God and, with wicked hands, you have crucified Him at Calvary. Well, I want you to know," Peter continues, "that this Jesus whom you crucified, God has raised Him from the dead. He has raised Him up! Because of His deity and the eternal decree of God, it is impossible that death should hold Him. We all are witnesses! This Jesus whom you crucified, God has made Him both Lord and Christ." That is preaching the Lordship of Christ to sinners.

Calvinists would do well to remember that a sinner does not

have to comprehend all the theological ramifications of the person and work of Christ in order to be saved. I was saved at age 16. I don't think I could intelligently compare and contrast the Calvinistic system with the Arminian system at that time. Furthermore, I had not decided whether I was an "infra" or "supra" Lapsarian in my views of God's decrees before my conversion!

Praise God! A sinner doesn't have to know everything about Christ in order to be saved. However, a sinner must know *some* things about Christ, and he must know them correctly to be saved. Intellectually, there must be a proper Christology. From the youngest to the eldest, a person must comprehend that Jesus is the Son of God; He died a substitutionary death; He was buried but was raised from the dead and He's alive and He is Lord! This is the gospel which Calvinists preach.

Not only must there be a proper Christology intellectually, but emotionally, there has to be a profound conviction. Notice verse 37: "Now when they heard this..."—that is, when they heard Peter's address—they were cut, convicted, pricked in their hearts, and they cried out saying, "Men and brethren what shall we do?" They interrupted Peter! I don't know what I'd do if on a Sunday morning in the middle of my sermon people just stood up and shouted, "Brother David you've said enough. I've got to be saved." I would like an opportunity to find out!

You will never convince me Peter was through preaching when he was interrupted. I believe he wasn't done for at least two reasons. First, Baptist preachers just don't get through that quickly. And second, the passage says, "that with many other words he did testify and exhort." He very likely had more to say. Jesus Christ—His person, His power, His passion, His resurrection, His exaltation, His Lordship—had been presented. And it is no accident that people were convicted of their sin. There is an unmistakable and undeniable correlation between a proper Christology and a profound conviction about sin in the human heart. You see, the more a person knows about the Lord Jesus—who He is and what

He's done at Calvary—the more deeply he will feel the weight of his sins and just condemnation before the Lord. Could it be that on occasions when there is so little conviction, Christ has been very poorly presented?

There must not only be a proper Christology and a profound conviction; but volitionally, there must be a powerful conversion. In verse 38, Peter responds to their query "what shall we do?" He says, "Repent and be baptized for the remission of sins, and ye shall receive the gift of the Holy Ghost." The commandment was to repent and to repent is to "turn about." It is a change of mind that leads to a change in conduct. You don't repent accidentally. It must be done on purpose. It requires an act of the will. I don't mean to imply that a man dead in sin has the natural capability to repent on his own. He might as well try to "will" the moon into cream cheese! However, when the Holy Spirit quickens, illumines and convicts, there is with the commandment the enabling to repent. What an experience!

A Proper Profession of Christ's Lordship.

Secondly, I want you to see that these people recognized the Lordship of Christ in their profession of Him at conversion. Verse 41 says, "Then they that gladly received His word were baptized..." In verse 38, Peter told them to "repent and be baptized in the name of Jesus Christ." Did you ever wonder why some of those brethren in the book of Acts were baptized in the name of Jesus Christ only? Now I don't claim to have the final word on this, but Dr. Lightfoot says, "These Jewish converts were baptized in the name of Jesus, instead of the Trinity, as a profession of their break with Judaism and it's religious and political institutions, and to demonstrate their absolute, total dependence and allegiance and loyalty to the Christ of God who was crucified, buried, and resurrected for them." I like that! That's what baptism ought to be. It should be a profession of one's faith in the Lord Jesus Christ, who was crucified and buried and resurrected. One has to be suspicious (but not judgmental) of those who claim to be saved but have no time or inclination to follow their Lord in the ordinance of baptism. It ought to be a profession of one's faith.

A Proper Practice of Christ's Lordship.

A religion that does not change the way you live your life will not save your soul and take you to heaven when you die. The converts in Acts 2 practiced the Lordship of Christ in their lives by being men of steadfast convictions, simple compassion, and by being spectacularly charismatic.

Verse 42 says these folks, who had been converted "continued steadfastly in the apostles doctrine." An old country preacher was preaching from this text. He didn't have any education so he offered this "homespun" explanation. He said, "When the Bible says they continued steadfastly, that means they didn't backslide right away!" In other words, they didn't join the church one Sunday morning and have company come in that afternoon and then not be able to make it out to the evening worship service. The next Sunday, they had to go out of town in their new car to visit with Granny out in the country and she needed help with the noon meal and they couldn't attend church out there. You know the ones. They visit much longer than they intended and by the time they got home late that Sunday afternoon (about 2:30), they were so worn and weary they couldn't make it back to the worship service that evening. And the following Wednesday, they had so looked forward to the mid-week Bible study and prayer time, but the little ten-year old boy came home with a high temperature of 98.7 and they didn't think he ought to be out in the night air!

The text says, "They continued steadfastly in the apostles' doctrine." This can mean one of two things. If it means that they continued in the "instructions" of the apostles, I like that. That means they went to Sunday School! On the other hand, if it means that "body of truth" expounded by the apostles, I like that also, for it means they were not uncomfortable or bored to tears during a study of the great doctrines of the Christian faith. Ultimately, what you believe determines how you behave.

They practiced their Christianity not only by being men of steadfast convictions but also by being men of simple compassion. Verses 44 and 45 say, "And all that believed were together, and had all things common; And sold their possessions and goods and parted them to all men, as every man had need." They recognized the need. They sold their possessions and goods and shared them with all men. Say what you want, but there is not a more scathing castigation of Southern Baptists in our day than this. We have so much of this world's goods and we see our brothers and sisters having need and have shut up our bowels of compassion against them. How dwells the love of God in us? Today, all across this great convention of ours, Southern Baptists with their thirty-six thousand churches and their almost fourteen million members still spend eighty-five cents out of every dollar on their own home base. There is not a more scathing castigation against us than that. But these men practiced the Lordship of Christ by being men of simple compassion.

We should not make communism out of this or fight against free enterprise with it. Instead, we need to just let the Bible say what it says. They had been converted, there was a need, and the Lordship of Christ meant that they practice simple compassion toward those in need.

They were spectacularly charismatic. We have allowed the neo-Pentecostals to rob us of the use of a perfectly good New Testament concept. Baptists who are saved are indwelt by the Spirit. Those who are indwelt by the Spirit are also gifted by the Spirit and they have in them a river of Living Water flowing out. This is what it means to be charismatic. Verses 46 and 47 say, "And they, continuing daily with one accord in the temple, and breaking bread from house to house, did eat their meat with gladness and singleness of heart. Praising God and having favor with all the people...." Have you ever wondered how they went about praising God? Do you suppose they went around shouting, "Hallelujah!" and lifting their heads toward heaven? I don't know for sure about that, but this I do know, wherever they were or whomever they were with, they just had something good and grand and glorious to say about Jesus. They went around bragging on Jesus!

Did you hear about the old country preacher who got to visit a big city church for the first time? He found a comfortable position on the padded pew. When the choir finished with the sevenfold "Amens" the pastor stood and began to read his sermon. Before long he said something good about the Lord. At that point, the old preacher just hollered out "Amen, brother! I believe that." The preacher lost his place! After awhile he regained his composure and continued to read his sermon. Before long he said something about heaven, how it's going to be when all of God's children get home; how that there will be no more sorrow, nor crying, nor death for the former things shall be wiped away. Once again, the old preacher got excited and just hollered out "Praise God, brother! I believe that." An usher came over and tapped him on the shoulder and said, "My brother, you are interrupting our service." The old preacher looked up at him with surprise and said, "But I was just praising the Lord." The usher said, "Yes, but you are bothering our preacher." The old fellow said, "But I've got religion. I was just praising the Lord." And the usher looked down at him rather sternly and said, "I don't care what you've got, you didn't get it here. Shut up!"

I know that wouldn't happen in your church. But I tell you, at some of the churches where I preach on Sunday morning, if some dear brother were to start thinking about what he used to be before he got saved, what he is now, and what he is going to be one of these days when Jesus comes back, and he stood up at a time not designated on the printed program for testimonies and began to say something like this:

> Naught have I gotten, but what I received.
> Grace hath bestowed it since I have believed.

Boasting excluded, pride I abase.
I'm only a sinner saved by grace.

Once I was foolish and sin ruled my heart.
Causing my footsteps from God to depart.
Jesus had found me, happy my case.
I'm now a sinner, saved by grace.

Tears unabated, no merit had I.
Mercy had saved me or else I must die.
Sin had alarmed me, fearing God's face.
But now the sinner, saved by grace.

Suffer a sinner whose heart overflows.
Loving his Savior, to tell what he knows.
Once more to tell it would I embrace,
I'm only a sinner saved by grace.

Only a sinner saved by grace,
only a sinner saved by grace.
This is my story, to God be the glory,
I'm only a sinner saved by grace.

I tell you, if this happened in some of our churches, the folks would go home with a crick in their necks because they turned around so quickly to see what on earth was happening.

I want to say something to us Calvinists here. We had better preach the truth about Jesus. We call it the doctrines of grace; we call it Calvinism; we can call it whatever we want to —just so it's the truth. I want to tell you that if our evangelism does not produce a proper perception of who Jesus is and a proper profession of Him at conversion, and cause the people to practice the Lordship of Christ in their Christianity, we haven't gotten the job done yet!

God help us to do it.

14.
THE SUFFICIENCY OF SCRIPTURE IN SALVATION
WALTER C. CHANTRY
1994 Southern Baptist Founders Conference

THIS evening we speak about the sufficiency of Scripture for man's salvation. Now hear the Word of God in Luke chapter 16, beginning at verse 19:

> There was a rich man who was dressed in purple and fine linen and lived in luxury every day. At his gate was laid a beggar named Lazarus, covered with sores and longing to eat what fell from the rich man's table. Even the dogs came and licked his sores.
>
> The time came when the beggar died and the angels came and carried him to Abraham's side. The rich man also died and was buried. In hell, where he was in torment, he looked up and saw Abraham far away with Lazarus by his side. So he called to him, "Father Abraham have pity on me and send Lazarus to dip the tip of his finger in water and cool my tongue, because I am in agony in this fire."
>
> But Abraham replied, "Son, remember that in your lifetime you received your good things while Lazarus received bad things but now he is comforted here and you are in agony. And besides all this, between us and you a great chasm has been fixed, so that those who want to go from here to you cannot, nor can anyone cross over from there to us." He answered, "Then I beg you father, send

Lazarus to my father's house, for I have five
brothers. Let him warn them, so that they will not
also come to this place of torment."
Abraham replied, "They have Moses and the
Prophets, let them listen to them."
"No, father Abraham," he said. "But if someone
from the dead goes to them they will repent."
He said to him, "If they do not listen to Moses
and the Prophets they will not be convinced even
if someone rises from the dead" (Luke 16:19-31).

These are the words of Jesus Christ. Some say it is a parable. Luke does not call it a parable. It is unusual that our Lord
should actually name a person within a parable. Whether this
is an actual case history or a parable, the lesson is still the
same.

Our Lord Jesus Christ is telling us about two men who died
so that you and I may know what the experience of death is
like. One man immediately enjoyed the pleasures of heaven
and the other immediately suffered the horrors of hell. These
two men illustrate the conscious experience of all who die.
There is no purgatory. There is no second chance after death.
There is no soul sleep. There is no such thing as annihilation
of the human soul. The Son of God is emphasizing that souls
do not die as bodies do. After death the souls of men enter,
and are consciously, intelligently aware of, heaven and hell.
Immediately!

The man who suffered the torments of hell held a conversation with Abraham. Abraham is the exemplar of the
believer. He is the father of those who have faith in Jesus
Christ who saves them from their sins. For all men have
sinned and deserve the wrath of God and deserve the sufferings of hell forever. But, in His mercy, God made a way of
escape for those who have broken His great holy law. And, if
anyone will trust in Jesus Christ for the forgiveness of sins he
will pass from death unto life and go to a place of pleasure
after death and not to one of torment. So Abraham's story in

Genesis is the example of the person whom God counts righteous on the basis of his faith in Jesus Christ.

The first conversation of the man in hell with Abraham was a prayer that he might be relieved of his torment which was seemingly unbearable. Abraham indicates to the man that that is impossible. Death fixes the destinies of men forever. In hell he is experiencing the justice of God and he will do so worlds without end, forever. His condition cannot change. There is no hope. There is a gulf that is fixed between those who are in the presence of Abraham because they believe in Christ as he did and those who are in hell. The man in hell, however, has five brothers as you see in verse 28—five brothers who are still alive in the world in which you and I walk. So he devises a scheme by which the five brothers will be saved. A man in hell devising a scheme of evangelism! Many human beings do the same. He imagines a way to deliver friends from the fate that he himself is experiencing in hell. Because the five brothers knew the poor, sickly, friendless man who lived at their gate and they knew that he had died, the man said, "Send this Lazarus back to them to show himself as one who has been raised from the dead and they will believe." He added, "Especially when he tells them about the torments of hell that I am now experiencing they will not come to this place as I have done." That's the wisdom of a man in hell. That's his proposal and his request.

From this arises a discussion between Abraham and the man in hell. Abraham in heaven argues one side and the man in hell argues another side. Abraham is defending the position of those who believe in God through our Lord Jesus Christ. The man in hell is arguing the position of those who do not believe and who finally perish. This argument is going on still, and it is important that you see what the argument is, and that you understand the difference between those who believe and those who do not believe. The difference is in their approach to evangelism and how a person can be saved. This conversation and argument is going on not only in the world of departed spirits but also in this world still. You will hear of it, and you will inevitably line up on one side or the other.

On the one side is Abraham and all who believe as he did. They hold to the sufficiency of Scripture to save a man from hell. In verse 29 Abraham says that the five living brothers have Moses and the Prophets—the authors of Old Testament Scripture. Moses wrote the first five books of the Scripture—the very foundation work of the Scripture—and the other Prophets wrote the rest of Old Testament Scripture. Abraham says the brothers have the Old Testament Bible—let them listen to what Moses and the Prophets had to say in the Old Testament Scriptures. Do you see Abraham's argument? The Old Testament Scriptures are sufficient to bring a man to saving faith in Jesus Christ. In verse 31 he says that if they will not respond to the Bible with faith, nothing else will do them any good, not even a miracle of resurrection before their very eyes. The question is, "Do you agree with Abraham?"

On the other side of the debate, in verse 27, the man in hell says "Send a dead man back to the world of the living to warn them." When Abraham says "they have Moses and the Prophets let them hear them" (verse 29) the man emphatically says, "no!" (verse 30). The Bible is not enough. He does not have confidence in the Bible. They need something more than the Bible if they are going to be saved.

Let's examine the attitude of the man in hell toward the Bible and toward human nature. For what he says about the Bible has something to say about human nature as well. He feels that the Bible is an ineffective book. You can't expect anyone to get serious about eternal life and fleeing from the wrath of God to come simply by reading the Scriptures and hearing sermons about the Scriptures. It is very interesting that he addresses Abraham as "Father Abraham" and Father Abraham agrees and says "My son" to the man in hell. Jesus is addressing this illustration to the Pharisees who were Jews and who were ethnically sons of Abraham. They could not imagine that the wrath of God would fall upon them. This man in the story is one who grew up in the synagogues where he had to memorize some of the Scriptures, where he heard the Scriptures taught and read week by week, and it never had any impact upon him so as to deliver him from hell. He thought he would never end up in that condition. He was a son of the Old Testament people of God. He lived in the biblical system and knew the rules of the system and knew the actual text of the Scriptures; but such a man lifted up his eyes in hell and called to Father Abraham who was far off with this great chasm fixed between them, which would never be crossed.

Sometimes even the children of ministers of the gospel, who are sons of Abraham in that natural sense of privilege and opportunity, are in the condition of going to hell. Perhaps all the sermons and discussions about the Bible are boring to them. People find sermons dull, and they become indifferent and unmoved by the Scriptures. If Scriptures do not save them, nothing will! But do you see what the man in hell is saying in the passage? He is saying that if the Scripture is all that you have to give to my five brothers, they are going to end up here too, because I had that and it didn't change me. In effect he is saying, from deep within his being, that it is understandable that he did not believe and that his brothers also have not yet believed. "I know my brothers, and they are a lot like I was. They are going to come here too unless something else is done for them other than what already has been done." In effect he is saying that his unbelief is excusable. "If I had seen a miracle that had thrilled me I would have believed. If I had heard a ghost come back from the dead talk to me I would have listened. If I had had an exciting preacher or been in a meeting where amazing things had happened then my destination would have been different. But all I had was the Bible. The Bible is all God gave me. I am a victim!"

Sounds like America doesn't it? "My brothers and I would have jumped at the opportunity to believe but all you gave us was the Bible." Abraham says, "let them hear Moses and the Prophets," and the man in hell says, "No!" Emphatically no! The system will not do! And, sad to say, there is much similar thought in the modern evangelical church today. It breaks our hearts.

The attitude is, we can't expect the world to be attracted to Christ by the Bible, by disciplined teaching of the Scriptures, by Bible memorization, by lessons on Bible stories in Sunday School and by sermons on the Bible in church. The belief is, we can't expect that. We can't expect that young people— teenagers especially—would be attracted to that. But if we use puppets and clowns they will come. If we use rock music they will be attracted. If we have contests in which we give out glittering prizes to the children they will believe. If we dress up the preacher in costumes or if we have drama and lead living animals through the church they will believe. If we get superstars to give their testimonies we will fill the church and they will believe. Anything to supplant the Bible. Anything! Just not the Bible alone, which was Abraham's position. This view says the Bible is not sufficient.

Do you know about the Vineyard movement and John Wimber who wrote the book, *Power Evangelism*? It was a thesis of John Wimber that the power which sweeps multitudes into the kingdom of God is not the Holy Spirit attending the Scriptures as they come to the intellect of a man who hears the Word of God. He said saving power comes from a direct experience of God in supernatural events which are non-rational and above mental activity. The sinner's resistance to the gospel is removed by these encounters so that miracles are *essential* to evangelism. As a matter of fact, in his book, *Power Evangelism*, Wimber said that when Paul preached at Athens he made a vital mistake which resulted in the fact that very few were converted. He said that when you read in Acts there weren't very many people converted in Athens and that's because Paul used the wrong message—all he did was preach the truth. But when he got to Corinth he performed miracles and there were many converts. So, John Wimber says, "When you are dealing with the unconverted you must have miracles." Is that not what much of the Charismatic movement has been after? "No, Father Abraham. Anything but the Bible alone!" If it be psychological techniques, sales techniques, informal and entertaining worship, etc. Many have adopted this mindset which was not foreign to a man who was in hell.

We do have, thankfully, many young people here, and I am sure that many of them are Christians. Do you tire of the Bible? If you think that the Scriptures are not sufficient for the salvation of sinners then let me ask, when did God ask a human being to pick the way in which salvation was to come to those who are lost? Do we have a right to say, "No! Not the Bible only," as this man in hell said?

Abraham represents all the men and women of faith in all ages. Remember that Abraham lived before any of the Scriptures were written. God did appear in Theophonies in those days, and He did occasionally speak from heaven to His people then. He certainly did reveal things to Abraham and things were passed down by word of mouth from what God had said in ages past. But Abraham had none of the Scriptures, and Abraham, the father of the faithful in heaven, was absolutely delighted with Moses and the Prophets. For Moses and the Prophets wrote as they were carried along by the Holy Spirit. It was not their private religious thoughts of what they had experienced. Bible words are living and powerful. They will not return empty but will accomplish exactly what God appointed them to do. For when God speaks, it is just as when He said, "Let there be light," and there was light. As we read in Psalm 19, these words give joy to the hearts of believers; they give light to the eyes; they endure forever; by them God's servants are warned; and in keeping them there is great reward in heaven (Psalm 19:8-11). Warned away from hell! Rewarded in heaven!

God has spoken to sinners. The Almighty has broken the silence of heaven, and He has spoken to sinners! How dare man say we need something other than the voice of God to save us! The Son of God Himself came down from heaven to add to what Moses and the prophets said. When He poured out His Holy Spirit upon His apostles, they wrote down in fuller measure still the gospel of saving grace. You have it all—Old Testament and New Testament—and our generation has the opportunity of reading it and holding the Book in their hands—reading it day by day, memorizing it, hearing it preached and going to classes where it is taught. There are people in the world today who have never had the Scriptures. There were people in other generations who lived and died without the Scriptures, without God's special revelation, His voice speaking to men in human language. What a condescension that He who made the heavens and the earth should speak in human language, conveying the thoughts of His heart and mind—that vast and infinite mind—in language that can be understood by man.

Furthermore, Abraham is expressing the Christian belief that the Bible is God's chosen means of saving all sinners who will escape hell. As the Apostle Paul said in Romans 10:17, "faith comes by hearing." It does not come by seeing people who were raised from the dead. "Faith comes by hearing," says God, "and hearing by the Word of God." In Romans 10 the context is hearing the Word of God as it is preached and Paul goes on to query, "How will they hear it unless someone is sent to preach it?" That is God's chosen means of saving those who believe. So men had better choose a church and a fellowship where the Scripture is central—a church where the Bible is preached and the prayers and the hymns are of biblical thoughts. Some of you who are ministers of the gospel know that there is no more difficult task that a minister faces than going to a church and hearing from here and there that the people expect this of the minister and they would like him to do that and they would like him to do the other thing. Poor young men coming out of seminary who thought that they were going to preach the Word. Everybody has a different expectation, and it is not that the law of truth should be upon their lips. Men should seek wisdom from the Word of God. It is not an easy thing to have a church that preaches the Word of God, but that is central. 2 Timothy 3:13-15 declares:

... Evil men and imposters will go from bad to

worse, deceiving and being deceived. But as for
you, continue in what you have learned and have
become convinced of,...and how from infancy
you have known the holy Scriptures, which are
able to make you wise to salvation through faith
in Christ Jesus.

God in mercy said He is going to deliver some sinners from
hell. They all deserve to go there. They all have broken His
commandments. They have all sinned in Adam, and all are
corrupt. They have multiplied their wickedness, they have
provoked God to His face; but He is going to save a large
multitude of sinners from hell, and He will do that for all who
believe on His Son Jesus Christ who died for their sins. How
will God bring men to faith in Jesus Christ? His divinely
chosen method is that faith will come by hearing and hearing
by the Word of God. The Word of God will be taken by
preachers to those who need to hear. Will those who hear
have to be scholars and geniuses in order to understand what
the Bible has to say? Will they have to have human experts
explain in great detail all that the Scriptures say when they
are preached? Psalm 19:7 tells us, "the law of the Lord is perfect reviving the soul. The statutes of the Lord are trustworthy, making wise the simple." A child can understand the
Scriptures. The simple can understand what is necessary to
know for salvation. The old London Confession of Faith says:

All things in Scripture are not alike plain in
themselves nor clear unto all. Yet those things
which are necessary to be known, believed and
observed for salvation are so clearly propounded
and opened in some place of Scripture or other
that not only the learned but the unlearned in a
due use of ordinary means may attain to a sufficient understanding of them.

It is all that the simple man needs for salvation. Simple and unlearned people come in contact with the Scriptures and pay attention and their hearts respond. I think there are pastors here who could bear witness that severely retarded people have responded to the gospel. I remember a young couple that came to our church. Neither of them had come from a Christian home or had been trained up in the Scriptures. They got married and they said to themselves, "Married people ought to belong to a church," and they chose the most liberal church in our town. Soon after they went to that church, the church offered a Bible study—a survey of the Bible. They looked at one another and said, "Well, if you belong to a church you ought to study the Bible." So, they went to the Bible study and they started at Genesis and the teacher said, "Now, you don't have to believe that God really created the world by a word," and with each miracle that came in the Scripture the teacher was saying, "Now of course we don't believe the miracles." He was saying we don't believe this and we don't believe that, but we are surveying the Bible. This young couple, as they read the Word of God, believed. They looked at one another and said, "We believe this and they don't. We have to find a church that believes this." They walked in the door of our church converted through the Scriptures. The Word of God is not bound and it does not take the wise to understand it. If they will pay attention they may understand sufficiently to be saved.

We notice also in the text that Abraham speaks about the hopeless condition of those who despise the Bible. If you are unresponsive to the Bible, it is a very bad sign. In verse 31 he said: "If they do not listen to Moses and the Prophets they will not be convinced if someone rises from the dead." They will not be convinced by anything else.

If the Spirit-filled, living Scriptures do not move a person to believe on Jesus Christ then nothing else will do it. Our gospel is the *power* of God to salvation to everyone who believes. It does not point us to the power, it *is* the power. Jesus said, "The words that I speak to you, they are Spirit and they are life" (John 6:63b). Now the preaching of the cross is, to those who perish, foolishness. But what does that say about the man who thinks it is foolishness? He is perishing! Psalm 119:155 says: "Salvation is far from the wicked for [or because] they seek not Thy statutes." Do you see how those things are put together? Salvation is far away from the wicked because they will not seek God's statutes. If they don't want to have anything to do with His Word they are far from salvation.

The smallest children have a game they call "hot and cold." One of the children will go out of the room while others hide an item somewhere. Then the child will come back in. If that child is getting closer to where that thing is hidden, the group will say, "you are getting warm, ...you are getting really warm, ...you are getting hot now." The seeking child will move in the other direction and the hiding children will say, "You're getting cool,...you're getting cold." Those who love the Scriptures are getting warm. They are on the trail of salvation and those who want nothing to do with the Word of God are far from salvation. Again, Psalm 119:174 put the two things together: "I long for your salvation, O Lord, and your law is my delight." If you want to be saved you will hold on to the Word of God. Surely preachers have to be convinced of the sufficiency of Scripture to save sinners; for there is no other effective means of bringing men to salvation in Jesus Christ.

Doesn't this break your heart, too, when you think of what is happening in America today? In its great "wisdom" America has said, "We don't want the Bible in the schools. We do not want the Scriptures taught or read to our children." It may date me as being very old, but when I grew up in the public schools I had the Scriptures read to me every morning. In English class every year we studied portions of the Scripture. Now I grant that the emphasis was on the literary value of those portions of God's Word, but we studied the Scripture carefully. In its "wisdom" America thinks it is wiser to be tolerant of any view at all than to give the children the Scriptures. Hell will welcome them all and the devil will be glad to send them off in that direction.

This puts a greater burden upon us. If a child is able to be made wise unto salvation through faith in Jesus Christ, as the Bible says, when they come to our Sunday School they ought to get the Scriptures. Have you ever sent your child off to Sunday School and hear a report back that the children really like this teacher because he sits for about the first half of the Sunday School hour and discusses the scores from the past week or what the sports heroes did? How tragic!

Does your Sunday School believe that a knowledge of the Bible can save those children? Do the teachers believe that God will save them through means—His Word? Do your Sunday School teachers believe that it is the *only* thing that can make them wise to salvation in Jesus Christ our Lord? Isaiah mentions that God at some time will speak with such clarity about the way that a person should walk that a wayfaring man, though a fool, could not err therein (Isaiah 35:8). And so we have Scriptures at our disposal, and we dare not adopt the theory of the man in hell. The Scriptures are sufficient to save the souls of men. They are God's chosen means and we need to side with Abraham and not with this other theory.

15.
THE DOCTRINES OF GRACE AND WORLD MISSIONS
GEORGE MARTIN
1996 Southern Baptist Founders Conference

Therefore I glory in Christ Jesus in my service to God. I will not venture to speak of anything except what Christ has accomplished through me, in leading the Gentiles to obey God, by what I have said and done— by the power of signs and miracles, through the power of the Spirit. So from Jerusalem all the way round to Illyricum, I have fully proclaimed the gospel of Christ. It has always been my ambition to preach the gospel where Christ was not known, so that I would not be building on someone else's foundation. Rather, as it is written: "Those who were not told about Him will see, and those who have not heard will understand" (Romans 15:17-21, NIV).

RECENTLY, after I had preached a sermon on the doctrine of justification in a very conservative, evangelical, Southern Baptist church, a member approached me and asked, "Brother George, do you really, believe that the sincere Buddhist, the sincere Muslim, and the sincere Hindu will not make it to heaven?" This person added, "I mean after all, they are just as sincere in their religions as we are; they hold their religious books, their holy books, in just as high esteem as we hold the Scriptures, the Bible. Who are we to say where they will end up?"

I have heard conversations about missions where a question is asked of people of other religions: "Are those people happy?" One might answer, "They appear to be so, at least on the outside." The response comes back, "Then why don't you leave them alone; why are you trying to convert them? They are happy, things are going pretty well for them, why rock the boat for them?"

About three years ago, Thomas Guterbock, in *The Stewardship Journal*, was examining the work of a number of Christian relief agencies and other ministry organizations, trying to gauge their commitment to world evangelization and world missions. These organizations were the primary agents to send food, be involved in disaster relief, and other such areas of practical ministry. Guterbock, who is a secular social scientist, commented, "If there may be other ways to heaven for the people of the third world, that is, other than Christ, then the imperative to evangelize is weakened as a logical result." I would modify his statement; the imperative to evangelize is not merely weakened, it is destroyed.

As the examples quoted above illustrate, there no longer is any real impetus for world-wide evangelization in many churches. In my introductory missions courses, the question often asked is: "Will those who have never heard the gospel ultimately be lost?" You might be amazed (or you might not) at the variety of answers students in college classes give to this question. Later I am going to read to you a conversation that took place in one of those classes as an example of some student thinking on this matter. But for now, we need to understand that these kinds of statements and questions betray a mindset that, at best, is ambivalent toward missions, and at worst, destroys missions and world evangelization of the lost.

Recently, I was pondering these things while reading from Andrew Fuller's journal. In his journal entry for July 5, 1780, Fuller wrote, "I longed in prayer tonight to be more useful; oh that God would do somewhat by me. Nor, I trust, is this from ambition, but from a pure desire of working for God, and the benefit of my fellow sinners." Fuller's desire to be useful, to work for God, corresponds perfectly with that of the apostle

Paul.

Paul's glory was in Christ Jesus (v. 17), and in his service to God. He declared, "I will not venture to speak of anything except what Christ has accomplished through me" (v. 18). His purpose was to lead the Gentiles to obey God. Both Fuller and Paul longed, first and foremost, to bring glory and honor to God through their lives and through their ministries. They also longed to rescue perishing sinners from judgment. Not a bad ambition, I'd say, to glorify God through the seeing of sinners saved and brought to Christ!

In our present text, Paul spoke more clearly about his ambition—those things he wanted to accomplish. He brought his ministry purpose into sharp focus; he then left the reader with no doubt as to what he wanted to accomplish.

There are several things that I am going to try to show from this text. First, I want you to see the general principle that guided and governed the life and the ministry of the apostle Paul. Second, to look at the specific working out of that principle in his life and ministry. Third, to point out the encouragement that motivated Paul and kept him going.

THE GENERAL PRINCIPLE GOVERNING PAUL'S LIFE

I want to contrast the general principle that governed the life and ministry of Paul with a principle that seems often to operate in so many of our lives, and I include myself in that group. Paul, first and foremost, gloried in Christ Jesus. He would speak only of that which Christ had accomplished through him and he spoke of this principle in these verses (among other places) by addressing the sinful pride of the Corinthian believers.

In 1 Corinthians 1, Paul wrote:

> Let him who boasts boast in the Lord. When I came to you brothers, I did not come with eloquence or superior wisdom as I proclaimed to you the testimony about God. For I resolved to know

> nothing while I was with you except Jesus Christ
> and Him crucified. I came to you in weakness
> and fear, and with much trembling. My message
> and my preaching were not with wise and persua-
> sive words, but with a demonstration of the Spir-
> it's power, so that your faith might not rest on
> men's wisdom, but on God's power (1 Corinthi-
> ans 1:31-2:5).

In yet another place Paul wrote, speaking of the life of
Christ, "We have this treasure in jars of clay, in bodies of
flesh that are easily broken, that are wasting away" (2 Corinthians 4:7).

Why did he speak this way? He was explaining that the all-
surpassing power is from God, not from us. If anything good
is accomplished by us or in our lives, it must be known that it
is God who has accomplished it. It is God who has enabled us.

Paul went on in 2 Corinthians 4 to talk about being pressed,
perplexed, persecuted, and struck down. He wrote about
death and suffering but he saw a purpose in it all. In the
closing verses of that chapter he wrote, "All this has taken
place for your benefit." What an astounding statement to the
man in the world, but the child of God understands it. Paul
explains that his suffering occurred so that the life of Jesus
also may be revealed, so that grace reaching more and more
people may cause thanksgiving to overflow to the glory of God.

Over and over again we see this principle operating in
Paul's life. More than anything else he desired to see his God
glorified and worshipped. Paul intended to preach the gospel
of Christ where it had not been heard so that God would be
served and Christ glorified. He had written to the Romans, in
the first chapter of that epistle, "I pray that now, at last, by
God's will, the way may be opened, for me to come to you."
Paul had long desired to preach the gospel in Rome and even
beyond, into Spain, to the far reaches of the then civilized
world. That was his ambition—not to build on the works and
foundations of other men but to preach the gospel where it

had never been heard. Paul would get to Rome—that great center of paganism and worldliness, the very center of the power that opposed Christianity—and he would do it no matter the cost.

Think for a moment about the closing sequence in the book of Acts. In those closing chapters, Luke is demonstrating for us something about this man, Paul.

In chapters 21 and 22, Paul is threatened in Jerusalem by the rioting masses and falsely accused of bringing Gentiles into the inner court of the temple. In this circumstance, what does he do? He testifies of his Lord.

In chapter 23, he is hauled before the hostile Sanhedrin, which wanted his death. What did he do? He preached about the resurrection of Jesus Christ.

In chapter 24, even though he had been at the mercy of Felix for two years, Paul nonetheless explained the Way and talked about the resurrection.

In chapter 25, when he appeared before Festus, he was unwavering in his exposition of Christ and His work.

In chapter 26, when he was brought before King Agrippa, Paul sought to persuade him to believe.

In chapter 27, while on his way to Rome, he endured hardship and shipwreck.

In chapter 28, while languishing in a Roman jail for 2 years, Paul still preached the kingdom of God and taught about the Lord Jesus Christ.

Folks, you put Paul before a rioting multitude and what does he do? He speaks of his Lord. You put him before hostile judges and kings, and what does he do? He speaks of his Lord. Paul stood before those who could take away his life in a moment; yet he was bold for the Lord Jesus Christ. Whether imprisoned, shipwrecked, or stranded on an island, he'll still preach. In thinking about Paul's ambition to preach the gospel where it had never been heard, do you see his perseverance? He will do it, no matter the cost.

It never seemed to occur to the apostle to ask, "What will this cost me?" It never came to his mind to ask, "What is in it for me or what will I have to give up in order to do this?" The Lord had directed him to Rome and to Rome he must go. To use the words of an old Dianna Ross song, "There ain't no mountain high enough, ain't no river wide enough," to keep Paul from getting to Rome. Do you see the perseverance of the apostle Paul?

In contrast to the apostle, it seems that the typical response today, even among many who are called to full-time ministry, goes something like, "Well, what will it cost? What exactly will I have to put up with? You know, that is a big undertaking. I have a family. I have this. I have that." By the way, we are talking about world missions—preaching the gospel to the uttermost parts of the earth. In case you were wondering, let me just tell you, it will cost you a great deal. It will cost more than you have ever imagined.

Imagine asking the apostle Paul, "What did it cost you to preach the gospel to Gentiles? What did you have to put up with?" His answer is "For me, to live is Christ, and to die is gain." Ask him, "Paul didn't you grow tired and weary? Didn't you miss so much?" Paul answers, " I have learned to be content, whatever the circumstances."

Ask the apostle about his sufferings and he would respond, "I consider my life worth nothing to me, if only I may finish the race and complete the task the Lord Jesus has given me, the task of testifying to the gospel of God's grace." The gospel must be preached and God must be glorified—that was Paul's passion and drive. It was the guiding principle of his life.

"I glory in Christ Jesus in my service to God, I will not venture to speak of anything except what Christ has accomplished, I have fully proclaimed the gospel of Christ." The governing principle of Paul's life was to see God glorified through the preaching of the gospel and the bringing of sinners to the Savior, Jesus Christ.

THE OUTWORKING OF THAT PRINCIPLE IN PAUL'S LIFE

Note that he is emphatic here when he says, "It has always

been my ambition." This is not a selfish, self-serving sort of ambition. Paul is not the type of person whom he describes in another place—one who, by persistence in doing good, seeks glory, honor, and immortality for himself. Paul is not serving himself or seeking fame for himself; his gaze is lifted higher than that.

Yes, there are those who dig for themselves cisterns which hold no water, and those manmade cisterns, which occasionally do hold water, are full of nothing but stagnant water that brings death and sickness. Paul's ambition is different. It's not that his name might be up in lights, nor that he might somehow or another be called the great apostle to the Gentiles, but along with Fuller, whom we quoted earlier, he had a pure desire of working for God and the benefit of his fellow sinners. Paul was obedient to the divine charge. It has always been the business of God, by the foolishness of preaching, to save those who believe. It is the gospel that is the power of God unto salvation, nothing else.

There are those today, who would do missions and evangelism by attempting to "meet perceived needs." Meeting perceived needs is an important concept in missiology today. While in a missionary meeting in Southeast Asia a few years ago, we were talking about how we might best evangelize the animists—those folks who believe that inanimate objects such as mountains, rocks, and trees are inhabited by evil spirits. Their whole lives are given over to appeasing evil spirits so they will not bother them. The question was asked, "How might we best evangelize these folks?" It seemed that most of the missionaries took the attitude: "Well, what we need to do is speak to their perceived needs. You don't want to speak about sin or their need for righteousness. No, these people are more concerned about those spirits out there that are going to get them. What we need to do is present Jesus as the great Spirit who can protect them from these other spirits." Some of us raised our hands and asked, "Is there no place for preaching about sin? What about the gospel?"

The apostle Paul had a different attitude than those who

would address only felt needs. He determined that he must preach the gospel whatever his audience thought it needed. He said, "I'm going to preach the gospel to them."

It is not enough to meet perceived needs. Everybody has them but the problem with lost man is that his perception is corrupted. He is blind and doesn't understand his real need.

When you go to the doctor with some sort of an illness, you expect to get some answers from him. What would you think if he heard your complaint and then asked you, "Well, what do you think you need?" And what would you do if he handed you his pad and let you write out the prescription? You wouldn't go back to him, would you?

Paul knew that the gospel is the power of God for salvation. We have this charge—to preach the gospel. Paul said that there was no other place for him to work in these regions. He saw that his work was done there. The gospel had been preached but it had not been preached beyond Rome and on into Spain.

Follow the unrelenting logic of this with me for a moment. Once the gospel is preached to a group of people it can be said that among those people the gospel is now known. If the ambition of the preacher stays the same, then he finds himself looking toward others who have not yet heard. He goes to them. He makes the gospel known, following those efforts by going to another group, and another and another, until in all places the gospel is known and Jesus Christ has been proclaimed. In other words, Paul was obedient to the vision of God Himself and to the instructions of our Lord to be witnesses in Jerusalem, and in all of Judah and Samaria and to the ends of the earth.

It seems to me that most preachers in America today possess an ambition completely opposite that of the apostle Paul. A couple of semesters ago at North Greenville College a student came into my office and wanted to talk about something related to some of his class work. Somehow or another, the conversation got turned around to missions. I just asked him, "What about the possibility of missions? Have you ever thought about it?" The response was, "Oh, no Dr. Martin. No, that is not for me. You see, the Lord has called me to work in the local church." And without much hesitation I responded, "You realize that there are local churches all over the world?" His jaw dropped open and there was silence for a few moments.

A week later, another student came in and somehow the conversation got turned around to missions. I asked him the same question: "Have you ever considered the possibility of missions?" He responded, "Dr. Martin, that's not for me. I don't think so. You see, the Lord has called me to work with youth." So I asked, "Have you ever thought about the fact that there are youth all over the world?"

Do you see how narrow our vision is? Missiologists tell us that in World A there are almost 2 billion people among whom the gospel has never been preached. Why do you think Paul possessed such an ambition to go to that world? Why did he possess such a drive? What drove Paul to preach in such places, to search them out, to give his all to get there and to proclaim the Good News when he got there? I'll tell you what it was. It was a settled conviction that without the gospel, men would die under condemnation and judgment without hope.

There is no theology, no soteriology, that so lends itself to going into new areas with the gospel as that which historically has been known as Calvinism. In line with the pluralistic emphasis of our day, increasingly the suggestion is made that Muslims, Jews, Hindus and others will ultimately be saved by virtue of their sincerity and following the light that they have. Of course we know that this absolutely destroys the urgency of missions and evangelism at the same time. There is not another theology that so angers men and so creates hostility toward the message and messenger. Herbert Kane, a missiologist of our day has written, "It is safe to say that the most offensive aspect of twentieth-century Christianity is it's exclusiveness" (*Understanding Christian Missions*, Baker, 1974, 1982, p. 105).

Folks, go out there and preach that there is only one way. Stand and declare that, and see what happens. You will hear, "How arrogant, how prideful you are in believing that you are the depository of all truth, that it is only your way or no way!" However, the following truths hold true all over the world: Men are lost and without hope by virtue of their sinfulness. There is a God who has determined to save. This God has made atonement in the person of and through the work of His Son, Jesus Christ. There is a God who does not simply offer salvation but actually makes alive and saves. There is a God who keeps to the end those who are His.

In short, if we are absolutely convinced that there is only one way, only one hope, we will not be silent nor will we be still. It is the gospel of Christ that is the power of God unto salvation. That gospel must be gotten into the hearts and minds of men, women, boys, and girls for them to be saved—no matter their circumstances, no matter their sincerity. It is the gospel that is the hope of mankind.

I want to tell you, a full-orbed, evangelical and biblical Calvinism is not a deterrent to world evangelization. Rather, it is the catalyst and driving force that will propel laborers into the fields already white unto harvest. There is no hope for those folks unless we take the gospel to them. How different from the view that often prevails today.

I had the following conversation one day with one of my students in a class on evangelism. I went immediately to my office after class and typed it out on the computer, thinking, "I need to save this one." The name has been changed to protect the not-so-innocent here, so we'll call him Ron.

During a class discussion about depravity, man's innate and natural condition, Ron raised his hand and said, "Dr. Martin, I was never a God-hater. Only after I accepted Jesus into my heart at age twelve did I come to understand that I was a sinner."

Professor (that was me): "Using your terminology, Ron, you are saying that you accepted Jesus into your heart and only later discovered yourself as a sinner? Is that correct?"

Ron: "Yes!"

Professor: "Then I have a question for you. Why did you accept Jesus into your heart?"

Ron: "What do you mean?"

Professor: "I mean, Ron, that if you accepted Jesus into your heart, you had to have some reason for doing so. What was that reason?"

Ron: "So that I could be saved."

Professor: "Saved from what?"

Ron: "From my sins."

Professor (by now I am scratching my head): "But you didn't know that you were a sinner! How could you have known you needed salvation? What motivation did you have for accepting Jesus into your heart? You didn't know you needed a Savior, so why did you do it?"

Ron: "That's not what I meant?"

Professor: "That's what you said!"

Ron: "Dr. Martin, you have to understand, I was not really disobeying God because I mean, I was not really against God, because I didn't know who He was, and as soon as a friend shared the gospel with me I accepted Jesus."

Professor: "Then you are saying that you were not really accountable before God because you didn't know who He was? Is that correct?"

Ron: "Yeah, something like that."

Professor: "And what if you had never heard the gospel?"

Ron: "That's my point, Dr. Martin. Before I heard the truth I never really had anything against God. I believe if I had gone through life without ever hearing the gospel, and thus without having the opportunity to accept Jesus, when I stood before God's heavenly throne on the day of judgment, that He would give me that opportunity."

Folks, this was a young man preparing for full-time Christian ministry in a Southern Baptist setting! Later, after class, two other students came to me (again the names are changed to protect their identities) They came in, and Ted was the spokesperson this time.

Ted: "Dr. Martin, I have a question for you."

Professor: "Go ahead."

Ted: "In responding to Ron in class you mentioned the accountability of all men before God. You also talked about missions and the work of the missionary in taking the gospel to the whole world because the whole world stands in need."

Professor: "That's correct."

Ted: "Well, what about those tribes who have never heard the gospel? Are you saying that they will go to hell?" (You have heard that question before!)

Professor: "Ted, why don't you read and study John 3, Romans 1," (I think I gave him a couple of other passages) "and then we can talk further about this."

Ted: "Yeah, you already mentioned those in class, but I want a straightforward answer. What about those who have never heard the gospel?"

Professor: "What do you think?"

Ted: "Well, I think that God does not hold them accountable, and because of their ignorance they will be in heaven."

Professor: "Then why send missionaries to them?"

Ted: "Because God wants heaven to be full. He wants as many people in heaven as possible."

Professor: "But Ted, according to your statements, those people will be better off if we didn't go to them with the gospel. By doing so, we make them accountable and at the same time, whittle down the number who will make it. After all, chances are pretty good that they will not all respond with repentance and faith. Don't you think we should just leave them alone?"

As a matter of fact, if we carry out this kind of reasoning what's the best thing we could do for them? Using absurdity to make the point, we might kill them! That way they will die in their ignorance and go to heaven! Isn't that plausible if we proceed on the basis of this logic?

Let's replay Paul's conversation with the Athenians from this sort of a pluralistic viewpoint that we have been talking about. Acts 17 would read:

Men of Athens, I see that in every way you are
very religious. I'm here to commend you and encourage you to keep on keeping on. Why, as I
walked around and observed all your religious
trappings and paraphernalia, I noticed that you've
covered all your bases. As a matter of fact, just in
case you have missed something vital, you even
have an altar with the inscription, "To an unknown God." You are in good shape. I came here
as an emissary from Yahweh, the God who has
created the world and everything in it, but I see
now that I can go on back home. You've got
everything under control. The God who has made
every nation of men, and having determined the
places and times where they will live, created me
as a Jew and created you as Greeks. He's just as
close to you as He is to me; even some of your
own poets have said, "We are His offspring."
Look, when we get down to it, there's really very
little that separates us religiously. As a matter of
fact, there is nothing of real substance that
distinguishes my religion from yours. I see that
now that I have been able to spend some time
with you. I was created by God; you were created
by God. I'm seeking God; you are seeking God. I
am doing the best I know how; you are doing the
best you know how. I'm sincere; you're sincere.
I'm OK; you're OK.

In a recent issue of *The Tie*, the publication of Southern
Seminary, Dr. Mohler wrote in his opening article ("Missions
at Risk: A Failure of Nerve") about the future of missions and
the failure of the American church:

At base, the issue is a failure of theological
nerve, a devastating loss of biblical and doctrinal
conviction. The result is retreat on the mission
fields of the world and regression on the home

front.

This loss of theological nerve is a fundamental failure of conviction. Put bluntly, many who claim to be Christians simply do not believe that anyone is lost. The essence of this belief is universalism, the belief that all persons will be saved, whether or not they have a saving relationship with Jesus Christ.

Given their commitment to the gospel, could evangelical Christians allow universalism to make inroads into their ranks? There are signs that this is now well underway. In the evangelical academy, some are advocating views well in line with the liberal, Protestant arguments of the mid-century. The challenge of pluralism has found many evangelicals with weak knees.

The pattern is not restricted to the academics, however. The most dangerous trend may be found in the pews of evangelical churches, where more and more Christians are willing to reject or compromise the uniqueness of Christ and His atonement, citing the apparent sincerity of those who worship other gods or no god at all.

Where will the church stand?

Dr. Mohler went on to write that, at a recent Urbanite Missions Conference where thousands of college-age Evangelicals were brought together, only a third of the participants indicated a belief that a person who does not hear the gospel is eternally lost. As one missionary veteran who attended responded, "If two-thirds of the most mission-minded young people in America do not affirm the lostness of mankind, the Great Commission is in serious trouble." Should these trends spread within the Southern Baptist Convention, we will be in serious trouble indeed.

Paul had a specific ambition, that is, to preach the gospel where it had never been heard. He knew that those who were without the gospel were lost, and that their only hope lay in the gospel. I'm not convinced that most professing Christians really believe this anymore. Maybe we are already in serious trouble, indeed. The general principle governing Paul's life and ministry was to bring glory to God through the preaching of the gospel and the bringing of sinners to Christ. The specific working out of that in his life was a determination to preach the gospel where it has never been heard.

THE ENCOURAGEMENT THAT KEPT PAUL GOING

My third point involves answering the question, "What was Paul's encouragement in all this?" It is found in verse 21. What drove him on? I am convinced that his vision and his ministry were based on the concept of God's sovereignty.

He quoted the prophet Isaiah, who wrote seven hundred years earlier: "Those who are not told about Him will see [not *may* see, but *will* see] and those who have not heard will understand." The prophet had asked, "Who has believed our report? And to whom has the arm of the Lord been revealed?" But before he asked the question, already he had given the answer, and it was an answer that both encouraged and emboldened him: "For what they were not told, they will see, what they had not heard, they will understand."

This is not the only time we find Paul and the other biblical writers speaking with such confidence. I remember him writing to the Roman believers, "I am not ashamed of the gospel, because it is the power of God for the salvation of everyone who believes, to the Jew first and also to the Gentile." What drove Paul on? What was his motivation? What was his encouragement?

Let's have another conversation with Paul: "Paul, why did you suffer? Why did you put up with all that you put up with? Why did you suffer those stonings and go back for more and more beatings, Paul? The mocking of the crowds that stood before you, terrible imprisonments, hunger, shipwreck, and all the other things that you had to put up with—Why? Why did you run the race with pain, leaving behind all? Paul, are you some sort of masochist? Why?"

We don't have to be left wondering the answer. Paul tells us in 2 Timothy 2:10, "I endure everything for the sake of the elect, that they too may obtain the salvation that is in Christ Jesus with eternal glory."

I am convinced that God has an elect people in every country, every tribe, every language group, and every nation around the world (Revelation 5:9-10). When my family and I first went to Southeast Asia as missionaries a number of our friends who knew something about my theology, but who themselves were not Calvinists, asked me this question: "Believing what you believe, why in the world would you go to all this trouble and move to the other side of the world and put up with all of that?" I didn't have any trouble responding to that question. I said, "We are going because we are convinced that Christ was slain and with His blood He has purchased for Himself men from every tribe and language, people and nation. In every nation God has a chosen people. He has always been, and today He remains, in the business of calling them out and saving them by the preaching of the gospel. We're going to Asia to get those folks."

Is that reasoning so difficult to understand? What part of that can people not understand? We are going over there to gather up some sheep. That's what drove Paul on and was his encouragement and motivation. Those who have not seen, are going to see, those who have not heard, are not only going hear, but they are going to understand. It is a given. It is going to happen by the preaching of the gospel.

PRACTICAL CONCERNS

It seems to me that if we have the same mindset as the apostle Paul, knowing that salvation is of the Lord, that there is only one way, only one name by which men might be saved, then several things will take place in our lives.

First, not only as missionaries, but as evangelists, pastors and laypeople, the first thing that we will notice happening in our lives is an increasing dependence upon God. I've often said a Calvinist is none other than a person who wholeheartedly agrees with the prophet Jonah when he said, "Salvation is of the Lord." Martin Luther, in that great hymn, "A Mighty Fortress is our God," wrote:

> A mighty fortress is our God,
> A bulwark never failing;
> Our helper, He amid the flood
> Of mortal ills prevailing;

Farther down he wrote:

> Did we in our own strength confide,
> Our striving would be losing;
> Were not the right Man on our side,
> The Man of God's own choosing;
> Dost ask who that may be?
> Christ Jesus it is He;
> Lord Sabaoth, His name,
> From age to age the same,
> And He must win the battle.

Spurgeon (*MTP*, 21:252) declared:

> It looks a task too gigantic, but the bare arm of God—only think of that—his sleeve rolled up, omnipotence itself made bare,—what cannot it accomplish? Stand back, devils! When God's bare arm comes into the fight, you will all run like dogs, for you know your Master. Stand back, heresies and schisms, evils and delusions; you will all disappear, for the Christ of God is mightier than you. Oh, believe it. Do not be downhearted and dispirited, do not run to new schemes and fancies and interpretations of prophecy. Go and preach Jesus Christ unto all the nations. Go and spread abroad the Saviour's

blessed name, for he is the world's only hope.

Second, we are going to discover that if we come to this thing with the mindset of Paul that we will find ourselves increasingly on our knees in prayer before God. If He is to do the work, if He is to bring in the harvest, then we must call upon Him and cry out to Him. I believe it was Hudson Taylor, a great missionary, who once wrote something like, "It is possible to move men solely by prayer to God." Solely by prayer. If the work is of God, we are going to find ourselves increasingly calling upon God and relying much more upon Him through prayer rather than contemporary schemes and methodologies.

Third, if we come at missions and evangelism with the mindset of Paul, we will have confidence that God will accomplish His will. That creates staying power for the missionary, the pastor, and the evangelist. C. D. Mallary was the first man asked to serve as corresponding secretary of the Foreign Mission Board. He was unable to serve because of ill health, but in preaching about the doctrine of election, he said:

> Is election [and we might here add the other doctrines of grace] unfavorable to efforts for the salvation of men? The farthest from it possible. It lies beneath the eternal rock of confidence and hope. If it were not true, we might well despair, but it is true, and therefore, our labors shall not be in vain in the Lord. The end is certain, as God has fixed upon definite results, and has prescribed the means which will infallibly conduct to the certain issue; with what joy may the spiritual husbandman thrust in his plowshare and sow his seed. With what immovable confidence may the missionary of the cross, in obedience to his ascended Savior, fly to distant lands, and proclaim in every valley and every hill, Oh ye dry bones, hear ye the word of the Lord! Victory he

knows will sooner or later come, and the assurance of victory nerves his arm and gladdens his heart amidst all the terrors of the battlefield.

Here is our confidence! Here is our staying power! Spurgeon once said, "Our business is to preach the gospel. We are to sow, whether a harvest follow or not; success is with God, service belongs to us." Again Luther in that great hymn declared:

> And, though this world with devils filled,
> Should threaten to undo us,
> We will not fear, for God hath willed,
> His truth to triumph through us.

Fourth, having the mindset and theology of the apostle Paul will lead us to truly effective means and methodologies in our preaching, evangelism, and missions. In the doctrines of grace we find the antidote to the modern decisionalist approaches to evangelism (which, by the way, are just as prevalent on the foreign fields as they are here in the states). In the modern decisionalist approaches to evangelism, a prospective convert is presented with several statements, pressed to affirm them vocally and then given quick assurance of salvation. The doctrines of grace are an antidote to that. When salvation is understood to be wholly of the Lord, this knowledge leads to a more consistently biblical evangelism and missiology, in which the claims of the gospel are pressed upon an individual, and God's Word, under the ministry of the Holy Spirit, is relied upon for the work of conversion.

I am a pragmatist. That's going to bother some of you. I'm a pragmatist because I want to use any and every methodology that accomplishes my goal. The key here is to define the goal. I want to bring folks to Christ. I don't care if a single person ever comes to the front of a church building, I want to know if he's been to the Master and to the foot of the cross. I don't care if a person has ever taken the hand of a pastor. I want to know if he has been touched by the Master's hand. We must determine the goal.

Finally, if we have the mindset and theology of the apostle Paul, we cannot remain in our slumber. Gerald Palmer, former Vice President of the mission section of the Home Mission Board, said that a belief in universalism was the primary reason so few Southern Baptists witnessed in their daily lives. In 1886, Arthur P. Pierson wrote, "Behind the shameful apathy and lethargy of the church that allows millions upon millions of human beings to go to their graves in ignorance of the gospel, there lies a practical doubt, if not denial, of their lost condition."

Beloved, many in our churches just do not believe that all without the gospel are really lost. Others believe that God will not ultimately judge and punish unbelievers. After all, they think, we need always to remember that God is love and nothing else. Remember, that is how Jonah rationalized away his responsibility. He went to preach to Nineveh and complained to the Lord when he saw that a revival happened. "Oh, Lord, is this not what I said when I was still at home? That is why I was so quick to flee to Tarshish, I knew that you are a gracious and compassionate God, slow to anger and abounding in love, a God who relents from sending calamity."

Is there any verse in all of Scripture that better depicts the mindset of many professing Christians today regarding the issues about which we are speaking? I can't think of one. "God is love"—we hear over and over and over again. The prevailing view is: "In the end everything is going to be OK. I'm OK; you're OK. God is not some terrible ogre," we're told. "Because He is a just and a gracious God, somehow, everything is going to work out." That seems to be the mindset. "Why go to so much effort? Why give so much? Why pray so unceasingly? Why should I get up and leave the comfort of my home and go?"

Again, nothing will shake us out of our slumber and lack of concern for world missions like a good dose of the doctrines of grace—to understand that men are lost, without hope and helpless and, unless the gospel gets to them, they will remain in that condition for all eternity. To truly understand those things will mean that we cannot sleep, we cannot remain still, we cannot remain quiet.

A number of years ago, one of the presidents of the Foreign Mission Board talked about those who should go to the foreign field. He said that first of all, those who *can* should go. (Some cannot because of physical disabilities and other matters.) Second, those who are *concerned* and *committed* should go. By this time, a lot of people in the congregation would become a bit anxious, thinking to themselves, "Well, there's nothing keeping me from going. I have to admit I'm concerned about it. I think I'm committed to taking the gospel to the lost." Perhaps beads of sweat would begin to come out; "Is he talking about me?" With his final point, that those who are *called*, should go, we might imagine the entire congregation thinking with relief, "Whew, boy, I'm off the hook!"

Many folks have gotten around their responsibility by waiting for some kind of supernatural and extraordinary call experience. I'm going to tell you something. The Word of God is full of instructions, already, for us to go into all the world with the gospel. I do not know how we can read it and be still.

16.
CLOSING WITH CHRIST
JIM ELLIFF

1998 Southern Baptist Founders Conference

W HEN modern evangelical churches seek to bring the unregenerate to Christ (and they should do so with passion), they often fall prey to a formula which produces disappointing results. The pattern runs something like this:

- Extending a public altar call.
- Praying "the sinner's prayer."
- Giving immediate verbal assurance that one is in Christ on the basis of the sinner's sincerity and the accuracy of the wording of the prayer.
- Immediate, or near immediate, public announcement that this person is now in Christ.
- Public baptism as a symbol of death to sin and life in Christ.

This pattern has been passed down and repeated because few are taking the necessary time to examine both its flight from Scriptural precedent and precept, and its dismal effect. When asked to give more careful consideration to its content and outcome, however, we are finding that many, thankfully, are rejecting this inept structure in favor of a better, more biblical one. The above list will seem familiar to every soul-loving believer, but the very evangelistic passion we have for our neighbors and unconverted family members should drive us to lay our present methods up against the truth for a well-needed examination. Like the short-of-breath fifty-year-old who has never been to the doctor, it is time for a major checkup.

What then is wrong with the above list?

First, there is no biblical precedent or command regarding a public altar call. Whatever might be said for its use, we cannot resort to the Bible for support. Jesus, nor Paul, nor any other early Christian leader used it. Did Jesus ask his listeners to come to the front after He preached the Sermon on the Mount? Did Paul say, "Every head bowed, every eye closed," as Luke quietly sang the invitation hymn on the Areopagus? Did Peter have seekers raise their hands as a sign of their interest in Christ at the end of the Pentecostal sermon?

Quickly it must be said that I espouse a *verbal* call to Christ in a most serious way and believe that the spoken invitation to come to Christ is a part of all gospel preaching. We "compel them to come in." When Moody failed to offer a public altar call on the evening of the Chicago fire, he stated a new resolve: "I learned that night [a lesson] which I have never forgotten; and that is, when I preach, to press Christ upon the people then and there, and try to bring them to a decision on the spot. I would rather have that right hand cut off than to give an audience a week now to decide what to do with Jesus." I could not agree more with his underlying sentiment, but this does not argue for an altar call. Evangelistic preaching does say, "Repent and trust Christ *now*." But there is nothing sacrosanct about getting people to occupy a certain piece of geography at the front of a building. Nor have I kept them from Christ by not having them respond to a public altar call. Rather I am offering them Christ without anything in between. I want nothing between their soul and the reality of Christ's offer. To put something in between is a practical sacramentalism.

Charles Grandison Finney (1792-1875) popularized this method through his mourner's bench. There was a person here or there that used it in an occasional manner prior to him, but he put it on the map. Reacting to Finneyism's ineptness, theologian Dabney commented, "We have come to coolly accept the fact that forty-five out of fifty will eventually apostatize [fall away]."

On the other side of Finney was the veteran evangelist Asahel Nettleton (d. 1844), whose converts stood. For instance, in Ashford, Connecticut there were eighty-two converts and only three spurious ones. In Rocky Hill, Connecticut, there were eighty-six converts and they all were standing strong after twenty-six years according to their pastor. Nettleton rigidly refused to offer public altar calls, believing that it prematurely reaped what would turn out to be false converts. C. H. Spurgeon, the Victorian "Prince of Preachers," thought similarly. The long-term history is consistent on this issue; you may and should examine it.

Attached to the altar call (and to personal evangelism) in this model is the use of "the sinner's prayer." What can be said about this? Is it found in the Bible? The sad truth is that it is not found anywhere but in the back of some evangelistic booklets. Yes the Scripture says, "whoever calls on the name of the Lord will be saved," but this means to evoke or place confidence in the name of Christ. The sinner may express genuine faith through a prayer, but to pray such a prayer is not the essence of the required response to the gospel invitation.

The typical "sinner's prayer" as evangelicals have come to express it, has three elements: 1) a mere acknowledgment of sin, which is not the same as *repentance;* 2) a belief in the act of Christ's death, which is far removed from trust in His person and work; and, 3) an "inviting Christ into the life." The last phrase hangs on nothing biblical (though John 1:12 and Revelation 3:20 are used, out of context, for its basis). It is considered, nonetheless, to be the pivotal and necessary instrument for becoming a true Christian. But God commands us to repentantly believe, not to "invite Christ into the life."

Following the above, immediate assurance is given to the one who prayed on the basis of the sincerity of the person and the accuracy of the prayer. But it is the Holy Spirit who gives assurance of life in Christ, not the evangelist (Romans 8:16). We are to relate the *basis* of assurance but leave the actual assuring to the Spirit. This is rarely practiced in modern evangelicalism. We prefer rather to take the place of the Spirit in assuring the prayer and therefore seal many in deception. It is not the efficacy of a prayer that saves; Christ alone saves. The well-quoted passage on assurance, 1 John 5:13 states: "These things I have written to you who believe in the name of the Son of God, that you may know that you have eternal life." "These things...written" are the tests in the rest of the letter which give a basis to determine if we are truly converted.

In many cases the next step is to publicly introduce the one who has prayed the sinner's prayer and has just been told that he or she is a Christian. I have cringed to find that some leaders turn around after five minutes of "Just as I Am" and announce that the persons coming forward are converted. Sometimes the person has not been known to the pastor until that moment! Regardless, his optimism is often not founded, since it has been proven that extremely high numbers of these never show any competent sign of being converted. I am not intimating that people cannot be saved immediately, but that our early acceptance of the persons coming forward has often led us to "eat our words" about their new life in Christ.

Finally, there is the last stage of public baptism. It is interesting to note that in much of evangelicalism that is Baptistic, the number supposedly "being saved" and those being baptized is vastly different. If a hundred were purportedly converted during some sort of evangelistic effort, then we might not baptize but thirty of them. But out of the thirty, as seen among Southern Baptists as an illustration, statistically only ten or eleven of those thirty (34%) would show up on a given Sunday morning and only four or five (12%) on a Sunday evening (in churches that have services at that time). They do not really love the brethren or the atmosphere of godliness. *All* of these, however, have prayed the prayer, walked the aisle, been told they are Christians by someone in authority, and were publicly declared to be such.

Would it not be better for a system to be reinstated that

comes closer to recognizing only the smaller number of *true* Christians? Is it love for the lost that will perpetuate practices producing such damning deception in so many or is it merely love for success? Or should we assume that most leaders have simply gone on with "business as usual" without ever thinking it through at all? I prefer to believe the latter is true in most cases. Whatever the motive, however, those deceived on our rolls are still damned.

The more biblical way of "closing with Christ" is to focus on the gospel itself, without props. Whereas the altar call method can be tacked on to just about anything, no matter how absent the gospel, the biblical method *demands* the hearing of the Word. "How will they believe without a preacher" (Romans 10:14). It is "by the will of God that they are begotten, *through the Word of truth*" (James 1:18, emphasis mine). They are "born again... *through the living and abiding Word of God*" (1 Peter 1:23, emphasis mine).

It is interesting to note that the Bible account focuses attention on the *object* of our faith, Jesus Christ, and His life and work, when presenting the gospel to those who do not believe. There is virtually no explanation of the nature of repentance and faith; merely its mention seems to be enough. Why is that so? It is because of this wonderful reality: When the Word is preached and the Spirit is at work, the sinner is brought to conviction of sin and he cannot love his sin any more. He *must* repent. And when the Word presents Christ as the only hope and the Spirit is at work in the sinner, he sees no refuge for his soul but Christ. He *must* believe. Where else could he possibly go?

What about those passages that deal with the nature of repentance and faith in detail? The Epistle of First John, James, and many other portions help the *professing* believer understand the nature of faith to test the quality of the faith he says he has. But on the main, evangelism, after laying out the awfulness of man and his sin, and the consequence and offense against God, should focus its gaze on Christ and His work on behalf of sinners. And the people simply believe.

There is no emphasis on anything else. They just believe. There is no laboring of mechanics or methods or perfectly worded prayers, or walks to the front. They believe because it is all they can do.

The New Tribes Mission has been instrumental in giving us the best of missiological tools in their chronological approach to working with tribal groups. They teach the Bible from its beginning, laying out each story in sequence without revealing what is beyond that point. When they come to Christ they do not present the gospel in its doctrinal entirety until it comes in the passage. In other words, they leave the person to experience the New Testament as it was experienced by those closest to Christ. In their video depiction of a tribal group in this process, the day to explain Christ's death comes. To the man, the New Guinea tribe visibly shows its sense of shame and remorse for the crucified Master. Three days pass before the group returns and then the resurrection is explained. In the midst of the presentation, an older man jumps to his feet and loudly exclaims, "EE-Taow," or "I believe." Others stand with the same exclamation, though this tribal group is normally reserved in its expressions. In time the whole tribe is chanting "EE-Taow, EE-Taow," and jumping up and down. This went on for an extended period of rejoicing. A tribe was re-born in a day!

Such a response, with varying degrees of emotion, is the nature of believing in the New Testament. It was entirely incidental whether anyone prayed a "sinner's prayer" or walked to another place to take someone's hand. The powerful Word had encountered the people through the invincible Holy Spirit. This is New Testament evangelism.

You may not agree with my assessment but it is my contention that our use of the altar call and the accouterment of a "sinner's prayer" is a sign of our lack of trust in God. Do we really believe that the *Spirit* convicts and regenerates, and that His *Gospel* preached and read is the ordained means He uses? Surely there is nothing unbiblical or non-evangelistic about the man who preaches the gospel forthrightly, prays earnestly, appeals urgently, and places his entire trust in God to do what only He can do.

17.
THE GLOBAL PRIORITY OF MISSIONS
JOHN PIPER

1999 Southern Baptist Founders Conference

Prayer:

> *"Lord, there have been signal evidences in my life that to be in this place this week was the right place to be and I thank you for them. And now as we finish I need your help this one more time to see truth and to say truth—to say it with an anointing from you that will bring it home "life-changingly"—to equip us to join Paul in filling up what is lacking in the afflictions of Jesus—that almost heretical sentence of Paul's that needs to be unfolded for the cause of world evangelization. So, Lord I ask you to come and help me to see the truth and to say the truth with power. Would you grant hearts to be opened. And though we have had wonderful hours together, I pray that this would be an extraordinary climax in which you work wonders for your Name among us and for the finishing of the Great Commission and the honoring of Jesus Christ among those unreached peoples in Indonesia, India, China, North Africa and the near East, not to mention the lost across the street and perhaps in our own families. Lord, do a great work in this hour—exceedingly, abundantly, beyond all that we can ask or think. And guard us from the evil one and all his distractions and distortions of truth. Guard my mouth from saying anything unhelpful, unbalanced, or wrong. I pray in Jesus' Name. Amen."*

INTRODUCTION: CHOOSING TO SUFFER

RICHARD Wurmbrand is a hero of mine because of how much he has suffered and the way he has engaged God's people for the suffering church. He is founder of Voice of the Martyrs. He came to our church one time. He took off his shoes and walked up onto the platform and sat down. He took off his shoes because during his fourteen years in prison they beat him so badly on his feet and tortured him in so many ways that it hurts his feet to keep shoes on and to stand. I felt like washing the feet of this man who speaks out of such extraordinary suffering. There are, of course, thousands in the world like him—people of whom this world is not worthy—in caves and unclothed and being mistreated in ways that we can't even imagine (Hebrews 11:38). Richard Wurmbrand told a story when he spoke at our church, and I want to tell it to you. He said that there was an Italian television newscaster who interviewed a Cistercian monk. The Cistercians are monks in the Catholic Church who take a vow of silence. They live their whole lives in silence except when they confess their sins to one another and sing together. Someone once interviewed one of the heads of the monastery (evidently he could speak outside) and the interviewer asked him, "What if you were to realize at the end of your life that atheism is true and that there is no God? Tell me, what if that were true?" The monk's reply was this: "Holiness, silence and sacrifice are beautiful in themselves. Even without promised reward I still will have used my life well."

In our American, modern twentieth-century, many people would stand in awe of that sentence and swoon with delight over such a wonderful answer. What struck me when I heard it was something different. I wondered why the Apostle Paul's answer was so radically different? In 1 Corinthians 15:19 Paul said, "If in this life only we have hoped in Christ, we are of all people most to be pitied." If Paul were asked the newscaster's question—"What if there is no God?—What if there is no resurrection?"—I believe he would have shaken his head and said, "I would have been an absolute pitiable fool to spend my life this way." My question is "Why?" Why these two radically different answers? Why wouldn't Paul say what I think many thousands of American evangelicals would say: "It has been a good life; if there is no God and I have been deluded, it still has been a good life"?

The gospel, in large measure, is being offered today on the ground of all the things it will do for you in this life. It will fix your marriage. It will make your business prosper. It might heal your bodily ailments. It helps you to reconcile with your enemies. It helps you have obedient children, and on and on and on. And, in fact, many of these things are true. To believe the gospel does help keep your marriage together. It does help you raise thankful children, and so on. The list of benefits in this age is really quite remarkable.

So is Paul's answer exemplary? Is that the way we are supposed to think, or is Paul's answer limited to the Apostles? He says, "If there is no resurrection, I am, of all people, most to be pitied." Could you say that at the end of your life after the nice house you had in the suburbs, the boat, the retirement plan, the 9-1-1 availability, the hospitals and doctors whose help you have gotten, the drugs that have relieved your pain? Can you say as Paul did—if this doesn't prove true and there is no resurrection to compensate, I was a fool to live this way?

In recent years I have been much drawn to the issue of suffering. When I wrote the second edition of *Desiring God* I added a chapter on suffering.[1] When I wrote *Future Grace* I ended it with a chapter on suffering.[2] To me, the most important chapter in my missions book, *Let the Nations Be Glad*, is the chapter on suffering.[3] I have been saying these things now for about nine years, trying to come to terms with

---

1 John Piper, "Suffering: The Sacrifice of Christian Hedonism," in *Desiring God: Meditations of a Christian Hedonist* (Sisters, OR: Multnomah, 1996), 212-238.
2 John Piper, "The Future Grace of Suffering," in *The Purifying Power of Living by Faith in FUTURE GRACE* (Sisters, OR: Multnomah, 1995), 341-350.
3 John Piper, "The Supremacy of God in Missions Through Suffering" in *Let the Nations Be Glad! The Supremacy of God in Missions* (Grand Rapids, MI: Baker, 1993), 71-112.

my life and my church and the ease of American Christianity. It is just so comfortable, so secure, so easy, and yet the tide of persecution and militancy in India is rising, particularly among Hindu and Islamic fundamentalists. Our American opposition is different from that.

Maybe this word in 1 Corinthians 15:19 is a call to check yourself as to the choices you are making. I remember sitting there listening to Richard Wurmbrand choose some peculiar questions to ask us. He said, "You know, don't you, that Jesus chose to suffer?" He *chose* to suffer. He *came* to suffer. He asked, "Are you willing to choose it?" And then he said something like, "If you knew that your wife was pregnant and your friend's wife was pregnant and one of you had to have a badly malformed child, would you choose to be the one?" Would you *choose* the child?

I feel encouraged in this regard because of what is happening in the lives of a few people in my church. We must remind ourselves that there are wonderful evidences of grace in even the worst of churches. There is wheat along with the tares! Wherever you see wonderful evidences of grace you should be heartened and encouraged by it. My associate, Rick, who was supposed to be here with me, standing at the Desiring God Ministries table handing out tapes and answering questions about the ministry, emailed me about three weeks ago and said, "John, my wife and I can't be at the conference because we will probably be in Russia." They are looking to adopt a Russian child. He told me, "We have found a one-year-old boy and he has a badly malformed cleft lip and palate." He sent me a picture of the child and his whole face is split open. You know how it looks before the surgery. Some of you have children like that. Rick said, "He is a year old and no surgery has been done yet. His mouth is just laid open and we are going to go get him and adopt him." While there will be joys, that is *choosing* pain.

Kyle and Sharon Hastings are a couple in our congregation with three children. Our church has gotten very involved with orphans in the Ukraine in recent days. The Ukrainian laws have changed enough recently so that hundreds and thousands of children are available for adoption. Kyle and Sharon saw a picture of a little girl about nine or ten years old with a little sister who was about six. Kyle and Sharon fell in love with them and began to communicate and asked if they were adoptable. They lived in an orphanage and had no parents, and the orphanage said "yes." Within months Kyle and Sharon had gone over and brought them back. Now picture this: The kids can't speak any English. Their formative years are over. Somebody (probably not a believer) has built these girls into what they are largely going to be. *That's* embracing pain.

I haven't had a telephone, television or radio here for four days now, so I have been totally isolated. But I have had the internet. I plugged my computer into the wall so I could go online and read the news. I read an article on the web about a new release of AIDS statistics from the southern part of Africa. I have heard these statistics from Christian agencies for several years now but there it was—not from any Christian agency, but on the secular news—there are six million AIDS orphans in sub-Sahara Africa. AIDS is wiping out cultures there. I learned somewhere that the challenge of one Wycliffe translator was to get his translation done before the tribe vanishes due to AIDS. He has spent fifteen years on it, and he's hoping somebody in the tribe will be left long enough to read the Bible before it is over.

AIDS is decimating whole languages and cultures. Who is going to do something? Imagine the prospect of six million children growing up without parents and the political destabilization that will bring in fifteen, twenty or thirty years. Will the church embrace the danger of AIDS? Will you bring AIDS orphans into your family? "But what if they have it and I prick my finger and what if, ... what if ... what if?" It is a thousand "what ifs" that keep us safe, secure and retreating into our little places where nobody embraces pain anymore. Wurmbrand asked, "Will you *choose* suffering?" It went home like a dagger to me and has caused me these eight or nine years to think about suffering.

In 1 Corinthians 15:32, Paul wrote, "If the dead are not raised, 'Let us eat and drink, for tomorrow we die.'" Now, don't misunderstand what he is saying there. To "eat, drink, and be merry" (cf. Luke 12:19) does not mean "let's all become drunks and gluttons and lechers." They're to be pitied just as much as those who spend their lives embracing pain for the gospel (if there is no resurrection). He's talking about ordinary people. When he says, "Let's just eat, drink, and be merry," he means eat a balanced diet, have some parties, play a little golf, have a good retirement, a nice secure home, and just be normal. If there is no resurrection, let's all just be normal Christians because it's the good life (as I read it off the American evangelical scene). How many American evangelicals embrace much pain *intentionally* taking risks with their family? How many are not on the mission field because Grandma says, "Don't you take my grandchild over there where he can get spinal malaria"? How many are off the mission field like a snap when the danger comes? How many believe there are "closed countries" when Paul would find that an inconceivable concept? "What's a closed country?" he might ask.

"Well," you respond, "they might beat you if you preach the gospel."

Paul might reply, "I got beat every time I preached the gospel. I have been in jail over and over. I bear in my body the marks of Jesus" (Galatians 6:17).

By referring to his body, I think he meant his back, having been hit with thirty-nine lashes five times in his life (2 Corinthians 11:24). Do you ever think about what his back looked like after thirty-nine lashes? Then it may have taken two or three months to heal. There might have been infection and they didn't know anything about antibiotics and then it happens a second time to the same back. It happens a third time. Same back. It happens a fourth time. Same back. It happens a fifth time. The same back. And, he never took a furlough. Wouldn't you, about the fourth time, say to God, "I'm trying my best. Protect me!"? We get mad at God so quickly in this country. Lose one child or get cancer and God's in the dock and we're the judge. If anybody could have put God in the dock, Paul would have. But Jesus came to Paul in Damascus and said to Ananias, "I will show him how much he must suffer for the sake of my Name" (Acts 9:16). He has a quota for you too. Are you running from it? Or are you embracing it?

When Paul says, "Let's eat, drink, and be merry," he really means "Let's just be ordinary, comfortable Christians." If that's the way you are, something is amiss. Eating, drinking, being merry. Paul evidently didn't see his relationship with Jesus as a means of maximizing his material securities and comforts here in this life. Otherwise, he would not have said, "We are of all men most to be pitied if there is no resurrection from the dead."

Paul said in 1 Corinthians 15:29-30, "If the dead are not raised ... why am I in danger every hour?" In other words, "I am *choosing* to imperil my life hourly because I *believe* that I am going to be raised to everlasting reward." If there is no resurrection, why am I in peril every hour? Then he added these words, "I protest, brothers, by my exaltation in you which I have in Christ Jesus our Lord, I die every day!" (1 Corinthians 15:31). He said, "I am of all men most to be pitied if there is no resurrection," because he was embracing a lifestyle which, if there were no reward beyond the grave with everlasting joy in the presence of Christ, he would have to say, "I am one colossal idiot to live the way I live."

Now, let's talk about idiocy and craziness. Go back to Kyle and Sharon Hastings for a moment. Kyle and Sharon, who adopted the two Ukrainian girls, could not afford to adopt and raise two more kids. They have a sod farm. Sod is not an easy business. It is seasonal and you have to make sure that you do it right. Weather can ruin it, and business is up and down. Life is hard. People said, "You've got three kids and a sod farm and you're going to adopt two more kids? Is this crazy?" His relatives said to him one Saturday night, "You're crazy!" and listed off all the disadvantages of adopting these girls.

Now, Kyle came to church the next morning pleading, "Lord speak to me. I've got to have peace about this." I was preaching through Hebrews 11: "By faith Abraham ... went out, not knowing where he was going" (v. 8). And then two verses later, "because he was looking for the city which has foundations, whose architect and builder is God" (v. 10). And I paused and I said, "He's crazy! ... Unless there is a city beyond the promised land." Kyle had ringing in his ears the words of his relative from the night before, "You're crazy!" Later he told me, "Your words went into me like the most wonderful thing I have ever heard in my life." He said, "I almost came straight up out of my pew." He went to Russia, got the girls and now they are living the crazy life. There will be much pain, there will be financial hardship, and who knows whether these girls will be faithful or become Christians, but he is doing a great and wonderful thing.

I said the first night that I was here that I am on a recruitment mission for martyrs, and I mean it. Revelation 6:11 says the Great Commission will not be finished or the age will not be consummated without that full number of martyrs that God has appointed coming in. Those who are under the altar right now, crying out, "How long, O Lord?" are robed, quieted, and given peace to wait until all their brothers come in who are to be killed for the name of Jesus. And some, I do believe, are in this room, and I am trying to strengthen you and encourage you not to become pathologically in love with pain. That can happen. I'm not too worried about that happening with most people, but it does to those who embrace a path of dangerous obedience—*dangerous* obedience—where you can bank on it that you are going to get in trouble. Paul said, "All who desire to live a godly life in Christ Jesus will be persecuted" (2 Timothy 3:12). That's a simple sentence. The fact that so many of us are not persecuted probably means that we have domesticated the word "godliness." Nobody is going to persecute you for not committing adultery, not lying, not stealing, not murdering and not coveting. You can obey all the Ten Commandments and not be persecuted. Is that godliness—to obey the Ten Commandments? Does anybody get persecuted for obeying the Ten Commandments? Not much. You get persecuted when you are so radically *God-centered* and *God-satisfied* that you adopt AIDS victims or you go into hard places where they might make fun of you at the bar or you cross the street to your neighbor who has always mocked Christianity and tell him about God. Godliness is *God-saturatedness* and *Godwardness* in all you do. It is not having an avoidance ethic. Most Christians live with an avoidance ethic. We don't go to movies, we don't dance, we don't tell lies, we don't commit adultery, we don't, don't, don't, don't, don't. But godliness is when you have an ethic that is driven to *penetrate* darkness and *penetrate* danger and *penetrate* strongholds.

I heard the brother last night pray about peoples in Indonesia. He said, "There are a few very dark places in Indonesia where it is so dangerous to go." I just shuttered because a mob of machete-wielding Muslims scares me to death! I saw the film, *Gandhi.* There were scenes in *Gandhi* that are probably tame compared to what people are watching today, but the mob scenes in this film where they beheaded a man are so vivid in my memory today that they color all my view of missions. They test me again and again whether I will have the grace at the moment of my own trial not to cave in. I believe there are special graces for that hour. If you feel very weak and incapable of enduring the loss of your life or your loved-one's life there will be a special grace. There will be. You need to cultivate a deep reliance on that grace while you have a chance.

COLOSSIANS 1:24: FILLING UP WHAT IS LACKING IN CHRIST'S AFFLICTIONS

Now let's go to the text in Colossians 1:24. Here is a kind of programmatic statement of the Apostle Paul about the *embrace* of suffering—the embrace of suffering on behalf of the elect. Let's just read this one verse: "Now I rejoice in my sufferings for your sake and in my flesh" (take that seriously, Paul's back, his skin)—"I do my share on behalf of His body" —(which is the church)—"in filling up what is lacking in Christ's afflictions."

What does it mean to "fill up what is lacking in Christ's afflictions"? I don't need to tell this group that you can't improve upon the merit of the cross. So, this is not a filling up of the *worth* of the sufferings of Christ or the *value* or the *sufficiency*, the *atoning sufficiency* of those sufferings. None of that is in his mind. What is "fill up what is lacking"?

How could the sufferings of Christ be spoken of as lacking anything? Let me try to explain. My first point from verse 24 is that completing what is lacking in the afflictions of Christ *means* getting those afflictions to the people for whom they were designed through the gospel of the sufferings of Christ. The second point is that Christ's afflictions are completed through Paul's suffering, through my suffering. In my *sufferings* I complete what is lacking. The third point is, I *rejoice* in this.

1. *Completing what is lacking in the afflictions of Christ means getting those afflictions to the people for whom they were designed through the gospel.*

Part of the answer to what is lacking in the sufferings or afflictions of Jesus for His own is the personal presentation *to* His own—the lost sheep that are not yet of the fold—of the sufferings for them which He paid. In other words, what is missing is the personal presentation *to* them of what He did *for* them. Why do I think that is what it means? Am I just making that up or are there some evidences of that in this text and its parallels? Here is the reason I am persuaded that Paul's "filling up what is lacking" is the *extension* of those sufferings *to* those *for* whom he suffered—both to gather in the elect and to bless, nurture and build up the elect.

There is a remarkable parallel in Philippians 2:30. Look at

The Global Priority Of Missions

this with me and try to nail down in your own confidence that we are not just guessing here about what Paul might have meant by "fill up what is lacking in Christ's afflictions." The words "fill-up" and "lacking" are two Greek words used together (*antanaplero ta husteremata*). They are not common words, but they are brought together in another place, Philippians 2:30. The saints at Philippi were a beloved church. They ministered to Paul now and again, and one of those times is mentioned in this passage. They had sent aid to Paul through Epaphroditus when Paul was in prison, probably in Rome. During the journey, or when he arrived in Rome, Epaphroditus risked his life to get whatever they sent— whether money, or clothes or books—from the Philippians to Paul. The Philippians were engaged in sacrificial giving. Epaphroditus became the mediator to take that personal, sacrificial gift from the Philippian church to the one for whom it was designed, namely Paul. Epaphroditus risked his life in the process and suffered and almost died. Philippians 2:27 says "he was sick to the point of death." Then in Philippians 2:29 Paul told how the church should honor Epaphroditus when he came back because he made such a remarkable risk of his life in order to complete their work. Now, the key comes in verse 30: "because he came close to death for the work of Christ" [that is, he risked, he did something dangerous, he suffered willingly] "risking his life to complete" (that is, fill up) "what was deficient (or lacking) in your service to me." So there you have an almost identical phrase. Epaphroditus suffered and risked his life to complete what was lacking in the Philippians' service to Paul.

What was lacking in their service to him? They had all the money together. They had all the clothes together. They had the books. They had the package wrapped. Their love was full. The sacrifice was made. What was lacking? The gift was prepared but there were some *miles* in between. There was some *danger* in between. There was some *mission movement* that had to take place here to finish the ministry.

Let me read to you the commentary of Marvin Vincent from

a hundred years ago. Vincent got it exactly right, I think. This is his commentary on this verse in Philippians 2: "The gift to Paul was a gift of the church as a body. It was a sacrificial offering of love. What was lacking was the church's presentation of this offering in person. This was impossible and Paul represents Epaphroditus as supplying this lack by his affectionate and zealous ministry."[4]

Now lets go back to Colossians 1:24 with this parallel—this verbal parallel. You have the same author, the same time, the same kind of situation, and you have, in the same Greek language, what is not a common construction. Therefore, I think we are warranted to say that something similar is meant in Colossians 1:24 where Paul says he fills up what is lacking in the afflictions of Christ. Christ prepared a love gift. He suffered to do it. What was missing was not the value in it; it is everything the people for whom it is designed need. Only one thing is lacking—it's got to get there. How shall they believe without a preacher and how shall they preach unless they are sent with this package of the cross and the gospel and the sacrificial offering of the blood. If they don't hear it, it is of no effect.

So, the meaning is, I fill up what is lacking by getting it to those for whom it is appointed. I hear Paul in Acts 18:10 where he is so scared at night and Christ in mercy comes to him and says, "Do not be afraid, but go on speaking ... because I have many people in this city" (Acts 18:9-10). In other words, the elect are there. "I'm going to bring them." They will hear the voice of the shepherd *speak* the word of the cross (John 10:16). Get it to them. It doesn't matter if they beat you the fourth time. *Speak it!*

---

4 Marvin Vincent, *Epistle to the Philippians and to Philemon*, I. C. C. (Edinburgh: T. & T. Clark, 1897), 78.

2. *Completing what is lacking in the afflictions of Christ means that in my own sufferings I complete what is lacking.*

Now, for the second observation. When I say that it doesn't matter if they beat you for the fourth time, understand that it is a lot more significant than that. Beating is not happenstance. Paul's beating at Philippi and being thrown into prison was not a wringing of God's hands as though things got out of control. This beating, I say it with fear and trembling, is an evangelistic missionary design of Christ. It is not only to get the sufferings of Christ from the cross to Indonesia but to get them there in the form of the suffering of the servant who carries them there.

Paul said in Galatians 6:17, "I bear on my body the marks of *Jesus*." There is a huge missionary theology of suffering in that sentence. It is not just through preaching that God gets the news of his sufferings there. I don't just stand before the people and say, "He suffered for you. If you will have it, it is yours effectively. Embrace the sufferings and they cover all your sins." That is *not* what this text says. This text says one thing more: In my *sufferings* in doing that, they arrive! This is how the Great Commission is going to be finished. That's why there is a number of martyrs appointed. That's why the American evangelical church has to have another message preached to it other than the "health, wealth and prosperity" gospel. That is why our running from need to security is so horrid and so contrary to what God is calling us to do.

We need hundreds of thousands of young people to swarm over the unreached peoples in the next few years. There is a picture I have in my mind. Have you ever pictured warfare in the Old Testament? Bullets are clean. They can rip half your face off—I know that—but by and large, "*ding*" and you're dead. It is clean and quick. Not back then. The first twenty thousand are hacked to pieces. They hack each other to pieces on both sides. So, if you were a soldier and you were appointed by Joab to go to the front today, you were history. There is no doubt about it. There are 120,000 Assyrians and

80,000 Jews and they all have machetes and spears and are coming together. This is horrible. That's what is going to happen to the first eighty thousand of the two hundred thousand. Are you ready, parents, to let them go? Are you willing, gray-hairs out there, to be among the number? Where is anybody saying to us, "It's going to cost many, many martyrs." I can't make this happen. You can't make this happen. Nobody can make this happen. But, a massive evangelical, cultural, shifting of the plates of the culture so that there rise up tens of thousands who no longer say, "You can't go to that country because they'll kill you if you go there." Suddenly something is going to happen. May it happen soon. Maranatha! Come, Lord Jesus! May it happen soon that there are tens of thousands who think totally differently about dying because they say, "To live is Christ and to die is gain." Let's go! Why should we live to age 30 when Jesus is on the other side of the sword?

Let me read you something. This article came from *Christianity Today* dated September 16, 1996.[5] It is the article written by Steve Saint, the son of Nate Saint—one of the five missionaries killed with nine-foot long spears through their backs and chests and necks in Ecuador in 1956. This article is amazing. I don't know if you have heard the latest on these subsequent things. They continually learn about what was going on behind the scenes when those men were murdered. I'm going to read one sentence that is mind-boggling. This shook me deeply. In fact, we have been in touch with Steve. I said to the guys at Desiring God Ministries, "Find this guy and read that sentence to him and say, 'is that a misprint? Do you believe what you said?'" They found him and called him and they asked him, "Do you believe that? Because if you do we are going to have you come speak to our conference one of these days." He said, "I do."

Here's the situation. He's been back to visit Ecuador now. He's written articles and has worked there some. Of course,

5 Steve Saint, "Did They Have to Die?" *Christianity Today*, September 16, 1996, Vol. 40, No. 10, 20-27.

his aunt Rachel has worked there. What he has found is that on the day of his dad's death it wasn't because of hostility toward outsiders that these men were speared. There was an intrigue about a young couple trying to elope and needing a scapegoat because they were found out. They blamed it on these outsiders. That's why these guys got speared to death. The story is all in here. A confluence of strange things that brought the timing to bear with five dead fathers of nine little children. They were all young, married men. After studying through the strange providence here, this is the sentence Steve Saint wrote as a climax: "As they described their recollections [all these people who were involved—he talked to them all], it occurred to me how incredibly unlikely it was that the Palm Beach killing [Palm Beach was the name of the strip where it all happened] took place at all. It is an anomaly that I cannot explain *outside of divine intervention*." When I read that I said, "Surely, that sentence got inverted." Surely, they meant to say, "Only divine intervention could have prevented such a thing." He said exactly the opposite. *Only* divine intervention could explain this killing.

God designed all the books of Elisabeth Elliot. God designed Chet Bitterman who also was shot in the chest and the thousands of volunteers who signed up in the next weeks to take his place. God designed the inspiration of Rachel Saint and all the women—the queens in the church—who didn't shake their fist in God's face, but who have gone on and spoken boldly, stayed in there, have been the Gladys Stains of their day.

Therefore, in my call to martyrdom or in my call to missions and completing the Great Commission, I have no rosy picture whatsoever to paint. Not because the devil is on a rampage, but because God designs that we extend the sufferings of Jesus and complete what is lacking in His afflictions. Not merely by preaching but by *suffering* with the *sufferings* of Jesus. We deliver the sufferings of Jesus in and through our own sufferings. And one of the reasons why we Christians aren't given the time of day in America is because people look at us and they see that we have exactly the same fears, anxieties and values they have, and it isn't the embrace of danger and risk and AIDS and mockery and shame. And, I am preaching to myself here with great earnestness because I want to be so different.

I blew it again in the airport coming down here. I said to somebody while sitting at the table the other day when he asked how he could pray for me, "Here's where I am. Here is the cutting edge in my little, teeny weenie, failure-filled life: would you pray Acts 5:41 into my life?" The Apostles were beaten and shamed publicly and sent out. Acts 5:41 says, "They went on their way ... rejoicing that they had been counted worthy to suffer shame for His name." The way I boil that down is to get the two words together so that it really hits home: *rejoice* to be *shamed*. Rejoice to be shamed. My prayer request as I leave in 10 minutes, is that you would pray, "As he goes, would you give to John Piper the authenticity of the things he says." So that when an occasion comes—in the Atlanta airport or on the plane or when I get home in my neighborhood—to be shamed, and it will feel attractive to me.

If that doesn't happen and we can't rejoice at shame, how are we going to finish the Great Commission? What about when beheadings will be required and tortures will be required? My wife is doing a talk to the women of our church on Dr. Helen Roseveare, medical missionary to the Belgian Congo. Nöel has been reading everything she ever wrote and we watched a video on Helen Roseveare. I sat there watching that video with Nöel, and Roseveare was describing in the most remarkably non-melodramatic way the Simba Revolution in 1964 when she and others were brutally and repeatedly raped and beaten. As the soldiers held them in bondage waiting to take them off to kill them, she said that they were telling the group how they were going to do it. "We're going to burn you, but before we burn you, we are going to skin you. We are going to take a big piece of skin off of you and eat it in front of you and then we'll burn you alive." That's what they were telling them before it happened. In that case it didn't happen, but that *has* happened! That picture, in fact, is on the front of Stephen Neill's paperback of *A History of Christian Missions*.[6] The picture of a man being filleted and his flesh being eaten while he is being burned to death. These things are going to happen. And *God* designs them.

So, get ready now not to get mad at God but rather to say, "I'm being counted *worthy*! I'm being counted worthy to *share* in the *sufferings* of Jesus!" 1 Peter 4:13, "Rejoice insofar as you share Christ's sufferings, that you may also rejoice and be glad when his glory is revealed." So, *future* grace is the key.[7] Setting your heart on *future* grace.

3. *Completing what is lacking in the afflictions of Christ means rejoicing in suffering.*

Let me close with one other word in verse 24. Some might say that last night's message and this message do not fit. Well, they didn't understand last night, which is why I have been adding chapters on suffering in everything I write, because I am being misunderstood—as I think every faithful minister of the gospel is misunderstood when he says radical things. Romans 6:1, "Let's just sin that grace may abound! That's what Paul says."

I didn't say anything about not suffering last night. I said "Pursue joy in God in everything you do," and what I am saying now is if you don't find your satisfaction in God and God alone, you will count Him as an enemy when He hands you over to the sword. But if He is your treasure and He is your all, you will say with Paul, "I count everything as loss and rubbish for the surpassing value of knowing Christ Jesus my Lord" (Philippians 3:8).

One thing will get you through the "craziness" of adopting AIDS orphans or going to serve in one of those dangerous places in Indonesia. The *one* thing that will motivate and sustain over the long haul that craziness is found in Hebrews 13.

6 Stephen Neill, *A History of Christian Missions*, 2nd edition (New York: Viking Press, 1994).
7 See John Piper, *Future Grace*.

Oh, I could spend many, many hours with you walking you through Hebrews 10, 11, 12, 13 on how to be radical in laying down your life for Jesus, but perhaps this is the best place to end. Hebrews 13:13-14 says: "So, let us go to Him outside the camp, bearing His reproach." Or another version, says: "Let us go *with* Him outside the camp bearing reproach *for* Him." That's what I have been calling for this morning. Let's go! Jesus went outside the safety to Golgotha and laid His life down. He said, "I send you forth as sheep in the midst of wolves" (Matthew 10:16). Now picture that. Use your imagination. It's not just wolf on sheep—that's bad enough—but you have a plurality of wolves here and you have one sheep. Sheep are absolutely helpless animals. They have no defense mechanism. They can only trust a Shepherd. That's their only hope, and if the shepherd doesn't show up, they have one hope—resurrection—that God can put the pieces back together out of the stomachs of the wolves. How are you going to do that? Verse 14 says: "For here we have no lasting city but we seek a city which is come."

You will go with Jesus to Indonesia, Ukraine, your neighborhood, the hard place across the aisle or across the street—wherever it takes you—go and embrace suffering and complete what is lacking in the sufferings of Christ (Colossians 1:24) *to the degree* that you are no longer a citizen of this world but your citizenship is in heaven from which we await a Savior—Jesus Christ the Lord, who will raise this lowly body and give it a body like His glorious body (Philippians 3:20-21). If that's not going to happen may God give you the grace to lead a life that is the most pitiable of all lives. If it is going to happen (and it will), may that mobilize you and empower you and sustain you to be an absolute *fool* in this age—a fool to your parents, a fool to grandparents (that you're taking your kids there), a fool to be adopting this kid, a fool to walk into *that* part of the city to speak the gospel or to rescue a girl in a cult, etc.

Be a *fool!* There are so many Christians choosing prudence. I almost loathe the word. Don't live a safe life. Live a risky life. Take chances which to God are no chances.

This slight, momentary affliction is preparing for us an eternal weight of glory beyond all comparison, as we look not to the things that are seen but to the things that are unseen. For the things that are seen are transient, but the things that are unseen are eternal" (2 Corinthians 4:17).

Embrace the slight! Five times on his back Paul was scourged. He called it momentary. A lifetime of affliction. That's what he meant. Slight means death and momentary means eighty years. *Embrace* it because there is an *eternity* of everlasting joy ready to make you a wise person, not a foolish one, in living that way.

18.
THE LAST FRONTIER
ANONYMOUS

1999 Southern Baptist Founders Conference

> Woe to him who builds a city with bloodshed and establishes a town by crime! Has not the LORD Almighty determined that the people's labor is only fuel for the fire, that the nations exhaust themselves for nothing? For the earth will be filled with the knowledge of the glory of the LORD as the waters cover the sea (Habakkuk 2: 12-14, NIV).

ONE of the things I love about Scripture, one of the glories of Scripture, is its honesty. The book of Habakkuk is a book of a complainer. The basic structure of this book is two complaints and a prayer. Complaint number one: "Judah is full of injustice, God. Why don't you do something?" And God says, "Ok, I will. I'm going to bring Babylon and destroy you." Complaint number two: "Wait a minute, your answer was worse than the problem." God's answer, "Wait until you see the whole picture." In 2:2-3 the Lord responds,

> And the LORD replied, "Write down the revelation and make it plain on tablets so that a herald may run with it. For the revelation awaits an appointed time; it speaks of the end and will not prove false. Though it linger, wait for it; it will certainly come and not delay."

And what is the final picture? We see it in 2:12-14, "The earth will be filled with the knowledge of the glory of the Lord as the waters cover the sea."

Now think about the prophet's environment. Internally, the people of God were being destroyed by corruption and idolatry. Josiah's reforms had not outlived him and already the people returned to ways that were utterly displeasing to God. Externally, the nation was facing impending disaster from Babylon and it is in this setting of internal corruption and external disaster that one of the most dramatic promises of Scripture is made. "The earth will be filled with the knowledge of the glory of the Lord as the waters cover the sea." It is a promise whose foundation is nothing less than the sovereignty of God Himself. Consider Habakkuk 1:6, "I am raising up the Babylonians, that ruthless and impetuous people." So much for superpower pretensions! Babylon may have thought it was in charge but it is God who raised up the Babylonians to do His will. In 2:13, it is the Lord Almighty who has determined judgment. The promise is based on the fact that whatever the condition of the people of God and international politics may be, God is sovereign and He is going to accomplish His purposes, not in spite of, but through everything that man can throw at the people of God.

The content of the promise is nothing less than the knowledge of God's glory. One of the most encouraging things that I am hearing right now that is coming out of our missionary learning centers is that people are being told that the point about missions is not us, the point is God. That is a pretty significant development within our organization. I just had a two-year journeyman join me as my administrative assistant. I was curious to find out what he learned when he had come through orientation and that is the one thing that stuck in his mind. He said, "This is not about me, this is not even about the nations, it's about God. He is the point and His glory is the content of the promises and everything else we do— evangelism, church planting, etc.—are all aimed at that end."

A time will come when all missionary effort will cease. A time will never come when worship ceases. As I heard at my own baccalaureate service from seminary, the whole point of what we are doing is to "recruit for the choir of heaven." But the scope of this is stunning because it is that "the whole earth will be filled with the knowledge of His glory." It is universal and overwhelming, "as waters cover the sea." Think about that literally (the sea is miles deep in places) and to that extent that "the earth will be filled with the knowledge of God's glory." That is the big picture. That is what God intends to do and you can see this from Genesis to Revelation. God's intention is nothing less than to entirely reclaim this planet for His glory.

Because of that perspective then the book of Habakkuk goes on to end in a prayer. But this time it is a prayer largely of praise and expresses joy in the face of reality. Remember, reality hasn't changed—Judah is still corrupt and the Babylonians are still coming, but the prayer at the end of Habakkuk is a glorious expression of praise to God and as a result of it, the prophet finds renewed strength for the task in the middle of one of the worst times in this nation's history; he knows how it's going to end. That is the big picture at which we are looking. In the face of corruption within the people of God, which is as true today as it was then, in the face of an external world of tyranny, injustice, and determined opposition to God and His work, God's agenda for human history is that "the earth be filled with the knowledge of His glory as overwhelmingly as waters cover the sea."

What is the current reality then? God gave this prophesy through the prophet centuries ago. Where do things stand now? What is the world like now? What are we doing about it? And perhaps most significantly, what should *you* be doing about it?

WHAT IS THE WORLD LIKE?

First, I want to give you a little history lesson on the history of missions. In the late eighteenth century, evangelical Christianity was largely confined to northwestern Europe and the eastern part of what is now the United States. There were other churches in other places but whether the gospel was heard is another matter. Then the modern missionary movement started with people like William Carey and others, largely as a movement to the coasts of the unreached world and the unreached world was just about everywhere. So you had people like Carey going to Calcutta, which is on the coast of India. You had Judson going to Burma and people going to the coast of China. There was a movement to the coasts to sort of beachhead for the gospel in places where Christ was not yet known.

The second wave occurred in about the middle of the nineteenth century when people began to realize, "Hey we've only touched the edge, we've only touched the fringe." So there was a substantial movement inland and many of the great faith missions were started in that time, indicated with that word "inland" in their title, specifically showing that we are not going to be content to stay on the coast where the foreign powers have their military bases, and it's safe; we are going inland. And hence, you had, Africa Inland Mission, Sudan Interior Mission, China Inland Mission that's now the Overseas Missionary Fellowship. There was this great move to go from the coasts where it was relatively safe to the inland. Many people lost their lives because they gave up the protection of the Colonial powers in that day.

That's the way things were for quite a while, until the great Lausanne Convention in 1974. Ralph Winter, in addressing that convention shook up people incredibly by, for the first time in a significantly public way, exposing the reality that we had not even touched a large portion of the human race. That yes, there was a church in just about every country (not all of them—there were at that point still about five with none in it), but there were "hidden peoples"—people groups hidden in these countries that no gospel witness had yet reached.

Where were Southern Baptists at this time? This was the 70's and we were where we had been for a long time—with our heads in the sand in the glorious splendor of our isolation. We were ignoring what the rest of the evangelical world was saying and things continued with business as usual. Then something really very radical happened in the mid 80's: the Board invited a man named David Barrett, one of the most significant missions researchers in the twentieth century, to join the Board.[1] He happens to be Anglican and British and our Board invited him to come as a consultant. The convention had adopted Bold Mission Thrust in 1976 and the goal was, more or less, the evangelization of the world and the Board wanted an outside observer to come in and see how we were doing. In essence, what Dr. Barrett said was, "You are not only not going to achieve Bold Mission Thrust, you are incapable of it. You are structurally incapable of fulfilling the Great Commission as things stand right now." To break it down, he came up with some categories that we have continued to use, along with much of the evangelical world, in thinking of the world not just as the world, but in three parts: World C, World B, and World A. World C is the "Christian" world (we use the term loosely). Dr. Barrett and I had some argument over this. He defines it as anyone who calls himself a Christian. I tend to think that probably God doesn't look at things quite the same way. This includes every denomination that has any affiliation of any sort with Christianity. Nevertheless, there is World C; it is the "Christian" world, where there is some affiliation or identity with the Christian faith. World B consists of those who do not in any way identify themselves as Christian but are around Christians and with a gospel witness accessible to them. Our missions efforts were all aimed either at World C— those who call themselves Christians but who have no lively faith in Christ—or at World B—those who are around Christians. The fact is that we were not doing anything at all for the last part, World A—that part of the world that not only had no identity with Christianity but also had no access to the gospel whatsoever.

---

1 "Board" refers to the International Mission Board of the Southern Baptist Convention (IMB), formerly known as the Foreign Mission Board.

World A-People Groups.

We had no structure to tackle World A at all. What is World A? It is, first of all, made up of people groups. When the Scripture refers to "nations" it is it not referring to political units, but it refers to "people groups." As Americans we sometimes have a very hard time grasping that because of the relative homogeneity of our society and the manner in which things sort of get blended together. Ethnic identity, compared to the rest of the world, is a fairly minor deal in this country. That is not the case in the rest of the world.

People groups are defined as distinct by virtue of language. You have no idea how blessed you are to live in a country where you can travel 3,000 miles and people speak almost the same language. We speak English and not only does our whole country speak English but most of the world is at least learning English. This is not the case in most countries. Did you know that in the country of India alone, according to their own statistics, there are 1,652 distinct languages in the country? Even a small country like Afghanistan, small as it is, has about 23 million people in it with 50 different languages spoken in that nation. Most educated men will speak one of two trade languages in Afghanistan. I said educated, though only seven percent of the population can read. So that tells you how extensive intercommunication is. In India, out of the 1,652 languages (according to the 1993 edition of *Operation World*),[2] only 46 have the Bible. An additional 35 have the New Testament and 60 more have portions of Scripture. That's out of 1,652 languages! Of the 50 languages in Afghanistan, one has the entire Bible, however it is in a dialect that most people cannot read. Two have the New Testament in an accessible form, out of fifty languages. If you don't speak the same language, you're not going to communicate the gospel. The linguistic diversity of the world is an astonishing thing.

People groups can also be distinguished by history and by

---

2 Patrick Johnstone, *Operation World*, (Grand Rapids, MI: Zondervan, 1993), 274.

religious heritage, even when language is held in common. A classic example that most people are now aware of to some extent is Yugoslavia. The Serbs, the Croats, and the Bosnian Muslims all speak the same language, Serbo-Croatian. But a Serb is Orthodox, a Croat is Roman Catholic, and a Muslim is obviously a Muslim. Actually, someone better put it, a Serb is someone who doesn't go to the Orthodox Church, a Croat is someone who doesn't go to the Catholic Church, and a Bosnian Muslim is someone who never goes to the Mosque. It's not even a matter of actual religious practice; it is a matter of identity and identity separates people. It all goes back to history and the conflict between the Ottoman Empire back in the early middle ages. Those people speak the same language but they hate each other and they have hated each other for a very long time. That's probably not going to end anytime soon because the blood vendettas have gone on from generation to generation to generation.

Again, as Americans we have very little sense of history and fail to realize that what happened in Kosovo in the fourteenth century is a crucial, deeply felt, emotional issue for every Serb because they are still living with the consequences of it. People are separated by history and by religious affiliation.

Sometimes people groups are separated by geography— where there are mountain ranges and deserts, and though people speak the same language, they simply have no access to one another. Sometimes political boundaries can end up dividing a people group. The people group that I was assigned to until the past year is a good example. The Soviets basically sealed their southern border. Previously, after the Bolshevik Revolution, the Soviets cut off all communication so that about half my people group was north of that border, half south of it, and they went their separate ways with even their languages diverging, all in the span of seventy years. So there are a number of ways in which people groups can be defined. The important thing to realize is that there are barriers to the natural expansion to the church all over the world, serious barriers—barriers that unless someone makes a point of crossing, the gospel will not reach beyond them.

Unreached people groups.

So, World A is made up of people groups and, more specifically, it's made up of unreached people groups. This again is one of the things that I can't stress enough because it's sometime difficult for Americans to grasp, but my part of the world is full of people groups that have few to no believers. The people group I worked with consists of 13 million people. When my wife and I arrived on the ground in 1992, we were the first Christian workers of any organization allowed in. Out of that 13 million, there was one known believer. One! There were no churches and there was not a Bible anyone could read, much less any other literature. There was absolutely nothing. That can be multiplied across Central Asia. Within Central Asia in 1992, when I began work in earnest after the fall of the Soviet Union, there was not a single people that had more than four believers in it. We're talking about a region that has about 100 million people in it with not a single people group having more than four believers. Bless the Lord, today there is not a single people group in Central Asia proper that has less than a couple of hundred believers. But still, that's only a few hundred out of a hundred million.

The reason it's in that condition is that it is made of unreached people groups in restricted access countries. I am responsible right now for a sub-region that spans fourteen countries and territories. There is not a single one of them where you can get a missionary visa. In every one of these, evangelism is either illegal or very highly restricted. Often, for example, it is okay to evangelize the Russians who remained behind after the Soviet Union collapsed because a Russian is, after all, a Christian in the minds of the local Muslims. For that matter, communism is "Christian" because communism is Russian and Russians are "Christians." People in most of the world cannot separate ethnic identity from religious identity. But evangelism among Muslims is illegal and not permitted. Bibles, literature and electronic media are highly restricted though it is permissible to bring a Russian Bible in, but not a Bible in one of the local languages. There is persecution, either official or unofficial, varying in intensity against local native believers. It can vary anywhere from losing your job to, in one country that is very dear to my heart, almost inevitably being killed.

Martyrdom.

Martyrdom is a serious thing. I think most of you know that there have been more martyrs for the Christian faith in the twentieth century than all previous centuries combined. It's one thing to read about it in a book, it is another thing when it happens to your friend. It is something to share the gospel with someone, knowing full well that the consequences of doing what you earnestly pray they do, may very well mean that they die. It puts us to shame. I had a seventeen-year-old boy that was from the most restricted country in my region that I had the privilege of being present when the Holy Spirit brought him into new life. And I remember asking what he thought would happen to him. He said, " Well, I don't think my father will kill me but I'm not sure. My neighbors certainly will kill me if they find out." Finally this seventeen-year-old kid looked at me and said, "If everything you said about Jesus is true and I now know that it is, then He is worth more than my life." Those were not pious words; they were the words of a seventeen-year-old boy who didn't know if he would be alive that night because of his stand for Christ. That is the world I live in. It's a world of authoritarian governments with no guarantee of civil liberties—governments that are not afraid to monitor or stop the work of the gospel.

We live in a place of unparalleled freedom here in the States but that is not the world in which my co-workers live in Central Asia. My wife was once on the phone with a co-worker when a voice broke in and said, "Would you please slow down, you are talking too fast, and we are having a hard time understanding you." We could usually hear the radio playing in the background of the KGB agent who was monitoring our phone calls. My mail would come to me opened with a letter opener and taped shut, just to let me know they had been reading it. Some of our co-workers were having troubles with their e-mails, so they went to the local e-mail server and said, "We've lost some of our messages." They replied, "Oh, no problem, we have them right over here," and handed them a disk with all of their e-mails on it—just to let us know that they read them all. One of my co-workers this past spring was on his way out of his country (I cannot name in a public setting any of these countries specifically) to a conference and he was stopped at the airport and strip-searched. He was taking out with him a disk that had on it the text of the children's Bible in his language that had just recently been translated. It was confiscated and lost. Some people were thrown out of his country as a result and his status is very tenuous at this point. In another part of our region, there were some folks who were working on the translation of the Scriptures for the first time ever into that language, when the police came in, confiscated the computers, all the disks, and all the work that had been done. The police arrested the believers, beat them and threw them in jail. They are still there; that was several months ago. In another very tough area, we were beginning to see some fruit for the first time ever and all the foreign workers that were there had their visas revoked, and all the believers were arrested and are still in jail. That's World A—a world of a bewildering variety of languages and people groups, who through history have had no access to the gospel and where there is a determined effort to keep things that way.

How big is it? Well, World A has three major blocks: the Muslims, the Hindus, and the Buddhists. There are one billion Muslims in the world. They make up 20% of the world's population and are growing quickly. There are 716 million Hindus, and they make up 13% of the world's population. There are 613 million Buddhists, and they make up 11% of the world's population. Now some of these folks do have access to the gospel, but not many. At the very least, World A comprises 25% of the world's population. The figure we use at the Board for all people groups of whatever size, that have yet to have a significant gospel witness is around 2,400 different people groups. Thirteen to fourteen years ago, we were doing nothing for any of them. Bless the Lord, today we are targeting eighty people groups—they are the largest eighty but that is 80 out of 2,400. This is the world that I'm working in, the world that God called me to and, I pray, that He calls many of you to, as well.

WHAT ARE WE GOING TO DO ABOUT IT?

What are we going to do about it? We are motivated and fueled by some basic convictions and I want to tell you that I am not just speaking for myself here. I have been a Calvinist for years. I was one when we joined the Board, they knew it, they took me anyway, and now suddenly I find that I am not even remotely alone. These are the kinds of convictions that underline and motivate what we are doing.

God's intention.

The first and most fundamental conviction is God's intention. God's intention for *the world* is to call to Himself a people from every tribe, tongue, people and nation. God's intention for *His church* is to make disciples from every tribe and tongue and people and nation. God's method for accomplishing his intention is the proclamation of His Word. "Faith comes by hearing and hearing by the Word of Christ," it's not just going to happen. It's going to happen by the means God has ordained and we are that means. There is none other.

No resistant people groups.

The second basic conviction is that there is no such thing as a resistant people group. One of the things that I often hear is, "You're working with Muslims? You can't work with Muslims, they are resistant!" It was asked last night and I really can't say it any better, "Are there degrees of being dead?" Is a Muslim in Central Asia any more dead than your unregenerate neighbor next door? Does it take any more of a miracle to bring my Muslim friend to Christ than it did to bring you or me to Christ? I don't think so. It is a miracle for any of us. If God has said He is going to call a people to Himself, it's going to happen. There is nothing that any human, or any demon in hell can do to stop it. Muslims are not resistant, *they are neglected.* The problem is with us. We have allowed ourselves to be so motivated by fear and an obsession with comfort, that we've stayed where it is safe. So the vast majority of all Muslims, to put it in human terms, have never had the chance to be resistant because we haven't taken the gospel to them. It was true a few years ago, bless the Lord, it is no longer true today, that only 2% of the Protestant missionary force in the world of all denominations combined was trying to reach Muslims that make up 20% of the world's population. God is doing a mighty work in our day. The numbers of our co-workers has increased greatly in my region of Central and Southern Asia alone. My massive region is one of fourteen in the world and has 26% of the world's population. Because a lot of those people are down in South Asia, it is broken up into sub-regions. I am responsible for the sub-region of Central Asia. In my region alone, two years ago, we had 214 total workers—that's long-term and short-term of two years or more. Today we have close to 500, so we have more than doubled in two years, and we now make up about 10% of the total force of the Board. You combine the other regions that are tackling World A and we probably make up about 20%, which is a big improvement over 2% but still that is only 20% trying to reach half the world's population.

There is no such thing as a resistant people. The only reality that matters is a sovereign God who is capable of taking a heart of stone and turning it into a heart of flesh. One who is capable of calling the dead to life and who has said that He would honor the preaching of His Word by calling a people to Himself through it. He will do it and He is doing it. What we are seeing over and over again is that when we go, God is waiting to use us to call people to Himself. And it's happening all over World A. We cannot publicize the statistics because we dare not publicize the statistics for fear of backlash on the part of governments and other forces. But the fact of the matter is that God is right now calling a people to Himself from among those that you would least expect. I wish I could tell you some stories, but it would get people killed if I did.

Taking the long-view.

The third basic conviction that fuels our obedience is the importance of taking the long view. Paul says, "One sows, another waters, but God makes the harvest." There has been, in my mind, some really, really, bizarre talk about a dichotomy between harvest fields and going to unreached peoples. The reason a harvest field is a harvest field is generally because there are those who have spent years laboring, sowing the seed, watering the ground, and picking up the stones. A classic example is Africa. You have heard about the explosion of the gospel in Sub-Saharan Africa. That explosion followed a century of seemingly fruitless labor on the part of missionaries. Sowing the seed, being faithful, sticking it out, being willing to persevere, and God was doing His slow, imperceptible work. When God had suddenly done all the preparation there was an explosive harvest and it continues to this day. We cannot expect to simply waltz into a place that has had no exposure whatsoever to the gospel and instantly have a harvest on our hands. It does happen sometimes; God is totally in control and He can do whatever He likes, but that doesn't seem to be the way He usually works. So we have to go in prepared to say, "I will give my life for all of my life, and if I see no fruit, that is God's business, not mine." Here again this runs so counter to the culture of the West today. It is very difficult to get members of my generation or those of the younger to commit to anything, even if it is good, for more than a few years. To say, "To really be effective, you need to go and be lost in an area, Kipling called 'the back of beyond' for the rest of your life, and you may see nothing or you may see God do something—that is not your business. Your business is to stick it out and be faithful and that's it." That's not an easy message for people to swallow, but we are convinced that without that perspective, without that attitude, we cannot expect to see God do through us what He intends to do. If He doesn't use us, He will raise up someone else.

Centrality of the church.

The fourth basic conviction that not only fuels what I am doing, but that I have also discovered increasingly fuels the work of our entire IMB, is the centrality of the church in the work of God. This is a major recent development. It wasn't too long ago, that if you asked anyone from what was then the Foreign Mission Board what our task was, they would have said, "Our task is evangelism." That is not what you hear now. It went from "our task is evangelism" to "our task is evangelism that results in churches." Now, it has gone from "our task is evangelism that results in churches" to "our task is evangelism that results in church planting movements that are totally out of our control, so that we can leave and go somewhere else." That is what we are after.

There is an encouraging revival in ecclesiology among our workers. Again, I have never really been secretive about what I believe, and what my convictions are, and so when I was asked by my regional leadership to spend a couple of hours at our recent region-wide annual meeting talking about the importance of the church, and then lead some workshop sessions to give a biblical ecclesiology to our workers, that said a great deal about the direction things are going. As I stood before a bunch of students from our "Two Plus Two Program" for seminaries that have folks do two years in seminary and then come two years to the field to finish their degree, the only negative comment I got was, "Why am I just now hearing this?" There was no resistance or resentment, in spite of giving a pretty detailed, extensive ecclesiology. There is a heart, a spirit, a thirst, to go back to the Scriptures and examine what the church is and to embrace its centrality in the work of God, recognizing that God actually has something to say about what it's supposed to be like. God's Word actually regulates the church and that's now accepted and embraced by our workers. Those are the basic convictions. Now there is a final, very important one.

The will of God.

Our fifth conviction is that no government on earth has the right to veto the expressed will of God. No government on earth has the right to tell us that we cannot fulfill the Great Commission within their borders. No government on earth can tell us, "You've got to stay out, we are going to keep our people in bondage to Satan." Though they may not grant us a missionary visa, which is their prerogative, they are not going to keep us out. We don't throw up our hands and say, "Well, until they agree that it's okay to obey God, we don't have to." What do we do? What do we do in this wonderful, weird world called World A?

The first thing we do is to start with the people group; that's our focus, our basic unit of operation. We assign a special kind of missionary called a "strategy coordinator." These aren't places we can just waltz into. We've got to figure out how to do it and how to do it right, so we assign someone whose first job is to learn everything they can about that people group, their setting, and what can be done. They must figure out how it is possible to get the witness of the gospel to that people.

As that person learns (it is usually a couple), they develop a comprehensive strategy that includes things like mobilizing massive prayer for those people and developing tools such as seeing to it that the Bible is translated. Almost everywhere we are working there is no Scripture to work with, so it is hard to begin. The *Jesus* film produced by Campus Crusade for Christ is an incredibly effective tool that basically puts the Gospel of Luke in video form. We try to get it dubbed into the language of the people we are working with. We also work with other agencies that do radio broadcasting to see how we can we get this language, this people, included in a regular radio broadcast of the gospel. The strategy coordinator works with other evangelical organizations in order to give a cooperative effort to the job. This has been a radical change.

I went to an inter-denominational seminary. One of the reasons why I was at first very reluctant to even consider our Board is because of its appalling reputation for isolationism. Those days are totally gone and dead now. As a matter of fact, at a conference we hold each year for all the organizations working in Central Asia, in almost all the people group partnerships, the organizer and facilitator of the partnership is one of our IMB workers, because we are passionately committed to not wasting effort and money in our attempts to bring the gospel to these people. The strategy coordinator determines modes of entry that we call "platforms." For instance, you can't go in as a missionary but they are perfectly willing to take doctors, engineers, teachers, nurses, or almost anything but preachers. They are willing to take you, knowing that you are a Christian, knowing you are coming motivated by the love of Christ, and knowing that when people ask you questions you are going to answer them. So, it's fine that I can't be a missionary but I can be a Christian, motivated by the love of Christ to share the good news of Jesus with people and to serve the people by, in my case, teaching English.

What we have discovered is that for years we had been allowing governments to keep us out. Sure they locked the front door but they left door back door wide open. Just about everywhere within my sub-region, with full honesty about our spiritual identity, we can get in. We are watched, we have to be careful and very discreet, but we can get in. So, the strategy coordinator looks at the big picture and thinks, how can we bring a full court press on this people group, to bring the gospel to them in every fashion and form, to penetrate every level of that society with the good news of Jesus Christ? The strategy coordinator determines the strategy, modes of entry, platforms to be used, writes job requests, recruits personnel and then goes with the team as a player/coach to implement that strategy. That is our basic means of approach. We can get in with the good news, we just have to do it intelligently.

We need people—this is the hard part. This is where *you* come in. What we need badly are workers. We need workers that are, as it were, "dually competent." We need people with a marketable secular skill of some sort but also competent in the ministry of the gospel. We haven't done too well at producing those types of doubly competent people. We will get folks that have good secular skills so that we can easily get them a job in the country, but all too often they don't have a clue how to share the gospel with somebody, and they certainly don't know much about the church and what needs to happen to establish it. Or we got folks that have good ministry training experience but can't demonstrate real integrity in their platform because they really don't know how to do anything but preach. What we need are folks with a sort of dual competency. It can be produced. People can be trained along those lines.

The joy and responsibility that we have in my part of the world is laying the initial foundation for the immerging church. It is incredible and amazing. It is amazing to see churches spring up where there has never, ever been a body of people worshiping Christ before. It is also very frightening because we realize that folks look at us—these new believers look at us—as the models for what the church is supposed to be. One of the things that frustrates me most due to the prohibition against traditional missionaries in my part of the world is that the folks that tend to be most attracted and sign on, particularly with other organizations, are folks that have very little theological training, very little biblical knowledge, and so foundations are being laid that we will regret for years to come.

Because our goal is to lay a good foundation, there are things we don't do. There are things that, for the sake of the integrity of the church and its spiritual health, we refuse to do. We do not pastor churches. Whenever one of our folks steps into the role of pastoring a local church, what we are saying is, "Only the well educated, wealthy Westerner can do this, I am afraid none of you are qualified." That is the message that comes across, whether we say it or not. What we find is that local leadership never springs up if we step into the leadership roles. We don't build buildings. I plead with you, please don't build buildings or pay to have buildings built for churches. The church did really well without buildings for the first 200 years or so of its existence. When foreign money comes in to build a building, church growth, of the healthy sort, tends to stop. We have seen it all over the world. As a region, we have made a comprehensive statement that we will never build a building. Our folks are in a persecution situation anyway, so they don't need to be visible. Churches meet in people's homes—sounds sort of familiar from the New Testament! Where foreign money comes in to build buildings, to subsidize salaries, the health of the indigenous, immerging church tends to go down the tubes.

We also don't institutionalize leadership training. We've seen that in parts of the world where the statement is made that for it to be a real church, you have to have a seminary-trained and ordained pastor. Pastors get sent off to the West, or the big city, and guess what? They never come back to the hard places. And if they do come back, they don't fit anymore and they are not really able to minister effectively. We strive to train people *in* ministry, and not train people *for* ministry. There is a world of difference between those two things because our goal is to leave. Our goal is not to stay there but to be available to God for starting something that gets out of control so that we don't need to be around anymore. Our goal is to establish a good enough foundation of biblical understanding that what we say we believe about the church can be true of them, too—that the local church can actually be autonomous.

We as Baptists have had far too great a tendency to act like we believe in congregational polity in America but like we believe in Episcopal polity across the ocean. Yet the same Holy Spirit that is capable of leading congregations here to the truth through His Word is just as capable of doing that overseas as well. And it is sheer racism on our part to act otherwise. Our goal is to leave. A lot of people talk about it, our goal is to actually do it, and bless the Lord, we already have one situation since we started our work in Central Asia in 1992 in which we've had one team that has redeployed elsewhere because they set a goal within this one particular people group of a church for every thousand within that people group, and they met the goal. They met the goal in the span of about five years. So they are somewhere else. We are not going to stick around to control those people. We prefer to leave Christ as Lord of those churches.

WHAT SHOULD YOU DO?

Pursue reformation of the church.

The first thing I plead with you to do is to pursue reformation of the church. For the sake of the reputation of the gospel overseas and for the sake of the quality of the workers we receive, I plead with you to pursue the reformation of the church. These two are not enemies; missions and reformation are best friends. Unless there is genuine reformation in the church our ability to continue pursuing what God has called us to is going to be severely compromised.

Learn about God's world.

The second thing I encourage you to do is to become a life-long learner about God's world. It is really kind of embarrassing how ignorant Americans are about geography. I meet people in Central Asia that can name all fifty states in America and then they will ask me, "What do most Americans think about _____?" (and they will name their country) and I have to tell them that 99% of all Americans don't have a clue that their country even exists. I encourage you to become a life-long learner about the world. Give the Holy Spirit weapons to use in your mind. I encourage you very strongly to get *Operation World*;[3] you will learn a lot about the world through it. Get a world map, put it up on your wall and start reading newspapers or magazines that actually talk about the world. I would commend *The Economist*, a British publication that has some of the best world news in it. Find out what is out there beyond our shores. Get to know missions. Read, if you haven't, *Let the Nations Be Glad!*[4] Read the new book, *The Church is Bigger Than You Think*.[5] Become a lifelong learner, not just about missionary support, but about missions and the role in which it takes place.

The call of God.

My third encouragement to you, and this is perhaps the most crucial of all addressed primarily to you pastors, is to come to grips with the call of God, and then take the lead in your churches. One of the most difficult things we face when we come back to the States is what we call "pastoral avoidance." The pastor is often the bottleneck that keeps a proper focus on missions from happening in the church. I think this is because pastors really haven't dealt with coming before God and asking why they have been called to obey the Great Commission by not going. It can be dangerous to deal with it. I had a friend who preached a mission sermon and his wife came forward in response, stating that she felt called to missions. He said, "What am I going to say to the congregation." She

3 Patrick Johnstone, *Operation World*.
4 John Piper, *Let the Nations Be Glad: The Supremacy of God in Missions*, (Grand Rapids, MI: Baker Books, 1993).
5 Patrick Johnstone, *The Church Is Bigger Than You Think*, (Great Britain: Christian Focus Publications, 1998).

unsympathetically said, "You're the pastor, you figure it out." They are serving in South Africa now.

HOW DO YOU OBEY THE GREAT COMMISSION?

You need first to come before God and not ask *if* you are called but *how* you are called. Acknowledge before God that you are called to obey the Great Commission, and the Great Commission does not just extend across the street; it extends around the world. Lay yourself open to go anywhere. I was one of those really stupid people that tried to set limits on what God could do with my life. When I accepted my call to the ministry—which is a really stupid way of putting it— when I finally gave into what God knew would happen anyway, I made a deal with God. The deal was, given the fact that I was obviously not the sort who was cut out for oversees service that I would stay in America and be a pastor. I have spent the last seven years in Central Asia. I have discovered is that living in a place where we had no heat in the winter and it was 14 degrees outside, living in a place where the electricity is off more than it is on, living in a place where you could spend all day hunting for something you need to buy, is where I'd much rather be than here. My family and I are mourning the fact that we have to be in the West right now, because that is where the office is. We don't want to be there. We want to be back where we were, home in Central Asia. The reason is clear: there is no greater joy than being on the cutting edge of what God is doing. I've had a far better life than any of you have had for the last seven years, being in one of the hardest places to live in the world. I plead with you not to set limits on what God can call you to do. In fact, I plead with you to say to God, "I'll go to the edge until You tell me that my role in fulfilling Your call to the edge, keeps me here." Until you have done that, you cannot be the kind of leader God is calling you to be within your congregation. Until you have dealt with that and know with certainty that being willing to go anywhere, God has called you to stay here, you cannot lead your congregation to be biblical in its fulfillment of the Great Commission. Settle the issue. Come to grips with the call of God and then, as He leads you, follow. If He leads you to stay, then take the lead in your church in making it a missions-minded and missions-oriented church.

Pray.

The way that you can do this is to transform your church's prayer life. It has been said, and I think that it is true, that in our prayer meetings we spend more time keeping the saints out of heaven than praying sinners into it. Prayer meeting should be one of the most dynamic times of the week, though it's usually not. I encourage you to incorporate prayer for the world in every level of your church life. Make your prayer meetings, not a time when the pastor prays a short prayer and then you really have Bible study, but a time when you get on your knees and do battle in prayer, doing battle for the world. I plead with you to pray for your workers on the field. We sorely need it. Spiritual warfare is real, but spiritual warfare is usually not what people think it is. The enemy doesn't need to do spectacular things since he has so many more effective tools, such as discouragement, dissention and distraction. When you live in a place where it can take eight hours to find light bulbs to buy (and I am not exaggerating) or you have to stand in line for three hours to pay your phone bill (and you have to do this every time you make an international phone call), it is easy just to get distracted by the busyness of life. We need your prayers. I plead with you to pray for your workers—that God would keep us focused and our minds fixed upon the reality of His glory and His sovereignty and not on the circumstances around us. Pray that God would keep us united and keep us pure.

One of the toughest things I have had to face coming into the responsibility I have now is dealing with the reality of sin on the part of missionaries. It has been heartbreaking—that is too mild of a word; it has been shattering. The enemy will do whatever is conveniently at hand to derail the work of God. We had the work in a city that is dearest to my heart nearly destroyed by immorality on the part of one of our workers. Pray for us, please. We desperately need it and so do the nations. You have the theology to pray correctly, to pray the kind of prayers we need; none of these wimpy prayers, "Oh please Lord bring people to the point of neutrality so they can decide for or against." Pray them into heaven! "Lord, change their hearts. Lord, break down barriers. Lord, change governments." I have prayed many times for a political ruler, "Lord, convert him or remove him." Pray powerfully and specifically for the nations that need to know the gospel. If you need material to pray about, give me your address and I'll see to it that you have it. Believe me, I have plenty of stuff that can be prayed about from our part of the world. One of my assignments for my new assistant is actually to put together a subregion wide comprehensive prayer guide. Realize that some of the prayer requests are deliberately vague to protect believers and workers. We can't name specific places or names but God knows the aim of your praying. I would really love to have the churches represented in this room focusing their prayers on our part of the world. Pray.

Give.

Give? Yes, I hadn't talked about it but I have to talk about money. We are the best-supported missionaries in the world and I am very appreciative to you and to all the congregations that support us. The Cooperative Program, the Lottie Moon Christmas Offering, make it possible for us to focus our attention on our task rather than raising support. It is estimated that the average faith missionary spends 40% of his or her time raising or maintaining support. We are free to spend that 40% of our time focusing on the task of bringing the good news of Jesus to the lost. God has been doing good things in our convention and the funding is up, but the needs are up even more. Again, my region more than doubled in the span of two years but our budget did not double. Our budget increased about 30% for a 100% increase in personnel. Given the kind of region we are, we find ourselves with the need to do first-time translations of the Bible, first time dubbings of the *Jesus* film into a new language, first-time broadcasts over the radio into a new language, and we have platform needs. I encourage you to examine what you do with your money and ask how it reflects what you think is important. There is a lot of stuff that we look at and say, "That would be nice, but we can't afford it," and I'm talking about stuff like translating the Bible for the first time or feeding people who are starving to death. I encourage you to give.

Go.

Finally, I encourage you to go. My prayer for this week is that out of the people sitting in this room God will raise up workers who will take the gospel where it has never been heard and I selfishly pray it happens in Central Asia. We pride ourselves as a denomination as having the largest mission board of any, but really it is a pretty pathetic showing, don't you agree? There are over 500 people in this room. There are more people in this room than there are Southern Baptists trying to reach the 1.3 billion in my region of Central and Southern Asia. If you take the number we claim to be Southern Baptist and the number of workers in the International Mission Board, what it boils down to is that it takes 3,000 Southern Baptists to produce one missionary. If you take a more realistic statistic it may drop to only 2,000 Southern Baptists to produce one missionary but that is also one of the worst percentages of any evangelical denomination.

So whom do we need? We need all ages, not just need the young. I live in a part of the world that has a much more biblical perspective on age than does America, for someone with white hair will be shown respect and listened to in a way that a kid like me will not. We need people who are willing to say that there is no such thing as retirement, that it's just an opportunity to devote full-time to taking the gospel to where it's never been heard. We need all professions. We can use preachers though we have to train them harder. We also need people with good secular skills that have been discipled well in their local church and are well equipped to share the gospel. But the key thing above everything else is that we need people who are humble and contrite of heart, who tremble at His Word. I'll take someone who's humble and teachable over someone who's talented, any day of the week. We need folks who are willing to say, "The gospel is worth more than my life," who are willing to say, "I will be obscure for the rest of my life if that's what it takes," who are willing to say, "I'll be inconvenienced for the rest of my life if that's what it takes, because the incredible joy of the gospel makes all the rest of that stuff look petty and pale and insignificant."

I plead with you, pursue reformation in your churches. Become a lifelong learner about God's world. Come to grips with God's call and take the lead in your church. Transform your church's prayer life. Give to the work of missions, and most of all, I plead with you to come. I am standing here, asking you to come over and help us. I pray that by the power of the Spirit, God will call some of you to do just that.

19.
REFORMATION AND MISSIONS
THOMAS K. ASCOL
1999 Southern Baptist Founders Conference

ROMANS 2:17-24

IN the latter part of the nineteenth century, an English Baptist pastor wrote a pamphlet in which he surveyed the state of Christianity in various countries. Although Europe was the obvious stronghold of the Christian faith at that time, this pastor said it was a "melancholy fact that the vices of Europeans have been communicated wherever they themselves have been; so that the religious state of even heathens has been rendered worse by intercourse with them" (page 64). He went on to observe in his pamphlet:

> Of those who bear the Christian name, a very great degree of ignorance and immorality abounds amongst them. There are Christians, so called, of the Greek and Armenian churches in all the Mahometan [i.e., Muslim] countries; but they are, if possible, more ignorant and vicious than the Mahometans themselves. The Georgian Christians, who are near the Caspian Sea, maintain themselves by selling their neighbors, relations, and children, for slaves to the Turks and Persians.... It is well known that most of the members of the Greek church are very ignorant. Papists also are in general ignorance of divine things and very vicious. Nor do the bulk of the church of England much exceed them, either in knowledge or holiness; and many errors, and

much looseness of conduct, are to be found among dissenters of all denominations. The Lutherans of Denmark, are much on par with the ecclesiastics in England; and the face of most Christian countries presents a dreadful scene of ignorance, hypocrisy, and profligacy. Various baneful, and pernicious errors appear to gain ground, in almost every part of Christendom; the truths of the gospel, and even the gospel itself, are attacked, and every method that the enemy can invent is employed to undermine the kingdom of our Lord Jesus Christ (pages 64-65).

This writer viewed the Christianity of his day as weak and ineffective. In fact, it was worse than ineffective because it worked at counter-purposes with the cause of Christ. In countries that were known as Christian the gospel had been forgotten and even attacked in the name of Christianity itself. Ignorance and immorality were rampant among those who called themselves followers of Christ. In their efforts to evangelize, Christians often left the unconverted people in a worse condition than they knew.

Who was this voice crying in the wilderness? Why was he so pessimistic? On what grounds was he compelled to put his thoughts in print?

The words belong to William Carey, and they come from the third chapter of his epic-making book published in 1792, entitled, *An Enquiry into the Obligation of Christians to Use Means for the Conversion of the Heathen.* That book has been called the "charter of the Protestant missionary movement" and Carey wrote it to motivate the Christians of his day to preach the gospel to all nations.

What Carey observed was a bleak spiritual picture—not only among the unevangelized nations of the world, but also in those lands with a long and significant Christian witness. Churches were weak. Christians were untaught and unholy. The truths of the gospel were being undermined by the very churches that professed to know and preach the gospel. Listen to the conclusion that Carey drew after assessing this distressing condition in his day:

> All these things are loud calls to Christians, and especially to ministers, to exert themselves to the utmost in their several spheres of action, and to try to enlarge them as much as possible.

Superficiality, ignorance, and immorality among the people of God, Carey says, are loud calls to Christians, especially to pastors, to exert themselves to the utmost in their churches and beyond. But for what purpose? To what end were they to give exertion? Carey knew the answer: For the reclamation of the gospel and the expansion of its work.

What William Carey recognized is something we need to see clearly in our day. The recovery of the gospel is reformation! The expansion of its work is missions! There is no incompatibility between the work of reformation at home and the work of missions abroad. In fact, there is a vital connection between the two. *Passion for missions demands a commitment to reformation.*

How much the gospel makes an impact abroad depends significantly upon the health of churches at home. Churches need to exemplify that which they would commend to others. This principle is established both positively and negatively throughout the Bible, especially in the New Testament.

In the positive sense, Jesus taught us that, as His followers, we are the light of the world. Collectively we are to regard ourselves as a city which is set upon a hill that cannot be hidden. Our light is to give light to the nations.

That certainly happened in the first century. A church was planted in Ephesus. We read in the book of Acts how Ephesus became a strategic foothold for the gospel through the work of that church. Through its members the message rapidly spread throughout all Asia (Acts 19). Also the church planted in Thessalonica was commended by Paul because of its spiritual health and vitality which spilled over into other regions of that land. He wrote in 1 Thessalonians 1:8-10:

> For from you the word of the Lord has sounded forth, not only in Macedonia and Achaia, but also in every place. Your faith toward God has gone out, so that we do not need to say anything. For they themselves declare concerning us what manner of entry we had to you, and how you turned to God from idols to serve the living and true God, and to wait for His Son from heaven, whom He raised from the dead, even Jesus who delivers us from the wrath to come.

This church, which Paul earlier had characterized as being filled with faith, hope, and love, sounded forth the gospel, by their reputation of how they lived and by their actions. Their living of the Word became the foundation of their proclamation of the Word throughout the world. The Thessalonian church was a healthy church and it had a broad impact. Its members followed a key principle: When spiritual vitality characterizes the home base, the gospel witness which goes out is strengthened.

But this principle also works in the other direction. Where there is a lack of spiritual health at home there will be a hindrance to the work of the gospel abroad. It is this negative aspect of the principle that I want to call to our attention by specifically looking to Paul's letter to the church at Rome.

> Indeed you are called a Jew, and rest on the law, and make your boast in God and know His will, and approve the things that are excellent, being instructed out of the law, and are confident that you yourself are a guide to the blind, a light to those who are in darkness, an instructor of the foolish, a teacher of babes, having the form of knowledge and truth in the law. You, therefore, who teach another, do you not teach yourself?

You who preach that a man should not steal, do you steal? You say, 'Do not commit adultery,' do you commit adultery? You who abhor idols, do you rob temples? You who make your boast in the law, do you dishonor God through breaking the law? For 'the name of God is blasphemed among the Gentiles because of you,' as it is written (Romans 2:17-24).

Verses 17 through 20 could be constructed as rhetorical questions, or, as the New King James Version seems to suggest, they could be statements—not completely accusatory ones, but somewhat critical in tone. Either way, the point is the same. Paul writes these words in the midst of building an argument for the doctrine of justification by faith alone. He is showing both Jews and Gentiles that they are all sinners before God, condemned by God's law, and in need of a salvation that comes only through grace and that will bring them into a right relationship with Jesus Christ, God's Son. Paul's argument in verses 17-24 demonstrates in a negative way the relationship between the advance of God's kingdom abroad and the spiritual health of God's people at home. Paul takes the Jews to task for failing to live up to the responsibilities and privileges which had been afforded them.

In verses 17-20 we see the great privileges of divine blessing that are set forth by the Apostle (albeit in an edgy way), but they are genuine privileges of God's blessing. We see first of all, in the first part of verse 17, that they are the people who bear the name of God. They have the distinction of being known as God's people, the Jews. This was a self-designation which, in the Jewish mind, encapsulated all of the prerogatives and all of the privileges which went with being God's chosen people.

Paul went on to speak of them "resting on the law." They took comfort in having God's law. They derived a sense of security from the fact that they were the ones to whom the law had been given. After all, doesn't Psalm 147 say that God "declares His Word to Jacob, His statutes and His judgments to Israel. He has not dealt thus with any other nation."

Paul then reminded them that they regarded their relationship with God as so wonderful that it was something to "boast about" at the very end of verse 17. I like the way the New International Version renders it "you brag about your relationship with God," as if they thought they themselves were responsible for it.

In verse 18, he showed how they claimed to have divine insight and knowledge which others did not have, thus making them rather self-assured regarding their calling in the world to be guides to the spiritually blind; light to those in spiritual darkness; teachers of the spiritually foolish and immature.

In other words, Paul described the Jews of his day in language which they themselves would have used, but there is what one writer calls a "latent irony" in the way that Paul addressed them. The Jews were indeed, called to be God's people. As such they were certainly blessed with many spiritual blessings. They enjoyed a special relationship with God. They had God's law. They possessed the covenant. To them the promises had been entrusted. They had a mission to the rest of the world. It was to the Jews that God gave the commandment to "proclaim the good news of His salvation from day to day, to declare His glory among the nations, His wonders among all people." They were the ones that were to "say to the nations, 'The Lord reigns'" (Psalm 96).

The Jews acknowledged all this, at least to some degree. In fact, the way that Paul addressed them in verses 17-20 suggests that they had a measure of pride and self-importance about this responsibility. They knew the true God. They possessed the only law of God. They were able to discern God's will, so naturally it rested upon them to be the teachers, the instructors, of others.

But what Paul said to the Jews in verses 17-20 was designed to set them up for the scathing indictment that followed. Beginning in verse 21 he laid out the devastating consequences of their spiritual hypocrisy. In verses 21-23 he exposed that hypocrisy by turning to a more accusatory tone and quizzing the Jews about their spiritual and moral conduct. It is as if he was saying to them in these verses, "You who have been so favored of God and who are so self-consciously in the position of being the stewards of His Word, declaring His Word to the world, how do you measure up to the things that you teach? Do you practice what you preach to others?"

In verses 21 and 22 he said, "You therefore, who teach another, do you teach yourself? You who preach the demands about stealing, do you steal? You who say you do not commit adultery, do you commit adultery? You who abhor idols, do you rob temples?"

The Apostle Paul used these four rhetorical questions to expose the specific hypocrisy among the Jews of his day. There is clear evidence that each one of these sins was being committed. He shows the inconsistency between that which they understood about themselves and proclaimed to others, and the reality of how they conducted themselves.

Then in verse 23 he turned to a sweeping accusation that categorically condemned the hypocrisy he had exposed in the immediately prior verses—that the Jews boasted of their possession and commitment to the law of God. They prided themselves in their unhesitating affirmation of the law being the very Word of God. They didn't wince at affirming the full authority of the Word of God. No doubt they would have affirmed its inerrancy and infallibility. They conscientiously embraced their own responsibility to make this Word known to the nations. Yet Paul castigated them in verse 23, "You who make your boast in the law, do you dishonor God through breaking the law?" The very God whose law they extolled with their lips was dishonored by their lives.

They were scrupulous in their devotion to His Word, zealous in their efforts to spread the Word of God to others, but grievously neglectful of applying that Word to themselves. In this instance Paul is following in the footsteps of the Old Testament prophet Nathan who stood before a slumbering, spiritually sick King David and said, "You are the man." That which you would do to others and have others do to you, you yourself are unwilling to do. The Jews, entrusted with God's Word, called to spread that Word, were living in ongoing disobedience to the Word.

Finally, in verse 24 Paul came to the conclusion of the point and described the consequences of their hypocrisy as devastating. "The name of God is blasphemed among the Gentiles because of you. You who boast of God, who take pride in your favored position as the people of God, who affirm the Word of God entrusted to you, do you not see that the *ethnesin*—the nations—blaspheme the name of your God because of the way you conduct yourselves!" In this verse Paul alludes to Isaiah 52:5, and also several passages in Ezekiel where God accused His Old Testament people of conducting themselves in a way that brought reproach upon His name that He had placed upon His people. The Jews were responsible for leading the nations to blaspheme God. The nations of the world were judging God on the basis of what they saw in the Jews. You can't blame them. The Jews claimed to be God's own people, the very children of God, the representatives of God, on the earth. They were His messengers and His family. The Gentiles judged God by their conduct and no doubt must have reasoned that if the family members, the children, are like this, the head of the family must also be like this. They tell us not to steal. They say we must not commit adultery. Yet they rob our temples and steal themselves and commit adultery. The God they worship must not be much of a God. They tell us that we must look to this law that they profess to honor, yet look at the consequences of this law in their own lives. There must not be much in this law that God has given to them.

John Murray comments on this verse: "The tragic irony is apparent. The Jews who claimed to be the leaders of the nation for the worship of the true God had become the instruments of provoking the nations to blasphemy." That wasn't their intention. Indeed, I think it's not too much to conclude that their intention was the exact opposite. They wanted, worked for, and desired to have the nations come to know their God. They even went to some effort to convert the Gentiles. They accepted the responsibility to be the stewards of God's Word, the instructors of it, even missionaries, to go out and make it known. Yet the work of spreading God's Word abroad was seriously hindered. Paul even suggests that it was overturned by the neglecting of spiritual lives at home. Instead of the nations being soundly converted, they were provoked into blasphemous thoughts of God.

Paul doesn't speak against their zeal. In later chapters he commends their zeal, but zeal to declare God's Word is never enough. Zeal must be based upon knowledge, truth, and a proper understanding of that Word. It must be matched with an ongoing application of that Word to our own lives.

Doesn't Jesus make the same point when He castigates the scribes and Pharisees in Matthew 23? He says, "Woe to you, scribes and Pharisees, hypocrites! For you travel land and sea to win one proselyte, and when he is won, you make him twice as much a son of hell as yourselves." It is an immeasurable tragedy when our evangelistic and missionary efforts leave the very people that we go to in a spiritually worse condition than we found them! That's precisely what happened in Jesus' day. It's what happened in Paul's day. It happened in William Carey's day. Brothers and sisters, it's happening in our day! The name of God is being blasphemed today among the nations because of the Christian church in America. Our great God of wonders, our Lord Jesus Christ, who bled for us, who came and revealed God's incredible love and grace for rebels, is being blasphemed among the nations.

A few years ago a missionary who works with Muslims told me about a conversation he had with an Afghani Mullah. When the Mullah discovered that the missionary was a Christian pastor, he asked him this question, "Is it true that you can have as many women as you want—like other Christians?" This Muslim leader's vision of moral decadence in "Christian America" and his awareness of immorality by

American ministers (who expressed sorrow only after they were caught) led him to believe that this Christian pastor must be able to be as immoral as he would want and with as many women as he would want.

If Christians are like a city set upon a hill, could it be that we who are part of the church of Jesus Christ in America should see ourselves as the highest peak in the range of modern nations? Whether we like it or not, we are highly visible to the world. A large percentage of the rest of the world, for good and for evil, judges Christianity and the Christian God by what it sees in America. Who is responsible for the moral degradation in America? We can all say "Amen" to criticism of the education system and how rotten it has become. We can all decry the politics of our land and how degenerate it is. But at least a very large, significant portion of the responsibility must be laid at the feet of the churches in America. We decry the immorality in our society, yet we wink at the same immorality within our churches. We declaim the loss of truth in our world, yet we do not guard the truth that has been entrusted to us in our churches.

If this is true, that the church in America bears incredible responsibility to the rest of the world because in God's providence we have a high profile before that world, then our concern for the work of the gospel among the nations must make us concerned for the reformation of the gospel here in America.

In a book entitled *The Call of the South* written in 1920 on the work of the gospel in the southern portion of the United States, the author, Victor Masters, records an incident that I find chilling. He says that in the year 1900 the Mikado, emperor of Japan, publicly stated his willingness to issue a decree which would make Christianity the state religion of his kingdom. He observed the work of Christian missionaries and he told his council that in observing the missionaries he had seen that their religion had been more helpful than any of the other religions that were being propagated in Japan. Some of his councilors suggested that before the decree was issued a deputation should be sent to the United States and Great Britain to measure how Christianity worked itself out within the borders of these sending countries. So the deputation traveled to Canada, the United States and Great Britain. They made notes of observations in the courts of law where they found justice often defeated. They noted that in the markets of trade and industry often reputed Christians were destroying each other in competitive business. They said they noticed something of a stench in American municipal government. They returned to Japan and wrote this report, "That while it may be true that the lives of the Christian missionaries among us is the purest of any of the advocates of religion in Japan, and the principles of Christianity taught by them are right and most helpful to our citizens, the people of the United States and Great Britain do not believe and practice the doctrines taught us by their Christian missionaries." Victor Masters, who recorded this incident, says, "Their deliberate refusal to adopt Christianity, after inspecting American and English life, is a severe arraignment on the effectiveness of our Christian teachings in our own land" (Victor I. Masters, *The Call of the South*, pages 213-214).

What if there had been more vital godliness in America and Great Britain at the turn of the century? While the Mikado's decree would not have made Japan a Christian nation, it would have opened up doors of opportunity for thousands of Christian teachers and missionaries to go in and to influence millions of Japanese.

John Stott has said, "No church can spread the gospel with any degree of integrity, let alone credibility, unless it has been visibly changed by the gospel it preaches. We need to look like what we are talking about. It is not enough to receive the gospel and pass it on; we must embody it in our common life of faith, love, joy, peace, righteousness and hope" (John Stott, *The Gospel and the End of Time,* page 44).

Brothers and sisters, do our churches look like what we are preaching about? Does the state of our own congregations commend the message of God's grace and love? Can we honestly stand before the world and declare the holiness of our God in light of the character in our own lives?

How can we expect the world to believe that our trinitarian God is Himself love when we can't even get along with one another? How can we call upon people to believe that God is holy if we are not holy? What makes us think that we can convince people that the God we know in Jesus Christ is blessed forever if our lives are not marked by genuine joy? Why should anyone believe that our Lord spiritually and morally transforms people if we who make that claim are no different from the world?

What must we do? Should we cool our hearts for the work of missions around the world and turn all of our efforts to the work of reformation at home? No! Never! What we must do is increase our passion to see the gospel carried to all peoples of the earth, and out of that passion—as an integral part of that passion—we must fully embrace the call of reformation here at home! Passion for missions demands a commitment to reformation.

There are many areas of reformation that are desperately needed among American evangelicals in general and Southern Baptist churches in particular. Much could be said about the sufficiency of Scripture; worship; or the doctrine of the church, its polity, its practices, its order and discipline. All of these and many others are worthy subjects for us to zero in on to refine our thoughts about the need of reformation, but in the interest of time and order of priority, let me limit myself to simply one area.

Where do we desperately need a reformation as evangelicals in America and as Southern Baptists? We need it in our understanding of conversion; what it means to be a Christian; how one becomes a Christian. We can no longer assume that all evangelicals agree on what it means to be a disciple of Jesus Christ or how a person becomes one. The Scripture is not ambiguous on this point. The Scripture says, "If any man is in Christ, he is a new creation, the old is passed away, all things become new" (2 Corinthians 5:17). John says, "Now by this we know that we know Him, if we keep His commandments. He who says, 'I know Him,' and does not keep His commandments, is a liar, and the truth is not in him" (1 John 2:4). Jesus said, "If you love Me, you will keep My commandments" (John 14:15).

We might have various nuances and differences of opinion in precisely what conversion means, but can we not all agree that being a Christian means something? Is there a difference between one who is a child of God and one who is simply of the world? It is a significant event when a person becomes a disciple of Christ. There is a difference between a converted man or woman and an unconverted person. They have different loves. They have different orientations of life. They have different objects of devotion. The notion that a person can be genuinely converted and yet have no discernible difference in inner or outer life has no biblical warrant. Yet there are countless millions of people on the rolls of our Baptist churches who have no discernible difference in their lives from the world. They are counted as converted though they don't have enough spiritual impulse to even show up among the people of God in worship once a year. Our understanding of what it means to be a Christian needs to be biblically reformed. We need a reformation of how a person becomes a Christian.

Related to that is our practice of evangelism. Walking an aisle, raising a hand, praying a prayer, taking a dip in a baptistry, does not effect conversion. We need to rediscover the doctrine of the new birth and look again to the Word of God to see what is meant by repentance and faith. If we are wrong regarding what it means to be right with God, and what is required for a person to get right with God, then we are poised not only to propagate spiritual confusion and disease at home, but also abroad as we send out confused people from our churches. And indeed, it is happening now.

Three years ago a well-known American Baptist preacher traveled to one of Russia's larger cities and conducted a two-week long crusade. He came home reporting that two thousand people had been converted at his campaign. Two people, a husband and a wife, who heard the reports were so overwhelmed with a sense of what God had done in this city that they took leave of absence from their jobs, got contact information for these two thousand converts, and traveled there intending to spend several months in the city following up with these converts and helping them get organized into churches. They were devastated by what they found, or rather, what they did not find. After weeks of searching, they could not locate even one of the supposed converts.

Five years ago a summer-long evangelistic emphasis in Albania was sponsored by American evangelical organizations. It was recorded back in the United States that 2,300 converts were made. The missionaries whose job it was to follow up on those converts in the northern region of Albania said that they could find only six people of the hundreds whose names they had been given who had even a slight interest in spiritual things. They heard of only a few more from the southern region of the country.

When severe doctrinal error regarding conversion is wedded to practical zeal in evangelistic and missionary emphasis the results are disastrous. Isn't this precisely the folly of the scribes and Pharisees? With zeal they traveled over their land and over their seas to make converts, yet Jesus said that when they did make a convert, they made him twice the child of hell as they themselves were. Why? Weren't the Pharisees sincere? Weren't they devoted to the cause. Absolutely! But at the same time they were dangerously wrong about the crucial issue of what makes a person right with God and how a person gets that way.

Recently the North American Mission Board's "specialist in evangelistic follow-up" stated that, based upon his observations, less than 1 in 10 people who make decisions as a result of Southern Baptist evangelism are active in Bible study one year later. He cited this observation as a part of his argument that we need to do a better job at "follow up." I appreciate his concern. I genuinely do. But might it be possible that follow up is not the issue but that we need to do a better job at evangelism?

If General Motors discovered that ninety percent of all of their automobiles that were manufactured weren't running a year later, what do you think they would do? Would they claim we must build better repair shops? Let us increase production so that we have more automobiles this year than we had last year? Let's open up plants in Africa and South America and China? Now all of these efforts are okay in their place, but none of them can justify ignoring the fundamental problem of needing to retool the manufacturing plant. Call out the engineers! Re-examine the schematics. Something's gone wrong. If we genuinely want to expand overseas, if we are genuinely concerned to see that productions increase, then we must retool at home.

In 1792, William Carey preached his deathless sermon before a group of pastors as he called upon them to move forward in the missionary work. He said, "Expect great things and attempt great things." His text for that sermon was Isaiah 54:2-3. In that passage God says to His people:

> Enlarge the place of your tent, And let them stretch out the curtains of your dwellings; Do not spare; Lengthen your cords, And strengthen your stakes. For you shall expand to the right and to the left, And your descendants will inherit the nations, And make the desolate cities inhabited.

Lengthen your cords *and* strengthen your stakes! Expand *and* deepen. Missions *and* reformation. Both are essential and neglect of either will result in unbalanced, unhealthy Christianity.

Some people charge us with the accusation that our concern for reformation is merely academic. You've heard the charges: "All these guys who like to engage in theological debate just like we did in seminary around the tables. They're just concerned in seeing if they can figure out precisely all the knotty, weighty theological questions that have plagued mankind throughout history. It's merely theological debate." They say that these kinds of discussions can be a distraction from the more important work of missions and evangelism. This kind of accusation betrays a false dichotomy. God Himself has joined together missions and reformation. What God has joined together, let no man put asunder. Passion for missions and commitment to reformation are not competing interests. Genuine passion for missions demands commitment to reformation.

In the last century Austin Phelps of Andover Seminary said, "If I were a missionary in Canton, China, my first prayer every morning would be for the success of American Home Missions, for the sake of Canton, China" (*Call of the South*, p. 217).

Reformation and missions go hand-in-hand. If we do not strengthen our churches at home, we will ultimately undermine the efforts of the gospel abroad. Do not shrink back from the hard work of reformation. Do not let others around you ignore its importance. Don't let anyone intimidate you into thinking that if you are concerned to order your life and see churches ordered by the Word of God, that somehow undermines the evangelistic missionary impulse that the gospel is to have in the world. Don't be so selfish with your time, Pastors. There are other pastors who need to think about the things you're thinking about. If you simply order your own life and your own church and you're not winsomely trying to come along your brother pastors to challenge them and encourage them to start thinking about these things, then you are not engaged enough in the work of reformation.

We must commit ourselves to a reordering of our personal lives by God's Word. Encourage this reordering in your church and in other churches among other brothers and sisters of the faith. We must work for reformation.

Can you imagine the accusation that God will make against those Jews on that great Day of Judgment, "My Name was blasphemed among the nations because of you"? The Name we love, the Name that God Himself is jealous of—it is for the sake of the Name that we send out our loved ones to the outer edges to live and die for Christ. It is for the sake of the Name that we have given our energies and our efforts to make Christ known. What a tragedy, what a travesty, it would be if it is said of us that because of our unwillingness to do the hard work of reformation, the nations blasphemed the Name of God.

Work for reformation. Do it for your own soul's sake. Do it for your children's sake. Do it for your children's children's sake. Do it for the people of China and South America and Africa and Asia, all of the peoples of the world. But do it first and foremost for the honor and glory of our God and of His Son Jesus Christ who bled for us to redeem us to God. It is His glory which unifies the great works of reformation and missions.

Lengthen your cords as never before! Go and call upon others to go. Send your best overseas. But don't forget to strengthen your stakes—that through you the name of God might be revered and not blasphemed among the nations.

PASTORAL/ECCLESIOLOGICAL

20.

THE VALUE OF *PILGRIM'S PROGRESS* IN PREACHING THE DOCTRINES OF GRACE

JIM GABLES

1983 Southern Baptist Founders Conference

WHEN I set out to preach through the book of *Pilgrim's Progress* on Sunday evenings, I had no idea it would take me two years and three months to complete it, but the Lord enabled us to persevere, and we are grateful for the fruit it produced. I want to get immediately into the subject today: "The Use or Value of *Pilgrim's Progress* in Preaching the Doctrines of Grace." Someone asked how I was going to condense seventy-two messages into one hour. I answered that I would approach it by using a three-point outline—I think that is the only way a good Southern Baptist can do it. If you do not have a three-point outline you have not been taught how to preach. My outline is:

1) The grace of God in Bunyan's life.
2) The grace of God in *Pilgrim's Progress*.
3) The grace of God in the minister of grace.

THE GRACE OF GOD IN BUNYAN'S LIFE

If I could pick one verse of Scripture from the Bible to commemorate the life and influence of John Bunyan today, I would choose Revelation 14:12-13:

> Here is the patience of the saints: here are they
> that keep the commandments of God, and the

faith of Jesus. And I heard a voice from heaven saying unto me, Write, Blessed are the dead which die in the Lord from henceforth: Yea, saith the Spirit, that they may rest from their labors; and their works do follow them.

Today, John Bunyan is resting from his labors, however, his works continue to follow him with great influence.

Bunyan was born in the year 1628 near Bedford, England into an extremely poor family, lacking many of the financial comforts of this world. He lived during a time of severe religious persecution by the established Church of England, which targeted anyone who dared to presume to preach without being licensed to do so by the Church of England.

This was the period known as the Puritan Era. Some individuals within the Church of England referred to as Puritans were attempting to restore the church to its original position as reflected in its Confession of Faith. Others believed that this could not be accomplished and left the Church of England while others were ousted from their pulpits. These men became known as Nonconformists or Separatists. The great issue of that day was the restoration of a dead church to its former first love. According to the letters to the seven churches in the Book of Revelation, departure was already beginning to manifest itself in the early New Testament age. Nevertheless God raised up some individuals to go back into the place where Satan's headquarters were and where Jezebel dwelt, and He gave them patience to call the people back to their first love. This was being attempted in the Church of England in the days of Bunyan as well. It was a time of confusion, and as far as Bunyan was concerned many churches were dead.

Fairly early in Bunyan's marriage he and his wife became the parents of four small children. Then the providence of God decreed for his wife to depart this earthly scene, leaving him alone to raise the four children, including a blind daughter named Mary. His first wife was taken from him when he seemingly needed her the most. He later remarried.

Bunyan was first imprisoned for preaching without a license in the year 1660 when he was thirty-two years old. His imprisonment would cover a span of twelve years. This means that at a time when his public ministry should have had most usefulness, he was taken out of the public eye and placed within the confines of a jail.

It was in this season that God's grace manifested itself in the writing of *Pilgrim's Progress.* In the darkest hour when from an earthly and human standpoint it seemed likely that Bunyan's life would go unnoticed, he developed the masterpiece known as *Pilgrim's Progress.*

God's greatest works of grace frequently come out of the most unlikely set of circumstances. You cannot bind the gospel. You cannot put it in prison. The Apostle Paul said he was bound but the gospel he preached was not bound. Truth crushed to the earth shall rise again. You may put it in prison but it will manifest its head again because God is still on the throne. God can open the doors of the prison gate like he did for Peter, and God can open the doors for the gospel and even bring it out of the cell. In fact, the most unlikely set of circumstances for producing success that could ever be seen is revealed in the cross of Jesus Christ. It appeared that the death of Jesus was the most unlikely way for God to bring victory over sin. Yet Jesus said, "You destroy this body and in three days I will raise it up again" (John 2:19). Out of the most unlikely set of circumstances, when sin was running rampant and by wicked hands men crucified the Lord of glory, God raised up and established the throne of His goodness upon the cross of Jesus Christ. May this be an encouragement to anyone laboring today under a difficult set of church circumstances. You may be ousted as was Bunyan. You may be poor as far as finances are concerned. You may have family problems. You may have denominational problems. You may have all sorts of grief and pain, but out of the most unlikely set of circumstances God is able to reach down and produce a work of grace in you that will glorify His Son, the Lord Jesus Christ. He did this in the life of John Bunyan. The most unlikely situation for a book to be written was in a prison cell. But you can't imprison the truth of God.

Let me also add—for any laboring under some pressing circumstances today—that God has the ability to replace your natural losses with added measures of grace to compensate for them. Bunyan was denied the natural comforts of this life but, at the same time, he was given insights into the character of God and the nature of man which I dare say have not been given to any of us here today. When God decrees to removes natural earthly comforts from us, He compensates for it with insights into the person and work of Jesus Christ. The next time you find yourself going down, and your outward man is perishing, remember that God will be faithful to renew the inner man, and He will give you insights which will enable you to speak forth out of the prison depths of your soul the eternal riches of Jesus Christ.

THE GRACE OF GOD IN PILGRIM'S PROGRESS

Now I want to touch upon the grace of God in *Pilgrim's Progress* itself. *Pilgrim's Progress* is an allegory that sets forth in poetic and pictorial form the Christian experience from conversion in Christ until his arrival into his eternal state, which Bunyan calls the Celestial City. Thus it is a pilgrimage between two worlds, this world and the world to come. *Pilgrim's Progress* reveals the true Christian experience as opposed to nominal Christianity. Bunyan had observed nominal Christianity all around him, but when he was removed from nominal Christianity in prison, he was exposed and shut up unto the Christianity expressed in the Bible. In this way, God revealed insights to him in that prison cell which enabled him to express for the layman's benefit—not just for preachers— the unsearchable riches of Christ concerning God's grace working in the practical experience of a Christian.

Someone asked me one time, "Brother Gables, what influenced you to deliver the series on *Pilgrim's Progress* in your church?" I responded that my church was in a reforming situation. I had preached the doctrines of grace and kept encountering the objector who said, "Well, I don't like doctrine. I don't care for doctrine. All you ever preach is doctrine." That is not a legitimate complaint because doctrine separated from life is a dangerous thing. But I didn't want it to be a "red herring" either. In answering this objection from some members of my own congregation, I said, "All right, if you don't care for doctrine then we will deal with experience. Come on Sunday night and we'll go through a book and look at the experience of a Christian." It did not surprise me that the same people who objected to the doctrines of grace objected to the experience of grace. One woman said it was too depressing. She never made it past the Slough of Despond. Do not let it be a "red herring" if you encounter a similar sentiment. If you preach the experience of a Christian in the Bible, the same objector will not care for that either. That is how we were led to introduce this series. At the same time on Sunday mornings we studied the whole counsel of God, the existence and attributes of God. On Sunday night we opened up the book of *Pilgrim's Progress* in a very informal fashion, and God was pleased to bless it in this way.

To understand the book itself, three things are necessary. First, you must understand the language of the Bible. You've got to speak the language of Zion. The reason why people in the pews today cannot understand the preaching of the Scriptures is that they are strangers to the language of Zion. They are exposed to bits and pieces, but they really do not understand the Scriptures. They may say they love the Bible, but they do not know how to express themselves in the language of the Bible. Therefore, it is essential that the Bible be understood in order to understand *Pilgrim's Progress*.

Second, you must possess a true experience of God's grace to understand *Pilgrim's Progress*. You'll fall off very quickly if you are a stranger to the grace of God. The book will leave you in confusion and you will not understand it. You must not only know the Bible but you must have personally experienced a work of saving grace to appreciate and understand it.

Third, you must understand Bunyan's personal theology. I am asked occasionally by individuals, "Can you give us some reference material? Where did you get all your material to help you to understand *Pilgrim's Progress?*" I have given it to you. My understanding of *Pilgrim's Progress* comes from the Scriptures, from my own personal experience in grace and from reading Bunyan's own personal theology.

I will never forget the time when I was in a Bible college and two hundred preachers had to take an English course. The English professor said we were going to study *Pilgrim's Progress* that semester, and it was an event to remember. After the end of the first semester, not a one of the two hundred preachers could understand what was going on in *Pilgrim's Progress.* It became so confusing that finally the teacher said, "Let's just drop this and get on to better things." They could not understand what was taking place in the writing of the book because they were unacquainted with the theology upon which it was based. We debated all kinds of questions: "When did Christian get saved? Did he get saved at the Straight Gate? Did he get saved at the cross? Did he lose his salvation on the Hill Difficulty? What in the world was going on? Who in the world was this man Bunyan?" They could not understand the theology. Therefore, they could not understand the book.

Pilgrim's Progress has been translated into one hundred ninety-eight languages and dialects and it is second only to the Bible in sales. But the primary reason why I believe God gave this book its great success is the practical reality of the characters and the events of the book. Beloved, you will find yourself somewhere in *Pilgrim's Progress.* Bunyan didn't deal with abstract people. He dealt with people with whom you relate every day. They are there, not only outside of you but also within you. They are running through your blood. They are real people, and Bunyan made them real because he understood that certain characteristics are fundamental to all human nature. Mark Twain, a native of my state of Missouri and a world traveler, made this statement: "I have never met a person anywhere in the world that I have not already met here in Hannibal, Missouri." From all indications Twain was not a Christian but he understood that human nature consists of some basic, fundamental characteristics.

Some young preachers who are here today are getting itchy feet and are at that stage where, in our Southern Baptist Convention, it is time for a pastoral change (every two or three years). They begin to get the idea that there must be a more fruitful field and better people somewhere else. They mistakenly think that when they find that, they will really be blessed and used of God. The truth of the matter is, the same human nature you find in your parish is the same over the hill in the next fellow's parish. If you go to Africa or Australia, wherever you go, you will find the same human nature, for we all came from Adam. It is your job to learn human nature and to know how to relate the Scriptures to the personalities you encounter. Rather than think you are going to find a better field somewhere else, you should consider that possibly God has put you in the prison cell of your present field to expose you to the Bible and to John Bunyan's *Pilgrim's Progress* to enable you to become a master in human nature and to know the people in your congregation. Maybe He is teaching you how to use the Scriptures to find them out and bring them to the light of the gospel where they will either be repelled and leave like Pliable and Obstinate, or they will lay hold with Faithful and Hopeful and make their way into the Celestial City. It is your job to become a master of human nature and learn it.

I discredit no educational process and I do not discredit at all the learning of behavioral sciences in books and colleges today. I believe, however, that you will become a master at understanding human nature by dedicating yourself to understand *Pilgrim's Progress* as well, because Bunyan himself had that understanding. It was the great John Owen who said that he would trade all of his learning for the ability to move people's hearts like Bunyan could. Study that book and become a master in human nature and the different characters that make up human nature.

THE GRACE OF GOD IN THE MINISTER OF GRACE

Now let's look at the grace of God in the minister of grace. Let us consider how to take advantage of the book *Pilgrim's Progress* in preaching the doctrines of grace. We are going to make it applicable and to describe the marks of a true gospel preacher in whom the grace of God has been made real.

I want to read to you from the section in the book that begins in the Interpreter's House. After Christian has been converted and is introduced to the Interpreter, who represents the teaching ministry of the Holy Spirit, he is led into a large house that has several different rooms. In the first room he sees a picture on the wall. I begin reading with this portion of the book:

> "Sir," said Christian, "I am a man that am come from the City of Destruction and am going to the Mount Zion and I was told by the man that stands at the gate at the head of this way that if I called here you would show me excellent things such as would be helpful to me on my journey." Then said the Interpreter, "Come in. I will show thee that which will be profitable to thee." So he commanded his man to light the candle and bid Christian follow him. So he led him into a private room and bid his man open a door the which, when he had done, Christian saw a picture of a very grave person hanging up against the wall. This was the fashion of it: he had eyes lifted up to heaven, the best of books in his hand, the law of truth was written upon his lips, the world was behind his back, he stood as if he pleaded with men and the crown of gold did hang over his head.
>
> Then said Christian, "What meaneth this?" The Interpreter said, "The man whose picture this is, is one of a thousand. He can beget children, travail in birth with children, and nurse

them when they are born. Whereas thou seest him with his eyes lifted up to heaven, the best of books in his hand, and the law of truth writ on his lips, it is to show thee that his work is to know and unfold dark things to sinners. Even as also thou seest him stand as if he pleaded with men, and whereas thou seest the world is cast behind him and a crown hangs over his head, that is to show thee that slighting and despising the things that are present for the love that he hath to his master's service, he is sure in the world that comes next to have glory for his reward. "Now," said the Interpreter, "I have showed thee this picture first because the man whose picture this is, is the only man whom the Lord of the place whither thou art going hath authorized to be thy guide in all difficult places thou mayest meet with in the way. Wherefore take good heed what I have showed thee and bear well in thy mind what thou hast seen lest in thy journey thou meet with some that pretend to lead thee right but their way goes down to death."

This is Bunyan's portrayal of the marks of a true gospel minister. In pictorial form he has given us the same information we find in biblical form in the book of 1 Timothy. Of Bunyan it is said that if you cut him anywhere he would bleed "bibline," that is to say, the Bible would come gushing out of him. That is certainly true because he based all of his characters on the Scriptures themselves.

This is a true saying, If a man desire the office of a bishop, he desireth a good work. A bishop then must be blameless, the husband of one wife, vigilant, sober, of good behavior, given to hospitality, apt to teach; Not given to wine, no striker, not greedy of filthy lucre; but patient, not a brawler, not covetous; One that ruleth well his own house,

having his children in subjection with all gravity;
(For if a man know not how to rule his own
house, how shall he take care of the church of
God?) Not a novice, lest being lifted up with pride
he fall into the condemnation of the devil. Moreover he must have a good report of them which
are without; lest he fall into reproach and the
snare of the devil (1 Timothy 3:1-7, KJV).

Bunyan has set before us in pictorial form the marks of a
true gospel preacher as described in the biblical language of
1 Timothy 3:1-7. This is in marked contrast to modern standards for what constitutes a gospel minister. It's the difference between day and night. We, as Baptists, have a cliché
that when we meet in our assemblies we discuss the three
"B's"—baptisms, budgets, and buildings. These are the marks
that have been superimposed upon the gospel ministry to determine whether a man will receive a call to a certain church.
In the average Baptist church the first thing the search committee would want to know is, "How large a church did you
have?" "How large a budget did you set?" and "How many
did you get baptized in the past year?" If a man can give a
glowing report that his church increased in attendance over
a period of time, and show how much his church budget was,
and how many people got wet in the baptistry, then the modern criteria for the call of a minister has been met. Yet this is
totally different from that which is set forth in the Bible and
that which Bunyan would have us consider. Rather than us
meeting upon the three B's of Baptists—baptisms, budgets
and buildings—we ought to meet on another three B's and
that is, Bunyan, Boyce and Broadus.

The Minister of Grace is Serious-Minded.

What are the marks Bunyan has set forth on the experience
of a true gospel minister? First of all, a minister of grace must
be a grave man as portrayed in the picture hanging on the
wall in Interpreter's house. The description that the apostle

Paul gave Timothy was that the minister is to be a sober and serious-minded man. Not that you never expose yourself to humor, but that you, who are called to the gospel ministry, are to manifest that you take your calling seriously before the Lord and before your fellow man. There is no place for a clown in gospel ministry.

Ephesians 5:18 exhorts us, "And be not drunk with wine, wherein is excess; but be filled with the Spirit." The emphasis on being filled with the Spirit is not on the charismatic phenomenon, but is given in contrast to what happens when a person becomes drunk with wine. He is no longer disciplined. He is no longer able to control his life in a sound fashion. He runs into riot and excessive usage and makes mistakes. But when a person is filled with the Spirit of God, then he is led into a life of discipline and self-denial whereby he will be able to hear clearly what God would say to him. So, be not drunk with wine, that is, always running into excesses and not really knowing what you are doing, but be filled with the Spirit of God that you might be able to manifest a disciplined lifestyle like that of the Savior.

In my fifteen years of preaching the doctrines of grace, the providence of God has brought me into contact with a tremendous number of young ministers. Many of those young men have come to embrace the doctrines of grace and remain faithful to them. But sadly, I have seen a great number of them embrace the doctrines of grace only as a fad. We are a faddish people in our American Christianity and we might as well confess that. Any new fad that comes along which we think can be used to give us a bigger building or a greater attendance, we will use. I want to warn you that the doctrines of grace are not a faddish thing to play with. If you try to play with them I can tell you what is going to happen. It will be the same thing that happened to the seven sons of Sceva in the book of Acts. When you go around trying to cast the demons out of your church with the doctrines of grace, you're going to run into the devil himself and he is going to say, "Jesus I know and Paul I know, but who do you think you are?" This is not something with which you can play.

You must not only grasp the doctrines of grace but they must grasp you, or else you will be like the stony ground hearer described in the parable of our Lord Jesus Christ, who at once embraced what they heard, but then when persecution because of the Word arose, at once left that position. I would encourage any of my hearers today who are in the gospel ministry, that if you are embracing the doctrines of grace, understand that this is not a new fad that God has given you just to make your church grow. It's not something somebody ran through a computer and said, "It's time for a revival of the doctrines of grace. We've tried everything else, let's try this." This is serious business and you will encounter opposition. You need to be anchored into the doctrines of grace. James 1:8 says, "A double-minded man is unstable in all of his ways. Set your affection on things above and not on things of this earth." So the first mark of a true gospel minister is that he takes his calling seriously.

The Minister of Grace Gets His Message and Motivation From God.

The second mark in the picture is that the man's eyes were lifted up to heaven. That is, he got his message and motivation for service from his view of God. He was not looking horizontally for his message. He was not the type of preacher who looks out upon the congregation and says, "Here is so and so, if I preach this here's what will happen." That kind of preacher becomes a political expert in knowing how to refrain from saying the wrong things. However, the man in the picture is not like that. He received his message and his motivation from heaven for the service of God.

In coming to the doctrines of grace out of an Arminian background, I had been taught to use an Arminian methodology in preaching. I've had clowns and hamburgers and I had gone the whole route to get people motivated to serve God. After embracing the doctrines of grace, not only did it empty my sermon file cabinet, but also my methods suddenly didn't seem to match my theology. After that I went through a four-year transition with hardly any methodology at all. I felt as if I couldn't freely exhort sinners because I didn't want to sound like an Arminian, so I was paralyzed. How do you keep yourself motivated? How do you get your people motivated? I think Bunyan has the key here. You must have your eye upon the glory of God and the face of Jesus Christ. You must have your eye upon heaven to receive His message and the motivation that comes from Him.

We pray in the Lord's Prayer, "Thy will be done here on earth as it is in heaven." Did you ever wonder how the will of God is done in heaven and what motivates the inhabitants of heaven to do the will of God? If that's the biblical pattern then we should know it, shouldn't we? Moses was given a pattern and instructions on Mount Sinai on how to erect all the things of the Tabernacle. If we believe the Bible to be the final rule of faith and practice, then surely God has something to say in His Word about how to motivate His people. It is not left up to our extra-biblical human wisdom to try to come up with some new campaign. The idea that we can go to Him for our faith but not our practice because He has left that up to ourselves is wrong. God has given us a heavenly pattern: "Thy will be done down here on earth as it is in heaven."

How is that pattern set forth? In Matthew 18:10 Jesus gives us a hint. "Take heed that ye despise not one of these little ones; for I say unto you, that in heaven the angels do always behold the face of my Father which is in heaven." The inhabitants of heaven have their attention on the face of God. In Luke 1:19 it is written, "And the angel answering said unto him, 'I am Gabriel, that stand in the presence of God; and am sent to speak unto thee, and to show thee these glad tidings'." So here we have the angels standing in the presence of God, waiting for a message from Him. When God gives them that message they are energized and motivated to go forth and deliver that message. If you want a fresh motivation, stand afresh, gazing upon the glory of God and the face of Jesus

Christ. The angels of God stand in His presence and gaze upon His face. Their hearts are so lavished with the beauty of God that immediately they gladly respond to do His will. It's a reflex—just like when the doctor hits your knee with that little hammer and your leg kicks. It is not an artificial motivation that we must have imposed upon us in order to get us to do something for a short period of time. This would only result in our running right back into the affairs of this world and having to be revived again. The motivation is found by gazing into the face of God and being carried away with His majesty so that immediately we do the will of God.

Let me give you a couple of Scripture passages to show that not only do the angels do this but that this is also what motivates the perfected saints in glory. Did you ever wonder why there will be no sin in the new heaven and the new earth? Human nature will be eradicated and all sin will be done away with. There are some means that God uses to do this. Look in Revelation 22:3 and see what motivates the perfected saints in glory in their eternal state to serve God. "And there shall be no more curse: but the throne of God and of the Lamb shall be in it; and His servants shall serve Him." Do you see the inseparable connection between seeing the glory of God's face and serving Him? When that grips you, you won't have to run off to some clinic twice a year to get motivated to preach. You won't need to have a clown get up and cheer, "Now, go get 'em!" You will stand there like the angel—and if He has you wait a hundred years you will stand there waiting—and as soon as He gives the message you are ready to go. It will not make any difference what the message is. It may be a message of comfort: "Go down there and tell that virgin she is going to have a baby." Wouldn't you have loved to have been that angel? It might be a message of adversity: "Go down there and take the lives of 185,000 Assyrians" or "Go down there and take the lives of those infants in Egypt." How would you like to have been that angel? The angels do not pick and choose the message or the motivation. How could a person go down there and take the firstborn? By looking in the face of God. When they see the face of God that makes it right. Why cannot people embrace the doctrines of God's sovereign grace? Because they think God is not right. They are not looking at the glory that is in the face of Jesus Christ. Motivation and the message come by having our eyes lifted up toward heaven.

The Minister of Grace Believes the Bible Comes From God.

The third mark that we see in the picture is that the man of God has the best of books in his hands. It is the best of books. This tells us that this man majors in Bible preaching. He believes that the final authority for all faith and practice is found in "thus saith the Lord." It is not what Pharisee so-and-so or Doctor so-and-so thinks, but Jesus came quoting the Scriptures. The response of the people was that "He teaches like no one we've ever seen."

The man who is going to minister the doctrines of grace must be convinced that this Book is a revelation of God given to us and that it is the final authority in all matters of faith and practice. If you are still wavering in that, then I would encourage you to get that settled before you start seeking out the doctrines of God's grace. Get it settled. Is this God's Book or is it a collection of human ideas about God?

> The cloak that I left at Troas with Carpus, when thou comest, bring with thee, and the books, but especially the parchments. (2 Timothy 4:13).

Have the best of books in your hands when you stand to preach the grace of God. "Study to show thyself approved unto God, a workman that needeth not to be ashamed, rightly dividing the word of truth" (2 Timothy 2:15).

The Minister of Grace Is Not Ashamed to Preach the Truth of God.

The next part of the picture painted by Bunyan was that the

man is seen as having the law of truth written upon his lips. This man loved the truth of God, and he was not ashamed to speak that truth. What he loved in his heart came out of his mouth. Jeremiah, at one time in his life, thought he would not preach what he believed. He said that the Word of God was like a burning fire within him. He could not contain himself. He loved the truth, and his lips expressed the truth.

The man of God loves the truth of God regardless of the cost. Someone says, "Oh, but it causes so much discord." One of the men of God said, "I am for peace, but when I speak they are for war" (Psalm 120:7). Have you ever had that experience? The preachers of the doctrines of grace, if they have the grace of God in them, are individuals who desire men to be reconciled to the peace of the cross. But, beloved, in order to bring a person to the point where the blood of Christ is applied in that cross, there's going to be some warfare going on between human nature and the remedy of God. You must bring a man down before he will ever be brought up. Love the truth of God.

Psalm 119:104 says, "Through thy precepts I get understanding: therefore I hate every false way." What causes you to be contentious when you contend for the faith that was once delivered unto the saints? The answer is that you esteem all the precepts of God to be right and that is why you oppose error. You cannot love the fine fruit of your garden without hating the weeds that are in the garden. You cannot love truth without hating error. Psalm 119:28 says, "Therefore I esteem all thy precepts concerning all things to be right; and I hate every false way." That is what gives the man of God the backbone to say, "I do not care what the Church of England says. I must preach what is right. Even if it puts me in a dungeon, I must preach what I believe because it is the truth of God. Even if it separates me from my family, I must preach that, because the love of truth is upon my lips."

The man of God must love the truth of God and he must proclaim that truth wherever he is. Wherever he finds wrong —whether it be with wife, children, congregation, country—

he must say, "This is not in accordance with the teachings of the Scriptures." May God give you wisdom and patience to be as harmless as doves and wise as serpents in so doing.

This man that Bunyan described had the law of truth written upon his lips. His prayer was from Psalm 120:2, "Deliver my soul, O GOD, from lying lips and a deceitful tongue." Is that your prayer as a gospel preacher? May God give us a love for the truth.

The Minister of Grace is a True Shepherd.

The man in the picture had the world behind his back. What does this mean? It simply means that he was no hireling. He was not like the character which Bunyan describes as By-ends, who used religion for personal advantage and self-gain. He was not a hireling. He was a true shepherd who cared for the sheep and would not flee when the wolves came. He loved the people of God and would give himself unselfishly for them. Paul, in grieving over one of his acquaintances said in 2 Timothy 4:10, "For Demas hath forsaken me, having loved this present world." Demas settled down in a comfortable lifestyle and said, "I'm going to believe the same things, but I'm just going to get a little comfort out of this life also."

Every so often I have individuals ask if I know of a place for them to preach. I ask what they are looking for, listen to their response, and can quickly read between the lines. They're looking for a little rural, country church where they can preach the doctrines of grace and have a $30,000 a year salary, a two-car garage, a boat, and a place where they can settle down and not cause any problems. There is no such place. God may give comforts in this life and, when He does, praise and thank Him. Earthly comforts are proper in their place, but if you set out to try to use the gospel of Jesus Christ as a float upon which to go through this world, my friend, you have left the gospel and you are using it for "by-ends" (selfish purposes).

Demas is described in *Pilgrim's Progress* as having been attracted by a silver mine. As they were on the way, suddenly Demas said, "Let's stop and go over there and dig in that mine." They had a long argument and Demas said, "Oh, well, I can get along with it if I am careful." Christian says, "No, no, we've been warned not to do this." Demas went on his way and he was followed up by By-Ends. Bunyan says they both fell into the pit. Beloved, you can turn on your TV set and watch Demas working in his silver mine—using the gospel for self-centered ends. He says, "Oh, my God is a great God! He can do whatsoever He wants to do, but you better send me your offering or else I'm going to go out of business. The only way in which God will work is through my kingdom and my ministry that I have erected to the glory of God. Send me your money!" If the Apostle Paul should come upon the scene today, he would say, "From such withdraw thyself, supposing that gain is godliness. Godliness with contentment is great gain." If you are going to set out to be the one man in a thousand to whom God is going to entrust the souls of people, make sure you have this world and present life behind your back. Get it behind your back and keep it there. Bunyan's man stood as he pleaded with men. He's a preacher. He said he knew how to beget children, how to travail like a handmaiden delivering the child out of the womb of grace. That is what God has called us to do. God begets children through His spiritual begetting but He has been pleased with the foolishness of preaching to allow us to be handmaidens to deliver the baby when he comes forth from the womb of regeneration. May God enable us to know how to beget spiritual children. The Apostle would say to the Corinthians, "For ye have ten thousand instructors in Christ, yet have you not many fathers, for in Christ Jesus I have begotten you through the gospel." In order to be one who can beget spiritual children, you must know the gospel and you must know how to expose the dark, mysterious things of the gospel to sinners.

At the start of the book when Pilgrim is setting out he is introduced to Evangelist, and God be praised that this man knew what he was doing. Pilgrim was all confused as to which way to go to get to the Celestial City. Evangelist said, "Do you see the Light over yonder hill?" Pilgrim said, "I think I do." Evangelist did not say, "Fill out this decision card." No, no! He said, "You go to the Light, continue to seek after the Light." That Light was the Scriptures, so continue to seek.

I read an article a few years ago that told how to conduct a citywide campaign. It gave a list of how to prepare the people, tell them what they were to pray, what they were to believe, and then it said show them how to make a decision. If you're going to receive Christ in His person, you must receive Him in His total person, and you must first know who He is. He's a Prophet who teaches the will of God. He's a Priest who intercedes for us, and He is a King and Lord to rule over our lives and tell us what the will of God is. We cannot receive a person without understanding something of that person.

So the Evangelist as portrayed by Bunyan was a man who knew how to beget children, how to travail in birth for children. The Apostle Paul said in the book of Galatians, "My little children, of whom I travail in birth again until Christ be formed in you." Yes, the Puritan method of evangelism and that of the New Testament was to call people to an experiential acquaintance with their sin and then to embrace the experiential remedy of the cross. They were not called just to give an intellectual assent to such questions as, "Are you a sinner?" and "Do you want to go to heaven?"

In a recent survey by a Catholic magazine, people were asked what they thought heaven would be like. Ninety-seven percent of them said they believed in heaven and eighty-three percent said they expected to go there. One lady wanted "an unlimited charge card." Another wanted "unlimited chocolate." Another wanted "a place in a celestial realm where we play lots of baseball." He said, "I can't wait to drive one of God's fast-balls into the upper deck."

I was taught that a prime method in avoiding the offense of the cross in witnessing is to begin with the person: "If you died right now would you want to go to heaven?" But beloved, you had better define what heaven is. It is not a box of chocolate. It is not a baseball field out of which to drive one of God's fast-balls. It is not an unlimited charge card. Heaven is a place where the servants of God shall serve Him. Everybody wants to go to "heaven!" But you had better make sure they have the heaven in mind that the Bible speaks of. "Do you see the light?" Evangelist asked. "Well, I'm not yet quite sure," Pilgrim replied. It is not your job to give that person assurance at that point. You point him on to the Light and you say, "Keep on looking and, by God's grace, the rays of glory will open up and the shackles of guilt and sin will fall off your back. Keep looking unto the Light."

The Minister of Grace Looks for His Reward in the Life to Come, Not This Life

Finally, the crown was over his head signifying that he looked for his reward not in this life but in the life to come. The Apostle Paul could say at the close of his earthly ministry in 2 Timothy 4, "I have fought a good fight, I have finished my course, I have kept the faith: Henceforth there is laid up for me a crown of righteousness," or a crown of right living. It is a place where I can be a perfect servant. Is that not your hope today? What is your hope of heaven? What is your hope of eternal life? Is it like the things that the surveyed individuals desired? Or is it a place where you shall be able to serve God without any indwelling sin? Is that not the hope of the believer? Christ in you, the hope of glory! When He comes we know we shall be like Him. What is He like? He is holy. We know that is our ambition right now, and if we are trying to apprehend that for which Jesus Christ has apprehended us, then we will strive on toward that mark, and a crown will be put upon our head. It will not be some big, three-layered crown made of fake gold. The crown of the servant of God is to be enabled to be the perfect servant. It is not that you will be able to sit on His right hand or the left, but how much service you will be able to give to your Master. That is the crown that the Christian is looking forward to. "Well done, thou good and faithful servant. Enter thou into the joy of the Lord" (Matthew 25:23).

CONCLUSION

What value can we gain from the person that Bunyan describes as a true gospel minister? He is one to whom the Lord of the Way said that this is the only person I will entrust the salvation of souls unto. Beloved, if our Baptist heritage is going to be restored in our day to a biblical standard of righteousness, then it will come only through God raising up men like the one described here in *Pilgrim's Progress* and in 1 Timothy 3. Only through committed men will His truth be restored and spread throughout our land like it was in the early nineteenth century when the Philadelphia Association sent missionaries down to the South. You ought to read what happened when they came down into General Baptist churches and began preaching the doctrines of grace as set forth in the Philadelphia Baptist Confession of Faith. One church after another was brought under the Lordship of Jesus Christ. That is the framework out of which Southern Baptists' heritage has come.

If truth is going to be restored in doctrine, and with the same missionary zeal, it must come by the grace of God raising up committed men who will stand in the gap, who will take their work seriously, have their eyes toward heaven, the best of books in their hands, the law of truth written upon their lips, the world behind their back as they stand and plead with men, expecting their reward to come not in this world but in the world to come. This Founders Conference came out of a little prayer meeting in a Texas motel room. May God raise up men that fit Bunyan's portrait of a true gospel minister.

21.
MINISTERIAL DEPRESSION
DAVID KINGDON
1990 Southern Baptist Founders Conference

INTRODUCTION

IN my introductory remarks I want to establish the fact of ministerial depression—it does exist. Second, I shall look at the experience of Jeremiah, the weeping prophet, because Jeremiah provides us with a biblical case history of ministerial depression. Third, I shall consider some important factors in the development of ministerial depression and, finally, I shall seek to offer some counsel regarding recovery from ministerial depression.

There are two main reasons why I have come to be occupied with this subject. The first is that I have become aware in recent years that a considerable number of God's ministering servants are subject to—I might even say afflicted with—depression. This is especially true in the middle years of their ministries, in the later thirties and forties. The second volume of the Dr. Martyn Lloyd-Jones biography by Iain Murray shows that the Doctor himself was no stranger to depression. Some have become so prostrated by depression as to have to give up the ministry entirely. The second reason why I have come to be occupied with this subject is a very personal one on which I will not dwell except to say that I am not a stranger to the experience of depression. I have known what it is like to walk in darkness with little or no light (Isaiah 50:10-11).

Depression is often acutely described in literature. Shakespeare makes Hamlet say,

> I have of late, but wherefore I know not, lost all of
> my mirth, forgone all custom of exercises, and in-
> deed, it goes so heavily with my disposition that
> this goodly frame, the earth it seems to me, a
> sterile promontory (Hamlet, Act II, Scene II,
> quoted, Jack Dominian, *Depression*, 15).

Jack Dominian, a contemporary psychiatrist, writes,

> Depression refers, first and foremost, to mood.
> This may vary from feelings of slight sadness to
> utter misery and dejection. Secondly it is used to
> bring together a variety of physical and psycholog-
> ical symptoms, which together constitute a syn-
> drome—the technical term for any collection of
> recognizable and repeatable symptoms. Finally,
> depression is used to indicate an illness which
> prevents the sufferer from functioning and re-
> quires active treatment to restore a body and
> mind to a state of health (op. cit., 8).

Now, both Shakespeare and Dominian are, of course, describing depression in general, but what of ministerial depression? By the use of the adjective "ministerial," I do not want
to suggest that ministers of the gospel suffer from a special
kind of depression that does not afflict other mortals. To take
such a view would be to forget that we are men of like passions as they. What I do want to suggest, however, is that
ministers of the gospel, with respect to their calling as ministers, are particularly prone to attacks of depression. Furthermore, I contend that the depression from which they can suffer has certain specific elements to it, which entitles us to use
the adjective "ministerial" to describe it.

A simple illustration will drive home the point I am making.
Not all persons who suffer from cartilage trouble are soccer
players, but many are, simply because the game they play
makes them liable to cartilage injuries. Just so, not all who

suffer from depression are ministers, but some are, because their vocation exposes them to its attacks in a particularly telling way. Should any of you still be unpersuaded that there is such a phenomenon rightly labeled "ministerial depression," the following quotations from Frank Lake's massive *Clinical Theology* should put the issue beyond doubt.

> In few occupations is a performance expected of a man which demands so much passivity and double talk in the face of hypocrisy and humbug, as that of a pastor.

Lake, a medical doctor who became a missionary, and then an ordained clergyman of the Church of England, writes out of a very long experience in the treating of depressed ministers. He goes on to say:

> He may be presented with the alternative of pleasing God or toadying to the strong in his congregation. To have given in makes him despise himself with such inner fury that he becomes depressed. This is particularly an occupational risk for free church ministers. A corrupt collective of laity, acting more obstructively as a group than they would dare as individuals, have him and his family by the scruff of the neck. As the representative of the congregation's ideal image of its religious side, the clergyman is permitted only a narrow range of deviation from the denominational pattern, He is paid to approve what they do. The congregation may anathematize the minister who shows anger where Christ showed anger—namely against the religious—or moves in compassion where Christ moved, towards the broken, the socially or sexually disgraced. He may work himself to the bone with little response or appreciation. The unmarried man is often lonely and isolated by his office. The married man has

so many demands made upon him for evening engagements that he becomes a stranger to his children. His wife may accept this strange arrangement with incredible spirit, but if she adopts the role of the manager in the home and the parish, to leave him time for other things, she may well lose her womanly attractiveness to him. If she becomes dispirited she cannot brighten her world with the results of a shopping spree. She dresses to the mood, and it may be dowdy. This brings a nemesis of its own when the husband in depression longs not for a manager, but for tenderness in a woman.

Lake continues,

Several times, within five minutes of the opening of an interview, a clergyman has told me with moving emphasis of the idyllic relationship between himself and his wife. At the end of a further hour or so the same man has shared in tears his despair of the wild fantasies that crowd his mind—passionate scenes with other women or young people of either sex. He is terrified that his mind is so little in control. He is bewildered at the fantasies he must in faithfulness report; in which he has stood at the gravesite of the same beloved wife and gone on to picture his next marriage to the perfect woman.

Comment is superfluous except to exclaim how vicious are the fiery darts of the evil one. They are pricked with deadly poison. How he knows where and when to strike!

BIBLICAL EXAMPLES OF MINISTERIAL DEPRESSION

Having established, I trust, the fact of the existence of a type of depression which may rightly be called "ministerial,"

I want now to raise the question as to whether we can find examples of ministerial depression within Holy Scripture. Is not Elijah, after Carmel, a good example? Did he not suffer a reaction so severe (1 Kings 19:4) that he fell into such despair that he longed for death to release him from it? Was not Jonah so angry with his God, and so full of pity for himself (Jonah 4:9) that he no longer wanted to live? Was not David so cast down by the oppression of the wicked (Psalm 55:6) that he cried out to God, "Oh, that I had wings like a dove! I would fly away and be at rest"?

Above all others is not Jeremiah, the weeping prophet, the classic example of ministerial depression recorded in the pages of Holy Writ? It is to him then that we shall now turn in order to learn something of ministerial depression. Jeremiah prophesied during the period when the dark night of God's judgment was fast descending upon Judah. The message he was given to declare was one of virtually unrelieved gloom. Much more than building and planting, he was called upon to root out, to pull down and to destroy (1:10). He was commissioned to announce judgment and to call for repentance. He was not even permitted by God to pray for the people of Judah (7:16). He had to tell them that their much-revered temple would be destroyed, meeting the same fate that had overtaken the shrine at Shiloh centuries earlier (7:4).

Deeply patriotic, yet so sure that catastrophe was imminent, Jeremiah brought the wrath of the inhabitants of Jerusalem upon his head by counseling submission to Babylon in order that they might escape the terrible times which they did experience when other counsels prevailed (25:9). He was a patriot who appeared as a traitor. He was a man of intense sympathy and tenderness of heart who was an outcast among his people. He was denied the company of a wife and the pleasure of children by the command of God (16:1-2) because of the impending disaster. So an intensely lonely man, Jeremiah, bursts out in complaints against the God who obliged him to be a prophet against his will. Jeremiah did not volunteer. God compelled him (1:4). Faithful prophet that he was, Jeremiah reveals to us the cost of faithfulness to his commission by the inner anguish and depression which he felt. He pours out his complaints to God in language of such passionate intensity that, while we understand it, we can scarcely bring ourselves to use it. Yet we may thank God that what Jeremiah hid from the people to whom he prophesied, he spoke to the God in whose Name he prophesied, and God, in His wisdom, has caused it to be preserved for our learning.

The first thing that we should notice about Jeremiah's depression is the depth of it. It clearly was not occasional. It was very deep and prolonged. So deep were the depths into which he had sunk that he cursed the day on which he was born (20:14). Jeremiah shows us here that these are not the blues of a preacher on Monday morning. They are the anguished cries of a deeply distressed prophet. This man was in the grip of a depression so deep that, in the words of Theo Laetsch, "there is a complete blackout of God's love and grace and mercy" (*Jeremiah*, page 178).

Next we remark the intensity of Jeremiah's depression. Jeremiah was a man of ardent, emotional temperament. He felt things deeply. He was not cold and calculating, so his outbursts against God were passionate, so passionate that their language verges on blasphemous. He even accused God of deception because he was so unhappy with his lot. He had stood firm against Pashhur the priest (20:1). Like a wall of brass he has not yielded an inch. But now in the solitude of his own house he pours out his heart to God. So intense are his feelings against his circumstances that he cries out in anguish against the God who had ordained them. He says to Him (20:7-8): "I am ridiculed all day long, everyone mocks me; whenever I speak I cry out proclaiming violence and destruction, so the word of the Lord has brought me insult and reproach all day long." The intense pressure of being a prophet in such a situation ground Jeremiah down. This man longs for sympathy and appreciation, but receives neither. His situation so overwhelms him that he charges God with having deceived him (20:7).

These words of Jeremiah are written not for our imitation but for our instruction and self-understanding. They tell us that ministerial depression can sometimes be so deep as to block out all sense of God's love, mercy and grace. There are times in our experience, dear brethren, when there is not even "light at the end of the tunnel" because we are not in a tunnel but in a tomb. Our anger and frustration at the constant grinding pressures of the ministry can be such that, like Jeremiah, we become so full of self-pity and anger that we start to take it out on God Himself.

There is something very profound here. Just as deeply depressed people take out their anger on those nearest and dearest to them, so Jeremiah takes it out on the God he loves and serves. His charge of deceit, of course, is without foundation, for God had very definitely warned him of the trials that his ministry would bring upon him in 1:18. To accuse the God who cannot lie of deceiving him is terrible indeed, but let us not be too quick to condemn Jeremiah. For in the furnace of the afflictions of our own ministries, blasphemous thoughts sometimes do arise in our hearts. We, however, conceal them whereas Jeremiah revealed his. He is disgusted with his office and he is dissatisfied with his God. He wants to escape from the constant pressure upon him, so he cries out with passionate intensity against God. Jeremiah's experience, strangely, is a comfort to the depressed minister of the gospel, for it declares to him that he is not as alone as he thought he was. He is not unique in his experience and more, though the servant of God may sink deeply into depression and utter terrible words, as Jeremiah did, yet he is not cast off by his God. Satan would persuade us that Jeremiah must surely have committed the unpardonable sin, but such is the mercy of God that Jeremiah is the prophet *par excellence* of the new covenant (31:31-34). The prophet who knew such depression is the messenger of the God of hope who declares that He will write His law upon the hearts of His people and blot out their sins forever. Yet Jeremiah must repent and not utter "worthless words" as he says in 15:19.

Next to be noticed is the way in which Jeremiah plunges from joy into the deepest gloom. One moment he calls upon himself to praise God and in the very next he curses the day he was born (20:13). It seems as if, for a moment, the sun breaks through the enveloping fog and Jeremiah's heart is cheered, but then the fog wraps around him again and despair grips him once more. How true this is to the experience of some of God's servants. For weeks, months maybe, they have struggled into their pulpits sunk in depression. Called to comfort their people they feel no comfort in their own souls. Then suddenly a ray of light shines and hope is revived. The depression is gone but, alas, only for a moment, and back they sink again to become more depressed because, for a brief moment, they had begun to taste that blessedness which once they knew when first they saw the Lord.

This taste of "what could be" in the midst of "what is" tortures Jeremiah. So troubled is he that he asks God in 15:18, "Why is my pain unending and my wound grievous and incurable? Will You be for me like a deceptive brook, like a spring that fails?" Is God going to be like a dried up stream that yields no water when it is most needed in the burning heat of summer? In his depression Jeremiah gives way to doubt, unbelief, despair. In God's presence there is no fullness of joy because God is absent. He is hidden. The light of His countenance shines for an instant and is gone, and the darkness is thicker than ever. No wonder then that God seems to the prophet like a deceptive brook, like a spring that fails. Let us notice here that Jeremiah does not at any point deny the existence of God in his depression. It is the void that he feels. It is the absence of God that is his great problem. It is the God who holds him to his duty, but denies him all enjoyment of His presence, that seems to cause his pain to be unending (15:17).

Fourth, there is a further aspect of Jeremiah's depression which we ought to notice, and this is the tension which exists between the demands of his prophetic office and his natural desires. Jeremiah did not want to be a prophet, yet God compelled him to be one. Sensitive soul that he was, he had to proclaim a message of impending calamity to a people who would not repent but derided him (20:7b). Isolated from the people he loved by the hand of God upon him, accused of sedition when he had at heart the deepest interests of the people, he longed to escape from the vocation that God had imposed upon him. He saw an easier life away from the pressures of the prophetic office and he longed for it. But God would not let Jeremiah have his way. He bound him to his office even though his whole being screamed out for relief from the intolerable burden that he was obliged to bear. Listen to the words he pours out to God: "Whenever I speak, I cry out proclaiming violence and destruction. So the word of the LORD has brought me insult and reproach all day long. But if I say, 'I will not mention Him or speak any more in His name,' His word is in my heart like a fire, a fire shut up in my bones. I am weary of holding it in; indeed I cannot" (Jeremiah 20:8-9).

What a tension is here! Jeremiah proclaims a message that brings him nothing but insult and reproach. But when he tries to be silent in order to spare himself further criticism, God forces him to speak. He hates preaching, yet he must preach. Some of us, I am sure, at times have felt just like Jeremiah. This preacher has. We could wish ourselves a thousand miles away from our pulpits because of the constant criticism of our hearers, yet to the pulpit we must go, worn down as we are because the Lord overpowers us and prevails (20:7).

Once, like Jeremiah, there was sweetness to the Word of God. We could say with him, "When Your words came I ate them. They were my joy and my heart's delight" (15:16). But now it may be, brother minister and fellow servant of Christ, that there is no honey, only God's Word in your heart, like a fire burning there. You try to suppress it but it comes out. You long for some sympathy, some appreciation from your hearers, but you cannot comfort them for they will not repent. You must go on proclaiming a message which they find unacceptable, and there is not a sign of repentance nor a glimmer of understanding to cheer you in your dark, dark days.

There remains one more aspect of Jeremiah's ministerial depression that we should notice. This is his profound spiritual isolation. Perhaps there are no words in all his complaining to God, which are as moving as these in 15:17: "I never sat in the company of revelers, never made merry with them; I sat alone because Your hand was on me and You had filled me with indignation." Denied the love and companionship of a wife and the pleasure of children, belonging to no school of prophets with whom he could have soul fellowship; misunderstood, maligned and persecuted by false prophets, accused of sedition when he was deeply patriotic, Jeremiah sat alone by the sovereign will of God.

Since Jeremiah's day many a minister of the gospel has had to do the same. Perhaps—despite his idiosyncrasies—the most notable modern example is that of A. W. Pink. As doors closed he sat alone more and more. He longed to preach but the opportunity was denied him. He, like Jeremiah, keenly felt his spiritual isolation. Writing on March 10, 1935, he declared, "It is now seven years since my dear wife and I partook of the Lord's supper. We feel it keenly and God means us and all His people to feel the awful character of the times in which we are living when the departure from the true faith is almost universal" (quoted in Iain H. Murray, *The Life of Arthur W. Pink*, 86).

These, then, are the most important aspects of the ministerial depression of the prophet Jeremiah. It was both deep and intense, leading him to pour out his heart in passionate complaint to God. It was lit by occasional shafts of light, but these did not dispel his depression for long. Torn apart by the demands of his prophetic office and his natural desires, he sat alone, having to endure a profound spiritual isolation from the people he loved.

IMPORTANT FACTORS IN THE DEVELOPMENT
OF MINISTERIAL DEPRESSION

In trying to understand ministerial depression it is neces

sary to analyze various factors that occur in ministers who suffer from it. I would not want to be understood, however, as meaning that all these factors occur in each particular case of ministerial depression, nor that equal weight is to be given to each of them. For a moment's reflection will surely persuade us that none of us are exactly the same. Hence it follows that some factors will be more influential in some cases and less in others.

First, it is generally agreed that temperament is a most important factor in depression. Writing of spiritual depression in general, Dr. Martyn Lloyd-Jones stated that he would, without hesitation, put temperament as its most important general cause (*Spiritual Depression,* 14). Temperament is not obliterated by the new birth. If a man is given to melancholy before his new birth he will be given to it afterwards. As Herbert Carson rightly observes, "We do not acquire different facial features when we are born again; no more do we acquire a new temperament" (*Facing Suffering,* 99). The new birth, introducing as it does the life of God into our soul, does give us hope, for now we begin the process of controlling our temperament instead of being controlled by it.

I think it is an observable fact that God in His wisdom does call into the ministry a not inconsiderable number of men of the introverted, introspective type of temperament. The introvert is a deeply sensitive person, able to enter into the feelings of others. He has an aversion for everything superficial. Whatever he undertakes he does thoroughly. He combines a rich emotional life with deep reflective thinking. He is therefore, as Hallesby has pointed out, "especially fitted for creative, intellectual work, both as an author and as a thinker" (*Temperament and the Christian Faith,* 41). He might have added that such men are also especially fitted to be pastors and preachers when called by God into the ministry. As Hallesby points out, the melancholic often feels himself called to enter an idealized and particularly difficult life work. Everyday life is too trivial for him. It falls far short of his ideal. But in his dream life he pictures a calling, a life work that comes up to his standards. These standards have nothing to do with providing a livelihood or making a profit. On the contrary, his life work must demand the utmost in sacrifice, self-denial and service. The relevance of Hallesby's remarks to our subject is obvious. The ideals of such a man can be shattered on the hard reality of the daily life of a minister of the Word of God. The experience can be so devastating that he sinks into a deep depression.

A second factor to which I would attach considerable importance is the physical. There is a tendency for ministers of the gospel to undervalue the influence that bodily states have upon the soul. Taken up as we are with matters of the spirit we often forget that man is a unity of body and soul, and that the body interacts with the soul and vice versa.

C. H. Spurgeon suffered a great deal from depression and it would appear that gout was its chief cause. That, at any rate, is the opinion of Dr. Martyn Lloyd-Jones, who was, of course, a physician by training. Of Spurgeon he says, "That great man was subject to spiritual depression and the main explanation in his case was undoubtedly the fact that he suffered from a gouty condition which finally killed him. He had to face this problem of spiritual depression often in a most acute form. A tendency toward acute depression is an unfailing accompaniment of the gout which he inherited from his forebears." I have known of a minister who suffered from depression for years and had to quit the ministry for a time. That depression was only alleviated when it was discovered that he had a malfunctioning thyroid gland.

As ministers we are also all too prone to neglect regular exercise, for ours is a largely sedentary occupation. If we would feed our people with the finest of wheat we must spend long hours in our studies. The result is that we can, if we neglect regular exercise, become sluggish and peculiarly liable to attacks of depression.

Furthermore, as ministers we are inclined to neglect the Sabbath principle. We labor hard on the Lord's Day, so hard that often we are wrung out at the day's end, and so strung out that we find difficulty in sleeping. Yet we have no real day set aside for *our* Sabbath rest, no day on which we may rest from our labors; so we suffer from the constant strain of overwork. Our psychical energy is constantly depleted and not often renewed. We are the worst of Sabbath breakers in the best of causes, with the result that we are not aware of the sinfulness of what we are doing—trying to be wiser than the loving Creator who gave us one day in seven to rest even from our ministerial labors.

Another aspect we must not neglect to mention is the widespread practice of preaching while on holiday. Sometimes the motive is financial—the preaching fees help to pay for a holiday we otherwise might not be able to afford. Sometimes we are simply weak. We are prevailed upon to preach when we should be resting and sitting under the Word ourselves. We are foolish if we do preach on holiday, for we shall not return to our labors as renewed and refreshed as we should be if we do so. We need to beware of Satan's devices. He does not trouble himself overmuch with bone-idle ministers, but he does seek to destroy conscientious ministers by depression resulting from overwork.

Another set of factors can be grouped under the general category of the pressures of the ministry. A very real pressure is that of loneliness. Those of you who are not preachers, do mark this and do pray for your pastor in this connection. Listen to Spurgeon: "Our position in the church will contribute to loneliness. A minister fully equipped for his work will usually be a spirit by himself, above, beyond and apart from others. The most loving of his people cannot enter into his peculiar thought, cares and temptations" *(Lectures to My Students,* First series, 170). Many a faithful minister plows a very lonely furrow. He may well have no spiritually-minded brother near to him to whom he can open his heart. Like Jeremiah, he sits alone without a familiar friend in whom he can repose his confidence.

Another pressure comes from a conscience that will not let

him rest. There is always more to be done—that extra visit; those few more pages to read; that letter to write. So the minister becomes a stranger to relaxation. He does not know what it is to rest in the Lord and to wait patiently for Him. He becomes a prey to sleeplessness and his conscience gives him no rest. So, utterly weary, he drags himself each day to perform his spiritual duties. He forgets the wisdom and the compassion of His Lord and Master when He said to His disciples, "Let us go into the desert and rest a while."

C. H. Spurgeon has some wise words for us to heed in this connection:

> The Master knows better than to exhaust his servants. Rest time is not waste time. It is economy to gather fresh strength. Look at the mower on a summer's day, with so much corn to cut down ere the sun sets, He pauses in his labor—is he a sluggard? He looks for his stone, and begins to draw it up and down on his scythe—is he wasting precious moments? While we are in this tabernacle we must every now and then cry halt and serve the Lord by holy inaction and consecrated leisure. Let no tender conscience doubt the lawfulness of going out of harness for a while, but learn from the experience of others the necessity and duty of taking timely rest (ibid., 174).

Yet another pressure comes from the demands of preaching itself. If you are conscientious in applying the Word of God to yourself before you preach it to others, you will become acutely conscious of the corruptions of your own heart. If you are not careful you will fall into depression. Satan will come and insinuate that such a hypocrite as you is a wicked charlatan for daring to stand before a congregation to set before them the demands of the living God. "You preach," says Satan, "on praying without ceasing, yet you pray so little yourself. You exhort people to bear their trials uncomplainingly, yet you moan at your own trials. You tell people to rejoice in the Lord, and look at you! You are cast down and you have been for weeks." Brethren, these fiery darts from the evil one stick, and they would soon bring us down all together. Such hypocrites do we feel ourselves to be, utterly unworthy of our God, and yet we have to preach to the servants of God whose consciences are sensitive. Preaching can be sheer agony when Satan brings such charges against us.

Early in his ministry Christmas Evans, that great Welsh Baptist preacher, knew the kind of depression which arises from a deep sense of unworthiness, exacerbated by a very tender conscience. Paxton Hood writes of him,

> He thought himself a mass of ignorance and sin; he desired to preach but he thought that such words as his must be useless to his hearers: as to the method of preaching he was greatly troubled. He thought by committing his sermons to memory he forfeited the gift of the Holy Spirit; so he says he changed his method, took a text without premeditation and preached what occurred to him at a time; but, he continues, if it was bad before it was worse now; so I thought God would have nothing to do with me as a preacher.

Paxton Hood continued,

> The young man was humbled; he entered every pulpit with dread; he thought he was such a one that his mere appearance in the pulpit would be quite sufficient to becloud the hearts of his hearers and to intercept the light from heaven [he only had one eye as a result of being involved in a fracas with some thugs]. It seems he had no close friends to whom he could talk; he was afraid if he laid bare the secrets of his heart, he would seem to be only a hypocrite; so he had to wrap up the bitter secrets of his soul in his own heart, and

drink of his bitter cup alone (Paxton Hood, *Christmas Evans—The Preacher of Wild Wales,* 52-53).

Pressure can come upon a minister in his home and bring him into the Slough of Despond. A beloved wife is often sick. Susannah Spurgeon, C. H. Spurgeon's wife, was never the same woman after the birth of their twin sons, Charles and Thomas. A minister's wife may be given to depression. Like William Carey's wife, she may accuse him unjustly of bringing all kinds of distresses upon her and the family. Sometimes the helpmeet is taken to heaven to leave behind a desolate shepherd. In his moving *Diary of Bereavement—A Record of Sorrow,* E. M. Blaiklock has this moving passage:

March 20, 1979, I think I tired myself too much last night and I failed to sleep. Perhaps today has been a reaction, a veritable Vale of Tears. I gave two lectures at Bible College and I think I thought and spoke without apparent stress. It was when I entered the empty home in the early afternoon that the desolation of life without her enveloped me like a shroud. If anyone ever reads this it will be perhaps to despise my frailty, rather than for others to understand how after fifty-eight weeks I can still sob and call to her. The grief will not abate, though in truth I have offered it to God for such an alchemy. What more must I learn? Dear God if there are deeper lessons awaiting, let me learn them soon and depart (page 53).

But sometimes, alas, a man of God has married a woman who is no helpmeet to him in the work, but rather the opposite. At home he finds no sympathy. The most extreme example I have ever come across is recorded in John Kennedy's most interesting volume, *The Days of the Fathers in Ross-Shire.* He writes of the wife of the Reverend James Fraser who was ordained minister of Alness in 1726, in Scotland. He was the author of a notable work *The Scripture Doctrine of Sanctification* and you will understand why when you read Kennedy's description of Fraser's wife:

> A cold, unfeeling, bold, unheeding, worldly woman was his wife. Never did her godly husband sit down to a comfortable meal in his own house. Often he would have fainted for sheer want of need for substance but for the considerate kindness of some of his parishioners. Even light and fire in his study was denied on the long, cold winter evenings, [this was the north of Scotland!] and as his study was his own place of refuge from the cruel scourge of his wife's tongue and temper, there, shivering and in the dark, he used to spend his winter evenings at home. Compelled to walk in order to keep warm, and accustomed to do so when preparing for the pulpit, he always kept his hands before him as feelers in the dark, to warn him of his approaching the wall at the other side of the room (Christian Focus Publications, 1979 edition, 43-44).

How the man kept with her is amazing. Being once at a presbytery dinner without his wife, amidst a group of moderates [that is, non-evangelical ministers], one of them proposed as a toast the health of their wives. Turning to Mr. Fraser he said, as he winked at his moderate companions, "You, of course, will cordially join in drinking to this toast."

"So I will and so I ought," Mr. Fraser said, "for mine has been a better wife to me than anyone of yours has been to you."

"How so?" they all exclaimed.

"She has sent me," was the reply, "seven times a day to my knees when I would not otherwise have gone. That is more than any of you can say of yours!"

Sometimes a child brings such grief to the heart of a minister that he is cast into depression for a season. A minister known to me in another country suffered from a time of prostration because his daughter had to get married. There is another pressure that I think is especially real today—and many a godly minister feels it. He preaches faithfully and he waters his sermons with much prayer, but he sees little fruit for his labors. However, not far away crowds flock to hear a man who claims a charismatic anointing of the Spirit. Now our godly minister suspects that the work is superficial, but if he ventures to suggest so he is either accused of envy of another's success or of quenching the Spirit. So he stays silent and before long some of his own flock leave him for the "Spirit-filled ministry" which is available in the other church. Feeling an utter failure, hurt and bewildered, he looks within to search out that secret sin in his heart that is grieving the Spirit. He becomes thoroughly depressed. If the depression goes unchecked he may well give up the ministry in deep disillusionment.

RECOVERY FROM MINISTERIAL DEPRESSION

I cannot do more than simply offer some brief pastoral counsels. These comments are not to be regarded as formulae which will automatically bring relief from ministerial depression, because ministerial depression may often be as slow in lifting as it is in coming. I would recommend to you Dr. Martyn Lloyd-Jones' *Spiritual Depression* and that tremendous book by the Puritan, Thomas Brooks, *Precious Remedies Against Satan's Devices*.

First, if you suffer from a melancholic temperament, learn to discipline it. When you feel yourself beginning to brood, center your thoughts upon the Lord Jesus Christ. Meditate upon His person, see Him as He gives Himself to others and then you will be less absorbed in yourself and less inclined to self-pity. Seek to bring every thought into captivity to Christ and start to live in the real world—the world that does not conform to your ideals because it is marred by sin. Make yourself a rule of life, which is within your ability to keep, so that you do not aim impossibly high. In this way you will overcome the paralysis of depression to which you will otherwise succumb.

Second, do not be afraid to complain to God when you are depressed. Jeremiah complained and God did not cast him off. David complained when his soul refused to be comforted (Psalm 77:2). Only the first three lines of Psalm 77 are a prayer. The rest is a complaint, though in the context of prayer. David complained of his distress. He poured out his heart to God about it. He told God just how he felt, and he hid nothing from Him. David's view of God allowed him to complain to God. He was not afraid that God would be offended.

Perhaps it rather shocks us that David, like Jeremiah, complained to God. There may be two reasons why we feel shocked. The first is that we may feel our depression is not worthy of God's notice. We tell ourselves we ought not to be depressed in any case, so we feel guilty of complaining. Moreover God is to us perhaps too majestic and too remote to listen to our complaints. But what a mistake we make if we think like this! He is not a remote God! He feeds birds. He clothes lilies. He marks the fall of the sparrow. If He heard "the prayers and supplications with strong crying and tears," which our Lord offered up to Him in the days of His flesh (Hebrews 5:7), then surely He will hear our groans as well. Beloved brethren, when we are sorely distressed, greatly cast down in the mire of depression, we need not hesitate to complain to our God. He will not stop up His ears for He is not that kind of God.

There may be another reason why we do not complain to God in distress and depression. We may have been taught, like all good Englishmen, to keep a stiff upper lip, never to give way, always to keep our emotions under rigid control. Here we make a profound mistake, for what we are really saying if we think like this, is that we are self-sufficient, we don't need to pour out our hearts to God, and we can get by without His help. David was a lot wiser than we often are. He was not a Stoic. He did not bottle up his anguish inside himself. He complained, he cried, he unburdened himself to his God, and in so doing, he found his burden lifted: "Cast thy burden upon the Lord and he will sustain you" (Psalm 55:22).

Third, remember the limitations of your bodily strength. If you are thoroughly tired in body then you will be in mind as well. Do not drive yourself on by sheer will power. Do not be afraid to go to your church officers and tell them that you must have a rest from your ministerial labor. It is better to do this sooner rather than later, before you are prostrated for a lengthy period. Sometimes we do not go to our church officers because of pride. We do not like to think that we have come to the end of our tether and we certainly don't want others to know that we have. Perhaps also we carry more burdens than we need because we refuse to delegate responsibility to others.

Fourth, find a brother minister to whom you can open your heart. He may not live near you but you can write. In former centuries godly ministers opened their hearts to each other in letters. Why should you not do the same? Why sit alone feeling utterly isolated when you could have the benefit of godly counsel and informed intercession. On the other hand, in God's good providence, the minister in whom you can confide may live near to you. Take advantage of God's providence. Enter into a covenant to have regular conversation on spiritual subjects. You will find that your soul will be refreshed. Let not Satan isolate you from your brother ministers so that, Elijah-like, in your depression you think that you are the only standard-bearer God has left on earth.

Finally, learn to live by faith. When we suffer from depression we so often forget the great truth of justification by faith. We often feel full of self-pity. Realize that self-pity arises from self-justification. We have tried and tried so hard and we have failed, so we pity ourselves. But what have we been trying to do? We have been trying to justify ourselves by works. That's why we pity ourselves. Do we not say to ourselves that we have been faithful in praying, in our preparation for preaching, in our pastoral visitation? And now look at what we are experiencing—constant pressure, lack of appreciation, depression, despair. Gerard Euabalong has made some profound remarks in connection with this tendency to "justify ourselves by law which ever threatens to cut us off from living by faith in God's justifying righteousness." Writing of the law, he says, "Instead of giving life it kills." This is clearly only manifest when it drives man to despair. But despair is merely the reverse aspect of blinded pride. One is just as fatal to man as the other. The mad attempts to cope alone with oneself and the world, with one's failure, and with death, and with the law, and the whole violence of the force by which it calls into question man's whole being—that is, the attempt to justify oneself—invariably means, either in the form of an explicit atheist conflict with God, or in the religious disguise of a pious attempt to justify oneself, a refusal to be made dependent upon God.

Euabalong quotes Luther in this connection:

> In this respect, there is not distinction between the Jews, the Papists and the Turks. Their rights are different but their hearts and thoughts are the same. That is, they say, "if I have acted in such and such a way, God will be well disposed toward me." The same feeling is found in the hearts of all men.(*Luther—An Introduction to His Thought,* 137-138).

So when in our depression we pity ourselves, we need to ask ourselves whether we have really learned what it is to live by faith. Is not self-pity the child of self-justification? Does not envy (the brother to self-pity), come and worsen the situation by making us envy those whose lines have fallen in more pleasant places than ours? Then again, consider the awareness of our ungodliness that threatens so often to drive us into deep depression. We feel as ministers of God's Word that we are so unworthy. When this happens, have we not forgotten that God justifies the ungodly (Romans 4:5)?

Now Satan does indeed charge us with ungodliness and so does our conscience, but God has justified us (Romans 8:33). He has pronounced His verdict of acquittal once and for all, so then we must meet the charges brought against us, especially the charge that we are ungodly (as indeed we are) by pointing not to God's work *in* us but to His work *for* us. Not to the degree of our sanctification, but to the alien righteousness of Christ—that eternal objective righteousness, which always avails the sinner. It is not to the degree of our sanctification that we must look, but to the completeness of God's justification. Who shall bring any charge against God's elect? It is God who justifies (Romans 8:34). We must accept our acceptance in the Beloved. We must ever look in faith to the substitutionary death, the resurrection, the glorious ascension and the prevailing intercession of our Savior. Who shall bring a charge against God's elect? It is God who justifies. Who is he who condemns? It is Christ who died and furthermore is also risen, Who is even at the right hand of God, Who also makes intercession for us. The way of joy is this: it is to look to God's work for us, outside of us.

The ultimate antidote to ministerial depression is found in the justifying righteousness of Christ. In this we must always rest. In this we must live, and we must preach it until we finish our course. We must preach out of our justification—"sinning yet justified," as Luther puts it. We must leave our depressions and consign them to the depths of the sea. Listen to John Newton:

> Though sin would fill me with distress,
> The throne of grace I dare address,
> For Jesus is my righteousness.
>
> Though faint my prayers and cold my love,
> My steadfast hope shall not remove
> While Jesus intercedes above.

Against me earth and hell combine
But on my side is power divine,
Jesus is all and He is mine.

That is enough, more than enough, to meet the slanders of Satan, the accusations of conscience, the weakness of the flesh and the gibes of the world. One more word, and this from my beloved Spurgeon:

> Between this and heaven there may be rougher weather yet, but it is all provided for by our Covenant Head. In nothing let us be turned aside from the path which the divine call has urged us to pursue. Come fair or come foul, the pulpit is our watch-tower and the ministry our warfare; be it ours, when we cannot see the face of our God, to trust unto the shadow of His wings (op. cit., 179).

22.
PREACHING IRRESISTIBLE GRACE
THOMAS J. NETTLES
1990 Southern Baptist Founders Conference

THE subject that I have been assigned is "Irresistible Grace." I want to ask, and seek to answer, the question: "What makes grace irresistible?" In what is the transforming power of grace? What is irresistible about it? Three passages serve as the background for this message. The first is Romans 8:1-9:

> Therefore, there is now no condemnation for those who are in Christ Jesus, because through Christ Jesus the law of the Spirit of life set me free from the law of sin and death. For what the law was powerless to do in that it was weakened by the sinful nature, God did by sending His own Son in the likeness of sinful man to be a sin offering. And so He condemned sin in sinful man, in order that the righteous requirements of the law might be fully met in us, who do not live according to the sinful nature but according to the Spirit. Those who live according to the sinful nature have their minds set on what that nature desires; but those who live in accordance with the Spirit have their minds set on what the Spirit desires. The mind of sinful man is death, but the mind controlled by the Spirit is life and peace; the sinful mind is hostile to God. It does not submit to God's law, nor can it do so. Those controlled by the sinful nature cannot please God.

You, however, are controlled not by the sinful nature but by the Spirit, if the Spirit of God lives in
you. And if anyone does not have the Spirit of
Christ, he does not belong to Christ.

The second is 1 Corinthians 1:30-2:5:

It is because of Him that you are in Christ Jesus,
who has become for us wisdom from God—that
is, our righteousness, holiness and redemption.
Therefore, as it is written: "Let him who boasts
boast in the Lord." When I came to you, brothers,
I did not come with eloquence or superior wisdom as I proclaimed to you the testimony about
God. For I resolved to know nothing while I was
with you except Jesus Christ and Him crucified.
I came to you in weakness and fear, and with
much trembling. My message and my preaching
were not with wise and persuasive words, but
with a demonstration of the Spirit's power, so
that your faith might not rest on men's wisdom,
but on God's power.

Relevant to the subject also is Paul's concise and startling
explanation of the foundation of ministerial encouragement
in 2 Corinthians 4:1-6:

Therefore, since through God's mercy we have
this ministry, we do not lose heart. Rather, we
have renounced secret and shameful ways; we do
not use deception, nor do we distort the word of
God. On the contrary, by setting forth the truth
plainly we commend ourselves to every man's
conscience in the sight of God. And even if our
gospel is veiled, it is veiled to those who are perishing. The god of this age has blinded the minds
of unbelievers, so that they cannot see the light of
the gospel of the glory of Christ, who is the image

of God. For we do not preach ourselves, but Jesus Christ as Lord, and ourselves as your servants for Jesus' sake. For God, who said, "Let light shine out of darkness," made His light shine in our hearts to give us the light of the knowledge of the glory of God in the face of Christ.

THE PERSUASIVE POWER OF THE PREACHER

What makes grace irresistible? Is it the earnestness and the insistence of the preacher that makes grace irresistible? We recognize much biblical data encourages us to be earnest and urgent and insistent in preaching. Ministers of the gospel have no excuse for a flaccid, lackadaisical, lazy, nonchalant approach to the preaching of the gospel. When the apostle Paul said that he did not come with wise and persuasive words, he referred to the schools of rhetoric that sought to gain adherence to themselves simply on the basis of their theories about oral communication. Paul said rhetorical technique has no power in producing a heart that is lovingly convinced of the gospel. One may be convinced of a philosophical position, or to follow one rhetorician over another, but sinners are never converted that way; such commitment does not come with wise and persuasive words.

The example of the apostle Paul tells us very clearly, however, that he was deeply involved in seeking to persuade men that Jesus was the Christ. He was deeply aware of the issues that were at stake—the eternality of condemnation and the infinite obligation that everyone has to love God. In 2 Corinthians 5:11, he said, "Knowing therefore, the fear of the Lord, we persuade men." And we see in the book of Acts the way that he conducted himself as he went to various towns to preach. He engaged in a persuasive ministry.

In Acts 17:2-4, speaking of the time Paul was in Thessalonica, Luke recorded, "As his custom was, Paul went into the synagogue, and on three Sabbath days he reasoned with them from the Scriptures, explaining and proving that the Christ had to suffer and rise from the dead. 'This Jesus I am proclaiming to you is the Christ,' he said. Some of the Jews were persuaded and joined Paul and Silas, as did a large number of God-fearing Greeks and not a few prominent women." He reasoned with them, he argued with them, he remonstrated with them. He sought to tell them that their views of life were not defensible, that they finally would fall flat, and that the Scriptures were inspired and spoke of a God who has revealed Himself in wrath and in mercy and is incarnated in the Lord Jesus Christ. He sought to convince them that this was true.

We see this also in verse 17 of this same chapter. Paul goes to Athens and he is now with the Greeks, and this verse tells us, "So he reasoned in the synagogues with the Jews and the God-fearing Greeks, as well as in the marketplace day by day with those who happened to be there." Then verse 18, "A group of Epicurean and Stoic philosophers began to dispute with him. Some of them asked, 'what is this babbler trying to say?'" Without hesitation he sought to convince them. Consequently, he went to the Areopogas and preached to them. He sought to persuade them that they were under the judgment of God, and that God would judge all men by this one Man, Jesus Christ. In Acts 18:4, Paul went to Corinth and we read, "Every Sabbath he reasoned in the synagogue, trying to persuade Jews and Greeks."

The same is true with respect to Apollos in Acts 18:24: "Meanwhile a Jew named Apollos, a native of Alexandria, came to Ephesus. He was a learned man, with a thorough knowledge of the Scriptures. He had been instructed in the way of the Lord, and he spoke with great fervor and taught about Jesus accurately, though he knew only the baptism of John." Verse 28 intensifies its representation of Apollos's zeal for the propagation of the gospel truth in recording, "For he vigorously refuted the Jews in public debate, proving, from the Scriptures that Jesus was the Christ." Apollos spoke with great fervor and he vigorously refuted the Jews; his intensity burns within these texts.

The image projected by these narratives is not of a man

who lies flat and lets words of the gospel roll out of his mouth like marbles would if he turned his face sideways. This depicts one whose life is involved in these most gripping issues of condemnation and redemption. It has the intensity of one who, seeing a child in a burning building, yells and screams to get the child out of the building and to safety. We should be no less earnest as we seek to persuade men to flee from the wrath to come!

We must tell all men, everywhere, that God commands them to repent, and if they do not repent, they will perish. Note the examples Jesus gave in Luke 13. People brought up to Him how Pilate had mixed the blood of the Jews with their sacrifices, and Jesus said, "I tell you, Nay: but, except ye repent, ye shall all likewise perish" (KJV). And then Jesus brought up a natural calamity that had occurred. The Tower of Siloam had fallen on some people and killed them. He viewed this as a judgment of God. He said, "Do you think they were more guilty than all the others living in Jerusalem? I tell you, no! But unless you repent, you too will all perish." He called people to repentance. He gave great examples of the coming judgment of God. We too must use persuasive means. Nothing can be more urgent than immediate repentance and faith.

But, even with all of that, the irresistibility of grace and the irresistibility of the gospel do not lie within any persuasive power of the preacher. Our texts tell us that even Paul could not rely on his skill, his knowledge, or his earnestness as a means of giving spiritual life. Much less could any method founded in ignorance, deceit, or manipulation be productive of spiritual life. The irresistibility of grace is neither produced nor aided by any psychological techniques we may employ. It does not lie with any salesmanship skills we may have acquired. It does not lie in the smooth, seamless techniques of evangelistic interviews that produce a minimum of "no" and a maximum of "yes" responses making the sealing prayer of decision an unobtrusive, pleasant, and natural ending to a lovely and friendly interview. Within such contrivances does not lie the irresistibility of grace, nor is it kin to biblical persuasion.

We persuade them of the truth of the gospel; we seek to persuade them, not rudely, that their way is wrong. It is false. It will lead them to hell! But then, finally, we gladly concede that it is in the hands of God—only He can give the results. We see this in 1 Corinthians 3:5-7. Paul has been speaking about the kind of loyalties the Corinthian church members had to different preachers. He said, "What, after all is Apollos? And what is Paul? Only servants, through whom you came to believe—as the Lord has assigned to each his task. I planted the seed, Apollos watered it, but God made it grow. So neither he who plants nor he who waters is anything, but only God, who makes things grow." Then, in verses 21-23, he said, "So then, no more boasting about men! All things are yours, whether Paul or Apollos or Cephas or the world or life or death or the present or the future—all are yours, and you are of Christ and Christ is of God." It is God that gives the increase and in the final analysis, when it comes to a person being born to the kingdom, men are nothing. One of our texts, 2 Corinthians 4:7, reminds us: "We have this treasure in jars of clay to show that this all surpassing power is from God and not from us."

So we must urge people to repentance and faith. Not to do so would be a faithless ministry. But it is an intrusion on the ministry and sovereign prerogative of the Holy Spirit to redefine faith for the sinner and lead him or her to think that faith consists of asking Jesus into your heart; indeed prescribing any form of prayer as the essential constituent of saving faith is tantamount to deceit. Saving faith might manifest itself in prayer or an earnest cry for Jesus to come into the heart. It may be found even in praying a prescribed form. Such forms, however, do not embody the essential constituent element of saving faith. If the heart has not been brought into congruity with all the contours of the gospel, no words (no matter how accurately articulated) will suffice. Saving faith is wrought in the heart of man by the Spirit of God and by Him alone.

THE WORD OF GOD

Now we press our inquiry further and ask if the action of the Word of God on the mind constitutes the irresistibility of grace? We see in many places in Scripture that regeneration is of such a nature that it cannot be conceived of as existing in the absence of the Word of God. In Romans 10:16-17, we read, "But not all the Israelites accepted the Good News. For Isaiah says, 'Lord, who has believed our message.' Consequently, faith comes from hearing the message, and the message is heard through the word of Christ." Faith comes through hearing.

1 Peter 1:22-25 shows clearly that where there is the new birth, there is the Word of God: "Now that you have purified yourselves by obeying the truth, so that you have sincere love for your brothers, love one another deeply from the heart. For you have been born again, not of perishable seed, but of imperishable, through the living and enduring word of God. For all men are like grass, and all their glory is like the flowers of the field; the grass withers and the flowers fall, but the word of the Lord stands forever. And this is the word that was preached to you."

In Hebrews 4:12 we read, "The word of God is living and active. Sharper than any double-edged sword, it penetrates even to the dividing soul and spirit, joints and marrow; it judges the thoughts and attitudes of the heart. Nothing in all creation is hidden from God's sight. Everything is uncovered and laid bare before the eyes of him to whom we must give account." The Word of God in its activity upon men is seen as living and active. James 1:18 says, "He chose to give us birth through the word of truth, that we might be a kind of first fruits of all that he created." The apostle Paul wrote to the Thessalonians that he knew God had acted upon them in a genuine way, stating in 1 Thessalonians 1:5, "Because our Gospel came to you not simply with words." As one person who has preached at this conference before says, "Now it says here that the gospel came not in word only, but it doesn't say it didn't come in word at all." It did come in word.

2 Thessalonians 2:13 says, "We ought always to thank God for you brothers, loved by the Lord, because from the beginning God chose you to be saved through the sanctifying work of the Spirit and through belief in the truth."

The Word of God is never absent where Scripture speaks of the new birth, regeneration. The lesson we should learn from that is, "Preach the word." One of the most powerful things I have read recently about the power of the word is Thomas Scott's work entitled *The Force of Truth*. The book presents Scott's testimony concerning the power that a close study of the Word of God had upon this man, bringing him out of the heresies of Socinianism and Arminianism into an orthodox understanding of Christ, out of his very shallow understanding of his own sinfulness into a full affirmation of his absolute depravity, and out of a rejection of those doctrines that he considered to be "enthusiastic" and "methodical" (a synonym for "Calvinistic" at that time), into the doctrines of grace. All of it came about through thorough study of the Word of God or "the force of truth," as he called it.

But, again, even as powerful as these passages of Scripture are, and even though the Word of God is a *sine qua non* of regeneration, regeneration is not simply the power of the Word of God, the power of truth itself, upon the mind of a man. You see, the point of Romans 10 is that the Jews have the Word of God and yet are not saved. They have heard but they have not believed. They were given a spirit of stupor, eyes so they could not see and ears so they could not hear (Romans 11:8).

In 1 Peter, the emphasis is the incorruptible seed and the necessity of true holiness resulting from one's confrontation with the Word. The incorruptible seed there is the Holy Spirit. Regeneration is the Holy Spirit, taking the Word of God and applying it to the mind. So the context is this: If the Word of God has acted upon you through the incorruptible seed, then there will be holiness of life. Hebrews 4, speaking of the Word of God, living and powerful and sharper than a two-edged sword, is in the context of those, who (in verse 2) have heard the gospel, but did not combine it with faith. It says, "For we also have had the gospel preached to us, just as they did; but the message they heard was of no value to them, because those who heard it did not combine it with faith." John 3, which speaks of the new birth, emphasizes the necessity of the Spirit's power attending the Word. We must be born of water and the Spirit. The water by analogy with John 7:38, 39 and Ephesians 5:26 denotes the Word of God in its cleansing power as energized by the Spirit. The Word speaks of righteousness and holiness. It reveals to us a holy God, a righteous kingdom, a just salvation, and a sinless heaven. It first instructs the mind to know that we will not be in fellowship with God nor enjoy His blessedness apart from true righteousness and holiness. But then, there are those who had such obvious revelations of truth, in their presence, before their eyes, that any person with an unbiased mind should have been converted and should have believed it; yet, they rejected it.

The truth is so desirable yet so antithetical to man's moral disposition that John could say, "Light has come into the world, and yet men loved darkness rather than light because their deeds were evil." Light is that thing that we should love and desire. Light when it comes in the darkness, allows us to see. It has come into the world, and men loved darkness rather than light! So, it is not the mere confrontation of truth or confrontation of the Word of God with the mind, that is the turning element in regeneration. It is not that that is irresistible.

1 Thessalonians speaks of the necessity of the Spirit's work in effecting God's eternal pleasure toward the sinners in whom He has chosen to delight. Paul was confident of their election because his gospel came "Not in word only, but also with the Holy Spirit and with much conviction." 2 Thessalonians 2 confirms this when he observes that they are loved of God and therefore have been chosen to salvation through "sanctification of the Spirit and the belief of the truth."

Also 2 Thessalonians 2 passes before us the distressing

truth that this Word that resulted in the sanctification of some unto belief of the truth was the same Word disbelieved by many others because they did not receive a love of the truth. Verse 9 unloads the dynamics of this radically different response: "The coming of the lawless one will be in accordance with the work of Satan displayed in all kinds of counterfeit miracles, signs and wonders and in every sort of evil that deceives those who are perishing. They perish because they refused to love the truth and so be saved. For this reason God sends them a powerful delusion so they will believe the lie and so that all will be condemned who have not believed the truth but have delighted in wickedness." A delight in wickedness makes the Word of God, in its exaltation of purity, holiness, and righteousness extremely distasteful.

So the Word of God is powerful, but it is not the bare Word of God impinging upon the mind of a man, that converts him. Rather, the gospel is veiled to those who are perishing. As our text reminds us, Paul, in preaching the gospel, said of those who are perishing, "the god of this world has blinded their minds." Romans 8 says that the mind of the flesh is enmity against God.

When unbelievers hear the law of God, that powerful word of the holiness of God, that law that would give life, they lack the ability and the disposition to obey it. It only condemns them. Their sinfulness makes the law powerless to give life; they hate the law and disobey it. In 1 Corinthians, we see that the man without the Spirit does not accept the things that come from the Spirit of God for they are foolishness to him. He cannot understand them because they are spiritually discerned.

Now, why can't they see the light of the gospel of the glory of Christ who is the image of God? Why can't someone see that? Why can't someone see the most glorious thing that is in existence, the one who is the sum of very being itself and who has all infinite perfections in Himself? Why can they not desire that? They neither see nor desire that because the god of this world has blinded their minds.

THE WRATH OF GOD

Many distinct elements in this gospel of the Word of God would in themselves irresistibly press an unbiased mind to faith. The truths of Scripture should be irresistible. Think for a moment of the awesome nature of condemnation. Consider the images in Micah 1, where the picture is given of the wrath of God as God comes forth in His holiness to a disobedient Israel. Micah 1:2 says, "Hear, O peoples, all of you, listen, O earth and all who are in it, that the Sovereign Lord may witness against you, the Lord from His holy temple." Now the prophet sees the Lord coming in His power and His holiness. "Look! The Lord is coming from His dwelling place; He comes down and treads the high places of the earth. The mountains melt beneath Him, and the valleys split apart, like wax before the fire, like water rushing down a slope. All of this is because of Jacob's transgression, because of the sins of house of Israel. What is Jacob's transgression? Is it not Samaria? What is Judah's high place? Is it not Jerusalem?" The prophet under the awful pressure of a clear revelation of God's righteous wrath assaults them with an irresistible call to repentance. Aren't you essentially all throughout yourself and even in your worship an abomination to God? And who will stand when He appears? The mountains will split apart. They will melt like wax. It will be like water running down hill. Nothing can resist God's wrath when it comes.

All those who are outside Christ are under condemnation, even a more aggravated condemnation. A vivid picture of the same wrath in the New Testament is found in 2 Thessalonians 1:8-10, which says of the Lord's return: "He will punish those who do not know God and do not obey the Gospel of our Lord Jesus. They will be punished with everlasting destruction and shut out from the presence of the Lord and from the majesty of His power on the day He comes to be glorified in His holy people." He comes with blazing fire and powerful angels.

No one can stand when He comes. You might try to brace yourself against it. The sinner might say that he can bear it for awhile. But it will be unbearable, and yet God will hold all of these beings in existence while He exhibits upon them wrath without mercy. Everything here in this life is tended with mercy. Every trial, every temptation, every bit of wrath, every punishment, every chastisement that comes has mercy connected with it. But in eternity, when those who are outside of Christ are experiencing the wrath of God, it will be without mercy. Irresistible, unbearable, and yet, they must sustain it to all eternity.

Such revelations give an irresistibility to the teaching about wrath, you might say. Such truths embedded within the passionate presentation of clear descriptive narrative ought to give reasons to the mind and motivation to the affections. A person with an unbiased mind who can perceive what that wrath of God must be should shutter before God, fall before Him, repent, and turn to Christ. But what in fact is the case? They say "It's not true. God's not like that," and "Not me. We just pass out of existence at death. That's all there is to it." Or maybe they say, "We come back and get another chance in another form."

There are all kinds of schemes that we invent to ignore the clarity of God's decree that it is appointed to man once to die and after that the judgment. The wrath of God is indeed unbearable. That should be an irresistible doctrine. But men are not converted on that. Some may become frightened in the same way that the demons in hell are frightened. Unconverted men would like to escape wrath the same way the demons in hell would like to escape it if they thought that they could. They might even meet a few requirements in the same way the demons in hell would if they thought it would do them any good. Such penitentiary repentance with the hope of parole does not produce disciples. Still they do not love the truth.

THE GLORY OF THE TRIUNE GOD

The Sovereign Lord.

There is an irresistibility in the glory of the Triune God. No one is sufficient to describe the glory of the Triune God. The question is asked many times in Isaiah 40. "To whom will you compare Me?" (Isaiah 40:25). God reveals Himself in great power and majesty to Isaiah, seeking to comfort the people. He speaks through the prophet in verse 9: "You who bring good tidings to Zion, go up on a high mountain. You who bring good tidings to Jerusalem, lift up your voice with a shout, lift it up, do not be afraid; say to the towns of Judah 'Here is your God!' See, the Sovereign Lord comes with power, and His arm rules for Him. See His reward is with Him and His recompense accompanies Him. He tends His flock like a Shepherd. He gathers the lambs in His arms and carries them close to His heart; and He gently leads those that have young." What could be more endearing and irresistible? The sovereign Lord, coming with power, gently leading those who have young.

Isaiah 40:18 says, "To whom, then, will you compare God? What image will you compare Him to?" The prophet then shows the irrational activity of those who make for themselves idols. He describes the beauty and majesty of God above all these things. Isaiah 40:25-28 says,

> "To whom will you compare Me? Or who is My equal?" says the Holy One. Lift your eyes and look to the heavens: Who created all these? He who brings out the starry hosts one by one, and calls them each by name. Because of His great power and mighty strength, not one of them is missing. Why do you say, O Jacob, and complain, O Israel, "My way is hidden from the Lord; my cause is disregarded by my God?" Do you not know? Have you not heard? The Lord is the everlasting God, the Creator of the ends of the earth. He will not grow tired or weary, and His understanding no one can fathom.

That should be irresistible, and I think to many of you it is.

You hear the words, and they give you a sense of awe, wonder, majesty and worship. But it is because you have been taught to love the truth. Even the glories of the Triune God, Holy Father, Holy Son, Holy Spirit, these Three in One, living in eternal glory, bliss, and excellence, enjoying a love relationship within Himself, having absolutely perfect communication, needing nothing outside Himself, an inexpressibly ineffable, Holy Being, inexpressible beauty, irresistible, and yet despised—even these glories don't make any sense to the natural mind. That which is compelling above all else is resisted.

The Person of Christ.

As an aspect of viewing the glory of the triune God, we could talk about the glory of the person of Christ. My, what a mysterious glory thrives in the person of Christ! The Word—the eternal Word—was made Flesh and dwelt among us. John testifies to having beheld His glory (the glory as of the only begotten of the Father), full of grace and truth. "No man has ever gone into heaven," Jesus said. Since Enoch and Elijah were taken to heaven, we conclude that Jesus meant by heaven the center of the manifestation of God's intrinsic, unapproachable glory. The one exception to this, however, is the Son of Man who came down from heaven. What do those words mean? The Son of Man who came down from heaven wasn't the Son of Man while He was in heaven. He had not come down from heaven while He was the Son of Man. He became the Son of Man at the moment He was conceived in the womb of the virgin Mary. Yet He uses the phrase "Son of Man" to describe Himself as coming down from heaven. What does He mean? He means now, in His person, something has happened that is mysterious. He is God and man in one person, indivisibly, so that, as He refers to Himself as in heaven, He uses a phrase that refers in particular to His incarnation.

That is a mystery, but it is beautiful. There is an indivisibility now to the union of the natures of Christ that guarantees an eternality to all of those who have union with Him. There is one mediator between God and man, the Man, Christ Jesus. Since by man, came death, by man came also the resurrection of the dead. God has said that all things will be put under the feet of man, but we do not see all things under his feet. We see Jesus and all things under Him.

How? There is a wonder to the incarnation, the glory of the person of Christ. God and Man, the image of God, as our text in 2 Corinthians 4 said. Hebrews says that He is the "brightness of His glory, the express image of His person." A wonder —oh, if we could fathom the depths of that—there would be something irresistible to it! Any person with an unbiased mind considering the glory of the incarnation of our Lord, seeing this majestic deity, as Hebrews 1 speaks about Him, and then going to Hebrews 5 and finding: "During the days of Jesus' life on earth He offered up loud cries and prayers and tears to the One who could save Him from death."

Is this the One that we say is the brightness of His glory, now offering up cries, prayers, with tears, and agony? Yes, the same One! The glory in His person. William Gadsby said:

> In the person of the Savior,
> All His majesty is seen!
> Here He shines, and shines forever.
> And, without a veil between,
> Worms approach Him,
> And rejoice in His dear Name.
> *("O What Matchless Condescension")*

That's irresistible, but even that is not the irresistibility of grace.

The Work of Christ.

Do you see how sinful we are? Do you see what kind of power we need to convert us, that even the glory and perfection of Christ's work is not irresistible. It should be irresistible, as we think of what the Lord Jesus Christ has done in His work. Hebrews 7 contains a phrase that I think is one of the most wonderful, marvelous, and instructive descriptions of His work in verse 26, "Such a High Priest meets our need."

Now, should preachers preach "need-centered" preaching? Without doubt! You've just got to know what the need is. "Such a High Priest meets our need." Our need is not to be popular. Our need is not to feel affirmed by everybody and to have a high self image. I think those things are great, and if they come along in the healing power of God, wonderful. But what is the need the Scripture talks about here? He meets our need. One who is holy, blameless, pure, set apart from sinners, exalted above the heavens, unlike other high priests, meets our need. He does not need to offer sacrifices day after day, first for His own sins, and then for the sins of the people. He sacrificed for their sins, once for all when He offered Himself.

We need someone who has lived a life of perfect obedience to the law of God, having in Himself the righteousness that we must have to stand before God, so that, in union with Him, we are declared not guilty.

> No condemnation now I dread;
>   Jesus, and all in Him is mine!
> Alive in Him, my living Head,
>   And clothed in righteousness divine.
> Bold I approach the eternal throne,
> And claim the crown through Christ my own.
> *("And Can It Be," Charles Wesley)*

One who is holy, blameless, pure, set apart from sinners, exalted above the heavens, that's what we need. We need forgiveness. We need someone who has died for us. Someone who has taken the wrath of God for us. Christ has died once for all. When He offered Himself, He met our need. For any person with an unbiased, unprejudiced mind, and who knows that he is under condemnation and is helpless to do anything about it, that should be irresistible to him. Yet, to those in a natural condition, that doctrine is not irresistible.

I trust it is irresistible to you. I pray that by God's grace, when you hear of the sacrifice of Christ and see Him bleeding and dying on the cross for sinners, it does something to you inside. I pray it makes you have at least some moment of deep resolution to live a life of holiness before God, to be pleasing to Him and full of gratitude to Him for this great sacrifice.

It is irresistible to those who have tasted that the Lord is precious, who have been convinced of it in their heart and have learned to love the truth. Gadsby again says,

> In His greatest work, redemption,
> See His glory in a blaze;
> Nor can angels ever mention
> Aught that more of God displays.
> Truth and mercy
> Here unite to endless days.
> *("O What Matchless Condescension")*

An irresistible doctrine, but that is not the irresistibility of grace. Why? Because they are holy doctrines. The doctrine of a Triune God is a holy doctrine. 1 Peter 1:15 says: "Just as He who called you is holy, so be holy in all you do; for it is written: 'Be holy because I am holy.'" Unholy men are not attracted to holy doctrines.

The Justice of God.

The doctrine of condemnation is a holy doctrine. Jonathan Edwards demonstrated this powerfully in a sermon entitled, "The Justice of God in the Condemnation of Sinners." Until we come to see clearly that God indeed is just in His condemnation, our level of conviction will not press us to Christ.

Our concern here is not a willingness to be damned to the glory of God. That is not a proper biblical concept. But one who has a true conviction of the ugly unholiness of sin will not seek to defend it and will sense intuitively the justice of

God in His punishment of sinners and will see with equal clarity that the sacrifice of Christ was necessary if any are to be forgiven. The pure holiness of Paul's phrase, "He who spared not His own Son, but delivered Him up for us all," becomes a holy wonder of infinite proportions seen in this light. Condemnation is a holy doctrine. It would not exist if God were not a holy God, and if it were not right and just for Him to hold sinners under eternal condemnation. All doctrines connected with it are holy.The person of Christ is a holy doctrine. The virgin birth is a holy doctrine. Christ's impeccability is a holy and necessary doctrine. Everything about the Person of Christ is a holy doctrine.

The work of Christ is a holy doctrine. He was born of a woman, born under the law, to redeem those who are under the law. His holy life of living in obedience to the law is a holy doctrine. Romans 8 describes Him when it says that "in Him the just requirements of the law are fulfilled." These are holy doctrines, and that is the reason unholy men are not drawn to God by them.

The more holy we conceive of these doctrines, the more we, as enemies of a holy God, will reject them. That which is unholy resists that which is holy; it's a reflex action. The brighter, the more glorious the sinner sees God is, the more he wants to escape from Him.

THE SOVEREIGN WORK OF THE HOLY SPIRIT

What then is it that draws us? In what lies the transforming power of grace? Is it the work of the Spirit, teaching us and then neutralizing us to allow us a hypothetical freedom to make a decision? I don't see any support for this in Scripture. Besides the absurdity of a moral agent being in a condition of utter neutrality concerning holiness, choice in such a condition is impossible; were it possible it would not be New Testament faith, for New Testament faith counts everything loss for the excellency of the knowledge of Christ Jesus. In addition, Scripture presents this transformation as a matter of omnipotent bestowal of life. Ephesians 2:5 says, while we are dead in trespasses and sins we are made alive. 1 John 3:7-10 teaches us that there is a planting of a seed in us,

> Dear children do not let anyone lead you astray. He who does what is right is righteous, just as He is righteous. He who does what is sinful is of the devil, because the devil has been sinning from the beginning. The reason the Son of God appeared was to destroy the devil's work. No one who is born of God, will continue to sin, because God's seed remains in him. He cannot go on sinning because he has been born of God.

The new birth, resurrection from death to life, creation, all of these are figures or analogies that tell us something has transpired that we cannot produce. We are not made neutral and then left to ourselves. We are created anew. We are born again. We are raised from the dead.

So what is irresistible grace? Irresistible grace is the mysterious and sovereign work of the Holy Spirit in which He so alters our moral disposition that the holy doctrines of the gospel become compelling and irresistible to us. We, therefore, submit to their truth and to the God of whom they speak.

That particular change must take place. No sinner in the natural condition will love any doctrine of the gospel and submit to any doctrine of the gospel before the moral disposition is changed. It is impossible. It is against the entire witness of Scripture. It is against the entire history of the sinfulness of man. Every evidence of the reaction of men to the miracles of Christ shows us this is so. The Word of God says that no man will turn himself from the flesh to the Spirit. All men will turn from spiritual things and hate them unless there is a moral change. And who makes that change? The Holy Spirit of God.

So, the new birth, the new creation, the divine seed, being

raised from death to life, is the work of the Spirit. Jonathon Edwards argues with an engaging spiritual brilliance for this very truth in a sermon entitled, "The Necessity of a Divine and Supernatural Light Immediately Imparted to the Soul of Man, Both a Biblical and a Rational Doctrine." It is built upon the confession of Peter at Caesarea Philippi when Jesus said to him, "Flesh and blood has not revealed this to you, but my Father who is in Heaven." That is irresistible grace. No person forced to do something against his will. None is drawn kicking and screaming into the kingdom. That analogy may be used at times when speaking of some moment prior to the new birth and has been used powerfully in a literary fashion. But it is this sovereign, secret, mysterious work of the Holy Spirit. He takes all the teachings of the Bible, and, by His grace, blowing where He wants, changes the moral disposition so that which was once hateful to us now appears our only hope. That which was hateful to us now appears to be our glory, something we should love. We have come to love the truth. We have seen the Kingdom of God.

So, what should we do? First, we should pray for the accompanying ministry of the Holy Spirit whenever we preach. "Not by might, nor by power, but by my Spirit," says the Lord. Second, we should preach the Word in such a way that its holiness is highlighted. God and man must be seen in true perspective. It does no good to the sinner when we hide the holiness of God. It is no part of the ministry of the gospel to seek to persuade men to close with Christ, when He is not perceived as a holy Christ, and men do not perceive themselves as unrighteous, unholy, men under condemnation. We must preach these doctrines in a way that highlights their holiness. Third, I think the admonition of the apostle Paul to Timothy is one on which to close. In 1 Timothy 4:7-8, Paul says to the young minister, "Train yourself to be godly. For physical training is of some value, but godliness has value for all things, holding promise for both the present life and the life to come." We end with verse 16: "Watch your life and your doctrine closely. Persevere in them, because if you do, you will save both yourself and your hearers." It is my prayer that the grace of God will become more and more irresistible to all of us.

23.
CORRECTIVE CHURCH DISCIPLINE
BILL ASCOL
1999 Southern Baptist Founders Conference

INTRODUCTION

I CAN remember it like it was yesterday—the spring of 1984. I was three months into my new pastorate and visiting with one of the church's deacons. He asked me if I had heard that the Sunday School Director (a married woman whose father was a retired Southern Baptist minister in our congregation and whose brother was vice-chairman of the deacons) had decided to divorce her husband and marry the pianist (a man who was a graduate of one of our seminaries, himself divorced and a deacon in the church). My knees buckled and I felt sick. Unknowingly, indeed, unwittingly, I had embarked on what Richard Belcher would later call a "journey in purity." I was about to enroll in an eight-year long course in church discipline that would be taught by what Ernie Reisinger calls "an odd teacher"—experience. She is odd because she gives you the test first, and then the lesson.

I summoned the "would be couple" to my study on Saturday morning and asked them if what I had heard was true—had they indeed discussed and planned to be married to each other? When they answered, "Yes" to my question, I informed them that they had sinned against the Lord Jesus' prohibition not to divide asunder what God had joined together. I further told them that they had violated the trust given to those who lead in the congregation and that they immediately would have to resign all positions of church leadership. I also admonished them to take definite steps at

405

once to break off their illegitimate relationship. They said they would think about it.

Needless to say, Sunday morning services were somewhat tense. On Monday morning the man showed up at my door at daybreak, with a friend, and manifested what appeared to be genuine repentance. I was euphoric. This is exactly how it is supposed to happen, I thought. But by Monday evening I was receiving phone calls telling me that plans were being made to sue me for slander and defamation of character. In the next eight years of ministry in that place I rode a roller-coaster of pastoral emotions: anger at the endless lies that were told about me; joy at the victories God gave us in the forward progress of reformation in that place; fear that I would be terminated as pastor and my wife and children left homeless; and peace, when the Lord confirmed on more than one occasion that this was His battle. Time and time again I ran the gauntlet of emotions from sadness, depression, confusion, and aloneness; to gladness, hopefulness, and confidence. I had the unspeakable privilege of seeing God raise up a body of believers who wanted their lives, their homes, and their church to be devoted to the glory of God and the exaltation of His Son, Jesus Christ. By God's grace a strong church was raised out of the ashes of an undisciplined congregation, and this body of believers stands today as a testimony to the power of God and His sovereign determination to purify a people for Himself.

The subject of corrective church discipline is something that I am absolutely convinced is both biblical and necessary. I believe John Dagg stated a profound truth when he asserted, "When discipline leaves the church, Christ goes with it."[1]

The urgency we feel today in the need to recover biblical corrective church discipline is made more pressing when one considers an article entitled, "Where Do Southern Bap-

---

1 John L., Dagg, *Manual of Theology and Church Order* (Harrisonburg, VA: Gano Books, 1982 reprint), 274.

tists Stand With Reference to Church Discipline?" that appeared thirty-nine years ago in the *Texas Baptist Standard.* Listen to this amazing observation made in 1959:

> A recent Southern Baptist survey discloses that for every 10 persons who join churches, 10 years later two are dead, one has dropped out of church, three have become non-resident, leaving only four of the 10 as local members. Of this four only two are active. This means that Southern Baptists are bringing under discipline only about 20 percent of the approximately 400,000 people they win per year.[2]

Note, when the author speaks of "bringing under discipline," he means getting them inside the church facility to teach them.

In 1962, James Leo Garrett stated,

> Baptists in the United States, and Southern Baptists in particular, are giving meager evidence of having today an ordered, disciplined churchmanship. This appears to be true whether one considers ethics, theology, or church order. Moral failures, which often are crimes as well as sins, increasingly occur among church members —Baptists and otherwise—and are reported in the public press. Even ordained ministers and other church leaders may experience such failures and no action by the congregation or by denominational bodies be taken...there is among Baptists widespread indifference toward the great Christian affirmations. While claiming to revere the Bible and to adhere to the New Testament as the basis of religious authority,

2 Bill G. West, "Where Do Southern Baptists Stand With Reference to Church Discipline?" *Texas Baptist Standard*, Dallas; July 23, 1959, 10.

Southern Baptists have been too little involved in the renewal of biblical theology. "[3]

Garrett went on to lament:

Inactive and nonparticipating church members and the problem of nonresident membership have become major Southern Baptist difficulties.[4]

And what is the remedy to these difficulties? The answer is found in following the Bible's teachings on the all but forgotten subject of corrective church discipline.

CHURCH DISCIPLINE: WHAT?

Even though we have lived to see something of a renewal in biblical theology, it still must be acknowledged that Southern Baptists, by and large, don't have much more concern about the recovery of corrective church discipline than they did when Garrett made his observations in the 1960s. I want to give you a working definition of church discipline. The words "discipline" and "disciple" come from the same Greek root, *manthano*, which means to develop, teach, or train. Thus the Great Commission of Christ is the basic commandment to the church in the matter of discipline. The church is to "disciple" all nations and then discipline them in all that Christ has commanded. Church discipline, in its full meaning, refers to the total instructional and developmental program of the church. This program is mainly positive but must include those more forceful steps prescribed by the New Testament for the protection of the church from schism and corruption and for the reclamation of erring

3 James Leo Garrett, *Baptist Church Discipline* (Nashville: Broadman Press, 1962); 1.
4 Ibid.

members."⁵ Now, clearly, when we talk about discipline there is *formative* discipline and there is *corrective* discipline. Formative discipline is going on all the time in churches. You are teaching, instructing, and leading people in learning to do whatsoever our Lord has commanded us to do. That is formative discipline.

What is meant by the term "corrective church discipline"? My definition is a complex sentence but I have tried to cram in it what I believe is the answer: Corrective church discipline, I believe, is the redemptive process ordained by God, taught by Jesus Christ, and practiced by the apostles; whereby, for the glory of God, the exalting of the name of Jesus Christ, the protection and well being of a congregation, and the good of his own soul, a disciple who has begun a path of sinful disregard for his covenant commitment might be brought to repentance, rescued from his sin, restored to fellowship with Christ, and recovered to the ministry of the church.

When practiced according to the precepts and pattern of the Scriptures in the Spirit of Jesus Christ, corrective church discipline functions not as a guillotine to hold over anyone, but rather as a banner of truth to be lifted in the midst of the assembly. It is not an accusatory charge pointed at a particular person, but rather a biblical challenge made to all. It is not a stone to be hurled in judgment, but rather an Ebenezer, a rock of testimony, erected in the midst of the church as a reminder of the serious obligations that attend our association with the redemptive mission of the church of the Lord Jesus Christ.

The Gospel of Matthew records five major discourses of Jesus Christ. The eighteenth chapter contains one of these. It is the pivotal passage in the gospel on relationships between brethren. The gospel at its heart is a message of rec-

---

5 West, "Where Do Southern Baptists Stand With Reference to Church Discipline?" *Texas Baptist Standard*, 10.

onciliation. In His death on the cross, Jesus Christ has leveled the middle wall of partition, thereby making a way for sinners to be reconciled to God and to fellow believers. Jesus Christ has made for Himself one new humanity from those who were previously alienated from God and all too prone to be alienated from one another. Generally when the need for discipline arises in a congregation, it does so because there has been some breach in relationships.

Recognition of this and a proper understanding of the teachings of Jesus in Matthew 18 are necessary in order to understand and implement corrective church discipline in the lives of congregated sinners saved by grace who are frailly attempting to relate to one another as redeemed ones. Jesus teaches us five lessons in this passage that tell us something about His heart and how He expects His people to relate to one another.

First, Jesus assigns greatness to humility (Matthew 18:1-5). It is not clear what triggered the debate over what constituted greatness in the kingdom of heaven. It is clear, however, that Jesus seized the opportunity to set a little child in the midst of the disciples and to tell them that they needed to be changed and live as humble men among one another.

Second, Jesus abhors offensive conduct (Matthew 18:6-9). If there was any question concerning Jesus' attitude toward the destructive nature of offensive behavior, that was completely removed by His assertion that a person would be better off drowned with a millstone around his neck than to live long enough to cause one of the little ones who believe in Him to sin. Acknowledging that offenses would inevitably come, He used the most severe language imaginable, as if to say, "Be sure that offenses do not come from you."

Third, Jesus adores every one of His sheep (Matthew 18:10-14). Why does Jesus find offensive conduct so offensive? Because He loves His sheep so much and earnestly longs for the well-being and safety of every one of them. Even if ninety-nine are safe, He will go to great lengths to recover the one who has gone astray. This is the heart of the

Savior, and it must be the heart of His followers.

Fourth, Jesus affords a plan for the recovery and reconciliation of His people when they go astray (Matthew 18:15-20). When an offense occurs between two professing believers who are functioning as brothers in Christ, it is important that the one who has been offended go to the offender and attempt to restore him to a reconciled relationship. If this attempt is unsuccessful, then others should be enlisted in the recovery effort. If this, too, fails, then the church must be notified so that it might be engaged in the recovery effort. If the joint energies and evangelical efforts of the congregation fail to move the erring brother so that he is led to repentance, then he must be regarded as one who has never repented. At this point the chief concern for the brother shifts from his being reconciled to a fellow believer to his need to be reconciled to God by the saving work of Jesus Christ. The authority to do this has been given by Jesus Christ Himself. The church that neglects this is derelict in its duties and demonstrates a lack of love for the sheep.

Fifth, Jesus admonishes His followers to forgive one another (Matthew 18:21-35). As if to emphasize that corrective church discipline is always undertaken with a view to the redemptive recovery of the erring brother, Jesus seized the occasion of Peter's question regarding forgiveness to set the whole matter into perspective. Because believers have been forgiven an enormous debt by the mercy of God, we ought always to be ready to forgive anyone who has sinned against us and repents of his sin. Failure to forgive in such a situation casts a cloud of suspicion over the unforgiving individual's experience of forgiveness from God. Jesus closes this passage on reconciled relationships with a warning that any who fail to forgive those who have sinned against them can expect nothing but torment in the life that is to come.

Jesus' teaching of corrective church discipline begins with the need for humility, ends with the need for a forgiving attitude, and is saturated throughout with a compassion for souls. This is the only proper climate in which corrective church discipline can be carried out in a way that pleases God.

CHURCH DISCIPLINE: WHY?

A question that inevitably arises when the subject of corrective church discipline is discussed, is: "Why do we need to do this when no one is perfect?" There are at least five answers to the question that arise from the Word of God. These answers must always be kept before those who are considering this weighty subject, and wisdom dictates that the order of these answers should not be changed.

The Scripture teaches it.

Both times that our Lord Jesus speaks of the church in the gospels (Matthew 16:18-19 & 18:15-20), he addresses the subject of church discipline and the church's God-given authority to "bind" and "loose." There are numerous passages throughout the New Testament that teach the propriety, indeed the necessity, of corrective church discipline. These passages will be considered later. For now suffice it to say that the sincere follower of Jesus Christ cannot ignore that the Savior Himself called His disciples to this practice.

The glory of God demands it.

We are to do all that we do in order to glorify God. His glory in the midst of the congregation should be the chief concern and primary motivating factor when the need for corrective church discipline arises (1 Corinthians 10:31; 2 Samuel 2:30; Romans 2:24). He will not share His glory with another. Nor will He manifest His glory in the midst of a people who so lightly regard His name, and the name of His dear Son.

The name of Jesus Christ upon the congregation requires it.

The church of Jesus Christ is to be comprised of disciples,

students who are willing to be taught and desirous to learn everything that Jesus has commanded us (Matthew 28:19-20). His name is mocked when His people carry on in sin (2 Corinthians 2:9, 17). The Puritan John Owen once stated, "This living Head will admit of no dead members in the building He is building."

The good of the body as a whole depends upon it.

Unlike the hyper-individualism that is so rampant in America, the Bible places the wellbeing of the whole above the interests of the individual (1 Corinthians 5:6-7). Those in a disciplined body are not only protected from the harm of erring members, but they themselves are deterred from sin (1 Timothy 5:20). As the Scots Confession stated, "vice is repressed and virtue nourished."[6] The little lambs in an assembly have the right to be protected by God's appointed under-shepherds from the ugly actions of goats and the destructive ways of wolves—even if such behavior manifests itself in the midst of the congregation. Furthermore, where corrective church discipline fails to be practiced, you can be sure that the enemy of our souls will embolden others to sin scandalously.

The well being of the erring individual is essential to it.

The individual is important, because he is a creature made in the image of God with a soul that will never die. He needs to be redemptively recovered—in fact, if discipline is undertaken with any other desire or goal in mind than to recover the wayward member, then no matter how meticulously the Scripture pattern is followed, that action cannot be called biblical corrective church discipline (cf. 1 Corinthians 5:5).

---

6 Daniel E.Wray, *Biblical Church Discipline* (Edinburgh: Banner of Truth, 1981), 4.

CHURCH DISCIPLINE: WHEN?

If the propriety of corrective church discipline is granted, and the reasons for engaging in it are embraced, then the question naturally arises: "When should corrective church discipline be practiced?" Generally speaking, when there is a breach of any type in the fellowship, steps should be taken to close that breach and recover the involved parties to a reconciled status.

> In each case, the cause of further discipline is impenitence. The person who will not repent of his sin is not living like a Christian. Only the repentant sinner can be counted as holy in Christ, and only the holy in Christ have a place in the fellowship of the saints (i.e. holy ones), as members of Christ's church. Therefore, regardless of what the offender's sin(s) might be, it is ultimately his impenitence that must exclude him from the church.[7]

Some examples of occasions when corrective church discipline should be undertaken are:

1. In cases of broken fellowship and unforgiveness (cf. Matthew 18:15-17).
2. In cases of unbelief and doctrinal error (cf., Romans 16:17-18).
3. In cases of divisive and disorderly conduct (cf., 2 Thessalonians 3:11-15).
4. In cases of immorality (1 Corinthians 5:1ff).
5. In cases of habitual neglect of involvement in the ministry of the church (Hebrews 10:25).

CHURCH DISCIPLINE: WHO?

Since all are sinners and no one is perfect, who are the proper

---

7 Ibid., 9.

subjects of corrective church discipline?

The immoral and those guilty of public scandal (Titus 1:16; 1 Corinthians 5).

"Those who live in habitual violation of biblical morality, and refuse to repent when admonished and rebuked, must be removed from church membership."[8]

Those who have departed from a cardinal doctrine of the faith (1 Timothy 1:19-20; 6:3-5; 2 John 7-11).

This does not mean that every member should be a finely-tuned theologian, but it does mean that every member should be in substantial agreement with the doctrines of the congregation to which he belongs, and no member should "knowingly reject any of those doctrines which the church considers essential and fundamental."[9]

Those who cause divisions in the body (Romans 16:17-18; Titus 3:10).

"Such persons must be watched, rebuked, and, if necessary, removed."[10]

Those who will not be reconciled to a fellow believer (Matthew 18:15-18).

"Though such offenses may begin in secret, they must ultimately result in public censure if the offender stubbornly refuses to repent."[11]

CHURCH DISCIPLINE: HOW?

When someone asks how corrective church discipline should

---

8 Ibid., 9.
9 Ibid., 9.
10 Ibid., 8.
11 Ibid., 8.

be undertaken, they usually are asking what steps should be taken to set the rescue and recovery mission in motion. The answer to such a question depends upon whether a personal or private offense is involved, or an offense of scandalous and perhaps public proportions. It is generally true that the response to personal or private offenses should follow the pattern set forth in Matthew 18:15-20. Very often offenses of a scandalous or public nature must be handled after the pattern given by the Apostle Paul to the church in Corinth (see 1 Corinthians 5:1ff). The church there had in its midst an immoral man whose circumstances were generally known. Paul called for immediate and swift action on the part of the church and made no suggestion that it was necessary for one person, or even two or three witnesses, to go and visit the man first. When in doubt, however, following the pattern of Matthew 18 is the better part of wisdom, even though it is not necessary to do so in every circumstance.

Admonition, Exhortation, Rebuke—either private or public (Matthew 18:15; Ephesians 5:11; 1 Timothy 5:20; 2 Timothy 4:2; Titus 1:9, 13, 2:15).

Admonition involves warning an individual of the danger of a particular attitude or tendency toward inappropriate conduct. This takes place oftentimes in the pastor's study, in private counsel, or with someone who may be in the early stages of a potentially destructive pattern (Romans 15:14; Colossians 3:16; 1 Thessalonians 5:14; 2 Thessalonians 3: 14-15; Titus 3:10-11).

Rebuke consists in pointing out sinful attitudes and/or actions of which an individual is actually guilty and calling upon that person to repent and bear fruit of a genuine change of heart and mind on the matter. Rebuke can take place privately or even publicly, depending upon the sphere in which the sinful conduct has occurred. If public rebuke is necessary, then it may be accompanied by suspension.

Suspension of voting privileges and admittance to the Lord's Table (implied by 1 Corinthians 11:27-32).

Suspension of voting privileges and admittance to the Lord's Supper may be necessary for a season as a tool to provoke someone to repent and return to a posture of faithfulness regarding congregational covenant commitments. For example, habitual absence to congregational worship services is not on a par with immorality or public drunkenness, but it is nonetheless a serious breach of faith. Such a person should not think that he or she can simply show up after a long absence and partake the Lord's Supper without eating and drinking condemnation upon himself. Nor should such a person think that he or she can simply show up at the next business meeting and participate in the conduct of the church's business with others who have been faithfully engaged in the ministry.

Suspension may also be necessary when someone who has been guilty of public sin or scandalous sin has shown hopeful signs of repentance and a season of time needs to pass to allow for the genuineness of the expression to be seen.

Excommunication (Matthew 18:17; 1 Corinthians 5:11, 13).

This most severe act of corrective church discipline is tantamount to the church saying, with tears, that inasmuch as the erring individual's life and conduct has taken on the pattern of that of an unconverted person, the church sadly agrees with the characterization of that lifestyle and concludes that the erring individual no longer should be considered a member of the congregation. Wray says,

> Thus this most severe of the forms of discipline excludes the offender from the church and from all the privileges of membership. However, while the person must certainly be excluded from the

Lord's Supper, he is not excluded from attendance upon the ministry of the Word preached
and taught, for even non-believers are welcome
to the public assemblies (1 Corinthians 14:23-
25).[12]

Since the goal of church discipline is reconciliation, recovery and restoration, it is

...not to be thought that excommunication is ir-
reversible, for the person who repents of his sin
and seeks God's cleansing and pardon is to be
welcomed back into the fellowship of the church
(2 Corinthians 2:6-8). Indeed, it is the responsibility of God's people to continue to pray for any
persons thus removed from fellowship that God
will bring them to repentance.[13]

The termination of a person's church membership once had a devastating, if not redemptive, impact upon the individual in question. Such is not always the case today. Because of the loose way in which many "churches" receive persons into membership, an excommunicated person who knows the various schedules of the churches in his area can, with a zealous determination, join four or five churches by nightfall on any given Sunday. This loose conduct on the part of other congregations does not, however, relieve those who are committed to corrective church discipline from the redemptive undertaking of this particular aspect of the Great Commission.

CHURCH DISCIPLINE: WHERE?

When any matter of corrective discipline takes on public dimensions (i.e., where it appears that suspension and/or ex-

12 Ibid., 8.
13 Ibid., 8.

communication is going to be inevitable), then the entire congregation should be made aware of and become involved in the process. Some make the mistake of confining the handling and administering of corrective church discipline to the elders and/or deacons. However, this unwise practice violates a principle of Baptist polity. The rule that should be followed is this: The same deliberative body that received the individual into the membership is the only one empowered to dismiss the individual from membership. This means that no group of elders, no body of deacons can, in and of themselves, remove anyone from membership. Our Lord Jesus Christ said, "Tell it to the church," and no one should ignore His command. When the erring individual repents and seeks forgiveness, it is the congregation's responsibility to receive him back and restore him to fellowship.

APPLICATION OF CORRECTIVE DISCIPLINE

Because we live in a day that is very litigious (i.e., very inclined to taking everything and everyone to court), pastors and church leaders must be very careful in leading a congregation to implement as a part of their church's doctrines and disciplines the biblical practice of redemptive, corrective church discipline. The following is a suggested list of action plans to take in teaching and leading a congregation on this matter. There is also a list of pitfalls to avoid once an individual, or group, or even congregation become convinced that in order to honor God in their midst the practice of redemptive, corrective church discipline must be a part of the warp and woof of a church's life together.

Action Plans.

First, teach your congregation (particularly your key leaders) the biblical material on the subject of redemptive, corrective church discipline. Seize the opportunity when preaching through the gospels or epistles to show how prominent such a posture was in the writings of the authors of

Holy Scripture. A series on Jesus' use of the term "church" will bring the congregation face to face with the concept of discipline (Matthew 16; Matthew 18). An exposition of 1 Corinthians presents the congregation, in the fifth chapter, with the Apostle Paul's exhortation concerning the handling of scandalous conduct in the church. A series on relationships preached from Matthew 18 (following the proposed five-point outline above or something similar) allows for a serious consideration of verses 15 through 20. Whatever it takes, familiarize your congregation with the biblical texts that address the subject.

In a more pointed way, disciple your spiritual leaders concerning the necessity of church discipline in order to have a biblically ordered congregation. Show them that just as formative discipline (teaching) is necessary, even so corrective discipline also is necessary for there to be a balanced growth among the members. Point out to them that families where corrective discipline is seldom or never practiced are almost always families marked by turmoil and chaos. Observe that the same is true in educational settings where teachers have the responsibility to teach students, but not the authority to correct their bad behavior.

Help your spiritual leaders to see the importance of recovering the biblical and Baptistic doctrine of a regenerate church membership. Teach them that only persons who give evidence of having become followers of Jesus Christ are entitled to membership in Baptist churches.

Second, make good literature available on the subject. Richard Belcher's excellent book entitled *A Journey in Purity* is a great place to begin reading about this subject, because the story is told in novel form. Daniel Wray's booklet on *Biblical Church Discipline* is brief but saturated with scriptural texts showing the soundness of this practice in the life of the church. More recently a book entitled *Polity* has been edited by Mark Dever and printed by the Center for Church Reform. It is a collection of ten historic Baptist documents addressing various aspects of corrective church discipline. The preponderance of literature available on the subject will go a long way to convince your leadership that the idea of corrective church discipline is certainly not new or cultic. If the spiritual leadership becomes convinced of the importance of this issue, the congregation will almost always follow in stride—if not immediately, at least ultimately.

Third, examine and evaluate your church's constitution, bylaws, covenant, and confession to make your congregation "judgment proof." While it is terrible to believe in the practice of corrective church discipline and not have a congregation agree with you, it is equally tragic to have a congregation agree with you on the importance of this matter and not have the documents in place to protect you (and them) from a devastating lawsuit that could bring irreparable harm to many. It is important from a legal standpoint that the documents by which your church undertakes its ministry include language that serves notice of your intent to practice corrective church discipline and that calls for the practice of redemptive, corrective church discipline. The church's constitution, bylaws, and covenant should reflect this belief and practice. Ideally, all of the members should have had an opportunity to agree to such a belief and practice, either when they joined the membership of the church or at some meeting designated for the ratification of these commitments. Ken Sande and Peacemakers Ministries is a great resource for the type of language that needs to be included in a church's constitution and bylaws. Part of a pastor's responsibility includes doing all he can to protect the congregation—that means even from law suits brought by disgruntled members who have been disciplined. We cannot keep people from suing us, but we can build in the necessary safe guards so that such lawsuits will not hold up in a court of law.

Fourth, unless you face a present scandalous, public sin that needs to be addressed immediately, begin your "journey in purity" with an effort to recover "non-resident" members, "resident inactive" members, etc. Work from the outer fringe and move toward the inner circle. Except for the occasional emotional attachment of someone for a near or distant relative, almost everyone recognizes that those who no longer live near enough to be a vital part of the worship services really have no part or lot in the ministry. Patiently attempt to contact every non-resident member. The sheer difficulty of locating some of these folks will make your point for you. Give time to "non-resident" members to respond to your correspondence by giving a reason they should continue to be considered as a vital member of the church. Though no valid meaningful reason exists for such a consideration, you should be prepared to see just how creative the human mind can be! Once a sufficient time has passed, their removal can come in an orderly process.

It is then time to move inward toward the "resident inactive" members. Those who have not attended over a long period of time should be contacted by mail and invited back to the congregation to which they say they belong. Appointments should be made to go and visit them and inquire as to what changed them from people who once attended worship (after all, they had to attend at least once to join) to people missing in action. Perhaps they have been offended by something or someone in the past. This becomes an opportunity to remove the offense and attempt reconciliation. If this does not prove helpful in their recovery, then the inactive member should be exhorted, admonished and warned (lovingly, of course—not harshly or censoriously) of the dangers of continuing in such a posture.

Through the years people have said to me over and over, "You mean to tell me that in order to be a Christian I *have* to come to church?" My response to this has always been, "I have never known any true Christian of whom it was said that he felt he *had* to come to church. Every true Christian I have ever known was very much like the psalmist who said, 'I was glad when they said unto me, let us go into the house of the Lord.'" The real question for these "inactive" members is, "Why don't you want to be among the people of God, worshipping God and studying His Word?"

After a reasonable period of time has been allowed for these folks to repent and return, if they fail to do so they should be notified in writing that if they do not give some valid reason why they should continue to be regarded as members of the church they will, with great sadness, be removed from the membership. The action will be nothing more than the congregation coming to a point of agreement with the non-attendee—he or she no longer wants to be involved in the ministry, therefore he or she shall not be considered a part of the ministry.

Once this long and tedious process has come near to completion, the faithful in the congregation will realize that not only has the sky not fallen, not only has the church building not collapsed, but rather God has given a spirit of enlivening to those who gather with a common experience of God's grace and a common commitment to glorify the Lord and advance His kingdom's cause.

Fifth, establish a paper trail in everything you do regarding the issue of corrective discipline. It is vitally important that copies of letters be filed, phone calls and visits be dated and documented and the substance of any conversation be written down in a "verbatim" whenever possible. While this will not keep false accusations from being hurled at those who are striving to please God, careful documentation may serve to expose the hollowness of the accusations.

Pitfalls to Avoid.

First, avoid giving the appearance of being impatient in the establishment and implementation of corrective church discipline. If you must be found to have erred, then err on the side of being too longsuffering, too forbearing, too patient, and too kind. Do not let someone (like a well-meaning outsider) pressure you into some manmade timetable. Don't use "patience" as an excuse to be lazy or to cover an unholy cowardice, but at all costs avoid impatience and impetuosity.

Second, avoid acting carelessly or emotionally. Move carefully and prayerfully in every aspect of the teaching and implementing of these matters. Act on biblical principle—dispassionately if possible. This subject provokes enough emotions without the pastors and other spiritual leaders adding their emotions to the mix.

Third, avoid acting angrily. Unrighteous anger is a sin, and public outbursts of anger are scandalous sins worthy of corrective discipline. When you manage to keep your head while those around you are losing theirs, your deportment will go a long way in convincing some who are sitting on the fence, the side of this issue on which they should align themselves. Let it be a settled conviction with you that angry outbursts will not serve God's purposes in advancing His righteousness as regards the establishment of corrective discipline.

Fourth, avoid acting without the overwhelming consensus of the church's leadership. Sometimes it is necessary to stand alone, but if at all possible patiently instruct the spiritual leadership in the congregation and lead them to become part of a godly consensus that sees the propriety and necessity of implementing corrective church discipline. Again it is important that you not give in to some outside pressure (real or imagined) that brings to bear some superficial timetable to "get this done." If God called you to be the pastor of the congregation, then you know better than anyone else the "pace" that your people can handle. You are a pastor—they are sheep. Lead them, don't drive them or bully them.

Fifth, avoid acting (or reacting) personally (i.e., to personal attacks against you). Do not take things personally. Any pastor who determines to lead his people in embracing and implementing corrective discipline will likely be called every name imaginable (and some that are not imaginable!). Realize that, because some do not like the content of the message but cannot refute its validity and the only thing they know to do is to assassinate the character of the messenger. Remember Jesus Christ, Who, when personally attacked, did not defend Himself. If truth is attacked, defend it valiantly.

If one of your brethren is verbally attacked, rise to defend his good name. But if you are verbally attacked and your character is maligned, bear the reproach by not returning in kind (and pray that God will raise up some godly brother who will defend you from such attacks).

Sixth, avoid acting without regard for established written procedures. It is unconscionable for a pastor to expose the people he pastors to unnecessary harm. As soon as is feasible, bring the church's documents into line with the practice in which you intend to lead the congregation in the area of redemptive, corrective church discipline.

Remember, if you act unwisely in this matter it very well may be that your efforts will fail. In all probability the very people who said that they did not believe in church discipline will discipline you by terminating you as their pastor. The hope of reformation coming to this congregation will be all but lost for the foreseeable future. It is worthy to note that John Calvin was in Geneva for almost a decade (in a very different set of circumstances from those of a pastor of a Baptist church) before he applied the doctrine of corrective discipline to the people under his charge.

CONCLUSION

Forty years ago today there appeared in the *Western Recorder* (the Baptist state newspaper for the Kentucky Baptist Convention), an article by Dr. James Leo Garrett (who was at the time Professor of Theology at The Southern Baptist Theological Seminary in Louisville) entitled, "Church Discipline: Lost, but Recoverable." In this article, Garrett declared,

> One of the most neglected and unpopular themes of our era is church discipline. To consider it one needs no crusading complex, but to do anything about it calls for a yearning to be a "prophet" rather than a "priest," the latter term

being translated, "an ecclesiastic," or, being interpreted, a drifter with the strongest current of the "status flow."[14]

Garrett further observed,

Church discipline, which was of so great concern to our forbearers in the gathered church tradition of Protestant Christianity, and this includes Baptists, no longer affects the lives or even is registered on the lips of their spiritual descendants.[15]

It struck me that at the same time Garrett (and a number of others like him) was sounding his clarion call for Baptists to return to their ecclesiological heritage by recovering the lost practice of corrective church discipline, there was a thirteen-year old boy growing up in Arkansas, about to be drawn into the sphere of influence and ministry of a Southern Baptist church. His name was William Jefferson Clinton (born August 19, 1946). Today he is perhaps America's most famous Southern Baptist. His personal life and public policies may gall some of us, but brethren, President Clinton is not the problem—he is a product of the problem. He was allowed to carry on his life of immorality all the while being treated as a "member in good standing" of a local Southern Baptist church.

So I leave you with this challenging thought. Who is growing up in the congregation you serve and what are you doing about it? Remember, disciple is not only a noun—it is also a verb. In the words of James Leo Garrett, "What do you say? Are you willing? May God so help us to do."[16]

---

14 James Leo Garrett, *"Church Discipline: Lost, but Recoverable,"* *Western Recorder*, Louisville, January 6, 1960.
15 Ibid.
16 Ibid.

24.
SHEPHERDING GOD'S FLOCK
ACTS 20:17-38
ROGER ELLSWORTH
2001 Southern Baptist Founders Conference

From Miletus he sent to Ephesus and called for the elders of the church. And when they had come to him, he said to them: "You know, from the first day that I came to Asia, in what manner I always lived among you, serving the Lord with all humility, with many tears and trials which happened to me by the plotting of the Jews; how I kept back nothing that was helpful, but proclaimed it to you, and taught you publicly and from house to house, testifying to Jews, and also to Greeks, repentance toward God and faith toward our Lord Jesus Christ.

And see, now I go bound in the spirit to Jerusalem, not knowing the things that will happen to me there, except that the Holy Spirit testifies in every city, saying that chains and tribulations await me. But none of these things move me; nor do I count my life dear to myself, so that I may finish my race with joy, and the ministry which I received from the Lord Jesus, to testify to the gospel of the grace of God.

And indeed, now I know that you all, among whom I have gone preaching the kingdom of God, will see my face no more. Therefore I testify to you this day that I [am] innocent of the blood of all [men]. For I have not shunned to declare to you the whole counsel of God. Therefore take heed to yourselves and to all the flock, among which the Holy Spirit has made you overseers, to shepherd the church of God which He purchased with His own blood. For I know this, that after my departure savage wolves will come in among you, not sparing the flock. Also from among yourselves men will rise up, speaking perverse things, to draw away the disciples after themselves. Therefore watch, and remember that for three years I did not cease to warn everyone night and day with tears.

So now, brethren, I commend you to God and to the word of His grace, which is able to build you up and give you an inheritance among all those who are sanctified. I have coveted no one's silver or gold or apparel. Yes, you yourselves know that these hands have provided for my necessities, and for those who were with me. I have shown you in every way, by laboring like this, that you must support the weak. And remember the words of the Lord Jesus, that He said, 'It is more blessed to give than to receive.'"

And when he had said these things, he knelt down and prayed with them all. Then they all wept freely, and fell on Paul's neck and kissed him, sorrowing most of all for the words which he spoke, that they would see his face no more. And they accompanied him to the ship (Acts 20:17-38).

WE have here one of the most powerful and riveting passages in all the Bible. Here the apostle Paul takes his leave of the Ephesian elders. Curtis Vaughan calls the message Paul delivered to these men "the most personal and most affectionate address which has come down to us from Paul." It falls into three parts:

• Paul's review of his own ministry among them (vv. 18-21). The key phrase in this section is "you know."

- Paul's announcement of the sufferings awaiting him (vv. 22-27). The key phrase in this section is "I know."
- Paul's charge or exhortation to the elders (vv. 28-35).

The chapter closes with a description of Paul's tearful parting from these men (vv. 36-38). The atmosphere was charged with emotion. The apostle was on his way to Jerusalem and the Holy Spirit had testified to him that "chains and tribulation" awaited him (vv. 22-23). The apostle knew that this would be his last meeting with these elders, that they would see his face no more (v. 25).

This account provides us with a wonderful basis for considering the theme "Shepherding God's Flock." I ask you to consider three things with me: the shepherd, the shepherd's flock, and the shepherd's neck.

THE SHEPHERD

In verse 28 the apostle says to these elders, "Take heed to yourselves." He would later issue the same exhortation to Timothy, "Take heed to yourself" (1 Timothy 4:16). The term "take heed" means, according to J. A. Alexander, "not mere attention but attendance, sedulous and anxious care." It means we are to develop the attitude which expects danger. It is to pick our way carefully so we can avoid the pitfalls and snares that are all around us.

The first object of the pastor's care must be himself. The shepherd must be aware that the well-being of his flock hinges on his own well-being. If the shepherd himself is sick or disabled, his flock is in trouble. Who now will feed the flock? Who will defend it? Who will care for its sick? Who will care for the little lambs?

How are we to apply this? If the pastor is *physically* ill some Sunday there is no problem in finding someone who can step in and fill the pulpit. However, if the pastor stands before his flock *spiritually* ill, how can they be properly fed and tended? Sadly, there are many pastors today who are spiritually ill in one way or another. They may be afflicted with:

- the disease of professionalism, that is, trafficking in unfelt truth.
- the disease of infatuation with the world's thinking and doing.
- the disease of selfish ambition that causes them to use the flock for their own advancement.
- the disease of materialism.
- the disease of untamed sexual desire.
- the disease of prayerlessness.

John R. W. Stott says shepherds "cannot care adequately for others if they neglect the care and culture of their own souls."

Many pastors these days have to say with the Shulamite in the Song of Solomon, "They made me the keeper of the vineyards, But my own vineyard I have not kept" (Song of Solomon 1:6b).

THE SHEPHERD'S FLOCK

The apostle also said, "take heed to all the flock among which the Holy Spirit has made you overseers, to shepherd the church of God which He purchased with His own blood" (v. 28). What an awesome charge this is! How can we ever hope to fulfill it?

Taking heed to the flock means taking heed to the nature of it and the privilege of shepherding it.

Have you noticed the Trinity in Paul's words? God the Father is here because the flock is the church of God. God the Son is here because the flock is purchased by His blood. God the Holy Spirit is here because the shepherds of the flock have been appointed by Him. Do you see the privilege of being a pastor? You are part of something that involves the triune God!

This inevitably leads us to a most important and vital conclusion, namely, it is not our flock. It is God's. We are not, therefore, to be "lords" over the flock (1 Peter 5:3). We are shepherds of the flock only in a secondary sense. We are undershepherds. Christ is the shepherd of the flock.

Taking heed to the flock means giving special care to what we feed it. There is, of course, no question about what constitutes the food with which we are to feed the sheep. It is the precious Word of God. This Word is sufficient for every member of the flock. It is milk for the very young and it is meat for the mature.

And no part of the shepherd's responsibility is more important than continually and systematically feeding his people the Word of God. This means he is to preach doctrinally. There is nothing more shameful and embarrassing than to hear a preacher ridicule and deride doctrine. He only shows that he has absolutely no understanding of doctrine or of the task of the preacher.

We remind ourselves that the apostle Paul not only urged Timothy to take heed to himself but also to his doctrine (1 Timothy 4:16). No man can adequately shepherd the flock of God who does not obey this command. We can do no better at this point than to look to Paul's ministry in Ephesus for a model of the type of ministry we are to practice. John Stott describes Paul's ministry in this way:

> He shared all possible truth with all possible people in all possible ways. He taught the whole gospel to the whole city with his whole strength. His pastoral example must have been an unfailing inspiration to the Ephesian pastors.

Taking heed to the flock means constantly watching for and guarding against predators. The apostle said, "For I know this, that after my departure savage wolves will come in among you, not sparing the flock" (v. 29). We know some of what took place after Paul's ministry. The Judaizers, with whom

Paul had so many confrontations, would continue to plague many of the churches for years to come. The Gnostics, against whom Paul had already battled, would exert a powerful influence over many churches. These represent, of course, only two of many heresies.

Some would have us believe that this part of Paul's exhortation to the Ephesian elders is completely without meaning or relevance for us. As far as they are concerned, there are no wolves menacing the flock today. But these only show a stunning lack of discernment. There are wolves aplenty today and no shepherd worth his salt can ignore them.

- The Judaizer wolf is still with us. The Judaizers taught that salvation was not a matter of trusting only in the finished work of the Lord Jesus Christ, but that one also had to be circumcised according to the law of Moses. The Judaizers, then, sought to mingle works with grace.

    How very many there are today who do the same! They turn their faith into a good work that they themselves do to earn salvation and add that to the grace of God.
- The Gnostic wolf is still with us, as well. The Gnostics claimed to have special knowledge or enlightenment granted by God. How many there are today who ignore the clear teachings of God's Word in order to embrace and advocate some teaching that God supposedly gave them!

In addition to having to deal with the same wolves with which Paul dealt, we find ourselves facing our own special wolves:

- The nice wolf: This wolf has invaded our churches to teach that the only thing one has to do to be saved is be nice and pleasant.
- The life-management wolf: This is the wolf that casts aside the traditional doctrinal understanding of various

passages and suggests that these passages were designed to convey truths that help us manage the crises and challenges of life. For example, the visit of Gabriel to Mary is in Scripture not, as you may suppose, to take us one step further down the road of redemption but to teach us how to deal with interruptions. Or, the story of David and Goliath is not in Scripture to show us how God raised up a deliverer for His people when true faith had faltered in Israel and, in so doing, to point us to Christ, but rather to show us how to kill the giants in our lives. The story of Isaac, Rebekah, Esau and Jacob is not in Scripture to show us how God sovereignly carried forth His plan of redemption by setting Jacob over Esau, but rather to give us clues on how to avoid having a dysfunctional family. And, of course, the ministry of Jesus has now become a rich resource for finding leadership principles.

It is time, in the parlance of the world, to call a spade a spade. The reason so many pastors have gone to this type of preaching is because they want to grow their churches and build a name for themselves, and they are convinced that preaching about sin, judgment, repentance and holiness will drive people away.

These wolves are savage because they all deprive people of the thing they need most—the saving truth of God.

THE SHEPHERD'S NECK

Another aspect of Paul's time with the Ephesian elders is found in verse 37, "Then they all wept freely and fell on Paul's neck and kissed him." There is a great deal of consolation in this scene. The apostle had declared the truth of God to these men, and as they looked upon him for the last time they realized how much they owed this man. Sure, their salvation was of God but God had used Paul as the instrument of His salvation. Overcome with emotion, they lined up and one after the other embraced and kissed Paul as they wept.

Some of you are undoubtedly deeply discouraged. You are trying to stand for the truth of God in an age that despises truth. And, as you preach, many of your congregation probably wonder why you seem to go out of your way to be such an odd number. They undoubtedly sit there saying, "Doesn't this poor fellow have enough sense to know he could gather a larger crowd if he would preach more timely and appealing topics? Doesn't he know that people today are far too sophisticated for this type of thing? Why does he insist on preaching things that only drive people away."

I offer each of you faithful preachers a word of encouragement. God's Word can and does save. And while you have your skeptics, I cannot help but believe God is using you to plant real faith in human hearts.

I see you now, faithful pastor, coming to the end of your journey. I see you coming into the presence of your Lord, and I hear him say, "Well done, good and faithful servant." And now I see behind Him a long line of people. And I hear you asking the Lord, "Who are these?" And the Lord says, "I will let them tell you." And so they come to you one after the other to embrace you, and yes, before the Lord finally wipes away every tear, to weep on your neck with gratitude and rejoicing that you faithfully declared to them the gospel of Jesus Christ. On that day you will be vindicated and you will be glad that you took heed to yourself and to the flock of God. You will be glad that you stood by the old gospel while others were forsaking it in droves. You will be glad that the sword of the Word clave to your hand. You will be glad that you preached the redeeming blood of Jesus Christ.

I urge you, then, my brother to not give up on the good work to which the Lord has called you. Keep preaching and keep laboring until you hear the Master's "well done" and you see in eternity the fruit of your faithful ministry.

I urge you to so preach that when you finally die the most fitting thing to put on your tomb will be the words etched on Spurgeon's:

E'er since by faith I saw the stream,
Thy flowing wounds supply,
Redeeming love has been my theme
And shall be til I die.

I urge you to so preach with these words from Charles Simeon ever fixed in your mind:

> Let us live for God, and for eternity; let us live as
> we shall wish we had lived when we shall stand
> before the judgment seat of Christ. Let us go for-
> ward in the path of duty, assured that the rest
> which awaits us will richly repay our labours, and
> the crown of righteousness our conflicts.

25.
REFORMING CHURCH MUSIC
KEN PULS

2001 Southern Baptist Founders Conference

O NE of the major issues confronting the church today is
music. Throughout history music has served the church
and helped shape its worship of God. In our day, however, it has become a pivotal issue. Whereas in the past, theology or pastoral leadership was the most distinguishing characteristic of worship, today *music* is the defining element for
many churchgoers. As more churches renew their interest in
worship, music is certain to continue as a dominant and perhaps volatile topic of discussion. The current emphasis on
music has produced some positive results—encouraging
churches to focus more attention on worship and to think
more about what they are singing in worship—but there are
negative results as well.

Many of us have watched with great concern as music has
forsaken its position of "handmaiden" to the preaching and
teaching of God's Word, and now in many churches appears
to be its "rival." That which God gave to be a blessing and encouragement to the church is now too often a source of contention, conflict, and controversy.

It is clear that many pastors and churches are struggling
with music. A few years ago I attended an evening service at
a Southern Baptist church where the pastor was seeking to
bring reformation. A guest preacher had been invited to come
and bring the message. I was very encouraged by the sound
expositional preaching, and by the service itself until the music director stood to announce the final hymn. As the music
began, I stood for a few moments in disbelief, wondering if

anyone else was aware of what was happening. Sure enough, by the time we started singing verse two, the pastor of the church realized that what we were singing contradicted much of what we had just heard in the message. He rushed to the front of the sanctuary, stopped the hymn in the middle of the verse, and then tried to bring the service to a graceful close.

This is but one instance of music gone awry in a church—a music director who was not with the pastor theologically, not in tune with the preaching, content to do his own thing, who ended up (perhaps unintentionally) undermining the ministry of the Word.

Potential of Music to Help or Hinder Ministry.

Music can have a great impact on the life of a church. I know of no other ministry in the church that has so great a potential to either help or hinder the pastoral ministry than music. Music has the potential to become an *obstacle* to worship—amusing, distracting, and entertaining the people; minimizing and trivializing the preaching of the Word; or worse contradicting and tearing it down. But music also has the potential to be a great *blessing*—supporting the pastor and undergirding the preaching and teaching ministry of church.

Music and Reformation.

How then can we effectively include music in our pursuit of reformation in the church? To answer this question, we will begin by looking briefly at the purpose of music in worship. We will then consider the following principles for evaluating and choosing music for worship, focusing on both the text and the tune: 1) Why the text/tune matters; 2) Questions to ask of the text/tune; 3) Two practical applications to pursue reformation.

THE PURPOSE OF MUSIC IN WORSHIP

God has purpose and intent in including music as an element of worship. The Bible has much to say about music and its role in worship. The following list summarizes seven roles that will help us define the purpose of music in worship.

1) Music is a primary means of praising God. The majority of references to music in the Bible, including verses that teach about music, as well as Psalms and other passages that are the texts to songs, are in the context of praising God. Through music we exalt, glorify, honor, bless, and adore God. We marvel at the perfection of His character, attributes, gifts, names, and works, ascribing to Him in song all that He is! *The Psalter* itself culminates in praise:

> Praise the LORD! Praise God in His sanctuary;
> Praise Him in His mighty firmament! Praise Him
> for His mighty acts; Praise Him according to His
> excellent greatness! (Psalm 150:1-2).

Music exists first and foremost to the glory and praise of God and Scripture convincingly bears this out.

2) Music is a primary means of giving thanks to God. Thanksgiving is a grateful acknowledgment or public confession of the goodness of God manifest in what He has done for His people. It is a grateful response to God for His deliverance, healing, forgiveness, salvation, and other blessings that He brings to us. Music accompanies thanksgiving in worship:

> Hallelujah! I will give thanks to the LORD with
> all my heart
> In the company of the upright and in the convo-
> cation (Psalm 111:1).

Thanksgiving is also sung in the context of evangelism:

> I will give thanks to You among the peoples, O
> Lord; I will sing praises to You among the nations
> (Psalm 57:9).

As with praise, references in Scripture to giving thanks most often occur in song.

3) Music serves as a means of prayer. Many of the songs and psalms of Scripture are addressed directly to God. David, for example, in Psalms 4 and 5 pours out his heart to God, brings petitions, and asks for help and mercy. Throughout the Psalter, psalmists lament over sorrows, anguish over difficulties, confess their sinfulness, rejoice over God's kindness, celebrate His goodness, and express numerous other emotions as they pour out their hearts before Him. Music can serve as invocation, petition, supplication, intercession, repentance, lamentation, and other forms of prayer, lifting our concerns before God.

4) Music serves as a means to proclaim truth. As we sing praise, thanksgiving, and prayer we voice our words to God, but music can also bring God's Word to us. We can sing the words of Scripture, Psalms and other passages set to music. We can also teach and admonish one another in song with the truths of Scripture. Psalm 1, for example, is a didactic song that teaches us the difference between the blessed and the ungodly. Music helps us to remember and meditate on the truths of Scripture. It serves along side preaching as a means of proclamation, edifying the church and evangelizing the lost, as it provides an emotional context in which we can interpret, understand, and express the truths of God's Word.

5) Music serves as a means of exhortation. Music lifts our words to God in prayer and brings God's Word to us in proclamation, but it can also voice our words to one another. Psalm 95, for example, is a call to worship. We exhort one another with the words:

Oh come, let us sing to the LORD!
Let us shout joyfully to the Rock of our salvation.
Let us come before His presence with thanksgiving;
Let us shout joyfully to Him with psalms
(Psalm 95:1-2).

Through music God's people speak to one another, stirring up one another to good works. Music can call us to worship, exhort us to love and serve one another, encourage us to live in obedience to God's Word, admonish us to flee from sin and pursue holiness, and enjoin us to go out and witness and share the gospel.

6) Music serves as a means to confess our faith. With music God's people can express common beliefs and doctrines as one voice. In the Old Testament Israel rehearsed their faith and history through music. Psalm 118, for example, is a public confession of the goodness and enduring mercy of God. The New Testament contains several confessional statements such as 2 Timothy 2:11 that many scholars believe are fragments of early hymns. Music provides an effective way to unite in declaring our confessions of faith. Perhaps the most notable example of this in church history is the "Doxology," written by Thomas Ken in 1709, a musical affirmation of the doctrine of the Trinity:

> Praise God from whom all blessings flow;
> Praise Him, all creatures here below;
> Praise Him above, ye heavenly host;
> Praise Father, Son, and Holy Ghost.

7) Finally, music serves as a means of enriching worship with beauty. According to Scripture, singing praise to God is pleasant and beautiful. Psalm 147:1 reads:

> Praise the LORD! For it is good to sing praises to
>   our God;
> For it is pleasant, and praise is beautiful.

It is good when we unite our voices together in singing to God. Music provides a beautiful garb in which we dress our words and actions in worship. It is a pleasant means of joining together to express our love and devotion to God in worship.

These are seven roles or functions of music that God affirms in His Word. God has commanded us to make music and included it in His design for worship. It is not the purpose of music to amuse, manipulate, or entertain us in worship. God has given us music that we might beautifully lift our praise, thanksgiving, and prayers to Him; that we might proclaim the truth of His Word, confess our faith, and exhort one another to good works as we gather in corporate worship.

PRINCIPLES FOR CHOOSING AND EVALUATING MUSIC FOR WORSHIP

PART 1: PRINCIPLES CONCERNING THE TEXT

Because God has given music a significant place in worship, it is essential that we evaluate and choose music carefully. We begin with the text.

Why the Text Matters.

The text matters because it voices the content of our worship. It carries our words to God as we offer praise, give thanks, and lift up prayers through song. It carries our words to one another as we exhort and admonish one another and confess together a common faith. More importantly it carries the Word of God to us as we proclaim, teach, and apply the truths of Scripture through our singing.

In John 4:23 Jesus taught that we must worship the Father in spirit and in truth. This is the essence of true worship. When Paul gives instruction to the church on music in Colossians 3:16 and in its parallel passage, Ephesians 5:18-21, he submits music to this important truth. In Ephesians Paul emphasizes worship in spirit:

> And stop getting drunk with wine in which is dissipation, but *be filled with the Spirit,* speaking to one another with psalms and hymns and spiritual songs, singing and making melody with your heart to the Lord, giving thanks always for every-

thing in the name of our Lord Jesus Christ unto God, indeed the Father (emphasis mine).

In Colossians 3:16 he focuses on worship in truth:

> *Let the Word of Christ dwell in you richly,* teaching and admonishing one another in all wisdom, with psalms, hymns, and spiritual songs, singing with grace in your hearts to the Lord; and in each word or deed you do, do all in the name of the Lord Jesus, giving thanks to God, even the Father, through Him (emphasis mine).

These two passages must be understood together. Worship and the music of worship must be rooted in the truth of God's Word and the work of His Spirit. Truth is inseparably tied to the work of God's Spirit. If we are to seek the truth, the Spirit must awaken us, quicken us, and enable us to come. It is the Spirit who indwells us and illumines our hearts and minds that we may grasp and understand and respond to the truth of God in His Word. In order for us to worship in truth, we need the revealed Word of God to be our light and point us to Christ. We need the Spirit of God to indwell us and illumine our understanding so we can know and apply the Word and live in its light.

As we plan our worship services and seek to choose music that will honor God and edify the church, our two priorities must be to: 1) Saturate our service and music with the Word of God; 2) Pray earnestly that God would manifest His presence in the power of His Spirit by giving us understanding of His Word.

If we desire to bring reformation to our church music, we must pursue music that will "let the Word of Christ dwell in us richly" and pray that the Spirit of God would illumine His Word to our hearts. "Letting the Word of Christ dwell in us richly," means we should:

1) Sing the words of Scripture (Psalms and other passages).
2) Sing words with substance, replete with the truths of Scripture.
3) Sing words that are in submission to Scripture, doctrinally sound, informed by, and conformed to the Word of God.
4) Sing words that are an appropriate response to God's Word, words that keep us focused on and accountable to the truth as it is proclaimed and applied.

What we sing before God matters! We are voicing our words in His presence and often actually addressing Him in prayer. In corporate worship we are also voicing our words in the midst of other believers, comforting, encouraging, and exhorting those around us. We may perhaps even be singing in the midst of unbelievers, bearing witness to them of the truth of the gospel. We must give attention to the text.

Questions to Ask of the Text.

1) As we evaluate the text, we can begin with questions of quality:

Are the words written well?
Are the words singable?
Are they poetically sound?

2) We should question the purpose of the text:

Why were the words written?
Do the words have a worthwhile and noble purpose?
Does the purpose of the text serve us in our worship?

3) We should question the message of the text:

What do the words communicate?
Will the congregation understand the words?
Is the message of the words conducive to worship?
Are the words biblically and doctrinally sound?

As we explore the text more deeply concerning its doctrine, we should ask:

1) What Scripture verses and passages are quoted or alluded to in the song?
2) What theological truths does the song teach?
    About God's natural revelation (creation)?
    About God's special revelation (the Scriptures)?
    About the Person and Work of God the Father? (God's presence, names, will, sovereignty, providence, attributes, etc.)
    About the Person and Work of God the Son?
    About the Person and Work of God the Holy Spirit?
    About humanity?
    About sin?
    About salvation?
    About Christian living?
    About evangelism?
    About the church?
    About the final judgment / heaven / hell?
    About worship?

These questions involve the content of our music, but the context is important as well.

3) How does the song fit into the worship service?
    Does it invite people into the presence of God?
    Does it focus our attention on God—His character, attributes, and works?
    Does it call upon God to meet His people in worship?

Does it declare and proclaim the truth of God's
Word?

Does it confess sin?

Does it rejoice in Christ and the forgiveness of sin?

Does it teach and expound the truth of God's Word?

Does it commission God's people to go out and live
in obedience?

Does it offer prayer and petition to God?

Does it declare the promises of God from His Word?

Is it an expression of praise or adoration to God?

Is it an expression of thanksgiving to God?

Does it voice our submission to God in obedience to
His Word?

As we corporately voice our songs before God, we must be
mindful and reverent in what are saying and doing!

How then can we practically "let the Word of Christ dwell
in us richly" in our music?

Two Practical Applications to Pursue Reformation.

1) We need to think theologically about church music and
choose music that is doctrinally substantial.

If we are to bring reformation to church music, we need to
choose music that is composed and designed to impart truth,
not just create an experience that feels good. We need to
choose music that has doctrinal substance and depth. We
need to ask questions and study our music according to theological content. We need to know and sing music that covers
a full range of theological topics.

There are truths that we need reminded of frequently. We
need to remember that our God is sovereign and in control of
all things. We need to dwell often on justification by faith
alone in Christ alone. We need to meditate on the imputed
righteousness of Christ. Music can be a great blessing as it
serves us in embedding these essential doctrines into our
thinking. What we sing feeds our soul. We must be careful
that our songs are spiritually healthy, theologically balanced,

and doctrinally rich.

2) We need to choose music that will support and under-gird the preaching and teaching of the church.

One of the major reasons why music has become such an area of contention in many churches today is because church music has become separated and disjointed from the teaching and preaching ministry of the church. In many churches the two almost seem in competition—the music seeking to out-shine and out do the sermon.

If we are to bring reformation to church music, music must once again return to being the "handmaiden" of the ministry of the Word, serving, supporting, and undergirding the preaching. This means we must choose music that helps the congregation begin thinking on the truths that are to be em-phasized in the message. It means singing a hymn following the message that is an appropriate response, one that holds the congregation accountable through song to what they have just heard and keeps them thinking about the truths taught and applied in the message.

For this to happen, church music needs the involvement of pastors and elders. Churches need fruitful communication between the one who preaches and the one who leads the music.

Pastors, one of the best ways you can help reform the music of your church is to be involved. Music is not an area of min-istry that you can afford to relinquish, even if you are not mu-sically gifted or trained. The music of your church needs your oversight and spiritual guidance. Communicate with your song leader or music minister. Let him know the goals and direction of your preaching. If your musicians need time to practice and rehearse (and most of us do), it may require you to plan ahead. Give your music minister advanced notice of the biblical texts and themes of your sermons. Then expect him to find hymns that will support and tie in to your mes-sage. Music has a great potential to bless your ministry as you teach and apply the Word of God. Pursue church music that will allow the Word of Christ to dwell in His church richly.

PRINCIPLES FOR CHOOSING AND EVALUATING
MUSIC FOR WORSHIP

PART 2: PRINCIPLES CONCERNING THE TUNE

The text is essential, but it is only part of the song. As we consider the music of the church we must not neglect the tune. Unfortunately there are many who, when they evaluate and think about music, believe that only the words matter. They conclude that the music accompanying the text is simply a matter of personal taste and is really of little or no significance. So long as the text is good, the tune is inconsequential.

Now I would readily agree that the words are the place to start. We must be diligent to peruse the text and think doctrinally and biblically about the text. But as a musician and a composer, I find the disregard for the music very disturbing. The tunes we use to accompany our words and our actions do matter.

Why the Tune Matters.

We must be sensitive to the way in which we wed music with words or music with actions, especially when our ultimate desire is to bring honor and praise to God in worship, as well as to edify, encourage, and teach one another as we sing together as a congregation. The music matters in at least three ways:

1) The music is the incarnation of the text. It is the garb in which we dress the text. The tune is how we present, experience, receive, and know the text. As we handle the precious truths of Scripture, and even the very words of Scripture, we must strive for the best our musical forms and styles can offer.
2) The music helps us interpret the text. It provides the emotional context in which we understand the words. Music powerfully effects how we interpret

the words. Through music we can sense if the
mood is serious, humorous, light, or reverent. The
character of the musical gestures, inflections and
movements in the tune will influence our interpretation of the text.
3) The music identifies the text. Once the tune and
text are yoked together they become identified with
one another. In time the music and words can
become closely associated. When we hear the tune,
the words come immediately to mind. Play, for example, the first six notes of "Holy, Holy, Holy." For
anyone who is familiar with that hymn, the hearing
of the notes brings the words immediately to mind.
Music serves to help us remember and embeds the
text in our being.

The tunes we use in worship can profoundly affect how we
receive, understand, and identify our words and actions. We
must not be satisfied with music simply because the words
are good. We must also give attention to the tune.

Questions to Ask of the Tune.

Some of the same questions we asked of the text, must also
be asked of the tune:

1) We must question the quality of the tune:
Is the music composed well?
Is the tune singable?
Does the tune represent the best our musical style
can offer?
2) We should question the purpose of the tune:
Why was the music composed?
Does the music have a worthwhile and noble
purpose?
Does the purpose of the music serve us in our
worship?

3) We should question the message of the tune:
What does the music communicate?
Is the message of the music conducive to worship?

Music is a language that communicates emotion and feeling, although it does not communicate the same way as a spoken language. Notes and chords are not combined to directly express emotions in the same way that letters are put together to make specific words to denote emotions (as J+O+Y=joy). Music conveys its message indirectly by reflecting and imitating gestures, inflections, and movements that are associated in human experience with specific emotions and feelings. For example, if a composer desires to convey the emotion of rage, he might make the movement of the notes agitated or violent. To create a feeling of peace, he might design the music to sound still and quiet with soft tones and little movement. By reflecting and imitating the gestures and movements of emotion, the music seems to take on the character of the emotion itself, both undergirding and inspiring the associated feelings, for it is these gestures, inflections, and movements that are the actual substance of emotion in human existence. We must be sensitive to the content of the tune and choose music that communicates emotions and feelings that are fitting and appropriate to worship.

As we consider the appropriateness of music to serve in worship, we should also ask:

1) What is the source of the tune?

Was the tune composed with the intent of accompanying worship? Did the tune spring from a Spirit-filled heart of a composer desiring to please God or did it arise from a dark, depraved heart of one seeking to promote ungodliness and sin? If the tune was originally composed with a purpose other than worship in mind, or composed to accompany and undergird a message unrelated to worship, we should not simply assume that it will be equally useful for worship. We must first hold the tune suspect and carefully consider its fitness as an expression of worship. Can the tune be used effectively as an accompaniment to the actions and words appropriate to worship? Are the musical gestures, musical inflections, and movement of the music conducive to worship?

2) What are the associations of the tune?

Are the associations of the music with other texts, other messages, or other purposes too strong to allow the tune to transfer into sacred use? For example, if I were writing the words to a call to worship, inviting people to come into the presence of God, I would not want to set the words to the tune of "Here Comes Santa Claus!" That is not to say that the tune is bad, evil, or even secular. It does however, at least here in America, have secular associations that make it entirely unfit for use in worship. The church must take great care in taking music from the world for its own use, especially when uniting music to Scripture. The associations of the songs with secular or even wicked contexts may be too strong to allow the music to be useful in the church.

3) What is the cultural setting of the tune?

The language of music is shared by people all over the world, but it is a language that exists in numerous dialects and with much variety across many cultures. We must be sensitive to cultural distinctions in music as we seek to fit music to specific words and actions. Missionaries, who go to foreign lands with unfamiliar dialects and unfamiliar styles of music, must be careful in choosing suitable words and tunes as they seek to proclaim truth. They cannot take indigenous music with no thought or examination, unite it with Christian words, and assume that it will communicate a clear message. Tunes that they choose to carry a message of peace may have connotations in those cultures with hatred or rebellion. Melodies that they find quite attractive may have strong associations with a false religion. If we are to make wise choices regarding church music, we must take time to learn about the culture around us and be aware of the musical styles and expressions of the culture.

How then can we practically improve our choice of music for worship?

Two Practical Applications to Pursue Reformation.

1) We need congruency between the text and the tune.

When choosing songs for worship, we must carefully consider how the music fits with the words it accompanies. If we desire music that will serve the text, we must choose music that is equally yoked to the text, communicating the same message. If the text and tune are congruent in their message, they will strengthen and undergird one another. If they are incongruent, they will distract and confuse. This can be seen in the example of two hymns from the 1991 *Baptist Hymnal*: "O Sacred Head, Now Wounded," sung to the tune PASSION CHORALE (#137), and "All Glory, Laud, and Honor," sung to the tune ST. THEODULPH (#126). Both hymns are equally yoked in text and tune. The tune PASSION CHORALE ably undergirds the grief and suffering so vivid in the text "O Sacred Head, Now Wounded" as it contemplates Christ's death on the cross. The tune ST. THEODULPH is joyful and uplifting—a fitting accompaniment to words that exalt Christ as King. The two tunes are also in same poetic meter (7.6.7.6.D.) so that the words could be exchanged; yet both texts would be ill served in doing so. The joy expressed in ST. THEODULPH is inappropriate for the somber reflection of Christ's suffering expressed in the text of "O Sacred Head, Now Wounded." Likewise, the heaviness and sorrow felt in PASSION CHORALE is contradictory to the uplifting praise offered in the text of "All Glory, Laud, and Honor."

As we evaluate church music, we must focus on the relationship between text and tune. Are the music and the words equally yoked to communicate a clear message suited to the purpose of worshipping God and edifying the church? Is the tune helpful or is it a hindrance as we try to understand and interpret the text? If the song accompanies an act of worship (such as praise, prayer, confession of sin), does the tune aid us or distract us? The musical gestures, inflections, and movements in the tune should communicate the same emotional and spiritual character of the text or action with which the tune is associated. Music should be submissive to the text or to the act of worship that it accompanies, not distract from it or call attention to itself.

2) Not all music or musical styles are appropriate for worship.

There are musical gestures, inflections, and movements that will always be out of place in worship. Many of us have had experiences with music in church that seemed inappropriate, out of place, or even trivial. Not all music is conducive to worship. Not all musical styles, especially those bred and nurtured outside of the church, can effectively carry the message of the gospel. If we find a tune, for example, that was composed to express feelings of hatred or rage, we should ask, "How useful can this tune be for worship?" We must admit that the world has many skillful composers who can create music that communicates such feelings very effectively. Can we really believe that we can take such music and simply by changing the words, use the same musical inflections, gestures, and movements to communicate biblical concepts of peace, obedience, and reverence?

The gospel is an eternal life or death issue. Its message is weighty and serious—inappropriate in the hands of clowns, entertainers, or frivolous music. Seeing people who are lost and going to hell should not be something the church finds amusing or treats in a light-hearted manner. If a man comes upon a house that is burning, he does not go inside and entice the occupants to come out by dancing a jig or singing a happy song. If the danger of the fire is real and the man actually cares about the lives that are inside the house, entertainment and frivolity will be farthest from his thoughts and actions. He will rush inside, warning and pleading with the occupants to flee for their lives. The reality of hell and eternal judgment is far more serious than a burning house, yet many evangelicals treat the gospel and its message as if it were a mere amusement or entertainment meant to entice the lost. We have freedom to create and enjoy music in a wide array of activities and venues. A church service, a football game, and a parade all include music that we can enjoy to the glory of God. But a worship service is not a football game or a parade. Each activity requires music suitable to its purpose. Music that we enjoy hearing at venues outside of the church may not be appropriate or fitting for the purpose of worship. In worship we are pursuing a well-defined purpose and seeking to communicate a clear message. As we choose music for worship, we must be wise in finding tunes that will serve as a suitable accompaniment to those thoughts, actions, and elements that Scripture affirms as appropriate for worship. In worship we are communing with the Sovereign God and proclaiming His Word. Our music should reflect the significance and importance of our endeavor.

A Proper Focus for Church Music.

As we evaluate, choose, and participate in church music, we must keep a proper focus. First and foremost, we must glorify God. Paul exhorts us in 1 Corinthians 10:31 to do all to the glory of God. In all our music, even music we enjoy simply for recreation, we are to seek first God's glory. Personal preferences and taste (our own and those of others in the church) must be submissive to this priority.

Secondly, we must choose music that will edify and encourage God's people. In 1 Corinthians 14:26 we are commanded "Let all things be done for edification." There is no room in the church for music that does not strengthen and build up the body of Christ. All music in corporate worship must be to the glory of God and for the good of the church.

Finally, we must choose music that reflects and displays the holiness and beauty of God. The music we use in worship and the way we use music in worship are vivid testimonies before the world of our understanding of God and our relationship to Him. If music is to serve us in proclaiming and bearing witness to the truth, we must choose both texts and tunes that join together in declaring the splendor and character of God.

This must be our focus as we consider the issue of reforming church music. We should not be asking, "What would I like to sing at church?" or "What would this group within the congregation most like to hear?" This approach centers the attention and priority on us and will most likely lead to contention and division. Rather, we should ask, "What music will most honor God and His Word? What will best edify His people? What will rightly declare His greatness to the world?" These are the questions that must motivate our choices if we are to include music in our pursuit of reformation.

HISTORICAL/BIOGRAPHICAL

26.
THE LIFE AND LABORS OF PATRICK HUES MELL
C. BEN MITCHELL
1983 Southern Baptist Founders Conference

L IKE the men and women of Hebrews 11 whose names are not even mentioned, there have been Southern Baptists who are little known to our generation, "of whom the world was not worthy" (Hebrews 11:38). Such a man was Patrick Hues Mell.

BIRTH AND EARLY YEARS

Born July 19, 1814, Patrick was the son of Major Benjamin Mell of Laurel Hill, Georgia, and Cynthia Sumner Mell of South Carolina. We know very little of Patrick's early years, except that he was the second of eight children. Young Patrick's father was a very wealthy man, though "sympathetic by nature, and generous to a fault."[1] So generous was he that he left his family very little after his death in 1828. Three years later Mrs. Mell died, leaving seventeen-year-old Pat responsible for the entire family.

> A mere youth without experience, he was forced to rely solely upon his native genius to provide a means of support for himself and dependent brothers and sisters. He gave up the small remnant of his share of the property...to the support of his brothers and sisters, and started out with the determination to obtain an education, and as

---

1 P. H. Mell, Jr., *Life of Patrick Hues Mell* (Louisville: Baptist Book Concern, 1895), 8.

far as possible recover the social position and
property that had been lost by his father's
misfortune.[2]

At this time Mell began his lifelong career of teaching. At
age seventeen, P. H. Mell taught primary school in a log hut
with a dirt floor in his birthplace of Walthourville, Georgia,
(approximately 50 miles southwest of Savannah).

Though Patrick's father never professed conversion, Mell's
early years were not without spiritual impressions. Dr. John
Jones, a classmate and later a Presbyterian minister, said of
Mell's upbringing,

> His mother was a woman of marked individuality
> of character, intellectual, and truly a Godly wom-
> an, brought up in the strictest mode of old Con-
> gregationalism, and, no doubt, perfectly familiar
> with the Westminster Shorter Catechism.[3]

An excerpt from a letter from Mrs. Mell to her son demonstrates her great concern for her son's soul (one should note
that by this time Mell evidently had aspirations toward the
gospel ministry):

> It is high time that you and I should communi-
> cate frequently and intimately and confidentially.
> If this is not to be expected by the time you have
> arrived at fifteen when is it to be looked for? On
> one account I have more anxiety, even dread on
> your behalf than for any of my children. Earnestly
> as I wish a son of mine to be a minister yet I
> tremble at the idea of educating and devoting a
> son to the sacred profession without previously
> satisfactory evidence that his own soul was right
> with God .... My heart burns *to see you* in every

---

2 Ibid., 10.
3 Ibid., 12.

sense of the word a true Christian.... You should
exercise a jealousy over yourself lest the trifles of
this world should deaden your feelings about the
grand questions: what are the chances of my salvation—what have I done—what must I do to be
saved? ... remember they that are Christ's have
crucified their affections and lusts—*crucify
yours.*[4]

Mrs. Mell's heart so yearned for her son's salvation that she
also wrote him the very next day.

I say this with anxiety, and write with fear, but I
say it with earnest prayers for the real conversion
of your soul to God, and with some hope that he
will hear the petition that I have endeavoured to
offer up for you for many years back. I will repeat.
I can never consent for you to study for the ministry until I have some satisfactory proof of your
heart being turned to God in holy consistency
and permanency of character.[5]

Mrs. Mell never lived to see her son converted for in 1831
the Lord took her; however, the seed of her prayers was not
sown in vain.

In the summer of 1832, Mell was baptized at North Newport Baptist Church in Liberty County, Georgia, by the pastor,
Josiah Samuel Law. The following year, due to the benefi-
cence of a wealthy gentleman, George W. Walthour, Mell was
enabled to enter the freshman class of Amherst College in
Massachusetts. Several events at Amherst testify that, though
baptized, Mell was not converted.

At Amherst things didn't go well between the
Southern boy and his Northern mentors. One of

---

4 Ibid., 13.
5 Ibid., 15.

them especially distasteful to Pat Mell was a Professor Fiske. Pat's southern blood boiled hot one Sunday when Professor Fiske was preaching. He made some derogatory remarks about Southerners. Pat walked out of the sanctuary and was condemned for disorderly conduct. Trouble arose again when Pat refused to divulge to the faculty the names of some of his fellow students accused of violating rules of the college. Threatened with expulsion, he was determined not to be intimidated and stood his ground to the last. Although he would not yield, the faculty decided not to expel him.[6]

But unknown to Mell, Dr. Fiske wrote to Pat's benefactor accusing the young Mell of wasting money which caused Mr. Walthour to withdraw his support from the young scholar. Hence, Mell could no longer afford to stay at Amherst. With little more than five dollars in his pocket, in 1835, Mell walked twenty-five miles to Springfield where he was able to secure a teaching position.

The next four years were filled with unrest for Pat Mell. Troubles and disappointments crowded in upon him. Even so, his buoyant spirit and sense of humor kept him from utter despair. From Springfield he moved to Hartford, Connecticut, where he became associate principal at the East Hartford High School. A year later in 1837, Mell returned to his Southern home and in a short time secured a principalship at Perry's Mill School in Tatnall County, Georgia. The following year he moved to Montgomery County where he taught at Ryal's school until, in February of 1839, he was offered the position of principal of the Oxford Classical and English School (which was a preparatory school for Emory College).

---

6 Spencer B. King, Jr., "Patrick Hues Mell: Preacher, Pedagogue, and Parliamentarian," *Baptist History and Heritage* 5 (October 1970), 187.

CONVERSION AND CALL TO THE MINISTRY

Though troubled, unsettled, and under the strain of several years of toil and struggle, a wise providence was watching over the young man. A merciful God held him in the hollow of His sovereign hand. A letter written on the twenty-fifth of February, 1839, to Josiah Samuel Law, who had baptized him eight years earlier, reveals that while at Oxford the prayers of his mother bore fruit in the life of her son.

Rev. and Dear Sir:
  You have no doubt been aware from your own observations, and from the testimony of others, notwithstanding you have received no confession from me of the fact, that I have been for some years past careless in regard to the interests of eternity, and a backslider from the faith I professed. When I gave up my hope I was absent from the state and did not inform you of it, as I thought (erroneously I have since been informed), there were but two ways, according to the rules of the church, by which my connection with it could be dissolved—one, by a dismission in regular standing, should I wish to connect myself with another body—and another by ex-communication. And I suppose the latter to be administered only when the member violated any of the obvious rules of *morality*—or at least as the church has instituted to regulate his *outward conduct.* My object in writing you at present is to ascertain whether my name is still on the church books so that I may be able to discover what my duty may be under the circumstances....
  The Lord has dealt mercifully with me and has been pleased to bring me from the most awful lengths of unbelief and to humiliate me at the foot of the Cross. And I think I can say that I have the firmest belief relying humbly upon his prom-

ises that he has for Christ's sake pardoned all my sins. It is almost more than I can realize, and when I consider who I am and what I have been and how I have trifled with this subject I am filled with astonishment that I can by possibility arrive at such a state of mind as to believe that I have passed from death unto life....

When I connected myself with the church I was entirely ignorant of the religion I was professing. This I say not to clear myself from the imputation of instability nor in any measure as an apology, but as an awful fact that I professed to believe in a God of whom I knew nothing....

Living by faith in Christ, laying hold of his promises and trusting him for their fulfillment, though read often and heard oftener—astonishing as it may seem to you—and it cannot surprise you more than it does me now, I never attached any idea as a part of the gospel plan and instead of seeking the witness of the Spirit of God which might bare witness with my spirit that I was born again, I looked to my own animal feelings for the proof of my acceptability with God—feelings which a pathetic story, theatrical representations, and harmony of sound have often since produced. And I was assured that all was right if I could succeed in exciting those feelings on rising from my bed in the morning and on retiring at night, especially if I could have them accompanied by a few tears. This, Sir, was my religion. This was the sandy foundation on which I built, and it was not to be wondered at that the waves of the world, beating on my house should overthrow it. The comforts of religion were to me but a name. I sought God's face, not because I loved him but because I feared him. I looked upon him not as one who could smile upon me and bless me too, but as an angry God who would punish

me for my sins. I renounced the world not because I saw its vanity compared with the things of
eternity, but because I felt myself compelled to
from motives of safety; and I am bound to believe
—though it was what I could not consent to confess to myself at the time—that if I had only been
assured that I had nothing to fear from God's
righteous indignation I should never have renounced them and connected myself with his
people. Such was my religious state when I left
home for college. And now I was placed in the
midst of new scenes and new associates—my attention and interest became absorbed by other
subjects. God and the things of eternity became
less and less interesting to me—my efforts to create a good state of feeling became less and less
strenuous with frequent intermissions. From indifference for my soul's salvation, I glided by an
imperceptible current to a distaste for the subject
—to a downright dislike for it and finally openly
and joyfully threw off the restraints that my religion has imposed upon me and buried myself in
the world. The failure to obtain that change of
heart which the Bible spoke of induced me to
question its reality and to believe at first that it
had its existence only in the heated imagination
of enthusiasts, and then that it was a cunningly
devised fable invented by priest-craft to gull the
simple and perpetuate its power. And thus the
Bible came to be viewed as an impostor and God's
people as deluders and deluded, and it only remained for me to consummate my unbelief by
doubting the existence of a God—Yes, with my
eyes upturned to the heavens, which declare his
glory, and open upon the beautiful material world
around me, which showeth his handywork, I said
in my heart, and rejoiced that I could say it:
There is no God. But my merciful Heavenly Fa-

ther has forgiven me that sin.

When I think of the awful depths of unbelief to which I had struggled, I am filled with amazement at the long suffering and mercy of God in that he did not suddenly cut me off or give me over to hardness of heart and blindness of mind to believe a lie. And now my whole heart became absorbed in the things of this world. God and religion were not thought of except to be blasphemed and sneered at—not openly; for motives of prudence induced me to conceal my state that I might not shock the minds of men and thus throw a barrier in the way of my temporal prospects. Ambition now took entire possession of my soul, a desire to rise above my fellows in mental state—not so much that I might be able to do more good, as that I might be a mark for all to gaze at. This, a desire to become great in the world, had been a *principle* with me from my earliest recollection, though I had the good sense to conceal it from my acquaintances generally, and often when I was a poor boy destitute of even the necessaries of life would I delight myself picturing in my imagination scenes of future grandeur and triumph in which I would be the actor. These were but dreams it is true, but dreams that expelled from my thoughts every thing that did not administer to them. And at the time I am speaking of my mind had become so spiritually darkened that could I have accomplished fame by it I verily believe I would have been willing to renounce without the slightest sinking of the heart thenceforth and forever all interest in the atonement of Christ whose very existence I doubted. Such was my state when a little more that a year ago I returned home.

But I have extended this already to an unbecoming length. It only remains for me to relate as briefly as possible the means by which my thoughts were again diverted to the things of eternity.—And here I have no signal interposition to relate, no *occurrence* to point out as having been instrumental in rousing me to a sense of my awful condition. But it pleased God that I should be placed in a situation where I could be frequently alone; where, by influences of his Holy Spirit he might turn my thoughts inward and the still small voice of conscience might be heard. The world, too, previous to this, had begun to assume rather a different aspect in my eye. Circumstances had happened which affected me, alone it is true, and which had made a deep impression on me. Experience had shown me that the affections of friends even who wished me well, could easily be alienated, and that from the world I was just as likely to receive censure for that which deserved commendation as the contrary During my absence from Georgia, all the time not devoted to the discharge of my duties had been spent in amusements or in company of which I possessed an unlimited command, and thus thoughts on religion had no opportunity of intruding themselves upon me. But after my return I engaged in business very much at the time against my own consent, in a part of the country that is very thinly settled, where there was not a single young person of my own age with whom I could associate; added to this was the fact that I was not in a situation to occupy my vacation time with books. So that certain hours every day I was left alone with myself. During these periods God was pleased to be near me and to induce such a train of thought as to show me the vanity of earthly things, and the weighty importance of things of eternity. The objections I had cherished against the existence of a God and the authenticity of the Scriptures, now that I had an opportunity of thinking calmly and without interruption, lost their weight. The more particularly so as I had no opportunity of noting the inconsistencies of professing Christians, and seldom heard the gospel preached. In this part of my experience there is nothing standing out distinct to which I can refer as the cause of any result which followed. I commenced teaching school in that place confessedly with the belief that the Bible was all a fable and even if true that it was never more to receive attention from me. And my steps that were imperceptible to me at the time and cannot be traced now I was brought to relinquish all my doubts and to feel that even from me the subject has an interest. But notwithstanding, for more than a year did I trifle with this subject. There was this doubt I had to solve, this mystery I had to look into, and I tried to satisfy myself with saying that Religion was a subject I could not understand. Then perhaps yielding to the influence of the moment I would retire to a private place and try to pray, and because I did not receive a miraculous manifestation of God's presence in my heart I would give up in despair and perhaps the next moment with a zest which would astonish myself, would join with the thoughtless in throwing ridicule on the Bible and Religion.

But not to multiply words. In this awful state did I continue until about three weeks ago when God was pleased to bring me like a little child to the foot of the cross, and I was led to pray him to save me in his own way. I know I am weak and unable to persevere if I depend upon myself; but Christ is strong and he has told me in his word, his grace will be sufficient for me. Let me beg an interest in your prayers, as I have no doubt I have already had. Pray for me that I may not again deceive myself but that I may build on the rock Christ Jesus.[7]

And thus we learn, from his own pen, how it was that redeeming grace laid hold on Pat Mell. Evidence that this change of heart was real came in Pat's desire to give his entire energies to the service of the King of kings and Lord of lords. Surely his dear mother's words echoed in his mind, "I can never consent for you to study for the ministry until I have some satisfactory proof of your heart being turned to God in holy consistency and permanency of character." The remainder of Mell's life was a living illustration of the constancy and diligence that attends the true call to the ministry. In writing to Pastor Law of his aspirations to the ministry of the Word, Mell acknowledged, "I know I am not fit for the office; but the preparation of the heart is with God and he can qualify me for it."[8] This belief that only God can qualify and equip a man for the gospel work was etched deeply into Mell's heart. In his first address to a graduating class (1843) at Mercer University, Mell said,

> Your hearts must be deeply imbued with the spirit of the Gospel. You must not only understand but feel those truths; not only recommend them to others but love them yourselves, and what is more, you must preach and strive in humble dependence upon Almighty aid.[9]

Mell also believed that for some men, himself in particular, formal theological training was part of God's means used to prepare His ministers. Though more education was Mell's aim, God was already guiding him toward a ministry and providing him with the requisite spiritual and intellectual materi-

---

7 P. H. Mell, Jr., *Life of Mell*, 33-39.
8 Ibid., 41.
9 P. H. Mell, "Professor Mell's Address, Delivered to the Graduating Class of the late Commencement," *The Christian Index*, August 18, 1843, 515.

als that make for a godly man and a preacher of great power.

In the late spring of 1840, less than a year after his call, Mell began preaching in the Oxford community under the license of the North Newport Church of Liberty County. During the weekdays Mell would teach at the prep school and on the Sabbaths he would preach in the destitute places in and around Oxford.

PASTORATES AND CAREER AT MERCER

In 1840 Mell married Lurene Howard Cooper—one of his former students at Ryal's Academy in Montgomery County, Georgia. Their union of twenty years was blessed with eight children and a love that saw them through both adversity and success.

On February 17, 1841, having been strongly endorsed by former Georgia Governor George M. Troup, P. H. Mell was elected to fill the chair of Ancient Languages at Mercer University, then located at Penfield some thirty-five miles from Athens. In October of the same year Mell was ordained to the gospel ministry by the North Newport Church, under imposition of the hands of B. M. Sanders, W. H. Stokes, and Otis Smith (then president of Mercer University). His ordination was called for by the Greensboro Baptist Church which Mell pastored for ten years following. W. H. Stokes preached the ordination sermon from the text of 2 Timothy 4:2, "Preach the Word." And preach the Word Mell did. One contemporary said of Mell,

> As a preacher Dr. Mell is strong, able, argumentative, and sound doctrinally, holding his audiences spell-bound by the clearness of his statements and the strength of his reasoning. His arguments, founded on sound premises, reach inevitable conclusions. On the grand doctrines of Christianity and especially the (so called) "five points" in theology, he is especially able. On the distinguish-

ing doctrines of his denomination he is particularly strong and conclusive, always refuting those who put themselves in opposition to him.[10]

When a year later, he addressed the graduating class at Mercer, Mell expressed his personal evaluation of much of the preaching of his day.

The demand for preaching that will excite, at once, all the faculties of mind and heart, is but limited, and I grieve to confess that the supply falls even short of the demand. The people are easily satisfied, and are patient, when, week after week, they hear the same first principles of the doctrine of Christ vociferated in their ears; and the preacher taking license from this to indulge his indolence, continues to substitute sound for substance, and to ring the same round of changes in their hearing.[11]

But to these young preachers he went on to say,

Penetrate, for yourselves into the inexhaustible mind of Gospel truth. It is necessary to your extensive and permanent usefulness, and, as educated ministers, you are bound to do so.[12]

Professor Mell's years at Mercer were spent, by and large, in usefulness and happiness. Under the eminent President John Leadley Dagg, Mell's "youth, health, and vigorous body enabled him to fill the position of disciplinarian with marked success."[13] It was while serving as Mercer University's disciplinarian that Mell received the nickname "Old Pat" from the

---

10 Samuel Boykin, "History of the Baptist Denomination in Georgia," (Atlanta: *The Christian Index*, 1881), 382.
11 P. H. Mell, "Address to Graduating Class," 516.
12 Ibid.
13 P. H. Mell, Jr., *Life of Mell*, 48.

students. One might think that the office of disciplinarian at a school for Baptist ministers would be a task of relative ease and complete safety. Such was not the case. One evening Professor Mell was called out by the noise of drunken university students on the street of Penfield. These students, armed with weighted sticks, threatened to beat Professor Mell for exposing some previous crime to the college authorities. As soon as Mell was able to see their faces, he announced himself, called them by name, and ordered them to go to their rooms and to report on the following morning to the President's office. When he turned to walk away, one of the students laid his loaded stick to Mell's head. Glancing off the side of his head, the stick landed soundly on his shoulder, temporarily paralyzing Mell's arm. The next day the young boy, sober and realizing what he had done, left the school without waiting to be expelled.

On another occasion, Mell's life was saved by rain-dampened gun powder, when a drunken student put a pistol to "Old Pat's" chest and pulled the trigger three times. The task of disciplinarian was not without its dangers. Still, Mell served well in this capacity.

From 1848 until sometime in 1880 Mell, along with his teaching responsibilities, pastored two, sometimes three churches. When in 1857 Mell took the office of Professor of Ancient Languages at the University of Georgia, "his agreement to come was with the stipulation that his professorial duties were not to interfere with his relationship to the churches which he pastored."[14]

In 1848, while still pastoring the Greensboro Church, Mell also accepted the Bairdstown Church in Green County. In 1852 he was called to take charge of the Antioch Church in Oglethorpe County as well. Realizing that these last two churches would occupy all of his time, he was compelled to dissolve his ten-year pastorate at Greensboro.

---

14 Robert Preston Brooks, *The University of Georgia* (Athens: The University of Georgia Press, 1956), 69.

Mell was a faithful and able pastor, as well as a powerful preacher. One of the members of the Antioch Church writes, after Mell's twenty-six-year pastorate there,

> I was impressed at once that he was a peace maker in the fullest and best meaning of that term. He did not seek to harmonize discords by leaving some points of the case unnoticed, others merely smoothed over or covered to ferment and burst forth in all their fury; his plan was the best; every point in dispute met on its own merits and upon principle, by which an adjustment could be made, and peace and harmony secured upon a solid basis.[15]

Another said of his pastoral abilities,

> As to his ministerial ability and usefulness, the success with which his efforts were crowned are sufficient answers even to the most fastidious criticisms to which his ministry might be subjected. As a pastor, in my judgment, I have yet to meet his equal. My kind regard and respect for him in the past were occasions for the remark that I worshipped him, and that I thought I would go to him when I died. In our memorial services I referred to this statement, and remarked that my attachment for him remained unabated and I was willing for my friends to consider that my desire was to go to him when I died, because I imagined he was very near to the Saviour, nearer in position, perhaps, than I hoped would be accorded me.[16]

Mell was not only a pastor, disciplinarian, and college pro-

15 P. H. Mell, Jr., *Life of Mell*, 55.
16 Ibid., 56-57.

fessor, but also an author. He held in his hand a ready pen whose ink flowed from 1851 until near his death.

Mell's first written work was his treatise on *Predestination and the Saints' Perseverance.* As seen earlier, Mell was an able exponent and a fearless defender of "the five-points of theology." Mrs. D. B. Fitzgerald, a member of the Antioch Church recalls,

> When first called to take charge of the church Dr. Mell found it in a sad state of confusion. He said a number of members were drifting off into Arminianism. He loved the truth too well to blow hot and cold with the same breath. If it was a *Baptist* church it must have doctrines peculiar to that denomination preached to it. And with that boldness, clearness, and vigor of speech that marked him, he preached to them the doctrines of predestination, election, free-grace, etc. He said it was always *his* business to preach the truth as he found it in God's word, and leave the matter there, feeling that God would take care of the results.[17]

His stated reason for writing *Predestination and the Saints' Perseverance* (which first appeared as a series of articles in *The Christian Index*) was to answer two printed sermons by Reverend Russel Reneau, which had been "extensively distributed through parts of Georgia and Tennessee, and [had] been lauded as a complete refutation of Calvinism."[18] Mell engaged in this written debate because he believed that the heart of the gospel was at stake. He did not believe that he was entering an esoteric discussion about some ancient controversy. This was very much a "live" issue.

17 Ibid., 58-59.
18 P. H. Mell, *Predestination and the Saints' Perseverance*, (Charleston: Southern Baptist Publication Society, 1851; reprint ed. Forth Worth: *The Wicket Gate*, 1983), iii.

I have been pained to notice, for some years past, on the part of some of our ministers, in some localities in the South, a disposition to waive the doctrines of Grace, in their public ministrations. While some have been entirely silent about them, and have even preached, though not ostensibly, doctrines not consistent with them, others have given them only a cold and half-hearted assent, and some few have openly derided and denounced them. This, in many cases, has resulted, doubtless, from a lack of information, and from an apprehension, therefore, that the doctrines of Grace are synonymous with Antinomianism.[19]

That Mell was no cold formalist and that his doctrines did not lead him to any kind of fatalism is seen in the fact that the Lord was pleased to send revival to the Antioch Church in 1852-1853. From this revival Mell's second treatise flowed, *Baptism In Its Mode and Subjects*.

This publication owes its existence to the following circumstances:—During the month of August last, the Lord blessed the church at Antioch, of which I am the pastor, with a season of refreshing from his presence. During its progress, we had, for nearly two weeks, daily occasion to administer the ordinance of baptism. As is my custom, I availed myself of the opportunity afforded, to address the people at the water's side on the subject....

Within a mile of Antioch is situated a Methodist Meeting House called "Centre." The next "Quarterly Conference" appointed the very estimable gentleman, Rev. Wm. J. Parks, the Presiding Elder, to preach a sermon on Baptism .... It was never publicly avowed, I believe, but it was

19 Ibid., iv.

generally understood, that it was to be a reply to
my remarks at the water's side.[20]

In addition to preaching on the subject of baptism, Rev.
Parks also distributed, in "Mell's Kingdom" (as the community came to be known), a number of works on infant baptism.
As a result the Antioch and Bairdstown churches requested,
at a regular business conference, that Mell publish his "very
instructive discourses ... on the subject of baptism." Thus,
again we see Mell thrown into controversy. We are told that
the book had a wide circulation and that it was instrumental
in changing several paedobaptists to the faith and belief of the
Baptist denomination.[21]
    While Mell never swerved an inch from the defense of the
truth, he was nevertheless very courteous to those who dif-
fered with him. The Scripture says,

> The Lord's bond-servant must not be quarrel-
> some, but kind to all, able to teach, patient when
> wronged, with gentleness correcting those who
> are in opposition if perhaps God may grant them
> repentance leading to the knowledge of the
> truth.... (2 Timothy 2:24, 25 NAS).

That this was the case with Pastor Mell is seen from the following description by his son,

> Among those who sat under his ministry for ten,
> twenty and twenty-five years were people of other
> denominations who were as warm and friendly as
> any he had. Some Methodist brethren attended
> every conference meeting as regularly as did
> those of his own flock, and it was a source of
> great pleasure to him. They might shake their

---

20 P. H. Mell, *Baptism In Its Mode and Subjects*, (Charleston: Southern Baptist Publication Society,
1853), v.
21 P. H. Mell, Jr., *Life of Mell*, 56.

heads at what they called his "hard doctrine," but they would shake his hand as cordially at the close of the sermon and they claimed a share of his visits as much as did the members of his own flock.[22]

PAUL AND BARNABAS AT MERCER?

The next several years following 1854 were tumultuous for Mell, Mercer University, and Georgia Baptists. In February of 1854, John Leadly Dagg let it be known that he thought the time had come for him to be released from the presidency of Mercer. Opposition to this course arose principally due to the apprehension of difficulty that might arise in the choice of a successor.[23] Almost prophetically the turmoil arose. A statement was purportedly given out that the reason for Dagg's resignation was due to his "failing strength." Dagg immediately registered his protest to this inaccurate statement.[24] Mell, believing that the stated reason for Dagg's resignation would do "great injustice to a capable and faithful officer," drew up a petition signed by all the professors (with the exception of Dr. N. M. Crawford, Professor of Theology) asking that Dagg not be retired on account of "failing strength." Nevertheless, the Board of Trustees received Dr. Dagg's resignation and very soon thereafter elected Professor Crawford to the position of President.

> There soon sprang up between Professor Mell and President Crawford a difference of opinion in regard to the duties belonging to each, which resulted in estrangement, and their resignations were offered to the Board.[25]

---

22 Ibid., 59.
23 John L. Dagg, "Autobiography" in *Manual of Theology and Church Order* (Harrisonburg, Virginia: Gano Books, 1982, reprint ed.), 49.
24 B. O. Ragsdale, *Story of Georgia Baptists*, Volume 1 (Atlanta: The Executive Committee of the Baptist Convention of the State of Georgia, 1932), 1:102.
25 P. H. Mell, Jr., *Life of Mell*, 77.

The ultimate end of this sad contention was similar to that in which Paul and Barnabas found themselves, and resulted in their departure from one another. Dr. Crawford was reinstated by the Board; Professors Mell, Dagg, and Hillyer resigned; and not until 1856 did things begin to settle. There is much that can be said about this controversy and much that must be left to conjecture.[26] Suffice it to say that no one's character was maligned during the tempest, especially not that of Mell. In the heat of the battle, Professor Mell was elected Moderator of the Georgia Baptist Association and offered the presidency of Mississippi College, the principalship of the Alabama Female Institute, and called as pastor to the First Baptist Church of Savannah, only the first of which he accepted.

Following his resignation as Professor of Ancient Languages at Mercer, the students of the University offered the following tribute to their beloved professor:

> At a meeting of twenty-nine students of Mercer University, in the Cicernian Hall, on Thursday evening, the 29th of November, the following resolutions were unanimously adopted:
> WHEREAS the pleasant relationship which Rev. P. H. Mell has heretofore sustained towards the Students of Mercer University, as Professor of Ancient Languages, not long exists,
> *Resolved,* That in his retirement he will carry with him our best wishes for his future happiness and the earnest desire that in whatever sphere his lot may be cast, his labors may be rewarded with the same eminent success that has attended them during his connexion with Mercer University.
> *Resolved,* That as a testimonial of the high esteem and admiration which we entertain towards

---

26 For the complete scenario see Ragsdale, *Story of Georgia Baptists*, 1:101-117 and P. H. Mell, Jr., *Life of Mell*, 76-102.

him, both as a man and as a laborious and competent Professor, we tender him a Gold-headed Cane, bearing the inscription: Prof. P. H. Mell, from Students of Mercer University.

Resolved, That the above proceedings be published in the Temperance Banner, Christian Index, and Tennessee Baptist.

A motion was made, and prevailed unanimously, that the meeting, on Saturday night thereafter, resolve itself into a Committee as the whole, and *en massa*, make the presentation in due form at the private residence of P. H. Mell.[27]

AT THE UNIVERSITY OF GEORGIA

By the time the tumultuous waters had been quieted, a year had passed. Somewhat battle-scarred and most certainly weary, Mell was elected by the Board of Trustees to the chair of Ancient Languages at the University of Georgia on December 11, 1856. He occupied this post until, in 1860, he was elected to the chair of Ethics and Metaphysics and made Vice-Chancellor of the University. In the interim Mell was elected President of the Georgia Baptist Convention, a position which he held for a total of twenty-four years. Also, Furman University conferred upon him the Doctor of Divinity degree in 1858. All seemed quiet for this space of three years, but in 1860 Mell was thrust again into the battle.

The publication of his third major treatise, *Corrective Church Discipline*, raised the ire of the growing number of Landmarkers in the Southern Baptist Convention. According to his son, Mell was asked by a number of Baptist leaders to "prepare a work on the subject [of church discipline] that would give a clear conception of the relationship existing between churches, and the status of the members of the church."[28] First published as a series of articles in the major

---

27 *The Christian Index*, Vol. 34, Dec. 13, 1855.
28 P. H. Mell, Jr., *Life of Mell*, 109.

Baptist papers of that day, *Corrective Church Discipline* was published later in book form by the Southern Baptist Publication Society in 1860. Though there is nothing in the superb treatise itself that would lead one to think it was a polemic against Landmarkism and especially against the treatment received by R. B. C. Howell of the First Baptist Church of Nashville, still, being published so soon after the Nashville trouble, everyone knew the target at which Mell had aimed. The publication of Mell's articles set off a journalistic debate in nearly all of the South's denominational papers. Professor A. H. Worrell of Talladega, Alabama, published a series of articles entitled "Review of Corrective Church Discipline" which sought to answer Mell's arguments from a Landmark position and only fanned the flames of controversy. Though some writers, as fallen men are often wont to do, engaged in character assassination, Mell remained courteous and tried always to address the issue, not the personality of the author.

When one writer tried to defend the Landmark position by taking verse after verse out of its scriptural context, Mell's only reply was,

> I see that my brother ... has attacked my last position and quoted certain Scripture to sustain his point. Now by my dear brother's course of reasoning I can prove anything from the Bible. I can prove that the brother ought to go and hang himself. Does not the Bible say "Judas Iscariot went out and hanged himself"? (Matthew 27:5) and does in not also say: "Go, and do thou likewise"? (Luke 10:37); "That thou doest, do quickly" (John 13:27).[29]

Thus, Mell was a staunch defender of Baptist principles and never let the opportunity pass to speak the truth in love against error. He had a keen sense of the ludicrous and he

---

29 Ibid., 114.

maintained a powerful ability to wield the weapon of sarcasm to make his point. The sharpening of the weapons of sarcasm and quick retort began even in his early years. As a young boy, he met the neighborhood bully on a narrow path on which the lad would not allow Mell to travel. Straddling the path the bully said, "I never give ground to a fool." Mell simply stepped aside and replied, "I do."[30]

The year following the publication of *Corrective Church Discipline*, the Civil War broke out. Being a strong sympathizer with the South, Mell was one of the first to offer his services to the defense of its cause. At the opening of the war a company of fighting men was organized called "Mell's Volunteers" (later "Mell's Riflement"). While preparations were being made to send the riflemen to the battle front in Virginia, Mell's wife died, forcing him to resign his commission. Not only did Mell lose his wife, but also in 1862 at Antietam, the bloodiest battle of the war, Mell lost his eldest son, Benjamin. The correspondence between Mell and the family who attended his son before his death is very touching.

Mell was married December 24, 1861, to Eliza E. Cooper of Screven County, Georgia, and fathered six children. In 1862 *Keep the Sabbath* was published as a tract to be distributed among the soldiers.

In 1863 two very important positions were bestowed upon Mell. First, he was elected colonel of a militia by the citizens of Athens, Georgia, for the purpose of defending the northern part of the state from invasion. One party on the committee for the citizens of Athens, upon learning that Mell was being considered for the position said, "Why he knows nothing about military affairs." To which another member replied, "I don't care for that, I am for Mell anyhow. For a man who can manage four hundred Baptists can do anything."[31] The second momentous event in Mell's life was his election in 1863 to the presidency of a denomination he helped build, the

30 King, "Preacher, Pedagogue, and Parliamentarian," 191.
31 P. H. Mell, Jr., *Life of Mell*, 144.

Southern Baptist Convention. Mell, who met with the others in Augusta in 1845, was to occupy the presidency of the Southern Baptist Convention for seventeen years. From 1863 to 1886, except for eight years of absence because of sickness, Mell presided over the convention.[32]

In January of 1866, with the scars of war etched upon his heart, Mell resumed his duties at the University of Georgia (the details of which are beyond the scope of this paper). Most importantly, Mell was convinced that there could be no separation of sacred and secular for the Christian. His labors at the University were performed as diligently unto the Lord as the work he undertook as pastor and Southern Baptist leader.

PRINCE OF PARLIAMENTARIANS

At the Southern Baptist Convention of 1867, meeting in Memphis, Tennessee, Mell was requested (by a resolution made by J. P. Boyce) to draw up a manual of parliamentary practice for the use of the denomination. A year later *A Manual of Parliamentary Practice* was published and adopted by the SBC. So wide-spread was the acceptance of this work that many legislative bodies adopted Mell's *Manual*, including the Georgia legislature. As parliamentarian and presiding officer Mell excelled, so much so that he wore the title "Prince of Parliamentarians." In *Parliamentary Law*, a text designed for the author's classes at Southern Seminary, F. H. Kerfoot acknowledges,

> During the first ten years that the author taught this subject he used as his textbook the manual on *Parliamentary Practice*, by President P. H. Mell. This is in many respects an excellent book. And it may well be supposed that the use of it for so many years must have left its impress upon the teacher, and hence upon the following pages

32 It is interesting to note that in the years of Mell's absence as president, J. P. Boyce presided over the denomination, and also, in the year of Mell's death, 1888, Boyce served as president of the SBC.

also.[33]

One visitor at the Southern Baptist Convention of 1866 commented upon Mell's abilities as a parliamentarian thusly,

> We think Dr. Mell the best presiding officer we have ever seen; and we heard many present at the Convention express the same opinion. He understands perfectly the duties of the position, and acts with that deliberation, promptness and firmness, yet with kindness, he held in check any who might be unruly, and enabled the humblest and most modest member of the Convention to gain the ear of the body. No press of business, or excitement incident to such meetings, when unexpected questions were sprung, could for a moment disconcert him. He impressed all with his peculiar fitness for the position which he so gracefully filled.[34]

Mell's personal charisma as president and presiding officer was seen when,

> At a certain meeting of the Southern Baptist Convention Dr. Mell called a brother to preside over the body over his temporary absence. Business moved along all right until some one made a motion that called many to their feet, all clamoring for recognition from the chair. The President hopelessly pounded on the desk for order, order, but there was no order. Dr. Mell was sent for by some one who recognized the importance of a cool headed man in the chair. He came back and quietly assumed charge of the chair. The gavel tapped lightly on the table, and instantly, as if by

---

33 F. H. Kerfoot, *Parliamentary Law*, (Nashville: Broadman Press, 1899), vi.
34 P. H. Mell, Jr., *Life of Mell*, 153-154.

magic, disorder ceased, groups of members that
had formed all of the house and were talking ex-
citedly and loudly, dispersed and sat down, and
the great body moved smoothly and orderly on
with its business as if it had been some vast piece
of machinery under the control of its master.[35]

Perhaps it was this great popularity as a parliamentarian
that so overshadowed his gifts and abilities as a pastor and
theologian, that has prevented more being known about Mell
in our own day.

MELL'S NERVOUS ATTACK

The years between 1871 and 1873 were very troublesome
for Mell. The weight of the churches upon him, the duties of
the university work, the denominational responsibilities, his
prolific pen, all contributed to what became known as Mell's
"nervous attack." In August 1871, while preaching at Bairdstown, Mell was seized by an attack that left him prostrate and
nearly ended his life. For over a year he was unable to do any
active work. Perhaps this was an instance of what we today
call ministerial burnout. Often Mell was heard to say, "Let me
wear out, not rust out."

Along with all of his responsibilities and duties, was it not
also his great burden for the souls of men that led to his attack? Several days before his debilitating seizure, Mell stood
in the pulpit of the Antioch Church and pleaded,

Must I leave you, as I found you, out of Christ?
Must all my arguments, my entreaties, my
prayers, be only so many millstones hanged about
your neck to drag you down into perdition? My
skirts are clear. I have warned you of God's righteous indignation. I have wooed you by the sweet-

---

35 Ibid., 159.

ness of Christ's love.[36]

Lifting his eyes he said solemnly,

> God is my witness. I have not shunned to declare
> unto you the whole counsel of God, but O how
> can I leave you. For many of you I feel it will be
> only a while till we shall hold sweet converse in a
> better world, but for you who have resisted the
> power of the Gospel so long, must I stand in judg-
> ment against you?[37]

I think Mell was impressed at this point that the time of his
own departure was at hand, but God wasn't pleased to take
him at this point.

After suffering for nearly a year it seems that instead of as-
pirin and water and plenty of bed rest the prescription of the
doctors then was a sea cruise. After a sea cruise and a year,
Mell again took up his labors for the University of Georgia and
his two churches with more vigor than before. Perhaps this
experience on the backside of the desert provided him with
more time for prayer and meditation because in 1876 his
book *The Doctrine of Prayer: Its Utility and Its Relationship
to Providence* was published.

December 12, 1887 Mell preached his last sermon. He
spoke on the doctrine of election from 2 Thessalonians 2:13.
On the fifteenth of the month he was forced to lay aside all of
his duties and seek rest in the southern part of Georgia. On
this day he wrote his son and said,

> My health is bad. I have broken myself down by
> overwork. My doctor orders me off for the recess.
> Many of the Trustees urge me to take a month's
> rest; but I cannot do so, my colleagues are already
> overworked, and my classes would suffer. There

36 Ibid., 179.
37 Ibid.

is no rest for me but in the grave.[38]

On the 26th of January 1888 Patrick Mell found his eternal rest in the arms of his loving heavenly Father. Three days before his death he was heard to say, "I've been a wonderful child of providence if not a child of grace."[39] His son spoke of Dr. Mell's last hours thusly:

> At intervals he said, "I commit my soul to God in Christ Jesus—Glory be to God." "Once I was dead but now am alive. In the other world I am thoroughly understood and thoroughly appreciated—thoroughly understood and thoroughly appreciated." He uttered these words just as written —repeating the last part of the sentence. It seemed to those who watched that he was permitted to penetrate the veil which hangs between this and the other world, and that he actually beheld the understanding and approving smile of his beloved Master's face.
> Just before breathing his last, he said: "Nearly home?" and made an effort to say something more, but failed. He then tried to fold his hands across his breast and died without a struggle—fell asleep in the arms of Jesus, for whom he had fought a valiant fight, and at the end of the many long years and a useful life was taken to his reward.[40]

Brothers and sisters, Patrick Hues Mell was a man of strong conviction. You see that in his writings and in the fact that every time that he was assailed by others he would only defend the truth in love. He wrote often of his theological position and held it without swerving. He was a man of deep com-

---

38 Ibid., 248.
39 Ibid., 249.
40 Ibid., 251.

passion. He stood and held the hands of many of his church members and wept with them over their sin. He pleaded with men to come to Christ. He was a man of rigorous discipline. Were to God that we would emulate men like Patrick Hues Mell; that we would have the love for the Savior that he had; that we would have the love for the church that he had; that we would have the love for communion with God that he had. He spent time in prayer and considered that he had lost many of this world's delights, yet that was nothing when compared to the glory and riches of the inheritance that awaited him in the Savior. May God help us to be men of like passions with P. H. Mell.

Prayer:

> *Our Father, we are moved at the life of your servant, Patrick Mell, yet if he were here we know that he would remind us that what he was, and what he is even now, he is by grace. We pray, oh God, that on our own hearts and minds you would establish such strong conviction, that deep compassion, that rigorous discipline, that love for the Savior and His church, as you did in him. Oh God, hear our prayer that our Convention would be once again turned unto thee as it was in the days of its founders. We do not worship them, nor the hour in which they lived, oh God, but we do ask that you would restore unto us the vision, the message and the hope that once belonged to the Southern Baptist Convention, that again we would be pleasing in your sight, for your glory and honor. In the matchless name of Christ, our Prophet, King and Redeemer, we pray. Amen.*

27.

THE LIFE AND DEVOTION OF DAIVD BRAINERD

JOHN THORNBURY

1985 Southern Baptist Founders Conference

IN this account I would like to share with you how I became interested in David Brainerd, provide a brief sketch of his life and Christian character, and show how the doctrines of grace influenced his life and ministry.

MY INTEREST IN DAVID BRAINERD

In 1962 the Banner of Truth Trust announced a missionary biography contest in which people all over the world could submit entries. Mine on David Braincrd was judged the second best. It appeared in a little book published by the Banner of Truth Trust called *Five Pioneer Missionaries*.

When I set out to write that essay, I knew nothing about David Brainerd except that he was an American. I began to search for books about him and found that there is quite a bit of material in print about this missionary. Ironically, around this same time, the Lord called me into a region of America where this man had preached to the Indians, namely the Susquehanna region of central Pennsylvania.

My essay aroused quite a bit of interest and a local historian filled in some details for me and explained some things I had not carefully considered. He pointed out that Opelholhaupung (as it was spelled by Brainerd), which I had mentioned in my book, is now the modern village of Wapwallopen, on the north branch of the Susquehanna not far north of Danville. And it was pointed out that Shaumoking, to which Brainerd

489

referred, was the important Indian village, Shamokin, which was on an island at the confluence of the west and north branches of the Susquehanna. The name Shamokin survives today in the town by that name, just north of Sunbury and in Shamokin Dam, which is about five miles south of where I live.

One interesting historical note: there was at the time that Brainerd lived in the mid-eighteenth century, a powerful Indian alliance known as the Six Nations or Iroquois Confederation. They controlled all the Indian tribes throughout New York, Pennsylvania, Maryland, Virginia, down even to the Carolinas—the borders of their archrivals, the Cherokees. The Six Nation Confederacy appointed a noble Indian chief to rule over the Delaware and the central Susquehanna valley. His name was Shikellamy. He is a very important figure in Indian culture and in the local traditions of my area. In fact there's a park named after Shikellamy, a local High School is named Shikellamy High School. I'm convinced that David Brainerd not only preached to this man, but may very well have sowed the seeds in his heart that led him to Christ. Brainerd visited Shamokin, the Indian capital on that little island in the confluence of the rivers, in 1745 and he mentions preaching to the Delaware chief though he doesn't call him by name. History tells us that three years later, Shikellamy went with the Moravians to Bethlehem where he became a Christian and died in the Christian faith. I believe it's very possible that David Brainerd's ministry may have had a part in bringing him to faith.

DAVID BRAINERD'S LIFE

David Brainerd was a missionary to the Indians. He is universally considered one of the greatest of the pioneer missionaries. His personal diary, edited and published by Jonathan Edwards, has probably done more to inspire missionary fervor than any other human production. Clifton Olmstead in *Religion in America* says, "His diary was widely read and probably more than any other work, aroused American interest in the Indian missionary effort, and later in home and foreign missionary undertakings." John Wesley printed and distributed an abbreviated version of the life of Brainerd to all his Methodist societies. His life moved William Carey, the apostle to India, and Henry Martyn who labored in Persia. Jim Elliot, who was killed with his flying missionary companions in 1956 by the Auca Indians, wrote in his journal, "Confession of pride suggested by David Brainerd's diary yesterday must become an hourly thing with me."

I suppose my favorite reference to Brainerd's impact on the lives of the godly is from the life of Robert Murray M'Cheyne. On June 27, 1832 as he poured over this life he wrote, "Life of David Brainerd. What a wonderful man, what conflicts, what depressions, desertions, strength, advancement, victories within my torn bosom! I cannot express what I think when I think of thee. Tonight more set upon missionary work than ever before." On the next day M'Cheyne wrote, "Oh, for Brainerd's humility and self and sin loathing dispositions." M'Cheyne later went to the Holy Land as a missionary.

David Brainerd was born in 1718 in Haddam, Connecticut, the son of Hezekiah and Dorothy Brainerd. His parents were godly people. In fact, his grandfather, Reverend Jeremiah Hobart, was a Puritan minister who fled persecution and came to America. David was taught to believe in an all-powerful God whom he reverenced. He tried to live a strict life and was faithful in attending church, prayer and reading the Bible, but he became self-righteous and trusted in his own works for salvation. In 1738 he became aware of his danger and under a deep sense of the wrath of God and a deep dejection, he fell into extreme conviction of sin. After a long struggle in July of 1739 he received peace and assurance through a spiritual vision of the glory of God.

He said that while walking in a solitary place, unspeakable glory opened to the view and apprehension of his soul. He said, "My soul rejoiced with joy unspeakable to see such a God, such a glorious Divine Being; and I was inwardly pleased and satisfied that He should be God over all for ever and ever. My soul was so captivated and delighted with the excellency, loveliness, greatness, and other perfections of God, that I was even swallowed up in Him."

He entered Yale in 1739 and was a brilliant student. While in college a conflict arose between the faculty and revivalists, such as the Tennent brothers and George Whitfield. Students were forbidden to attend the revival meetings. The more reserved, intellectual leaders considered Whitfield and his associates to be wildfire enthusiasts. Brainerd joined the revivalists and imbibed something of their judgmental attitude towards what was called the "standing clergy." The revivalists felt that the standing clergy was mired in dead orthodoxy. In an unguarded moment Brainerd was talking privately to another student leaning against a chair and said, concerning a professor who had just prayed very pathetically, "He has no more grace than this chair." He was expelled from school because of this remark and that expulsion cast a cloud over him that exacerbated his battle with depression the rest of his life.

Shortly after leaving school he decided to become a missionary to the Indians and he was approved by a Scottish Presbyterian Missionary Society for this work. He first labored in an Indian settlement near the Hudson River in New York where he got a taste of the hardships of living in the wilderness. Following this he traveled south to the Forks of the Delaware, near modern Lehigh, Pennsylvania, where he labored for about a year.

The Indians in these two places were respectful toward the young missionary but there was little result. In 1745 he went to an Indian settlement at Crossweeksung, New Jersey where his preaching took hold with power on the hearts of the savages. A kind of Pentecostal awakening took place, resulting in about one hundred and thirty conversions. Brainerd described one meeting,

> The power of God seemed to descend upon the
> assembly like a rushing mighty wind, and with an

astonishing energy bore down all before it. I stood amazed at the influence that seized the audience almost universally, and could compare it to nothing more aptly than the irresistible force of a mighty torrent, or swelling deluge, that with its insupportable weight and pressure bears down and sweeps before it whatever is in its way. Almost all persons of all ages were bowed down with concern together, and scarce one was able to withstand the shock of this surprising operation. Old men and women, who had been drunken wretches for many years, and some little children, not more than six or seven years of age, appeared in distress for their souls, as well as persons of middle age. And it was apparent these children (some of them at least) were not merely frightened with seeing the general concern, but were made sensible of their danger, the badness of their hearts, and their misery without Christ, as some of them expressed it. The most stubborn hearts were now obliged to bow.

A thorough change in behavior came about through Brainerd's ministry among the Indians. They gave up their superstitions and idolatry and became devoted to the gospel of Jesus Christ. Problems such as drunkenness, dishonesty, and immorality were, in large measure, corrected through the influence of his biblical teaching. Brainerd became the spiritual shepherd of these Indians, whom he formed into a stable Christian community at Cranberry, New Jersey. He was not only a pastor but a legal advisor, agent and general overseer as they became civilized.

The spiritual awakening among the Indians was remarkable—especially so when we consider that Brainerd spoke through an interpreter who was himself often intoxicated. Brainerd made four trips into central Pennsylvania to preach to the Delaware Indians along the Susquehanna. He was always accompanied by an interpreter, a fellow preacher, or in

HISTORICAL/BIOGRAPHICAL

the case of the last trip, some of the Christian Indians in New Jersey. Occasionally he would see signs of attention and seriousness among these tribes like that at Cranberry, but he never experienced the same success in leading them to Christ. On his last trip, tuberculosis, with which he had been afflicted for some time, began to ravage his body. The hardships of wilderness life, sleeping out in the cold, improper food, and fatigue began to take their toll. From July to October 1747, as an invalid, Brainerd stayed in the home of Jonathan Edwards, where he was cared for by Jerusha, Edwards' daughter. David and Jerusha were kindred spirits and would have married but both died—David in October and Jerusha the following February.

Brainerd left his diary in the hands of Edwards who came to admire his devotion to Christ and theological perception. He saw immediately its autobiographical value and published parts of it with his editorial notes. This classic is still is in print.

DAVID BRAINERD'S CHRISTIAN CHARACTER

As I turn to Brainerd's Christian character, consider that here is a twenty-five year old man recently expelled from college and, for awhile, a fugitive from justice, having to hide from the authorities in New Haven, who set out on a mission to convert the American Indians. After five years he died with tuberculosis. During his travels of this period (1743-1747) he wrote down his feelings and experiences in a diary. This diary was printed and in the two hundred plus years since that time, it has radically changed the world. I say this because untold thousands of missionaries have been inspired and motivated by reading this diary and as a result, they have preached the gospel to millions who have been converted to Christ.

Now let me clear up some matters about Brainerd's personality traits and experiences. I do not state nor has anyone stated, least of all Jonathan Edwards, that Brainerd was a perfect Christian model. There is only one such model and that is our Lord Jesus Christ. David Brainerd was no doubt too often dejected and melancholy. That was a personality trait that ran in his family. It was exacerbated by the situation in which he found himself after being expelled. I believe we would all agree, however, that the Lord often does wonderful things in and through Christians who are extremely introspective and self-critical. Among these might be included Moses, David, Madam Guyon and C. H. Spurgeon. A melancholy disposition is itself neither good nor bad; it can be run to excess or it can be God's field in which rare graces are planted. I do not say that all of Brainerd's conduct, particularly his critical remark in college, are above reproach, although I think the punishment was rather severe. How many of us could stand before such severity? David himself later admitted his fault and begged to be reinstated into college. In fact, he wrote a lengthy apology saying, "I humbly confess that herein I have sinned against God and acted contrary to the rules of His word." But the intransigent college officials would not bend.

What I do believe, however, along with many thousands of godly preachers, scholars and other Christians in the two hundred years since Brainerd lived, is that the Lord revealed His glory and grace in a special and remarkable way to David Brainerd. It is clear when we read his journal that some of the most beautiful and rare traits of Christian character are found in this missionary. Hosts of people have been inspired, encouraged, rebuked, taught and prodded on to a life of service to God by reading Brainerd's memoirs.

In studying Brainerd, there are five specific manifestations of grace evident in his character and life.

First, he adored the triune God and delighted in Him. Pick out any page in his diary and you will see that this is true. His spirit longed for the fellowship of God; he panted for it. In 1742 he wrote, "When I really enjoy God and I feel my desires of Him the more insatiable and my thirsting after holiness the more unquenchable, the Lord will not allow me to feel as though I were fully satisfied and supplied, but keeps me still reaching forward." In 1743 he wrote, "Oh I feel that if there is no God, though I might live forever here and enjoy not only this but all other worlds I should be ten thousand times more miserable than a reptile." In 1744, after a time of prayer, he said, "I was delighted with the divine glory and happiness and rejoiced that God was God and that He was unchangeably possessed of glory and blessedness." This no doubt accounts in part for his often-expressed desire to leave this world and go to heaven. In 1746, he said,

> Never felt more sedateness, divine serenity and composure of mind. Could freely have left the dearest earthly thread for the society of angels and spirits of just men made perfect. ... I viewed the emptiness and unsatisfactory nature of the most desirable earthly objects, any further than God is seen in them. And longed for a life of spirituality and inward purity: without which I saw there be no true pleasure.

Second, Brainerd had an overpowering sense of his own sinfulness and unworthiness. The godly in all ages have acknowledged their consciousness of ill desert and depravity. Job said, "Behold, I am vile." David acknowledged, "There is no soundness in my flesh nor is there any health in my bones because of my sin. For my iniquities have gone over my head: like a heavy burden they are too heavy for me." Paul exclaimed, "Oh wretched man that I am! Who shall deliver me from this body of death?" Superficial religionists might read such statements and conclude that these men were arch criminals. Not so! These were the godliest people of their day.

In 1742, Brainerd wrote, "No poor creature stands in need of divine grace more than I and none abuse it more than I have and still do." On April 13, 1743, he wrote, "My heart was overwhelmed within me; I verily thought I was the meanest, vilest, most helpless, guilty, ignorant, benighted creature living. And yet I knew what God had done for my soul, at the same time. Sometimes I was assaulted with damping doubts and fears whether it was possible for such a wretch as I to be in a state of grace."

After his success as a missionary he was, of course, commended and praised. He responded:

> Oh, me thought, if God's people knew me as God knows, they would not think so highly of my zeal and resolution for God as perhaps now they do! I could not but desire that they should see how heartless and irresolute I was, that they be undeceived and "not think of me about that which they ought to think." And yet I thought if they saw the uttermost of my flatness and unfaithfulness, the smallness of my courage and resolution for God, they would be ready to shut me out of their doors as unworthy of the company or friendship of Christians.

This attitude, of course, reflects his Puritan theology with its emphasis on the strictness of the law, the holiness of God, the depravity of human nature.

Third, not only did Brainerd adore God and see his own sinfulness, but he longed for holiness. He wrote in 1742, "My soul seems to breathe after holiness; a life of constant devotedness to God." He wrote in 1743, "Had some intense and passionate breathings of soul after holiness, and very clear manifestations of it, of my utter inability to procure or work it in my self; it is wholly owing to the power of God. Oh with what tenderness the love and desire of holiness fills the soul." In 1744 he wrote, "My soul was exceedingly grieved for sin and pride and longed for holiness; and it wounded my heart deeply, yet sweetly, to think how much I had abused a kind God. I longed to be perfectly holy that I might not grieve a gracious God."

Fourth, David Brainerd felt a remarkable contempt for the gains, glory, and pleasures of the world. In 1743 he penned these words,

> The whole world appears to me like a huge vacuum, a vast empty place whence nothing desirable or at least satisfactory can possibly be derived and I long daily to die more and more to it; even though I obtain not that comfort from spiritual things which I earnestly desire. Worldly pleasures, such as flow from greatness, riches, honor, and sensual gratifications are infinitely worse than none. May the Lord deliver us more and more from these vanities.

He wrote in 1744, "Life itself now appeared but an empty bubble. The riches, honors, and common enjoyments of life appeared extremely tasteless. I longed to be perpetually and entirely crucified to all things here below by the cross of Christ."

Fifth, he lived in dependence upon God and resignation to His will though in pain. Though in difficult circumstances, he resigned his soul to the Lord. Again in 1744, "My soul is sweetly resigned to God's disposal of me in every regard: and I saw that nothing had happened but what was best for me." It was my privilege a few years ago to go to New Jersey and visit the Tennent Church in Freehold. I saw the original building where William Tennent, the brother of Gilbert, preached. There is an altar along the front of the church where it is said that David Brainerd served communion to his Indians. After visiting that church, he said, "Oh, that I could fill up all my time whether in the house or by the way for God. I was enabled, I think, this day, to give up my soul to God, and put over all his concerns into His hands and found some real consolation of the thought of being entirely at the divine disposal." He wrote in 1746,

Was made sensible of utter inability to preach without divine help: and was in some good measure willing to leave it with God to give or withhold assistance as He saw would be most for His own glory. ... Afterwards, was pleased to think that God reigneth; and thought I could never be uneasy with any of His dispensations, but must be entirely satisfied, whatever trials He should cause me and His church to encounter.

DAVID BRAINERD AS AN EVANGELIST

David Brainerd was an evangelist, or, as I would call him, a "soul winner." When Brainerd went to New York to preach to the Indians in 1743 he embarked on a mission that was as difficult as one can imagine. The Native Americans, not withstanding some noble qualities, were in the truest sense of the word, pagans. As I pointed out in my essay on Brainerd, they did not believe in one supreme God but had a strange and confused notion of a plurality of invisible deities under a variety of forms and shapes to which they paid homage. They also paid superstitious reverence to beasts, birds, fishes and reptiles upon which they fancied invisible beings that bestowed great powers. Brainerd once saw an Indian burn fine tobacco for incense in order to appease the wrath of the god who presided over rattlesnakes and was supposedly angered because one of them had been killed by a fellow-Indian. If you've ever read any Indian stories you know they practically worshiped rattlesnakes.

The Indians were ruled over by powwows, meaning conjurers or diviners, who were supposed to have the power of foretelling future events, healing the sick, or charming, enchanting, and poisoning others by their magic divinations. One of these powwows was converted under Brainerd's ministry and he told how he received his power. In a vision he imagined he was admitted into the presence of a great man in a world above and a vast distance from the earth. He was clothed with the day, yea, with the brightest day he ever saw. This man in that brightest of all days sent his shadow to be with the Indian to guide him on earth. The powwow said the shadow always was with him and told him how and where to hunt. He was always successful when he followed the direction of the shadow. Always!

Brainerd regarded this as one of Satan's lying-wonders to hold the Indians in spiritual slavery. Brainerd mentioned other hindrances to ministering to the Indians such as their inconvenient situation, savage manners and unhappy method of living. He said,

> I have been often obliged to preach in their houses in cold and windy weather, when they have been full of smoke and cinders as well as unspeakably filthy: which has many times thrown me into violent sick headaches. While I have been preaching, their children frequently cried to such a degree that I could scarce be heard and their pagan mothers would take no time to care for or quiet them. At the same time, perhaps, some have been laughing and mocking divine truths; others were playing with the dogs, whittling sticks and the like.

How would you like to pastor a church like that?

Brainerd spoke of other strong obstacles in winning the Indians to Christ. Such inveterate qualities as indolence, drunkenness and revenge made them prejudiced against the gospel. They were wary of white people because the white people they had met often cheated them and lied to them. They were suspicious of any apparent good intentions of white people, believing the real design was to make slaves out of them like the Negroes.

In light of such seemingly insurmountable difficulties it is no wonder that Brainerd wrote in August 1746,

Scarce ever saw more clearly than this day that it is God's work to convert souls and especially poor heathens. I knew I could not touch them; I saw I could only speak to dry bones, but could give them no sense of what I said. My eyes were up to God for help. I could say the work was His and if done, the glory would be His.

But in spite of the spiritual darkness of the savages, the communication problems he had, and his own failing health, Brainerd pressed on in the mission to which God had called him. He labored faithfully, depending upon God and he was rewarded by seeing many Indians converted. In a great measure he witnessed their pagan customs change. In October 1745 he wrote,

There was at this time a very agreeable melting spread throughout the whole assembly. I think I scarce ever saw a more desirable affection in any number of people in my entire life. There was scarcely a dry eye to be seen among them; and yet nothing boisterous or unseemly, nothing that tended to disturb the public worship; but rather to encourage and excite a Christian ardour and spirit of devotion.

He also said,

I could not but earnestly wish that numbers of God's people had been present at this time to see and hear these things which I am sure must refresh the heart of every true lover of Zion's interest. To see those who were very lately savage pagans and idolaters, having no hope and without God in the world, now filled with a sense of divine love and grace and worshipping the Father in spirit and in truth, as numbers have appeared to do, and was not a little effecting; and especially

to see them appear so tender and humble as well
as lively, fervent and devote in the divine service.

After the awakening at Crossweeksung, the Indians gave up
their idolatrous practices and became sober and responsible
Christians. They were civilized and reformed, but only after
the Holy Spirit worked in their hearts through the gospel.

BRAINERD'S METHODS OF PREACHING AND TEACHING

What methods, what type of preaching, what kind of spiritual work, preceded such an amazing work of God?

First, in considering David Brainerd as an evangelist or soul
winner, his concern was not merely to do good to the Indians,
but the impelling motive of his labor was the advancement of
Christ's kingdom. In 1742, he wrote, "Oh that the kingdom of
the dear Savior might come with power and the healing waters of the sanctuary spread far and wide for the healing of
the nations." He wrote in 1743, "My soul was concerned not
so much for souls as such, but rather for Christ's kingdom
that it might appear in the world that God might be known to
be God in the whole world." He again wrote in 1744, "To an
eye of reason, everything that respects the conversion of the
heathen is as dark as midnight and yet I cannot but hope in
God for the accomplishment of something glorious among
them. My soul longs for the advancement of the Redeemer's
kingdom on earth." Again in 1744, "I exceedingly long that
God would get to Himself a name among the heathen." Isn't
that great? "Indeed I had no notion of joy from this world. I
cared not where or how I lived or what hardships I went
through so that I could but gain souls to Christ."

These quotations show an important aspect of the theology
of the First Great Awakening. It is this: gospel preaching is
kingdom work! And the conversion of sinners is the extension
of Christ's kingdom. Edwards, Brainerd, Bellamy, Hopkins
and the Tennents emphasized that God has a kingdom now
and that it is exercised through the mediatorial headship of

Jesus Christ. They proclaimed that the gospel is not merely the proclamation of a remedy for sin, which men are to accept, but it is a mandate for men to bow to sovereign rule. The evangelist is an ambassador from heaven representing a King who says you must yield to His lordship.

This view of evangelism and missions prevailed in large measure in the first two great awakenings and in evangelical churches until the time of the Civil War. This outlook contrasts sharply with much modern evangelical theology which states that Christ came to establish a political and earthly kingdom which was rejected; now we are in a virtual kingdomless gap period. Christ has gone back to heaven without a kingdom and shall come again the second time when, hopefully, He will be more successful. Whether one believes that Christ is now King will inevitably affect one's attitude toward evangelism. The classic view that the spiritual kingdom of Christ is now in force is accompanied by a strong message of the law and repentance, which is usually missing from the theory that the kingdom of Christ is only a future reality.

Edwards and Brainerd preached that sinners are rebels and must lay down their arms of rebellion and yield to God, but this lack of emphasis in the modern pulpit on the Kingship of Christ has resulted in an anemic sort of evangelism. Sinners are told to accept Christ as their personal Savior but there is no brokenness over sin or surrender to Christ. There is a vigor and strength in the type of evangelism and missions which views gospel preaching as an attack on the kingdom of darkness and a mandate to occupy the world in the name of Christ!

Second, in considering his work as an evangelist, the spiritual awakening among the Indians was presided over by many months of patient, persevering prayer on Brainerd's part. In 1742 Brainerd wrote,

> At night the Lord visited me marvelously in prayer. I think my soul never was in such agony before. I felt no restraint for the treasures of di-

vine grace were opened to me. I wrestled for absent friends, for the ingathering of souls, for multitudes of poor souls, and for many that I thought
were the children of God personally and many
distant places, I was in such agony ... that I was
all over wet with sweat, but yet it seemed to me
that I had wasted away the day and done nothing.
Oh my dear Savior did sweat blood for poor souls!
I longed for more compassion towards them.

In 1744 he acknowledged, "In prayer I was exceedingly enlarged ... I was in such anguish, and pleaded with so much
earnestness and importunity that when I arose from my
knees I felt extremely weak and overcome." He wrote in
1744, "Endeavored to spend the day in fasting and prayer to
implore the divine blessing, more especially upon my poor
people and in particular I sought for converting grace for my
interpreter."

It is only fair to say that Brainerd often complained in his
diary of deadness, listlessness, and coldness in prayer. He did
not always have such fervor or earnestness as just described.
But when he felt cold and abandoned by God in prayer work,
he grieved and sought help from God to continue to plead
with power and prayer.

There can be no doubt that there is a connection between
Brainerd's success as a missionary and his wrestlings with
God in prayer. The Bible teaches and history demonstrates
that spiritual battles are won on one's knees. Jonathan Edwards saw a relationship between Brainerd's faithfulness in
prayer and the blessings he experienced. As he introduced
Brainerd's material, recounting the 1745 awakening at Crossweeksung, he said,

Long had he agonized in prayer and travailed in
birth for their conversion. Often had he cherished the hope of witnessing that desirable event
only to find that hope yield to fear and end in dis-

appointment. But after a patient continuance in prayer, in labor and in suffering as it were through a long night, at length he is permitted to behold the dawning of the day. "Weeping continuous for a night, but joy comes in the morning." He went forth weeping bearing precious seed: and now he comes rejoicing bringing his sheaves with him.

Pastors, evangelists, Christian workers, what an example is David Brainerd for us all! If we were as diligent in prayer work as he was, it would no doubt make a difference in our ministries! The promises that Brainerd claimed are still in the Bible waiting for simple believing Christians to claim them. The intensity of his devotion to the Lord rebukes us and also should encourage and inspire us to follow in his steps. We do not minister to savage Indians with their primitive customs, idolatry, and false religion. We do not have to preach through drunken interpreters. Our calling is to a sophisticated American culture—a scientific age. Our people have their televisions, automobiles, VCR's and computers, but people today are just as blind and hardhearted as the Indians of the American colonies. Superstition and false religion are just as prevalent though in a more subtle form. The Indians worshipped snakes and demon spirits; we worship status, bank accounts, and political power! But the God who broke the hearts of the savages can break the hearts of yuppies of modern America. Do you believe it? To say that He can't or won't is to deny that God is immutable.

The preaching of Jesus Christ and His cross were the great instrument of bringing the Indians to salvation. My copy of Brainerd's diary is volume 10 of the works of Jonathan Edwards, printed in New York in 1830. It contains the funeral address of Edwards and also Brainerd's ordination sermon by Ebenezer Pemberton, who was pastor of the Presbyterian Church in New York City. His text at the ordination service was Luke 14:23, "The Lord said unto the servant, 'Go out into the highways and hedges and compel them to come in, that my house may be filled.'" In this excellent message, Pemberton explained what is to be the theme of a gospel preacher. How can we compel them to come in? First, he said by showing them their guilt and danger. But secondly, he said, we are to compel them to come in by a lively representation of the power and grace of our Almighty Redeemer. Not all the thunders and terror of curses from Mt. Evil, not all the thunderous "wrath revealed from Heaven against the ungodly," not all the anguish and horror of a wounded spirit in an awakened sinner, are able to produce an unfeigned and effectual compliance with the gospel terms of mercy. The ministry of the law can only give the knowledge of sin, rouse the sinner's conscience and awaken his fears. It is the dispensation of grace that sanctifies and saves the soul. Conviction gives us a sight of our sin and misery. It inclines us to "flee from the wrath to come" and disposes us to submit to the gospel message of salvation "by grace alone through faith."

Pemberton said,

> It is not the office of preacher to be perpetually employed in the language of terror or exhaust their strength and zeal in awakening and distressing subjects. No! But it is their distinguishing character that they are ministers of the gospel! So it is their peculiar business to preach the unsearchable riches of Christ; the person, the offices, the love of the great Redeemer, the merits of His obedience, the purchases of His cross, the victories of His resurrection, the triumphs of His ascension, the prevalence of His intercession, the power of His Spirit, the greatness of His salvation, the freedoms of His grace, these are the chosen and delightful subjects of their discourses.

This is what Brainerd heard on that warm June morning when he was ordained and he carried out to the letter these instructions.

In June of 1746, in a report to the missionary society which sponsored him, he explained how he went about evangelizing the Indians. He said,

> I have often times remarked with admiration that whatever subject I have been treating upon, after having spent time sufficient to explain and illustrate the truths contained therein I have been naturally and easily led to Christ as the substance of every subject. If I treated of the Being and the glorious perfections of God, I was thence naturally led to discourse of Christ as the only way to the Father. If I attempted to open the deplorable misery of our fallen estate, it was natural from thence to show the necessity of Christ to undertake for us, to atone for our sins, and to redeem us from the power of them. If I taught the commands of God and showed our violation of them, this brought me in the most easy and natural way to speak of and recommend the Lord Jesus Christ as one who had "magnified the law" which we had broken and had "become the end of it for righteousness to everyone that believes." Never did I find so much freedom and assistance in making all the various lines of my discourses meet together and center in Christ as I have frequently done among these Indians.

Brainerd attributed the spiritual deliverance of the Indians to the proclamation of the free grace of God in Christ. He said,

> It was remarkable from time to time, that when I was favored with any special freedom in discoursing of the ability and willingness of Christ to save sinners and the "need in which they stood of such a Savior," it was then the greatest appear-

ance of divine power in awakening numbers of secure souls, promoting convictions, and comforting the distressed.

THE DOCTRINES OF GRACE IN BRAINERD'S LIFE AND MINISTRY

I now turn to the impact of the doctrines of grace on the life and ministry of our subject. Jonathan Edwards was the great promoter and interpreter of Brainerd's teachings and ministry. In his reflections on Brainerd's diary he delightfully emphasized the wholesome and beneficial impact of Calvinistic theology on David Brainerd. He said,

> It is further observable that this religion all along operated in such a manner as tended to confirm his mind in the doctrines of God's absolute sovereignty, man's universal and entire dependence on God's power and grace, etc. The more his religion prevailed in his heart and the fuller he had of divine love and of clear and delightful views of spiritual things and the more his heart was engaged in God's service, the more sensible he was of the certainty and the excellency and importance of these truths and the more he was affected with them and rejoiced in them.

In other words, the closer Brainerd got to the Lord the more his love flamed up to God, the more he loved the doctrines of grace. Devotion and doctrine go together. Then Edwards asked, "Can the Arminians produce an instance, within this age, and so plainly within our reach and view, of such a reformation, such a transformation of a man to spiritual devotion, heavenly mindedness, and true Christian morality, in one who lived without these things, on the basis of their principles and through the influence of their doctrine?" Good question.

The doctrines of grace were the instrument of Brainerd's

conversion. He had an intellectual grasp of man's total depravity, the effectual nature of Christ's redeeming work and God's electing grace, even before his conversion. These truths humbled him and caused him to seek God. Most of us, you know, come to them afterwards. Not him! Wrestling with the sovereignty of God was a part of his humiliation and conviction even before he was converted. He explains in his diary how four things irritated him before he was saved: 1) The strictness of the divine law. 2) The fact that faith alone was a condition of salvation. 3) The fact that he couldn't find out what faith was or how he could get it. And finally, 4) The sovereignty of God. He said, "I could not bear that it should be wholly at God's pleasure, to save or damn me, just as He would. That passage, Romans 9:11-23, was a constant vexation to me." After he was converted his attitude changed and these truths became precious.

Brainerd's sense of unworthiness should be seen in light of his grasp of God's greatness, sovereignty and glory. Edwards commented, "He saw clearly that whatever he enjoyed better than hell was of free grace." Brainerd said,

> I am now more sensible than ever that God alone
> is the author and finisher of our faith; that the
> whole and every part of sanctification and every
> good word, work, or thought found in me is the
> affect of His power and grace; that "without Him
> I can do nothing" in the strictest sense and that
> He works in us to will and do of His good pleasure and from no other motive. Oh, how amazing
> it is, that people can talk so much about man's
> power and goodness, when if God did not hold us
> back every moment we would be devil's incarnate!

The doctrines of grace—particularly the power and right of God to convert a sinner—was a source of encouragement to him during his missionary labor. Arminians argue that Calvinistic teachings discourage soul winning and cause Christian workers to be slothful, dead and heartless. How often we've heard, "If I believed those doctrines I would not try to win souls; I would not preach; I would not pray," etc. The life and the ministry of David Brainerd is a blazing contradiction to such objections. He testified and his life proved that the doctrines of grace drove him forth to preach and encouraged him in difficult times. He said,

> I was assisted in prayer for my dear Christian friends and brothers whom I apprehended to be Christians, but was more concerned especially for the poor heathen and those of my charge, and was enabled to be instant in prayer for them and hopeful that God would bow the Heavens and come down for their salvation. It seemed to me that there could be no impediment sufficient to obstruct that glorious work, seeing the living God as I strongly hoped, was engaged for it.

Discouraging? Does your Calvinism cause you not to pray? Brainerd writes,

> While I was riding I had a deep sense of the greatness and difficulty of my work and my soul seemed to rely wholly upon God for success in the diligent and faithful use of means. Saw with the greatest certainty that the arm of the Lord must be revealed for the help of these poor heathens if ever they are ever delivered from the bondage of the power of darkness.

Finally, the doctrines of grace produced a spiritual awakening among the Indians and were the instrument of moral reformation among them. I have met people who discount the accounts of the great awakening. They say, "Ah, it didn't happen; couldn't happen. The revival accounts are exaggerations."

I don't believe it's so, brethren. I don't believe Edwards and Nettleton were lying when they told about what happened. Eyewitnesses were there. I don't believe Brainerd was lying about what happened among those Indians. It was the doctrines of grace that awoke those Indians from their pagan slumber. Brainerd declared,

> The very method of preaching which is best suited to awaken in mankind a sense and lively apprehension of their depravity and misery in a *fallen state,*—to excite them earnestly to seek after a change of heart, and to *fly for refuge* to free and sovereign grace in Christ, as the only hope set before them is like to be most *successful* toward the reformation of their *external* conduct.

Again, Brainerd said,

> When these truths were formed at heart there was now no vice unreformed, no external duty neglected. Drunkenness, the darling vice, was broken off from and scarce an instance of it known among my hearers for months together. The abusive practice of husband and wives and putting away each other and taking others in their stead was quickly reformed, so that there are three or four couples who have voluntarily dismissed those whom he had wrongfully taken and now live together in love and peace. The same might be said of all other vicious practices. The reformation was general and all springing from the internal influence of divine truths upon their hearts, and not from any external restraints or because they heard these vices particularly exposed and repeatedly spoken against.

In other words, the dead leaves fell off in the spring when the sap of God's glory touched their hearts.

Brainerd used the catechetical method of teaching, based on the Scriptures and the Westminster Shorter Catechism. He wrote,

> There has been a wonderful thirst after Christian knowledge prevailing among them in general and eager desire of being instructed in Christian doctrines and manners, this has prompted them to ask many pertinent as well as important questions; the answers to which attended much to enlighten their minds and promote their knowledge in divine things. Many of the doctrines which I have delivered, they have queried me about in order to gain further light and insight into them, particularly the doctrine of predestination and have from time to time manifested a good understanding of them by their answers to the questions proposed to them in my catechetical lectures.

I'd like to leave you today with a challenge: First, if you've never read David Brainerd's memoirs, get it and read it. Second, I call upon each of you here to dedicate your life to the glory of God like David Brainerd and to leave here with a desire to spread the kingdom of the Lord Jesus Christ through the conversion of sinners. Third, I call upon you to be men and women of prayer. Get on your knees and pray over your problems. Pray that God would fill you with compassion and broken hearts over our modern day American problems, and take away your bitterness and anger. Finally, I call upon you today to preach Jesus Christ and Him crucified. And may the fire of the Almighty fall upon us as it did those pagan savages. I close with the words of this great hymn by Reginald Heber:

> The Son of God goes forth to war, a Kingly crown
>   to gain;
> His blood red banner streams afar: Who follows
>   in His train?

Who best can drink His cup of woe, triumphant
over pain,
Who patient bears His cross below, he follows in
His train.

That martyr first, whose eagle eye could pierce
beyond the grave,
Who saw His master in the sky, and called on
Him to save.
Like Him, with pardon on His tongue, in midst of
mortal pain,
He prayed for them that did the wrong: Who
follows in His train?

A noble army, men and boys, the matron and the
maid,
Around the Savior's throne rejoice, in robes of
light arrayed.
They climbed the steep ascent of heaven, through
peril, toil, and pain;
O God, to us may grace be given, to follow in their
train.

28.
A BIOGRAPHICAL SKETCH OF JOHN A. BROADUS

BILL ASCOL

1989 Southern Baptist Founders Conference

In 1895 the Southern Baptist denomination celebrated its fiftieth Anniversary in Washington, D. C. The Protestant churches in D. C., made their pulpits available to the Southern Baptist men who were there for the annual SBC meeting. In the midst of the convention, Dr. W. H. Whitsitt, president of the Southern Baptist Theological Seminary in Louisville, Kentucky, gave an address entitled "A Retrospect." It was a survey of the first fifty years of the Southern Baptist denomination. His concluding words hint at the vision which early Southern Baptists entertained for their convention of churches:

> When the convention was holding its opening session in Augusta there was a lad just turned 18 years resting under the quiet shades of Culpepper in far distant Virginia. He was unknown to fame, possibly no member of the body had ever heard his name. In due time he appeared upon the scene and for a period of 30 years played the role of our Great Commoner. For 30 years he was the leading force in our councils and history, yet throughout that entire period he did not occupy the smallest office directly in the gist of the convention. This year of our jubilee with all its life and gladness has been sadly darkened by his departure. On the 17th of March devout men car-

515

ried him to his burial and made great lamentation over him. The foremost leader of our history, great in the might of his gentleness, has passed away from us, but his fame and usefulness shall go and grow throughout the years and ages. When you who sit here shall be aged and feeble men and women, little children will gather about your knees with reverence and delight to look upon one who has seen and heard and spoken with John A. Broadus.[1]

This statement reflects the hope that those who founded this denomination had for future generations. But it grieves me to think that less than 150 years after the founding of the denomination, less than 100 years after Whitsitt made these remarks, John Albert Broadus remains a stranger to most Southern Baptists.

HIS LIFE

The Broaddus family (spelled with two d's) came to Green Island, Virginia in the early 1700s in the person of Edward Broaddus who was John Broadus' great-great-grandfather. He had come from a Welsh family of Anglo-Saxon descent. The family name was originally *Broadhurst*, but it had become Anglicized and then Americanized to Broaddus. The way that one "d" disappeared from the name, the story is told, is that an eccentric uncle decried the unnecessary use of letters. He saw the second "d" as serving no purpose and so it was dropped.

Though John Albert's family followed his lead, not all of the Broaddus clan did. Dr. William F. Broaddus, who was a pastor in Fredericksburg, Virginia, was in the process of a building program and he told the young man in charge of building the

1 W. H. Whitsitt, "Fiftieth Anniversary of the Southern Baptist Convention," *Proceedings of the Southern Baptist Convention* (March 1895), 20.

pews to be sure and put on his pew the "dd." This man was aghast that the pastor would so flaunt his Doctor of Divinity that he did not even put the pastor's name on the pew and it remained without a name until Dr. Broaddus' meaning was clarified.

John Broadus was born January 24, 1827 to Major Edmund Broadus and his wife Nancy Simms Broadus. John was the youngest of four children. James Madison, Martha and Caroline were the three eldest siblings. It is interesting to note that James P. Boyce was born 13 days before John Broadus. They did not meet, however, until many years later. John Albert Broadus was named after two of his mother's brothers: John Simms, a doctor, and Albert Simms, a schoolteacher who would make a tremendous mark upon the life of young John.

When John Broadus was fifteen years old his uncle, William F. Broaddus, wrote to Edmund, John's father, and said, "Then let's hope that someone in our family is destined to be a prodigy and, as our day is nearly past, take it for granted that the next generation will be favored with his presence."[2] Some time after this John's sister, Martha, wrote to one of the cousins, "I think your little cousin John will be the brightest star of the Broadus family."[3]

At the age of five John began his education under Mr. Albert Tutt who had a field school. In that setting John became very proficient in spelling. From the age of eight Broadus was taught at home under the tutelage of his sister, Martha. Under her instruction, he became a tremendous reader. His sister exposed him to a great range of subjects, including religion. He began reading the *Religious Herald* during childhood and continued this practice throughout his life. When John was ten years old, his father, Major Edmund Broadus, opened a school and taught John for two years.

In 1839, after his father returned to politics, John enrolled

---

2 A. T. Robertson, *The Life and Letters of John A. Broadus*, (Harrisonburg, VA: Gano Books, 1987), 10.
3 Ibid., 20.

in a school taught by his uncle, Mr. Albert Simms and under
his leadership John became an outstanding Latin scholar.
Without a doubt this proficiency opened to him the doors of
other language study, chief among them being New Testament Greek. When visiting Europe many years later, John
took the occasion while in Rome to write a letter in Latin to
his uncle Albert, who responded in turn with his own letter
written in Latin. John stayed under Mr. Simms except for one
year when it became necessary for him to manage the farm
for a season. He graduated from Mr. Simms' school at the age
of sixteen without fanfare. He arrived at home one day with
his trunk containing all his belongings. His father was
alarmed by such an abrupt appearance and thought that perhaps John had been thrown out of school for being disobedient. So Edmund Broadus checked into the matter with Albert
Simms who told him, "The boy has learned everything I can
teach him. I can't teach him anymore."[4]

While John was still in school a protracted meeting was
conducted at Mt. Poney Baptist Church, Culpepper Court-
house, by Reverend Charles A. Lewis of Kentucky along with
the aid of Reverend Barnett Grimsley. At this meeting John
Broadus was converted. While under conviction, and feeling
unable to take hold of the promises of the Scripture concerning those who had come to Christ, a friend quoted to him
John 6:37, "All that the Father giveth me shall come to me,
and him that cometh to me I will in no wise cast out," repeating to John, "'In no wise cast out.' Can't you take hold of
that, John?" Indeed he did as the light of heaven opened
upon his soul and he was saved, seeing that Christ had died
for him and called him unto Himself. He was soon baptized
into the membership of the Mt. Poney Baptist Church and
shortly after that moved his membership to the New Salem
church where his family attended.

---

4 Ibid., 33.

At the age of seventeen Broadus began to teach as a tutor in the home of William Sowers at Rose Hill, Clarke County, Virginia. He was a good teacher, though very young. The next year he undertook a teaching assignment in Woodley, Virginia, staying part time in the home of Dr. Llewelyn Kerfoot, the father of F. H. Kerfoot, who later became a great Southern Baptist theologian in his own right.

It was during this period of John's life, while making preparation to study medicine, that God made clear to him that he was to give his life to preaching the gospel. In August of 1846 Dr. A. M. Poindexter came to the area. He preached on the parable of the talents. Years later, at Dr. Poindexter's funeral, Broadus told the story of his call to the ministry:

> Presently he spoke of consecrating one's mental gifts and possible attainment to the work of the ministry. He seemed to clear up all difficulties pertaining to the subject. He swept away all the disguise of self-delusion, all the excuses of fancy humility. He held up the thought that the greatest sacrifices and toils possible to a minister's lifetime would be a hundred-fold repaid if he should be the instrument of saving one soul.

Doubtless the sermon had many more important results that have not been recorded, but when a break in the services came young Broadus sought out his pastor and with choking voice said, "Brother Grimsley, the question is decided, I must try to be a preacher."[5]

In the fall of 1846, Broadus entered the University of Virginia where he established himself immediately as an outstanding scholar. He became one of the university's favorite sons. At various intervals throughout the rest of his life, he would be sought after by his alma mater to serve in one capacity or another. One of his professors said of him, "If genius

---

5 Ibid., 53.

is the ability and willingness to do hard work, Broadus was a genius."

During his university career he met Maria Harrison, daughter of Dr. Gessner Harrison, his favorite professor. Maria would take long walks with him to help him improve his health. Their friendship blossomed into love and they were married after his graduation from the university.

The university was not all joy and gladness for him, however. In June, at the end of his first year of studies, his mother died suddenly. He was able to enter the bedroom just in time to speak with her as she passed away. Then in June of 1850, two days prior to his graduation from the university, his father died. John was scheduled to deliver the valedictory address for his class. Instead he had to graduate *in abstencia* and the address was never given. So powerful was the address, however, that it was printed in the university magazine and was entitled, "Human Society in Its Relation to Natural Theology." It was a tribute to the influence of Dr. William McGuffey, another of John's professors.

On November 13, 1850 John and Maria were married. Their union was blessed with three children: Eliza Summerville, Annie Harrison, and Maria Louisa who lived less than four years. Before their seventh anniversary Mrs. Broadus died suddenly at the age of twenty-six. For fifteen months John bore various responsibilities as a pastor and a father without the comfort and help of a wife.

Later he married Charlotte Eleanor Sinclair who became his companion throughout the remainder of his days. Five children were born to this union: Samuel Sinclair Broadus, who was known as S. S. Broadus; Boyce Broadus; Alice Virginia Broadus; Mellie Broadus, a child who died early in infancy; and then Ella Thomas Broadus who would later marry Dr. A. T. Robertson.

His Labors

John Broadus wore many different hats in the course of his

life's labors. It has already been mentioned that he taught school. He also served as a tutor in the home of General J. H. Cocke of Virginia after his graduation from the university. He had not forgotten his call to the ministry. Rather, tutoring allowed him to spend a year studying at his own pace. Later on, as a professor in the seminary, Broadus would often encourage his students who had opportunity, to take a year off before they engaged themselves in their labors. He counseled young students planning to enter college to do the same. He said it was a very valuable year in his life.

In 1851 the opportunity came for him to pastor. He had preached his first sermon on June 4, 1849 at the Mt. Eagle Presbyterian Church to supply for Dr. William McGuffey. Dr. McGuffey had become ill and needed someone to supply on a short notice so he asked young Broadus. The college senior took the congregation by storm. He captured the hearts of the members of the Mt. Eagle church as they compared the young, fiery, eloquent Broadus with Dr. McGuffey, whose sermons were considered by many to be stale and predictable. In September 1851 Broadus was called to be the pastor of the Charlottesville Baptist Church. He accepted this call at a time when the University of Virginia was pleading with him to consider a teaching position. By taking the Charlottesville pastorate Broadus knew that he could pastor the church and at the same time teach part time as an instructor in Latin and Greek under his dear friend, Dr. Gessner Harrison.

During the pastorate at Charlottesville Broadus helped establish the Albemarle Female Institute. It was the only one of its kind and the young preacher brought to it some very interesting innovations in education. He and Professor Hart placed a high emphasis on piety at the institute. One student, who entered in 1857, was particularly known for her "devil-may-care" attitude. Her name was Charlotte Diggs Moon. In December 1858, however, the prayers of Lottie's Christian friends were answered. Broadus was holding a series of evangelistic meetings directed to the students in Charlottesville and a group of Albemarle Female Institute students held a sunrise inquiry meeting in support of the efforts. Lottie's name was on that prayer list. To the girls' great surprise Lottie attended the prayer meeting and got into an earnest, private conversation with John Broadus. Soon after, she confessed Christ as her Lord and Savior and was baptized into the membership of the Charlottesville Baptist Church by Broadus himself. John Broadus had a tremendous impact on the life of Lottie Moon and there is good reason to believe that she shared similar theological convictions with the pastor who pointed her to the Savior.

Broadus had a pastor's heart though he often felt very inadequate for the task of shepherding the people of God. Once while on a journey away from his field of labor he wrote to his wife, sharing with her his concerns for the congregation,

> Oh that I could see sinners among my people converted. It lies like a burden on my heart the thought that there are so many unconverted men and women who look to me for almost their only instruction. So many on the road to hell with no voice but mine to warn them of their danger and invite them to Jesus. Alas, how cold have been my warmest feelings, how dull my most earnest appeals. The Lord in mercy forgive me that so often, so constantly I have neglected my duty. I know that I am not fit to be the instrument of good. The Lord take me and fashion and temper me and then use me for His glory. Pray much for me that the love of Christ may subdue the deceitfulness and rebelliousness of my heart, and a zeal for His glory and pity for poor perishing souls may lead me to work more faithfully in the Master's vineyard. Pray for the divine blessing upon my preaching, especially upon the poor sermon of next Sunday night. Dear Maria, do not fail to

pray.[6]

Broadus took the work of the ministry very seriously. He saw his duty as a pastor as one with sober implications for this life as well as the life to come.

During this same period of ministry Broadus was developing as a great preacher—very eloquent, very articulate and very powerful. A small example of his pulpit genius was evidenced when he was preaching on the ministry of the Apostle Paul from Acts 20:

> What a scene was that. This great and inspired man speaking to the people both publicly and from house to house, warning them with tears. Telling them of God's amazing love and His tremendous wrath, of their guilt, their helpless condemnation and the one way of salvation. Christians, too, he warned of the false teachers that should enter from without like grievous wolves into the fold and that should rise up among themselves. He would weep as he entreated them to hold fast the truth as it is in Jesus, to adorn their profession, to live for the salvation of men and the glory of God. Thus night and day for three years he ceased not to warn everyone with tears. Why should not Paul weep and every creature and every Christian weep? See the condition of our fellowmen, our friends, our kindred, as depicted not by our wild fancy or morbid fear, but by the calm teachings of the Word of God. They are condemned already. The wrath of God abideth on them. Their steps take hold on hell. Can we half realize what is meant by these fearful sayings and not weep? But worse, we tell them of the Savior who died that we might live and ever lives

---

6 Ibid., 103.

to save. We tell them of free pardon, of full salvation to every penitent believer in Him, of His redeeming love, His gracious invitations and precious promises. We tell of eternal bliss and eternal woe at their own imminent and increasing danger. We urge all that is terrible in God's wrath and all that is moving in His mercy and they look at us calmly. They turn away as unconcerned, as though it were all a trifle or a dream. Oh, where is our pity, where our love that we do not weep tears of blood, that we do not say with the psalmist, "Rivers of water run down mine eyes because they keep not thy law." It is well that the gospel induces tenderness since the preacher has to speak such awful truth. It is no light thing to look into the eyes of one you know and respect and love and charge him with being a vile sinner, charge selfishness and pride and pervading ungodliness upon what he accounts his best actions. To warn him of the wrath to come. To bid him tremble lest he receive deserved damnation. And reflect now what will be his unavailing remorse if in hell he should lift up his eyes being in torment. It is well that the gospel, which along with its promise of salvation to the believer, requires us to say, "He that believeth not shall be damned." It is well that such a gospel should also inspire that feeling of tenderness with which the painful duty ought to be performed.[7]

On more than one occasion those who heard him preach observed that Broadus spoke as if he was speaking directly to each member of the congregation. It was as if he took each hearer into the inner circle of his confidence.

He served as pastor for a season at Charlottesville Baptist

---

7 John A. Broadus, *Sermons and Addresses* (New York, NY: Hodder & Stoughton, 1886), 149-150.

Church and then was called to serve as chaplain at the University of Virginia. It was a temporary work, a two-year term, as the chaplaincy rotated among the different denominations. He took the position at the insistence of J. B. Taylor and J. B. Jeter and made arrangements for an associate pastor to come and labor in the Charlottesville church, handling the preaching duties in the absence of Broadus for the next two years. His term as chaplain was a time of great harvest, though Broadus, in reflecting upon it, was somewhat disappointed. He did not discover in the chaplaincy what he thought he would find in the way of an opportunity for increased theological study. He found the demands upon his time as great or greater than they had been in the pastorate. But his ministry as a chaplain was certainly not in vain as evidenced by a situation that occurred when he was on a trip to Texas years later.

> While preaching in Texas, John Broadus was informed that a lady desired an interview with him. He made an appointment and she came, leading a little boy about 11 years of age by her side. She soon informed the doctor that her husband, now deceased, was a student in the University of Virginia when the preacher was a chaplain there. He was awakened and led to Christ through Broadus' sermons. The man was in the habit, before she became acquainted with him, of repeating many of the sentences of those sermons in his father's family. When they married he would rehearse to her the thoughts that made such a deep impression on his mind. Since his death, the widow and mother had been teaching the preacher's words to the little boy. When Broadus was told this, in response later on he said, "The heart of a preacher might well melt in his bosom at the story. To think that your poor words, which you yourself had wholly forgotten, which you could never have imagined had vitality enough for that, had been

repeated among strangers, had been repeated by the young man to his parents, repeated by the young widow to the child. Your poor words thus mighty because they were God's truth you were trying to speak and because you had humbly sought God's blessing."[8]

At the same time that John Broadus returned to the work of the ministry at Charlottesville, James P. Boyce, having recently finished at Princeton, became the pastor at Columbia, South Carolina. William Williams, recently graduated from Harvard, assumed pastoral work in Alabama. Basil Manly, Jr., having studied at Newton and then at Princeton, and having pastored in Alabama, had come to Richmond as pastor of the First Baptist Church there. The providential timing of God is intriguing because in 1857 the messengers of the Southern Baptist Convention meeting in Louisville had appointed a committee to investigate the feasibility of establishing a theological seminary for Baptists in the south. This committee was made up of James P. Boyce, John A. Broadus, Basil Manly, Jr., E. T. Winkler and William Williams. On February 15, 1858, Broadus received a letter from Manly (the committee members had been assigned different responsibilities and were working on their respective assignments) and Manly was encouraging Broadus to pay him a visit. Manly's letter read in part, "In speaking of the abstract of doctrines and principles [Manly had been assigned the responsibility of drafting those] if you will come down we can have a chat about our work committed to us—that *creed*, schedule of theological studies, etc." It is worth observing that Basil Manly, the author of the abstract of principles, referred to that document as "that *creed*."[9]

The two men did meet and on May 1, 1858, Southern Baptists held an Educational Convention in Greenville, South

---

8 Robertson, *The Life and Letters of John A. Broadus*, 143.
9 Ibid., 147-148.

Carolina. It was at this meeting that the Southern Baptist Theological Seminary was formally established. It was decided that the seminary would be located in Greenville, South Carolina. It was also at this meeting that the four professors were elected: James P. Boyce, John A. Broadus, Basil Manly, Jr., and E. T. Winkler. The fifth professor, A. M. Poindexter, was added shortly thereafter. John Broadus found himself once again in great straits as to what to do. When his congregation in Charlottesville became aware that he had been approached about the possibility of serving in the seminary, they were in a great uproar. A petition was circulated, signed by many members of the church, pleading with him to stay and continue his pastoral labors. The pressure brought to bear upon Broadus by the congregation was great. Basil Manly, Jr., however, brought his own brand of pressure in a letter which essentially said, "If you refuse to go to the seminary, then it will fail, it will not come to pass." An excerpt from that letter stated,

> So far as I can see, the real decision [whether or not there will be a seminary] rests with you. If you decline, I think Poindexter will. If he and you decline, I certainly shall, then Winkler will feel unwilling to leave his church, even if he could otherwise be induced to go, and even Boyce, left alone, will feel himself compelled to look rather cheerlessly for new associates.[10]

Amazingly, Broadus declined and the whole matter of the seminary remained in limbo for about a year. Almost a year later two letters came to Broadus from James P. Boyce—one dated March 29 and the other April 11. The first letter informed Broadus that he was still being considered by the committee as a professor of the seminary and they were not willing to consider anyone else for the position. Broadus re-

---

10 Ibid., 150.

sponded with a brief letter saying, in essence, "If you will keep it completely under your hat and not tell anyone, I will consider. This must not get out." Boyce responded immediately with another letter. Included was an extract from a letter that Basil Manly had written to Boyce:

> The prospects of the theological school have been shaded, at least, by failing to obtain the officers we've sought and to commence business last fall. The trustees are to hold their first meeting in Richmond at the time of the approaching anniversary. Make another failure and you will see what will come of it.[11]

Boyce then exhorted Broadus with the following challenge:

> If you cannot fully consent to a lifetime work, try it for a while in order to inaugurate the matter. Your simple name will be a tower of strength to us; and when we are once started, if you find it not congenial, you can return to the pastorate.[12]

To this appeal Broadus responded, "if elected I am willing to go. May God graciously direct and bless, and if I have erred in my judgment, may he overrule, to the glory of his name."[13] It was not long after this when John Broadus, Basil Manly, William Williams and James P. Boyce were elected to the seminary, that Broadus and Manly received honorary doctorates from Richmond College. They were not as yet Doctors of Divinity so Richmond College conferred these degrees upon them. One man wrote to Broadus, stating, "I see you have been doctored and I want you to know I had nothing to do with it." Some were not very fond of such a practice. Later

---

11 Ibid., 158.
12 Ibid., 158.
13 Ibid., 159.

William and Mary College gave Broadus an honorary doctorate. Many years later, while Dr. Broadus was speaking at the 250th anniversary of Harvard, he had yet another doctorate conferred upon him.

Having come to a resolution of the matter concerning his willingness to teach at The Southern Baptist Theological Seminary, Broadus' face was set like flint toward Greenville, South Carolina and he entered upon a labor that would consume his time and energies for the remaining thirty-six years of his life. The only intervals of his service to the seminary would be brought about by the ravages of war and his declining physical health. Even then, though physically hindered, his heart, mind and soul were thoroughly invested in the advance of the gospel through the ministry of the seminary.

When the seminary held its first commencement (May 28, 1860), it seemed that a bright future might lay ahead for the progress and prosperity of the institution except for one concern: the gathering storm clouds of war which hung on the horizon over the south. War between the North and South became increasingly inevitable. It is interesting to note that Broadus and Boyce were strong anti-secessionists. They did not want to see the South secede. Williams was a strong secessionist and Manly was a mild secessionist. The position of these men on that subject did not affect their fellowship, however, nor their common desire to see the seminary become a useful institution. When the southern states seceded from the Union, Broadus and the others determined to do all they could to aid the southern cause. If they could have gotten their way, they would have continued the operation of the seminary, but the provisional government of Jefferson Davis made it mandatory that all students, even theological students, resign their studies and go to war.

Dr. Boyce became a chaplain in the Confederate Army and the other professors tried to keep the seminary going, supporting themselves through supply preaching in various country churches. Dr. Broadus was approached and asked to write an evangelistic tract to be used among the soldiers in the

Confederate Army. (The reader may not be aware that there was a great revival that occurred among the armies of the south. God saved many of these young men.) He wrote a tract entitled, "We are Praying for You at Home." The following excerpt gives a sense of the evangelistic passion of Broadus:

> We pray for the cause—that just and glorious cause—in which you so nobly struggle, that it may please God to make you triumphant, and that we may have independence and peace...We know it must be hard for you, amid the distractions of camp life, the alternate excitement and ennui, the absence of home influences and the associations of the sanctuary, to fix mind and heart on things above. We do not doubt the nobleness of your impulses, or the sincerity of your frequent resolutions to do right, nor do we exaggerate the temptations of a soldier's life. It is no reproach on your manliness, and no assumption of superiority on our part, to utter the mournful truth, that spiritually man is always and everywhere weak; that you wrestle against outnumbering and overpowering spiritual foes. We pray that you may be inclined and enabled to commit your soul to the divine Savior, who died to redeem us, and ever lives to intercede for us, and who with yearning love is ever saying, "Come unto me." We pray that the Holy Spirit may thoroughly change your heart, bringing you truly to hate sin, and love holiness, and may graciously strengthen you to withstand temptation, and give you more and more the mastery over yourself, and the victory over every enemy of your soul. Whether it be appointed you to fall soon in battle, or years hence to die at home, may God in mercy forbid that you should live in impenitence and die in your sins. Whether we are to sit with you again around our own fireside, and "take sweet counsel together as

we walk to the house of God in company," or are
to meet you no more on earth, oh, may God in his
mercy save us from an eternal separation![14]

When General Stonewall Jackson was made aware of John
Broadus' availability and his talent, he sent an urgent summons for Broadus to become a missionary to the Southern army, which he did. He preached very effectively in the Confederate camp and God gave him a harvest of souls, as reported
on several occasions.

There is a postscript to Broadus' years in the War Between
the States. It is important to add that in 1863 he returned to
Greenville and until 1866 he served as corresponding secretary to the Sunday School Board of the Southern Baptist Convention—a board that was established chiefly by the combined labors of Broadus and Manly. The name "Broadman
Press" is derived from a combination of their last names.

When Broadus first came to the seminary it was agreed that
he would teach two new departments: New Testament Interpretation in English and Greek and Homiletics—a course that
John Broadus entitled, "On the Preparation and Delivery of
Sermons." This same title would later be given to his great
work on homiletics. Not only had his teaching been interrupted by the war, but the financially hard times made it necessary for Broadus to take on the pastorates of the Clear Spring
Church, the Cedar Grove Church, the Williamston Church
(all in 1863) and then in 1864 he added to that the Siloam
Church. He had the great burden of four pastorates as well as
the responsibility of trying to get the seminary going again.

John Broadus saw preaching as preeminent in training
young men for the ministry. In his "Preparation and Delivery
of Sermons" he made this statement about the importance of
the preeminence of preaching:

---

14 Ibid., 190.

The great appointed means of spreading the good
tidings of salvation through Christ is preaching,
words spoken whether to the individual, or to the
assembly. And this, nothing can supercede. *Printing* has become a mighty agency for good and for
evil; and Christians should employ it, with the utmost diligence and in every possible way, for the
spread of truth. But printing can never take the
place of a living word. When a man who is apt in
teaching, whose soul is on fire with the truth
which he trusts has saved him and hopes will
save others, speaks to his fellowmen, face to face,
eye to eye and the electric sympathies flash to
and fro between him and his hearers, till they lift
each other up, higher and higher, into the intens-
est thought, and the most impassioned emotion—
higher and yet higher, till they are borne as on
chariots of fire above the world—there is a power
to move men, to influence character, life, destiny,
such as no printed page can ever possess.[15]

Broadus was a "preacher's preacher" and placed high value
and great stock in the ministry of preaching. It came through
in his seminary teaching whether he was teaching homiletics
or New Testament.

In 1869 Dr. Broadus' health began to weaken severely and
two actions were taken by the Board of Trustees and the administration of the seminary in an effort to provide Broadus
with some relief. First, Dr. Crawford Howell Toy was elected
to the faculty. This allowed Dr. Manly to give over some of his
responsibilities to Dr. Toy, and Dr. Manly, in turn, took up
some of Dr. Broadus' responsibilities. Second, Broadus was
encouraged to travel abroad. For one full year he traveled
throughout Europe. It was thought that this would afford him

---

15 John A. Broadus, *A Treatise on the Preparation and Delivery of Sermons* (New York, NY: George
H. Doran Company, 1898), 2.

opportunities of increasing health as well as expand and further his scholarship. A. T. Robertson records this of Broadus' visit with Charles Spurgeon:

> When he visited the Metropolitan Tabernacle in London, he had this to say, "I was greatly delighted with Spurgeon, especially with his conduct of public worship... The whole thing—house, congregation, order, worship, preaching, was as nearly up to my ideal as I ever expect to see in this life. Of course Spurgeon has his faults and deficiencies, but he is a wonderful man."[16]

Broadus further observed, "Then he preaches the real gospel, and God blesses him."[17]

Concerning his visit to Geneva:

> At Geneva I made some effort one afternoon to find places associated with Calvin, and it was curious to see how little could be found... An admirer of Calvin (and assuredly I belong to that class) might liken the case to that of Christianity itself, whose original abodes have long been occupied by its enemies, leaving few genuine memorials beyond the mere natural locality, but which thus only the more vindicates its character as not local and sensuous.[18]

Some time after Broadus returned from Europe, it became evident that the seminary had to move in order to survive. In June of 1877 it was decided that the seminary would relocate to Louisville, Kentucky. The wisdom of this was seen by the fact that the largest number of students who had ever been enrolled at Greenville was sixty-seven. In the opening session

---

16 Robertson, *The Life and Letters of John A. Broadus*, 243.
17 Ibid., 243.
18 Ibid., 275-276.

at Louisville there were eighty-eight students.

May 10, 1879, marked a sad day in the history of the seminary. Dr. Crawford Howell Toy had been steadily embracing the views of higher criticism. He had begun to call into question the inspiration and authority of the Scriptures. As a result of this it became necessary for him to resign from the seminary. This event devastated both Broadus and Boyce. They said their young jewel was gone. Yet, these men placed such a high value on truth and believed that we are called of God to "buy the truth and sell it not" that they were willing to put on a "train-to-nowhere" one of their dearest friends, rather than keep him and compromise the gospel at that institution.

In 1883 Dr. Broadus was perhaps at the height of his career. Through his untiring labor the seminary had become the recipient of considerable endowments and he was gaining a reputation for himself as a consummate theological scholar. In addition "to Anglo-Saxon, Latin, Greek, and Hebrew, he had added a proficiency in German, French, Spanish, Italian, Gothic, Coptic, and modern Greek. He had made himself a specialist in homiletics, in the English Bible, in New Testament history, exegesis, in Greek, in textual criticism, in patristic Greek, and hymnology (English and foreign). His 'Preparation and Delivery of Sermons' [which had appeared in 1870] had become the standard and most popular work on the subject."[19]

On June 27, 1884, the faculty of the Southern Seminary sent birthday greetings to Charles Haddon Spurgeon on his fiftieth birthday, a portion of which stated:

> The undersigned professors in the Southern Baptist Theological Seminary, beg leave to offer respectful and hearty congratulations on your fiftieth birthday ... Especially we delight to think how

---

19 Ibid., 337.

nobly you have defended and diffused the doctrines of grace; how in an age so eager for novelty
and marked by such loosening of belief you have
through long years kept the English-speaking
world for your audience while never turning aside
from the old-fashioned gospel.[20]

By 1887 the seminary professor's life had reached a fren-
zied pitch as more and more people called for his services. He
was in demand as a pulpit supply, as an interim pastor, and
would spend his summers filling the pastorates in New York
and New Jersey. Constant demands were made on his time.
People were writing him all the time wanting information, re-
questing his services, inviting him to attend various meetings
to preach. His *Commentary on Matthew* appeared that year
and was hailed as the best of its kind on the gospel of Matthew. Annie Armstrong wrote him from Baltimore pleading
with him to make available his Baptist catechism for supple-
mental Sunday School material. Given the theological bent of
Broadus' catechism, one cannot help but wonder what Annie
Armstrong's own theological convictions must have been.

In 1889 the man who did not seek prominence or position,
found himself shouldered with the responsibility of serving
the seminary as its president. The honor came to him in a
most grievous way, however, as his dearest friend in all of life,
Dr. James P. Boyce, had passed away December 28, 1888.
This was a great blow to Broadus and he wrote to Basil Manly
saying, "I shall be constantly needing your advice, about
measures and men, about great things and small. Now that
Boyce is gone, I value your advice in Seminary matters beyond that of all other men."[21] Yet in the providence of God he
only had thirteen months to lean on him. On January 31,
1892, Basil Manly passed away (the same day that Charles
Spurgeon had died in England).

---

20 Ibid., 341-342.
21 Ibid., 375.

The end was drawing near for Broadus himself. He knew that his health was failing. Increasingly he needed to take trips to the springs for the water that seemed to arrest his condition. He developed a heart disease and this proved to be the beginning of the end. After an attack of pleurisy on Friday, March 8, John Broadus came to the end of the course, having fought a good fight, having kept the faith. He died on Saturday, March 16, 1895. Ten days prior to his death he had managed to attend his New Testament class and lecture. Listen to his parting words (the last words his students heard him say),

> Young gentlemen, if this were the last time I should ever be permitted to address you, I would feel amply repaid for consuming the whole hour in endeavoring to impress upon you these two things, *true piety* and, like Apollos, to be men *"Mighty in the Scriptures."*[22]

The labors of John Broadus were many and mighty and they left their mark indelibly upon Southern Baptists of succeeding generations.

HIS LEGACY

The legacy of John Broadus is perhaps best viewed from the vantage point of his theology and his personal example. Rightly undertaken, such a view would give a clear portrait of Broadus' applied theology.

John Broadus' theology was in the mainstream of reformed thought, being thoroughly Baptistic and unashamedly Calvinistic in his understanding of biblical Christianity. Some nine months after he had graduated from the University of Virginia, John wrote to his uncle, Reverend Andrew Broaddus, asking him "how far should Calvinism be carried?" His uncle

---

22 Ibid., 430.

replied:

> I know but little about "isms," and desire to "know nothing among the people but Jesus Christ and him crucified." My plan has been, since I have been in the ministry, to avoid as much as possible all controversy on religious subjects. In this course I have enjoyed, no doubt, far more peace of mind than I should have done had I been a controversialist. It is a point well settled in my mind that God always acts in accordance with an eternal purpose, else how can many portions of his word be reconciled? I am also well convinced that Christ and the apostles, in their appeals to mankind, recognized no impediment in the way of any, but called upon "all men everywhere to repent." Now because I cannot fathom the mystery connected with God's sovereignty and man's accountability, I must not run into fatalism, as some do; but the safe plan, in my judgment, is that of Christ and his apostles, alluded to above.[23]

Somehow Broadus managed to follow the advice of his uncle and hold to his solid biblical orthodoxy and yet avoid major controversies in his life. When he did find himself involved in controversy it was more often than not by virtue of his association with James P. Boyce.

Broadus had a high degree of respect for the theology of John Calvin, Frances Turretin, Charles Hodge, John L. Dagg, and James P. Boyce. Concerning Calvin and Turretin, he said,

> Several great departments of systematic theology seem to me more thoroughly discussed and luminously stated by Turretin's noble work than by

---

23 Ibid., 89.

any other of the great theologians. The people
who sneer at what is called Calvinism might as
well sneer at Mont Blanc.

He wrote this when he was over in Europe and he could see
Mont Blanc, the chief peak in all of the Alps, some three
miles high.

We are not in the least bound to defend all of
Calvin's opinions or actions, but I do not see how
any one who really understands the Greek of the
Apostle Paul or the Latin of Calvin and Turretin
can fail to see that these latter did but interpret
and formulate substantially what the former
teaches.[24]

Concerning Francis Turretin's treatise on Theology, Broadus said: "For one who sympathizes with what we call the Calvinistic, or Augustinian, type of Theology, this work is in certain important respects unrivalled."[25]

Though Broadus himself never studied under Charles
Hodge, he had a great respect for the Princeton professor's
theology. Broadus also recognized what a privilege it had been
for Boyce and Manly to have studied under Hodge and he
said,

[It was a] great privilege to be directed and up-
borne by such a teacher in studying that exalted
system of Pauline truth which is technically
called Calvinism, which compels an earnest student to profound thinking, and, when pursued
with a combination of systematic thought and fervent experience, makes him at home among the
most inspiring and ennobling views of God and of

24 Ibid., 396-397.
25 John A. Broadus, *Memoir of James Petigru Boyce* (New York, NY: A. C. Armstrong and Son, 1893), 268.

the universe he has made.[26]

Broadus had a great degree of admiration for John Dagg and his writings. He said of Dagg, "Dr. Dagg was a man of great ability and lovable character. His works are worthy of thorough study, especially his small volume, *A Manual of Theology*, which is remarkable for clear statement of the profoundest truths, and for devotional sweetness." Broadus went on to say "that after toiling much in his early years, as a pastor over Knapp and Turretin, Dwight and Andrew Fuller, and other elaborate theologians, he found this manual a delight," feeling all through his life "the pleasing impulse it gave to theological inquiry and reflection."[27]

Of course he had great esteem for James P. Boyce, his dearest friend on the earth, fellow laborer in the gospel, his counselor and instructor. He said of Dr. Boyce's class in Systematic Theology, "You had to know your Systematic Theology or you could not recite it to Dr. Boyce. And though the young men were generally rank Arminians when they came to the Seminary, few went through this course under him without being converted to his strong Calvinistic views."[28]

Concerning Boyce's *Abstract of Systematic Theology*, Broadus said:

> Dr. Boyce's work is indeed thoroughly in accord with the system of theological opinion commonly called Calvinism. This is believed by many of us to be really the teaching of the Apostle Paul, as elaborated by Augustine, and systematized and defended by Calvin. It is a body of truth that compels men to *think*—in itself a great advantage. The objections to it are believed to grow out of either misapprehension, or misapplication through

26 Ibid., 73.
27 John L. Dagg, *Manual of Theology and Church Order* (Harrisonburg, VA: Gano Books, 1982), second page of Preface.
28 James P. Boyce, *Abstract of Systematic Theology* (nc: np, 1887), xxi.

wrong inferences. Men assume predestination and election, and then deny human freedom and responsibility; or they assume human freedom and accountability, and then deny predestination and election—in either case because they cannot fully reconcile these two sides of theological truth; thus making our capacity to harmonize things the limit of possible truth, and the criterion of Scripture interpretation. The world of matter is kept in equilibrium by the antagonism of physical forces, and the world of truth in like manner through countervailing facts and principles. Whatever theoretical position may be held, no truly devout man actually lives in practical neglect of either divine sovereignty or human responsibility. The blindest "Hardshell," who has "no message to the unconverted," does not neglect to plough his corn; the most ultra and heated Arminian believes in the doctrines of grace whenever he grows earnest in prayer.[29]

Speaking again, on the *Abstract of Systematic Theology,* Broadus said:

It is designed as a text-book for classes, is in like manner well suited to careful private study. Nothing is more useful to a thorough-going student than to take some first-class book on a great subject and master it completely, chapter by chapter, paragraph by paragraph, so that he can state the exact line of thought in any portion to himself or to some patiently sympathetic friend... If now to Boyce's Abstract a minister will add such a copious work as Strong's *Systematic Theology,* he will possess a very admirable theological apparatus—

---

29 Broadus, *Memoir of James Petigru Boyce,* 310.

and both works from American Baptists.[30]

Commenting on the value of Dr. Boyce's tracts and printed sermons, Broadus said, "One of special interest to ministers treats 'The Value of a Complete and Accurate Knowledge of the Doctrines of Grace to the Successful Preaching of the Gospel.'"[31]

Broadus was not simply an admirer of the doctrines of others however; he admired the theology of these men because he himself embraced the same convictions. This can be demonstrated exegetically, catechetically, and homiletically: Exegetically his commitment to the doctrines of grace can be seen through his commentary on Matthew's gospel; catechetically this same commitment comes through in his *Catechism of Bible Teaching;* and homiletically the same commitment can be demonstrated from an excerpt or two of his printed sermons and addresses.

Exegetically.

It was predicted by some that Broadus' commentary on Matthew would probably become the chief commentary in the *American Commentary* set. Let's consider his comments on several verses from Matthew 11 beginning with Verse 25 which states, "At that time Jesus answered and said, I thank thee, O Father, Lord of heaven and earth, because thou hast hid these things from the wise and prudent, and hast revealed them unto babes." Broadus observed,

> It is the Sovereign of the universe that does this; who shall hesitate to acknowledge that what he does is right?[32]

---

30 Ibid., 310.
31 Ibid., 313.
32 Alvah Hovey, Editor, *An American Commentary on the New Testament*, Volume 1, "Commentary on the Gospel of Matthew," by John A. Broadus, (Philadelphia, PA: The American Baptist Publication Society, 1886), 251.

Of verse 26, "Even so, Father: for so it seemed good in thy sight," Broadus commented,

> Our Lord acknowledges the propriety of the sovereign Father's course, and praises him for it. Whatever pleases God ought to please us.[33]

Verse 27 reads, "All things are delivered unto me of my Father: and no man knoweth the Son, but the Father; neither knoweth any man the Father, save the Son, and *he* to whomsoever the Son will reveal *him*." Broadus wrote,

> At some past time...perhaps, when the covenant of redemption was formed in eternity—all things were committed to him,...[34]

Then speaking of the vanity of men in trying to come to God on their own, Broadus said,

> All their wisdom and intelligence will not avail to gain a true knowledge of the Father, unless the Son chooses to reveal him to them.[35]

Regarding verse 28, "Come unto me, all ye that labour and are heavy laden, and I will give you rest." Broadus observed,

> Notice how the invitation follows immediately upon the statement that no one knows the Father but the Son, and he to whomsoever the Son chooses to reveal him. To his mind [the mind of Jesus] there was no contradiction between sovereign, electing grace and the free invitations of the gospel.[36]

---

33 Ibid., 252.
34 Ibid.
35 Ibid.
36 Ibid., 253.

Concerning the purpose of Christ's death, Broadus considered the substitutionary nature of the atonement and also the specific design of Christ's death when commenting on Matthew 20:28, which states, "Even as the Son of man came not to be ministered unto, but to minister, and to give his life a ransom for many."

> The preposition rendered "for" necessarily means "instead of," involving substitution, a vicarious death. When objectors ... require us to prove otherwise that Christ's death was vicarious, then it is well to remember that here (and also in Mark) the preposition is *anti*, which no one can possibly deny to have, and necessarily, the meaning "instead of."
> ... Christ's atoning death made it compatible with the divine justice that all should be saved if they would accept it on that ground; and in that sense he "gave himself a ransom for all" (1 Timothy 2:6), "tasted death for every man" (Hebrews 2:9), but his death was never expected, nor divinely designed, actually to secure the salvation of all, and so in the sense of specific purpose he came "to give his life a ransom for many." "Sufficient for all," Broadus says, "effectual for many."[37]

Broadus also recognized the biblical balance needed in properly addressing the divine side and human side of salvation, when commenting on Matthew 22:14, "For many are called, but few are chosen."

> This selection [choosing] of the actually saved may be looked at from two sides. From the divine side, we see that the Scriptures teach an eternal

---

37 Ibid., 418-419.

election of men to eternal life, simply out of God's good pleasure. There you have unconditional, eternal election. From a human side we see that those persons attain the blessings of salvation through Christ who accept the gospel invitation and obey the gospel commandment. It is doubtful whether our minds can combine both sides in a single view, but we must not for that reason deny either of them to be true. The few who are chosen give proof of it [of their having been chosen] by accepting the call and behaving accordingly. These enjoy the feast of salvation, gladly honor the Son of God and humbly ascribe all to sovereign grace.[38]

Like most Baptists of his day, Broadus also recognized that a proper understanding of and appreciation for predestination was critical to a proper understanding of the perseverance and preservation of the saints.

Catechetically.

Broadus' catechism is replete with his commitment to the doctrines of grace. A few questions will suffice to illustrate this.

Q. Does God act according to the purposes formed beforehand?
A. God has always intended to do whatever he does.[39]

Q. What is Christ doing for us now?
A. Christ dwells in his people, intercedes for them and controls all things for their good.[40]

---

38 Ibid., 450.
39 Tom J. Nettles, Editor, *Baptist Catechisms*, (nc: np, 1983), 250.
40 Ibid., 257.

Q. What was Christ's chief work as Savior?
A. Christ died and rose again for his people.[41]

Q. What is meant by the word "regeneration"?
A. Regeneration is God's causing a person to be born again.[42]

Q. Does faith come before the new birth?
A. No, it is the new heart that truly repents and believes.[43]

Q. Does God give his renewing Spirit as he sees proper?
A. Yes, God gives his renewing Spirit to those whom he always purposed to save.[44]

Homiletically.

Broadus delivered an address in 1874 to the students at Southern Seminary on "The American Baptist Ministry of A. D. 1774." In this address he said:

> The great Scripture doctrines of depravity, atonement and regeneration were almost unknown to many of their hearers, and disputed by many others. And so the preacher felt called continually to preach these and the related doctrines, proving and enforcing them by liberal [generous] quotations from the text of Scripture. Whenever men cease to preach these great doctrines of the Bible, drawing them directly from the fountain head, believing something definite, knowing what they believe and why they believe it, and how to prove it from the Inspired Word, then the pulpit soon loses its power.[45]

---

41 Ibid., 260.
42 Ibid., 263.
43 Ibid.
44 Ibid.
45 Broadus, *Sermons and Addresses*, 244.

Broadus was adamant in his desire to demonstrate that the doctrines of grace do not promote complacency. In a sermon from Romans 9:3, entitled "Intense Concern for the Salvation of Others," Broadus said,

> Concern for the salvation of others is not prevented by a belief in what we call the doctrines of grace; is not prevented by believing in divine sovereignty, and predestination and election. Many persons intensely dislike the ideas which are expressed by these phrases. Many persons shrink away from ever accepting them, because those ideas are in their minds associated with the notion of stolid indifference. They say if predestination be true, then it follows that a man cannot do anything for his own salvation; that if he is to be saved he will be saved, and he has nothing to do with it, and need not care, nor need any one else care. Now, this does not at all follow, and I will prove that it does not follow, by the fact that Paul himself, the great oracle of this doctrine in the Scripture, has uttered these words of burning passionate concern for the salvation of others, so close by the passages in which he has taught the doctrines in question.[46]

Broadus continued in a compelling way to show how Paul had taught previously in Romans 8 that "whom He did predestinate, them He also called." He then cited a subsequent passage in Romans 9 that teaches, "Jacob I loved and Esau I hated." Broadus then stated, "Look here they are and Paul said in the midst of this, 'I want to see my brethren saved.'" Broadus suggested that the difficulty with these passages comes

---

46 Ibid., 116-117.

when men in many cases "draw unwarranted emphases from the teachings of the Bible and then cast all the odium of those inferences upon the truths from which we draw them."[47]

A word needs to be said about Broadus' doctrine of the church. He wrote a pamphlet entitled, "The Duty of Baptists to Teach Their Distinctive Views."

> We hold that the Christian Church ought to consist only of persons making a credible profession of conversion, of faith in Christ ... Maintaining that none should be received as church members unless they give credible evidence of conversion, we also hold in theory that none should be retained in membership who do not lead a godly life; that if a man fails to show his faith by works, he should cease to make profession of faith. Some of our own people appear at times to forget that strict church discipline is a necessary part of the Baptist view as to church membership.[48]

THE LESSONS

Several helpful lessons can be drawn from the life, labors, and legacy of John Broadus.

First, we need to be balanced in our theology. When you read Broadus' sermons and addresses, it is clear that he was balanced. He held together that wondrous system of truth we call Calvinism, with continual outstretched hands, pleading with sinners to come to Christ. That may seem contradictory to some, but it does not matter. That posture reflects the proper biblical balance in a ministry.

Second, we need to learn that we ought to be faithful in our labor then usefulness will find us and influence will flow from us. Broadus never sought to "position himself" in any way in

---

47 Ibid., 118.
48 John A. Broadus, "The Duty of Baptists to Teach Their Distinctive Views" (Philadelphia: The American Baptist Publication Society, nd.), 6-7.

his denomination in order to be more useful to it. He was faithful to the labor God had given him and usefulness found him and influence flowed from him. We need to learn that today. We have a tendency to think, "If I could just get in with this group, if I could lay low and blend in ..." Be faithful where you have been planted, men. Was Broadus not involved in Associations? Certainly, he was but it doesn't appear that he was ever any kind of kingpin in his association. Was he involved in the National or State Conventions? Certainly, but not as one who held office. That is not wrong. If you are sought out for such a position of influence, then take it if the Lord so leads. But to put yourself in a spot so that the likelihood of that would increase is to turn your back on your primary labor. Broadus did not do this and we can learn from him that if we are faithful where we are, usefulness will find us.

Third, be personable. Broadus touched people of every segment of society. When he died a Jewish rabbi in Louisville said of him, "...when I learned to know and revere in Broadus a Christian, my conception of Christianity and my attitude toward it underwent a complete change. Broadus was the precious fruit by which I learned to judge of the tree of Christianity."[49] He had what I would call a "sanctified congeniality." We all need to be congenial. We don't need to be back-slappers and hail-fellows-well-met, but we can be congenial. We need to be more so, meeting people where they are. Our gospel is offensive enough, we don't need to make it more so by our obnoxious personalities.

Fourth, always maintain fervor for the souls of the lost. Whether looking at the aged John Broadus before he died, longing to see people saved, longing to see his students be mighty in the Scriptures, or whether considering John Broadus, the University student signing the autograph book of one of his fellow students, one consistent marks shines through—

---

49 Robertson, *The Life and Letters of John A. Broadus*, 438.

an earnest desire to see souls come to a saving knowledge of Jesus Christ. In the autograph book of a man who was known as very intelligent on campus, but not a Christian, Broadus simply wrote, "One thing thou lackest." Years later, from Texas, there came a letter from Dr. P. M. Matthews to John Broadus saying, "You may not even remember years ago you wrote in my autograph book 'One thing thou lackest' and I want you to know that I have found that thing."[50] May God give us a continual concern for the lost who are all around us.

Fifth, make preaching central to your ministry. Don't ever apologize for making the preaching of the gospel central to your times of worship. There is a movement underway across evangelicalism that constitutes a practical abandonment in the confidence of preaching. Some would have us believe that to this generation preaching has become passé. Don't fall into that trap. Preach the Word. This is God's ordained means through which sinners are saved. John Broadus said it this way, when delivering the Lyman Beecher lectures at Yale University in 1889:

> For the most part our hope of usefulness in the world is through you. Preach your best before God, for your own sakes, and then think of us and preach a little better still.[51]

This is a conference on the Faith of the Founders. When you go back to your pulpits this Sunday and the various labors God has given you, preach your very best before God for your own sake. You will give an account of that one day. Once you've done that, then think of Broadus, Boyce, these men who have gone before, and preach a little better still.

---

50 Ibid., 339-340.
51 Ibid., 337.

29.
A BIOGRAPHICAL SKETCH OF RICHARD FULLER
DON WHITNEY

1991 Southern Baptist Founders Conference

HISTORICAL CONTEXT

WHAT first attracted me to Richard Fuller was the unusual and evident blessing of God upon his pastoral ministry during the War between the States. In 1847 Fuller left his native South Carolina to become pastor of the Seventh Baptist Church in Baltimore. Before and during the war, Maryland was divided in its sympathies. In the presidential election of 1860, it was the Southern candidate, John Breckinridge, who carried the state, not Abraham Lincoln. The first Union soldiers on their way to Washington were mobbed in Richard Fuller's city. Maryland might have seceded had not Governor Thomas Hicks established martial law and called on Federal troops to help maintain order. Consequently, it did stay in the Union.

Now imagine pastoring not only when there is a War between the States of your country, but also when your own state is divided over that war. Worse than that, imagine pastoring a church in which some of the members have sons fighting in one army, and others have sons fighting in the opposing army.

Consider what it must have been like in mid-September, 1862 on the first Sunday after the Battle of Antietam. At Sharpsburg, less than 60 miles from Seventh Baptist Church, more than 28,000 soldiers were killed or wounded in one of the bloodiest days of the war. Half of the dead wore blue, half of them wore gray. Imagine walking into the pulpit on that Lord's Day and having a congregation looking at you, many of them feverishly wondering if a notice was on its way informing them that their son had been killed. Imagine the task of preaching to and pastoring the people that Sunday when they are glancing across the aisle and wondering if that man's son had killed their son that week, and if not, will he kill him next week. That's what Richard Fuller did. That was his task Sunday after Sunday through thirteen tense years before the war and then week after bloody week during those agonizing and anxious years of the war itself.

But most amazing of all is that during more than two decades when the entire nation was torn asunder, and especially during those four years when every emotion in the hearts of parents, wives, sisters, sons and daughters tempted them to harbor bitterness and a divisive spirit, the fellowship of Seventh Baptist Church in Baltimore under the preaching of Richard Fuller not only remained united, it actually *grew* from 87 members to an astonishing 1,200. There is much we can learn from the life and preaching of a man like that.

EARLY LIFE AND STUDENT DAYS

Fuller was born in April, 1804, in the town of Beaufort, which is near the coast at the southern tip of South Carolina. Richard was the ninth of the ten children given to Thomas and Elizabeth Fuller, all ultimately gave evidence of salvation. His father was converted only the year before Richard was born, but he established a Godly heritage for his family. For example, the third child, Harriet, "lived so constantly in prayer, that, in the preparation of her body for burial they found her knees to have become hardened from habitual kneeling, as tradition reports that the knees of the beloved

John were callous like those of the camel."[1]

Fuller grew into an athletic man. He loved the outdoors— he was a hunter, a fisherman and an excellent horseman. He reveled in the opportunities he had to be on the ocean, whether it was crossing the Atlantic to Europe or sailing up the eastern seaboard. Throughout his life he loved walking which was his daily exercise.

He enrolled at Harvard in 1820 at the age of 16, which was considered an unusually young age for acceptance even then. Despite his age, Fuller became one of the best students in his class. One of the evidences of his scholarship was his ability to take part in a dialogue in Greek at the beginning of his junior year. But at the end of that semester he developed what was described as a hemorrhage of the lungs. It was apparently a case of tuberculosis and it affected him the rest of his life. He was forced to leave school but he stayed in Massachusetts spending a year recuperating at Northampton, the town made famous by Jonathan Edwards.

There in the winter of 1823 he first experienced what Edwards would have called the first awakenings of the soul. He wrote about it to Dr. W. B. Sprague, author of a well-known volume on revival, saying his mind "awoke from its oblivious sleep."[2] It would be some nine years later before Fuller was converted but the Holy Spirit continued to manifest occasional evidences of His convicting power. One such occurrence happened after Fuller had returned home to South Carolina. He was lying on a couch in his mother's room when one of the family members saw him "convulsed with weeping." When asked if he was hurting he replied, "No, I am overpowered with a sense of the goodness of God to me."[3] Would to God that we would see more such work of the Holy Spirit in our day!

Although able to attend Harvard for only two and a half

---

1 J. H. Cuthbert, *Life of Richard Fuller* (New York: Sheldon and Company, 1879), 25.
2 Ibid., 63.
3 Ibid.

years, his academic standing with the faculty was so high that they voted in an unusual action to give him a degree with the class of 1824. He was not, however, an unbalanced intellectual, too serious for fun. After his death, one friend wrote, "I went with Dr. Fuller to his old room at Harvard which he had not visited since he left college. He was, as he always was, 'grave and gay,'—sad as he recounted old memories, and then bright and cheerful as he told of his college-scrapes. 'See!' said he, 'there are the very shot-holes where I used to sit and amuse myself with a pistol at the mice as they ran across the room.'"[4]

Of his days back in Beaufort, Fuller's biographer, nephew J. H. Cuthbert, says of him, "He was always a gentleman, easy in manner, ready in wit, brilliant in conversation. In dress he was scrupulously neat. He loved horseback-exercise as much as Napoleon did, and was an excellent rider.... With these advantages and equipments, it is not surprising to learn that young Fuller was a great favorite with the (fairer) sex. One of his sisters reported some little maneuvers of his, which his biographer must record,—how Richard would get her to ask some girls to spend the evening, when, dressing himself with great neatness and care, he would stroll out, and, after the party had assembled, stroll in and surprise them with an easy, nonchalant air, as if it were all a matter of moonshine; a little light skirmishing, as to which let him that is without sin cast the first stone."[5]

Through self-study, Fuller was admitted to the bar at age 21. He established his own practice and was quite a successful attorney. He married his wife, Charlotte, in August, 1831 when he was 27. They would have three daughters. He loved his girls dearly and their love for him testifies to his faithfulness to his responsibilities as a father. On his deathbed, his youngest daughter Florence, now grown, said to him,

---

4 Ibid., 43.
5 Ibid., 44-45.

"My darling father, I will die for you." Fuller said, "No, my child, live for me and for Jesus."[6]

CONVERSION

A few years before his conversion Fuller had been called by a Baptist minister named Benjamin Scriven to come to his bedside as he lay dying. Scriven pleaded with the young lawyer to come to Christ and Fuller was deeply moved. He made a profession of faith and joined the Episcopal Church, the most influential church in Beaufort. After a study of the subject he became convinced that New Testament baptism was by immersion so he was baptized in a river by the Episcopal rector. A day or two after his immersion a fellow townsman said to him, "So, Fuller, I see you arc a kind of mongrel Baptist." In a reaction quickly regretted, Beaufort's newest church member knocked the man senseless with one punch. This created, as Cuthbert says, "no little stir in the quiet little town."[7]

But in October, 1831, shortly after his marriage, Fuller experienced genuine conversion and its fruit—a changed life. During that year and the next, revival swept through the Carolinas and Georgia. Cuthbert described it as "a work of great power, that moved whole communities 'as the trees of the wood are moved with the wind'."[8] In the midst of that movement of God, an evangelist named Daniel Baker came to Beaufort. According to Fuller's biography, "When Mr. Baker came to town, it was the same extraordinary influence.... The whole town was a holy place. The meetings were held alternately in the Episcopal and Baptist churches.... The work was remarkable, not only in the number and soundness of the conversions, but in its triumphs among the higher classes of society. Men of talent, culture, and wealth were

---

6 Ibid., 61.
7 Ibid., 65.
8 Ibid., 67.

brought to Christ."[9] One of those men was the successful attorney, Richard Fuller.

In the family Bible, Fuller wrote this account of his conversion:

> R. Fuller, "born again" Thursday, 26th October, 1831. I had from childhood (long before I attached any definite meaning to the words) prayed to God for this change,—for a new heart. During a severe fit of illness (in the year 1827, I think) I felt what I now believe to have been the working of God's Holy Spirit; and, for a while after convalescence, I took pleasure in the service of the dear Redeemer. I also made a profession of religion. The work, however, if begun, was imperfect. The world soon re-asserted and resumed its control. My life for years was now spent amidst vanity and folly and sin. Pride and evil passions prevailed. Nay, in my heart I attempted to vindicate them; though I felt the folly and guilt of such pleas, even when reason would seem to have approved them. All this while my "goodness" was like Ephraim's. I felt satisfied I had never experienced that change without which a man cannot enter the kingdom of heaven. For this I prayed without ceasing. Glory to God! I found at last what I sought, and was filled with a joy which I can never express,—"unspeakable, and full of glory." Creation seemed full of God. The trees, the leaves, the earth, the sky, all things seemed to utter his praises. For days I could neither eat nor sleep. I lived upon the love of God shed abroad in my heart, and the name of Jesus shed light and fragrance over every thing. These ecstatic feelings have now passed away (they would have rendered me unfit to live in such a world); but I am still

---

9 Ibid., 67-68.

filled with the peace of God, which "passes all understanding." This change (the new birth) I felt under no excitement, but while on my knees in the company of many gathered for prayer. I knelt down trembling, but in a moment was so melted and filled with wonderful emotions, that I did little more than sob and weep. When I arose, I was hardly conscious of what had passed. My heart and soul were running over with love and joy and praise. I make this record, in hopes, when I am gone, it may cause a serious thought in those who read it.[10]

PASTORATE AT BEAUFORT

Afterwards, Fuller quickly came to the conviction that baptism was not only by immersion, but that it was for believers. So he presented himself for baptism in the Baptist church and announced his sense of call into the gospel ministry. He was ordained quickly, within a year. Later that same year, 1832, he was called as pastor of the Beaufort Baptist Church where he labored for fifteen years.

The church flourished during Fuller's ministry there and a large, new building was erected. He soon developed a reputation as one of the most influential preachers in the southeast. Young men preparing for ministry surrounded him and were trained by him. But the two best-known events during his ministry in South Carolina were written debates involving Catholicism and slavery.

In 1839 Fuller, who had visited Rome three years earlier, responded to a letter in the *Charleston Courier* by Catholic Bishop John England. This inaugurated a newspaper debate over some claims of the Roman Catholic hierarchy. Their letters to each other were read in many newspapers on both sides of the Atlantic. But even while the controversy raged,

10 Ibid., 69.

both men were able to maintain a friendship on matters outside the debate. And when England died shortly thereafter, *The Catholic Mirror* of Baltimore noted how Fuller came to Charleston to view the body.

DEBATE ON SLAVERY

Unfortunately, the event for which Fuller is remembered most today is his newspaper debate in the mid-1840's with fellow-Baptist Francis Wayland over the subject of slavery in the Scriptures. The debate was published in the book *Domestic Slavery Considered as a Scriptural Institution*. Like the famous evangelist George Whitefield a hundred years earlier, Richard Fuller was a slave-owner. In this public discussion between friends, Fuller argued—and Wayland conceded—that the Bible nowhere prohibits slavery. Wayland was surely right, however, in asserting that there are principles in the New Testament which necessitate the extinction of the practice.

As misguided as some of this thinking was, however, Fuller's heart was always in the right place. Surely not even a slave owner in Scripture could be named who was kinder to those slaves in his household than was Richard Fuller. Many of his slaves were inherited, and he was much loved by all of them. In one of the letters of the debate he offered to free his slaves to Wayland or any other reader who could give him "bond and security" that their condition would be improved but no one took up his offer. Furthermore, there are some other facts that are never mentioned in this connection. According to Thomas Armitage's *A History of the Baptists*, when Fuller became pastor of the Baptist church in Beaufort its condition was described as "feeble. But under his faithful care it increased to about 200 white persons and 2400 colored."[11] Shortly after he entered into the pastorate of that church he

---

11 Thomas Armitage, *A History of the Baptists*, vol. 2 (New York: Bryan, Taylor and Co., 1890; reprint ed., Watertown, WI: Baptist Heritage Press, 1988), 760.

wrote to a friend, "I had resolved, when first called to the ministry, to confine my labors wholly to our colored population. I was prevented by the hand of God."[12] Most remarkable of all, throughout his entire fifteen-year ministry in Beaufort he never accepted the salary offered to him, devoting all of it when allowed to do so, for what he called "the spiritual instruction of the slaves."[13]

PASTORATES IN BALTIMORE

In 1847 Fuller accepted the pastorate of the Seventh Baptist Church in Baltimore. He accepted the call on the condition that the church buy another piece of property and begin construction on a new building before he came. This they did and the church thrived, as mentioned earlier, throughout those turbulent years before and during the War. In 1871 Fuller led the church to build a building in the northwest part of Baltimore for the establishment of a new mission, the Eutaw Place Baptist Church. As soon as the building was dedicated the new group extended a call to Fuller to be their pastor. So he left the 1,200 member Seventh Baptist Church after twenty-four years and was one of the 131 charter members of the new fellowship. At the end of his final five years of ministry, the church had a total of 452 members.

He preached his last sermon at Eutaw Place on September 24, 1876. He had endured for some time what he called a fire in his shoulder which would probably be diagnosed today as cancer. In his last weeks one growth was removed but another lump quickly appeared. On the morning of October 20, Richard Fuller entered the Celestial City of his God. His last words were, "Who'll preach Jesus?"[14]

FULLER AS A PREACHER

Fuller's dying words bear testimony to what he lived for—to

12 Cuthbert, *Life of Richard Fuller*,105.
13 Ibid., 157.
14 Ibid.

preach Jesus. His biographer contends that "As a preacher of the gospel and a good minister of Jesus Christ, he must rank with the foremost of this or of any age."[15] W. T. Brantly, Fuller's successor at Seventh Baptist Church in Baltimore and the preacher at Fuller's funeral added, "And the glory of his preaching was that Jesus was the constant theme.... Whether the text was selected from the prophecies or the histories, the proverbs or the epistles, the psalms or the gospels, the sermon was always fragrant with the precious odor of Christ."[16] Cathcart's *Baptist Encyclopedia* says of his Christ-centered proclamation, "Dr. Fuller as a preacher had but few peers."[17]

Perhaps Richard Fuller's distinction in the pulpit can best be seen in the influence of his preaching at the annual meetings of the Southern Baptist Convention. He had already addressed the last two meetings of the old Triennial Convention when he was asked to preach the very first annual sermon of the Southern Baptist Convention in 1846. "In the subsequent meetings of the Southern Baptist Convention," writes Cuthbert, "it was generally understood that Dr. Fuller was to occupy on Sunday morning the pulpit of the church with which the body met. There were many able and devoted men present equal to any occasion; but they, as well as the community, were anxious to hear Richard Fuller. It was not unusual in this way for him to preach in the evening as well as in the morning of the great day of the feast."[18] And as far as I have been able to tell, Fuller did preach at one time or another at every annual meeting of the SBC at least until the meeting at Raleigh in 1872, totaling upwards of twenty-six consecutive years of preaching to the gathered messengers of our denomination. Some men said they traveled to the convention for the sole purpose of hearing Fuller preach.

---

15 Cuthbert, *Life of Richard Fuller*, 313.
16 W. T. Brantly, *Richard Fuller: Recollections of His Life and Character* (Baltimore, MD: J. I. Weish-ampel, Jr., 1876), 6.
17 William Cathcart, ed., *The Baptist Encyclopedia* (Philadelphia: Louis H. Everts, 1881; reprint ed., Paris, AR: *The Baptist Standard Bearer*, 1988), 424.
18 Cuthbert, *Life of Richard Fuller*, 181.

THE IMPORTANCE OF PREACHING

He also spoke on behalf of needy Southern Baptist causes. Two of his most influential appearances before the convention were on behalf of the Southern Baptist Theological Seminary, then at Greenville, SC, and for the Home Mission Board. When the convention met in Macon in 1869 a newspaper gave this report of his appeal: "He loved the seminary, because they there teach the students to preach Jesus. The Bible is written in other languages; and we Baptists should see to it that we have men able to interpret them, and to state and defend our particular views.... How important that these mighty interests should not be committed to ignoramuses!"[19] In Raleigh in 1872 he spoke of being touched by the need of home missions when he had walked the previous day among the graves of soldiers from the recent war. In what must have been an emotional moment he asked, "Will we not send the gospel to their widows and orphans?" He went on to appeal for more missionary work among the former slaves.

In addition to his preaching before the convention, we should not forget his other denominational service. Fuller was the third president of the SBC, chosen twice as the man to lead the convention in what may have been the most difficult terms of office ever (1859-1861 and 1861-1863). The *Encyclopedia of Southern Baptists* records his role in this little-known fact: "He was leader of the Provisional Board in Baltimore, which carried on foreign missions work during the Civil War when the Foreign Mission Board in Richmond was cut off from communication with missionaries in China and Africa, and funds from the South were not available."[20]

He loved our denomination and worked for it but preaching was Richard Fuller's first love in the ministry and it was to this work that he gave his best and longest hours. This is not to imply that he was a great preacher who stayed aloof from

---

19 Cuthbert, *Life of Richard Fuller*, 186-187.
20 *Encyclopedia of Southern Baptists*, vol. 1, (Nashville, TN: Broadman Press, 1958).

people. He once admonished an inexperienced pastor, "Young man, don't you know you can't succeed anywhere without visiting?"[21] But the heartbeat of his ministry was the proclamation of the Word of God. And though he was unusually gifted by God, one should not conclude that Fuller coasted into pulpit effectiveness. Commentator William Newell said of him at Harvard that "His brilliant talent was united with great power of work, with close and indefatigable study."[22] Of his later ministry Newell observed, "He was certainly a gifted and powerful preacher whose success, however, was due quite as much to his full and elaborate preparation of thought for his subject as to his readiness of speech."[23]

Fuller gave three days' preparation to his messages. "Monday morning by nine o'clock," he would sometimes say, "I have my texts for next Sunday. I am at work on the morning sermon until Thursday: the rest of the week I give to the second. Then, if something occurs to you in the pulpit, say it."[24] Cuthbert adds at this point, "Some of his own happiest sentences were in this way strictly extemporaneous; but they came with him, as they must with every one, from the momentum of a previous and thorough preparation."[25] His preparation was so thorough that in the latter part of his ministry he preached without a single note.

APPLICATORY PREACHING

It is impossible to appreciate fully the preaching of Richard Fuller without focusing specifically on his masterful use of application. As part of my doctoral studies I examined the use of application in the sermons of ten well-known Southern Baptist preachers—five living and five deceased. One of those

21 Cuthbert, *Life of Richard Fuller*, 172.
22 Ibid., 38.
23 Ibid., 39.
24 Ibid., 320-321.
25 Ibid., 321.

whom I studied was Richard Fuller. I discovered that in terms of the sheer number of applications of the text in his messages, Richard Fuller consistently ranked higher than any other preacher I studied. This includes some modern men who are considered unusually relevant and practical preachers by today's pragmatic standards.

We need to learn from Richard Fuller how to be doctrinal preachers who clearly demonstrate the application of the doctrines we preach. Fuller's sermons were heavy with theology on one side and equally weighted with the practical outworkings of that theology on the other. Notice the doctrinal titles of some of his sermons: "Predestination," "The Law and the Gospel," "The True Christian," 'The Judgment," "Mortification of Sin."[26] Richard Fuller preached the deep things of God, yet he always showed the difference these doctrines make and how we should respond to them. For instance, there are no less than thirteen practical applications in his sermon on predestination. In one of these applications he said,

> Let us pray for grace that we may acquiesce in all the mysteries of God's sovereignty, and yet hold inviolate all the strenuous activities of the life of faith.... Take prayer, for example. God promises to answer prayer, and we know he does answer prayer. Let us not perplex ourselves by curious speculations as to the manner in which our petitions can be granted, and how the prevalence of our supplications can consort with God's unchangeableness.[27]

Fuller teaches us that no matter how well we explain a doctrine, we do not preach it until we apply it.

---

26 Richard Fuller, *Sermons by Richard Fuller* (Balltimore: John F. Weishampel, Jr., 1877).
27 Ibid., 27.

What Fuller did is true of all great preaching. His younger contemporary, John A. Broadus wrote, "The application in a sermon is not merely an appendage to the discussion or a subordinate part of it, but is the main thing to be done."[28] Broadus then quotes Spurgeon's statement, "Where the application begins, there the sermon begins."[29]

METHODS OF APPLICATION

Fuller used four different methods of applying his message to the lives of his listeners. The method he used most often we may call the principal method. This means he applied the text in terms of a principle. In a lengthy application in his sermon, "Fellowship in Christ's Sufferings," Fuller makes his point by setting forth biblical principles on suffering:

> "We all suffer by the will of God;" it is plain that he means us to pass through this ordeal. A single fact is conclusive on this point; it is, that in our bodies, minds, hearts there are exquisite capacities for pain as well as pleasure. God intends that we shall experience sorrow and anguish, or he would not have opened this source of bitterness in the very centre of our being. As man, Jesus was "made perfect through suffering;" and it is through the same austere discipline that we are to reach the true dignity and glory of our nature —to "come unto a perfect man, unto the measure of the stature of the fulness of Christ".... The religion of Jesus is designed to confer upon us a good far superior to any present enjoyment. To secure this good, afflictions are indispensable. And therefore in the Gospel system our sorrows are preferments; chastisements are the expres-

28 John A. Broadus, *On the Preparation and Delivery of Sermons* (1870; 4th reprint ed., Vernon L. Stanfield, San Francisco: Harper and Row, 1979), 165.
29 Ibid., 165.

sions of God's love. Afflictions are indeed the only blessings bestowed without being asked for—so necessary are they. And what the Bible declares is confirmed for every child of God. He feels that afflictions are distinctions. For him there is in sanctified suffering an alchemy which turns everything into gold.[30]

These statements, in principal form, on Philippians 3:10 cause us immediately to identify with the implications of this verse.

A second method he used in applying the Scriptures is the directive method. This method is more straightforward. By it Fuller tells his hearers what action they should take. Regarding predestination he asks, "What are we to do? It is evident that there is only one hope left us. We must confess our absolute blindness, and procure a guide who comprehends all the dark intricacies; one in whom we have perfect confidence; who can and will conduct us safely; and we must surrender ourselves to him."[31]

Then there is the illustrative method of applying the message. This is the use of an illustration not necessarily to clarify the explanation of a text, but to clarify its application. Fuller does this in his sermon, "Danger to the Soul from Lawful Things":

> God gives us temporal blessings "richly to enjoy;" but to set our affections upon any earthly objects so as to make them essential to our highest happiness, this is at once a mistake and a sin. An impatient restlessness to possess them; a pining after them as if they were our life, in the temper of Rachel when she exclaimed, "Give me children, or I die;"—this shows clearly that our hearts are

30 Fuller, *Sermons,* 270-271.
31 Ibid., 18.

given up to idolatry; and unless mercifully withheld, such objects will cause our souls to come to
grief, and to sad experience.[32]

A fourth method, which Fuller employs less frequently than
the others but with great effect, is the interrogative method.
By asking one or more questions he presses the truth of
Scripture right into the heart of his hearers. Near the end of
his sermon on predestination he says to the unconverted in
his congregation,

> If you are bent on self-destruction—if no entreat-
> ies from God ... no solicitation of the Spirit, ... no
> fears of your Saviour can stop you—at least do
> not insult Heaven by pretending that you are
> waiting for more effectual influences. This plea
> admits that you feel some strivings of the Holy
> Ghost; why do you not comply with these? Why
> resist these, and desire more powerful move-
> ments? What is this, but openly to proclaim that
> you ... are resolved to strive against your Maker,
> to yield nothing to him willingly, to defy him as
> long as you can, and only to submit to a sad ne-
> cessity when he shall compel you? Is there any
> thing in Revelation—do you seriously think there
> is any thing in the secret counsels of eternity—to
> justify the hope that God will thus be appeased?
> What, my beloved friend, what can you expect
> from such deliberate, unrelenting opposition to
> the Sovereign of the Universe?[33]

A further point to be noted about Fuller's use of application
is his tendency to apply a text throughout the sermon as well
as at the end. He knew that if he did not begin showing the

---

32 Ibid., 39.
33 Ibid., 30.

text's relevance in his introduction and continue to do so throughout the message, there might not be anyone listening by the time he came to apply it all at the end.

A century after Fuller, Martyn Lloyd-Jones argued for continuous application in his classic work, *Preaching and Preachers:*

> But as you have presented your message in this way it is important that you should have been applying what you have been saying as you go along. There are many ways of doing this. You can do so by asking questions and answering them, or in various other ways; but you must apply the message as you go along. This again shows that you are not just lecturing, that you are not dealing with an abstract or academic or theoretical matter; but that this is a living matter which is of real concern to the people in the whole of their life and being. So you must keep on applying what you are saying.[34]

However, in the great tradition of the Puritans and later of Lloyd-Jones himself, Fuller often had a separate section of application at the end of his message. Many of the Puritan preachers would say they had finished expounding the doctrine found in their text and now they had come to its "uses." Fuller sometimes made a similar formal transition to a separate part of his message devoted exclusively to application. Near the end of his sermon, "The Law and the Gospel," he announced, "I have now finished the discussion of this subject. Many reflections are suggested."[35]

Lloyd-Jones practiced and encouraged the same approach: "When you have ended the reason and the argument, and have arrived at this climax, you apply it all again. This can be

---

34 D. Martyn Lloyd-Jones, *Preaching and Preachers* (Grand Rapids, MI: Zondervan, 1971), 77.
35 Fuller, *Sermons,* 108.

done in the form of an exhortation which again may take the form of a series of questions, or a series of terse statements. But it is vital to the sermon that it should always end on this note of application or of exhortation."[36]

CONCLUDING LESSONS

What lessons can be learned from the preaching ministry of Richard Fuller? At least three immediately suggest themselves. First, good preaching requires devotion to application. Fuller's preaching was powerful because it was practical. It was mighty because it mattered. He never assumed that people would automatically understand the possible applications of a text to their situations. He knew that for the nails of Scripture to be well-driven he should use the hammer of application to fix them into people's lives. Broadus said it tersely: "If there is no summons, there is no sermon."[37]

Second, good preaching requires devotion to Christ-centered declaration. When Paul reminded the Corinthians of the focus of his initial ministry among them, he described it this way: "For I determined to know nothing among you except Jesus Christ, and Him crucified" (1 Corinthians 2:2). Apostolic preaching—which Fuller exemplified—centered on the Person and work of Jesus Christ. Everything the apostles preached was in some sense an expression or extension of that same message. Third, good preaching requires devotion to preparation. As uniquely gifted as Richard Fuller was, everyone agreed that it was his study and preparation that distinguished him as a preacher. Thomas Armitage acknowledged this as well:

> As a preacher Dr. Fuller was appreciated throughout the nation, for he found but one answer to the question, How can a man preach with

---

36 Lloyd-Jones, *Preaching and Preachers*, 77-78.
37 Broadus, *Preparation and Delivery of Sermons*, 165.

power? He believed the word of God with all his soul and walked with its Author continually... . To this he added the most painstaking study to ascertain by every form of help what the Scriptures required him to preach. Aside from the dutiful visitation of the sick and sorrowful, and other indispensable duties, his mind was bent upon the divine results of the coming Sabbath.[38]

At his funeral it was said of Fuller, "Great gifts were not used by our brother as a substitute for diligence in his calling. As a workman for Christ he proved himself a great man. From early manhood up to threescore years and ten, he led a life singularly laborious."[39] His usefulness over many years came through the discipline of intentional, life-long diligence in study.

In a day when preaching is being increasingly judged as irrelevant, and many who make a start in the ministry do not finish there, Richard Fuller's legacy provides a much needed challenge. May God raise up men of like faith and diligence in our own generation.

---

38 Armitage, *A History of the Baptists,* 761.
39 Brantly, *Richard Fuller,* 7.

30.
THE LIFE AND MISSION
OF WILLIAM CAREY—PART 1
TIMOTHY GEORGE
1992 Southern Baptist Founders Conference

THE section of Isaiah in which chapter 54 is found reverberates with missionary zeal. Isaiah 54 was a chapter of particular importance in the life and the formation of William Carey. The first five verses provided the text for the most famous missionary sermon perhaps since Peter gave that great message on the Day of Pentecost. Clearly it was the great missionary trumpet call to the Particular Calvinistic Baptists of England who in 1792 launched what we call the Modern Missionary Movement. Listen to God's Word:

> "Sing, O barren woman, you who never bore a child; burst into song, shout for joy, you who never were in labor; because more are the children of the desolate woman than of her who has a husband," says the LORD. "Enlarge the place of your tent, stretch your tent curtains wide, do not hold back; lengthen your cords, strengthen your stakes. For you will spread out to the right and to the left, your descendents will dispossess nations and settle in their desolate cities.
> "Do not be afraid; you will not suffer shame. Do not fear disgrace; you will not be humiliated. You will forget the shame of your youth and remember no more the reproach of your widowhood. For your Maker is your husband—the LORD Almighty is his name—the Holy One of Israel is your Redeemer; he is called the God of

all the earth" (Isaiah 54:1-5, NIV).

CAREY'S EARLY LIFE

William Carey was born on August 17, 1761 in Paulerspury, a tiny, little village of only 800 inhabitants hidden in a tiny corner of Northamptonshire in the midlands region of England.

The year of Carey's birth was an important year. 1761 witnessed the death of William Law. Law was one of the great spiritual writers of that century, and his book, *A Serious Call to a Devout and Holy Life*, is still in print today. Also in 1761, John Wesley was 58 years of age. It may be that young Carey was taken to hear Wesley preach, as he came through that part of England on one of his many itinerate missions.

In that same year, in fact in the very month that William Carey was born, another great preacher of the eighteenth century (perhaps the greatest preacher of that century or any century), George Whitfield, was making his way across the Atlantic Ocean. This was his sixth trip from Old England to New England. He would preach up and down the Eastern seacoast from Maine to Georgia. George Whitfield, the first Trans-Atlantic evangelist, ignited the fires of awakening and revival throughout the American colonies. Whitfield would make two more such trips before his eventual death in New England. He was buried in Newburyport, Massachusetts.

The year 1761 was also an interesting time on the continent of Europe. In Vienna there was a child prodigy, Wolfgang Amadeus Mozart. He was producing his first symphony at age five. Matters of musical significance were happening in London too. In Westminster Abbey the crowds were trickling in to hear Handel's Messiah. It was the age of Boswell and Doctor Johnson, of Jane Austin and Robert Burns, of Gibbon and Burke, and Wedgewood and Chippendale.

It was an age of cultural flourishing in Georgian England but it was also an age of violence. Six months before Carey was born, the last outpost of the French empire in the subcontinent of India surrendered to the British fleet at Pondi-cherry, assuring that for nearly two centuries the sun would not set on the Union Jack. The year before Carey was born, 1760, a new king ascended the throne of England. George III was his name. He would reign for 60 years, longer than any other monarch in the history of the realm (with the only exception being his remarkable granddaughter, Victoria, who reigned for 63 years in the nineteenth century). But these great events of national and international importance made no dent whatsoever in that tiny hamlet of Paulerspury in Northamptonshire in 1761. Life went on much as it had for centuries.

William Carey was born into a very humble family. His fa-ther Edmond was a weaver. A few years after William was born Edmond became the schoolmaster of that village and moved to another house at the end of the town. This was very important because it meant there were books in the humble cottage in which young William grew up. Later he said that he was accustomed to reading the Scriptures from his infancy.

However, it was not his father Edmond who had the de-cisive influence on his early years. Rather, it was his father's brother, his Uncle Peter. Peter had been away fighting for the British army in America in what we call the French and Indi-an War. He had seen the evidence of the slave trade on the high seas. He had adventure stories to tell and had come back to this tiny hamlet to spend his latter years tending a garden. When the day's work was done and the shadows were falling, the family would gather around the fireplace to hear Uncle Peter tell stories of fighting against the French in Quebec and the Indians in North America, of sailing the high seas, as well as other adventures. The romance of his stories lit a fire in the heart and imagination of young William that there was a world beyond the bounds of his village. It was also to his Uncle Peter that he owed his love for plants and gardening that he would carry with him to the end of his life.

In all likelihood William would have ended up like most boys did in that and similar villages—as an agricultural laborer, a common farmer, tilling the soil, raising fruits and vegetables to sustain the minimum standard of life in that era—except for the fact that when he was age seven, he contracted a severe disease of the skin. There was no diagnosing what really might have been his problem but they knew that exposure to the sun greatly irritated his skin. So it was necessary for his parents to find for him an occupation which could be undertaken indoors where the beams of the sun could not irritate this terrible skin condition. In the neighboring village of Hackleton there was a man named Clarke Nichols who was looking for an apprentice to work in his shoe shop. And so it was that the parents of William Carey apprenticed their son to work with Nichols as a cobbler, learning the trade of making shoes.

It was in the context of being an apprentice to Clarke Nichols, learning how to make shoes as well as other leather items, that Carey met probably the most important single person in his life—a person of whom not a single one of you here has ever heard (unless you have read my book on Carey). He was John Warr. Warr was also an apprentice to Nichols but he had recently been converted to Christ through attending a dissenting meeting, and he was ablaze with zeal to share his newfound faith in Christ. So he began daily to witness to his new apprentice friend, William Carey. Carey admitted later on in life that he was, as a young boy and teenager in that part of England, given to lying and swearing. He further acknowledged that he was rowdy in the company of ringers and football players, as well as in the society of the blacksmith shop.

As Warr witnessed to him, young William came to see that it wasn't so much a question of whether his sins were big ones or little ones. Rather the question was whether or not he had sinned before a holy and righteous God.

He could not find quiet in his soul. Oh, he tried to dismiss it. "Heaven and hell were both out of my sight, and as for saving and damning, they were lost in my thoughts," he said. But he couldn't get away from it and John Warr would not leave him alone. Daily, in the close company of that cobbler shop, he continued to share with William the newfound faith he had discovered in Jesus Christ and to give him books to read. Even at that young age, William was a voracious reader and remarkable in his gift to learn languages.

One of the books that Warr gave him was in Dutch. Carey couldn't read Dutch but he borrowed a Dutch grammar from someone in a neighboring village and within two weeks he had taught himself enough Dutch to read and understand that book. This is a remarkable feat for anyone, much less an unlearned teenager! But God had given William Carey a remarkable ability with languages.

It was in the context of that cobbler shop that he eventually was brought to a personal and saving faith in Jesus Christ as his own Lord and Savior. As he described it, better than we can describe it, he was brought "to depend on a crucified Savior for pardon and salvation; and to seek a system of doctrines in the Word of God." Faith was born in William Carey in this remarkable way.

The first thing that he wanted to do was to see his family converted. So he would go back home to Paulerspury and ask permission to lead in family prayers. All the evidence we have is that he was a young man whose zeal sometimes outran his patience. His sister Polly was always fond of William—they had a very close relationship. Even after William moved to India, he corresponded regularly with Polly, who became an invalid later in life. But she recalled those early days when young William would come home and lead in family prayers. She says, "Often have I felt my pride rise when he was engaged in prayer, at the mention of those words in Isaiah 'that all our righteousness was like filthy rags.' I did not think he thought his so, but looked on me and the family as filthy, not himself and his party."

Well, maybe Carey had something to learn of how to do evangelism, but his zeal was unmistakable. About ten years after that event, when he had seen every member of his family come to faith in Christ through his patient and persistent witness, he wrote the following letter to his parents:

> Religion is far from being a dry and formal round
> [of] mere externals. When we pray, 'tis to the Al-
> mighty Governor of heaven and earth. When we
> hear a sermon, it is for eternity. The solemn
> thought we are accountable immortals should on
> all occasions possess our minds. Probationers for
> an eternal world, how should we live? [I think
> that is one of the greatest lines I have ever read in
> a letter.] By nature children of wrath and under
> condemnation, how earnestly should we sue for
> mercy!. . .Repentance is absolutely necessary for
> salvation. . . .I hope all my dear relations know
> the truth of these observations by their own ex-
> perience.

It was shortly after his conversion, in this context of seeking, that William joined himself to a group of dissenters. His
father was the schoolmaster in the village and so, per force,
a member of the Church of England. But William had come
to see that there was a like precious faith held in common by
those on the margins of society known as the dissenters or the
non-conformists of England.

This takes us back to the century before Carey was born, to
the year 1662. This was the year when the Stuart monarchy
had been restored in England following the Civil War and the
brief interregnum of Oliver Cromwell. With the restoration of
the Stuart monarchy in 1662, Parliament passed an Act of
Uniformity requiring conscription to the *Book of Common
Prayer* for all who would be ministers within the realm of
England. There were two thousand ministers who refused to
subscribe to the *Book of Common Prayer*, and thereby began
this tradition of dissent and non-conformity. Some of the
leading ministers in the land were in that two thousand, including the maternal grandfather of Charles and John Wesley, the Reverend Samuel Annesley. New laws were passed by

parliament, such as the Clarendon Code which imposed penalties including imprisonment and harassment for those who refused to conform. Even after 1688, when William and Mary of Orange came to the throne of England and there was at least a minimal statutory freedom of worship granted, it was still the case that those who refused to join the Church of England were persecuted, discriminated against and made the objects of grave prejudice.

One church member said that these dissenters were miscreants "begat in rebellion, born in sedition, and nursed in faction." In fact it wasn't until 1871 that they finally were admitted into the universities of Oxford and Cambridge. So, William Carey, in joining himself with these dissenters, was taking his stand with those who stood at the margins of society. They were discriminated against, persecuted, harassed and inevitably looked down upon by the established religion of the land.

Even after becoming a dissenter there was a restlessness in Carcy as he read and studied the Scriptures, particularly the New Testament and especially on the subject of baptism. Through the study of the Bible, Carey became convinced that the infant baptism he had received in the parish church of his native village was not a biblical baptism and that baptism was only for believers who have closed with Christ through repentance and faith. So he sought out one of the leading Baptists in that part of the world, John Ryland Sr., and applied to him for baptism in the College Lane Church of Northhampton. Ryland Sr. appointed his son, John Ryland, Jr. to deal with the young nondescript shoemaker and after a period of extensive study, instruction, and prayer, it came to the point of baptism for William Carey. He was baptized on a Sunday morning, in October 1783. Later, John Ryland, Jr., who actually baptized Carey, recorded the following lines in his diary:

> On October 5, 1783, I baptized in the Nene, just
> beyond Doddridge's meeting-house, a poor journeyman-shoemaker, little thinking that before

nine years elapsed he would prove the first instrument of forming a Society for sending missionaries from England to the heathen world, and
much less that later he would become professor
of languages in an Oriental college, and the
translator of the Scriptures into eleven different
tongues.

William Carey was a new baptized Baptist now, and he began to sense that the Lord was leading him to a commitment
to Christian ministry. So he applied for membership in a
church that was nearer his home and his cobbler shop. It was
a church in Olney, pastored by a great Baptist leader named
John Sutcliff. Sutcliff was a native of Yorkshire who had studied at the British Baptist Academy, the first theological seminary founded by the Baptists of England. He had come to this
village of Olney with a great burden and he desired to train a
new generation of faithful ministers of the gospel. So he welcomed with enthusiasm this approach from Carey and spent
hours counseling with him, finally bringing him before the
church for examination and consideration of his request that
he be licensed to preach the gospel.

The church minute book at what is now the Sutcliff Baptist
Church—the Baptist Meeting house as it would have been
known then—records the following result of that business
session: "W. Carey, in consequence of a request from the
Church, preached this evening. After which it was resolved
...that he should engage again on suitable occasion for sometime before us, in order that further trial may be made of his
ministerial Gifts." Translated into modern vernacular, "No
Way!" They refused to license William Carey to preach! Now
that is a remarkable fact.

What is even more remarkable is the attitude Carey took
away from what must have been a shattering, disappointing
experience. Most of us, had we encountered a negative, dis-
qualifying experience such as that, so early and tender in our
ministry, would have turned away with no thought of pur-

suing it again, or more likely, gone down the road and started our own church irrespective of what those stuffy Baptists at Olney thought. But that wasn't at all what Carey did. He followed the advice given by Sutcliff and the Olney church. He realized he wasn't ready yet to undertake this awesome responsibility of carrying on the ministry of the gospel. So he subjected himself to a further trial of his gifts.

He began to preach—in homes sometimes, out of doors on other occasions, and in various churches to which he would be called. A year or so later, the church at Olney did indeed call him back and license him to preach the glorious gospel of Jesus Christ. Carey had met, as they said in their record book, "to our unanimous satisfaction" the obvious and evident blessing of God on his ministerial abilities. And they sent him forth wherever God in His providence might call him.

Now I think we have something to learn from this experience of Carey and his close call, so to speak, with the Olney congregation—that we be careful in licensing and sending forth ministers of the gospel. More is required than zeal, desire, a sweet smile, or even an M.Div. from Beeson Divinity School before one is ready to be sent forth to preach.

Carey was called to pastor his first church in the village of Moulton. The chapel in which Carey preached is still standing, along with the little cottage where he lived and the little shoe shop he kept, because he had to be what we would call today a "bi-vocational" pastor. Those poor Baptists of Moulton, could not support William and his growing family, for he had taken a wife already and had two children when his family moved to Moulton.

Carey wrote a letter at this time to a man named John Stanger, a Baptist pastor in Kent who had been present at Carey's own ordination. In this letter, Carey set forth his ideal of the Christian ministry and the motive of his own pastoral work. I think again it is a model for those of us who would be ministers of the gospel today. Carey said:

> [The minister] should keep up the character of a

teacher, an overlooker, at all times; and in the
chimney corner, as well as the pulpit....The importance of those things that we have to do with,
ought always to impress our minds, in our private
studies, our addresses to God, and our labours in
the pulpit. The word of God! What need to pray
much and study closely, to give ourselves wholly
to those great things, that we may not speak falsely of God. The word of truth! Every particle of it
is infinitely precious. O that we may never trifle
with so important things. The souls of men! Eternal things! All of the utmost moment, their value
beyond estimation, their danger beyond conception, and their duration equal with eternity.
These, my dear friend, we have to do with; these
we must give an account of....Pray for me and
God help me to pray for you.

Integrity, diligence, commitment and compassion are the
characteristics that stand out in the life of that young Baptist
pastor in Moulton. I said he was a bi-vocational pastor, making shoes on the side. Actually, he was a tri-vocational pastor
because even making shoes was not enough to keep bread on
the table, and so he also had to keep a school. He was a
schoolmaster, and students came to learn how to read, write
and count from this village shoemaker and Baptist pastor. It
was in this context that William Carey began to look out on
the world beyond him and to have a burden for that wider
world beyond the bounds of Northampton and even his native
England.

Carey would read anything he could get his hands on—any
report of missionary activity from the Moravians or the Pie-
tists of Germany who had pioneered carrying the gospel
around the world. Anything, any word, any news, he would
greedily devour. He also at this time began to read the journals of Captain James Cook. Captain Cook sailed around the
world, into the South Sea Islands, and discovered Australia.

Reports of Captain Cook's journals were now being circulated in England and Carey read and devoured them. Inside him grew the conviction that somehow the gospel had to be taken to these people in far-off lands.

In those days, teachers were short on supplies and so in order to teach geography to the students, Carey took a football (more like what we would call a soccer ball or round ball) and a marker, and drew on the ball the lines of the continents and nations of the world. It substituted for a globe as well as a soccer ball. There is a story that one day Carey had been teaching his students the geography of the world and the different continents and islands. As he held that globe in his hand, he began to weep and cry. The students, no doubt, must have thought it very unusual for the schoolmaster to be crying over a geography lesson. But they heard him say, "And they are pagans, pagans!" For Carey, those lines on the globe were not simply demarcations of continents and islands and nations. They were places where people lived, people who had never heard the name of Jesus Christ. And Carey wept before his students when he considered that.

He drew a map of the world and put it up above his cobbler shop. Andrew Fuller tells about riding down from the city of Kettering and visiting Carey there and seeing this remarkable, homemade map of the world. As Carey would make shoes, he would look up and see the representation of the globe. He had written on it not only the names of the different nations, but the estimated population of each and the various religious traditions of each.

So he had the world before him every single moment he was laboring in the cobbler shop, praying to God that there would be an awakening and a revival. So it was that Carey was led to share with others this burden and compassion that somehow the gospel should be carried to the ends of the world. Andrew Fuller tells us that Carey would not leave him alone, that every time he and other fellow ministers saw Carey, this was the topic of conversation.

TWO PRECURSORS TO THE MISSIONARY AWAKENING

Now I want to address this passage in Isaiah 54 and Carey's great "Deathless Sermon" which he preached before the Baptist Association of Northampton. But, before doing that, I want to say a word about two other movements that led up to and, in a way, opened the door for the great missionary awakening that God was to use Carey to bring about.

A Call to Prayer.

The first movement was a call to prayer. In 1748 in Boston, Massachusetts, a new book by Jonathan Edwards came off the press, entitled, *An Humble Attempt to Promote an Explicit Agreement and Visible Union of God's People Through the World, in Extraordinary Prayer, for the Revival of Religion, and the Advancement of Christ's Kingdom on Earth, Pursuant to Scripture Promises and Prophesies Concerning the Last Time.* Now they knew how to write book titles in those days! Edwards wrote this book in response to a request that he had received from some ministers in the Church of Scotland, particularly a man named John Erskine, who had written and asked him to write a book which would be a call to prayer for the ministers of Scotland. It was to be a call to Christian unity in prayer and for revival. This was the result, this "humble attempt" by Jonathan Edwards. It was sent to Scotland and apparently proved useful for a few years. There was a revival of religion in Edinburgh, Dundee and several of the cities of Scotland. This book contributed to that but you don't hear very much of it anymore. In fact, the book went out of print and it didn't seem to be quoted or cited by anyone for a long time.

Almost three decades later John Erskine, now a very aged minister in the Church of Scotland, received a letter from John Sutcliff, the Baptist pastor of Olney. Sutcliff said to Erskine, "We Baptists down here in England are so poor, and we have so few resources, could you please send us some good gospel literature, even things that you no longer use but that you have read. We would be glad to receive them and would put them to profitable use."

Well, John Erskine went up to his attic and dusted off his shelves and picked up a few books he probably hadn't read in twenty or thirty years. Among them was Jonathan Edwards' *An Humble Attempt.* He packaged it off to Sutcliff along with a few other things. Sutcliff opened it and as he read it his heart was set on fire by what his eyes saw on the page! He felt that God was calling him to issue a call for prayer, just as Jonathan Edwards had in 1748 when the book was first published.

In 1784, these very words are uttered by John Sutcliff after reading this book by Jonathan Edwards before the Baptist pastors of Northampton:

> The grand object of prayer is to be that the Holy Spirit may be poured down on our ministers and churches, that sinners may be converted, the saints edified, the interest of religion revived, and the name of God glorified. At the same time remember, we trust you will not confine your requests to your own societies; or to your own immediate connection; let the whole interest of the Redeemer be affectionately remembered, and the spread of the Gospel to the most distant parts of the habitable globe be the object of your most fervent requests.

It was a clarion call for the Baptists of Northampton to unite themselves together in fervent prayer for world evangelization and world missions. This was in 1784, the year after William Carey had been baptized in the river Nene and the Baptist churches in that association began to meet regularly on the first Tuesday of every month for a prayer meeting. And let me tell you, it was a prayer meeting! Sometimes our prayer meetings today consist of little more than fellowship together, sometimes a little devotion and maybe a little business meeting. But these folks gathered to *pray*. They prayed for revival —that God would open up the doors of their own hearts for revival.

For nearly ten years before Carey and his family finally set sail for India in 1793, the Baptist churches of Northampton had been pouring out their hearts to God in regular, fervent and united prayer for missions, awakening and revival. Carey acknowledged that had this not occurred, there never would have been the impetus and open door that God provided for him. So one of the things that preceded Carey's great missionary call, was a revival of prayer on the part of God's people.

A Revival of Theology.

The second great precursor to the Baptist missionary movement was a revival of theology. Since the seventeenth century, Baptists in England had been divided into two different groups.

There were the General Baptists, that is, Arminian Baptists who traced their lineage back to John Smyth and Thomas Helwys. Early on in the seventeenth century, the General Baptists had been greatly used of God in evangelism and missions but by the eighteenth century the vast majority of General Baptist churches were no longer aggressively evangelistic in winning many to faith in Christ and planting churches. Rather, they had been swept away in the tide of rationalistic theology. Many of them had even come to the point of denying the deity of Christ and the doctrine of the Trinity. Indeed, a large number of General Baptists had become Unitarians, so the General Baptist movement at this time in England was at perhaps its lowest ebb. Later in the eighteenth century there was something of an evangelical revival among these General Baptists led by a man named Dan Taylor. This revival was known as the "New Connexion." But by the time Carey came on the scene, the General Baptists were, by and large, given over to Unitarian theology and some ceased to be Baptists altogether.

The second group of Baptists—the dominant group numerically as far back as the early seventeenth century—were the Particular Baptists. They were the Calvinistic Baptists of England. They adhered to the theology as set forth in the First London Confession of 1644 and then the Second London Confession of 1677 and 1689. They adhered without reservation to what Andrew Fuller and others called "the discriminating doctrines of grace." The Particular Baptists were, by and large, the mainstay of the Baptist denomination in England.

It was the Particular Baptist denomination that Carey himself joined when he was baptized by John Ryland, Jr. in the river Nene. But of late, there had arisen within this Particular, Calvinist Baptist movement, hyper-Calvinism, a theology that Andrew Fuller called "false Calvinism." False Calvinism was opposed to the Calvinism Fuller believed, which he referred to as "strict Calvinism."

The dispute had to do with the propriety of preaching the gospel and calling on sinners to repent. The false Calvinists taught and believed that it was wrong for sinners to be admonished to repent of their sins and turn to Christ. Later, Charles Haddon Spurgeon would say of it, "This was the theology which chilled our churches to the very soul." This false Calvinism was the very theology against which Andrew Fuller and William Carey would react.

Carey was greatly influenced here by Fuller, and Fuller again by Jonathan Edwards. Edwards had published *An Inquiry Into The Freedom Of The Will* in which basically he tried to show (and I think did show successfully) that there was no inherent contradiction between evangelism and Calvinism. He showed that there was no contradiction between the universal obligation of all who hear the gospel to repent and believe in Christ and the sovereign decision of God to save those whom He had chosen to save before the foundations of the world. The failure to believe, Edwards argued, was the result of a perverted human will, and the distinction that Jonathan Edwards made between natural and moral ability became the key which unlocked for Andrew Fuller the mystery of divine sovereignty and human responsibility. He wanted to assert both without compromising either and this he did in a book published in 1785 entitled, *The Gospel Worthy of All Acceptation*. In that book, Fuller set forth the following six propositions, which formed the core of the missionary theology that under-girded William Carey in the English Particular Baptists' early missionary effort:

1. Unconverted sinners are commanded, exhorted, and invited to believe in Christ for salvation.
2. Everyone is bound to receive what God reveals.
3. The Gospel, though a message of pure grace, requires the obedient response of faith.
4. The lack of faith is a heinous sin, which is described in the Scriptures as human depravity.
5. God has threatened and inflicted the most awful punishments on sinners for their not believing on the Lord Jesus Christ.
6. The Bible requires of all persons certain spiritual exercises which are represented as their duty. These include repentance and faith, no less than the requirement to love God, fear God, and glorify God. That no one can accomplish these things apart from the bestowal of the Holy Spirit is clear. Nonetheless, the ob-

ligation remains. In this respect, man's duty, and God's gift are the same thing seen from different perspectives.

This was a Calvinistic theology that did not in any respect compromise any of the discriminating doctrines of grace. It was fully in accord with the Second London Confession of 1689 and, indeed, we might say with the Westminster Confession and the Synod of Dort before that. But it nonetheless had to overcome the resistance of what Fuller called false Calvinism—the idea that the promiscuous preaching of the gospel is something that is inappropriate for believers.

William Carey was to develop his missionary insight out of these basic truths. If sinners are obliged to repent and believe in Christ, he asked, was there not another obligation to be considered? Were not Christians—themselves delivered from darkness into light—most urgently obliged to present the claims of Christ to those who had never heard? Fuller was the theologian, Carey the visionary and activist of the Missionary Awakening.

EXPECT GREAT THINGS FROM GOD, ATTEMPT GREAT THINGS FOR GOD!

Theology and vision came together in perhaps the most famous incident in his life and the one that is always written about in various biographies of Carey. It occurred at a ministers' meeting in Northampton, presided over by John Ryland, Sr., the venerable Baptist leader of that part of England. Following their prayer and Scripture study the floor was opened for topics for discussion and Carey himself raised the issue of whether indeed the gospel should not be carried to the ends of earth so that God would use it for the conversion of the lost and the heathen who had never heard. John Ryland, Sr. said to him, "Young man, sit down! When God wants to convert the heathen He will do it without your aid or mine."

Now, as a matter of fact, God did do it without Ryland, Sr.'s aid, but He did not do it without William Carey's aid. Carey was asked to preach the annual associational sermon. At the appointed time, the Northamptonshire Baptist Association met in Nottingham at Friar Lane Chapel. The place was packed and crowded as it was the last day, the climactic moment when the concluding sermon of the association meeting would be preached.

Carey took his text from Isaiah 54—a remarkable passage of Scripture. It begins with an exhortation from God: "Sing, O barren woman, you who never bore a child, burst into song, shout for joy, you who never were in labor." The passage presents the picture of a woman, a widow, for her husband has been carried away into captivity to Babylon, and she is desolate. She has no one to care for her in her old age. She sits by the gates of Jerusalem in dust and ashes, mourning, crying, lamenting her terrible estate. But God says to her, "Sing, O barren woman, burst into song, and shout for joy" because God has something very special in store for you. And then the Word of the Lord, "Enlarge the place of your tents, stretch your tent curtains wide, do not hold back, lengthen your cords, strengthen your stakes." Move out! Claim this great victory for God! Don't sit there in desolation and pity but attempt something tremendous for God. It was out of that text that Carey came with that marvelous watchword, "Expect great things from God! Attempt great things for God."

Now it would seem to be the counsel of folly to be saying this to such a woman. She had no family, she had no husband, no children, no support, no means of living. How could she possibly enlarge the place of her tent or stretch her tent curtains wide? She didn't even have a tent with curtains! She was sitting, mourning in the ashes at the gate of Jerusalem's defeat. But the Word of the Lord came, "Do not be afraid. Fear not, fear not!"

That tremendous word of Isaiah is repeated again and again in these great chapters, "Do not be afraid. Do not fear disgrace." Why not? "For your Maker is your husband, the

LORD Almighty is His name." God is calling you to attempt great things and expect great things, but you are not asked to go in your own power or your own strength! Your Maker is your Husband. He will provide for you far better than any earthly husband could. The LORD Almighty is His name, His sovereignty, His omnipotence, His power, His greatness, His holiness, His almightiness. The Holy One of Israel is your Redeemer. He is called the God of all the earth. Not just the God of the Baptists of Northampton, and not just the God of the Christians in England, but the God of all the earth. This was the challenge and the charge that William Carey delivered at that associational meeting. Expect great things and attempt great things.

John Ryland, Jr. was present, and he said, "Had all the people lifted up their voice and wept, as the children of Israel did at Bochim, I should not have wondered, so clearly did Carey prove the criminality of our supineness in the cause of God."

Well, the sermon was over, and whatever they said in those days to indicate it was a good sermon was said, but now it was time to get back on their horses and go home. The associational meeting was over and it seemed that the meeting was about to be dismissed without any plan of action, but Carey reached up and took hold of the sleeve of Andrew Fuller, his friend, who was moderating that meeting. He said, in an imploring voice that could be heard throughout the whole building, "Is nothing again to be done, sir? Is nothing again to be done?" It was not exactly a response you could ignore. They had to do something. Do you know what they did? They appointed a committee! You know, the best way to kill any good idea is to appoint a committee to study it.

They appointed a study committee thinking, "Perhaps that will satisfy brother Carey—he's a bit of a zealot you know. These things are wonderful. It is a great exposition of Isaiah 54 and we will consider this." The committee resolved that a plan be prepared for the next ministers meeting at Kettering for forming a "Baptist Society for Propagating the Gospel Among the Heathen." That's what it was called.

But Carey would not let that committee alone. He met with them, pleaded with them, and pumped them with all the new information he had gathered. So when they met in the city of Kettering, October 2, 1792, to consider this request from the association, Carey was there and he had with him all the recent mission sheets from the Moravians. The Moravians were those who would go anywhere. They lived what we sing in one of our missionary hymns, "From Greenland's icy mountains, to the tropic climes." The Moravians were those who would go and preach the gospel to Eskimos in Greenland or to the slaves in the West Indies. Carey brought with him the reports of these Moravians and said, "Listen, brethren, look at what the Moravians are doing. If the Moravians can do this, should the Baptists be one step behind?"

He was trying to shame them into doing something by showing them what the Moravians were doing. Finally, under Carey's insistence and their own burdening hearts that were beginning to catch something of his vision, they agreed to form a Particular Baptist Society for the Propagation of the Gospel Among the Heathens. On that evening they took up their first missionary offering. It was taken in a snuffbox which has been preserved to this day. You can go see it at the Baptist Missionary Society Headquarters in Oxford. A snuffbox! It contained 13 pounds, 2 shillings and 6 sixpence. That was the result of their missionary offering but it was the first fruits of what became a great, great harvest for God.

The day came for Carey's departure. They met again at Olney, the church where Carey had been originally denied ordination but then later ordained, the church where John Sutcliff, his dear mentor and friend, was pastor. Carey preached a final farewell sermon to all those who had come together. He preached from Romans 12:1-2. He would be the living sacrifice that Paul calls forth to carry the gospel to far away India. And then they stood to sing a hymn.

And must I part with all I have, Jesus, Jesus my
Lord for Thee.

> This is my joy, since Thou hast done much more
>   than this for me.
> Yes let it go, one look from Thee will more than
>   make amends
> For all the losses I sustain of credit, riches,
>   friends.

He must have pondered those first four words of the second verse "Yes, let it go" because his wife refused to go with him. His father thought he was crazy and the Baptist "bigwigs" in London who had heard about this hair-brained scheme refused to support it. They thought nothing would come of it. Carey was saying goodbye to all of that.

> Yes let it go, one look from Thee will more than
>   make amends
> For all the losses I sustain of credit, riches,
>   friends.

That's the kind of commitment that stands at the fountainhead of the great Baptist Missionary Movement—a movement we are a part of and that we can claim as our own. If we are serious about the gospel and the missionary obligation that William Carey put forth at such great price to himself, it may also be necessary for us to say, "Yes, let it go."

31.
THE LIFE AND MISSION
OF WILLIAM CAREY—PART 2
TIMOTHY GEORGE
1992 Southern Baptist Founders Conference

IN concluding this study on the life and mission of William Carey, two different aspects need to be considered. The first is Carey's plan for missions which he set forth in his *Enquiry*, this great little masterpiece that Carey wrote and published in 1792.

The second pertains to some of the aspects of his ministry in India and particularly some of the great themes and principles that stand out in his forty-one years of uninterrupted missionary service. What can we learn today from the legacy of William Carey? The study of these great men of God from ages past should never be motivated by merely antiquarian interest. They are given to us as a part of that great cloud of witnesses that we might learn from them, and that we ourselves might run that race that is set before us with endurance and patience, looking unto Jesus most of all, but also unto those who have come before us in the family of faith.

CAREY'S PLAN FOR MISSIONS

William Carey set forth his ideas of missionary service in a book called *An Enquiry into the Use Of Means for the Spreading of the Gospel to the Heathen*. It is not a very long book. It forms an appendix in my Carey biography. There are several presuppositions that underlie his approach to missions.

The last five words in the first paragraph of this little book set the tone for his whole approach and theology of missions. He speaks of "the character of God Himself." This is what motivated William Carey.

There is no doubt that Carey had great compassion for the millions and millions of people in the world who are lost and perishing, inasmuch as he would weep when he looked at a globe, remembering that pagans were lost without any knowledge of Jesus Christ. But it was not primarily that fact alone which motivated him to leave everything behind and go halfway around the world to bear witness to Jesus Christ. Rather, it was the character of God Himself.

The God we serve and the God who has redeemed us is a missionary God. He is a God who in no way was obligated to save the world. The idea that God was obligated to save is still an idea that we hear preached and taught from time to time, but it is totally erroneous. God would have been not one wit less God, less just or less powerful, had He consigned the entire world to perdition. He didn't have to redeem us. But out of His great love and over-splashing mercy He chose to redeem us. That is what the doctrine of election in the Bible is all about. God Himself is first and foremost the Missionary with a capital "M" and all of us who follow His command are missionaries with a small "m."

A few years ago, David Wells, whom I think is one of the finest theologians in America today, published a little book called *God the Evangelist.* I recommend it to you as a wonderful little primer on biblical evangelism. God is the evangelist—not you, or me, or Billy Graham, or R. F. Gates, or anybody else. God is the One who really draws men and women out of sin and unto Himself, and God is the Missionary. Unless God is the One who goes and carries the message Himself by His Spirit, everything that we do is in vain. William Carey knew and believed that and staked his life upon that—the character of God Himself.

Another presupposition underlying Carey's plan for missions involves the history of salvation. In his introduction to the *Enquiry,* Carey masterfully reviews the history of salvation beginning with creation, the fall, the various stages of apostasy and repentance that we read of in the Old Testament, culminating in the appearance on earth of the Messiah, Jesus Christ, our Lord. His birth, His life, His death, His resurrection, His ascension, and the promise of His coming again— this is the gospel, the good news that God has invaded our planet and come among us as one of us. Carey reviews that in a sweeping introduction to the *Enquiry* and then he continues that survey in the history of the church. We sometimes think of William Carey as the first missionary or the "Father of Modern Missions" and there is a sense in which that is certainly a well-deserved title. But Carey didn't see himself as a lone ranger or as the first one ever to go forth. He saw himself in continuity with those faithful men and women of God of ages past who had born witness to the gospel of grace in an age of darkness and apostasy. He saw himself in continuity with the Reformers of the sixteenth century.

I have a chapter in my book entitled "The New Reformation," and there is a sense in which I feel that is the best way to understand the life and mission of Carey as well as the whole great missionary awakening that he inaugurated. It was a return to, a furtherance of, an extension of, the great principles of biblical Christianity that were recovered in the sixteenth-century reformation of the church. In many respects that was true and Carey saw himself in continuity with Luther, Calvin, Wycliffe and those who had come before him, bearing witness in difficult days.

We must see ourselves in this way as well. We must not think of ourselves as the first to have invented the gospel, or the first even to have thought of a way to carry the gospel into the world. We belong to this great chain of believers and witnesses. We can learn from them and they are a part of the same great movement of God that we belong to as well.

Carey emphasized the imperative of the great commission: "Go ye into all the world and preach the gospel to every creature." He challenged the hyper-Calvinism that prevailed in certain circles of Particular Baptist life in that day. There were often occasions when some of those dear brothers and sisters would come together in a service and they would actually sing anti-missionary hymns. It's hard for us to imagine. We sing these great missionary hymns, "O Zion Haste" and many others like it but they would actually sing anti-missionary hymns! One of them went like this:

> Go ye into all the world,
> The Lord of old did say,
> But now where He has placed thee,
> There He would have thee stay.

The idea, you see, was that the great commission had expired with the death of the apostles and that it was no longer relevant in the life of the church today. Carey said, "There is no statute of limitations on the Great Commission. 'Go ye' means you, and it means me, and it means now." He took the imperative word of Jesus to heart.

He also dealt in this *Enquiry* with certain practical objections to missions. One example is, "Oh, it's so far away. The distance alone would prohibit our carrying the gospel to those in far off lands." Carey says, "Look at the merchants. They sail the seven seas in the tall ships carrying wool and cheese and all kinds of goods. Shouldn't we be willing to do as much as they for the sake of eternal souls?"

Somebody else says, "They're so uncivilized over there. How could you go into such an uncivilized place?" Carey replied, "Just think what England was like before they brought the gospel here, and what it is like today." Here William Carey showed himself not to be a pious idealist, but to be a very hard-nosed practical Christian. He said, "It is not enough just to go out and trust the Lord. Along with the Bible, you need to take some instruments of agriculture, you need to take a shovel, and a plow, and some seed, and corn, and learn how to cultivate a piece of ground so you can sustain yourself in that far off land."

"What about the languages, they are so different?" Carey

responds to this objection, "Anybody with a good dictionary can learn a language in two weeks. I've done it." Well, he may have been exaggerating a little bit there. At least some of our students struggle a little more than two weeks with Greek and Hebrew, but he has a point.

"What about the fulfillment of prophesy?" There were those who said, "Well, yes, we need to carry the gospel in all the world, but there are some prophesies, that haven't been fulfilled yet. What about Revelation 11 and these two witnesses that are foretold?" Carey says, "There is not a single prophesy in the Word of God that prevents us from carrying the gospel to the furthest corner of the world." Indeed, the last year of his ministry at his church in Harvey Lane in Leicester, William Carey spent an entire year preaching expository sermons through the book of Revelation though not a one of them has survived.

I would give my eye-teeth if I could go to England and find somewhere a cache of those sermon notes on the book of Revelation. Whatever his eschatological views, he was certain that we don't have to sit around waiting for the two witnesses to appear or for something else to happen in the book of Revelation in order to go to all the world.

Carey then took up another objection that we still hear today: "This would be a fine thing to do, but we have work enough at home. Why should we go off to India, or Africa, or the South Sea Islands, when we have work enough at home?" Carey of course admitted that indeed there were lost people everywhere, but what about those who have never heard about Jesus Christ for the first time and who have never seen a Bible? Shouldn't we carry the Word of God to them and proclaim the same gospel of grace to those who have never heard?

Carey suggested that perhaps God was opening a door for them to go. He surveyed the whole world and concluded that there were 731 million people in the world, more than half of whom were pagans, more than one fifth of whom were Muslim, and many others Papists, lost in the errors of the church of Rome. Even when factoring in the Anglicans, Lutherans, and the Dissenters, including Baptists, Carey believed that the vastness of the error left no excuse to stay at home. What can Christians do? Pray. This was the driving conviction behind the prayer revival that preceded Carey's mission. Also plan. Plan carefully. That is why Carey compiled all these statistics and carefully studied the different populations and climates of the different continents. This enables us to go forth with the very best plan that we can have under God as we do mission work.

Give. Carey said that if every Christian would tithe his income, we could carry the gospel around the world. Give liberally and give sacrificially.

Finally, Carey said Christians could go. Now, up until this point, Carey himself had not particularly committed his own life to be a missionary. He had called the church to this great awakening, and he had set forth a plan in his *Enquiry*, but would Carey go himself? He was meeting now with this little missionary committee that the Particular Baptists had brought together in England. Carey was focusing particularly on the South Sea Islands and Tahiti. He had read about that in Captain Cook's journal and that's where he thought that they should send the first missionaries. Then Carey received a letter from a man he had never heard of before. His name was John Thomas, a person with whom Carey's life would be linked in a very providential way. Thomas was a doctor. In fact, he was the first medical missionary and he had actually gone to India and served one stint as a missionary there. Actually, he hadn't gone as a missionary because that was illegal. He had gone as a chaplain and tried to work with the Anglicans there but had fallen out of favor with them.

John Thomas was one of those people who is so creative, so energetic, so zealous, so sincere, and sometimes just so plain stupid. Thomas was quixotic. He didn't seem to sail on an even keel and would perhaps prove to be as much of a burden as a blessing in the long run to Carey. But in any event, God used John Thomas to bring into Carey's heart the vision of a mission to India.

It was January 9,1793, about four months after this little committee had been formed in Kettering. They met together and Carey preached in the morning on Revelation 22:12, the words of Jesus, "'Behold I come quickly, and my reward is with me,' says the Lord." The afternoon was given to prayer and then the evening came when they had to decide what they would do. Carey presented this challenge by reading the letter from John Thomas regarding the need for the mission to India where an associate was needed to go back with Thomas to plant the gospel. Everybody in the group asked Carey, "Will you go?" The minutes record very simply and powerfully that he readily answered in the affirmative.

It was his moment of commitment, his moment of decision, and he said, "Yes." From that time on, his face was set like flint for Jerusalem and he could not turn back. Andrew Fuller was present that evening, and he said later on, "From Mr. Thomas's accounts, we saw there was a gold mine in India, but It seemed almost as deep as the center of the earth. Who will venture to explore it? 'I will go down,' said Mr. Carey to his brethren, 'but remember that you must hold the ropes.'" Fuller responded, "We solemnly engage to do so; nor while we live, shall we desert him."

The way in which Carey's actual voyage to India came about is a remarkable story. I won't go into detail, but his church was not at all willing for him to go at first. He had come to Leicester to minister when the church was in a shambles. God had blessed the ministry. They had added a new wing on the church and the pews were packed. Things were going great. And now, would God call their pastor to just leave all the revival they were experiencing at Harvey Lane Church to go halfway around the world? It was a hard thing for his church to let him go.

Then his family, particularly his wife, Dorothy, refused to go. Dorothy has sometimes been given a short shrift in Carey biographies; however, I tried to treat her a little more sympathetically and to look at it from her point of view. Here she was, married to a man who had been eking out a living as a cobbler. They had three sons, and now she discovered, the very same time that she was expecting their fourth (two little girls had already died in infancy and early years of childhood), that her husband feels God is leading them to go all the way around the world with no means of support and no promised income. Dorothy refused to go.

Carey said to her, "Alright, you stay here. I'll go and I'll take little Felix. [Felix was his eldest son, who was eight years old at the time.] He and I will go and we'll plant the work there, and then I'll come back and get you."

So, William Carey, his son Felix, John Thomas, and his family set out for India, leaving behind Carey's wife and the rest of the family. They got as far as the Isle of Wight. They had to wait there, because there was a war with France going on and they had to have a convoy of ships so they could sail together. While they were waiting, already admitted on the ship and ready to sail for India, there was a knock at their cabin one night. It was the bailiff, the sheriff! He had come to arrest John Thomas who had skipped out on some debts that he owed. So the captain of the ship said "off with you," and he threw off John Thomas, William Carey and his little son. Mrs. Thomas and their children sailed on to India. John Thomas, William Carey, and Felix Carey were left behind. What were they to do? It seemed that God had slammed the door of providence in their face.

Well, they stored their belongings and baggage in Portsmouth and traveled to London. Carey had the idea to walk to India. He said, "Okay, if I can't get a ride on a ship, I'll walk. I'll cross the English Channel and I'll just make out across land. I'll just walk to India." And he was dead serious.

Here again, John Thomas showed himself to be a little more street smart than that. He went to the coffee houses in London and began to ask people, "Is there any ship headed for India that we might get passage on?" Of course this was very unusual and irregular, but someone gave him the name of a ship. It was a Danish ship that was expected any moment in the straits of Dover.

Hope sprang again in their hearts. William and Felix dashed off in a coach to their home in Northampton for one last farewell. Carey pleaded with his wife to go but again, she refused. They were going to get their final belongings and head for Dover when John Thomas said, "No, we must go back and implore her again to come." So they went back that night and John Thomas said to her, "Unless you go to India, you will never see your family again." It was too much. Dorothy said, "Alright, I'll go, but only if I can take my sister with me." Her sister, whose name was Kitty, also agreed to go.

So they set out for Dover and made the ship as it was sailing out into the straits of Dover. Off they headed for India, this rag-tag, illegal band of missionaries, brought together in such a marvelous way.

Carey wrote in his journal as the ship set sail from the white cliffs of Dover. Looking at that verdant countryside as the shadows of evening fell, he wrote, "This, I hope, was a day of joy to my soul. I was returned to take all my family with me, and to enjoy all the blessings which I had surrendered up to God. This is an Ebenezer which I raise to God and I hope to be strengthened whenever I reflect upon it." Every single person in that little missionary party onboard that little Danish ship would die in India without ever setting eyes on their native land, the only exception being Kitty, the sister of Dorothy.

On board the ship, Carey immediately began to entreat Thomas to teach him the Bengali language. So on that long journey from England to India, day after day, he would learn the basic language and grammar of the Bengali tongue. He wrote in his diary, "I am very desirous that my children may pursue the same work [of translating the Scriptures into the languages of the world]; and now intend to bring up one in the study of Sanskrit, and another of Persian. O, may God give them grace to fit them for the work!"

One of the remarkable things about William Carey is that every single one of his surviving children became a faithful missionary witness of the gospel. This says something of the care that their father placed in them even from the time they were nursing infants, as one of them, little Jabez, was when they set sail from England.

CAREY'S MINISTRY IN INDIA

Carey's ministry in India can be divided into three periods chronologically.

1793-1800: A time of struggle and beginnings, when Carey was often laboring alone in great distress and against tremendous difficulties.

1800-1814: The Golden Age of Carey's ministry in India. It was at this time when he gathered around him at the little colony of Serampore a team of fellow missionaries, equally devoted as he to the evangelization of India. Among them were William Ward, the printer of that community, and Joshua and Hannah Marshman, who ran the schools and were great evangelists with Carey in the work. This was a time of growth and prosperity.

1814-1834: The last two decades of Carey's life. This was a time of consolidation in the midst of increasing struggle and difficulty, as the forces of dissipation began to work themselves out in the mission. 1814 is the key year, because that is the year in which Andrew Fuller died in England. As long as Fuller was alive, at least one of the rope holders was steady and persevering. But once Fuller died, and particularly after the other friends who had known Carey (like John Ryland, Jr. and John Sutcliff) began to pass away, a new generation came which knew not William Carey. There came to be increasing tension between the mission in Serampore and the Baptist Mission Society back in England. Eventually there was a rupture in that relationship and a schism that caused Carey great, great pain to the day he died.

Looking at this whole scope of forty-one years without a furlough, without ever returning to his native land but of constant, incessant, persevering labor for the Lord in India, what stands out as the great principles of Carey's ministry? Three of them deserve serious consideration.

A Faithful Walk in the Face of Adversity.

The first great principle of Carey's ministry is a faithful walk with God in the face of adversity. Carey faced many challenging difficulties. The missionary group entered India as illegal aliens. In those days India was under the control of the East India Company which held a monopoly on all comings and goings out of India and they refused to allow anyone to go to India as a missionary. It wasn't until 1813 when William Wilberforce and other great evangelical leaders of Parliament passed the India Bill that India was opened up in some measure to those who would actually go as bona fide missionaries.

In this earlier time, however, Carey's party was refused a permit to enter the country. So when the ship arrived at the mouth of the Hooghly River, Carey and his little missionary party had to be led off the ship and put on little dinghies. Then they traveled under cover of night into the Port of Calcutta lest they be discovered and sent back to England.

All through the first years of Carey's ministry he was on a most precarious basis as an illegal alien in a country where he had no legal right to be ministering the gospel. In addition to that, there was the grinding poverty and the physical danger. Having to support his wife and growing family with basically no wherewithal to do that, after a year or so of trying to eke out a living in Calcutta, he moved them to a place called Debhatta, some thirty or forty miles to the east. It was in a place known as the Sundarbans, and this is how he described that region of the country where he moved his family in 1794:

> The Sundarbans are a land of monsters dire. The rivers swarm with hideous alligators, which we often see basking on the shores, or rather imbedded in the mud, of which the banks consist; tigers of the fiercest kind pass and repass every night

over the ground where the people are at work in the day; and snakes of monstrous size and deadly poison abound.

This is where he was trying to eke out a living with all the dangers of a jungle teeming with threatening animals all about him. Carey did move north to a place called Mudnabatty where he was appointed again, through the good offices of John Thomas, as a plantation director for an indigo plant. Here things again were very, very bad.

Carey's little son Peter caught a terrible fever and lingered until finally he died at age five. This was a severe blow to Carey and particularly to Dorothy Carey. They themselves had to dress the body of their son for burial because no native would touch a dead body. It was a violation of the caste system.

In a sense, Dorothy Carey herself never recovered from the death of their son Peter. They had another son, Jonathan, a year or so later, but from the time of Peter's death, she continued steadily to decline and deteriorate until she lost whatever sanity she had when she left England. She began to make wild accusations against her husband, false accusations of having affairs with other women and things that were so far from the truth that they were preposterous to those who heard them. Finally she began to threaten not only her life, but the lives of others. She tried to kill Carey on at least one occasion. She had to be bound to a chair and often held against her will until finally she died in 1807, thus ending the sad, sad story of Dorothy Carey. All the while Carey was faithful in his support of her. He could have put her in what was known in those days as an insane asylum, but it was a terrible place and he knew it. So he himself provided care for her until her death in 1807.

Other trials included the rupture with the Baptist Missionary Society and the desertion of John Thomas. On one day Thomas would want to go out and win the world and on another day he had taken a job 25 miles down the river and spent all their money. It was up and down, and a great frustration for Carey.

What sustained him during this time? Well, during these days he confided in his diary the emotional strain of his spiritual struggles: "In this wilderness, O how my soul wanders! I thirst, but find nothing to drink. O Lord, I beseech thee, deliver my soul! ... Feel very much degenerated in my soul; scarcely any heart for God."

What sustained him during those days? The Sabbaths were especially difficult. He had been a pastor of a loving, affirming, growing church back in Leicester. Now he was on the edge of a jungle, thousands of miles away. Sometimes it required two years to get a letter from home. There was no contact with fellow believers, his wife was depressed and deteriorating, his children were often sick and one of them dead, and there was no steady way to make an income. He said one March 16 day, "Such another Sabbath I hope I should never pass. What a hell it would be to be always with those who fear not God."

What sustained him during those days? The Word of God sustained him. The Scriptures he would read in the various languages he was learning until they soaked into his very soul. Prayer also sustained him during those days. Every Sabbath day he would mark the time on the calendar when he knew that back in England the believers in the little church where he had pastored and those of like mind were praying for him. Whenever that was, whatever time of the day it was in India, when they were praying back in England, Carey would stop and spend that time in meditation and prayer. He felt great sustenance in knowing that at that very moment the throne of heaven was being besought by those who loved him and had sent him forth in the name of Christ.

Godly readings sustained him. Outside of the Scriptures, the book which meant the most to Carey in the difficult days was the *Diary of David Brainerd*, which had been edited by Jonathan Edwards. It was Edwards' edited version of Brainerd's *Diary* that Carey read and reread and reread again, because, of course, Brainerd too, experienced some of those same travails in his soul that Carey knew in India. If William Carey was the Father of Modern Missions, Andrew Fuller was the Stepfather, and Jonathan Edwards the Grandfather.

Through it all, Carey had a faithful walk in the face of adversity. Why should we think it will be any different for us? Charles Haddon Spurgeon, near the end of his life, looked back over his own great difficulties, the depression that he experienced from time to time, the controversies in which he was engaged, and the attacks which he sustained, and he said,

> All the way to heaven we shall only get there by the skin of our teeth. We shall not go to heaven sailing along with sails swelling to the breeze like seabirds with their fair white wings, but we shall proceed full often with sails rent to ribbons, with masts creaking, and the ship's pump at work both by night and day. We shall reach the City at the shutting of the gate, but not an hour before.

We need to hear those words and we need to tell them to young ministers when we send them forth into the battle. We need to remind ourselves that God did not call us to a luxury liner, but to a battle ship. That's not salvation by works. There's not anybody in the history of the Christian church who believed more in the sovereignty of God and the grace of God than Charles Haddon Spurgeon. It's the grace of God, however, that puts us in the thick of the fight. But the grace of God also sustains us for every battle that we must encounter. William Carey experienced that in his life again and again. He said in his diary, "I feel that it is good to commit my soul, my body, and my all into the hands of God. Then the world appears little, the promises great, and God an all-sufficient portion." A faithful walk in the face of adversity.

An Uncompromised Gospel In a Culture of Pluralism.

The second great principle in Carey's life and ministry was an uncompromised gospel in a culture of pluralism. Now pluralism is a word that we hear rather often today and it is frequently presented as something new and unheard of in the history of the church. It is often spoken of as something that we must face as no one has ever faced it before. That isn't really true. Pluralism is as old as the Ten Commandments, where God said, "You shall have no other gods before me." Pluralism is as old as Elijah on Mt. Carmel when he faced the prophets of Baal and said to the children of Israel, "Choose this day which god you're going to serve."

Pluralism is not new. William Carey faced pluralism in a major way when he went to India, for there was hardly any other nation on the face of the earth more religious than India. The people were mainly Hindu, but also many millions were Muslim, and they were devoutly religious.

What would Carey do today if he were governed by some of the principles which guide our modern missiological thinking going into a place like that? Would he try to establish a point of contact with some of those folks, maybe think about all the good in their religion and point to that so there could be a basis for discussion? Well, this is what he said to a group of Hindus: "I told them that their books were like a loaf of bread, in which was a considerable quantity of good flour, but also a very malignant poison, which made the whole so poisonous that whoever should eat of it would die." That was William Carey's approach. Then he went on to present the suitableness and glory of the gospel, focusing on the infinitely great sacrifice for the infinite guilt of sinful men offered by Christ on the cross.

Eternal life and the benefits of grace are to be found in Christ alone. It is a free salvation for poor and perishing sinners. He didn't try to water down the gospel to the lowest common denominator. He preached the theme of this Founders conference—a whole Gospel for a lost and dying world, a world that was going straight to hell. William Carey did not shrink back from talking and preaching and teaching about hell. There was a great deal of misunderstanding about hell because the Hindus believed in the transmigration of souls. They saw life on earth as one stage in a long process of begetting and becoming through which the soul passes on its way to Nirvana, the ultimate release from desire and death, when the individual's self is absorbed into the great impersonal force of the universe. That was their belief and before reaching that stage the soul might have to pass through as many as seven heavens and twenty-one hells. So when he preached hell to them, they understood it in the context of their own Hindu mythology about this great transmigration of souls.

In one of his sermons Carey mentioned hell as the ultimate destiny of unbelievers and several of his hearers stayed to talk with him about it. One of them said, "I suppose sir, that we shall be treated there as we would at the Dinagepore jail." Carey answered, "No. In prison, only the body can be afflicted, but in hell the soul. A person may escape from prison but not from hell. Death puts an end to imprisonment, but in hell they shall never die. There God's wrath will be poured upon them for ever, and they must dwell in endless fire."

Why did Carey preach like that? Because he wanted to offend people? Because he wanted to turn people off? No. He preached that way because it was true. He preached that way because he had no choice to preach anything other than the gospel of God's grace reflected in the death of Christ who experienced hell itself on the cross. He would travel back and forth in his little boat from village to village. For seven years he preached faithfully without seeing one single convert to his ministry. Imagine that! Some mission boards would send him packing back home. He said, "I feel as a farmer does about his crop. Sometimes I think the seed is springing, a little blast and my hopes are gone like a cloud. There were only weeds which appeared, or if a little corn sprung up it quickly dies, being either choked with the weeds or parched up by the sun of persecution. Yet I still hope in God and will go forth in His strength and make mention of His righteousness, even of His only." He did just that for seven years until finally there came a great day of rejoicing when a carpenter named Krishna Pal heard the gospel, responded to it and finally came to saving faith in Jesus Christ.

There had been some professions of faith before this but Carey refused to baptize them unless they were willing to break caste and eat a common meal with other believers. He said, "The renunciation of caste is a means to test the sincerity of new converts." He wrote back to Fuller in England and asked his advice about that and Fuller said he was doing the right thing. "A willingness to lose caste may be as great a proof of sincerity with you as with anything that our converts [in England] can offer to be with us." What was so important about breaking caste and eating together? Jesus did that in the gospels. He ate, and that shared meal represented the common faith of Jesus Christ, which transcended all of those distinctions imposed by society and politics and social status. William Carey said, "Unless you are willing to eat a meal together and to renounce caste, you will not be baptized."

Finally Krishna Pal came to that point of commitment where he was willing to do that on December 28, 1800, the last Sunday of the year and the turn of the new century. They were now in Serampore, the new community. This is how it is recorded.

> After our English Service, at which I preached on baptism, we went to the riverside, immediately opposite our gate when the Governor, a number of Europeans and Portuguese, and many Hindus and Mohammedans attended. We sang in Bengali, "Jesus and shall it ever be?" Carey then spoke in Bengali, particularly declaring that we did not think the water sacred, but water only, [because of course the Hindus have this idea of the magical potency of the Ganges River and its sacred power to wash away their guilt. Carey had to

make it very clear that when we baptize somebody
it is not because the water is sacred, it is water
only] and that the one from amongst them about
to be baptized professed by this act to put off all
sins...and to put on Christ.
After prayer, he went down to the bank into the
water, taking Felix in his right hand, and baptized
him. Then Krishna went down and was baptized,
the words in Bengali. All was silence. The Governor could not restrain his tears, and almost every
one seemed struck by the solemnity of this new
ordinance. I never saw in the most orderly congregation in England, anything more impressive.
"Ye gods of stone and clay, did ye not tremble
when in the Triune Name one soul shook you
from his feet as dust?"

Carey rejoiced and wrote in his diary that he thanked God
for having permitted him to desecrate the Ganges by baptizing
the first Hindu believer. By 1821 the missionaries had baptized over 1,400 new Christians, more than one half of them
Indians. Carey was faithful, he persevered, and he proclaimed
an uncompromised gospel in a culture of pluralism.

Deep Humility Despite the Accolades of Man.

Finally, his life was characterized by a deep humility despite
the accolades of man. Carey had a peculiar custom. Every
year on his birthday he would write a letter to one of his children, looking back over his life. It was a kind of retrospective
of the past year, looking at his walk with God. In the year
1819, he wrote to his son, Jabez. By this time, consider what
Carey had done. He had pioneered the way for this missionary movement in England to India. He had established dozens and dozens of churches up and down the Ganges delta.
He had established hundreds of schools where Indian children were being taught and translated the Scriptures into
more than twenty different languages. He said to his son Ja-

bez in his birthday letter, "I am this day 58, but how little I have done for God."

That is not a false humility. That is the response of someone who knows that his measure is not to be judged in comparison to somebody else, (to some other pastor, to some other missionary), but before the judgment bar of God to whom he must give an account for the stewardship with which he had been entrusted. In 1831, when he was seventy years old, he wrote in his birthday letter,

> I am this day 70 years old, a monument of divine mercy and goodness, though on a review of my life I find much, very much, for which I ought to be humbled in the dust. My direct and positive sins are innumerable. My negligence in the Lord's work has been great. I have not promoted His cause, nor sought His glory and honor as I ought. Notwithstanding all of this I am spared unto now, retained still in the work. I wish to be more entirely devoted to the service of my Lord, more completely sanctified, more habitually exercising all the Christian graces, and bringing forth the fruits of righteousness to the praise and honor of that Savior that gave His life, a sacrifice of sin.

Humility, despite the accolades of man.

Back in England he heard they were collecting relics from his early life—shoes he made when he was a cobbler, the sign he used to put up outside his cobbler shop, some samples of his handwriting. The Carey cult was already beginning. Carey got wind of this in India and said, "God forbid that they would collect any of my mortal remains!" Alexander Duff, the great missionary from Scotland, spent a long time with Carey during his dying days. As he was about to leave, Carey summoned him back to his bedside and whispered in his ear, "Do not speak of Doctor Carey, Doctor Carey. Speak instead of Doctor

Carey's Savior." That was the heart of this man and that is why God used him in such a tremendous way.

Well, his death came, and it came in a very unexpected way though he was seventy-three years old. It was June 9, 1834. Throughout his long life, he had taken great comfort in the hymns of Isaac Watts. One of his great requests was that a couplet from one of his favorite Watts' hymns, and nothing more, be inscribed on the stone slab that would mark his grave:

> A wretched, poor, and helpless worm,
> On Thy kind arms I fall.

One of those who spoke at his funeral, a young missionary also from Scotland, named John Leechman, said (and I think Carey undoubtedly would have approved):

> And now what shall we do? God has taken up our Elijah to heaven. He has taken our master from our head today. But we must not be discouraged. The God of missions lives forever. His cause must go on. The gates of death, the removal of the most eminent, will not impede its progress, nor prevent its success. Come: we have something also to do than mourn and be dispirited. With our departed leader all is well. He has finished his course gloriously. But the work now descends on us. Oh, for a double portion of the divine Spirit.

May God speak to each of us through the life and witness of his servant, William Carey.

32.
THE VALUE OF PURITANS FOR SBC MINISTRY

MARK DEVER

1995 Southern Baptist Founders Conference

*W*ANTED! *A pastor. Not particularly theological. Committed to the success of the church. A humorous risk-taker with a big personality. Perhaps slightly irreverent at times but with a driving ambition. Committed first and foremost to success in discovering and meeting the needs of the congregation. Master of a wide array of self-help and recovery programs and yet at the same time easy on himself and others. Acceptance, tolerance and sociability a must. Also, should value more emotionally engaging and non-cognitive aspects of worship, the centrality of self-expression and the great power of brief sermons.*

Brothers in the pastoral ministry, could you answer such an ad? Have you ever attempted to answer such an ad? I am delighted for the opportunity to have a conference like this, where we celebrate the faith of our Southern Baptist fathers in the faith. Those Southern Baptist fathers in the faith themselves had fathers in the faith and I am here to talk for a brief time about the fathers in the faith of *our* fathers in the faith —the Puritans.

There is a regrettable, general stereotype of the Puritans. The Puritans, generally, are not the kind of people who would draw a crowd, except perhaps at the Founders Conference. The Puritans are the kind of people that one would tend to avoid. The Puritans are the kind of people whose books you would pick up only if you were having trouble going to sleep.

The Puritans are known as being somewhat harsh—a people you would be uncomfortable sitting next to on an airplane if you were on a long journey. I won't go on with the stereotype. Any of you who are into the doctrines of grace understand. You run into that when you begin to talk about them in your associations and among your friends. But we know better than that.

At the same time there is our own far different stereotype of a Puritan. Our stereotype of a Puritan is that they are wonderful. If you have any trouble with a ministry go buy a Puritan book and the problem will clear up. If you just buy more and more Banner of Truth books to put on your shelves then your ministry will improve forthwith. Well, that is a bit closer to the truth but still, as many of our sagging shelves could sadly tell, it is not simply the purchasing of the volumes but the reading of them. Sadly, not even the reading of them merely but the understanding of them and the ingesting of them and putting them into pastoral practice that can give us what we need in our ministry.

Many times when I mention the Puritans, or people talk to me about the Puritans, one of the main difficulties they run into is that Puritans are simply difficult to grasp. Not that they are difficult to grasp in the sense of buying them but, for the most part, they are difficult to read and understand. I admit that, and I love the Puritans.

Let me give you a tip on reading the Puritans. It takes much longer, but read them out loud. Almost all of these Puritan volumes were sermons. They didn't sit around writing books so much, although they did some, but most of them are compilations of sermons, and they work best when you read them out loud. My dear wife has suffered through many a Puritan volume and has been edified by it. Sibbes is her absolute favorite. So I encourage you if you are reading a Puritan work and come to a difficult section and you're having trouble understanding it, don't pretend you understand it and keep reading. No, wrestle with those ten pages. Get a hold of those ten pages. Read them out loud several times if you have to.

One of the great advantages of the Puritan period is that they were less pressed for time than we are. They would take longer over something. They would linger over it. Would it not profit us to do the same?

THEOLOGY IS GOOD, ESPECIALLY GOOD THEOLOGY!

I was brought up with the idea that theology and zeal for Christian growth didn't go well together. If one wanted to grow in holiness and be zealous, then one shouldn't concern one's self with doctrine. You see, "people fuss and fight over doctrine." It is a standard line often given to those young in the faith. It's why some grow concerned when young believers start getting involved in doctrine. The first thing I learned from the Puritans, that has been very helpful for me as a minister, is that theology is good—especially good theology!

Most of the Puritans happily taught what we call reformed or Calvinist theology and not because they wanted allegiance to the Reformation or to John Calvin. Many of them would disagree with John Calvin on some particular matters. But they felt, as a people who had answered the remonstrances of the Arminians at the Synod of Dort in 1618, that it was important that we understand that people are, by nature, spiritually dead. They thought it was important that we understand what the Bible very clearly teaches—that our salvation is completely and fundamentally based upon an action initiated by God and not us. They felt it was important that we understand that Christ did not die in vain, but that He died as a substitute—willingly giving His life and laying it down for His sheep. We need to understand that conversion happens, fundamentally, not because a person chooses, but because of the gracious enabling work of the Holy Spirit of God. They understood that in those whom God calls, He will complete His work. God not only will justify them but He will sanctify and finally, glorify them. This is the theology that is very clearly applied by the Puritans and is extremely helpful. If you attempt to do pastoral ministry without it your ministry will suffer.

THE GRACE-CENTEREDNESS OF THE GOSPEL

From the Puritans we learn something of the grace-centeredness of the gospel. In every aspect of the minister's understanding of Christianity—of living as a Christian, and particularly functioning as a pastor—the Puritans help us to see how grace is at the very center of everything. It is at the center of the system of doctrine that the Puritans adhered to. God's grace is at the center—not our zeal, not our sincerity, nor our knowledge, our efforts, or our own holiness.

Grace is also at the center of our worship. We have emotionally moving and engaging worship, not simply in order to have emotionally moving and engaging worship but rather, because our hearts are engaged with the truth of God and of His grace in the gospel. Because of what He's done for us in Christ, the spark of God's grace ignites the flame of gratitude in our hearts and the more we perceive it the brighter it burns.

Grace also then begins to mark our interactions with others in the body. There is little room for self-righteousness in a minister who has read with much sympathy the works of the Puritans—because, the Puritans understood the works of God's Holy Spirit in His Word. Instead, what characterizes the person's ministry who has been touched by God and knows the grace of the Holy Spirit in his own life, is a graciousness with others. If you don't see that graciousness with others, perhaps that suggests that person hasn't really comprehended God's own graciousness and patience and mercy to them. Jesus told many parables about this and the Puritans had a good sense of it. Sometimes when we stand up and make our doctrine clearly known we are charged with arrogance. That should not be. Anyone who claims to be in Christ by grace alone and is characterized by arrogance either doesn't understand grace or possibly has not truly experienced it. Learn from the Puritans how everything we do—in theology, in worship, in our care for others as pastors—is to be marked by the grace of God.

THE CHURCH IS THE LORD'S

It goes to follow that the church is God's. It's not the minister's. Christ's kingdom is not an effect. Christ's kingdom is utterly victorious around the world. We've already had the decisive battle at the cross and God, through His Holy Spirit, is employing us in a "mopping-up" exercise. I need not worry that I must make my church the largest there is in order for Christ's kingdom to succeed. Christ's kingdom will succeed. Not because of me, but because of Christ. A faithful understanding that the church is God's fundamentally, and not the minister's, leader's, or even the congregation's is clear in the Puritans.

When we stand in the desk of God and preach the Word, we have an awful ministry to perform. Awful, not in the modern sense, as something we want to avoid or something that tastes bad, but in the sense that it fills us with awe and reverence at the seriousness of the task. It is said that in his sermons, William Perkins used to pronounce the word "damned" with such an emphasis that it left a soulful echo in his auditor's ears. When he was a catechist in Christ's College and expounding the commandments, he applied them so honed to the conscience as was able to make his "hearer's hearts fall down and their hairs almost stand upright."

The church is God's and, therefore, there must be an accountability for the task. Brothers, do you realize the seriousness of our accountability to God? If the church really is His, then perhaps He appeals to us in some of the same ways as we see Him speaking to Saul in Acts 9 when He knocked him off his horse. What did the risen Christ say to Saul? "Saul, Saul, why have you been persecuting—[not my church]—Me?" If the Lord Jesus Christ identifies Himself that closely with His church then do you not think He will hold us accountable? John Brown wrote some advice in a letter of pa-ternal counsel to one of his students who was newly ordained as a pastor over a small congregation. He said, "I know the vanity of your heart and that you will feel mortified that your congregation is very small in comparison with those of your brethren around you, but assure yourself on the word of an old man, that when you come to give an account of them to the Lord Christ at His judgment seat, you will think you have had enough."

Because the church is God's, we must have humility in the task. The pastoral ministry especially, is not a place for training self-promoters. It is a place for great humility. Therefore, since the church is God's, there should be a sense of His presence in the task of pastoral ministry. Brothers, you gain a sense of that privilege of the task in reading the Puritans. Again, William Perkins felt it was a great privilege, while he was in the Cambridge College, to go to the jail in Cambridge to witness to those who had been condemned to death. He felt it was a great privilege to be used in God's ministry.

THE IMPORTANCE OF PASTORAL CARE

From the Puritans we learn about the importance of pastoral care in evangelism. They were patient in their evangelism. It involved that awkward combination of truth—saying that the demands of following Christ were utterly total and complete to the cost limit of the disciple; yet at the same time it was urgent that one must cough up this cost now. You find in the gospels this strange combination in Jesus: an urgency for the gospel and the complete cost. We are never asked to give up anything in following the Lord for which He doesn't richly repay us. Many of our Puritan forefathers knew that and they paid for it heavily with their lives and in various other ways.

Perkins was very clear in the demands of discipleship. One of his people was condemned to death for a crime and he started to climb up the gallows from the jail in Cambridge. He felt so wrought in his heart with terror at the thought of dying that he physically couldn't make it up the steps. Perkins brought him back down the steps and he didn't tell him about the love of God. Isn't that what we might think to do? He told him about the terror of facing God apart from Christ—the terror of facing God apart from repentance and true faith in Christ. For some time, Perkins unfolded this to the prisoner until he broke out in tears of despair and death. When Perkins saw that despair, he brought him the gospel of Christ. He told him about the salvation there is in Jesus Christ. He had tears of joy and would happily meet his Maker. The Puritans knew something of pastoral care in evangelism.

They also understood the assurance of salvation. The Puritans did not quote 1 John 1:9 to anyone who ever asked whether it was a sin to wonder if he was a Christian. That's a wonderful verse but it's misapplied if you use it in your congregation to instruct people not to follow Paul's exhortation to examine ourselves to see if we are in the faith. The Puritans were patient in examining people's salvation. They considered it very, very carefully. Many of them—Richard Greenham, William Perkins, Richard Baxter—became known as "excellent surgeons of the soul" in the area of pastoral care and visitation. Richard Baxter is one who is particularly known for this because of his book, *The Reformed Pastor.* Many of you will have read it, but if you haven't I strongly encourage you to do so. Baxter had a wonderful ministry of pastoral visitation where annually he would visit every member of the congregation and have a serious talk with them about the state of their souls. Not just about how their children were getting on physically or at school. Not just about how they felt about the programs in church. Not just about the extension they just put on their house, but about the state of their souls. There is much to be learned of pastoral care from the Puritans.

DISCIPLINE IS IMPORTANT

When Richard Greenham would be up sick during the night (which was frequent) his manner was, as much as he possibly could, to spend the time in meditation and prayer. William Perkins, while dying a painful death, heard one friend praying for mitigation of his pain—that there would be less of it. Perkins said, "Pray not for an ease of my torments, but for an increase of my patience." These men are regularly described as "painful" as in painstaking. They personally took great pains of discipline. They probably were pretty careful about simple things that would affect anything in the quality of their ministry. They spared no pains. They were suspicious of ease and pleasure and the luxuries of the world in a way that is utterly alien to our society.

Consequently they were also concerned with discipline in the church. The name Puritan was given to them in derision because they wanted the church to be more pure. They were concerned over errors in doctrine in the church. They were concerned over lapses in the discipleship of her members. The importance of discipline in pastoral ministry is clearly seen in the Puritans.

THE CENTRALITY OF PREACHING

From the Puritans we can learn something of the centrality of preaching. They worked very, very hard at their preaching to be both accurate and accessible. The story is told of Thomas Manton who had gone to preach in London before the Lord Mayor. He was wearing his academic robes and as he was walking down the street after preaching, someone came up to him and tugged at his cloak and asked him if he was the gentleman who had just preached before the Lord Mayor. Manton replied that he was and the man said to him, "Sir, I came with hopes of getting some good to my soul but I was greatly disappointed for I could not understand a great deal of what you said. You were quite above me." The doctor replied with tears, "Friend, if I did not give you a sermon, you have given me one and by the grace of God I will never play the fool to preach before my Lord Mayor in such a manner again." Here was a man with one of the best educations you could ask for, who was more concerned with whether he had done good to the simple soul who pulled on his sleeve than whether he had impressed the Lord Mayor of London.

The Puritans were painful in their preaching and their preparations for it, to make sure that it was accurate and accessible. It is said of Perkins that his sermons were "not so plain but that the piously-learned could admire them, nor so learned but that the plain could understand them." A couple years ago I gave an overview of Puritan theology at a church in London. I mentioned that in the Puritan period a common gift from congregations to their ministers was a piece of wrought iron fashioned in the shape of a circle that comes out of the pulpit. They actually held an hourglass. Those were gifts from the congregation to the minister. The minister would be granted one or usually two turns of the hourglass for his sermon. When I mentioned this, one woman raised her hand and asked how much time that left for worship in the service. Well, I understood and appreciated her question. She wanted to worship the Lord and that is a good and godly thing. I told her that prayer is very important and music can be important, but the fundamental of worship is people hearing the Word of God read and preached and responding to it.

If you do a study of any of the Greek words in the New Testament you will find that that is what worship is biblically. The Puritans knew that the very center of worship is our hearing the Word of God and responding to it. Not hearing only. That is condemned as wrong by Paul and James and, most of all, our Lord. We don't want to create a race of "sermon-tasters." Hearing and responding to the Word of God is the very center of Christian worship and the Puritans were clear on this. Therefore, do you know what implication that should have on our schedules as pastors? It should mean that our preparation becomes central in our schedules. Thomas Manton would sometimes transcribe his sermons more than once, and this before the age of computers, going over them again and again trying to make them a little better here or there. He would sometimes stay up all Saturday night re-writing a sermon. If he would go to bed Saturday night and wake up in the middle of the night with a thought he would often get back up and stay up for an hour re-writing a section of his sermon. Richard Greenham's constant course was to preach twice on the Lord's day and before the evening sermon to catechize the young people of the parish. His manner was also to preach on Mondays, Tuesdays, and Wednesdays, and on Thursdays to again catechize the youth. Again on Friday, he would preach to his people. He preached on weekdays so that the people might have the better opportunity to attend upon his ministry. His course was to be in the pulpit in the morning as soon as he could see well. He was so earnest and took such extraordinary pains in his preaching that his shirt would usually be as wet with sweat as if he had been drenched in water. So he was forced, as soon as he came out of the pulpit, to change his clothes.

I don't know what that means for you and your schedule, but for me it has meant trying to give myself as much time as possible on Fridays, and even more so on Saturdays, to my Sunday morning sermon. Very practically, it means trying to block out large parts of my schedule to work on one sermon. The centrality of preaching was evident with the Puritans.

THE IMPORTANCE OF PUBLIC PRAYER

Certainly the Puritans thought it was important to pray in private, and there's wonderful literature on that, but I think I have personally learned from them of the importance of public prayer. This is something to which our evangelical culture in America often gives little thought. We value spontaneity and seem to think that sincerity and casualness are the height of the relationship we can have with the Lord. To be thoughtful and careful about our expression is considered to be mere formalism—too great a danger that we rather not do it. The Puritans spent almost as much time preparing their prayers as they would their sermons because they felt it a great privilege to lead the people of God before the throne of

God. The book *The Valley of Vision,* edited by Banner of Truth, is a collection of prayers. They are some of the most moving prayers I have ever encountered and are just filled with a sense of the presence of God. If you know of someone whom you would like to introduce to a more fully biblical view of God, you might try the back door. Give them a book of prayers. *The Valley of Vision* contains so much of the reverence of God and appreciation for His grace that you might find it helpful for friends.

THE IMPORTANCE OF EDUCATION

Have you ever wondered why aren't there any more Puritans today? When did they stop? Well, there's no certain time they stopped. J. I. Packer, when he teaches his course on Puritanism, says the Puritan period ended about 1700, and I agree. Packer suggests that the reason why they stopped is that after 1662 in England you could no longer have access to a university education without subscribing to the Thirty Nine Articles and the *Book of Common Prayer.* If you could not conscientiously be an Anglican, you could no longer have a university education. What happened to the Anglican Church was that things became so polarized that most of the people who held to the doctrines of grace felt conscience-bound to leave the church in 1662 or during the twenty years thereafter. Consequently the very places that had fed the Puritan movement were emptied of them. William Perkins had been educated at Christ's College Cambridge, his mentor Richard Greenham was educated at Pembroke College Cambridge. The Puritans had the finest of educations yet they also had the personal character to continue to apply themselves to their studies even after obtaining those educations. Their educations were not lulled and laid on. They were enticements to continued and greater usefulness. Richard Greenham studied very hard, rising both winter and summer at four o'clock in the morning to pursue his studies.

Realizing that education was not just important for ministers but also for members is one of the reasons they took their sermons so seriously. They realized that in preaching their sermons well they would be educating the church. That's why they would encourage families to rehearse the sermons at the dinner table. I suggest reading a passage of Scripture and discussing it. Perhaps the passage preached on. One of the practical things I thought of in our church, that we have not done yet, is to begin having small groups meet through the week for Bible study and use as a passage the sermon text from the previous Sunday morning. The hard spadework would have been done for them already. They could then use that passage as the meat that they would work on in smaller groups in terms of application.

The Puritans encouraged Scripture reading. It wasn't unusual to find people reading many, many chapters a day. That's why they encouraged afternoon lectures. It was very common at one o'clock on Sunday afternoon, after they had been in church and before they would be in church again at 3:30, to have a lecture. They wanted everything they could get, and Sunday was a market day for the soul. They wanted to take in as much as they could. That's why there was continuous catechizing and teaching again.

Baxter used regular visitation. Greenham's manner was, beside his public preaching and catechizing, to walk out into the fields and confer with his neighbors as they were at the plow. Have you ever visited your people at work? Go have lunch with them. Read something with them. Pray over them. Pray with them about their non-Christian friends at work. Realize that it is important that they be educated in understanding the grace of God so that they come to understand more of the living God and the great grace that is revealed in Christ in their own lives and the desperate need of those with whom they work.

THE PERSONAL RESPONSIBILITY OF PASTORS
IN TRAINING MINISTERS

I appreciate what the Lord is doing in our seminaries. I

think at the end of the day the problem has not been with the seminaries, it has been with the churches. The seminaries can only do what the churches allow. Brothers, if you are a pastor, you and I are the under-shepherds—the ones to train the church. It is our responsibility to train ministers of the coming generation. Seminaries can be useful, but fundamentally God's Holy Spirit uses the church to train the minister.

It was very common for the Puritans to train young ministers by having them live with them in their homes—sometimes two, three, even four. Some would live there for a few weeks, some for a few months, and some for years. Informal networks of people from schools to colleges were set up so that if you knew a young, promising lad who evidenced God in his life, seemed to be sensitive to spiritual matters, and felt called to the gospel ministry, you would know where to send him to school because there already was a godly person there from whom he could learn—someone to take him under his wing. From there you knew where to send him to college and then where to send him to work at a church under a faithful pastor. That's what I want to see all across our Convention. That's what I want to see all across the church—godly churches with a burden to raise up godly ministers; using the seminaries for the glory of God, but realizing it is the church's God-given responsibility to educate and train ministers.

THE IMPORTANCE OF STRATEGY AND TRUST

Some people think that if you are a Calvinist it means you're lazy. They think if the Lord determines things, all the pressure is off you to do anything. That may be some of your experiences, but it has not been mine. The more I understand what God has done for me, the more heightened is my sense of being a steward of God's incredible work in Christ. So I am not surprised when I read the Puritans and find them strategizing again and again. Richard Greenham was the instrument and means under God, we read, to encourage and train up many godly ministers. He strategized to do this. He also used his money to help the poor. He would work out very complicated ways of buying some extra surplus corn when the harvest was good, keeping it back and selling it below market prices, even below his cost, in order to be able to provide for the poor. He knew God was sovereign over the harvest. He knew God saw the sparrow fall but he had a heart for the family that was hungry. So he strategized to be able to see how he could alleviate the situation simply by helping out.

So the Puritans strategized for the ministry. They came up with a whole series of afternoon lectures. They couldn't get into the pulpits of the established churches, so they started getting little endowments to pay a lecturer to come at one o'clock. He wouldn't be the minister of the church usually. Sometimes he would preach contrary to the minister of the church, but they would give a little endowment to establish a lectureship at one o'clock. They would choose key market towns where people would come, like a supermarket these days, to buy their goods on a certain day of the week and they would have public lectures there in the market square during that time. They would pay for them.

The Puritans would strategize where they wanted to be in order to reach the populace of England with the gospel, but at the same time as they strategized they trusted. They knew the battle was the Lord's. That's why they could be content to stay in a place longer than two and a half years. They could be content to stay in small places for their whole lives. Greenham stayed in the little village of Drayton, outside of Cambridge, for twenty years before going to London. Even when he went to London he was "very careful," he wrote before his remove, "to get an honest able man to succeed him in that place."

The Puritans were willing to lay down their lives for the sheep in so many ways. They were put to the choice in 1662 of going against their conscience or being cast out of their pulpits and positions at great personal expense to themselves. There was no welfare system, just a small stipend that they would be given but they would be forever removed from the ministry that had been their lives and they couldn't live near the place where they had ministered. Over 2000 of them decided to choose resignation from the Church of England on a single Sunday. The press, a few years ago, was full of controversy over women's ordination in the Church of England, how many people would be resigning and how this would be the greatest schism in the Church of England. Obviously none of those press writers had read anything from the seventeenth century. These people in the seventeenth century didn't talk about it and get on national news shows about it and threaten, they simply, humbly, in good conscience and great pains, resigned the only way they knew to make a living. And they did so out of faithfulness to the gospel, out of love for the very people they were committed to feed. That's why when the great plague hit London in 1665 and so many of the paid ministers were getting out of town so they wouldn't get infected, the very ministers who had been thrown from their pulpits started heading into London because there were men and women who needed to hear the gospel of Christ. The Puritans had a godly combination of trust and strategy.

THE IMPORTANCE OF A BELIEVING CONGREGATION

Finally, I must share with you something I learned by default. The Puritan that I studied for my dissertation was Richard Sibbes who was committed to the established church. He was committed to infant baptism and he was committed to the Episcopal structure. I learned through studying Sibbes— whom I love deeply and look forward to meeting—the importance of being in a believing congregation. In studying the Puritans, I learned by negative example the importance of rejecting a doctrine which would include in the church people who do not claim regeneration. I say this gingerly because I have perhaps more friends who are Presbyterian than Baptist, but believer baptism is something that I think I have learned by seeing the opposite among so many of the Puritans. I'm not surprised that by the late seventeenth century so many of the pulpits had run down into a kind of moralism. If you assume that everyone within your hearing who has had vows made for them is therefore, under special obligation to obey the commands of God, you run the risk of throwing yokes on people that God has not put there. If they have not had the new birth they cannot live the new life.

Also, I've learned something about the importance of a congregational church polity. In the Westminster Assembly there was a great argument over what polity we should follow. Will it be Presbyterian style? There were some who advocated an Episcopalian style. Or should it be a Congregational style? The Congregationalists argued valiantly and they lost overwhelmingly. But the basic argument that I think holds sway both biblically and in my own experience, is this: pastoral authority and responsibility must be tied to pastoral relationship. That was the argument that Goodwin used at the Westminster Assembly in the grand debate. When you break it down it is that pastoral authority must be tied to pastoral relationship. He is right in that and we can learn by negative example when that is not followed.

I encourage you to go and read the Puritans. You don't have to buy seventeen volumes your first time. Buy a few that are recommended to you by people who know and take the time to read them carefully. Read them out loud to your spouse or to somebody in the church that you are trying to disciple or work with. Come to groups and discuss them together and pray that the Lord will teach you of the value of that with which we have been entrusted—the stewardship of the ministry of the Word of God.

Let me close by sharing with you one of the prayers from *The Valley of Vision*:

O my Lord,
Let not my ministry be approved only by men,
or merely win the esteem and affections of
people;

But do the work of grace in their hearts, call in thy elect, seal and edify the regenerate ones, and command eternal blessings on their souls.

Save me from self-opinion and self-seeking;

Water the hearts of those who hear thy word, that seed sown in weakness may be raised in power;

Cause me and those that hear me to behold thee here in the light of special faith; and hereafter in the blaze of endless glory;

Make my every sermon a means to grace myself, and help me to experience the power of thy dying love, for thy blood is balm, thy presence bliss, thy smile heaven, thy cross the place where truth and mercy meet.

Look upon the doubts and discouragements of my ministry and keep me from self-importance; I beg pardon for my many sins, omissions, infirmities, as a man, as a minister;

Command thy blessing on my weak, unworthy labors, and on the message of salvation given;

Stay with thy people, and may thy presence be their portion and mine.

When I preach to others let not my words be merely elegant and masterly, my reasoning polished and refined, my performance powerless and tasteless, but may I exalt thee and humble sinners.

O Lord of power and grace, all hearts are in thy hands, all events at thy disposal, set the seal of thy almighty will upon my ministry.

33.
THE HISTORY OF SOUTHERN BAPTIST PREACHING
MARK COPPENGER
1995 Southern Baptist Founders Conference

INTRODUCTION

B Y the most conservative estimates the Southern Baptist Convention has had at least 88,000 preachers over its 151-year history. Even after the growth patterns of the denomination are taken into consideration, it is still safe to estimate that during the last century-and-a-half, more than 120 million Southern Baptist sermons were preached![1]

In light of this, it is impossible for anyone to presume to summarize exhaustively the history of Southern Baptist preaching in any respect. This article is no exception. It is, rather, a survey based upon the examination of several hundred sermon-collection books in the Southern Baptist Historical Commission library.

In reading through these sermons, an interesting connection suggested itself. It is presented here not so much as a theory, but as a program for study. Could it be that the per-

---

1 In 1845, there were about 4,000 Southern Baptist churches. Fifty years later that number had grown to 18,000. In 1945 there were 26,000 and by 1995 the total was approximately 40,000. Assuming one preacher per church, and each preacher preaching for 50 years, the convention has had at least 88,000 preachers. Assuming further that a whole new shift has just reported to work at our 40,000 churches, we shall count only the 48,000 who have gone before. If each of those preached an average of once per Sunday for their 50 years of ministry, we have 2,500 sermons per preacher (M. E. Dodd is reported to have preached 18,000 times! See T. W. Gayer, "Monroe Elmon Dodd," *Encyclopedia of Southern Baptists,* mg. Ed., Norman Cox [Nashville: Broadman, 1958], 378). This makes a total of 120 million sermons from 48,000 preachers for our first 150 years. Of course, these are extremely conservative numbers. There are more preachers than churches and more sermons than Sunday morning sermons. And the turnover of preachers is much greater.

ception of lost mankind's character and capability are improving in our preaching, much as they have in our doctrinal statements? Could it be that the unregenerate are being progressively perceived as less depraved? The evidence indicates that there has been an ascent of lost man in the thinking of Southern Baptists over the course of their history.

Does preaching generate the confessions? Or do the confessions shape the preaching? Or does it work both ways? To what extent does one influence the other? While these questions cannot be answered with absolute certainty, the parallels are worth watching.

When we read the 1859 *Abstract of Principles* of Southern Seminary, we find that lost man inherits a "nature corrupt and wholly opposed to God and His law." Sixty-six years later, the first *Baptist Faith and Message* said men "inherit a nature corrupt and in bondage to sin." The 1963 revision stated that men "inherit a nature and an environment inclined toward sin." One wonders how a fresh revision might read in the year 2025? If the theological trajectory remains the same, perhaps in the 21st century men will be said to "inherit a nature open to sin as an option."

While there have probably been millions of Southern Baptist sermons preached, relatively few have found their way into print. And relatively few of those have found their way into our historical library. Still, that collection makes for an interesting sample.

ANTE-BELLUM PREACHING

Ante-bellum preacher Charles D. Mallary explains the doctrines of grace in his sermon on Ephesians 1:3,4, "The Doctrine of Election."[2] This founding trustee of Mercer University defined election as:

---

2 C. D. Mallary, "The Doctrine of Election," *The Georgia Pulpit*, Robert Fleming, ed. (Richmond: H. K. Allyson, 1847), 176.

God's free, sovereign, eternal and unchangeable purpose to glorify the perfections of his character in the salvation of a definite number of the human family by Jesus Christ, without regard to any foreseen merit or good works on their part, as the ground or condition of this choice.[3]

His account of depravity serves as a clear benchmark of early Southern Baptist views:

The scriptural doctrine of depravity is not that every man is as bad as he possibly can be, for there may be indefinite progression in guilt:—nor that one man is necessarily as wicked as another, — for there may be as many shades of depravity as there are sinners in the universe. But it teaches us that man, by nature, is destitute of all holy principles and desires; that there is nothing in his character which is pleasing in the sight of God; that being alienated in his heart from God, corrupt in the very fountain of action, in the temper and spirit of his mind, all the actions that he performs, even those which are in themselves excellent and lovely, are still the service of an alien and a rebel, and consequently an abomination in the sight of heaven. Every imagination of the thought of his heart is only evil continually.[4]

In this light, he went on to observe, "The want of power is the want of will.... the sinner's inability is the sinner's crime."[5] Mallary, a trustee of Mercer University from its founding in 1833 until his death in 1864, represented main-stream Baptist thinking in his day.

Virginia pastor Addison Hall joined in this grim assessment of

---

3 Ibid., 178.
4 Ibid., 180.
5 Ibid., 181.

unregenerate man in a sermon specifically addressing the topic:

> The doctrine of human depravity is fundamental, and lies at the very foundation of the Christian Religion; insomuch as a practical conviction of its truth, may be considered as the first step towards the reception of the offered mercy of the gospel. By it we understand that man by nature is wholly corrupt and depraved; not only destitute of love to his Creator, but actually opposed to his laws, and at war with his perfections: that man's whole nature and attributes, animal, intellectual, and moral, are perverted. His understanding is darkened, his imagination beclouded, his memory impaired, his reason dethroned, his will perverse, his conscience defiled, his affections estranged, his heart polluted. In his thought he is impure, in his words filthy, in his actions vile. In short, that he is 'earthly, sensual, devilish.'...This humiliating doctrine is confirmed by the history of all nations and religions, whether Pagan, Mahommedan, Jewish, or Christian; else why those scenes of war, of rapine, and blood-shed, that fill the pages of history, sacred and profane? ... A steadfast conviction of this doctrine is necessary, to tear away from self-righteous man the leaf-covering of his own righteousness, and to make him see himself in all his native deformity and pollution, that so he may duly value the atoning righteousness of the Lord Jesus Christ.[6]

Georgia pastor J. H. T. Kilpatrick answered a variety of objections to the doctrines of grace, He responded to those who charge that the doctrine of human depravity diminishes human responsibility:

---

6 Addison Hall, "Doctrine of Human Depravity," *The Baptist Pulpit of the United States*, ed., Edward H. Fletcher (New York: Edward H. Fletcher, 1853), 133-36.

Others, again, excuse themselves thus: they say it is their nature to sin, and they cannot see how any one can be blamed for acting according to his nature; and especially as he got this nature from another. Therefore, such persons appear to think they are quite excusable in sinning against God; purely, because it is their nature to do so; but let us try this mode of reasoning and see whether it will do. Suppose a man is arraigned in a court of justice for the crime of larceny, and his attorney or counselor urges before the court and jury, as his only plea of exoneration: that this poor unfortunate man is a thief by nature; it is his nature to steal, and that he always had been a thief at heart, &c. , and moreover, his father was a thief, and this man, poor fellow, is just like his father; and therefore, he hopes the court and jury will find a verdict of acquittal for the prisoner; in as much as it is his nature to steal, &c. We ask, what do you think of such a plea as this? Do you think it would stand? Or rather, do you not think this man intended, through his counselor, to insult the court, and sink himself still lower, if possible, in the estimation of all who know him? Make the application, my dear objector, and tremble before God for having insulted him in like manner."[7]

Our first president, W. B. Johnson, similarly had little patience for the lost who refused to take responsibility for their own spiritual destiny:

Now, now, O fellow-sinners, you have it in your power to place yourselves under influences that are spiritual and saving; or under influences that are carnal and damning. You can read the Bible,

---

7 James Hall Tenner Kilpatrick, "God's Willingness to Save Sinners," *The Georgia Pulpit*, ed., Robert Fleming (Richmond: H. K. Allyson, 1847), 123-24.

or the book of infidelity; the sermon of truth, or
the novel of fiction; you can attend the party of
sinful pleasure, or the meeting for holy prayer;
you can go to the midnight revel, or to the house
of God. You can lift up the prayer of the publican,
or the howl of the bacchanal. You can utter the
praise of the Most High, or belch out the blasphemy of the arch fiend. How solemn the responsibilities that are upon you![8]

Returning to Kilpatrick, we find a lack of enthusiasm for
much that appears to be religious interest within lost man:

Here is a man, for instance, who is very sick, he
greatly dreads to die; his physician proposes to
him to take a potion of very nauseous medicine,
the patient is perfectly willing, and greatly desires
the medicine. We ask, Is it really, the medicine
the man wants, independent of its effects? O no,
the medicine itself is disagreeable; it is the good
effects of the medicine which is really the object
of his desire. He wants to live, and he only desires
the medicine as the means of obtaining the end.
This, perhaps, unfolds the secret of your situation. If so, you are only a legalist; and it has not
been religion you have been wanting all the while,
but its good effects. If you will examine yourself
closely, perhaps you will find that so far from having desired religion on account of what it is in its
own nature, you have in reality been desiring it
only as a kind of necessary evil, which you did not
want, only as a means of obtaining certain
wished-for ends.... We see a great many persons
who appear to be greatly concerned about keeping out of hell and getting to heaven, while they

8 W. B. Johnson, "Free Agency of Man," *The Baptist Pulpit of the United States*, ed., Joseph Belcher
(New York: Edward H. Fletcher, 1853), 125-127.

appear to be very little concerned about sin and holiness.[9]

In an 1860 sermon collection, Reverend W. T. Ussery of Union University underscored the magnitude of man's lostness with these words:

> It may take more power to redeem fallen man than it did to create this material world. It required the combined power and wisdom of the God-head to save man, while the Father merely spoke this world into existence.... If the great, rich and eternal grace of God is required to save the human soul, how deep, inevitable and universal must be human depravity?[10]

Parenthetically, we should note that Calvinist apologists were just as hard on hyper-Calvinist's as they were toward Arminians. Adiel Sherwood, who organized the theology department at Mercer and wrote the resolution that resulted in the formation of the Georgia convention, called hyper-Calvinists "anti-nomians."

In a sermon entitled, "The Covenant of Redemption," he spoke of the doctrines of grace as "the system which acknowledges God as the author of salvation, the Spirit as the agent, and Christians as the means." In his estimation, it was "the only scriptural system."[11] But he was opposed to hyper-Calvinism, which scorned means:

> Anti-nomians have been so fearful of trenching upon the Lord's prerogative of converting sinners, or that the set time to favor Zion had not arrived, that they have attempted but little.... If they had been guided by the scriptures, they would have

---

9 Ibid., 130.
10 W. T. Ussery, "Grace," *Sermons* (Union University, 1860), 159,164.
11 Ibid., "The Covenant of Redemption," 90.

been "up and doing" long ago, for the same commission which authorizes them to labor in their own neighborhoods,—not only gives liberty, but presses the duty of preaching "the gospel to every creature."[12]

LATE NINETEENTH CENTURY PREACHING

After the war, toward the end of the century, there is still an allegiance to the notion of total depravity, but the preachers seem more concerned than their predecessors to mention "freedom." Consider Thomas Skinner's remarkable statement of depravity, of the bondage of the lost man's heart. But then note the closing qualifier.

The unconverted sinner's heart is fortified in his weakness, is desperately set in him to do evil, and all that converted men can do is to break upon them, as the sea breaks on the rocky shore. It is the sea that is sent back while the rock stands firm. There are scores of men who live for the flesh, and yet live in the full light of truth; men that are familiar with every statement and argument of the Scriptures; men that have known and seen much of the power of God in revivals, and yet there is within them that fixed, rooted, toughened life of sin that refuses to yield itself to any power which can be wielded merely by the hands of men.

If the Christian's strength be in the Lord and not in himself, then the Christless person must needs be poor, impotent creature, void of all strength to do anything towards its own salvation. The Holy Spirit works in the saving of a sinner without impairing the freedom of the human

---

12 Ibid.

will.[13]

W. P. Walker offered a similar account, with a strong statement of depravity: "In this slavery the mind is blinded, that truth cannot be seen. The affections are perverted that the truth is hated, and the will is paralyzed that it cannot be obeyed."[14] Given this "helpless and hopeless" condition, Walker noted the necessity of the Holy Spirit: "with his aid we can turn to God."[15] It may be significant that he says "with his aid" rather than "by his power."

This milder statement of the Holy Spirit's role accords with his claim: "There is no coercion in matters of religion. God's revelation to man is sufficient to convince his judgment, conquer his will, and win his love."[16] The listener is left to wonder what this could mean. On one level, it is surely false. Any number of people are exposed to God's manifold revelation of Himself—through the declaration of the heavens, the testimony of natural law, and the clear preaching of the gospel. Many refuse to respond to this revelation. Or is he speaking of an elective/irresistible "revelation"? If so, then why put it so? If he means simply that no one is dragged kicking and screaming into heaven, then that is true enough, but against whom is he arguing? If it means that somehow depraved man achieves saving heights of spiritual perception so that he might choose God on his own, then he makes his earlier statement of man's helplessness confusing.

It seems that the cords of man's bondage are just loose enough that he, Houdini-like, can, with the Holy Spirit's whispered urgings, swell his wrists and work enough slack to break free and grasp God.

As perplexing as this prose may be, it does show the tension

---

13 Thomas E. Skinner, "Conversion," *Sermons, Addresses and Reminiscences* (Raleigh: Edwards & Broughton, 1894), 91.
14 W. P. Walker, "Abandoned of the Lord," *The Southern Baptist Pulpit*, ed., J. F. Love (Philadelphia: American Baptist Publication Society, 1895), 311.
15 Ibid., 310.
16 Ibid., 306.

involved in trying to hold to the biblical doctrine of total depravity while answering to the philosophical theme of freedom. As is noted below, some later preachers utterly abandoned the doctrine of total depravity and the tension collapsed.

EARLY TWENTIETH CENTURY PREACHING

Shortly after the turn of the century, there are clear signs of lost man's progress in Southern Baptist preaching. C. B. Williams, dean and professor of Greek New Testament and New Testament Theology at Southwestern argued that "man is worth saving morally and spiritually. This is his chief glory. Then let us build more churches, more Sunday schools, let us send forth more evangelists and missionaries to save this lofty being called man, spiritually and morally, in order that he may be lifted to the side of God in the Kingdom, through Jesus Christ, whose grace shall transform his character and light his life, until at last he may be like God Himself."[17]

Of course, the Bible teaches that man is a "little lower than the angels," that he is "fearfully and wonderfully made," but it does seem a bit much to speak of salvation as lifting a lofty being yet higher.

Williams is a fascinating and disturbing character. He seemed right susceptible to modern expressions. In "The Worth of a Man," he said "I believe in eugenics, the science of noble birth, the science which says we can produce a higher race by proper birth and by proper parentage."[18] In "Christianity for the Twentieth Century," he embraced a popular slogan ordinarily associated with theological liberalism: "This teaching of the New Testament on the fatherhood of God and the brotherhood of man must be basal in the twentieth century Christianity."[19]

---

17 C. B. Williams, "The Worth of Man," *Citizens of Two Worlds* (New York: Fleming H. Revell, 1919), 42.
18 Ibid., 41.
19 Ibid., 137.

Despite his qualifiers and links to Scripture, these words reveal a man who is overeager to make Christianity "relevant." By this standard, talk of total depravity did not fare so well in his day.

In the same era, Southwestern Seminary president L. R. Scarborough suggested a good measure of freedom for lost man, building a sermon on Revelation 3:20 in the Laodicean letter, "Behold, I stand at the door and knock." Despite the fact that this letter is directed toward one of the seven churches, Scarborough calls it "the simplest explanation of the plan of salvation encompassed in so brief a statement within the lids of God's Book."[20]

MID-TWENTIETH CENTURY PREACHING

By the 1930's, the Reformed perspectives that permeated earlier Southern Baptist preaching had declined in influence. Southern Seminary president E. Y. Mullins, seemingly at odds with the anthropological article of the *Abstract of Principles*, preached these words:

> You may choose to believe in God or choose not to believe. Again the choice is in the highest degree momentous. You may freely will to believe in God. Indeed, when we look at the spiritual nature of man closely it becomes quite evident that he is so made that faith is the natural or normal expression of his nature. There are certain deep instincts in him which cannot be evaded. They impel us to believe in God.... In all these deeper impulses we find a vindication of his right to believe in God. Faith in God is his inalienable right. The instinct of thought and of conscience, the instinct of prayer and of suffering, the instinct of courage

---

20 L. R. Scarborough, "The Savior Knocking at the Door," *The Tears of Jesus* (Nashville: Baptist Sunday School Board, 1922), 75.

and of hope—all these vindicate man's right to
believe. The whole make and trend of his soul im-
pels him to God.[21]

A "right to believe?" What a curious construction, so unlike
ordinary discourse. Stranger yet is M. E. Dodd's sermon on
John 3:16, one of a series of sermons he preached on various
3:16's. He began with "'GOD SO LOVED'—did not hate. It
does not say, 'I believe in you.' He does. It does not say, 'I
trust you.' He does...."[22] The point seems to be that God believes in and trusts mankind.

Texas executive secretary R. C. Campbell expressed similar
enthusiasm in his sermon on Psalm 8:4, "God's Estimate of
Man": "God sees in us the ability to overcome our selfish desires and inclinations. It is an inspiring sight to see an individual who   forgets   himself   in   unselfish   service   for
humanity."[23]

Well, it is true that there are stirring stories of non-Christian Medal-of-Honor winners who threw themselves on gre-
nades for their buddies, and of unbelieving parents who
slaved to give their kids an opportunity for a better life. But
does the Bible justify speaking so sweepingly and generously
of man's capabilities at the deepest level of motivation?

W. T. Conner, longtime theology professor at Southwestern
Seminary, similarly mitigated man's depravity:

> Jesus regarded men as sinful—all men—but
> He did not believe that men were fixed in their
> sinful state. He knew the love of God toward
> men, and He believed in the possibility of
> winning men to a favorable response to God's
> grace.... Jesus did not believe, then, that man
> could lift himself out of his sinful state in his own

21 Edgar Young Mullins, "The Right to Believe," *Faith in the Modern World* (Nashville: Baptist Sunday School Board, 1930), 11-12, 21.
22 M. E. Dodd, "John 3:16," *Three:Sixteens* (Grand Rapids: Eerdmans, 1936), 31.
23 R. C. Campbell, "God's Estimate of Man," *Youth & Yokes* (Nashville: Broadman, 1938), 57.

strength, but He did believe that men could respond to God's grace and let God lift them out of their sins. It is true that this response was one that was won from the man by the grace of God offering to save man. Yet it was man's response. And Jesus counted on such a response on the part of sinful men. To some extent that was what He was finding. He welcomed such a response. He eagerly watched for it. He said there was rejoicing over it in the presence of the angels in heaven.

In befriending sinners, then, Jesus was not compromising with their sins. He was offering them a friendship that was calculated to win them from their evil ways.[24]

It seems a little strange to talk about Jesus' "believing," "counting on," "eagerly watching," and "calculating." Doesn't Jesus more nearly work in the realm of "knowing" and "effecting?" Intentionally or not, Conner presents a picture of man who, while not perfect, is perfectly open to the overtures of an amiable, gift-bearing divinity.

Moving into the 1940's, many other spokesmen for the liberty and even honor of lost men are easily found. M. F. Ewton of First Baptist Church, Seminole, Oklahoma, drew this boundary line:

God cannot go beyond man himself. Men are free moral agents, having the right and power of choice. Man can choose the highest heights of heaven or the lowest depths of hell. God will not, God cannot force men to love and serve Him because forced service is slavery. If men love and serve the Most High God, they will do it willingly.

24 W. T. Conner, "Jesus, The Friend of Sinners," *The Christ We Need* (Grand Rapids: Zondervan, 1938), 45.

> By the promptings of the Holy Spirit, by the faith-
> ful preaching of the Word, and by the testimony
> of Christian friends, the issue of eternal impor-
> tance has been placed before you.... Your soul
> will perish in the regions of the damned unless
> you will to do the will of God. God cannot go be-
> yond your own heart and its desire. If you remain
> hard of heart and stiff of neck then there is noth-
> ing that God can do. The matter rests with you.[25]

Is it not more appropriate to speak of the "promptings of
the Holy Spirit" in the lives of the saints? For the lost, it
would seem to involve more than prompting, for they have
not yet consented to be actors in Kingdom drama.

Llew Northern, in his Broadman sermon book, *Simple Salvation*, claimed,

> There is a longing in every man for acquaintance-
> ship with the divine. This quality of man's nature
> may not always be known, but it is universally
> real. The further one advances in the progressive
> elements of life the more he feels the need of
> something that cannot be defined by the ordinary
> rules of expression and realized by the use that is
> made of material accomplishments.[26]

Now, it is easy to argue that men want security, significance, and heaven, but it is quite another thing to say that
they want God as Lord. In Northern's sermon, we find little
trace of the notion of man as a hardened rebel. And what
could Northern mean by "advances in the progressive elements of life?" If he means, "advances in spiritual sensitivity,"
then his statement is trivially true. If he means, "advances in
the arts, sciences, and civic virtues," then his statement is de-

---

25 M. F. Ewton, "Limits Beyond Which God Cannot Go," *Cardinal Truths* (Self-published, 1947), 48.
26 Llew C. Northern, "Man's Quest for God," *Simple Salvation* (Nashville: Broadman, 1940), 99.

monstrably false. Indeed, as men count themselves more progressive, enlightened, educated, and esteemed, they are prime candidates for spiritually ruinous pride.

Not surprisingly, the Jesus who seeks this advanced man is more supplicant than Sovereign.

> In Jesus' standing at the door of the hearts of men knocking, one is struck with the valid significance of a symbol of man's character by finding that the Lord Jesus respects the privacy of the human soul. He does not batter his way into this privacy, nor resent a kind of barrier between man and him. Quite gently and lovingly he comes to the heart's door and knocks.... He would enter to cheer, to counsel, to instruct. He would have an abiding place within the heart. He will await the opening of the door.[27]

South Carolina pastor W. P. Hall elaborated on the posture of the seeking Jesus in this fashion: "About what was Jesus optimistic? He was hopeful about His words enduring, the redemption and transformation of human personality, and the coming of His kingdom."[28] "If He had not been hopeful about redeeming lost men, He would not have come and sacrificed so much in order to do it."[29] An optimistic and hopeful Jesus? Well, yes. But should not more be said?

In another 1940's Broadman book, *Christ and Human Liberty*, Adiel Moncrief spoke of Jesus' view of man in these terms: "Belief in human liberty and in man's free institutions involves the greatest measure of faith in man. Jesus has that measure of faith in man. He believes in the boundless possibilities of mankind to become free sons of God."[30]

---

27 Ibid., 89-90.
28 W. P. Hall, "The Optimism of Jesus," *Walking With God* (Grand Rapids: Zondervan, 1940), 89.
29 Ibid., 91.
30 Adiel Moncrief, "Christ and Human Liberty," *The Loving Christ in the Life of Today* (Nashville: Broadman, 1941), 21.

Jesus has "faith in man." Had their been a denominational press 100 years earlier in 1840, it's doubtful that this expression would have received much play.

Broadman also published a 1940's collection by Zeno Wall, one in which he describes the Holy Spirit's work in salvation in these terms: "A sinner is hard of hearing. He, in fact, would never hear if the Lord did not unstop his ears. The Holy Spirit, therefore, takes the initiative in our salvation by unstopping our ears." Wall then goes on to say, "When you open your heart's door and bid the Lord to come in, you will experience something that you cannot explain."[31]

It's remarkable how strong the imagery of Revelation 3:20 plays in Southern Baptist evangelistic preaching. In this sermon, the sinner is portrayed as sitting in the house of his soul, deaf to noise of the Savior's knock. Perhaps "violating his privacy," the Holy Spirit slips in and clears his hearing. But then the question stands, why should the sinner want to answer instead of recoiling in fear or irritation, as some folks do when we go out on church visitation? Is hearing enough to prompt opening? It's not a bad image as far as it goes, but it leaves the question of will untouched.

Moving into the 1950's, we find yet other voices raised against the Reformed view of lost man. In a "Baptist Hour" sermon, Roy McClain declared that there are "no elect people."[32] He pictured a wistful God who ever renews his invitation. "He puts perfume in the flowers with the hope that you will someday ask why."[33]

This God has done what He can, and now He waits hopefully for us to pick up on His cues.

Of course, one speaks of the Baptist Hour, Herschel Hobbs comes readily to mind. This venerable Southern Baptist statesman was emphatic in stressing human freedom over

---

31 Zeno Wall, "Experimental Religion," *Verities of the Gospel* (Nashville: Broadman, 1946), 5.
32 Roy O. McClain, "The Great Supper, God's Broken Heart," *Stoop and Drink* (Ft. Worth: Radio and Television Commission, 1955), 17.
33 Ibid., 21.

human bondage: "The devil and God held an election to determine whether or not you would be saved or lost. The devil voted against you, and God voted for you. So the vote was a tie. It is up to you to cast the deciding vote."[34]

Everyone is familiar with the practice of watching election returns, waiting to see how the vote went. It's difficult to imagine God's doing this sort of thing, even if done eons in advance of the actual vote.

To close the 50's we turn to yet another Broadman Book, *Southern Baptist Preaching.* In it Carlyle Marney's sermon on "The New Birth" provides the most generous view of man yet. Speaking of inquiring Nicodemus, he said, "He is blind with the awful spiritual blindness of all men who know only religious habit. He is blind to the indwelling Spirit, blind to his freedom, to his responsibility, to his spiritual destiny, and to the inner light."[35] Unless Marney is arguing that the inquiring Nicodemus was already regenerate, he pictures a lost man indwelt by the Holy Spirit—one who needs a happy discovery more than a conversion.

CONTEMPORARY PREACHING

In the late 1970's, Broadman's fourth volume of *Award Winning Sermons* featured a sermon by Clay Warf on the prodigal son. Warf draws from William Hull in describing "the waiting of God as one that is filled with an agony compounded with fear and hope—each day hoping for the son's return yet each moment filled with fear that the son may destroy himself in the far country. But the fact is that no matter how close in pursuit of us God may be, he still chooses to wait until we turn and reach out to take his hand."[36]

---

34 Herschel Hobbs, "God's Election Day," sermon preached on The Baptist Hour, 8 October, 1967, Beam International, 18, No. 5 (May 1967), 23-24.
35 Carlyle Marney, "The New Birth," *Southern Baptist Preaching,* ed., H. C. Brown, Jr. (Nashville: Broadman, 1959), 133-134.
36 Clay Warf, "The God of the Lost," *Award Winning Sermons,* ed. James Barry (Nashville: Broadman, 1979), 109.

What are we to make of this Heavenly Father wracked with fear that His son may not return? Never mind predestination. Whatever happened to prescience?

Warf applies this parable to every person, but in what sense do lost people possess sonship, prodigal or not?

In the 1970's, Southern Seminary professor Frank Stagg continued the assault on Reformed thinking in Southern Baptist life:

> The 'Achilles heel' of 'predestination,' besides its monstrous and fallacious view of God as arbitrary, is that what it offers as 'salvation' is really destruction. Were God to determine that some be 'saved' and some be 'lost,' there would be no meaningful difference between the two groups or fates. Both groups would be lost. Both would be reduced to the status of things, objects manipulated. Salvation is not salvation for a person unless personhood itself be preserved. That is why Jesus asked the cripple, 'Do you wish to become well?'[37]

I fail to take the offense Dr. Stagg suggests I ought to take. Believing that I was an incurably self-indulgent, spiritually dead creature, I have nothing but gratitude to God for giving me a new heart and a heavenly destiny. These changes seem to me to constitute a "meaningful difference." If this is destruction, then may we see more of it!

Of course, a "person" is one who wills, who acts according to values and principles, and believers have all the personhood one could ever want, Stagg's claims notwithstanding. Stagg's lost man seems much finer than the lost man pictured the *Abstract of Principles*, which Stagg signed under some necessarily arcane interpretation.

---

37 Frank Stagg, "A Whole Man Made Well," *The Struggle for Meaning* (Valley Forge: Judson, 1977), 73-74.

NOTABLE EXCEPTIONS

In fairness, it should be noted that Southern Baptist preaching does not chart a simple trajectory from total to lesser depravity. All along the way, there have been both words of esteem for lost man's capacities and, on the other hand, dismissive judgments on those alleged capacities. The question is not, then, one of discrete and exclusive eras, but of the shifting center of mass.

J. R. Graves was an early dissident from the Reformed view of man. In his 1847 sermon on the "The Sovereignty of God," he said:

> The doctrine of eternal and unconditional election, and reprobation as taught by Calvin, and assented to by many professed Christians, we utterly repudiate—it finds no place in our faith and affections. It is as contrary to our reason as to our understanding of the Word of God.... Either He will save some, who disbelieve the truth, and damn some who love our Lord Jesus Christ; or He must invincibly force some to love Him and some to hate Him, so that He might damn them. Both of which suppositions are contrary to the plain construction and spirit of the Bible, and effectually destroy all human accountability and moral agency.[38]

He went on the say that all predestination was based on foreknowledge, and then suggested that those foreknown to choose Christ were those of more worthy character.

> Did He dispossess Himself for the time of His omniscience, close His eyes, and decree a certain quantity, instead of a certain character, for salva-

---

38 J. R. Graves, "The Sovereignty of God," *Satan Dethroned* (New York: Fleming H. Revell, 1939), 47-48.

> tion? Impossible for eternal wisdom thus to act!
> What would you think of that man before whom
> was set a large measure full of gold coins and
> pieces of tin of the same size and, being freely of-
> fered all he chose, should—instead of carefully
> selecting the gold—should shut his eyes and be
> satisfied with clutching a handful of whatever
> kind it might be! Would an infinitely wise God
> thus discern between the righteous and the wick-
> ed?[39]

So Graves compared those who would ultimately be saved
to gold coins on account of their superior moral character.
These are the ones with the sensitivity to recognize the wor-
thiness of Christ, and so, naturally turn to Him. Seeing their
virtuous choice, God affirms this choice in advance—hence,
predestination.

Graves acknowledged that the Bible teaches that the lost
man is a slave to sin, but he asks, "Cannot the slave wish for
freedom and release?" He goes on, "The slave may wish in
vain, but the sinner has a deliverer to rescue him when he
wishes. So to him the freedom of thought and of choice is still
left."[40]

The problem with this image is that the master imprisons
the literal slave. The spiritual slave imprisons himself.

Just as there were early Baptists who mitigated depravity,
there are modern Baptists who underscore it. One could
hardly imagine a more sober account of fallen man than this
one offered by the incomparable R. G. Lee:

> My own definition of the grace of God is this:
> the unlimited and unmerited favor given to the
> utterly undeserving. Let us think of the strength
> of grace. Sin is very powerful in this world. Sin is

39 Ibid., 49.
40 Ibid., 71-72.

powerful as an opiate in the will. Sin is powerful as a frenzy in the imagination. Sin is powerful as a poison in the heart. Sin is powerful as a madness in the brain. Sin is powerful as a desert breath that drinks up all spiritual dews. Sin is powerful as the sum of all terrors. Sin is powerful as the quintessence of all horrors. Sin is powerful to devastate, to doom, to damn.[41]

Here is the sinner's only hope, although, until quickened by the Spirit of grace, he does not know it. No man can rescue himself from the tyranny of sin. Men may reform, but they cannot regenerate themselves. Men may give up their crimes and their vices, but they cannot, by their own strength, give up their sins. Can the Ethiopian change his skin? No. Can the leopard eliminate his spots? No.[42]

Elsewhere, Lee said, in contrast to Marney:

Nicodemus was blind and blind to the fact that he was blind. Nicodemus was ignorant—and ignorant of the fact of his ignorance. Nicodemus was dead—and dead to the fact that he was dead. Nicodemus was lost—and lost to the fact that he was lost. He did not know that unless men are converted and become as little children—not masters in scholarship, not philosophers of the academic grove—they cannot see the Kingdom of God.[43] Adam, the federal head of the race, plunged into sin and carried the whole human race with him.... Nothing but regeneration will save this generation.[44]

---

41 R. G. Lee, "The Grace of God," *Heart to Heart* (Nashville: Broadman, 1977), 141.

42 Ibid., 143.

43 Ibid., 54.

44 Ibid., 58.

652   HISTORICAL/BIOGRAPHICAL

Regeneration is the great change which God works in the soul when He brings it into life, when He raises it from the death of sin to the life of righteousness. It is the change wrought when the love of the world is changed into the love of God; when pride is dethroned and humility enthroned; when passion is changed into meekness; when hatred, envy, and malice are changed into a sincere and tender love for all mankind.

It is the change whereby the earthly, sensual, devilish mind is turned into the mind that was in Christ. The new birth is not the old nature altered, reformed, or reinvigorated, but a being born from above....[45]

It is not that the natural man is ignorant and needs instruction, feeble and needs invigorating, sickly and needs doctoring. His case is far more. He is spiritually lifeless, and needs quickening—a spiritual corpse which needs bringing from death to life.[46]

The necessity of the new birth is shown in that the human heart is "deceitful above all things and desperately wicked" (Jeremiah 17:9), is affected with a malady which no example can cure, no philosophy can change, no ritualistic formulas or religious ceremonies can reach and change.

I repeat, the natural man, in his unregenerate state, cannot understand the things of the Spirit (I Corinthians 2:14). He is blind (II Corinthians 4:4); he is dead in trespasses and sins (Ephesians 2:1-3); his understanding is darkened (Ephesians 4:18-19); full of evil thought (Genesis 6:5, Jeremiah 17:9), and unable to please God (Romans 8:8).

Therefore, as all who believe the Word of God

45 Ibid., 61
46 Ibid., 65.

know, a new birth, even a birth from above, is needed because of the depravity of human nature.[47]

So the unregenerate man has the eyes of his understanding darkened in respect to spiritual and saving truth. The stars of gospel truth shine brightly in the firmament of the word of God, but the lost man does not see them.[48]

And again, "The gospel is hated and rejected as foolishness until the direct power of the Spirit changes the governing disposition of the heart."[49]

Consider yet another "counter-culture" 20th century voice. J. Frank Norris' view of man required that even saving faith must come as a gift:

> Now the New Birth, the Regeneration act, is not a human act, it is a Divine act. That's God's side. Now, repentance and faith are graces given of God, and they are an act of the human.... Now, don't be worried, if you get one of the two, you will have the other. They are both from the human side. The Divine side is the new Birth.... So it is, which do you have first, repentance or faith? If you have one you have the other. Both are—let me emphasize, both are gifts from God.[50]

One final example is drawn from our contemporary, W. A. Criswell, who pulls no punches on the helplessness of lost man:

> We are dead. We are corpses. We are born in that death. We are born in sin, even conceived in sin. All of our propensities and affinities flow in

---

47 Ibid., 68.
48 Ibid., 69.
49 Ibid., 73.
50 J. Frank Norris, "The New Birth," *The Gospel of Dynamite* (Ft. Worth, 1933), 28-9.

the direction of sin. We are by nature set in a fallen direction. Have you ever stood by the mighty Niagara? The great river falls over that precipice. It naturally does. It is uncoerced. It falls by nature. It cannot rise. It does not rise. It falls and each drop of water pushes the other over the rim of that great falls. We are set in a fallen direction.... I am bound, paralyzed between two steel rails, one, my fleshly lust and the other, my fallen will. And I stand in the path of an inevitable judgment, inexorable death. I'm like a man paralyzed between two steel rails and thundering down on me is a great chain of cars.... I can stand and preach to a dead corpse and say, "Don't you see?" But a corpse doesn't see. I can lift up my voice and say to a dead corpse, "Don't you understand?" But a dead corpse does not understand. I can say to a dead corpse, "Don't you hear?" But a dead corpse does not hear. It cannot will itself to a quickened life. It cannot choose, it cannot see, it cannot hear, it cannot think, it cannot understand. It is dead.... The initiation of our salvation, of our calling, of our regeneration, of our new birth, of our salvation is in God and not in us. Consequently, our new birth, our regeneration, our calling is a gift of God.... Now, when I read this in the Bible, and I look in my heart, is it confirmed in my experience? It is. And not only in mine, but in every man who has ever come to know Jesus as his savior. A man or a woman. Everyone of us.... Those old, great hymns of long ago were just like that. Isaac Watts wrote the song you sang just a moment ago.

Why was I made to hear thy voice
And enter while there's room
When thousands make a wretched choice
And rather starve than come?

Twas the same love that spread the feast
That sweetly forced me in
Else I'd still refuse to taste
And perish in my sin....

In like manner, long years ago, Josiah Conger wrote this hymn,

'Tis not that I did choose thee,
For Lord that could not be.
This heart would still refuse thee,
But thou has chosen me.[51]

CONCLUSION

It is a pity that such preaching is scarcer than it once was. While few deny the reality of human free agency (else what sense could we make of the conscious rejection or acceptance of the gospel?), it seems that today, the "freedom" of the lost has been magnified at the expense of their "bondage." Unlike the founders of the Southern Baptist Convention, some have come to view lost people as discriminating shoppers, whose failure to buy is due to our failure at marketing.

It is good to note that man's will is free in the sense that his choices flow freely from his character or nature, whether regenerate or unregenerate. But today the spiritual freedom of fallen man is being woefully overrated and, consequently, saving grace is being tragically underrated.

Let us not underestimate our own freedom to address this imbalance, to the magnification of God's grace and the praise of His glory.

---

51 W. A. Criswell, Transcribed from the cassette tape, "The Bible Kind of Salvation: Romans 9:15-16."

34.

THE PURITANS AND THE RECOVERY OF THE LORD'S DAY

ERROLL HULSE

2002 Southern Baptist Founders Conference

THAT there is such a thing as a special day is indicated in Revelation 1:10 where the apostle John says, "On the Lord's Day I was in the Spirit."

Te kuriake hemera literally means "the Lordly day," "Lordly" being an adjective which describes the day. It is the day as against all other days over which the Lord exercises His Lordship, a day marked out from all other days. He is Lord of all days but this day is set apart for Him and so it is "the Lordly day."

I will presently describe the contest over whether there is indeed a whole day which belongs in a special sense to the Lord. But first note that the idea of one day in seven being set apart has been with us from the creation of the world. The Hebrew practice of resting on the seventh day influenced all the surrounding nations. Josephus said, "There is not any city of the Grecians, not any of the barbarians, not any nation whatever, whither our custom of resting on the Sabbath day has not come."[1] Philo said, "For that day is the festival, not of one city or one country, but of all the earth."[2]

Generally speaking, by the fourth century the day of rest had changed from the seventh day to the first day of the

---

1 Robert Cox, *The Literature of the Sabbath*, vol 1, (Maclachlan & Stewart: London, 1865), 116. Literature on the sabbath question is massive. This is illustrated by the fact that the references to books and articles on the sabbath compile into two volumes by Robert Cox which can be found in the Dr. Williams Library in London.
2 Ibid., 117.

week, called the Lord's Day, which custom has prevailed in all the world ever since. This is a subject that spans human history and is described in the Bible from Genesis to Revelation. Is the whole day to be separated from our other activities, both secular and recreational? Is the whole day to be devoted to the Lord or only part of it?

In order to address that question we need to be aware of the development of the Medieval Sabbath which prevailed for hundreds of years before the Reformation and then for the most part right through the 16th century.

THE MEDIEVAL SABBATH[3]

The Medieval doctrine taught that there should be an observation of the Lord's Day by attending the mass which was also called "divine service." After that the rest of the day was for recreations. Since Sunday was the only regular day of leisure in medieval culture, apart from frequent saints' days and feast days, the population seized Sundays to have fairs, markets, football and parties at which ale flowed freely. Thus Sabbaths were often riotous occasions.

It can be argued that the ecclesiastical and political establishment (remember society was sacral, Church and State worked hand in hand) compromised higher views of the use of Sunday in an attempt to get people to attend church just once. In practice the day began with divine service (the mass) after which recreations followed in the church yard or anywhere nearby that was convenient. The problem of absenteeism has always been present with national Churches. It is the problem which continues to harass the Roman Catholic and Anglican communities. A man is encouraged to attend early

---

3 For an excellent treatment of this subject see James T. Dennison, "The Puritan Doctrine of the Sabbath," *Banner of Truth* magazine. The complete indices for the *Banner of Truth* magazine from 1955 to 2001 are obtainable from THE FINDER the diskette being available from The Christian Bookshop, Alfred Place, Aberystwyth, SY23 2BS, UK. The indices include the monthly *Banner of Truth* magazine as well as the bi-monthly magazine *Reformation Today* from 1970 to 2001 and the Westminster/Puritan Conference papers from 1956 to 2001. The latter are being published in the USA by Presbyterian and Reformed Publishers.

morning mass on Sunday after which he is free the whole day for golf or bowling, or if he is a family man to spend time for recreation with his family.

Now the medieval doctrine supporting this practice was that, unlike the other nine commandments in the Decalogue, the fourth commandment is a mix of moral and ceremonial law. The nine commandments were entirely moral but not the fourth. The Saturday of the fourth commandment applied to the Jews and it now has been entirely abolished. The day has changed to the first day of the week so apart from spending some time in the worship of God we are free to spend the rest of the day as we please.

The medieval doctrine found no authority for Sabbath practice in the New Testament. According to the medieval view nothing is prescribed by Christ or His apostles for how Sunday is to be employed. The New Testament is silent. There are no instructions or precepts to go by. Therefore it belongs to the Church to prescribe Sunday times and customs of worship.

This medieval doctrine and practice prevailed in England. In 1618 and 1633 anti-sabbatarian manifestos were published by the Church of England with royal approval. It was required that these manifestos called "the Book of Sports" be read in all the churches. These manifestos were detested by the Puritans and some Puritans were persecuted for refusing to read them in church.

I summarize the medieval doctrine inherited by the Church of England:

> The fourth commandment is part moral and part ceremonial. That day is now abrogated. The only injunction that applies now is that we set apart some time for the worship of God. The Lord's Day possesses no *de jure* [divine law] principle which applies to us because the New Testament is silent on the issue. The Sabbath is not a creation ordinance and Genesis 2:3, the example of

God resting on the seventh day, does not apply to us.[4]

With medieval practice firmly in place we can now understand the descriptions given by some of the Puritans of social life in England.

For instance Richard Baxter recalled the distractions experienced by his family when he was growing up in an English village:

> We could not on the Lord's Day either read a chapter, or pray, or sing a psalm, or catechise or instruct a servant, but for the noise of the piper and taber, and shouting in the streets continually in our ears, and we were the common scorn of the rabble in the streets, and we were called Puritans, precisionists, hypocrites because we chose on the Lord's day to read the Scriptures rather than do what they did.[5]

Philip Stubbs in 1583 described the moral and religious evils of his day and of the Lord's Day asserting that "the people spend their time frequenting bawdy stage plays, interludes, playing May games, frequenting church ales,—and spend their time in piping, dancing, dicing, carding, bowling, tennis playing, hawking, hunting and such like—also in keeping of fairs and markets, and in football playing and in other like devilish pastimes."

THE PURITAN SABBATH[6]

A truly remarkable contribution to the history of Great

---

4 The Church of England doctrine (the Prelatic view) is expounded by writers such as Peter Heylyn, David Primerose, Christopher Dow, and Francis White.

5 Daniel Neal, *History of the Puritans*, vol. 1 (Harper Brothers: New York, 1843), 560.

6 For a detailed account of the positions of both the Reformers and the English Puritans see my work *Sanctifying the Lord's Day, Reformed and Puritan Attitudes*, in Westminster Conference Papers for 1981, and for further details see reference 3 above.

Britain, and through Great Britain to many other countries in the world, was the retrieval of the Lord's Day Sabbath from Medieval doctrine and practice.

This was brought about by the triumph of the Word of God over the authority and custom of Church policy, tradition and pragmatism. The driving force and engine by which the Puritans achieved their objective was the exegesis of Scripture.

Puritan expositors went straight to the heart of the matter, namely, the Sabbath *is* a creation ordinance (Genesis 2:1-3). The essential meaning of "sabbath" is rest but rest with a qualitative significance. Reflection is implied. "God saw all that he had made and it was very good" (Genesis 1:31). Puritan expositors proceeded from Genesis and the creation straight to the fourth commandment to demonstrate that the first word of the fourth commandment is "Remember." Remember what happened at the beginning. Do not forget that in perpetuity, that is for always, the Lord has set aside one day in seven for rest from all work apart from works of necessity. The Sabbath they showed was coterminous with the created order. It is an integral part of created order. It is generic inasmuch as it applied not only to our first parents but to all their offspring. Man is not created to labor incessantly. There are six days for work but the seventh is to be set apart and made holy for the Lord.

There was nothing ceremonial about the Sabbath when it was instituted at the creation. Later under the Mosaic law the Jews were given statutes and details about how they were to keep the Sabbath. Those details of a ceremonial nature do not apply to us in the new covenant era. The Puritans observed that the fourth commandment as stated in the Decalogue is entirely moral like all the other nine. They affirmed the unity of the Decalogue in stating universal moral law on tables of stones (Deuteronomy 4:13). There are Ten Words not Nine. The fourth is not out of line with the other commandments. It, like all the others, is purely moral in character with no ceremonial reference whatsoever. In Moses' commentary on the Decalogue in Deuteronomy 5:1-21 he reminds Israel that they were liberated from slavery in Egypt. The same principle of redemption applies to us. We are rescued from slavery and need to celebrate our freedom by worshipping the Lord. Remember that Pharaoh loathed the idea that the Israelites should be free to go and worship the Lord apart from the work commitments that he enforced. Freedom from drudgery is required in the fourth commandment for all the family, for all the servants in the household, and for all the animals, the plough oxen and the donkeys as beasts of burden. There must be a full day of rest for all alike.

The Puritans' position is that Exodus 20:8 does not specify a particular day of the week. They rejected the view of the Seventh Day Sabbatarians (who have as their equivalent the Seventh Day Adventists today). The point at issue is not legalistic, that is, that the importance of the matter attaches to a certain day. It is a moral issue of one in seven that is vital. The fourth commandment does not assign a specific day of the week but stresses the importance of setting aside one day in seven. That day was Saturday from Sinai, when the Lord gave a double portion of manna, to after the resurrection of our Lord, who is Lord of the Sabbath and who invested that day with further special significance and meaning in His resurrection. But from His resurrection until His return it will still be one in seven, and even when He has set up the new earth and heavens, that same principle, according to Isaiah 66:23, will still pertain.

For the Puritans, the New Testament is not silent about the Sabbath or Lord's Day. Our Lord set for us an example, with works of necessity (Matthew 12:1-8), worship (Luke 4:16), and works of mercy (Matthew 12:10-13; Luke 13:10-17; 14:1-5 and John 5:1-18).

HOW DID THE PURITAN SABBATH COME TO PREVAIL?

The Puritans' ideal of the Lord's Day triumphed in the churches after the Civil Wars of 1642-1648 and made a pervasively massive impact after that. Even to this day in secular

Britain, in which great efforts by the liberal establishment have been to secularize Sunday, it still remains the practice of the large magnates of business and banking to be shut. It is only in recent years that Sunday has been overrun by sport.

The English Puritans are unique in their achievement to establish the Lord's Day. Before them the early sixteenth-century reformers, William Tyndale, John Frith and Martin Luther, took the fourth commandment as ceremonial and accepted more or less the status quo. Luther was opposed to the Roman Catholic saints days and holy days, and the practice of these made him resistant to making any day special.

John Calvin, Heinrich Bullinger and Zacharias Ursinus took the fourth commandment to be both ceremonial and moral. Calvin stressed the need to make the Lord's Day special and devote the whole day to God. The churches that followed in Calvin's teaching have been noted for strict Sabbath observance. Scotland is one example and the Dutch Reformed churches in South Africa is another.

However, the continental reformers did not develop detailed exegesis on the point like the English Puritans. Richard Baxter apologized for them and said, "You must remember they came newly out of popery."

The story of the change can be traced to Richard Greenham (1531-1591), who influenced his son-in-law, Nicholas Bownde. Bownde preached on the subject of the Sabbath in 1586. He then marshalled the Sabbath-law arguments in a book which he published in 1595. This was a straightforward and balanced work on the text of the fourth commandment. It became enormously influential, appearing in an expanded edition in 1606. According to historian Daniel Neal, "A mighty reformation was wrought."

Bownde proclaimed that the commandment to rest was a moral and perpetually binding law. To follow studies, do worldly business, or engage in recreations or pleasures such as shooting, hawking, tennis playing, fencing and bowling was discouraged. "Men must not come to church with their bows and arrows."

Bownde's brother-in-law, John Dod, nicknamed John Decalogue Dod, published his work on the Ten Commandments later. The book was very popular, going to forty editions. Concerning harvesting on Sunday Dod wrote, "'What about reaping our harvests endangered by ill weather?' ask some. 'Trust in providence' is the reply. Better we hazard some part of our estate than the wrath of God fall on us."

Two members of the Westminster Assembly, Daniel Cawdrey and Herbert Palmer, collaborated to produce *Sabbatum Redivivum—The Christian Sabbath Vindicated* (1645). In two volumes this work came to 1050 pages. The authors began by establishing the distinction between ceremonial, judicial and moral law, and early defined what they meant by "moral." Solemn worship they upheld as a moral and perpetual obligation. The fourth commandment, being part of the first table, they asserted as being moral and perpetual. In 1655 a significant work by Thomas Shepard, the New England Puritan, was published. Shepard expounded the morality, change of day, beginning of, and sanctification of, the Sabbath.

The Westminster Confession and *Second London Baptist Confession of Faith of 1689* (chapter 22, paragraphs 7 and 8) bring together the main ligaments of the Puritan teaching as follows:

> As it is a law of nature applicable to all, that a proportion of time, determined by God, should be allocated for the worship of God, so, by his Word, he has particularly appointed one day in seven to be kept as a holy sabbath to himself. The commandment to this effect is positive, moral, and of perpetual application. It is binding upon all men in all ages. From the beginning of the world to the resurrection of Christ the sabbath was the last day of the week, but when Christ's resurrection took place it was changed to the first day of the week, which is called the Lord's Day. It is to be continued to the world's end as the Christian sabbath, the observance of the seventh day being

abolished.

Men keep the sabbath holy to the Lord when, having duly prepared their hearts and settled their mundane affairs beforehand, for the sake of the Lord's command they set aside all works, words and thoughts that pertain to their worldly employment and recreations, and devote the whole of the Lord's day to the public and private exercise of God's worship, and to the duties of necessity and mercy.

In 1668 *The Practical Sabbatarian* appeared. This was a 787-page exposition of instructions on the duties of Sabbath observance written by John Wells of St Olave Jewry, London. Wells was one of the ministers ejected in 1662. His work is an exposition of Isaiah 58:13-14. He contended that sports and recreation on the Lord's Day easily remove the sweetness of the Word and are the debasements of spiritual mercies. The law of nature requires a total abstinence from all works of labor and pleasure during the time allotted and consecrated to God's service (pages 26-28). The very essence of the day, argues Wells, is apartness, or holiness, from the other days: "Shall men fix days for themselves," he asked "and shall not God have one?" We must prepare for this day: "Was not Mary Magdalene last at the cross and first at the sepulchre?" And then he stressed the delight of the Lord's Day: "Joy suits no person so much as the saint and no day so well as the Sabbath." In support he quoted Psalm 118:24 (KJV): "This is the day which the Lord hath made; we will rejoice and be glad in it." Between morning and evening service he advised that we indulge in "luscious, sweet, holy discourse."

A typical outline of advice for preparation and conduct for Sunday runs like this:

1. Prepare well for the Lord's Day by prayer and meditation. "If you would leave your heart with God on Saturday night," says Swinnock, "you should find it with

him on the Lord's Day morning. Go seasonably to bed
so that you may not be sleepy on the Lord's Day."

2. Heads of homes should gather their families in good
time on Sunday mornings and prepare them all to receive maximum spiritual edification throughout the
day. Public worship is central on the Lord's Day.

3. Heads of families should make sure that the sermon
materials are retained. Encourage lively discussion
and repetition of the main heads of the exposition at
the meal table.

4. Seek to retain the teachings received and the blessings of the Lord's Day during the week that has begun.

It is misguided to think that Puritan teaching on the Lord's
Day is only negative. It is negative in the sense that we must
forsake pleasuring ourselves and rather seek the Lord's will
for the best use of His day, but the power of Puritan teaching
lies in its expressions of enjoyment of, and zeal for, the Lord's
Day. The advantages of this day well spent are enormous.
Thomas Watson called it "the market-day of the soul" and we
can see from the following quotations the zeal that Watson
felt for the Lord's Day:

The sabbath is market-day of the soul, the
cream of time. It is the day of Christ's rising from
the grave, and the Holy Ghost's descending upon
the earth. It is perfumed with the sweet odour of
prayer, which goes up to heaven as incense. On
this day the manna falls, that is, angel's food.
This is the soul's festival day, on which the graces
act their part: the other days of the week are most
employed about earth, this day about heaven;
then you gather straw, now pearls. Now Christ
takes the soul up to the mount, and gives it trans-
figuring sights of glory. Now he leads his spouse
into the wine-cellar, and displays the banner of

his love. Now he gives her his spiced wine, and the juice of the pomegranate (S. of S. 2:4; 8:2).

The Lord usually reveals himself more to the soul on this day. The apostle John was in the Spirit on the Lord's Day (Rev. 1:10). He was carried up on this day in divine raptures toward heaven. This day a Christian is in the heights; he walks with God and takes as it were a turn with him in heaven (1 John 1:3). On this day holy affections are quickened; the stock of grace is improved; corruptions are weakened; and Satan falls like lightning before the majesty of the Word. Christ wrought most of his miracles upon the Sabbath; so he does still: dead souls are raised and hearts of stone are made flesh. How highly should we esteem and reverence this day! It is more precious than rubies. God has anointed it with the oil of gladness above its fellows. On the sabbath we are doing angels' work. Our tongues are tuned to God's praises. The sabbath on earth is a shadow and type of the glorious rest and eternal Sabbath we hope for in heaven, when God shall be the temple, and the Lamb shall be the light of it (Rev. 21:22-23).[7]

APPLICATION

Two attitudes are to be avoided. The first is the mentality of legalism. The Lord's Day can be destroyed the way the Pharisees destroyed the Jewish Sabbath by excessive and small-minded legislation. Every household needs leadership and ground rules but these need to be constructed so that the day is a day of rest, joy and spiritual advantage.

The way many believers keep the middle part of the day is to entertain friends making the major preparation for that on Saturday evening.

---

7 Thomas Watson, *Ten Commandments* (Banner of Truth Trust: London, 1965), 97.

A second attitude to be avoided is antinomianism that is to behave as though this day did not matter and make it the same as the other days.

The most important contribution we can make is to apply the doctrine of adoption to the Lord's Day. We are the sons and daughters of God. If we apply ourselves positively and creatively to this day to use it to show that we do love Him with all our hearts, minds, souls and bodies, then according to the promise of Isaiah 58:14 we will find joy in the LORD and He will "cause us to cause us to ride on the heights of the land and to feast on the inheritance of our father Jacob."

SCRIPTURE INDEX*

---

* Some Scripture references have been supplied by the index compiler where none appear in the text.
—No indication is made when a reference appears more than once on the same page.—An asterisk
(*) beside page numbers indicate texts which are the subjects of presentations.